Bloy and Parry's
Principles of Criminal Law

Fourth Edition

Cavendish
Publishing
Limited

London • Sydney

Bloy and Parry's

Principles of Criminal Law

Fourth Edition

Mike Molan BA, LLM, Barrister
Head of the Law Division, South Bank University

Denis Lanser LLB, Dip Crim
Lecturer in Law, Staffordshire University

Professor Duncan Bloy BA, LLM, PGCE,
Academic Director, Forté-IRI, Singapore

Cavendish
Publishing
Limited

London • Sydney

Fourth edition first published in Great Britain 2000 by Cavendish Publishing Limited, The Glass House, Wharton Street, London WC1X 9PX.

Telephone: +44 (0)20 7278 8000   Facsimile: +44 (0)20 7278 8080

Email: info@cavendishpublishing.com

Website: www.cavendishpublishing.com

    First edition   1994
    Second edition   1996
    Third edition   1997
    Fourth edition   2000

British Library Cataloguing in Publication Data
Molan, Michael T
Bloy and Parry's Principles of criminal law – 4th ed – (Principles of law series)
1 Criminal law – England 2 Criminal law – Wales
I Title II Lanser, Denis III Bloy, Duncan J IV Parry, Philip V Principles of criminal law
345.4'2

ISBN 1 85941 580 6

Printed and bound in Great Britain

PREFACE

The three years since the publication of the third edition of this book has seen a significant amount of government activity in the areas of criminal justice, but very little by way of legislative reform of the substantive criminal law. In this period, the Crime Sentences Act 1997, the Crime and Disorder Act 1998 and the Youth Justice and Criminal Evidence Act 1999 have all made appearances to varying degrees of critical acclaim. The legislation that may yet prove to have the most impact on the substantive law is the Human Rights Act 1998, with the majority of provisions having come into effect on 2 October 2000.

This book therefore endeavours to reflect judicial decision making in this period, together with proposals for reform of the criminal law contained in various publications, such as the Law Commission, *Consultation Paper on Fraud and Deception* (1999) and the Home Office, *Consultation Paper on Reforming the Law on Involuntary Manslaughter* (2000), and raises the question of whether or not the nation needs a criminal code. It does not focus on the procedural or sentencing areas of the criminal law as these are rarely, if ever, dealt with in detail as part of a university level criminal law syllabus.

Duncan Bloy would like to thank his co-authors who have undertaken the vast majority of the work associated with the revision of the text. He also wishes to thank Cara Annett at Cavendish Publishing for her forbearance over the last few months.

Mike Molan and Denis Lanser would like to extend their thanks to Cara Annett and Sonny Leong at Cavendish Publishing for encouraging their involvement in this fourth edition. Mike would like to thank Alison for taking care of business so that he had the time to do the writing and Denis would like to thank Melanie for all her support and assistance.

We have stated the law as at 1 October 2000.

Mike Molan
Denis Lanser
Duncan Bloy
October 2000

CONTENTS

Contents

TABLE OF CASES

TABLE OF STATUTES

TABLE OF ABBREVIATIONS

AA	Abortion Act 1967
AAA	Accessories and Abettors Act 1861
AVTA	Aggravated Vehicle-Taking Act 1992
CA	Children Act 1989
CYPA	Children and Young Persons Act 1933
CMA	Computer Misuse Act 1990
CApA	Criminal Appeal Act 1968
CAtA	Criminal Attempts Act 1981
CDA	Criminal Damage Act 1971
CJA	Criminal Justice Act 1967/1972/1982/1988/1991/1993
CJPOA	Criminal Justice and Public Order Act 1994
CLwA	Criminal Law Act 1967/1977
CLRC	Criminal Law Revision Committee
CLA	Criminal Lunatics Act 1800
CP(I)A	Criminal Procedure (Insanity) Act 1964
CP(IUP)A	Criminal Procedure (Insanity and Unfitness to Plead) Act 1991
HSWA	Health and Safety at Work Act 1974
HA	Homicide Act 1957
HFEA	Human Fertilisation and Embryology Act 1990
IA	Infanticide Act 1938
IL(P)A	Infant Life (Preservation) Act 1929
LA	Licensing Act 1872
MHA	Mental Health Act 1983
OAPA	Offences Against the Person Act 1861
PVS	persistent vegetative state
PHA	Protection from Harassment Act 1997
RTA	Road Traffic Act 1988

SOA	Sexual Offences Act 1956/1993
SO(A)A	Sexual Offences (Amendment) Act 1976
TA	Theft Act 1968/1978
T(A)A	Theft (Amendment) Act 1996
WTA	Wireless and Telegraphy Act 1949

CHAPTER 1

AN INTRODUCTION TO
THE STUDY OF CRIMINAL LAW

1.1   Coverage of the book

This book has been written specifically for students studying criminal law as part of their undergraduate or CPE studies. It examines the general principles of the subject and then looks at selected specific crimes. The selection has been undertaken on the basis of those crimes which make the greatest impact on the life of the citizen and those which take up the majority of court time. It does not attempt to offer a comprehensive review of the several thousand crimes which do not fall into either category but we believe that having studied the general principles of criminal liability the student will be able to employ the same approach to these other crimes and be in a position to subject them to detailed analysis.

We have not included chapters on sentencing or criminal procedure. This is not because we consider these subjects unimportant but for the functional reason that there is simply not enough time on most criminal law courses to deal with these matters. Criminal law is a particularly interesting and challenging subject and we wish to avoid over-burdening the student. They are in any event best studied in the final year of the undergraduate programme and many universities now offer courses in evidence, criminology, criminal litigation and sentencing at this point in the academic programme.

However, the subject cannot be properly understood without regard to the context in which the rules originate and in which they are applied by the courts and so we have included sections concerned with such fundamental questions as the purpose of the criminal law, the function of the judge and the jury, the burden and the standard of proof, and the right to appeal. We have also attempted to explain how criminal offences are classified and the implications of the classification for the mode of trial and for the defendant.

1.2   A criminal law for the new millennium

What can be reasonably expected from the criminal law at the start of the new millennium? It is a system that is under the microscope at various levels and for a number of well documented reasons. In December 1999, the Lord Chancellor announced a Criminal Courts Review to be undertaken by Auld LJ. Its purpose is to:

> ... review ... the practices and procedures of, and the rules of evidence applied by, the criminal courts at every level, with a view to ensuring that they deliver justice fairly, by streamlining all their processes, increasing their efficiency and

strengthening the effectiveness of their relationships with others across the whole of the criminal justice system, and having regard to the interests of all parties including victims and witnesses, thereby promoting public confidence in the rule of law.

Reading the terms of reference, one is entitled to wonder whether there is anything *right* with the criminal justice system. The implication is there for all to see that the current practice and procedures may not be delivering 'justice fairly' and that public confidence in the rule of law is waning. There are indeed those who believe that the task set for Auld LJ and his team is an impossible one (see Zander, M, 'What on earth is Lord Justice Auld supposed to do?' [2000] Crim LR 419).

However, this book focuses on the substantive law and is not primarily concerned with practice and procedure. Nevertheless, all is not well with the principles of criminal law. One is entitled to assume that, as a very minimum, they should be certain, consistent and accessible. One might refer to these as 'benchmark criteria'. Yet note the comments of Sir Henry Brooke, a former chairman of the Law Commission who is on record as stating that the law in many areas 'is a disgrace, when judged in terms of simplicity, clarity and accessibility' ((1994) 158 JP 158). Much time will be spent considering the meaning of some of the most fundamental fault terms which determine whether or not a defendant can be found guilty of a serious crime, that is, based on a finding of the defendant acting either intentionally or recklessly. These terms have been the subject of widespread debate and no little uncertainty in recent years, leading to confusion in the minds of judges, lawyers and students. Even when clarity has seemingly been established, as in the House of Lords decision in *Woollin* (1998), academic comment has once gain opened up old wounds regarding the place of 'indirect intention' in the law of murder (see Chapter 3 and the article by Professor A Norrie, 'After *Woollin*' [1999] Crim LR 532).

The defence of self-defence has been plunged into the spotlight as a result of the publicity generated by the *Tony Martin* case where the defendant shot and killed an intruder at his remote farmhouse late at night. The media portrayed the case in a light favourable to the defendant and there continues to be a groundswell of public opinion supporting the action that Martin took on that fateful night. When pleaded, self-defence is an 'all or nothing' defence, in the sense that, where successful, it leads to an complete acquittal; if rejected, the defendant is found guilty of murder. If one accepts the argument that the degree of culpability may vary on a case by case basis then there is a strong argument for accepting that self-defence could in certain circumstances lead the defendant to be found guilty of manslaughter. The issue, though, is not a new one. As long ago as 1989, the House of Lords Select Committee on Murder and Life Imprisonment proposed the introduction of a special defence to murder. Where excessive force was used in circumstances where it was reasonable to use some force in self-defence, then a jury could return a verdict of guilty of manslaughter rather than murder. It will be interesting to see whether the Government will move to change the law now that the Human Rights Act 1998 is in force. Article 2 of the European Convention on Human Rights (the right to life) is not violated if force is used that is no more than *absolutely necessary*. This could lead to the defence becoming more restricted in its ambit and, therefore, the pressure for the introduction of a special defence could become irresistible (see Chapter 7).

Some will regard uncertainty as a necessary prerequisite to moving the law forward, and it is also true that the frontiers of criminality are continually moving. However, it represents a significant departure from the view that the law should be a pre-established and well known body of rules that governs our behaviour and which clearly tells us what we may or may not do. It transgresses one of the justifications for punishment, which is that, because ignorance of the law is no defence, the law should be accessible, certain and easily knowable.

Richard Buxton ('The Human Rights Act and the substantive criminal law' [2000] Crim LR 331) tells us that there are two types are of reason why certainty is desirable in the criminal law. First, the citizen is entitled to know what he can or cannot do and, as such, is entitled to be protected from the arbitrariness of State action that must 'attend punishment for breaches of a law that is erratic in its operation'. Secondly, uncertainty in, or difficulty of access to, the criminal law leads to unpredictability in the outcome of criminal trials, which in turn extends the length of trials and increases expense.

The answer, suggests Buxton, is a long overdue criminal code:

> [There is an] almost universal desire that the present jumble of ancient statutes, more modern accretions to them, and acres of judicial pronouncements, should be replaced by a criminal code that would set out the criminal law in rational, accessible and modern language.

Why might the criminal law in many areas be considered a disgrace? Some of the more important reasons are:

- judicial law making;

- the role of the House of Lords as the final appellate court;

- lack of general agreement as to the purpose of the criminal law; and

- inadequate machinery for law reform.

1.3 Judicial law making

The late Professor Glanville Williams was of the opinion that judges are strongly influenced by their own ideas of what conduct should or should not be allowed and thus engage in extending and creating new law (*Textbook of Criminal Law*, 2nd edn, 1983, p 14). In some ways, of course, this creative characteristic is inherent in the common law and can be a force for positive social change. Consider for example the decision in *R* (1991), where the House of Lords changed the existing law and held for the first time that a husband was capable, in law, of raping his wife (see Chapter 10). Whilst this decision to overturn a rule of law dating back 300 years was accepted as being long overdue, only weeks before the House made its landmark ruling, the Law Commission was of the view that such a significant deviation from the current law should require legislative intervention (Law Commission, Working Paper 116, para 2.08).

It should also be understood that much of this law making is directed at people who would be regarded as seriously anti-social in any society, for example, people who devise new methods of stealing other people's money using new technology. But the problem still remains that the judges, particularly senior judges, regularly step beyond the bounds of their legitimate law making powers and create uncertainty in the law (consider, for example, the House of Lords cases of *Metropolitan Police Commissioner v Caldwell* (1981), in Chapter 3; *Shivpuri* (1986), in Chapter 5; and *Gomez* (1993), in Chapter 8). It is also far from clear whether judges, as opposed to Parliament or law reform agencies, are qualified or equipped to engage in law reform. They are not for most purposes accountable for the results of their decisions; they have little if any training in the social policy and economic implications of their decisions; and these issues will almost certainly not have been fully argued before the court prior to the decision. Contrast this style of law making with that adopted by the Law Commission, where their carefully considered final report will usually have been preceded by a detailed consultation paper distributed to all parties with an interest in the criminal justice system. The comments received will inform the final report, which will then, if all goes well, be subjected to detailed parliamentary scrutiny.

But what of the rules of precedent and statutory interpretation – surely they prevent judicial law making? In theory, the rules should prevent judicial law making but, in practice, they are only partly successful. In *C (A Minor) v DPP* (1995), the Divisional Court had overturned an ancient rule of law to the effect that before a child aged between 10 and 14 years could be found guilty of committing a crime the prosecution had to prove that the child knew that the act was 'seriously wrong'. The court decided that this rule no longer applied since it had become outdated in the changed conditions of modern society. The House of Lords reversed this decision. Lord Lowry held that such an important change should only be made by Parliament. He referred to five 'aids to navigation' for judges tempted to embark on the uncertain sea of judicial law making. Judges should be cautious:

- where the solution is doubtful;

- where Parliament has declined to legislate;

- where the matter is not purely legal but involves disputed social policy;

- where intervention involves setting aside fundamental doctrine; or

- where a change would not be sure to produce finality or certainty.

According to these criteria, much judicial law making in recent years indicates that the judges were lacking in caution! Little wonder then that Lord Mackay of Clashfern, then Lord Chancellor, still felt the need publicly to caution judges against taking it on themselves to overcome defects in the law. His view is that the judge's duty is 'to apply the law as he finds it, not to seek to rectify perceived inadequacies by the use of creative interpretation ... when deficiencies in the law become apparent it is for Parliament to respond ...' ((1997) *The Times*, 14 March).

Of course, judges often need to interpret the words of a statute because the words are ambiguous or unclear. Here, it is perfectly legitimate for the court to consider the legislative purpose, having regard to parliamentary materials, providing, according to Lord Browne-Wilkinson in the House of Lords' case of *Pepper v Hart* (1993), that:

(a) [the] legislation is ambiguous or obscure, or leads to an absurdity;

(b) the material relied upon consists of one or more statements by a minister or other promoter of the Bill, together if necessary with such other parliamentary material as is necessary to understand such statements, and their effect;

(c) the statements relied on are clear.

Courts may, and frequently do, consult reports of the Law Commission and other law reform agencies to discover the state of pre-existing law and the mischief which the statute was designed to remedy. If this fails to resolve the doubt then the benefit of any significant ambiguity will be given to the defendant (*AG's Reference (No 1 of 1988)* (1989)).

1.4   The role of the House of Lords as the final appellate court

The House of Lords is in a unique position to influence and shape the law because all the appeals before it must concern matters of general public importance (s 34 of the Criminal Appeal Act 1968) and the purpose of the appeal is not, therefore, confined to dispensing justice in the individual case. And yet one leading academic has categorised the House as having 'a dismal record in criminal cases' (Smith, JC [1981] Crim LR 392) and a second has called for its criminal jurisdiction to be abolished (Professor Glanville Williams [1981] Crim LR 580).

One of the primary aims of the House of Lords ought to be to produce certainty in the law. But can it do this when there might be up to five contradictory speeches? Look, for example, at their Lordships' decisions in the important cases of *Reid* (1992) concerned with the meaning of 'recklessness'; and *Hyam v DPP* (1975) concerned with the meaning of 'intention'. Try to ascertain the *ratio decidendi*. You will find this a formidable task as have many other students, lawyers, academics and, yes, judges. However, it would be wrong to suggest that the House is never unanimous in its decision making. The specific intent rule in respect of the defence of drunkenness was upheld by seven judges in *DPP v Majewski* (1976), and the House in *Woollin* (1998) was unanimous in allowing the defendant's appeal after a misdirection by the trial judge as to the meaning of 'intention' in the law of murder. The latter case is interesting because two of the five Law Lords, while agreeing that the appeal should be allowed, did not go so far as to endorse the sentiments of Lords Steyn and Hope who delivered the major speeches. This, though, should not be taken as a sign that the authority of the decision is in any way diminished.

Another problem facing the House of Lords is if counsel choose not to rely on or indeed argue a particular point of public importance because they believe their chance of success to be greater by relying upon another point. The result might be that a good opportunity to clarify the law on an important matter may be lost.

But the fundamental problem, according to Professor ATH Smith, 'is their failure to articulate goals for the criminal process [and] that their Lordships' collective ambivalence of purpose has frustrated a coherent treatment of the issues of general public importance' ((1984) 47 MLR 133). He contrasts their role with that of the American Law Institutes' Model Penal Code (1962, Art 11.02) which clearly states the objectives of criminal law in the US:

(a) to forbid and prevent conduct that unjustifiably and inexcusably inflicts or threatens substantial harm to individual or public interests;

(b) to subject to public control persons whose conduct indicates that they are disposed to commit crimes;

(c) to safeguard conduct that is without fault from condemnation as criminal;

(d) to give fair warning of the nature of the conduct declared to be an offence;

(e) to differentiate on reasonable grounds between serious and minor offences.

> By comparison with this, the response of the House of Lords has been one-dimensional. It tends to see itself as being above all the guardian of the public interest whose function is to prevent harm to the public. Where this purpose conflicts with others identified by the Model Penal Code, the interests of the defendant himself, or the demands of logic and principle, the House of Lords will act so as to protect its conception of social welfare [p 143].

The result is that the House of Lords has not managed to identify purposes other than the loosely defined 'protection of society'.

1.5   The purpose of the criminal law

It may be easy to criticise senior judges but does society itself have a clear idea as to the aims or purpose of the criminal law, particularly in the area of morality? Two opposing views are traditionally argued. First, the 'libertarian' view which is that self-protection and to prevent harm to others is the only justification for interfering with the liberty of others (see JS Mills's essay 'On liberty' (1859), 1974, Harmondsworth: Penguin). Lord Wolfenden's *Report of the Committee on Homosexual Offences and Prostitution* (Cmnd 247, 1957) broadly agreed when it recommended that homosexual acts between consenting adults in private should no longer be a criminal offence. Wolfenden thought that the function of the law was to 'preserve public order and decency, to protect the citizen from that which is offensive or injurious and to provide sufficient safeguards against exploitation and the corruption of others, particularly those who are especially vulnerable' (para 13). The Committee's view was that there remains a realm of private morality and immorality with which the criminal law ought not to concern itself.

Contrast the libertarian approach with that of the 'authoritarian' view as represented by Lord Devlin, in *The Enforcement of Morals*, 1965, Oxford: Oxford UP. Lord Devlin felt that even apart from self-protection, 'there are acts so gross and outrageous that they must be prevented at any cost', and that 'the suppression of vice is as much the law's business as the suppression of subversive activities'. He was, in effect, criticising Wolfenden's conception of a private morality with which the criminal law ought not to be concerned.

Let us examine some of the cases where this problem has presented itself. In *Shaw v DPP* (1961), the appellant published a booklet with the object of assisting prostitutes. It contained the names, addresses, 'phone numbers and description of various specialist perversions in which particular prostitutes were willing to engage. Mr Shaw had been found guilty at the Old Bailey of, *inter alia*, 'conspiracy to corrupt public morals'. He now appealed on the grounds that such a crime did not exist! In the result he was unsuccessful and his conviction was upheld. Lord Simonds, with whom the majority agreed, was:

> ... at a loss to understand how it can be said either that the law does not recognise a conspiracy to corrupt public morals or that, though there may not be an exact precedent for such a conspiracy as this case reveals, it does not fall fairly within the general words by which it is described. The fallacy in the argument that was addressed to us lay in the attempt to exclude from the scope of general words acts well calculated to corrupt public morals just because they had not been committed or had not been brought to the notice of the court before. It is not thus that the common law has developed. We are, perhaps, more accustomed to hear this matter discussed on the question whether such and such a transaction is contrary to public policy. At once the

controversy arises. On the one hand, it is said that it is not possible in the 20th century for the court to create a new head of public policy, on the other, it is said that this is but a new example of a well-established head. In the sphere of criminal law, I entertain no doubt that there remains in the courts of law a residual power to enforce the supreme and fundamental purpose of the law, to conserve not only the safety and order but also the moral welfare of the state, and that it is their duty to guard it against attacks which may be the more insidious because they are novel and unprepared for. That is the broad head (call it public policy it you wish) within which the present indictment falls [p 452].

Lord Simonds was, in other words, reserving the right of the judges to expand the frontiers of criminality when, in their opinion, the circumstances so demanded.

Lord Reid, on the other hand, disagreed:

Even if there is still a vestigial power of this kind, it ought not, in my view, to be used unless there appears to be general agreement that the offence to which it is applied ought to be criminal if committed by an individual. Notoriously there are wide differences of opinion today how far the law ought to punish immoral acts which are not done in the face of the public. Some think that the law already goes too far, some that it does not go far enough. Parliament is the proper place, and I am firmly of opinion the only proper place, to settle that. When there is sufficient support from public opinion, Parliament does not hesitate to intervene. Where Parliament fears to tread it is not for the courts to rush in.

... In my judgment, this House is in no way bound and ought not to sanction the extension of 'public mischief' to any new field, and certainly not if such extension would be in any way controversial. Public mischief is the criminal counterpart of public policy, and the criminal law ought to be even more hesitant than the civil law in founding on it in some new aspect [p 457].

He was, however, in a minority of one.

Since this case, the judges have denied themselves the power to create new offences. In *Knuller v DPP* (1972), the House of Lords denied the existence of any residual power they may have had to create new offences – all they could do was recognise the applicability of established offences to new circumstances to which they were relevant (Lord Simon of Glaisdale, p 932). In addition the House of Lords has acknowledged its power to create new defences (see Lord Mustill's comments in *Kingston* (1994)). However, this is the formal position. In practice we have already seen that matters are not quite as clear as the above cases would have us believe. In the case of *R* (1991), the House of Lords still felt able to declare that a man was capable in law of raping his wife – a classic example of judicial law making.

1.6   A way forward – codification of the law?

Most other common law and civil jurisdictions have long accepted that the judicial process is unsuitable for major law reform and that many of the problems that we have examined would be most suitably remedied by the comprehensive codification of the criminal law. The Criminal Law Reform Committee was established in 1959 and the Law Commission in 1965 to keep the law under review and to suggest reform, but much of their work was piecemeal and failed to address the problem of judicial uncertainty. A major event in the history of English criminal law occurred, therefore, in 1985 when the Law Commission produced a first draft of a proposed codification of the law written by a team of academics headed by Professor JC Smith. It set out the aims of codification as being to improve the accessibility, comprehensibility, consistency and certainty of the criminal law (Vol 1, para 2.1). The (proposed) code would do this by:

- bringing within one set of covers, most of the important offences;

- establishing a dictionary of key fault terms (for example, 'intention', 'recklessness') which Parliament henceforth would be presumed to have intended unless they indicated to the contrary;

- providing a draft Bill encompassing its recommendations;

- incorporating not only the existing law but also recommendations for reform made by law reform bodies.

The team attempted to draft the code in such a way as to prevent the judiciary creating new offences or resurrecting old one's but yet allowing them to extend the law providing the extension stayed within the boundaries of the proscriptive clause. In other words, it clearly indicated to the judiciary just how far they could go in defining the frontiers of criminality when dealing with novel forms of behaviour. The importance of the proposal is, therefore, that it:

> ... makes a symbolic statement about the constitutional relationship of Parliament and the courts, it requires a judicial deference to the legislative will greater than that which the courts have often shown to isolated and sporadic pieces of legislation [Vol 1, para 2.2].

The Law Commission took the view that it would not be unduly restrictive and hinder the development of the common law because evidence from other jurisdictions indicated that judges still retained a considerable amount of flexibility within the parameters of the code's provisions.

A period of consultation followed the publication of the proposal which included the establishment of eight circuit scrutiny groups each headed by a circuit judge and whose membership included representatives of those who were likely to be professional users of a code. The weight of opinion was strongly in favour of codification. The eventual result of the consultation was the publication in 1989 of *A Criminal Code for England and Wales* in two volumes (Law Com 177). This was described by the editor of the *Criminal Law Review* as 'an impressive piece of work' ([1989] Crim LR 393). The proposals would, if implemented, cover about 90–95% of the work of the criminal courts.

The proposed code was broadly welcomed by most of those involved in the criminal justice system although, as might be expected with such an ambitious exercise, criticisms have been made by a number of commentators. Much of it is to the effect that it goes further than merely codifying existing law and encompasses a substantial body of law reform. The Law Commission used as the basis for its proposals for reform its own previous reports, those of the Criminal Law Revision Committee and the Butler Committee on Mentally Abnormal Offenders (1975). It decided to incorporate reforms (Vol 1, para 3.30):

- when there was an inconsistency which represented a conflict of policies and where a choice had to be made to produce a coherent law;

- where otherwise it would be restating 'rules of an arbitrary nature fulfilling no rational purpose';

- where there had been a recent official report recommending reforms.

A second criticism is that the Code team may have maximised the certainty of language and minimised the inventiveness of judges (Wells, C, 'Restatement or reform' [1986] Crim LR 314).

So far as the future of the codification project is concerned, this will, inevitably depend upon the will of Parliament to devote sufficient time to debating the proposals. It has shown a distinct unwillingness to do this. The Commission's response has been to produce 'mini-codifications' in relation to specific areas of criminal law in the hope that this will be more attractive to Parliament. In the main, they have omitted some of the more controversial proposals. See, for example:

- *Legislating the Criminal Code: Offences Against the Person and General Principles*, Law Com 218, 1993;

- *Legislating the Criminal Code: Intoxication and Criminal Liability*, Law Com 229, 1995;

- *Legislating the Criminal Code: Involuntary Manslaughter*, Law Com 237, 1996.

This decision by the Law Commission has been described by Professor ATH Smith as 'a failure of nerve' ([1992] Crim LR 397) whilst Simon Gardner, writing in relation to the offences against the person proposals, has criticised them as involving 'a substantial but selective agenda of change in the law' ((1992) 55 MLR 839).

These developments highlight a fundamental problem with criminal law reform. Brooke LJ (as he now is) vividly described his experience upon assuming the chairmanship of the Law Commission:

> I must describe the scene that confronted me in January 1993. The Commission had an enviable reputation among the cognoscenti for the quality of its proposals for eliminating unfairness and illogicalities in the law. Sometimes its reports involved policy proposals that were unacceptable to the government of the day, or were years ahead of their time. But much more often its reports – and those of the Criminal Law Revision Committee – were being shelved because there was no effective machinery for taking them forward, and because there was no general perception, particularly among non-lawyers, that there was anything much wrong with the criminal law that needed reform, let alone that large sums of money were being wasted, and countless unfairnesses perpetrated, because important parts of our basic criminal law were so difficult to access. There were a lot of powerful autonomous bodies each parading their own views, a general antipathy to intellectual solutions or to anything resembling a carefully co-ordinated approach to some fairly intractable problems, and above all, nobody seemed to be accepting personal responsibility for sorting out the muddle [[1995] Crim LR 913, p 915].

The House of Commons has no dedicated mechanism for examining proposals for criminal law reform on a routine basis. This is because the House of Commons regards almost every such proposal as *prima facie* controversial. As the pressure on parliamentary time is so great, the result is that, as Brooke LJ put it, 'no government is ever likely to put aside much of this precious time for technical law reform Bills, however desperately they are needed by those who have to make the criminal law work, since they will win few votes and advance few ministers' reputations' ([1995] Crim LR 913, p 918). The Commission's own preference is for a type of 'fast track' procedure for dealing with its reports in the form of a joint committee of both Houses of Parliament. This would combine the legal expertise of the House of Lords with the political considerations present in the Commons. Until this occurs we can only agree with the comment:

> ... the Law Commission has produced a steady flow of Bills designed to bring order to the ragged edges of the legal system. Most deserve speedy implementation; all deserve scrutiny. The neglect of the Commission's labours does justice and the taxpayer, a disservice [(1997) *The Times*, 14 March].

A clear example of the dilatoriness of government is to be found in respect of the Law Commission's *Report on Involuntary Manslaughter* (Law Com 237, 1996). It is only recently that the Government's response appeared in print. The Home Office Consultation Paper, *Reforming the Law on Involuntary Manslaughter: The Government's Proposals* (April 2000), invites views on a number of proposals emanating from the Law Commission Report of 1996. What is somewhat galling is the fact that the Government appears to accept the Law Commission's Report in principle and agrees with the majority of the proposals. Why, therefore, take four years to publish a consultation paper? The Editorial to the July 2000 issue of the *Criminal Law Review* comments:

> We trust that it will not take another four years for decisions to be made about matters which the Home Office paper seeks consultation.

The speed at which the Home Office worked on this area of law is in stark contrast to the Law Commission's response to the Home Office's request in April 1998 for it to examine the law on fraud and make recommendations for its improvement, while making it comprehensible to juries. The Commission produced a Consultation Paper, *Legislating the Criminal Code: Fraud and Deception* (Law Com 155, 1999, London: The Stationery Office) in spring 1999.

We are no nearer a criminal code in this country than we were at the time of writing the last edition of this book. Now, there are voices being raised advocating the need for a code of criminal procedure (see Spencer, JR, 'The case for a code of criminal procedure' [2000] Crim LR 519). As Spencer says:

> In many respects, the case for a code of criminal procedure is the same as the case for a code of criminal law. Criminal procedure and substantive criminal law are in reality two sides of the same coin. Together, they contain the rules under which the State can strip the citizen of his reputation, his property, his liberty and – until recently – his life ... you would expect these two areas of law to be clearly formulated and made publicly accessible in codes.

One welcome innovation in this period has been the creation of the Criminal Cases Review Commission, set up in April 1997 with the remit to investigate alleged miscarriages of justice. There is evidence to suggest that the Commission has been 'widely accepted, in theory and in practice ... [and is] ... a great improvement on its predecessors, the C3 Department of the Home Office and an equivalent unit in the Northern Ireland Office' (James, A, Taylor, N and Walker, C, 'Criminal Cases Review Commission: economy, effectiveness and justice' [2000] Crim LR 140).

1.7 The decision to criminalise conduct

This is a complex matter. Professor Ashworth's view is that 'political opportunism and power, both linked to the prevailing political culture of the country' is the main determinant (*Principles of Criminal Law*, 2nd edn, 1995, Oxford: Clarendon, p 55) but traditionally commentators have asked two questions:

- is the conduct *harmful* to individuals or to society?; and

- is the conduct *immoral*?

If the answer to both questions is 'yes' then the conduct is considered *prima facie* suitable for criminalisation. But this traditional view is too simplistic to be helpful to the student because some acts are both immoral and harmful and yet have not been criminalised (for example, adultery), whilst others are neither immoral nor harmful and yet are crimes (for example, failure to wear a seat belt and some other 'victimless' crimes).

The law does not criminalise all immoral acts because:

- difficulties of proof (many such acts occur in private and in the absence of independent witnesses);

- difficulties of definition (take the example of the husband whose wife deserted him many years ago and who has now found a new partner. If he engages in sexual intercourse, do we really wish to see him punished as an 'adulterer'?);

- rules of morality are sometimes difficult to enforce without infringing the individual's right to privacy;

- the civil law sometimes provides an adequate remedy to the parties affected by the conduct (for example, the deserted wife);

- in any event, how do we ascertain prevailing 'moral opinion' given the deep divisions within modern society?

Lord Devlin has argued that an act should be criminalised if it incurs 'the deep disgust' of the right-minded individual (*Enforcement of Morals*, 1965, Oxford: Oxford UP) but as HLA Hart has pointed out: what if the right minded man's opinion is based upon ignorance, superstition or misunderstanding? (*Law, Liberty and Morality*, 1963, Oxford: Oxford UP.) It is arguable that if Lord Devlin's view prevailed law making powers would, in effect, be delegated to the proprietors of popular tabloid newspapers – a horrible thought! On the other hand, if the law makers move too far away from the values of the 'right minded man' we face the danger of a loss of respect for the rule of law itself amongst the general populace – an equally horrible thought!

Perhaps the most useful and practical contribution to the debate about what conduct ought to be criminalised has been made by the American academic Herbert Packer. He suggests the following criteria in addition to immorality and harm being caused to a person or property (*The Limits of the Criminal Sanction*, 1968, Stanford, CA: Stanford UP):

- most people view the conduct as socially threatening;

- the conduct is not condoned by a significant section of society;

- criminalisation is not inconsistent with the goals of punishment;

- suppressing the conduct will not inhibit socially desirable conduct;

- it may be dealt with through even-handed and non-discriminatory enforcement;

- controlling the behaviour will not expose the criminal justice system to severe qualitative or quantitive strains;

- there are no reasonable alternatives to the criminal sanction for dealing with it;

- the costs of enforcement are not prohibitive.

Look at the case of *Brown* (1993), in Chapter 10, where the House of Lords was called upon to decide whether men engaged in homosexual sado-masochistic acts could, by their consent, give each other a valid defence to charges of assault occasioning actual bodily harm contrary to s 47 of the Offences Against the Person Act 1861. In this case, consent was present, there was no permanent injury, no medical attention sought, no complaint to the police, the acts were carried out in private and there was no profit motive. Notice how the issue divided the House of Lords with three judges deciding that the consent given was no defence to such a charge but with two judges dissenting and regarding the acts as essentially a matter of private sexual relations for which a valid consent could be given (depending upon the degree of harm inflicted). Note that all five judges had little difficulty in thinking that professional boxers were capable of giving each other a valid consent to charges of assault even though the principal purpose of a boxing match is to render the opponent unconscious and/or inflict grievous bodily harm! A useful exercise is for the student to apply Packer's framework to the facts of *Brown* in order to determine whether the majority or minority view is to be preferred. We wonder whether the reader agrees with us that near the margins of human behaviour the decision to criminalise particular acts is random.

1.8   The definition of a crime

Professor Ashworth has written: 'The chief concern of the criminal law is seriously anti-social behaviour. But the notion that English criminal law is only concerned with serious anti-social acts must be abandoned as one considers the broader canvas of criminal liability. There are many offences for which any element of stigma is diluted almost to vanishing point' (*Principles of Criminal Law*, 3rd edn, 1999, Oxford: Clarendon, p 1). What, then, are the unique characteristics of a crime? How do we define a particular act as being criminal? Believe it or not this can be a very difficult question to answer. The act may or may not cause harm or be immoral. It is difficult to isolate unique characteristics other than procedural differences which exist between criminal and civil proceedings. For example, any citizen can, in general, bring a private criminal prosecution even though that particular citizen has not suffered personally as a result of the act whilst in civil cases usually only the 'victim' may sue. Professor Kenny has, therefore, defined a crime as, 'an act capable of being followed by criminal proceedings having one of the types of outcome (punishment, etc) known to follow these proceedings' (*Outlines of Criminal Law*, 15th edn, 1936, Cambridge: Cambridge UP, p 16). Kenny would urge us to look at the statute to try to identify a procedural issue indicating whether the prescribed act constituted a criminal or civil wrong. If, for example, the statute indicated that the matter was to be heard in the Crown Court or that the remedy was a fine or term of imprisonment then this would be a fair indication that it was a crime. The defendant would thus be entitled to the benefit of the rules of evidence, rules of procedure, legal aid, rights of appeal, etc, applicable to the criminal law.

Nicola Lacey and Celia Wells, in *Reconstructing the Criminal Law* (2nd edn, 1998, London: Butterworths), argue that the:

> ... intangible phenomenon of *'public opinion'* and, perhaps more importantly, perceptions of that phenomenon, are enormously influential. The politicians who are involved in the legislative process are ultimately accountable to the populace and are therefore liable to be influenced by what they think are prevailing opinions [p 63].

The willingness of various interest groups in the UK to take to the streets in the fuel tax demonstrations in September 2000 indicates that the public will not always exert their influence through the accepted constitutional channels. At the time of writing, it is not clear whether or not the Government will change the law in order to reduce the amount of tax on fuel but, if they were to do so, it would be as a direct response to the public opinion voiced by the demonstrators.

1.9   Classification of offences: explanation of terms

Throughout this book reference will be made to terms unique to the criminal law. It is important that the student understands them because that understanding will give an enhanced appreciation of the nature of the crime the defendant is facing and of the procedure which determines the court in which the case will be heard. This in turn will determine the appeal procedure. The majority of criminal law reports are reports of appeals.

Most crimes are, today, statutory offences although many of them have their origins in the common law. Surprisingly perhaps, some of the most serious crimes such as murder and manslaughter are still common law offences.

For procedural purposes crimes are classified, according to the Sched 1 to the Interpretation Act 1978, as:

(a) 'indictable offence' means an offence which ... is triable on indictment;

(b) 'summary offence' means an offence which is triable only summarily;

(c) 'offence triable either way' means an offence which ... is triable either on indictment or summarily.

Generally, *summary offences* are the least serious and can only be heard in the local magistrates' court and without a jury. *Indictable* (pronounced inditeable) *offences* are the most serious and can only be heard before a judge and jury in the Crown Court. *Either way offences* are those which are capable of being tried either in the magistrates' court or Crown Court. They tend to be offences which encompass a very broad range of criminal behaviour. Take theft for example. At one end of the spectrum of seriousness, this includes the 12 year old who steals a packet of sweets from a supermarket; at the other end, it could include a multi-million pound theft from a bank by a defendant with a lengthy criminal record. It would be incongruous if the proceedings which followed were the same in both cases. Hence theft is triable either way. The decision as to venue is made by the magistrates' court having regard to all the circumstances of the case and the wishes of the prosecution and the accused (s 17 of the Magistrates' Courts Act 1980). However, if the magistrates decide to retain jurisdiction over the case (and deny the accused the right to a trial by jury) the accused must consent. Thus, the accused can insist on a trial by jury. The Divisional Court has issued detailed guidelines setting out the factors which may make an either way offence more suitable for trial on indictment. They should usually be heard in the magistrates' court unless they contain various kinds of aggravating factors or the maximum sentence of the magistrates' court is insufficient. This is currently generally six months imprisonment and/or £5,000 fine (see *Practice Note (National Mode of Trial Guidelines) (1990)*).

In May 1999, the Home Secretary announced that he intended to abolish the right of the defendant to elect jury trial for a number of 'either way' offences. Perhaps understandably, given the long standing nature of the right, the proposals have encountered significant opposition from lawyers and civil liberties groups. At the time of writing, the proposal has not become law and is unlikely to do so.

Section 1 of the Criminal Justice Act (CJA) 1967 abolished the distinction between *felonies* (serious offences) and *misdemeanours* (less serious offences) and provided that both should be governed by the law previously applicable to misdemeanours. This is most significant in relation to secondary participation in crime which will be dealt with in Chapter 4. The CJA 1967 introduced a new classification of arrestable and non-arrestable offences, that is, offences in relation to which a power of arrest exists without a warrant and those which do require a warrant. Section 2 has now been replaced by s 24 of the Police and Criminal Evidence Act 1984, which defines an arrestable offence as those offences for which the sentence is fixed by law (murder, treason, piracy) or for which a person can be sentenced to five years imprisonment or more.

1.10   Rights to appeal

It is important to understand the appeal process because much of the criminal law has been established by the results of appeal decisions. Of particular importance are appeals from the Crown Court to the Court of Appeal where the grounds of the appeal may be that the trial judge failed accurately to explain the law to the jury in the summing-up (the 'direction' to the jury) at the end of the case.

The right to appeal and the grounds of appeal depend upon the trial venue.

Summary trials

The defendant or the prosecution can appeal *by way of case stated* to the Divisional Court of the Queen's Bench Division on the ground that the magistrates' court exceeded its jurisdiction or, more commonly, misunderstood or misapplied the law. The appeal will normally be heard by two or three Courts of Appeal or High Court judges. Either side may further appeal to the House of Lords if the Divisional Court certifies the point of law involved as being of general public importance and either the Divisional Court or the House of Lords grants leave to appeal. Cases in the House of Lords are normally decided by five Lords of Appeal in Ordinary (Law Lords).

A defendant may also appeal against conviction to the Crown Court which sits for these purposes with a single circuit judge assisted by (usually) two lay magistrates. There is no jury involved in the proceedings.

Trials on indictment

The defendant can appeal to the Court of Appeal (Criminal Division) only on the ground that the conviction was 'unsafe' (s 2(1) of the Criminal Appeal Act 1995) and only with the permission of the trial judge or leave of the Court of Appeal. The appeal may be heard by two or three judges of the Court of Appeal but currently is more likely to heard by one Court of Appeal judge together with one judge from the High Court and one senior circuit judge. If the defendant was acquitted at the original trial, the Attorney General may appeal to the Court of Appeal for a ruling on a point of law although the defendant's acquittal stands. This procedure accounts for the large number of important cases in this book with references such as *AG's Reference (No 1 of 1992)* (1993). The Attorney General may also appeal to the Court of Appeal if he considers that a sentence given at the Crown Court was unduly lenient and wrong in law. The court is then in a position to pronounce a 'guideline sentence' which trial judges thereafter are expected to follow (s 35 of the CJA 1988). It is also possible for a person convicted at the Crown Court to appeal against the sentence imposed. However, leave to appeal is required and the Court of

Appeal may substitute any sentence that would have been available to the Crown Court.

Either side may further appeal to the House of Lords on a point of law if the Court of Appeal has certified the point as being of general public importance and either the Court of Appeal or the House of Lords has granted leave to appeal.

The Criminal Cases Review Commission was established under the Criminal Appeal Act 1995 and its role is to investigate cases involving an alleged miscarriage of justice and to refer the case, if appropriate, to the Court of Appeal.

1.11   Burden of proof and standard of proof

It is a fundamental principle of English law that a person is innocent of any criminal offence until proven guilty. The *burden of proving* the defendant's guilt falls upon the prosecution who must prove to the satisfaction of the jury (or magistrates') that the accused is guilty *beyond reasonable doubt* (this is referred to as the *standard of proof*). It is not for the accused person to prove his or her innocence and the accused is entitled to the benefit of any doubt as to his or her guilt. As Lord Sankey LC stated in the leading case of *Woolmington v DPP* (1935):

> No matter what the charge or where the trial, the principle that the prosecution must prove the guilt of the prisoner is part of the common law of England and no attempt to whittle it down can be entertained [p 482].

Ashworth and Blake have argued that 'from time to time English judges have articulated fundamental principles which they believe to underlie criminal law and procedure' ([1996] Crim LR 306). These include the privilege against self-incrimination, the need for the prosecution to prove a guilty mind and, of course, the 'golden thread' acknowledged by Viscount Sankey that the prosecution must prove the prisoner's guilt. However, it should be noted that, in a parliamentary democracy, any of these fundamental rights can be withdrawn, and Ashworth and Blake consider that: 'Developments in recent years have cast grave doubt on the existence of these "fundamental principles".'

However, if the defendant raises a defence to the charge, for example, provocation, duress, self-defence, the law usually places an *evidential burden* on him to provide some credible evidence to substantiate the claim. At this point, the prosecution is then required to prove 'beyond reasonable doubt' that the defendant is not in fact entitled to the benefit of the defence. In a small number of exceptional cases (chiefly, insanity and diminished responsibility – see Chapters 7 and 6 respectively) the law places the burden of proof squarely on the shoulders of the defendant to prove that he or she was suffering from this affliction but the standard of proof here is that used in the civil courts, 'on a balance of probabilities' (*Carr-Briant* (1943)).

1.12   The trial and the role of the judge and jury

The trial commences with the prosecution presenting its evidence. This might be a combination of live witnesses, scientific evidence (for example, finger prints) and documentary evidence (for example, a written statement made by the defendant to a police officer). At the conclusion of the prosecution's case, the defence is entitled to argue that it has 'no case to answer' because the prosecution has failed to make out even a *prima facie* case. If the judge (or magistrates') decide that a case has in fact been made out, the defence then presents its own evidence and again this might be a combination of witnesses and documentary evidence. At the conclusion of this part of the trial, the judge's task is then to 'sum up' for the jury. This involves summarising the evidence from both sides and highlighting those parts most relevant to the jury's task of deciding the guilt or innocence of the accused. This would include identifying weak or contradictory evidence which had been presented during the trial. The judge will then explain the relevant principles of law to the jury. For example, if the accused has admitted killing the victim but has raised the defence of provocation, the judge will explain the legal constituents of this defence. As Chapter 6 explains, this will involve outlining s 3 of the Homicide Act 1957 and several leading cases which have interpreted and clarified the meaning of this defence. The judge will then ask the jury to retire and reach a conclusion on the factual evidence they have heard and then to relate this to the legal issues that have been laid before them. If the jury find the defendant guilty, they are discharged by the judge who then goes on to decide the appropriate sentence. The jury play no part in the sentencing process.

1.13   Approaching the study of criminal law

We suggest that the best method to analyse particular crimes and to answer problem questions is as follows:

*   carefully examine the statutory definition of the offence;

*   identify the different elements separating them into *actus reus* (see Chapter 2) and *mens rea* (see Chapter 3);

*   identify any further explanatory provisions in the statute relating to each element (for example, the statute may define particular words);

*   examine the leading case(s) in relation to both elements to ensure a sound understanding of how the law is currently defined and applied by the courts;

- consider whether any defence may be available to the defendant. This might be a general defence arguable in relation to all crimes, for example, insanity, or relevant only to a specific crime, for example, provocation can only be a defence to murder.

There are dangers if the student fails to adopt a structured approach to the study of criminal law. First, it is easy to fall into the trap of deciding upon the defendant's guilt or innocence in advance of the analysis, usually on the basis of 'instinct', revulsion or 'gut reaction'. This may, or may not, be in accordance with the law. Secondly, a failure to carry out this basic research may mean that the law is misunderstood, is out of date or that an important part of the problem is ignored, for example, the existence of a defence.

Take theft for example. The basic definition is found in s 1(1) of the Theft Act (TA) 1968: 'A person is guilty of theft if he dishonestly appropriates property belonging to another with the intention of permanently depriving the other of it ...' Consider the question: 'Is it possible in law to steal one's own property?' 'Instinct' and, on the face of it, s 1 would both indicate that the answer must be no. However, s 5(1) of the TA 1968 defines 'belonging to another' as follows: 'Property shall be regarded as belonging to any person having possession or control of it, or having in it any proprietary right or interest ...'

The answer to the question is clearly not as simple as might have first been thought. Further research will reveal the Court of Appeal decision of *Turner (No 2)* (1971). In this case, the appellant had taken his car to a garage for repairs. The repairs were completed and the car left outside the garage overnight awaiting collection by the owner. Unknown to the garage proprietor, Mr Brown, the appellant had a spare set of keys which he used to remove his car from the garage without Mr Brown's consent and having omitted to pay for the repairs which had been carried out. He was found guilty of theft by a jury and the Court of Appeal dismissed his appeal. This conclusion was only possible because the words of s 1 of the TA 1968 were qualified by s 5 of the TA 1968.

How does one identify the different elements of the crime and divide them into the *actus reus* and *mens rea*? A full analysis of these terms will be found in Chapters 2 and 3 respectively. In outline, however, the *actus reus* consists of those aspects of the definition of the crime which relate to the defendant's conduct or the consequences or circumstances of the defendant's act. *Mens rea* refers directly or indirectly to the mental element which the prosecution must usually prove in relation to the defendant in order to secure a conviction. In relation to the basic definition of 'theft' contained in s 1 of the TA 1968:

Actus reus words are:

- appropriates; and

- property belonging to another.

Mens rea words are:

- dishonestly;

- intention of permanently depriving the other of it.

Do not forget to consider the possibility of a defence being available. The defendant may admit to having 'stolen' sweets from a local shop but what if he was intoxicated at the time he took the sweets? What if he was 11 years of age? What of the student in halls of residence who enters his best friend's room in order to borrow some sugar only to find the friend absent but the sugar bowl on the desk. If the student removes the sugar, is he guilty of theft or could he rely on s 2(1)(b) of the TA 1968 and claim that he appropriated the sugar, '... in the belief that he would have the [owner's] consent if the [owner] knew of the appropriation and the circumstances in which it had taken place?' (see Chapter 8 for the answer).

The message is clear: there is no substitute for a structured and methodical approach to the study of the criminal law. It is not enough merely to rely on a textbook.

1.14 Keeping up to date with the law

Most students find criminal law to be an exciting and challenging subject but it can also be frustrating at times as a result of its tendency to change very quickly as a consequence of new statutes and appellate decisions. The Law Commission has produced a large body of work in recent years and most commentators agree that its reports and consultation papers are of an excellent standard. They often provide a thorough and critical review of the law in a particular area, sometimes compare English law with that of other jurisdictions, and propose reforms. For the serious student or the practitioner who seeks a detailed appreciation of the criminal law, their reports and papers are essential reading. Throughout this book you will be referred to the work of the Law Commission. It is vital to keep abreast of current developments and the best method of doing this is by regularly perusing the *Criminal Law Review* published monthly and available in every university law library. It contains helpful case notes which not only analyse the decision in the case but often, in addition, compare and contrast the decision with the previous law and with the recommendations of law reform bodies such as the Law Commission. It also contains articles on current issues affecting the criminal law and the criminal justice system. The *Criminal Law Review* also appeals to judges, practising lawyers and other professionals with a serious interest in the criminal law.

There are often themes running through the pages of the *Criminal Law Review*. One that you should pay particular attention to is the impact on the criminal law of the Human Rights Act 1998, which came into force on 2 October

2000. The potential impact of the Act on the substantive criminal has already been much discussed by contributors to the *Review*, but ultimately it is the judges and politicians that will decide whether Arden J's provocative title to her article in the June 1999 issue proves to be prophetic ('Criminal law at the crossroads' [1999] Crim LR 439). Her view is that codification of the substantive criminal law offers the best way of ensuring compliance with the Human Rights Act 1998. She states:

> The criminal law faces a choice. The choice is between having a strategy and an overall vision of a well considered, consistent, coherent and modern criminal law on the one hand, and on the other hand patching up an area of law which is already seriously defective and out of date under a policy of mend and make do. The right choice is obvious. But it needs courage and political will. It needs the support of the judiciary and the profession. It will also take time and effort, but ... it is the only course that will lead to the real improvement in the criminal law that we would all like to see.

A new code for a new millennium? We wait in eager anticipation.

AN INTRODUCTION TO
THE STUDY OF CRIMINAL LAW

Criminal law in the 1990s

Criminal law should be certain, consistent and accessible. There is now widespread concern that the law satisfies none of these criteria. This is due in large measure to judicial law making, a lack of general agreement as to the purpose of criminal law and inadequate machinery for law reform. Codification of the law would largely meet these problems and the Law Commission published a proposed codification in 1989. The proposal had been preceded by widespread consultation with all those professionally involved in the criminal law. However, Parliament has failed to allocate time in order to consider codification and as a result the Law Commission has published a series of 'mini-codes' in the belief that they will be more appealing to politicians. Unfortunately, this tactic has also failed and proposals for law reform have been largely ignored during the 1990s.

Defining conduct as criminal

The decision to criminalise conduct is traditionally taken when a particular activity is both immoral and harmful to people or property. However, there are many exceptions and acts can be identified which meet both criteria and yet which are not classified as criminal. Conversely, other acts do not meet either criteria and yet are classed as criminal. It is in fact difficult to define unique characteristics of a 'crime' other than by reference to the nature of the proceedings which follow the commission of the act.

Classification of offences

The great majority of crimes are statutory offences and they are classified as being either indictable, summary or either way offences. This classification determines the court in which the case will be heard (and whether or not a jury will be involved) and any rights to appeal which may exist.

Burden of proof

It is important to understand what is meant by the burden of proof and the standard of proof and upon whom the burden is placed. This is particularly relevant when the defendant wishes to argue that he or she is entitled to the benefit of a defence. Similarly, it is important to understand the roles of the judge and jury in a trial and the terms used throughout this book to describe their role such as 'model direction' or the judge's 'summing up'.

Studying criminal law

A structured approach is provided for the study of this complex, fascinating but rapidly changing subject. This will lead the student away from the trap of deciding problem questions on the basis of 'instinct' and will ensure that the correct law is fully understood and applied to legal problems. In order to keep up to date students are urged to regularly consult the *Criminal Law Review* and the reports and consultation papers published by the Law Commission.

CHAPTER 2

ACTUS REUS

2.1 Introduction

The prosecution's task is to demonstrate to the jury (or magistrates) beyond reasonable doubt:

- that the defendant brought about the prohibited act, omission or state of affairs. This is called the *actus reus*;

- that the defendant did this with the state of mind prescribed by the definition of the crime. This is called the *mens rea*; and

- that the defendant is not entitled to the benefit of any defence which may have been argued on his or her behalf.

Traditionally, this is encapsulated in the Latin maxim, *actus non facit reum, nisi mens sit rea*, which means that an act does not make a person guilty of committing an offence unless the mind is legally blameworthy. The use of this expression has been criticised as likely to mislead those involved in the study and operation of the criminal law, not least by Lord Diplock in his speech in *Miller* (1983). He pointed out that as long ago as 1889 the eminent criminal lawyer Stephen J in *Tolson* 'condemned the phrase as likely to mislead ...'. Lord Diplock considered that 'it naturally suggests that, apart from all particular definitions of crimes, such a thing exists as a *"mens rea"*, or "guilty mind", which is always expressly or by implication involved in every definition. This is obviously not the case, for the mental elements of different crimes differ widely'. While acknowledging that Stephen J was criticising the phrase *mens rea* he believed that *actus reus* is equally liable to mislead since 'it suggests that some positive act on the part of the accused is needed to make him guilty of a crime and that a failure or omission to act is insufficient to give rise to criminal liability unless some express provision in the statute that creates the offence so provides' (p 979).

Lord Diplock thought it preferable to think and speak about the prohibited *conduct* of the defendant and his state of mind at the time of the conduct instead of speaking of *actus reus* and *mens rea*. However, these two expressions are now firmly established and commonly used by those professionally involved in the criminal law and they are a convenient way of referring to the differing requirements of the definitions of particular crimes. The Law Commission, in its (proposed) draft Criminal Code (*A Criminal Code for England and Wales*, Law Com 177, 1989), preferred the expressions *external elements*, in place of *actus reus*, and *fault elements*, in place of *mens rea*, and used them throughout the work. Whichever terms are preferred, it is important to note that they are merely convenient tools of analysis for the lawyer. At the conclusion of the trial, what matters is that the prosecution have established that all the ingredients contained within the definition of the crime have been satisfied; it matters not whether the ingredients are categorised as *actus reus/external elements, mens rea/fault elements* or in any other way.

2.2 Circumstances required by the definition of the crime

The prosecution must always prove the 'external elements' if they are to succeed in their task. These elements might include:

- positive acts on the part of the defendant; or

- in some circumstances, *omitting to act*; or

- (very rarely) being involved in a *state of affairs*.

It is, therefore, incorrect to state that the *actus reus* refers merely to 'the guilty *act'*.

The importance of proving the *actus reus* is illustrated by the case of *Deller* (1952). The defendant was convicted of obtaining a car by false pretences (now s 15 of the Theft Act (TA) 1968). When obtaining some property, he had made statements which he thought were untrue. It turned out that in fact the statements were true. Despite his best efforts Mr Deller had in fact spoken the truth! Whilst he certainly possessed the *mens rea*, the *actus reus* (that he made false pretences) was missing and he was, therefore, entitled to be acquitted (today he would almost certainly be guilty of attempting to obtain property by deception contrary to the Criminal Attempts Act 1981 – see Chapter 5).

Any analysis of the *actus reus* must, therefore, take account of the fact that particular conduct may only be forbidden in the particular *circumstances* required by the definition of the crime. With theft, for example, the prosecution must prove that the property belonged to another; with rape that the victim did not consent to sexual intercourse with the defendant; with handling stolen goods that the goods are indeed stolen. The case of *Haughton v Smith* (1975) graphically illustrates this point. Police stopped a van on a motorway and found it contained stolen goods. The officers decided to allow the driver to continue his journey. The defendant delivered the goods to others who intended to receive them and to dispose of them. The defendant was convicted of attempting to handle stolen goods contrary to s 22 of the TA 1968. He successfully appealed to the House of Lords on the basis that at the time he attempted to handle the goods they were no longer stolen because the police had earlier taken effective charge of them.

2.2.1 Result and conduct crimes

A further dimension of the analysis of the *actus reus* is the distinction often drawn between result crimes and conduct crimes. It is important, therefore, when considering a particular crime, to consider not only the circumstances required by the definition, but also whether it is a result or conduct crime. In *Miller* (1983), Lord Diplock referred to *arson* contrary to s 1(3) of the Criminal Damage Act (CDA) 1971 as an example of a result crime. This he defined as a crime which is not complete unless and until the conduct of the accused has *caused* property belonging to another to be destroyed or damaged. He went on to emphasise that with all result crimes the 'conduct of the accused that is *causative* to the result may consist not only of his doing physical acts ... but also of ... failing to take measures' (p 980).

An example of a *conduct* crime is the offence of dangerous driving contrary to s 2 of the Road Traffic Act (RTA) 1988 (as substituted by the RTA 1991). It is clear from the wording of the offence that the *actus reus* of dangerous driving is driving a mechanically propelled vehicle on a road or other place. Nothing more needs to be established and there is certainly no need to show that any dire consequence ensued. However, for the crime to be completed reference needs to be made to the circumstances. The driving must be *dangerous* and s 2A(1) and (2) make it clear that what is deemed to be *dangerous* is to be largely assessed by using the objective standard of the 'competent and careful driver'. Obviously, to drive a car is not a crime but to do so in such a way that the conduct is dangerous inevitably establishes the offence.

2.2.2 Justification

Sometimes the law allows some form of justification for the act which the defendant committed, for example, the use of force in self-defence renders the accused's conduct lawful (see below, 7.7, for further details). Is this justification to be classed as part of the *actus reus* or *mens rea*? For practical purposes, it is best regarded as being part of the *mens rea* and therefore if a justification exists it is preferable to consider this to be a situation where no *mens rea* was present. What if the defendant was unaware of the facts giving rise to the justification? Is his conduct still justified in law? The answer is 'no'. In *Dadson* (1850), the defendant was a police officer who shot a man escaping from a wood from where he had stolen timber. At that time, it was lawful to shoot an escaping felon. The victim was in fact a felon because he had several previous convictions for theft but this was unknown to the policeman. He was convicted of unlawfully wounding the felon with intent to commit grievous bodily harm. Dadson pleaded justification, that is, what he had done was justified in law; the law allowed escaping felons to be shot and this was all he had done. His appeal was dismissed because the court for Crown Cases Reserved held that his act could only be justified if he was aware of the facts which gave rise to the defence and here he was not.

The Law Commission's view is to be found in cl 27 of *Legislating the Criminal Code: Draft Criminal Law Bill* (Law Com 218, 1993) which adopts the *Dadson* principle. The Law Commission originally proposed in its 1989 (proposed) codification of the criminal law to engage in law reform and reverse the *Dadson* principle but eventually concluded that:

> Although opinion was not unanimous on consultation, we think it right to maintain this long-standing common law rule. Citizens who react unreasonably to circumstances should not be exculpated by the accident of facts of which they were unaware [para 39.11].

2.2.3 The *actus reus* must always be voluntary

In *Bratty v AG for Northern Ireland* (1963), Lord Denning stated that: '... the requirement that it should be a voluntary act is essential ... in every criminal case.' This requirement applies to all crimes including those classed as *strict liability* offences where the prosecution do not have to prove *mens rea* in relation to one or more aspects of the *actus reus* (see Chapter 3). A car driver would not, therefore, be guilty of a driving offence if he suffered a heart attack or was attacked by a swarm of bees as a result of which he crashed into a second vehicle because his actions would have been involuntary and an essential element of *actus reus* of such offences would be missing. However, the courts are concerned to ensure that involuntary conduct is kept within narrow boundaries and emphasise the importance of the absence of fault on the part of the defendant. For example, if the car driver was prone to heart attacks and had experienced heart tremors shortly before the accident but had continued driving, it is unlikely he would be able successfully to demonstrate the absence of *actus reus*. In these circumstances, he should have immediately stopped the car and sought help.

2.2.4 State of affairs cases

It is often suggested that there is an exception to the rule that the *actus reus* must be voluntary and this concerns so called 'state of affairs' cases. Here, it is said, a person has acted involuntarily and yet still been convicted. Consider the two leading cases of *Larsonneur* (1933) and *Winzar v Chief Constable of Kent* (1983). In the former case, Ms Larsonneur, a French citizen, was granted leave to enter the UK on 14 March 1933. On 22 March, the permission was varied and she was required to leave the UK by the end of that day. The appellant *chose* to travel to Eire. Whilst there she was deported by the Irish police and taken by them, and against her will, back to the UK where she was immediately detained by police officers at the port of entry. She was convicted under the Aliens Order 1920 in that, she, 'being an alien to whom leave to land in the UK had been refused, was found in the UK'. Her appeal was unsuccessful despite her claim that she lacked both the *mens rea* and the *actus reus*! Lord Hewart CJ held during the course of a short and terse judgment that the manner of her return to the UK was 'perfectly immaterial'. All that mattered was that 'she was found here' and 'was in the class of person whose landing had been prohibited ... by reason of the fact that she had violated the condition on her passport' (pp 78–79).

Not every commentator has chosen to criticise the judgment, however. D Lanham, for example, concluded that Ms Larsonneur was, to a significant extent, the author of her own misfortune and that whilst:

> ... no one could claim that *Larsonneur* stood as a shining example of English jurisprudence ..., it can hardly be regarded as the last word in judicial depravity. If Ms Larsonneur had been dragged kicking and screaming from France into the UK by kidnappers and the same judgment had been given by the Court of Criminal Appeal, the defence of unforeseeable compulsion would truly have been excluded and the case would be the worst blot on the pages of the modern criminal law. But she wasn't, it wasn't and it isn't [[1976] Crim LR 276].

A similar case in our judgment is *Winzar v Chief Constable of Kent* (1983). Here, the appellant had been convicted of having been found drunk in the highway and fined £15. Winzar had been taken to hospital on a stretcher but was there diagnosed as being merely drunk and told to leave. This he declined to do and was found slumped in a corridor. The police were summoned and they carried him to a police car parked on the road outside the hospital. His appeal to the Divisional Court was on the grounds:

- he was not 'found on the highway' as he had been carried to the police car;

- his presence on 'the highway' was momentary;

- he was not there of his own volition.

Robert Goff LJ upheld the conviction because in his judgment all that mattered was that:

- a person is in a public place or highway;

- he is drunk;

- he is perceived to be there and to be drunk.

Here, Winzar was found guilty of an offence which was in fact procured by the police! It can be argued of course that if a drunken man refuses to leave a hospital after repeated requests to do so it is inevitable that the police will be called and that if their requests to him to leave are declined they will remove him by force. Perhaps Winzar, as with Ms Larsonneur, was at least partly the author of his own misfortune.

In our opinion, cases such as these, rare though they may be, are 'result driven' and are decided primarily on the grounds of what the judges consider to be 'policy'.

2.3   Non-insane automatism

A further qualification must be introduced into any discussion of the importance of the voluntary nature of the *actus reus* and this concerns 'non-insane automatism'. This has been described as 'a modern catchphrase [to describe] an involuntary movement of the body or limbs of a person' (*Watmore and Jenkins* (1962)). Imagine that a dental patient kicks out whilst recovering from an anaesthetic and injures the dentist. This *prima facie* is the *actus reus* of one of the charges contained within the Offences Against the Person Act 1861. The charge could be defeated on the ground not only that the prosecution would be unable to prove the *mens rea* requirement of the offence but also on the ground that as the act was involuntary the defendant had not committed the *actus reus* – it took place whilst the defendant was in a state of automatism.

Of course, it might be thought that so long as the defendant escapes conviction it does not matter whether this is because the prosecution are unable to prove the existence of either the *mens rea* or *actus reus*. In fact, it does matter because, as will be seen in Chapter 3, many criminal offences are categorised as offences of *strict liability* which means that the prosecution do not have to prove mens rea in relation to one or more aspects of the *actus reus*. If automatism was considered to be a part of the *mens rea,* it follows that in crimes such as these the defendant might not escape conviction.

The basic principles were outlined by Lord Denning in *Bratty v AG for Northern Ireland* (1963), drawing support from Lord Sankey LC in *Woolmington v DPP* (1935), where he said:

> ... when dealing with a murder case the Crown must prove (a) death as the result of a voluntary act of the accused and (b) the malice of the accused.

Lord Denning continued:

> No act is punishable if it is done involuntarily: and an involuntary act in this context – some people nowadays prefer to speak of it as 'automatism' – means an act which is done by the muscles without any control by the mind such as a spasm, a reflex action or a convulsion; or an act done by a person who is not conscious of what he is doing such as an act done while suffering from concussion or whilst sleepwalking.

In practice, automatism is closely related to the defence of insanity and works within a narrow sphere because any *automatic* behaviour which results from a *disease of the mind* results in the actor being found 'not guilty by reason of insanity' (as a result of the *M'Naghten* Rules of 1843 – see Chapter 7). The law distinguishes between 'external factors' responsible for the automatic behaviour and 'internal factors', the former potentially leading to an acquittal, whilst the latter is liable to result in detention in a secure hospital. Insanity and non-insane automatism are thus mutually exclusive defences. As Nicola Padfield has noted, 'the legal definition of both automatism and insanity bear little relationship to their medical counterparts. Indeed, insanity is not a medical concept and automatism only exists in medical texts in relation to some forms of epilepsy' ([1989] CLJ 354). Little wonder that Lawton LJ has described the whole area as a 'quagmire seldom entered nowadays save by those in desperate need of some sort of defence' (*Quick* (1973)).

The distinction between external and internal factors is supposed to distinguish between those who suffer from 'one-off' problems and who pose no future threat to society and those who due to a continuing medical condition are likely to experience the problem again and re-offend. Unsurprisingly, defendants often go to great lengths to avoid pleading the insanity defence and risking committal to a secure hospital. The distinction can and does lead to injustice. In *Quick*, the defendant was a diabetic charged with causing actual bodily harm whilst in a hypoglycaemic state (low blood sugar) brought on by taking his insulin and failing to eat properly. His defence was that of automatism but the trial judge ruled that the evidence amounted to a defence of insanity. The defendant at this point changed his plea to guilty and was then sentenced. He now appealed on the ground that the judge's ruling was wrong and that a diabetic in a temporary condition of hypoglycaemia was not whilst in that condition suffering from any defect of reason from disease of the mind. The Court of Appeal quashed his conviction on the ground that an *external* factor was in fact responsible for his act, that is, the taking of the insulin. It held that a malfunctioning of the mind does not occur if it is caused 'by the application to the body of some external factor such as violence, drugs including anaesthetics, alcohol and hypnotic influences'. The court drew a distinction between a person suffering from a hypoglycaemia condition such as Mr Quick and a person suffering from a hyperglycaemia condition (excessive blood sugar). The court held that the former case was caused by the external factor of taking insulin whilst the latter was caused by an internal defect (and the fact that it was treated and controlled by insulin was deemed to be irrelevant!) N Padfield has posed the obvious question, 'why should [a] failure to eat be less likely to recur than [a] failure to take ... insulin?' ([1989] CLJ 354, p 356).

Sleepwalking is also now regarded as an internal factor (despite Lord Denning's opinion in *Bratty*). In *Burgess* (1991), the defendant and his female friend both fell asleep while watching television in her flat. She awoke to find Burgess attacking her. She screamed and as a result, 'he seemed to come to his senses' and showed great remorse. He was charged with wounding with intent and he raised the defence of lack of *mens rea* because, he said, at the time of the act he was sleepwalking and this constituted non-insane automatism. The trial judge ruled that this amounted to a plea of 'not guilty by reason of insanity' and ordered him to be detained in a secure hospital. He appealed on the basis that the judge's ruling was incorrect. The Court of Appeal dismissed the appeal Lord Lane CJ stating:

> One can perhaps narrow the field of inquiry still further by eliminating what are sometimes called the 'external factors' such as concussion caused by a blow on the head. There were no such factors here. Whatever the cause may have been, it was an 'internal' cause. The possible disappointment or frustration caused by unrequited love is not to be equated with something such as concussion. On this aspect of the case, we respectfully adopt what was said by Martin JA giving the judgment of the court in the Ontario Court of Appeal in *R v Rabey* (1977) which was approved by a majority in the Supreme Court of Canada (see [1980] 2 SCR 513, p 519) [where the facts bore a similarity to those in the instant case, although the diagnosis was different]:
>
> > Any malfunctioning of the mind, or mental disorder having its source primarily in some subjective condition or weakness internal to the accused (whether fully understood or not), may be a 'disease of the mind' if it prevents the accused from knowing what he is doing, but transient disturbances of consciousness due to certain specific external factors do not fall within the concept of disease of the mind ... In my view, the ordinary stresses and disappointments of life which are the common lot of mankind do not constitute an external cause constituting an explanation for a malfunctioning of the mind which takes it out of the category of a 'disease of the mind'. To hold otherwise would deprive the concept of an external factor of any real meaning.

Epilepsy is also classed as an internal factor. The House of Lords dealt with this condition in *Sullivan* (1984). Mr Sullivan suffered from epilepsy. There had been a period in his life when he was subject to major seizures but medication had lessened their intensity and at the time of the relevant conduct he was proved to suffer minor seizures known as petit mal, perhaps once or twice each week. On the day in question he was chatting to elderly neighbours when he was suddenly overcome by a seizure. One of the neighbours, a Mr Payne, aged 80, was kicked by the appellant and required hospital treatment. The prosecution accepted that he had no recollection of the events but the trial judge ruled that his defence was one of insanity and not automatism which Sullivan's counsel had wished to establish. As a consequence of that ruling, the defendant pleaded guilty to assault occasioning actual bodily harm. He appealed against the judge's ruling. Lord Diplock in giving the decision of the House considered the law relating to insanity and held that the word 'mind' in the *M'Naghten* Rules 'is used in the ordinary sense of the mental faculties of reason, memory and understanding'. Therefore:

> If the effect of a disease is to impair these faculties so severely as to have either of the consequences referred to in the latter part of the Rules, it matters not

whether the aetiology of the impairment is organic, as in epilepsy, or functional, or whether the impairment itself is permanent or transient and intermittent, provided that it subsisted at the time of the commission of the act.

Lord Diplock ended his speech by saying, 'sympathise though I do with the appellant, I see no other course open to your Lordships than to dismiss this appeal' (p 677).

In *Bratty v AG for Northern Ireland* (1963), Lord Denning emphasised that an act is not to be regarded as involuntary if the person was conscious but nevertheless could not control his actions (irresistible impulse) or could not remember after the event exactly what had taken place. There must be a total destruction of voluntary control. In *AG's Reference (No 2 of 1992)* (1993), it was alleged that the defendant, a lorry driver, had fallen asleep at the wheel of his lorry and had collided with a stationary vehicle on the hard shoulder of a motorway which resulted in two people losing their lives. He had been driving for some 350 miles and had been at the wheel for approximately six out of the preceding 12 hours. He had taken the regulation meal and rest breaks. His defence was that he had no awareness of what was taking place until the very last moment due to being in a trance-like state induced by driving for long distances on 'straight, flat, featureless motorways'. Expert medical evidence supported the contention. The defence claim was that he was in a state of automatism. The trial judge left the defence to the jury, which acquitted. The Attorney General referred to the Court of Appeal the question whether the defence was open to the respondent. The court held that the condition known as 'driving without awareness' could not support the defence of automatism. Lord Taylor CJ stated:

> In our judgment, the 'proper evidential foundation' was not laid in this case by ... [the] evidence of driving without awareness ... The defence of automatism requires that there was a total destruction of voluntary control on the defendant's part. Impaired, reduced or partial control is not enough. [Expert evidence] suggested that he would be able to steer the vehicle and usually to react and return to full awareness when confronted by significant stimuli.

The court relied upon the decisions in *Watmore v Jenkins* (1962) and *Robert v Ramsbottom* (1980). In the former case, Winn J referred to the need for 'such a complete destruction of voluntary control as could constitute in law automatism', and in the latter case, the court accepted the proposition that 'one cannot accept as exculpation anything less than total loss of consciousness'.

In *Broome v Perkins* (1987), the defendant had been charged with driving without due care and attention. He had driven his vehicle erratically for some six miles. His conviction was upheld even though there was evidence to establish that he was suffering from hypoglycaemia (low blood sugar) he must have been exercising conscious control of the vehicle, even though imperfectly, in order to have manoeuvred the vehicle reasonably successfully over such a distance. This case had been criticised by the Law Commission (*A Criminal Code for England and Wales*, Law Com 177, 1989, Vol 2, para 11.4) and was distinguished in *T* (1989). In this case, T, a young French woman, stabbed another woman in the course of a robbery. It was later established that she was suffering from post-traumatic stress as a result of having been raped three days prior to her arrest. The Crown argued that she must have had some control over her actions to be able to open the blade of the knife prior to the stabbing. It was held that the case could be distinguished on the basis that T had been in a 'dream', whereas in *Broome v Perkins* there had been partial control. It is perhaps reassuring that the court thought that the categories of automatism are not closed, although there are no real signs of them being widened.

2.3.1   Self-induced automatism

The position in relation to self-induced automatism was originally established in *Quick* (1973). The Court of Appeal held, in the case of a diabetic who had failed to eat properly and who had consumed too much alcohol after taking his insulin, that 'a self-induced incapacity will not excuse ... nor will one which could have been reasonably foreseen as a result of either doing or omitting to do something, as, for example, taking alcohol against medical advice after using ... prescribed drugs or failing to have regular meals while taking insulin' (although the conviction was reversed on the ground that the defence ought to have been left to the jury to decide at the trial). The position has become more complicated since this case, however, as a result of *Bailey* (1983). The current position is dependent upon whether the crime the defendant is alleged to have committed is classed by the courts as one of *specific intent or basic intent*. As will be seen in Chapter 3, the former is one where the prosecution must establish that the defendant *intended* to bring about the prohibited result, whereas the latter may be committed *recklessly*, that is, the defendant has knowingly engaged in risk-taking activity (with the exception of s 1 of the CDA 1971, where recklessness has an alternative, objective meaning). A defendant cannot be guilty of a crime requiring specific intent if he or she was suffering from automatism, even if it was self-induced. Where the crime is one of basic intent, however, and the automatism was induced by the voluntary consumption of drink or drugs or was otherwise self-induced, then the defendant has no defence even if the effect of the intoxication was to deprive him of *mens rea*. This is because subjective awareness on the part of the defendant that, for example, consuming drugs or failing to eat properly may render him uncontrolled, aggressive or unpredictable amounts to recklessness on his part and thus he is liable for crimes of basic intent where recklessness suffices for the *mens rea*. Griffiths LJ in *Bailey* (1983) stated the law as follows:

> The question in each case will be whether the prosecution have proved the necessary element of recklessness ... if the accused knows that his actions or inactions are likely to make him aggressive ... with the result that he may cause

some injury ... and he persists in the action or takes no remedial action ... it will be open to the jury to find that he was reckless [p 765].

It follows that if the defendant was taking medically prescribed drugs and was *unaware* that it would make him or her aggressive then he may be able successfully to plead automatism. In *Hardie* (1984), the defendant consumed several valium tablets which belonged to his former girlfriend. He was unaware of the effect of this drug. He started a fire in his friend's flat and was convicted of damaging property with intent to endanger life contrary to s 1(2) of the CDA 1971. His appeal was allowed. Parker LJ stated:

> In the present instance, the defence was that the Valium was taken for the purpose of calming the nerves only, that it was old stock and that the appellant was told it would do him no harm. There was no evidence that it was known to the appellant or even generally known that the taking of Valium in the quantity taken would be liable to render a person aggressive or incapable of appreciating risks to others or have other side effects such that its self-administration would itself have an element of recklessness. It is true that Valium is a drug and it is true that it was taken deliberately and not taken on medical prescription, but the drug is, in our view, wholly different in kind from drugs which are liable to cause unpredictability or aggressiveness. It may well be that the taking of a sedative or soporific drug will, in certain circumstances, be no answer, for example in a case of reckless driving, but if the effect of a drug is merely soporific or sedative the taking of it, even in some excessive quantity, cannot in the ordinary way raise a *conclusive* presumption against the admission of proof of intoxication for the purpose of disproving *mens rea* in ordinary crimes, such as would be the case with alcoholic intoxication or incapacity or automatism resulting from the self-administration of dangerous drugs.

2.3.2   Reform

The law is clearly in need of reform in this area. The Butler Committee on Mentally Abnormal Offenders (Cmnd 6244, 1975) recommended radical reforms and most of its proposals have been adopted by the Law Commission in its proposed Criminal Code. The Commission's proposals would, if enacted, effectively abolish the distinction between internal and external factors.

Clause 33(1) proposes that:

A person is not guilty of an offence if:

(a) he acts in a state of automatism, that is, his act:

   (i) is a spasm or convulsion; or

   (ii) occurs while he is in a condition (whether of sleep, unconsciousness, impaired consciousness or otherwise depriving him of effective control of the act; and

(b) the act or condition is the result neither of anything done or omitted with the fault required for the offence nor of voluntary intoxication.

However, to deal with the defendant who still poses a continuing 'threat' to others cl 34 provides that a defendant acquitted under cl 33 would be the subject of a 'mental disorder' verdict and the court would still have wide and flexible sentencing powers (which would include the power to compel the individual to receive in-hospital medical treatment). If Parliament adopted these proposals, many of the problems experienced by those suffering from some kind of mental disorder short of insanity would be alleviated and the defence would cease to be the 'quagmire of law' identified by Lawton LJ in *Quick* as long ago as 1973 (for a detailed analysis of the Law Commission's proposals, see Pt 2 of the proposed Criminal Code (*A Criminal Code for England and Wales*, Law Com 177, 1989).

2.4　Causation

Many find causation a complex area because, as will be seen, it is often difficult to identify strict *principles* of law. Judges often seem to be strongly influenced by policy considerations. The authors of the leading work explain the problem as follows:

> For writers of the first school 'policy' is just a name for an immense variety of considerations which do weigh and should weigh with courts considering the question of the existence or extent of responsibility. No exhaustive enumeration can be given of such factors and no general principles can be laid down as to how a balance should be struck between them. Policy, on this interpretation, is atomised: the courts must focus attention on the precise way in which harm has eventuated in a particular case, and then ask and answer, in a more or less intuitive fashion, whether or not on these particular facts a defendant should be held responsible. The court's function is to pass judgments acceptable to society for their time and place on these matters, and general policies can never take the place of judgment [Hart, HLA and Honoré, T, *Causation in the Law*, 2nd edn, 1985, Oxford: OUP, p 103].

Given the emphasis placed on the role of *fault* in determining criminal liability it is perhaps an unsurprising proposition that the prosecution must prove beyond reasonable doubt, in relation to result crimes, that the defendant *caused* the prohibited consequence. This involves demonstrating that:

- the defendant's conduct was the *factual* cause of the prohibited consequence; and

- the defendant's conduct *in law* caused the consequence.

Normally, the prosecution will not have a problem in demonstrating an unbroken link or causal chain but cases are sometimes argued by the defence on the basis that the chain of causation has been broken and that the defendant should not be held responsible in law for the consequence. In these cases, according to *Pagett* (1983):

> ... it is for the judge to direct the jury ... in the most simple terms, in accordance with the legal principles which they have to apply. It would then fall to the jury to decide the relevant factual issues which, identified with reference to those legal principles, will lead to the conclusion whether or not the prosecution have established the guilt of the accused [*per* Robert Goff LJ, p 290].

Nicola Padfield, in her article 'Clean water and muddy causation' ([1995] Crim LR 683), identifies three rules of causation established by the various authorities over the years. The first, she says, is the need to establish 'factual causation', that is, 'it must be established that the (consequence) would not have resulted "but for" the accused's conduct'. Secondly, it must be shown that the accused's act must be 'more than a minimal cause' of the consequence. The third rule of causation relates to the recognition by the courts of a *novus actus interveniens* 'which absolves the defendant of liability. Examples include outrageously incompetent medical treatment, self-neglect by the victim, or naturally occurring unpredictable events'.

Most cases where causation is called into question relate to homicide and therefore the examples which are to be reviewed should also be re-examined when investigating the law relating to homicide in Chapter 6.

It has been stated above that a potent argument often advanced by defence counsel is that an intervening event has severed the chain of causation thus removing the burden of responsibility from the shoulders of the accused. For example, D is involved in a fight with P and as a consequence D strikes P a blow which renders him unconscious. An ambulance is called, and as it speeds P to hospital it is involved in a traffic accident which results in the death of the driver and patient. For the sake of simplicity, let us assume that the ambulance driver bears no responsibility for the accident it having being caused solely by the fact that the front tyres blew out as a result of a defect in the manufacturing process. Is D responsible for P's death? One fact is clear: P would still be alive *but for* his involvement in the fight and if he had not been hit by D.

The principle of law to be applied is well established and has been considered in *Cheshire* (1991), which applied the comments of Goff LJ in *Pagett* (1983). The following points emerge from the judgment:

- in cases of homicide, it is rarely necessary to give the jury any direction on causation as such;

- how a victim comes by his death is not usually in dispute: it is usually other matters which are in dispute, for example, did the accused have the necessary intent?;

- the established principle to put to the jury is that, in law, 'the accused's act need not be the sole cause or even the main cause of the victim's death, it being enough that his act contributed *significantly* to that result', and that the actions of the defendant were an 'operative, proximate or substantial cause of the *actus reus*';

• it is possible for there to be more than one cause of a result and two or more people can be independently liable in respect of the same harm;

• occasionally, specific issues of causation may arise particularly where the act of the accused 'constitutes a *causa qua non* of (or necessary condition for) the death of the victim ...'. Nevertheless, the intervention of a third person may be regarded as the sole cause of death. Lawyers are used to referring to this as a *novus actus interveniens*. The Latin term has become a 'term of art' and is used to indicate that the intervening act is so independent of the act of the accused that it should, in law, be regarded as the sole cause of death.

In *Pagett*, for example, the defendant shot at armed police whilst using his pregnant girlfriend as a shield. The girl was killed by shots fired at the defendant by the police. He was acquitted of the murder of the girl but convicted of her manslaughter. He appealed on the ground, *inter alia*, that on the question of causation the trial judge erred in directing the jury that it was for him to decide as a matter of law and not for the jury whether the defendant's act caused or was a cause of the girl's death. The Court of Appeal rejected his appeal and held that the act of the police officer was 'a reasonable act performed for the purpose of self-defence'. As it had been caused by the defendant's own acts, it did not operate as a *novus actus interveniens* and thus he was liable for the death of the victim.

Poor medical treatment after the defendant's initial unlawful act is often alleged to be a *novus actus interveniens*. In *Jordan* (1956), the appellant stabbed the victim in a cafe and the victim died eight days later in hospital. The defendant now sought to introduce further medical evidence to demonstrate that the wound was not the cause of death. The court found that the stab wound had penetrated the victim's intestine in two places but that it had mainly healed at the time of death. To prevent infection he was given an antibiotic but he soon displayed signs of intolerance to the drug and it was withdrawn. Unfortunately, the next day a different doctor ordered that the treatment be resumed and as a result the victim died from broncho-pneumonia. The court held:

> We are disposed to accept it as the law that death resulting from any normal treatment employed to deal with a felonious injury may be regarded as caused by the ... injury ... it is sufficient to point out here that this was not normal treatment.

Accordingly the conviction was quashed.

Not surprisingly the case led to concern within the medical profession that this was placing too much emphasis on the treatment given by medical staff and diverting attention away from the wrongdoer whose actions had led to the need for medical attention in the first place. Whilst never having been expressly overruled, it has been described as 'a very peculiar case' (*Blaue* (1975)) and is therefore best considered to be an unusual case and to be confined to its facts.

Much more representative of the law today is *Smith* (1959) where the Courts Martial Appeal Court distinguished *Jordan* and upheld the defendant's conviction for murder. Here, an army doctor failed to diagnose the victims pierced lung which resulted from a fight between two soldiers. The evidence suggested that the treatment given to the soldier was 'thoroughly bad and might well have affected his chances of recovery'. Nevertheless, the court dismissed his appeal. Lord Parker CJ stating that:

> ... if at the time of death the original wound is still an operating cause and a substantial cause, then the death can properly be said to be the result of the wound, albeit that some other cause of death is also operating. Only if it can be said that the original wound is merely the setting in which another cause operates can it be said that the death does not result from the wound. Putting it another way, only if the second cause is so overwhelming as to make the original wound merely part of the history can it be said that death does not flow from the wound [p 198].

In *Malcherek; Steel* (1981), two cases which raised the same question, both defendants were convicted of murder. They appealed on the basis that the doctors, by switching off life support equipment as a result of their belief that the victims were brain dead, were the cause of death and not the appellants. The court dismissed their appeals Lord Lane CJ making it clear that:

> ... if treatment is given *bona fide* by competent and careful medical practitioners, then evidence will not be admissible to show that the treatment would not have been administered in the same way by other medical practitioners ... The fact that the victim has died despite or because of medical treatment for the initial injury given by careful and skilled medical practitioners will not exonerate the original assailant from responsibility for the death.

Thus, the fact that medical treatment was inadequate or even negligent will not necessarily relieve the accused of liability for his or her actions. In *Cheshire* (1991), Beldam LJ referred to the Australian case of *Evans and Gardiner (No 2)* (1976) as an illustration of how difficult it can be to shift the burden of responsibility onto medical practitioners. In that case, the appellants had stabbed the victim but death had not occurred for nearly a year during which time he had 'resumed an apparently healthy life'. The cause of death was a stricture of the small bowel which is a not uncommon occurrence after surgery carried out to repair stab wounds. Should the doctors have diagnosed the problem and taken remedial action? Was their failure tantamount to negligence? The Supreme Court of Victoria applied the accepted English test by posing the question whether the original act was still an 'operating and substantial cause of death' – taken from the *dictum* of Parker CJ in *Smith* (1959) – and concluded that it was.

In *Cheshire* (1991), the appellant shot his victim in the thigh and stomach. Whilst being treated in hospital the victim developed respiratory problems and was given a tracheotomy. At his trial a medical witness suggested that the original wounds were no longer life-threatening and that his chances of survival were good. Indeed, it was suggested that medical negligence had caused the victim's death. The court dismissed the appeal, Beldam LJ stating:

> Even though the negligence of the treatment ... was the immediate cause of his death, the jury should not regard it as excluding the responsibility of the accused unless the negligent treatment was so independent of his acts, and in itself so potent in causing death, that they regard the contribution made by his acts as insignificant ... it is not the function of the jury to evaluate competing causes so as to choose which is dominant provided they are satisfied that the accused's acts can fairly be said to have made a significant contribution to the victim's death.

A new dimension to the medical treatment cases arose in *McKechnie* (1992) where the wound prevented medical treatment for an independent condition which would have saved the victim's life. The accused had attacked the victim causing severe brain damage. Soon after his admission to hospital it was discovered that he had a duodenal ulcer but the medical opinion was that because of his injuries no attempt should be made to operate on the ulcer. Five weeks later the ulcer burst and as a result the victim died. The trial judge had directed the jury that they must be convinced that the injuries to the head had significantly contributed to his death. He also stressed that they must be satisfied that the medical decision not to operate was reasonable. The Court of Appeal found nothing wrong with this direction and in light of the strong wording in *Cheshire* this must be regarded as correct. Presumably, there was nothing 'extraordinary and unusual' in the decision not to operate nor in the medical treatment that ensued following his admission to hospital. The beating the victim received at McKechnie's hands put him in a position where he was unable to receive the necessary treatment and in principle there seems to be no difference between this and the case where the defendant's act results in the victim receiving medical treatment from which he dies.

The *Smith* case focuses attention on the words *operating* and *substantial*, and in *Cato* (1976) Lord Widgery CJ made the following comment:

> ... it was not necessary for the prosecution to prove that the heroin was the only cause of the death. As a matter of law, it was sufficient if the prosecution could establish that it was a cause, provided it was a cause outside the *de minimis* range, and effectively bearing on the acceleration of the moment of the victim's death.

In *Kimsey* (1996), the Court of Appeal relied on its own decision in *Hennigan* (1971) in a case of causing death by reckless driving. *Hennigan* is authority for the proposition that there is no requirement that the accused's driving be a substantial cause of the accident so long as it was 'something more than *de minimis*'. The recorder at the trial had directed the jury using the words 'slight or trifling link' and this was held to be an acceptable and 'useful' way to avoid using the term *de minimis*.

Various points have emerged from the case law in addition to the ones outlined above. Some cases are unique because of their own particular circumstances but they nevertheless add to the body of knowledge surrounding the principle. It was decided in *Dalby* (1982) that the accused's supply of the drug diconal to the deceased, albeit an unlawful act, was not a *cause* of his death. The act of *supply* had not caused immediate injury and it could not be maintained that the supply was a substantial cause of death. The deceased had injected himself with the drug and this action and not the *supply* was the cause of his death. It could be argued that without the original supply of the drug the deceased might still be alive today and therefore the supply contributed to the death. However, the supplier of any object which has the potential to cause death would be at risk if it is to be accepted that culpability stems from the supply.

In *Dalby's* case, the supplier did not force the victim to inject himself. It might be thought that the victim's decision to indulge in the behaviour amounts to the *novus actus interveniens* that breaks the chain of causation in law. Unfortunately, the principles applicable are far from clear, as the Court of Appeal decision in *Kennedy* (1999) illustrates. This was another case where the accused supplied the deceased with heroin for the deceased to administer to himself with fatal consequences. The Court of Appeal upheld the conviction for manslaughter on the basis that the case was distinguishable from *Dalby*. The accused had gone beyond mere supply. By preparing the syringe and handing it to the deceased, the accused had encouraged and/or assisted the deceased in the act of self-administration. Is this distinction sustainable? The Court of Appeal accepted that *Dalby* was still good law, but surely the supply of drugs in that case could be seen as an encouragement to consume them? More significant is the objection that (possession offences aside) the self-administration of a lethal, or potentially lethal, quantity of drugs is no longer a criminal offence (see the Suicide Act 1961). Hence, it is difficult to see what unlawful act the accused in *Kennedy* was encouraging. Different considerations based on a duty of care argument might arise if the accused had supplied a minor or mental defective with drugs, but that was not the case in *Kennedy*.

Rather, the ruling reflects a policy consideration, discernible in many decisions, that an accused ought not normally to be able to escape legal liability for his actions by citing the actions of his victim as a *novus actus interveniens*.

Instructive in this context is the Court of Appeal decision in *Blaue* (1975) which confirmed the applicability of the civil law principle that 'one takes one's victim as one finds him' to the criminal law of causation (this is often referred to as the 'thin skull rule'). If there is something unusual about the physical, mental or emotional make-up of the victim so that the consequence is much more serious than the defendant foresaw, or could have foreseen, then this is irrelevant so far as the *actus reus* is concerned and the defendant is considered to have caused the consequence. In this case, the deceased had been stabbed and required a blood transfusion if her life was to be saved. The woman was a Jehovah's Witness and refused to contemplate a blood transfusion and died a few hours later. Counsel argued that if her decision not to have a blood transfusion was unreasonable then it should be held that the chain of causation had been broken. But, pondered Lawton LJ, reasonable by whose standards?

> Those of the Jehovah's Witnesses? Humanists? Roman Catholics? Protestants of Anglo-Saxon descent? The man on the Clapham omnibus? ... It has long been the policy of the law that those who use violence on other people must take their victims as they find them. This in our judgment means the whole man, not just the physical man. It does not lie in the mouth of the assailant to say that the victim's religious beliefs which inhibited him from accepting certain kinds of treatment were unreasonable. The question for decision is what caused her death. The answer is the stab wound. The fact that the victim refused to stop this end coming about did not break the causal connection between the act and the death [p 1415].

It must be emphasised that this type of issue had been before the courts as long ago as 1841 in *Holland*, where the victim of an assault had rejected the surgeon's advice that in order to prevent complications developing he ought to have his finger amputated. Within a fortnight, the victim had died as a result of lockjaw. Maule J directed the jury to the effect that the assailant could not avoid liability on the basis that his victim could have avoided death by taking greater care of himself.

In these cases, the victim made a conscious, presumably reflective and reasoned decision. There will, however, be situations where the victim has acted on the spur of the moment, perhaps in a panic and without the opportunity for mature reflection, in response to real or imagined circumstances which the victim would prefer to avoid. If in taking this avoiding action death occurs should responsibility rest with the victim or the defendant? There is a clear link between the defendant's actions and the consequence but are there sufficient links to complete the chain of causation? This problem has been the subject of analysis by the Court of Appeal in *Williams* (1992). The deceased had been hitchhiking to a festival in Glastonbury and was offered a lift in a car driven by Williams and containing two friends. Five miles later the deceased jumped from the car and died from head injuries sustained by falling onto the road. The car was travelling at about 30 mph. Evidence was adduced to establish that as he jumped from the moving car an object, thought to be his wallet, flew into the air. The Crown's case was that the occupants of the car had made to rob the deceased and he had sought to take avoiding action. The Court of Appeal was of the opinion that the deceased's conduct had to be proportionate to the gravity of the threat otherwise the deceased's conduct would amount to a voluntary act, a *novus actus interveniens*, which would break the chain of causation. Stuart-Smith LJ expressed the test to be:

> ... the nature of the threat is of importance considering both the foreseeability of harm to the victim from the threat and the question of whether the deceased's conduct was proportionate to the threat; that is to say that it was within the ambit of reasonableness and not so daft as to make his own voluntary act one which amounted to a *novus actus interveniens* and consequently broke the chain of causation.

The learned judge emphasised, however, that:

> It should of course be borne in mind that a victim may in the agony of the moment do the wrong thing ... and the fact that in the agony of the moment he may act without thought and deliberation [p 191].

In the result, the failure of the trial judge to give any direction to the jury on the matter of causation was held by the Court of Appeal to amount to a misdirection and the conviction was quashed.

In *Roberts* (1971), the victim jumped from the defendants car in order to escape from his sexual advances. The car was travelling between 20 and 40 mph and she sustained injuries. The defendant was convicted of assault occasioning actual bodily harm and he appealed on the basis that there was a lack of causation. His appeal was dismissed because the victim's actions were a natural consequence of the attack and a likely reaction in the circumstances she found herself in.

It is, therefore, incumbent upon trial judges to give a direction on causation, in such circumstances, which should be in these terms:

- Was it reasonably foreseeable that some harm albeit not serious harm, was likely to result from the defendant's threat?

- In addition, was the *reaction* one which might have been expected from someone in that situation, taking account of any particular characteristic and the fact that one might act instinctively in the circumstances?

- There is no need to establish that the accused foresaw the victim's actions, although the objective test of reasonable foresight is based on what a reasonable person in the accused's situation (excluding his personal characteristics) would have foreseen (see *Majoram* (1999))

What of the rape victim who subsequently commits suicide? Could the rapist also be convicted of her murder? There has never been a successful prosecution in England and the problems of proof for the prosecution would be formidable (it would have to be proved, for example, that the victim would not have killed herself but for the rape). However, it is submitted that the case law would support such a conviction. This could be either on the *Blaue* principle that a defendant takes his victim as he finds her, or on the *Williams* foreseeability test. *Dear* (1996) appears to support this view. Here, following allegations by the appellant's 12 year old daughter that the deceased had sexually assaulted her, the appellant badly injured the deceased with the result that he was hospitalised. He died two days later and there was some evidence to suggest that he had committed suicide, presumably because of his shame and remorse. The appellant argued that the suicide acted as a *novus actus interveniens* and that his conviction for murder should be overturned. The Court of Appeal dismissed his appeal on the basis that the question which had been left to the jury, simply whether the injuries inflicted by the appellant were an 'operating and substantial' cause of the death, was correct and that the jury had been perfectly entitled to conclude that the answer was 'yes'.

2.4.1   Reform

This area has not been subjected to comprehensive law reform consideration either by the Law Commission or the Criminal Law Revision Committee. The Commission's (proposed) codification of the criminal law (*A Criminal Code for England and Wales*, Law Com 177, 1989) sought in these circumstances simply to restate the existing common law principles. Clause 17 provides:

> (1) A person causes a result which is an element of an offence when:
>
>> (a) he does an act which makes a more than negligible contribution to its occurrence; or
>>
>> (b) he omits to do an act which might prevent its occurrence and which he is under a duty to do according to the law relating to the offence.
>
> (2) A person does not cause a result where, after he does such an act or makes such an omission, an act or event occurs:
>
>> (a) which is the immediate and sufficient cause of the result;
>>
>> (b) which he did not foresee; and
>>
>> (c) which could not in the circumstances reasonably have been foreseen.

The codification team debated whether the code should contain a provision on causation at all, because two types of objection had been received as a result of the consultation exercise held between 1985 and 1989. These were, first, that such a provision was unnecessary because causation is a matter of fact for the jury to decide; and, secondly, that such a definition would provoke unproductive argument among the jury (Vol 2, para 7.20). The Commission decided in the event to include cl 17 because it felt that a failure to include it would necessitate trial judges going back to the common law principles and thus one of the principal aims of codification – to state the known law clearly – would be defeated (para 7.21). They felt that judges would be well able to explain the meaning of the clause in language suitable to the jury's needs and that this would not produce any more confusion than exists at the present time.

For a detailed and well argued critique of cl 17, see Professor Glanville Williams's article, '*Finus* for *novus actus*' ([1989] CLJ 391). For a strong defence of the proposal, see Professor JC Smith and the late Professor B Hogan, *Criminal Law Cases and Materials* (7th edn, 1999, London: Butterworths, pp 46–49).

English law is similar to American law so far as causation is concerned. The American Law Institute's Model Penal Code (1962) provides:

Section 2.03

(1) Conduct is the cause of a result when:

    (a) it is an antecedent but for which the result in question would not have occurred; and

    (b) the relationship between the conduct and the result satisfies any additional causal requirements imposed by the Code or by the law defining the offence.

(2) When purposely or knowingly causing a particular result is an element of an offence, the element is not established if the actual result is not within the purpose or the contemplation of the actor unless:

    ...

    (b) the actual result involves the same kind of injury or harm as that designed or contemplated and is not too remote or accidental in its occurrence to have a just bearing on the actor's liability or on the gravity of his offence.

Issues of disputed causation are, therefore, left to the jury's sense of 'justice'.

Since 1989, the Law Commission has given further consideration to aspects of causation in its *Report on Involuntary Manslaughter* (Law Com 237, 1996) where it recommended a new offence of corporate killing based upon management failure by a corporate body. It recommended that corporate liability should arise if the failure was the cause or one of the causes of a person's death. The Commission took the view that the ordinary rules of causation would be inadequate to link the decision making processes of corporate bodies with the ultimate consequence of death. The risk would be that the management failure would simply be regarded as a 'stage already set' and thus the corporation itself would avoid liability. The Commission is adamant that even though the management failure is not the immediate cause of death, liability ought not to be avoided unless a jury accepts that the intervening act or omission of an *individual* is a complete *novus actus interveniens* (see Chapter 6 for a more detailed discussion of the report).

2.5　Omissions

The general rule is that there is no liability for omissions unless either the statute creating the offence has been interpreted by the courts as creating such liability or the omission comes within one of the common law exceptions to the rule. As Stephen J stated in 1887:

> A sees B drowning and is able to save him by holding out his hand. A abstains from doing so in order that B may be drowned. A has committed no offence! [*Digest of the Criminal Law*].

The court will look at a particular statutory word or phrase and decide whether it is capable of creating liability for omitting to act. Parliament has established many positive duties to act and they usually present few problems. Examples of such crimes:

- failing to report a road traffic accident (s 170 of the RTA 1988);

- failure to provide a police officer with a specimen of breath (s 6 of the RTA 1988);

- failure to provide for a child in one's care in terms of food, clothing and medical care (s 1(2) of the Children and Young Persons Act 1933).

These are all examples of crimes where Parliament's wishes are perfectly clear. But this is often not the case. In *Shama* (1990), for example, the defendant was convicted under s 17(1)(a) of the TA 1968 for falsifying a document when he had *omitted* to fill in a form which it was his statutory duty to complete. Section 17(1)(a) provides that a defendant is liable if he 'destroys, defaces, conceals or *falsifies* any ... document made or required for any accountancy purpose'. In *Firth* (1990), a doctor was convicted of deceiving a hospital contrary to s 2 of the TA 1978, when he failed to inform the hospital authority that some of his patients were being treated privately and were not NHS patients. Section 2 makes it an offence, *inter alia*, 'to dishonestly *secure* the remission of ... any existing liability to make a payment, whether his own liability or another's'. Words such as 'obstructing a highway' (*Gully v Smith* (1883)) and 'misconduct' are other examples which the courts have held capable of creating liability for omission. 'Causing' (*Price v Cromack* (1975)), 'harbouring' (*Darch v Weight* (1984)) and 'assisting the doing' (*Brown* (1970)), on the other hand, have been held to exclude liability. Other words, such as 'act', have been held to be capable of both interpretations. Compare *Yuthiwattana* (1984) with *Ahmad* (1986). Both are concerned with the meaning of 'act' as found in s 1(3) of the Protection from Eviction Act 1977. The former case held that the offence was capable of creating liability for omission, whilst the latter adopted a more strict approach to statutory interpretation and decided the opposite. The result is a degree of uncertainty in this area of the law.

The common law contains a number of important exceptions to the general rule. Whilst they are best approached as separate instances of areas in which the courts have established a positive duty to act, they tend to share a common theme – the defendant has assumed a responsibility, creating an expectation in the minds of others that he will act. The exceptions are:

- Certain categories of people are under a positive duty to act

  Captains of ships for example are required to take reasonable steps to protect the lives of their passengers and crew. A parent is under a positive duty to feed and ensure the welfare of his or her children. In *Downes* (1875) a parent declined to summon medical help to his very sick child on religious grounds and the child subsequently died. The parent was convicted of manslaughter.

- *Contract* can create a positive duty to act

  Lifeguards at a swimming pool for example, are under a positive duty to act. In *Pittwood* (1902), a railway crossing keeper negligently left the crossing gates open as a result of which the driver of a hay cart was killed by a train. He was convicted of manslaughter.

- *Public office* can create a positive duty to act

  In *Dytham* (1979), a police officer was convicted of the common law offence of wilfully and without reasonable excuse neglecting to perform his duty. The defendant had been on duty outside a nightclub at 1 am and witnessed a violent assault outside the club by a bouncer from which the victim subsequently died. He took no steps to intervene and drove away from the scene. The basis of the charge was that he had omitted to take any steps to preserve the peace or to protect the victim and to bring the bouncer to justice – all of which his duty demanded he attempt to do (it will be seen in Chapter 6 that it is arguable that the defendant could also have been convicted of manslaughter).

- A defendant who is responsible for *creating a dangerous situation* has a duty to prevent a prohibited result occurring

  In *Miller* (1983), the defendant was a squatter who lay on a mattress in a house and fell asleep with a lighted cigarette in his hand. He awoke to find the mattress on fire and he responded by simply going to the next room and resuming his slumbers. The house caught fire and was damaged. He was charged with arson contrary to s 1 and (3) of the CDA 1971 ('damaged by fire a house ... intending to do damage to such property or reckless as to whether such property would be damaged'). The House of Lords dismissed his appeal Lord Diplock stating:

  > I see no rational ground for excluding from conduct capable of giving rise to criminal liability, conduct which consists of failing to take measures that lie within one's powers to counteract a danger that one has oneself created ...

Currently, however, the most important issues arising before the courts in this area are the duties placed upon volunteer carers and medical practitioners.

2.5.1 Duty of volunteer carers

Problems can arise in the situation where a person voluntarily assumes a responsibility towards another person and then fails to cut in accordance with that duty. This is a particularly challenging problem in an era of a rapidly ageing population where the relatives of elderly people increasingly feel obliged to provide a degree of help and support. The question arises as to the standard of care such carers are obliged to provide and the consequences of failing to meet that standard if the elderly person – who may be very frail, ill and confused – dies. Is the carer (who may have been reluctant to assume any responsibility both before and during the assumption of responsibility) guilty of manslaughter?

Consider the leading case of *Stone and Dobinson* (1977). Stone, who was 67 years old, cohabited with Dobinson, aged 43. The latter was described as 'ineffectual and inadequate'. Mr Stone was partially deaf, nearly blind and of low intelligence. They both looked after Stone's mentally subnormal son. Stone's 61 year old sister, Fanny, came to live with them. Fanny suffered from anorexia nervosa and had very little to do with the rest of the family. She spent most of her time alone in her room, although she sometimes cooked herself some food when Stone and Dobinson visited the pub. In the spring of 1975, the defendants unsuccessfully attempted to contact Fanny's doctor but they walked to the wrong village. In July, she was ill and confined to bed and Mrs Dobinson and a neighbour gave her a bedbath. Both defendants were incapable of using telephones and a neighbour was unsuccessful in getting a local doctor to visit her. The sister died in August and a pathologist's report indicated she must have been in serious need of medical attention. The defendants were both convicted of manslaughter and appealed on the basis that they had not assumed a duty of care in relation to her. They argued the point on the basis that Fanny had come to the house as a lodger and that due to her own eccentricity she became infirm and immobile and unable to look after herself. The court dismissed their appeal Geoffrey Lane LJ commenting that:

> ... whether Fanny was a lodger or not she was a blood relative of the appellant; she was occupying a room in his house; Dobinson had undertaken the duty of trying to wash her; of taking such food to her as she required ... This was not a situation analogous to the drowning stranger. They did make efforts to care ... The jury was entitled to find a duty had been assumed.

On the face of it, few would disagree with this judgment. It is in fact largely a restatement of Lord Coleridge CJ in *Instan* (1893) where he said:

> It would not be correct to say that every moral obligation involves a legal duty; but every legal duty is founded on a moral obligation. A legal duty is nothing else than the enforcing by law of that which is a moral obligation without legal enforcement.

But this analysis presupposes that the carer *freely chooses* to assume a duty of care and then neglected to adequately discharge it. What if the carer felt he or she had little real choice because the elderly and infirm relative had nowhere else to go, or, simply refused to go elsewhere? What if the carer provides a room on the clear understanding that the 'lodger' is to be solely responsible for his or her own health and welfare? What if the carer is himself old, infirm, sick and barely able to cope with his own problems never mind anybody else's? How can the carer *give up* a duty once assumed? Inform the Social Services Department? What if Social Services have run out of money and are unable to provide the sick person with alternative accommodation? As Professor Brian Hogan commented:

> What is disturbing about *Stone* is that the evidence hardly supported the inference that these two elderly [one was 43!] incompetents had taken it upon themselves to discharge the onerous task of looking after the sister. Did they really kill the sister? ['Omissions and a duty myth', in Smith, P (ed), *Criminal Law: Essays in Honour of JC Smith*, 1987, London: Butterworths].

A second point arising from the case law is that as we have seen, it takes very little for the law to place this duty of care on the carers shoulders. Simply providing a room might be enough particularly if the person involved is a relative. The more one does for somebody in Fanny's position the more likely it is that a voluntary duty will have been assumed. Conversely, the more harsh and uncaring a person is the less likely is he to assume such a duty!

If a duty of care has arisen the question arises as to whether the victim can relieve a relative of his common law obligations. The answer is unclear as the only authority is the first-instance case of *Smith* (1979). In this case, Mrs Smith was very suspicious of doctors and asked her husband not to seek medical assistance for her after she had experienced a stillbirth at home. Mr Smith complied with her request but her condition deteriorated and she died. He was charged with manslaughter (although acquitted as the jury were unable to reach a verdict). In his summing up to the jury, the judge placed considerable emphasis on the ability of the wife to engage in rational decision making. If 'not too ill it may be reasonable to abide by her wishes. On the other hand, if she appeared desperately ill, then whatever she may say it might be right to override'.

2.5.2 Duty of medical practitioners

The role of and duties owed by medical practitioners have been subjected to judicial scrutiny by the House of Lords in *Airedale NHS Trust v Bland* (1993). In this civil law case, the judges had to decide whether a young man who had suffered 'catastrophic and irreversible' brain damage in the Hillsborough football stadium disaster and was being fed artificially *via* a nasogastric tube should cease to have this life-sustaining treatment with the inevitable result that death would occur a few days later. He had been in this persistent vegetative state (PVS) for some three years and it was agreed that there was no hope of improvement or recovery. He displayed no cognitive functions, sight, hearing, capacity to feel pain, move his limbs or communicate in any way. It was submitted that by starting and continuing to feed and treat Anthony Bland, the doctors had undertaken a duty to provide medical treatment for an indefinite period. If this is so then to withdraw artificial feeding which would be treated as an omission rather than a positive act, would constitute murder. The counter argument is that when treatment started it was possible that recovery might occur and therefore it was in the patient's best interests that it should continue. However, when all hope of recovery had been abandoned it was not in his best interests to be kept alive. The result was that the justification for what was a non-consensual regime of treatment had disappeared and the doctors were not under a duty to provide nourishment. It followed that failure to do so did not amount to a breach of any duty and so could not be a criminal offence. This latter argument was accepted by the House of Lords. As Lord Mustill put it:

> Absent the duty, the omission to perform what had previously been a duty will no longer be a breach of the criminal law.

The House of Lords held that:

- there was no absolute rule that a patient's life had to be prolonged regardless of circumstances and that respect for human dignity had to be considered;

- the wishes of the patient must be considered. Where the patient is incapable of giving an informed consent, treatment may be provided if it is in the patient's best interests;

- if the treatment is futile there is no duty on the doctor to continue it if it is not in the patient's best interests.

The House of Lords held unanimously that medical staff could discontinue the treatment except for the purpose of enabling Mr Bland to die with maximum dignity and with the least distress.

It should also be noted that doctors are expected to act in accordance with any relevant professional guidelines and to seek the opinion of the Family Division of the High Court before discontinuing the treatment (see *Official Solicitors' Practice Note* (1994)).

It is also worth examining Lord Mustill's speech, where he refers to the role of acts and omissions in the criminal law. Lord Mustill speaks of the 'morally and intellectually dubious distinction between acts and omissions' and illustrates it by showing that an act resulting in death, done without lawful excuse and with the requisite intent, is murder, whereas an *omission* to act leading to the same result and with the same intent is 'in general no offence at all'. Crucially he acknowledges that the law is unclear on when a duty should be held to exist and goes on to comment that 'the current state of the law is unsatisfactory both morally and intellectually, as shown by the troubling case of *Stone*'. Be that as it may, the distinction between acts and omissions exists and the judiciary must give effect to it. The law on omissions is in an unsatisfactory state and the House acknowledged the difficulty. This leads to the conclusion that if a doctor gives his PVS patient a lethal injection then that is murder on the basis that he has performed a positive act with the necessary intent, but it is no offence it he omits to continue to feed the patient with death the inevitable consequence. In a similar vein, why is it not possible to assault or wound someone by omission when it is possible to kill them? The defendant in *Fagan v Metropolitan Police Commissioner* (1969) who accidentally drove his car onto a policeman's foot and left it there was found guilty of assaulting a police officer in the execution of his duty not because he *omitted* to remove it but on the basis that this was a continuous act.

2.6   The continuous act theory

Finally, reference has been made in this chapter to the importance of the *Miller* decision. This case decides that if the accused has done something which creates a dangerous situation then he is under a duty to prevent a particular result from occurring.

The House of Lords considered liability in the context of the continuous act and duty theories. The former is based upon the assumption that a crime is complete once the *mens rea* supervenes upon the continuing act. So, in *Fagan*, the *actus reus* commenced when the car was driven onto the policeman's foot and continued until the car was removed. If during that period the defendant intended to allow it to remain there or was reckless as to whether or not it remained there then the crime would be complete. The Court of Appeal favoured this approach in *Miller*. The mattress smouldered for a considerable period before setting alight. The defendant then became aware of the situation and chose to do nothing. At that moment the *mens rea* coincided with the *actus reus* and the crime was then complete. However, the House of Lords preferred the duty theory to found liability. Miller had created the danger albeit inadvertently. Once he became aware of the situation he was under a duty to limit the damage as far as reasonably possible. His failure to react in a positive way was evidence of the breach of duty. (Note that Lord Diplock preferred the word 'responsibility' rather than the breach of duty.) This approach has the advantage of avoiding a decision on whether certain conduct is deemed 'continuing' for the purpose of the *actus reus* element of a crime. In *Kaitamaki* (1985) and *Cooper v Schaub* (1994), it was held for the purposes of the law of rape that penetration was a continuing act. Therefore, if a man continues to penetrate a woman after she has withdrawn consent, then he commits rape, always assuming the other elements of the definition of the crime are present.

Miller did not deliberately set the mattress alight. A charitable interpretation is that it was merely an accident and therefore no fault element was present. The duty theory identifies the fault *via* the breach of duty rather than any fault at the outset of the escapade. The disadvantage of the breach of duty theory, however, is that, as has been pointed out by Professor B Hogan, 'it is likely to mislead a jury into thinking of duties in other than legal terms; into a consideration of the immorality of particular conduct; into convicting the defendant merely for his callousness ... To introduce an imprecise, ill defined concept of "duty" into the equation only serves to confuse the issue'. ('Omissions and a duty myth', in Smith, P (ed), *Criminal Law: Essays in Honour of JC Smith*, 1987, London: Butterworths). He would prefer a judicial approach based upon causation and which simply examines all the conduct of the defendant and asks the question, did the defendant *cause* the *actus reus* and do so with the relevant *mens rea*?

2.7 Reform

In the first draft of its proposed codification of the criminal law (Law Com 143, 1985), the Law Commission proposed to confine omissions to the more serious crimes involving offences against the person. However, as a result of the consultation exercise which followed, the Law Commission decided not to engage in elaborate law reform because it was too fraught with legal technical difficulties (their deliberations were informed by Professor Glanville Williams, 'What should the Code do about omissions?' ([1987] LS 92)). Hence, 'we have found ourselves unable to include a provision relating to omissions in our draft Bill' (Vol 2, para 7.9). The result is cl 16, which merely restates existing law ('references in this Act to an "act", shall, where the context permits, be read as including references to the omission, state of affairs or occurrence ...').

English law is similar to that prevailing in the United States (American Law Institute, Model Penal Code, 1962, s 2.01(3)).

The problems involved with reforming this area of the law are:

- It is often difficult to distinguish between an act and an omission. For example, if a doctor withdraws life-saving medication from a newly-born and profoundly-handicapped baby who then dies, is this an act on the doctor's part or an omission?

- A general duty to act might impose liability on a large number of people and over-extend the frontiers of criminality. For example, if a large crowd of spectators at a football match observe a fight taking place and fail to take any action to stop it are they *all* to be guilty of an offence? In *Stone and*

Dobinson, ought the neighbour who helped wash Fanny also be liable for manslaughter?

- A general duty to act might cause people to over-interfere in their neighbour's business. For example if you passed the authors' houses and heard young children crying and in distress (a not uncommon occurrence!) should you notify the police? If you fail to do so and a child subsequently suffers injury at the hands of one of the authors ought you to be a party to our crime?

- A general duty to act might give rise to problems with causation. Take the man identified by Stephen J who observes another man drowning and who could save him merely by holding out his hand but declines to do so. It is difficult to say the man died *but for* the defendant's failure to save him. The real reason he died was because he fell into the water or was carried away by the current – neither of which is in any way the fault of the defendant. More important in practice, however, are cases involving a failure to provide medical help. It might be very difficult for the prosecution to prove, beyond reasonable doubt, that the consequence, for example, death, would not have occurred at that particular time and in that particular manner, had medical help been sought.

ACTUS REUS

The requirement for the prosecution to prove the external elements of the act and that it was committed voluntarily

Actus reus refers to the external elements of an act (or in some cases an omission) together with circumstances and consequences required to establish the prohibited conduct elements of an offence. The prosecution must always prove these external elements if they are to succeed in their task and this applies even in the case of crimes classified as offences of strict liability.

The *actus reus* must be a voluntary act on the part of the defendant. In most cases this presents few problems. However, an exception concerns what is known as non-insane automatism. This consists of an involuntary movement of a person's body or limbs. The law attempts to identify the reason for the involuntary behaviour. If it is due to an 'external' factor, the actor's behaviour is excused because of its involuntary nature. But if the reason for the act relates to an 'internal factor' caused by a 'disease of the mind' the actor will be found to be not guilty by reason of insanity and might well face detention in a secure hospital. This can lead to injustice – particularly in the case of those suffering from epilepsy or diabetes. The Law Commission has published proposals designed both to alleviate this injustice and to protect society from people who pose a potential future threat. Parliament has yet to consider them.

Causation

Causation can sometimes pose particular problems for students. It consists of a requirement that the prosecutor demonstrate that the defendant's conduct *caused* the prohibited result, that is, it would not have occurred 'but for' the defendant's conduct. Sometimes the defence claims that an intervening act occurred at some point between the commission of the initial act and the prohibited result, for example, the defendant might admit stabbing the victim but claim that the cause of the victim's death was the negligence of medical staff in the hospital where the victim was taken for treatment. The law is very reluctant to admit such claims. It is enough to ensure conviction if the defendant's acts were a significant cause of the prohibited result. They do not have to be the sole cause or even the main cause provided that they are not now 'merely part of the history'.

Liability for omissions

The general rule is that there is no liability for omissions but there are many common law and statutory exceptions to this rule. Liability for omissions can cause particular problems for those who voluntarily assume the care of another (for example, elderly relatives) and for medical personnel who wish to discontinue life-preserving treatment for patients. The law is in urgent need of reform but the Law Commission has decided not to engage in reform at the present time because the area is too fraught with legal difficulties.

CHAPTER 3

THE MENTAL ELEMENT – *MENS REA*

3.1   Introduction

We saw in Chapter 2 that the prosecution must prove that the defendant brought about the prohibited act (or in some cases an omission or state of affairs). The prosecution's next task is to prove that the defendant did this with the state of mind prescribed by the definition of the crime. This is usually referred to as the *mens rea*, but is sometimes also described as the 'fault element' or 'mental element'. However, some caution is necessary here because 'fault' may be defined more broadly than *mens rea* or 'mental element'. So, there is no doubt that negligence is 'fault' but, traditionally, it is not included within the definition of *mens rea*. At common law, *mens rea* usually means intention or recklessness. If the prosecution merely has to prove negligence to establish the further element for liability, then the offence is one which requires proof of fault but not of *mens rea*. Yet, such distinctions cannot be made with absolute conviction, since the courts have recognised a concept of 'objective' recklessness which very closely resembles negligence. As Nicola Lacey observed in her article, 'A clear concept of intention: elusive or illusory?':

> *Mens rea* is the (not entirely happy) umbrella term used by most criminal law scholars to refer to a range of practical attitudes or states of mind on the defendant's part, which form part of the definition of many offences' [(1993) 56 MLR 621].

There is a large number of offences in which the prosecution does not have to prove any further fault element at all, neither *mens rea* nor even negligence. These are known as offences of *strict liability* (though, confusingly, judges sometimes refer to *absolute liability* which, as explained in 3.8, below, is an even harsher form of liability).

The focus of this chapter will be:

*   intention;

*   recklessness;

*   offences of strict liability.

Negligence will be considered in Chapter 6 in the context of involuntary manslaughter.

Judicial attempts at ascribing definitive meanings to these everyday English words have been fraught with difficulty. Lord Simon referred to these difficulties in *DPP for Northern Ireland v Lynch* (1975):

A principal difficulty in this branch of the law is the chaotic terminology, whether in judgments, academic writings or statutes ... 'will, ... motive, purpose ... specific intention' ... such terms which do indeed overlap in certain contexts, seem frequently to be used interchangeably, without definition, and regardless that in some cases the legal usage is a term of art differing from the popular usage [p 688].

It is suggested that there are two principal reasons for the constantly changing meanings of these key words and expressions with the consequent confusion for all those professionally involved in the criminal law:

(a) because for the courts to adopt the standard dictionary definition of these terms would exclude from criminal liability a number of defendants whom the judiciary believe ought not to be excluded;

(b) a lack of confidence amongst a number of senior judges in the ability of juries to understand complex evidence and to be able to discern truth from falsehood in some cases. The result is that some defendants are acquitted whom judges believe ought not to have been.

3.2   Motive

Before analysing *mens rea* words it is vital to understand the role of motive in proving *mens rea*, because a common mistake is to confuse these two, separate matters. Motive, be it good or bad, is generally said to be irrelevant. Take a so called 'mercy killer' who the jury believe acted from what he understood to be the highest motives when he gave his terminally ill wife, at her own request, a fatal dose of drugs intending that her horrific suffering might cease and that she die quickly and with dignity. This man is guilty in law of murder and will be sentenced to (mandatory) life imprisonment unless he has a defence available to him (see Chapters 6 and 7). His motive in killing his wife is irrelevant and he will be treated in precisely the same way as the armed robber who kills a security guard in cold blood. In *Chandler v DPP* (1964), for example, Campaign for Nuclear Disarmament activists planned a 'sit-in' at a military airfield in order to prevent aircraft movements. They were convicted under s 1 of the Official Secrets Act 1911 which makes it an offence, 'If any person for any purpose prejudicial to the safety or interests of the state: (a) approaches ... any prohibited place ...'. The airfield was a prohibited place. They appealed to the House of Lords on the ground that their campaign and their actions were in fact in the interests of the state and of the entire UK population and that they consequently had no guilty motive. The House of Lords dismissed their appeal on the ground that their motives were irrelevant and did not alter the nature or content of the offence; all that mattered was that they had planned to enter and obstruct the operational use of the airfield.

Conversely, bad motives do not of themselves affect the *mens rea*. In *Cunningham* (1957), the defendant wrenched a gas meter from the gas pipes in a cellar in order to steal the money contained within. Unknown to the defendant, his actions fractured the gas pipe and gas escaped and entered the bedroom of a house on the adjoining side of the wall. The result was that the occupant inhaled gas and suffered injury. Cunningham was convicted of s 23 of the Offences Against the Person Act (OAPA) 1861: '... unlawfully and *maliciously* causing to be administered ... any ... poison or noxious thing ... so as to endanger life ... or to inflict grievous bodily harm.' The trial judge had directed the jury that 'malicious' meant 'wicked'. The jury convicted him presumably on the basis that he had acted wickedly. The Court of Criminal Appeal allowed his appeal holding that 'malicious' is not the same as 'wicked'. 'Malicious' required that the defendant either *intended* to administer the noxious substance (which he clearly did not) or, without intending to do this he nevertheless foresaw that by fracturing the pipe the prohibited consequences might occur (and again he may not have foreseen this result).

On the other hand, as Lord Radcliffe conceded in *Chandler v DPP*:

> All controversies about motives or intentions or purposes are apt to become involved through confusion of the meaning of the different terms and it is perhaps not difficult to show by analysis that the ideas conveyed by these respective words merge into each other without a clear line of differentiation.

The case of *Steane* (1947) is sometimes mentioned as an example where the facts and circumstances of the case were so unusual that they led the court to confuse intention with motive. Steane was a British actor working in Germany at the outbreak of the Second World War. His wife and two sons lived in Germany. He was arrested, threatened and beaten by the Gestapo who wished him to broadcast radio propaganda on the German Broadcasting System and to produce films. He was told that if he failed to comply he and his family would be placed in a concentration camp. He eventually acceded to the demand solely because he wished to save his wife and sons. After the war, he was convicted, under reg 2A of the Defence (General) Regulations 1939, 'of doing acts likely to assist the enemy with intent to assist the enemy'. Were his actions consistent with those of a man intending to aid the German war effort? He could only save his family by broadcasting and thereby assisting the enemy. Lord Goddard CJ compared his case to British prisoners of war in the power of the Japanese who helped build the Burma military railway during the War. 'It would be unnecessary surely in their case to consider any of the necessities of [the defence of] duress because no jury would find that merely by doing this work they were intending to assist the enemy.' The court allowed his appeal and quashed his conviction despite the fact that he possessed what is called 'oblique' intention (see below, 3.3.2). Lord Goddard would have been able to achieve the same result if he had found that Steane had in fact intended to assist the enemy but that the defence of duress was available to him (see Chapter 7).

In reality, motive is only irrelevant to criminal liability if we define motive in a very narrow way and ignore the fact that the law adopts a variety of devices to attribute significance to all kinds of reasons for which defendants act. In effect, the law has pre-selected some reasons or 'motives', and has excluded all others:

- An offence may actually require proof of a particular motive as part of the elements of the offence. For example, the Crime and Disorder Act 1998 contains provisions which make the commission of various non-fatal offences, harassment, criminal damage and some public order offences separate and more serious offences where they are *racially aggravated*. For these purposes, s 28 states that an offence is racially aggravated if immediately before, or during, or immediately after the commission of the offence, the offender demonstrates hostility towards the victim based on the victim's membership (actual or presumed by the offender) of a racial group, *or if the offence is motivated wholly or partly by hostility towards members of a racial group based on their membership of that group.*

- An offence may include an element in its definition which permits an enquiry into the defendant's reasons for his acts which cannot be contained within notions of intention or recklessness. Examples are 'dishonesty' in theft and related offences and 'unwarranted' (demand with menaces) in blackmail.

- Specific or general defences may be available which enable the defendant to justify or excuse his acts and the harm caused. The law considers his reasons for his acts to be sufficiently acceptable. Examples are to be found in 'lawful excuse' for criminal damage, the abortion of a foetus by a doctor because it was necessary to do so to prevent grave permanent injury to the physical or mental health of the mother, and acts in self-defence or under duress or duress of circumstances.

Apart from its relevance in this way, motive may be very important:

- as evidence at trial tending to demonstrate the accused's guilt;

- at the sentencing stage.

3.3 Intention

Parliament has not defined this term and yet many of the most serious crimes carry the requirement that the prosecution should prove beyond all reasonable doubt that the accused intended the consequence proscribed by law. Therefore, the definition of murder demands that the accused must have intended to kill or intended to cause grievous bodily harm. Theft requires, in addition to dishonesty, that the defendant *intended* permanently to deprive the owner of his property. One who attempts to commit a crime is guilty under s 1 of the Criminal Attempts Act 1981 only if 'with *intent* to commit an offence ... he does something more than merely preparatory to the commission of the offence'. The person who enters a building as a trespasser commits the offence of burglary (s 9(1)(a) of the Theft Act 1968) only if he has the *intent* to commit theft, rape, criminal damage or grievous bodily harm.

The *Oxford English Dictionary* defines intention in this way: '... that which is intended or purposed; a purpose or design; ultimate purpose; the aim of an action ...' How is intention defined by the courts? There are two aspects to this question.

3.3.1 Where a consequence is wanted for its own sake

This is often called *direct intention* and is relatively easy to define. If a particular consequence prohibited by the law is wanted for its own sake then clearly the consequence is intended by the actor. If the actor is fighting an opponent and is trying his best seriously to injure that person then he clearly *intends* serious injury. He may still intend serious injury if he realises that his chances of success are less than 100%. In fact, it is not simply that a belief in a 100% chance of success is not required. It will make sense to say that he intends as long as he thinks that there is *some* chance of success, however small. For example, if he appreciates that his opponent is a much more skilled fighter than himself but nevertheless he keeps on trying to knock the opponent unconscious, he still *intends* serious injury to the victim.

3.3.2 Consequences foreseen but not wanted

Problems arise however where the actor does not have an aim, purpose, goal or desire to cause a prohibited consequence, but he realises that he will cause it, or is almost certain to cause it, if he goes ahead and pursues his true aim or purpose. Examples discussed below include *Hyam v DPP*, *Hancock and Shankland* and *Nedrick*. In some cases, it is difficult to discern any particular aim or purpose underlying the actor's conduct, and yet he too realises that he will cause or is almost certain to cause a prohibited consequence if he engages in that conduct. Examples discussed below include *Moloney* and *Woollin*.

There is no doubt that this is a different state of mind from that of an actor who aims to cause a prohibited consequence, but, viewed as a matter of the actor's blameworthiness for causing the prohibited consequence, it is strongly arguable that there is no great difference between the two states of mind. Consequently, foresight of this kind without aim or purpose is often included within the definition of intention by calling it *oblique intention*. Take the example of a defendant who insures a package scheduled to travel on a transatlantic plane and who conceals a bomb in the package timed to explode in mid-flight. He does this in order to claim on the insurance policy. The defendant bears no personal animosity towards the passengers and crew. Indeed, he has no idea whatsoever as to their identity and might actually prefer that they did not die.

However, he realises that in order to achieve his goal of collecting the insurance money it is inevitable that the passengers and crew will die when the bomb explodes. Does the defendant *intend* to kill them? The dictionary definition of intention confines its meaning to what is called *direct intention*, that is, where a consequence is wanted for its own sake. If the law confined its definition in this way, the defendant, who does not seek the fatalities for their own sake, would not be guilty of murder. This would strike most of us as wholly unreasonable and likely to lead to a loss of respect for the rule of law. Thus, the meaning of the word has been 'stretched' by the judges to encompass this kind of behaviour. However, defining the precise limits of *oblique intent* has caused the judiciary considerable problems.

An analysis of 'intention' can best be achieved by focusing on six cases which, if analysed chronologically, help to illustrate the dilemma which has faced the judiciary over the last 40 years. The cases are: *DPP v Smith* (1961); *Hyam v DPP* (1974); *Moloney* (1985); *Hancock and Shankland* (1986); *Nedrick* (1986); *Woollin* (1998).

DPP v Smith and the objective approach

The *Smith* case was authority for the proposition that intention should be assessed *objectively*, that is, by reference to the *foresight* of the reasonable man and not by proof that the defendant actually foresaw the particular consequence of his actions. Smith was the driver of a car which contained stolen goods. He was ordered by a police officer to leave his vehicle. Smith panicked and accelerated away with the police officer still holding onto the car. At a speed thought to be in the region of 60 mph the officer was thrown from the car and fell under the wheels of an oncoming vehicle causing his death. The House of Lords concluded that a person could be taken to have foreseen the nature and probable consequences to flow from his actions (or presumably inaction). If the jury concluded that a reasonable man would foresee the consequence then, despite any protestations to the contrary, the defendant could be said to have intended that consequence. Viscount Kilmuir said:

> The only test available ... is what the ordinary responsible man would, in all the circumstances of the case, have contemplated as the natural and probable result ... .

This case was authority therefore for the view that the intent required for the crime of murder (an intention to cause death or serious bodily harm) was purely objective. It mattered not that the defendant did not foresee the prohibited consequence of his act. The decision was subjected to enormous criticism and many judges were seriously concerned at the width of the judgment. The matter was referred to the Law Commission who reported in 1967 (*Imputed Criminal Intent: DPP v Smith*, Law Com 10). The Commission recommended the adoption of a subjective test with the jury free to infer intent from the totality of the evidence they had heard. This led to Parliament eventually, but arguably unsuccessfully, seeking to prevent a person being convicted of a crime requiring intent even though he did not in reality foresee the outcome of his conduct. Section 8 of the Criminal Justice Act (CJA) 1967, provides that:

> A court or jury, in determining whether a person has committed an offence:
>
> (a) shall not be bound in law to infer that he intended or foresaw a result of his actions by reason only of its being a natural and probable consequence of those actions; but
>
> (b) shall decide whether he did intend or foresee that result by reference to all the evidence, drawing such inferences from the evidence as appear proper in the circumstances.

Section 8 has since been confirmed as an evidential provision only and not one which amended the substantive law. It can be argued that the section did not reverse the decision in *Smith* although plainly that is what Parliament thought it was doing, as was confirmed by subsequent judicial pronouncement (see *Wallett* (1968) and Lord Hailsham in *Hyam v DPP* (1974)). It is of interest to note that, in *Frankland* (1987), the Privy Council (composed of five Law Lords) declared *Smith* to have been wrongly decided. However, decisions of the Council cannot overrule decisions of the House of Lords.

Hyam v DPP and foresight of high probability

In *Hyam v DPP* (1974), a strong House of Lords (Lords Hailsham LC, Dilhorne, Diplock, Cross, Kilbrandon) engaged in detailed analysis of the *mens rea* for murder and, in particular, of the degree of foresight of the prohibited consequence it was necessary for the defendant to possess in order to incur liability. Ought he to be:

- *virtually certain* that the consequence would occur; or

- would an appreciation that the consequence would be *highly likely* to occur be enough; or

- would mere *likelihood* or ordinary *probability* be enough?

In this case, the appellant had been a man's mistress for some time but the relationship had largely ceased because the woman was suffering from medical problems. Her lover commenced a relationship with another woman, Mrs Booth, and Mrs Hyam became jealous. Eventually she drove to her rival's house and set fire to it at 2.30 am by pouring petrol through the letterbox and setting it alight. She then drove home. She did not warn the occupants of the house or call the emergency services. As a result two of her rival's daughters were killed. She admitted to the police that she knew what she had done was very dangerous but that she did not intend to cause death or serious harm to any person; she wished only to frighten or scare Mrs Booth into leaving the district in order that she could recommence her relationship with Mr Jones, her former lover. She was convicted of murder. The House held (Lords Diplock and Kilbrandon dissenting) that a person murdered another if he knowingly committed an act:

- which was aimed at someone; and

- was committed with the intention of causing death or serious bodily injury.

But, Lord Hailsham stated, intention can also exist:

> ... where the defendant knows that there is a serious risk that death or serious bodily harm will ensue from his acts and he commits those acts deliberately and without lawful excuse with the intention to expose a potential victim to that risk as the result of those acts. It does not matter in such circumstances whether the defendant desires those consequences to ensue or not.

Lord Hailsham was of the view that only evidence that the accused foresaw the consequence as a 'moral certainty' would be sufficient evidence from which to conclude that she intended that consequence. Viscount Dilhorne said:

> A man may do an act with a number of intentions. If he does it deliberately and intentionally, knowing when he does it that it is *highly probable* that grievous bodily harm will result, I think most people would say and be justified in saying that whatever other intentions he may have had as well, he at least intended grievous bodily harm.

Lord Diplock took the 'uncomplicated view' that:

> No distinction is to be drawn ... between the state of mind of one who does an act because he desires it to produce a particular evil consequence and the state of mind of one who does the act knowing full well that it is likely to produce that consequence although it may not be the object he was seeking to achieve by doing the act.

The following passages taken from the judgment of James LJ in *Mohan* (1975) illustrate the deep division of opinion held by the judiciary at this time as to how the word intention should be defined. Judges in the Court of Appeal rejected the view that the *Hyam* meaning of intention was applicable throughout the criminal law. Having reviewed the speeches in *Hyam* James LJ went on to comment:

> We do not find in the speeches of their Lordships in *Hyam* anything which binds us to hold that *mens rea* in the offence of *attempt* is proved by establishing beyond reasonable doubt that the accused knew or correctly foresaw that the consequences of his act unless interrupted would 'as a high degree of probability', or would be 'likely' to, be the commission of the complete offence
> ...

He went on to state:

> ... evidence of knowledge of likely consequences, or from which knowledge of likely consequences can be inferred, is evidence by which intent may be established but it is not, in relation to the offence of attempt, to be equated with intent. If the jury find such knowledge established they may and using common sense, they probably will find intent proved, but it is not the case that they must do so [p 200].

Similarly, in *Belfon* (1976), Wien J stated that:

> ... we do not find ... in any of their speeches of their Lordships in *Hyam's* case anything which obliges us to hold that the 'intent' in wounding with intent is proved by foresight that serious injury is *likely* to result from a deliberate act.

Moloney, Hancock and Shankland, Nedrick – foresight as evidence of intention

Clearly, the judges in *Mohan and Belfon* saw foresight not as *intent*, but merely *evidence* from which a jury might, or might not, infer intent. Such disarray amongst the judiciary was evident throughout the 1970s, and an attempt was made to introduce clarity to the debate in two significant House of Lords' cases in the mid-1980s. In both *Moloney* (1985) and *Hancock and Shankland* (1986), the House of Lords considered the relationship between foresight of consequence and proof of intention. In the former case, the defendant tragically killed his stepfather with whom he had 'enjoyed a happy and loving relationship'. Death occurred as a result of a contest between the two men to see who was the faster at loading a shotgun. Moloney was then challenged by his stepfather to fire the gun which he did, killing him instantly. Both men had been drinking. The House of Lords in allowing his appeal against a murder conviction was of the opinion that knowledge of foresight of consequences was at best 'material from which the jury, properly directed, may infer intention when considering a crime of ... intent'. It was clearly stated that the trial judge should seek to avoid any 'elaboration or paraphrase of what is meant by intent ... and should leave to the jury's good sense the question as to whether the accused acted with the necessary intent'. Lord Bridge, who gave the leading speech, with which his brethren concurred, purported to create guidelines for juries in the few cases where it is necessary to direct a jury by reference to foresight of consequences. These cases would be those where the defendant's purpose was something other than causing death or serious bodily harm but where one of these results is an inevitable or probable consequence. The jury should be invited to consider:

- whether the consequence which had to be proved was the 'natural consequence' of the accused's act; and

- whether the accused foresaw that it would be a natural consequence of his act.

If positive answers to both these issues were agreed by the jury then it would be 'proper' for them to *draw the inference* if they so wished that the accused intended that consequence. It is advisable to note that, in Lord Bridge's view, in such circumstances juries *may* rather than *must* reach the conclusion that intention is proved, because foresight of consequences is no more than evidence of the existence of the intent.

The significance of *Moloney* was that it marked a shift away from attempts to define intention for juries to a recognition that intention was a matter for the 'good sense' of the jury. At Cardiff Crown Court in May 1985, Mann J used the *Moloney* guidelines in his summing up to the jury in the case of *Hancock and Shankland* (1986). The defendants, striking miners, were accused of murdering a taxi driver who had been driving a miner to work during the bitter dispute of 1984. A concrete block weighing 46 lbs and measuring 18 x 9 x 5 inches was thrown over the parapet of a bridge in an endeavour, it was claimed, to block the road and thus prevent the man from getting to work. Sadly, it hit the taxi, with fatal consequences for the driver. They pleaded guilty to manslaughter but the Crown was not prepared to proceed on that basis. The jury convicted them of murder but the Court of Appeal substituted convictions of manslaughter on the grounds that the *Moloney* guidelines, as they stood, were unsafe and misleading because they contained no definition of what was meant by 'natural consequence'. The Crown appealed. In the event the appeal was dismissed. If one accepts that the intention was to block the road and frighten the occupants of the taxi, then the defendants' desire or purpose was not to cause grievous bodily harm or death. Therefore, foresight became a vital factor in the equation. Lord Scarman, commenting on the guidelines, felt that the jury may not have gained much assistance because of the absence of any guidance 'as to the relevance or weight of the probability factor in determining whether they should, or could properly, infer from foresight of a consequence ... the intent to bring about that consequence'. The *Moloney* guidelines referred only to *natural* consequences flowing from the act and ignored the matter of probability although Lord Bridge did suggest that 'if a consequence is natural, it is really otiose to speak of it as also being probable'.

The House of Lords considered that it was possible that a jury might understand *natural consequence* as indicating something which followed in an unbroken causal chain from the initial event whether it was highly likely or not. This is not to say that Lord Bridge denied the importance of probability as he commented after reviewing decided cases on specific intent that 'the probability of the consequence taken to have been foreseen must be little short of overwhelming before it will suffice to establish the necessary intent'. The fact remains that the guidelines did not refer to probability and Lord Scarman concluded that they were defective 'and should not be used as they stand without further guidance'.

In approaching the issue of intent one should not ignore *Moloney*. As Lord Scarman points out, the case did 'clarify the law ... in view of the history of confusion in this branch of the law'. Therefore, the following points need to be noted about the *Moloney / Hancock and Shankland* approach:

- the mental element in murder is a specific intent, that is, to kill or cause serious bodily harm;

- 'foresight of consequence is no more than evidence of the existence of intent; it must be considered, and its weight assessed, together with all the evidence in the case. Foresight does not necessarily imply the existence of intention, though it may be a fact from which ... a jury may think it right to infer the necessary intent'; and

- the probability of the result of an act is a matter for the jury to consider in seeking to determine whether or not the result was intended '... the degree of probability of death or serious injury resulting from the act done may be critically important. Its importance will depend upon the degree of probability ... and ... the greater the probability of a consequence the more likely it is that the consequence was foreseen and that if the consequence was foreseen the greater the probability is that the consequence was also intended'.

This issue of the degree of foresight required by the defendant was pursued further by Lord Lane CJ in *Nedrick* (1986). The facts were essentially the same as those in *Hyam*. The Court of Appeal had the benefit of Lord Scarman's speech in *Hancock and Shankland* and Lord Lane asserted that a jury should be directed to consider:

- how probable was the consequence which resulted from the defendant's act; and

- whether he foresaw that consequence.

From this, it follows that if the defendant does not appreciate that the consequence (death or serious bodily harm in this case) is *likely* to result from his act, he cannot have intended to bring it about. If, however, he believed there was a risk of the consequence occurring, the jury would have to consider the probability of that consequence occurring and his foresight of it. No degree of probability is specified but it would be unlikely that a jury would infer intention except on proof of foresight of a very high degree, perhaps of virtual certainty. However, Lord Lane did not leave it at that. He concluded his judgment by stating that:

> Where the charge is murder ... the jury should be directed that they are *not entitled* to infer the necessary intention, unless they feel sure that death or serious bodily harm was a virtual certainty (barring some unforeseen intervention) as a result of the defendant's actions and that the defendant appreciated that such was the case.

Of course, this *does* specify a minimum degree of probability which must exist and which the defendant must foresee before the jury is *entitled* to infer intention. It is inconsistent with Lord Lane's earlier pronouncement (in which he went so far as to say that, if a defendant thought that he was exposing a victim only to a *slight risk* of being killed, 'then it may be easy for the jury to conclude that he did not intend to bring about that result'). In *Moloney*, as interpreted by Lord Scarman in *Hancock and Shankland*, this was a matter of evidence to be handled by the jury. If Lord Lane's final pronouncement in *Nedrick* was accepted as the correct one, then, though the jury had not lost its discretion on whether or not to draw the inference, it was being told as a matter of law that it could only do so if first satisfied that the defendant had foreseen with virtual certainty. This approach had the merit that it sought to draw as sharp a line as possible between intention and recklessness, insisting that foresight of nothing less than overwhelming probability (virtual certainty) would permit intention to be inferred. Risk taking involving foresight of lesser degrees of probability would be the province of recklessness.

Even so, just as different juries may in practice interpret a term such as virtual certainty in different ways, so judges in this area cannot be relied upon to maintain consistency of language in directing juries. The danger that the line marking the boundary between intention and recklessness would be eroded was well exemplified by the decision in *Walker and Hayles* (1990). The charge was attempted murder for which intention must be proved. The trial judge had used the words 'very high degree of probability' on at least three occasions when responding to a jury question as to what would amount to an intent to kill. The appeal against conviction was based upon the assertion that the jury would have been confused into believing that a high degree of probability of death could be equated with an intent to kill. It was said that the judge should have used the words *virtually certain* in cases where the simple direction as to *mens rea* was not enough. On a charge of attempted murder, the prosecution must prove an intent to kill (serious bodily harm not being sufficient). In the event, it was decided that there was little if any difference between what was highly probable and virtually certain to occur, and therefore the use of the words 'a very high degree of probability' did not amount to a misdirection. The process of erosion seemed to have gathered pace when the Court of Appeal in *Woollin* (1997) refused to reject the trial judge's direction to the jury that an inference of intention could be drawn from proof of foresight of a *substantial risk*, a term redolent of recklessness if ever there was one.

To summarise the position before the decision of the House of Lords in *Woollin*, the most recent of the six cases:

- neither Parliament nor the courts had supplied any clear definition of intention. It is likely that intention was constituted by an aim or purpose to cause a result. *Desiring* a result was also intention but it was not necessary to prove desire. Where the actor had an aim or purpose, he was only required to foresee some chance of success. He did not need to foresee any high degree of probability of success;

- in the absence of aim or purpose to cause the result, the actor's foresight that he would or might cause the result was not *in itself* an intention to cause the result. So, to call foresight of virtual certainty (or any lesser degree of probability) oblique *intention* was misleading. As *Moloney, Hancock and Shankland, Nedrick* and the later decision in *Scalley* (1995) all loudly proclaimed, whatever intention was, it did not include foresight of consequences alone;

- in those cases where there was foresight of a consequence without aim or purpose to cause that consequence, a jury was *entitled* but not *bound* to infer intention from proof of such foresight. The House of Lords in *Moloney* and *Hancock* had not specified foresight of a minimum degree of probability, but the Court of Appeal in *Nedrick* asserted that the jury must be satisfied that the defendant foresaw the consequence as *virtually certain*. However, in *Walker and Hayles*, the Court of Appeal reluctantly accepted the formula, *'very highly probable'* as an alternative expression for virtual certainty, and, before being overruled by the House of Lords, the Court of Appeal in *Woollin* was prepared to countenance *'substantial risk'*. Wherever the line was drawn, any lesser degree of probability was neither intention nor evidence from which intention could be inferred;

- it was unnecessary to give the jury anything other than simple guidance in straightforward intention cases. More complicated guidance should only be given in cases raising difficult issues of foresight.

Criticisms of the *Moloney, Hancock and Shankland* and *Nedrick* approach

The lack of any clear definition of intention did not cause problems where the defendant had an aim or purpose to cause the consequence, but it created a good deal of confusion in the problematic 'foresight' cases. Juries were being invited to infer one state of mind (intention) from another state of mind (foresight of virtual certainty) without being told what intention was. Moreover, since intention probably meant aim or purpose, it was difficult to understand how such a state of mind could be inferred from foresight in those cases where the jury had probably ruled out aim or purpose in the first place. In this context, it is as well to remember that the foresight cases were those in which the defendant did not appear to have an aim or purpose to cause the consequence. As Lord Lane said in his judgment in *Nedrick*:

> ... if the jury are satisfied that at the material time the defendant recognised that death or serious harm would be virtually certain ... then that is a fact from which they may find it easy to infer that he intended to kill or do serious bodily harm, *even though he may not have had any desire to achieve that result.*

Small wonder, perhaps, that Lord Lane stated in an extra-judicial capacity to the House of Lords Select Committee on Murder in 1989 that '*Nedrick* was not as clear as it should have been'.

The process of inferring intention was subjected to very strong academic criticism. The gist of this criticism was that, since foresight of virtual certainty should be regarded as included within intention (in other words, it *is* intention, albeit oblique), there is no further state of mind to be inferred. Thus, Professor Glanville Williams asserted:

> The proper view is that intention includes not only desire of consequence (purpose) but also foresight of certainty of the consequence, *as a matter of legal definition*. What the jury infer from the facts is the defendant's direct intention or foresight of a consequence as certain; there is no additional element to be 'inferred' [(1989) 105 LQR 387].

Similarly, Professor Andrew Ashworth explained:

> What the courts probably meant to say is that intention includes both purpose and foresight with regard to a particular consequence occurring in the ordinary course of events ... the evidential process of drawing inferences – which is basic to every case where the defendant does not confess, since one cannot see into another person's mind – should not be confused with the legal definition of intention [*Principles of Criminal Law*, 1991, Oxford: Clarendon, pp 150–51].

A perhaps less important, but nonetheless puzzling, aspect of Lord Lane's judgment in *Nedrick* was his assertion that, before the jury could infer intention from foresight of virtual certainty, they had to be satisfied not only that the defendant foresaw such virtual certainty, but also that the consequence actually was virtually certain to occur. Whilst *foresight* of virtual certainty would generally imply that a consequence *was* virtually certain, it is the defendant's state of mind which is in issue. If he went ahead with an action in the belief that a consequence was virtually certain to result, the fact that it was not (for reasons perhaps unknown to him) would make no difference to the degree of blameworthiness which he bore. If, after all, it did occur, then his liability ought to be exactly the same as in the case where he foresaw with virtual certainty and the outcome was a virtually certainty.

Woollin and foresight of virtual certainty as intention

In 1998, in the case of *Woollin*, the House of Lords had yet another opportunity to bring some coherence to the approach to the meaning of intention. The defendant had been left with the task of feeding his three month old baby son. He admitted that he had 'lost his cool' when the baby started to choke on his food. He had shaken him and then, in a fit of rage or frustration, had thrown him in the direction of his pram which was standing against the wall some three or four feet away. He knew that the baby's head had hit something hard (the wall or, possibly, the floor) but denied intending to throw him against the wall or wanting him to die or suffer serious injury. The trial judge directed the jury that they might infer intention if they were satisfied that when he threw the baby, the defendant appreciated that there was a '*substantial risk*' of causing serious harm. The Court of Appeal rejected the defendant's contention that 'substantial risk' was merely a test of recklessness and that the judge should have used the phrase 'virtual certainty'. The question put to their Lordships on a further appeal to the House of Lords was whether in murder, where there is no direct evidence that the defendant's purpose was to kill or inflict serious injury on the victim, it is necessary to direct the jury that they may only infer an intent to do serious injury if they are satisfied: (a) that serious bodily harm was a virtually certain consequence of the defendant's voluntary act; and (b) that the defendant appreciated that fact. In other words, was the *Nedrick* direction correct?

Their Lordships were unanimous in quashing the conviction for murder and substituting a conviction for manslaughter. Lords Hope, Nolan and Steyn were agreed upon the reasons for doing so and they are contained within Lord Steyn's speech. Lords Browne-Wilkinson and Hoffman expressed agreement only with the result and gave no indication of their reasons for doing so. Lord Steyn rejected the trial judge's use of the phrase 'substantial risk' since it blurred the line between intention and recklessness. He upheld the validity of the *Nedrick* direction but made modifications to it. First, the jury should not be asked to consider the two questions which Lord Lane derived from Lord Scarman's speech in *Hancock and Shankland*, namely, how probable was the consequence which resulted from the defendant's act, and, did the accused foresee that consequence (see the discussion of *Nedrick*, above)? Secondly, instead of being invited to '*infer*' intention from proof of foresight of virtual certainty, the jury should be invited to '*find*' it from such proof. Thirdly, he stated that Lord Lane's suggestion that there may be an irresistible inference that a man intends a result which he knows for all practical purposes to be an inevitable consequence of his actions was not part of the direction. Consequently, the amended direction now reads:

> Where the charge is murder and in the rare cases where the simple direction is not enough, the jury should be directed that they are not entitled to find the necessary intention, unless they feel sure that death or serious bodily harm was a virtual certainty (barring some unforeseen intervention) as a result of the defendant's actions and that the defendant appreciated that such was the case. The decision is one for the jury to be reached on a consideration of all the evidence.

The elimination of the first two questions removes the logical inconsistency evident in Lord Lane's judgment in *Nedrick* between allowing the jury to deliberate on the whole range of probability and requiring them to be satisfied that the defendant foresaw nothing less than virtual certainty. It is important to note that, in making the second modification, replacing *infer* by *find*, Lord Steyn specifically referred to and accepted the criticisms of the '*infer*' formula expressed by commentators such as Professor Glanville Williams and Professor Ashworth (see above). The clear message of this modification, therefore, seems to be that Lord Steyn accepted that foresight of virtual certainty is intention, not merely evidence of intention. This message is reinforced by other comments made by Lord Steyn. For instance, he said of the original *Nedrick* direction: 'The effect ... is that a result foreseen as virtually certain is an intended result.' Similarly, he pointed out that 'in *Moloney* Lord Bridge said that if a person foresees the probability of a consequence as little short of overwhelming, this "will suffice to *establish* the necessary intent"' (Lord Steyn's emphasis).

Does this mean that it is now finally decided that intention in English criminal law comprises both direct and oblique intention, so that a jury which decides that the defendant foresaw the virtual certainty of a consequence without aiming to cause it, having a purpose to cause it, or desiring to cause it, nevertheless has *found* that he intended it? No reader who has studied the discussion thus far will be surprised to learn that the answer must still be 'not necessarily'. The correct interpretation of the decision in *Woollin* remains in doubt and clarification by subsequent cases is still awaited. The major difficulty arises from the fact that Lord Steyn adopted the *Nedrick* direction, albeit with modifications. The *Nedrick* direction was based on the premise that the jury's role was to *infer* intention. It assumed that, since foresight of virtual certainty was not in itself intention, it was within the jury's discretion to infer or not to infer, even though they were satisfied that the defendant foresaw virtual certainty. The sole restriction on this discretion was that it only became available to the jury when they *were* satisfied that the defendant foresaw virtual certainty. If they were not satisfied of that they were *not entitled* to infer intention. If satisfied, they were *entitled* but *not obliged* to infer intention. The modified direction continues to use the language of *entitlement* where, in truth, if foresight of virtual certainty *is* intention the jury is *obliged* to find intention, not merely entitled to do so. The argument currently advanced by those who deny that *Woollin* has declared that foresight of virtual certainty is intention (for example, Mirfield, P [1999] Crim LR 246) is that, just as in pre-*Woollin* days, *not being entitled* to find intention unless satisfied of foresight of virtual certainty inevitably implies *being entitled not* to find intention, even if satisfied of foresight of virtual certainty. In response, it might be objected that the one does not inevitably imply the other and that it is open to judges to interpret the direction according to the new perspective introduced by the modification to *'find'*. Lord Steyn's continued insistence that 'the decision is one for the jury to be reached on a consideration of all the evidence' is not incompatible with this view, since the jury retains the responsibility for deciding whether the defendant did foresee virtual certainty.

Other doubts about the effect of *Woollin* arise because Lords Browne-Wilkinson and Hoffman did not express any support for Lord Steyn's reasoning and because Lord Steyn himself was clear that he was discussing intention only in relation to the offence of murder: '... it does not follow that "intent" necessarily has precisely the same meaning in every context in the criminal law.' It should also be noted that, in approving the rest of the *Nedrick* direction, Lord Steyn appears to perpetuate the difficulties arising out of Lord

Lane's suggestion that death or serious bodily harm must actually *be* a virtual certainty rather than merely be *foreseen* by the defendant to be such.

Reform

The struggle of the courts over the last 40 years to devise a coherent approach to the meaning of intention, and the fact that, even after *Woollin*, it is impossible to be confident about accurately interpreting that approach, suggest that a statutory definition of intention is desirable. Attempts to provide such a definition have now been made on a number of occasions. In its 1989 draft Criminal Code (*A Criminal Code for England and Wales*, Law Com 177, cl 18(b)), the Law Commission offered the following definition:

> ... a person acts intentionally with respect to a ... result when he acts either in order to bring it about or being aware that it will occur in the ordinary course of events.

This definition was criticised on the grounds both that it was under-inclusive and over-inclusive. It did not catch the terrorist bomber who knew that he would cause death if the bomb went off but who also knew that the bomb had only a 50% chance of exploding, because he was not 'aware that it will occur in the ordinary course of events'. Conversely, it allegedly did catch the person who acted from the best of motives but who knew that death would occur in the ordinary course of events, such as a father who throws his young son off the top of a blazing block of flats in a vain attempt to save his life.

In response, the Law Commission produced a revised definition in its report, *Offences Against the Person and General Principles* (Law Com 218, 1993). According to this definition, a person acts intentionally with respect to a result when:

(a) it is his purpose to cause it; or

(b) although it is not his purpose to cause it, he knows that it would occur in the ordinary course of events if he were to succeed in his purpose of causing some other result.

This definition was substantially reproduced in the Home Office Consultation Paper of 1998 dealing with proposed reform of the law on offences against the person. The second limb includes the bomber and excludes the desperate father. Yet, Professor JC Smith considered that even this improved version was defective. Considering the facts of *Woollin*, Professor Smith argued that, even if it could be proved that the father foresaw the virtual certainty of the baby's death or serious injury, he would not have intended it on this definition because he did not have a purpose to cause it and did not have any other purpose sufficient to fall within the second limb of the definition (he argued that Woollin was merely venting his anger, which is not a purpose to cause a result). In consequence, Professor Smith has suggested that the second limb should be amended to read, 'he knows that it *will occur in the ordinary course of events,* or that it would do so if he were to succeed in his purpose of causing some other result'. This amendment would certainly deal with the *Woollin* issue but surely at the cost of once again endangering the desperate father.

Of course, if *Woollin* is interpreted as ruling that foresight of virtual certainty is intention, then it can be argued that the courts have already succeeded in defining intention in much the same way as in this proposed statutory definition. This depends in part on whether *foresight of virtual certainty* can be equated with *knowledge that a result will occur in the ordinary course of events.* In his speech in *Woollin,* Lord Steyn certainly considered that the two were 'very similar'.

In his article, 'After *Woollin'* ([1999] Crim LR 532), Professor A Norrie has suggested that a clear definition of intention which includes foresight of virtual certainty (either derived from *Woollin* or from a statutory provision) will raise further problems. He argues that it will be too narrow to include cases which should be included, such as *Hyam v DPP,* and yet may be too broad in including cases which should not be included, such as *Steane,* or cases in which doctors act out of medical necessity. In putting this argument, he takes the view that there is a moral dimension in judgments about liability for an offence such as murder which depends on good and bad motives and which cannot be captured in the language of intention and foresight. As long as the jury were given the discretion whether or not to infer intention, they could reflect society's moral perceptions in the exercise of that discretion. This remains the case if Lord Steyn's reformulation of the *Nedrick* direction has not removed that discretion. If it has done so, or if a statutory definition were to do so, then some other way would have to be found to reflect moral perceptions, so as at the least to absolve those with sufficiently good motives. Professor Norrie is not even convinced that *Woollin* has put an end to the possibility that liability in murder may yet be founded on foresight of high probability rather than of virtual certainty:

> Another case with different moral facts, reflecting a more manifest malice, could well let the *Hyam* genie out of the bottle. Indeed, the broader spirit of *Hyam* has always lurked within the indirect intention cases even when they have denied it, and this is as true of *Woollin* as the others.

Specific, basic and ulterior intent

Such is the commitment to establishing intention as a key determiner of fault that certain crimes are designated as *specific intent* offences. The term was recognised at the highest level in *DPP v Beard* (1920), where Lord Birkenhead dealing with the relevance of a plea of intoxication in respect of a brutal killing said: '... that where a specific intent is an essential element in the offence ... drunkenness ... should be taken into consideration ...'

Lord Birkenhead later referred to specific intent as meaning simply the intent required to constitute the particular crime. However, though Lord Simon attempted, in *DPP v Majewski* (1976), to provide a more detailed exposition of what is meant by *specific intent*, it cannot be said that he was successful or that his approach has been adopted. He tried to argue that specific intent required an element of *purpose*, but this is at odds with the actual requirements of crimes considered to be specific intent offences. In truth, no clear meaning of the term has emerged and no principle seems to underlie the designation of crimes as requiring proof of specific intent.

In practice, *specific intent* crimes need to be distinguished from *basic intent* crimes mainly because intoxication is, as we shall see in Chapter 7, normally a defence for crimes of *specific* intent but not for those of *basic* intent. Lord Simon in *DPP v Morgan* (1975) stated that basic intent crimes are those where the *mens rea* does not 'go beyond the *actus reus*'. He cites assault as an example where the consequence is 'very closely connected with the act'. The *actus reus* is 'an act which causes another person to apprehend immediate and unlawful violence. The *mens rea* corresponds exactly'. The problem with Lord Simon's view, however, is that his exposition does not always neatly fit in with the decided cases. Take for example, murder where the *mens rea* is an intention to kill or commit grievous bodily harm. This is universally agreed by the case law to be a crime of *specific* intent. However, with this crime the *mens rea* not only fails to extend beyond the *actus reus* but actually falls short of it in the case of a defendant who intended only to commit grievous bodily harm to the victim! Similarly with s 18 of the OAPA 1861. This is categorised as a crime of *specific* intent despite the fact that this is not a crime where the *mens rea* extends beyond the *actus reus*. When attempting to identify a crime of *specific intent*, best practice is to refer to the leading case(s) to see how the crime has been categorised by the courts.

Thus murder, s 18 of the OAPA 1861, theft and attempts are *specific intent* crimes; manslaughter, rape, criminal damage and ss 20 and 47 of the OAPA 1861 are crimes of basic intent. As a rule of thumb, those crimes requiring intent to be proved in relation to one element of the *actus reus* fit into the former category whilst those having either intent or recklessness as part of the definition fit into the latter. This means that in the case of a crime of *basic intent* the prosecution need not prove intention. Proof that the defendant acted recklessly will be enough.

A further term, *ulterior intent*, is evident in some case reports. This is taken to refer to definitions of crime where the *mens rea* goes beyond an element of the *actus reus*, that is, the *mens rea* of the crime requires the prosecution to prove that the defendant intended to produce a consequence beyond the *actus reus* of the crime. Burglary will serve as an example where the *actus reus* is complete once a person enters a building or part thereof as a trespasser. However, there is a further requirement ulterior to the *actus reus* which demands an *intent* to commit one of four crimes (theft, grievous bodily harm, rape, unlawful damage). It is this element to which the label ulterior intent is attached. *Specific intent* crimes may, of course, incorporate *ulterior intent*, as with burglary which does not include recklessness as part of the required *mens rea*.

3.4   Recklessness

Recklessness suffices for most crimes where the prosecution need to prove *mens rea* in relation to at least one element of the *actus reus*. As with intention Parliament has yet to define this key fault term and so the task has been left to the courts. The *Concise Oxford Dictionary* defines the term as 'lacking caution, regardless of consequences, rash, heedless of danger'.

Traditionally, the term has been taken to mean the deliberate and conscious taking of an unreasonable risk by the defendant. The defendant realises that if he carries out a particular act or fails to do so he is taking a risk that a particular consequence or result will occur. It does not matter that he has no particular wish or desire that it will occur; all that matters is that the defendant realises that he is engaging in risky activity.

The risk must not be one which he would be justified in taking and the courts judge this objectively on the basis of the social utility of the act. For example, a surgeon developing a new form of surgical procedure for seriously-ill patients may take a large risk when performing an operation but if the operation goes badly and the patient dies the courts would be unlikely to find that he acted recklessly, at least if there was no safer alternative procedure available. The court would balance the very high social utility value of his acts (assessed objectively) against the risk he took. They would almost certainly conclude that the former outweighed the latter and that he had not, therefore, acted recklessly. Contrast the surgeon with the armed political terrorist who robs a bank in an effort to secure funds for his organisation. In order only to attract the attention of staff and customers, he fires his pistol into the ceiling, but unfortunately the bullet ricochets from the ceiling and wounds a customer. Let us suppose that expert evidence presented at the subsequent trial suggests that the statistical chance of this happening was very small indeed. Was the terrorist reckless? Yes, because here the court would judge the social utility value of his act as nil and therefore *any* risk of injury associated with the act would constitute recklessness on his part. He would, therefore, be guilty of an offence under the OAPA 1861 for which recklessness sufficed for the *mens rea*.

But what of the person who simply gave no thought to the consequences of his action and therefore did not appreciate that he was taking a risk? Is this person reckless? This has been a major dilemma for the judges since the early 1980s. It had been assumed prior to the decision in *Metropolitan Police Commissioner v Caldwell* (1981) that the approach to the assessment of recklessness should be a subjective one. The decision of the Court of Criminal

Appeal in *Cunningham* (1957) is the major authority for this assertion. The court was concerned with the meaning of 'malicious'. The modern word superseding malicious is reckless. The court adopted the principle contained in Professor Kenny's *Outlines of Criminal Law* (15th edn, 1936, Cambridge: Cambridge UP) that malice was not synonymous with wickedness but required either intention or 'recklessness as to whether such harm should occur or not (that is, the *accused had foreseen* that the particular kind of harm might be done and had yet gone on to take the risk of it)'. Thus, the foundation was laid for the proposition that recklessness should be assessed subjectively. This was confirmed more than 20 years later by the Court of Appeal in *Stephenson* (1979) the facts of which invite us to examine our own views on whether or not a person who is schizophrenic should be facing criminal charges. The appellant had crept into a hollow in the side of a large haystack to sleep, but feeling cold he had lit a fire of twigs and straw inside the hollow. Needless to say the stack caught alight and damage amounting to £3,000 was caused. It is obvious that the ordinary person would be likely to foresee the immediate consequence of such an action and presumably if he or she did not desist then one would have no difficulty establishing culpability. Section 1 of the Criminal Damage Act (CDA) 1971 requires evidence that property belonging to another was damaged or destroyed by the accused either intentionally or being 'reckless as to whether any such property would be destroyed or damaged'. The judge directed the jury that the defendant could be found guilty if 'he closed his mind to the *obvious* fact of risk from his act'. They convicted. The Court of Appeal, in allowing the appeal against conviction, confirmed that the correct test of recklessness (at least for the purposes s 1 of the CDA 1971) was *subjective* in the sense that the *accused* must be proved to have foreseen the risk of damage from his act. If such knowledge or foresight was present, then liability would not be avoided simply by suppressing or closing one's mind to the risk. If the accused was suffering from a mental abnormality which affected his ability to foresee the risk, then this was an issue for the jury to consider in deciding whether or not the risk had been appreciated. *Cunningham* was applied by the Court of Appeal and this unequivocal statement appears in the judgment of Geoffrey Lane LJ:

> We wish to make it clear that the test remains subjective, that the knowledge or appreciation of risk of some damage must have entered the defendant's mind even though he may have suppressed it or driven it out.

It is difficult to imagine a clearer statement of principle. This approach endorsed the Law Commission's view expressed in its 1970 Working Paper, *General Principles: The Mental Element in Crime* (Law Com 30), and little evidence exists to show that the test did not work well or that it was a particular cause of concern for those professionally involved in the criminal law.

However, the House of Lords believed it necessary to depart from the subjective approach in the leading cases of *Caldwell* (1981) and *Lawrence* (1981), decisions which have heralded uncertainty as to how the word should be defined ever since. Each judgment was delivered by a separate division of the House of Lords on the same day. In *Caldwell*, the defendant had a grievance against the owner of a hotel and he set fire to the hotel. The fire was discovered before serious damage occurred. He was convicted of arson under s 1(1) and (2) of the CDA 1971. At his trial, he had pleaded guilty to the s 1(1) charge of intentionally or recklessly damaging the property of another, but not guilty to the more serious charge of damaging property with intent to endanger life or being reckless whether life would be endangered. His defence was that he was so drunk at the time of the act that the thought that he might be endangering the lives of the guests had never crossed his mind. He successfully appealed to the Court of Appeal but the prosecution appealed to the House of Lords on the basis that intoxication was no defence to a charge under s 1(2). This led the House of Lords to consider the meaning of recklessness in detail because (as will be seen below, 7.3) intoxication is usually a defence for crimes where the *mens rea* requirement is intention but not where recklessness suffices for the *mens rea*. The House of Lords was divided. Lords Keith and Roskill agreed with Lord Diplock that:

> ... recklessness covers a whole range of states of mind from failing to give any thought at all to whether or not there is any risk of those harmful consequences, to recognising the existence of the risk and nevertheless deciding to ignore it ... Neither state of mind seems to me to be less blameworthy than the other; but if the difference between the two constitutes the difference between what does and what does not ... amount to a guilty state of mind for the purposes of [the Act] it would not be a practical distinction for use in trial by jury. The only person who knows what the accused's mental processes were is the accused himself ... If [he] gives evidence that because of his ... drunkenness the risk of particular harmful consequences of his acts simply did not occur to him, a jury would find it hard to be satisfied beyond reasonable doubt that his true mental process was not that, but was the slightly different mental process required [by] *Cunningham* ... *mens rea* is by definition, a state of mind of the accused himself ... it cannot be the mental state of some non-existent, hypothetical person.

> ... a person is reckless [for the purposes of s 1(1) of the CDA 1971] if (1) he does an act which in fact creates an obvious risk that property will be destroyed or damaged, and (2) when he does that act he either has not given any thought to the possibility of there being any such risk or has recognised that there was some risk involved and has nonetheless gone on to do it. That would be a proper direction to the jury.

It is interesting to examine the views of his two dissenting colleagues. Lord Edmund Davies (with whom Lord Wilberforce concurred) expressed the opinion that:

> ... I have to say that I am in respectful but profound disagreement ...

and that:

... unlike negligence which has to be judged objectively, recklessness involves foresight of consequences, combined with an objective judgment of the reasonableness of the risk taken.

Lawrence (1981) was an equally significant judgment and this time the House of Lords was united in its decision. The *Caldwell* definition of recklessness was applied to the *actus reus* of the offence of causing death by reckless driving (this offence has been superseded by s 1 of the Road Traffic Act (RTA) 1988 which created the offence of causing death by dangerous driving). The facts of *Lawrence* were that the defendant was riding his motor cycle along a street in Lowestoft in Suffolk. In so doing, he collided with a pedestrian who was crossing the road. The road was subject to a speed limit of 30 mph. It was the prosecution's case that the motor cycle was being driven at a speed of between 60 and 80 mph. The defence case was that the speed was probably between 30 and 40 mph. The jury, having heard the evidence, had to choose between the two versions of events and eventually returned, by a majority of 11:1, a verdict of guilty. The direction to the jury had sought to combine statements from two cases, *Murphy* (1980) and *Stephenson* (1979). Each had dealt with the issue of recklessness; the former in the context of reckless driving and the latter dealing with criminal damage contrary to s 1 of the CDA 1971. The *Murphy* direction was in the following terms:

> A driver is guilty of driving recklessly if he deliberately disregards the obligation to drive with due care and attention or is indifferent whether or not he does so and thereby creates a risk of an accident which a driver driving with due care and attention would not create [[1980] 2 All ER 325, p 329e].

It will be clear that the *Murphy* direction is essentially adopting a subjective approach to the assessment of what constitutes reckless behaviour. A person must give at least a modicum of thought in order to be indifferent to a consequence or circumstance, that is, a person cannot be 'indifferent' to something which has never crossed his mind. The *Stephenson* direction is very positive in its support of the subjective approach. Nevertheless, *Stephenson* was overruled by *Caldwell*.

However, there still remains the issue of a defendant who fails to give *any* thought to either the circumstances or likely consequences of his actions. A person may decide to ride his motor cycle at 60 mph but give no thought whatsoever to the possibility that injury to health or damage to property may result from his decision to drive at high speed. *Lawrence* held that when giving an instruction to the jury on what is meant by reckless driving the judge should tell them that they must be satisfied, first, that the defendant was in fact driving in such a manner as to create an obvious and serious risk of causing physical injury to some other person or of doing substantial damage to property. Secondly, that when consideration was being given to the matter of a defendant's failure to give thought to an obvious and serious risk what matters is that the risk would be obvious to the ordinary prudent person, not the accused. Support for this conclusion comes from Lord Diplock's speech where he refers to the ordinary prudent person on two occasions:

> Recklessness on the part of the doer of an act presupposes that there is something in the circumstances that would have drawn the attention of an ordinary prudent individual to the possibility that his act was capable of causing ... serious harmful consequences ... and that the risk of those harmful consequences occurring was not so slight that an ordinary prudent individual would feel justified in treating them as negligible.

So in answer to the question 'obvious to whom?' the answer is the reasonable or ordinary person – not the accused. In the result, Lawrence's appeal was dismissed. Lord Diplock was concerned with the position of the person who failed to give thought to an obvious risk and, if there was an *obvious* risk, the defendant was guilty. It makes no difference whether he realised there was a risk or not. 'Not giving thought' is classed as a state of mind. Professors JC Smith and Brian Hogan have pointed out that:

> ... once the obvious (and serious) risk is proved, there seems to be only one way out for the defendant. He can escape liability only if he [can introduce some evidence that he] considered the matter and decided that there was no risk, or a 'negligible' risk [*Criminal Law*, 9th edn, 1999, London: Butterworths, p 65].

The impact of the decisions was immediate, harsh and confusing. PR Glazebrook commented:

> The present generation of Law Lords is unlikely to admit that a great mistake has been made. But it seems probable that their successors, fortified perhaps by amending legislation, will look back on these cases ... and condemn them ... as a disaster [[1984] CLJ 5].

Professor JC Smith described the two cases as 'pathetically inadequate' ([1984] Crim LR 393) and Professor Glanville Williams as 'slap happy and profoundly regrettable' ([1981] Crim LR 581). These are strong words but justified, in our opinion, because the decisions created considerable uncertainty as to the meaning of one of the key fault terms in the criminal law. Professor Smith has written that 'many judges have reported that, when they give the *Caldwell/Lawrence* direction the juror's eyes glaze'. Lord Browne-Wilkinson in *Reid* (1992) observed, 'Although after long and careful analysis of Lord Diplock's direction with the help of very skilled counsel I have, *I think*, understood it, and find it legally correct, I cannot believe that a direction in that abstract conceptual form is very helpful to a jury' (emphasis added). As Smith has observed, 'if that is the reaction of so eminent a judge, what hope has the average juror?' ([1992] Crim LR 821).

Much of this uncertainty has been as a result of the Court of Appeal feeling obliged progressively to depart from Lord Diplock's direction in relation to specific crimes. In *Pigg* (1982), Lord Lane CJ purported to apply *Caldwell* on a charge of attempted rape. The issue of recklessness arose as a result of s 1 of the Sexual Offences (Amendment) Act (SO(A)A) 1976 which required that a person must either intend to have intercourse without consent or be 'reckless as to whether that person consents to it'. In delivering the judgment of the court, the Lord Chief Justice, Lord Lane, said:

> ... so far as rape is concerned, a man is reckless if either he was indifferent and gave no thought to the possibility that the woman might not be consenting in circumstance where if any thought had been given to the matter it would have been obvious that there was a risk she was not, or he was aware of the possibility that she might not be consenting but nevertheless persisted regardless of whether she consented or not.

The difficulty with this statement is that it expects the prosecution to prove that the defendant is both indifferent *and* fails to give thought to the issue of consent. As has already been stated, how can a person be indifferent to something he has not considered?

The whole issue of recklessness in rape has developed since *Pigg* on the basis that *Caldwell* recklessness is inappropriate to the offence despite, of course, it being found in a modern criminal statute to which, according to Lord Diplock, the new definition ought to apply. In *Satnam S; Kewal S* (1983), the Court of Appeal accepted that there was ambiguity in the *Pigg* direction and was of the opinion that the use of the word 'obvious' might mislead juries into believing that an objective test should be used when considering recklessness in the context of rape. The law on rape had been clearly stated in the case of *DPP v Morgan* (1976) and the SO(A)A was deemed to be declaratory of the existing law as determined in *Morgan*. The case confirmed that if the accused in fact honestly believed that the woman consented, irrespective of whether or not that belief was based upon reasonable grounds, then the essential element of *mens rea* would be absent and he could not be convicted of the offence. Thus *Cunningham* recklessness applies to the law of rape and a defendant is guilty only if he was subjectively aware of the possibility that the victim might not be consenting and yet nevertheless proceeded to engage in sexual intercourse. It therefore follows that the 'failure to give thought' element contained in *Caldwell* has no relevance to this offence (see Chapter 10). A similar approach was adopted with regard to the offence of indecent assault in *Kimber* (1983) with Lawton LJ urging acceptance of the proposition that the 'state of mind' aptly described in the colloquial expression, 'couldn't care less', amounted to recklessness in law.

It has been steadfastly maintained that *Caldwell* and *Lawrence* have no application to offences requiring malice, and *Cunningham* recklessness will apply to s 20 of the OAPA 1861. In *W (A Minor) v Dolbey* (1983), the defendant, who was 15 years old, possessed an air gun and pointed it at a friend telling him 'there is nothing in the gun; I have got no pellets'. He fired and his friend was wounded. He was charged with unlawful and malicious wounding contrary to s 20. It was found as fact that he believed the gun to have been unloaded because he thought he had used his last pellet while shooting at bottles earlier in the day; that he had not opened the gun; third, that he had ignored the risk that the gun might be loaded. It was concluded by the justices that he had been reckless and they convicted. His appeal was allowed on the basis that *Cunningham* was still the authority to be applied and this approach has been confirmed by the subsequent House of Lords' decision in *Savage; Parmenter* (1991). Therefore, in order to obtain a conviction, it would have to be shown that on the facts known to the defendant at the time, he actually foresaw that a particular kind of harm might be done to his victim. If someone honestly believes that a gun is not loaded, then the consequences could not have been foreseen and the defendant could not be found to have acted maliciously. However, if he had pointed his gun at his friend's property, discharged it and caused criminal damage (within the meaning of the CDA 1971), say to a window, then *Caldwell* would apply if he had failed to give thought to the possible consequences of his actions, providing the ordinary person would have given thought and the risk of damage to property was obvious. Recklessness, therefore, has a variable meaning depending upon the offence in question. This was confirmed in the House of Lords' decision of *Reid* (1992) despite Lord Roskill's view in *Seymour* (1983) that the *Caldwell/Lawrence* meaning should be used throughout the criminal law, 'unless Parliament has otherwise ordained'.

The potential harshness of the *Caldwell* decision is illustrated by the case of *Elliott v C*, where a 14 year old girl who was a member of the remedial class at her school set fire to a carpet in a garden shed after staying out all night without sleep. The fire flared up out of control and destroyed the shed. It was accepted that, because of her age and general understanding, and in view of her physical condition on the night, she might not have appreciated the risk of burning down the shed by dropping lighted matches onto white spirit which she had poured onto the carpet. In the magistrates' court, the argument was accepted that Lord Diplock in *Caldwell* had been referring to a risk which would have been obvious to the particular defendant if she had given any thought to the matter, and she was found not guilty. Goff LJ, in allowing the prosecutor's appeal, reluctantly followed the reasoning that the arbiter of risk in circumstances where thought had not been given was *not* the defendant but the ordinary prudent person. The harshness, acknowledged by the court, is in finding someone with limited mental capacity guilty of a crime which requires blameworthy conduct, that is, *mens rea* in its fullest sense. As Goff LJ said:

> I agree with the conclusion reached by Glidewell J, but I do so simply because I believe myself constrained to do so by authority ... I would be lacking in candour if I were to conceal my unhappiness about the conclusion which I feel compelled to reach.

Presumably, Goff LJ, like the present writers, was questioning the purpose of labelling this particular girl a 'criminal'.

Nor is the ordinary prudent person to be bestowed with any of the characteristics of the accused (*R (Stephen Malcolm)* (1984)). This is in direct contradiction to the development of the law on provocation which, since *Camplin* (1978), has allowed juries to take account of age, sex and any other relevant characteristics of the accused in deciding whether or not a reasonable person would have lost his or her self-control (see Chapter 6). Similarly, the ordinary prudent individual possesses no particular expertise. As Tucker J stated in *Sangha* (1988):

> Is it proved that an ordinary, prudent individual would have perceived an obvious risk that property would be damaged ...? The ordinary prudent bystander is not deemed to be invested with expert knowledge relating to the construction of the property nor to have the benefit of hindsight.

On the other hand, if the defendant holds himself out as possessing specialist knowledge, for example, surgeon, then in terms of appreciation of the risk he will be compared to a 'reasonable' member of his peer group and not the ordinary prudent individual (*P & O European Ferries (Dover) Ltd* (1990)). If the defendant's failure to appreciate an obvious risk was due to intoxication as a result of consuming drugs not generally thought to be dangerous, for example, valium, then he will not be considered to have acted recklessly: *Hardie* (1984) (see above, 2.3.1).

3.4.1 Ruling out the risk

In *W (A Minor) v Dolbey* (1983), the defendant had adverted to the possibility that the gun was loaded and concluded, albeit without checking, that it was not. This situation, where thought is given to the potential risk, but after due consideration the defendant proceeds having dismissed the possibility of an unwanted consequence arising as non-existent, became known as the 'lacuna'. It does not fit into either strand of *Caldwell* recklessness. With subjective recklessness, the actor contemplates the risk and then goes ahead, having recognised that a risk exists; in the case of objective recklessness the person has to be proved to have given no thought to the possibility of risk. While the lacuna has been acknowledged by academics, the judiciary is far from positive in its attitude towards recognition. In *Chief Constable of Avon and Somerset Constabulary v Shimmen* (1986), the respondent was charged with destroying a shop window contrary to s 1(1) of the CDA 1971. He had proceeded to demonstrate to friends a particular form of Korean martial arts in which he was trained and qualified. Despite warnings that he might cause damage, he made as if to kick the window. He claimed to have 'weighed up the odds and thought he had eliminated as much risk as possible by missing the window by two inches instead of two millimetres'. The magistrates' dismissed the charge and the prosecution appealed by way of case stated. The Queen's Bench Divisional Court concluded that the respondent had been reckless in that he had created an obvious risk that the property would be damaged, recognised the risk and went on to take it. The appeal was allowed and the case remitted back to the magistrates' with a direction to convict. It was clear that Shimmen had recognised there was a risk, but had failed to take adequate precautions to eliminate it. Professor Glanville Williams made the pertinent comment that:

> This was a case where the defendant needed to be cross-examined. 'Would you have kicked with such force towards ... your baby's head relying on your ability to stop within an inch of it? No? Then you knew that there was *some* risk of your boot travelling further than you intended.' A person may be convinced of his own skill and yet know that on rare ... occasions it may fail him ['The unresolved problem of recklessness' (1988) 8 LS 74, p 75].

If, however, D believes that he has eliminated all risk by some, in fact inadequate, precaution he cannot be held reckless. However, the Court of Appeal showed no inclination to accept this argument in *Merrick* (1995). The defendant had removed old cable television cabling with the consent of the owner of the property and in so doing had exposed live wiring for a period of some six minutes. He admitted that he was aware this was dangerous but believed there would be no actual risk and would not have undertaken the work if he had not been competent to do so. He was convicted of damaging property, being reckless as to whether life was endangered contrary to s 1(2) of the CDA 1971. On appeal, it was maintained that his situation did not fall within the ambit of the *Caldwell* definition of recklessness. He had considered the risk and had gone ahead believing there to be no danger in what he was doing. The Court of Appeal drew a clear distinction between avoiding a risk and taking steps to remedy a risk which had already been created. Any steps which are taken must be aimed at preventing the risk, rather than remedying it once it had arisen. In his commentary on the case, Professor JC Smith maintains that the distinction drawn by the Court of Appeal is 'unsound' ([1995] Crim LR 802, p 805). If one draws a parallel with *Miller* (see above, 2.6) the defendant having created the danger is under a duty to remedy it. If he palpably fails to take adequate steps to rectify the problem, then given that he is aware of the danger he could be said to be reckless to the extent that he is failing to comply with his 'duty' or 'responsibility'. It is arguable that the courts are seeking to establish a policy designed to deter individuals from creating dangerous situations in the first place and thereby absolving them of the responsibility to assess risk after the event. The actions perpetrated by Shimmen and Merrick really have little or no utility value at all and certainly no benefit was likely to accrue to the shopkeeper in the former case nor the property owner in the latter.

Shimmen is not a lacuna case simply because the defendant realised there was a risk, whereas the true lacuna operates where the defendant considers the situation and concludes there is no risk if the conduct is undertaken. Professor

Smith in his commentary on *Merrick* concludes: 'There is no doubt that the so called lacuna exists in the propositions stated by Lord Diplock in *Caldwell* ... and the decision of the House of Lords' in *Reid* (1992).' In *Reid*, Lord Goff asked, in the context of the old offence of causing death by reckless driving, what of the case of a defendant who considers the possibility of risk but concludes that there is none? This might happen where the driver is genuinely mistaken in respect of some crucial information, for example he believes he is driving in a two-way street when in fact it is one way. The act is objectively dangerous, but is it reckless? The driver does not consider there to be a risk because he is labouring under a genuine mistake of fact. Lord Goff goes on to say:

> If that was indeed the case, his driving might well not be described as reckless, though such cases are likely to be rare. It has been suggested that there is therefore a 'loophole' or 'lacuna' in Lord Diplock's definition of recklessness. I feel bound to say that I ... regard these expressions as misleading ... it is not in every case where the defendant is in fact driving dangerously that he should be held to be driving recklessly [p 690(h)].

The lacuna may well exist, as suggested by the decision in *Reid*, but as yet there has been no unequivocal endorsement by the courts.

3.4.2 The future of recklessness

What of the future of recklessness? The House of Lords considered the matter in *Reid* (1992). In this case, the appellant was convicted of causing death by reckless driving, with the judge giving a *Lawrence* direction to the jury on the meaning of driving recklessly. The House of Lords refused to take the opportunity to overrule *Lawrence*, because as Lord Keith of Kinkel opined:

> Those who fail to display the requisite degree of self-discipline through failing to give any thought to the possibility of the serious risks they are creating may reasonably be regarded as no less blameworthy than those who consciously appreciate a risk but nevertheless go on to take it. The word 'reckless' in its ordinary meaning is apt to embrace the former category no less than the latter, and I feel no doubt that Parliament by its use intended to cover both of them.

However, the *Lawrence* direction was modified by Lord Goff, supported by Lord Browne-Wilkinson, to the extent that the driving should be in such a manner as to create a *serious* risk of causing physical injury or damage to property. Lord Goff expressed the view that, 'the requirement that the risk be obvious ... cannot be relevant where the defendant is in fact aware that there is some kind of relevant risk' (p 691). This must, of course, be correct if the accused recognised that there was some risk of the type mentioned and nevertheless went on to take it. In this situation there is simply no need to invoke the foresight of the ordinary prudent person because the accused has acknowledged the existence of a serious risk of harmful consequences. On the other hand, it is still vital to refer to the risk being obvious if the accused failed to address his mind to the possibility of risk. In *P & O European Ferries (Dover) Ltd* (1990), the judge held there was no evidence of recklessness because of the absence of evidence of an 'obvious' risk that dire consequences would ensue if the ferry sailed with its bow doors open. Thus, a defendant is culpable as a result of failing to appreciate what ordinary people would foresee as obvious. A direction to the jury on a criminal damage charge should now be phrased, according to Smith and Hogan (*Criminal Law*, 9th edn, 1999, London: Butterworths, p 63) in the following terms:

> The jury must be sure that:
>
> (i)   D did an act which created a *serious* risk that property would be destroyed or damaged; and
>
> (ii) either (a) he recognised that there was some risk of that kind involved but nevertheless went on to take it; or (b) that, despite the fact that he was acting in such a manner, he did not even address his mind to the possibility of there being any such risk, and the risk was in fact *obvious*.

Rather more intriguing is the suggestion by Lord Keith that 'inadvertence to risk is no less a subjective state of mind than is disregard of a recognised risk'. He justified this statement by arguing that 'if there is nothing to go upon apart from what actually happened', then it would be impossible for a jury to decide which state of mind was present. The defendant's chance of acquittal is possible only if he did give thought to the possibility of risk and concluded there was none, that is, the lacuna argument. To recognise the existence of the risk and go ahead will lead to *mens rea* being established as will failure to give thought providing a *serious* risk has been created and it would have been *obvious* to the ordinary prudent person.

There are also some suggestions in *Reid* that some of the harshness created by *Caldwell/Lawrence* might be alleviated if the defendant failed to recognise an obvious and serious risk because he or she lacked the capacity to recognise it, for example, illness, shock, mental incapacity (see in particular the speech of Lord Keith, p 675 and Lord Goff, p 690). However, this possible means of avoiding some of the harshness of objective recklessness appears to be limited. In *Coles* (1995), the Court of Appeal affirmed the decision of the trial judge not to admit evidence of a young person's low average mental capacity. This is likely to mean that pre-existing incapacity such as that in *Elliott v C* (1983) will not be affected and that this particular form of injustice will continue. It might be possible to argue however, that an incapacity which was not in existence prior to the *actus reus* could be introduced and the defendant's foresight compared not with that of the ordinary prudent individual but with a person of his or her own capacity and capability (see further, Field, S and Lynn, M, 'Capacity, recklessness and the House of Lords' [1993] Crim LR 127).

Reid applies the *Lawrence* (1981) test. *Caldwell* and *Lawrence* are virtually indistinguishable in terms of principle and therefore it is arguable that *Reid* should be equally applicable to the offence of criminal damage. *Seymour* (1983) had considered the *Caldwell/Lawrence* definitions and applied them to the offence of manslaughter on the basis that the legal ingredients of the common law offence of manslaughter (when caused by poor driving) and the statutory offence of causing death by reckless driving were the same. It is, however, no longer necessary to consider whether *Reid* should apply to the common law offence. The House of Lords overruled the *Seymour* decision in *Adomako* (1994) on the basis that the underlying statutory provisions pertinent to the decision have now been repealed. While *Reid* is an important decision, it does highlight many of the difficulties experienced with the concept of recklessness since *Caldwell* in 1981. Lords Keith and Ackner appear to support the *Lawrence* direction without modification, whereas Lords Browne-Wilkinson and Goff favoured omitting the word 'obvious'. The *ratio* on this point at least remains obscure. However three Law Lords agreed that the meaning of *reckless* could well vary by reference to the particular statutory context. The result is that the *Caldwell/Lawrence* meaning of recklessness is confined for most practical purposes to offences under the CDA 1971.

3.4.3   Reform

The Law Commission in its report, *Legislating the Criminal Code: Offences Against the Person and General Principles* (Law Com 218, 1993, para 10.1), was of the view that 'much of the debate in both *Caldwell* and in *Reid* was occasioned by the fact that neither in the CDA 1971 nor in the RTA 1988 was the term "reckless" defined. Both courts were, therefore, led to speculate on the normal, usual or natural meaning of that word'. The Commission is clearly of the view that it is imperative that a statutory definition of recklessness be established. Paragraph 10.2 puts it this way:

> Indeed, the history of attempts to expound an undefined 'recklessness' ... reinforces our view, which was also that of the CLRC [Criminal Law Revision Committee] that statutory definition of the term is essential. As the CLRC put it, discussing both intention and recklessness: 'If the law is to be consistently applied, [these terms] cannot be left to a jury or magistrates as "ordinary words of the English language."' That is particularly so of the word reckless, which in its undefined form has a wide and far from generally agreed range of meanings. Possible dictionary synonyms include 'careless, regardless or heedless of the possible consequences of one's act'; 'heedlessness of risk (non-advertence)'; but also simply negligent or inattentive. Left to its own devices, therefore, a jury asked to think in terms of undefined recklessness might well apply nothing more than the civil, tortious, standard of liability.

The Law Commission therefore proposed the following definition of 'recklessly':

> A person acts recklessly with respect to:

(i)   a circumstance, when he is aware of a risk that it exists or will exist; and

(ii)   a result, when he is aware of a risk that it will occur, and it is unreasonable, having regard to the circumstances known to him, to take that risk [cl 1].

This proposed definition is exactly the same as that contained in the proposed 1989 draft Criminal Code (*A Criminal Code for England and Wales*, Law Com 177, 1989, cl 18(c)) (apart from a minor textual readjustment).

We make one final point before leaving recklessness. It is important to understand that fault terms such as intention and recklessness do not exist independently of the specific crime of which they form a part. There is no crime called 'intention' or 'recklessness'. But there are specific crimes where the prosecution are required to prove that the defendant possessed the *mens rea* required by the offence.

3.5   Other key words

We have analysed the meaning of intention and recklessness but how have the courts interpreted other words commonly found in statutory offences?

Wilfully

This word is frequently found in statutes but unfortunately the courts have not been entirely consistent in their interpretation. The leading case is *Sheppard* (1980) where the House of Lords was called upon to interpret s 1(1) of the Children and Young Persons Act 1933, which provides that: 'If any person who has ... authority, charge or care of any child or young person ... *wilfully* assaults, ill-treats, neglects, abandons, or exposes him ... in a manner likely to cause him unnecessary suffering or injury to health ... that person shall be guilty ...' This case involved a failure to provide medical aid to a child and Lord Diplock suggested that the following direction to the jury should be provided by the judge:

> ... on a charge of wilful neglect of a child ... by failing to provide medical aid the jury must be satisfied (1) that the child did in fact need medical aid at the time at which the parent is charged with failing to provide it (the *actus reus*) and (2) either that the parent was aware at that time that the child's health might be at risk if it were not provided with medical aid, or that the parent's unawareness of this fact was due to his not caring whether his child's health were at risk or not (the *mens rea*).

'Wilfully' is therefore a *mens rea* word and covers both intention and recklessness. However, in a number of cases the courts have limited this requirement to merely one part of the *actus reus* and not to the other. In *Maidstone BC v Mortimer* (1980), the defendant was convicted of *wilfully* destroying a tree in contravention of a preservation order. The Divisional Court held that 'wilfulness' only applied to the destruction of the tree; it was irrelevant to his conviction that he had in fact no knowledge that a preservation order was in existence.

Knowingly

'Knowingly' is a *mens rea* word and includes a defendant who:

- Knows something is true or is virtually certain that it is true (as with intention it is irrelevant that it is not the defendant's aim, wish, purpose or desire that the prohibited act occur or circumstance exist).

- Is wilfully blind to the truth. Lord Bridge defined wilful blindness in *Westminster CC v Croyal Grange Ltd* (1986) as, 'the defendant ... deliberately shut his eyes to the obvious or refrained from enquiring because he suspected the truth but did not want to have his suspicions confirmed' (p 359).

When 'knowingly' is found in a statute it normally applies to each element of the *actus reus* of the offence.

Permits

This word has been the subject of considerable judicial uncertainty and it is therefore difficult to state with confidence whether it is a *mens rea* word or not. In *James & Son Ltd v Smee* (1955), a case concerned with *permitting* a person to use a vehicle with defective brakes, the Divisional Court held that the word 'in our opinion, imports a state of mind' and did not denote an offence not requiring *mens rea*. On the other hand, the same court held in *DPP v Fisher* (1992), in relation to the offence of driving without insurance, that the only *mens rea* the prosecution need prove was that the owner permitted some other person to drive his vehicle. It was unnecessary to prove knowledge that the driver permitted to drive was uninsured.

Perhaps the answer to this confusing situation is that the meaning which the courts attach to the word depends upon the seriousness of the offence; the more serious the more likely it is that the courts will find the word requires *mens rea*.

3.6   Transferred malice

The *mens rea* of an offence must of necessity relate to the *actus reus* in order for liability to follow. However in some circumstances the legal requirements of the offence may be present but the result of having carried out the *actus reus* is not what the defendant (D) intended. He may have shot at A intending to kill him but missed and killed B. B may in fact be a person against whom he had no animosity whatsoever. Nevertheless, a human being has lost his life and it must be determined if D is legally to be held responsible. Examples abound to illustrate the principle of transferred malice which is the idea that the intent held by D against A can be transferred to B in order to sustain a conviction against D. In *Mitchell* (1983), Staughton J reinforced the point:

> We can see no reason of policy for holding that an act calculated to harm A cannot be manslaughter if it in fact kills B. The criminality of the doer of the act is precisely the same whether it is A or B who dies. A person who throws a stone at A is just as guilty if, instead of hitting and killing A it hits and kills B.

In this case, the defendant had intentionally assaulted a man in a post office queue which caused the man to stumble against a frail 89 year old woman who fell and later died following an operation to treat the injuries she sustained. The Court of Appeal upheld Mitchell's conviction for manslaughter.

Precise liability will inevitably depend on the *mens rea* of the defendant. Two leading 19th century authorities support the principle of transferred malice. In *Latimer* (1886), the defendant hit out at another man (C) with his belt, which glanced off him and struck and wounded R who was standing nearby. Even though the jury found that R was hit accidentally, the *mens rea* held by Latimer towards C was held to be capable of being transferred and he was found guilty of malicious wounding contrary to s 20 of the OAPA 1861. Here the two crimes involved were the same and the principle will only apply in such circumstances. This means that the prosecution cannot join the *mens rea* of one type of offence with the *actus reus* of a different type of offence. The principle applies only when the *actus reus* and *mens rea* of the same crime are present. This point is well illustrated by the second of the cases, *Pembliton* (1874). P, who was involved in an altercation outside a public house, threw a stone at the persons with whom he had been fighting. It missed them and broke a window. Undoubtedly, whilst he did intend an offence of violence, he did not intend to break the window and his conviction for malicious damage was quashed because there was no evidence that he possessed the *mens rea* in relation to the *actus reus* he had caused. Putting this case into a modern context would result in a charge of criminal damage and if in the circumstances P was found to have acted recklessly in relation to the criminal damage then a conviction could be achieved, as it apparently could have been under the Malicious Damage Act 1861 if there had been evidence from which it could have been proved that D was reckless.

Transferred malice has caused a number of problems in relation to the defendant who intentionally causes serious injury to a pregnant woman, who subsequently gives birth to a child who later dies as a result of the initial injury to the mother. In *AG's Reference (No 3 of 1994)* ((1997)), the defendant had stabbed his girlfriend who was to his knowledge pregnant with his child. She survived the attack but gave birth to a grossly premature baby. The knife had penetrated the foetus although when the child died some four months later it was from lung condition unrelated to the knife attack. The respondent was charged with murder. The trial judge ruled that he should be acquitted on the ground that no conviction for murder or manslaughter was possible in law. The Attorney General referred the matter to the Court of Appeal under s 36(1) of the CJA 1972. The court held that a murder or manslaughter conviction could be secured providing the child had been born alive; that it enjoyed an existence separate from that of the mother; and that the original attack had been a substantial cause of death. In relation to murder, the court held that the prosecution must prove that the defendant intended to kill the mother or to cause her serious bodily harm, the foetus prior to birth being viewed as an integral part of the mother.

The case was referred to the House of Lords which held that whilst the defendant could be convicted of the crime of unlawful and dangerous act manslaughter (see below, 6.8.1) he could not be convicted of murder. The House rejected the Attorney General's argument that it was possible to add together the malice towards the mother (which started a chain of events leading towards a premature birth) and the coming to fruition of those events in the death of the baby after having been born alive. All judges agreed with Lord Mustill that:

> ... the doctrine of transferred malice harked back to a concept of general malice that a wrongful act displayed a malevolence which could be attached to any adverse consequence, which had long been out of date. To apply the doctrine to the facts of this case would be ... not a 'transfer' but to create a new malice which never existed before.

The House of Lords was unwilling to extend the law to a case where the defendant had acted without an intent to injure either the foetus or the child it would become. To do so would, in fact, require a double transfer of malice. First, from the mother to the foetus, and then from the foetus to the child as yet unborn. 'Then one would have to deploy the fiction ... which converted an intention to commit serious harm into the *mens rea* of murder. That was too much.' Additionally Lord Mustill expressed the opinion that:

> ... even on a narrow approach the argument [that the doctrine of transferred malice should apply] broke down. The effect of transferred malice was that the intended victim and the actual victim were treated as if they were one, as if the latter had been the intended victim from the start. To make any sense of that process there had to be some compatibility between the original intention and the actual occurrence and that was what one found in the cases. There was no such compatibility here.

The House of Lords held, therefore, that the *mens rea* for murder was not present.

In relation to the question of unlawful act manslaughter, however, Lord Hope stated that providing the other elements were satisfied (see below, 6.8.1) the question was simply one of causation (see above, 2.4) and that there was no need to involve the doctrine of transferred malice in cases such as this.

3.6.1   Reform

The Law Commission considered both transferred malice and transferred defences in its proposed draft Criminal Code (*A Criminal Code for England and Wales,* Law Com 177, 1989) and decided in favour of a general provision in relation to transferred fault (cl 24). Its recommendations have since been slightly modified to take account of developments in the law of recklessness and now appear in cl 32 of *Legislating the Criminal Code: Offences Against the Person and General Principles* (Law Com 218, 1993):

> (1)   In determining whether a person is guilty of an offence, his intention to cause, or his awareness of a risk that he will cause, a result in relation to a person or thing capable of being the victim or subject-matter of the offence shall be treated as an intention to cause or, as the case may be, an awareness of the risk that he will cause, that result in relation to any other person or thing affected by his conduct.
>
> (2)   Any defence on which a person might have relied on a charge of an offence in relation to a person or thing within his contemplation is open to him on a charge of the same offence in relation to a person or thing not within his contemplation.

The Commission considered such a provision necessary because, as they explained in para 42.1 of the report:

> Where a person intends to affect one person or thing (X) and actually affects another (Y), he may be charged with an offence of attempt in relation to X; or it may be possible to satisfy a court or jury that he was reckless with respect to Y. But an attempt charge may be impossible (where it is not known until trial that the defendant claims to have had X and not Y in contemplation); or inappropriate (as not describing the harm done adequately for labelling or sentencing purposes). Moreover, recklessness with respect to Y may be insufficient to establish the offence or incapable of being proved. The rule stated by [cl 32] overcomes these difficulties.

3.7   Coincidence of *actus reus* and *mens rea*

In the overwhelming majority of cases the *mens rea* and the *actus reus* will coincide in the sense that at the time the consequence occurred the accused possessed the requisite mental element.

Reference has already been made to the continuous act theory (see above, 2.6) and in these circumstances the crime is deemed to be complete once the *mens rea* is evident at any time whilst the act continues. For example, the Judicial Committee of the Privy Council decided in *Kaitamaki* (1985) that in the context of the law of rape, sexual intercourse is a continuing act starting at the moment sexual intercourse commences and finishing when it stops and that, if penetration continues when the consent has been withdrawn part way through the act, then the crime is complete. The assumption in this type of case is that the intercourse is consensual at the outset, but consent, for whatever reason, is then revoked. The celebrated case of *Fagan v Metropolitan Police Commissioner* (1968) also illustrates the general point.

Fagan had been told by a police officer to park his car against the kerb. In attempting this manoeuvre, Fagan drove the car onto the policeman's foot. Despite several requests to remove it the appellant left it there, until finally reversing off the constable's foot. He was charged with assaulting a police officer in the execution of his duty. Fagan claimed that the act was unintentional and that, of course, may have been true. What is also beyond doubt is that he realised the car was on the officer's foot and he deliberately chose to leave it there, telling the constable in no uncertain terms that he would have to be patient. The Court of Appeal was of the opinion that it was unnecessary for the *mens rea* to be present at the inception of the *actus reus*, taking the view that it 'can be superimposed on an existing act'. The court sought to draw a distinction between a completed act where any later *mens rea* will not complete a crime and a continuing act where the subsequent *mens rea* will result in a crime being committed. In this case, the car was driven onto the foot and the appellant knew what had happened before turning off the ignition. The act could, therefore, be said to have continued certainly until the engine was cut, during which period the evidence of his intention to leave it there was clearly articulated. (This case must now be read together with the *Miller* (1983) decision (see above, 2.6)).

Other circumstances may arise where one is dealing with more than one act or transaction, usually where the defendant(s) are carrying out a preconceived plan. In *Thabo Meli* (1954), the appellants acting in concert lured a man into a hut and attacked him. Believing him to be dead they took his body and rolled it over a cliff hoping to make it appear that he had died accidentally. It transpired that at the time he was pushed over the cliff he was still alive and died from exposure while lying unconscious at the foot of the cliff. It was argued for the appellants that two acts had been carried out, the attack in the hut when there was clear intent to kill and the second in pushing the victim over the cliff when there was no intent to kill as they believed him already to be dead. It was maintained that the first act did not cause death and that the second, which did, was not accompanied by the *mens rea* of murder although they could be guilty of manslaughter. The Privy Council upheld the conviction for murder because it was:

... impossible to divide up what was really one series of acts in this way. There is no doubt that the accused set out to do all these acts in order to achieve their plan, and as parts of their plan; and it is much too refined a ground of judgement to say that, because they were under a misapprehension at one stage and thought that their guilty purpose had been achieved before, in fact, it was achieved, therefore they are to escape the penalties of the law.

Similar reasoning was applied in *Church* (1966), although in that case there was no antecedent plan. The appellant had taken a woman to his van where sexual relations were attempted. He was unable to satisfy her and she slapped his face as a result of which a fight ensued and he rendered her unconscious. He attempted to revive her for approximately 30 minutes but failed. He then panicked and threw her body into a nearby river. It was proved that she had died by drowning. The Court of Criminal Appeal applying the reasoning in *Thabo Meli* thought there to be a series of acts which culminated in death. However, it cannot be said that *at the outset* he intended to kill or cause grievous bodily harm otherwise the conviction would have been for murder. It is thus difficult to isolate the series of acts which culminated in death. The only act which brought about death was the disposal of the body into the river, there being no evidence whatsoever of any prior thought that this chain of events would unfold. He went to the van with Mrs Nott for sexual pleasure, she taunted him and struck him first and to say that any of his actions were designed to cause death is hardly an accurate reflection of what took place. This is a case which is better examined in light of the *Miller* decision, that is, having created a dangerous situation he failed in his duty to render assistance. A manslaughter conviction is certainly sustainable.

However, all this should now be read in light of the Court of Appeal decision in *Le Brun* (1991), where *Church* was applied to convict a husband of the manslaughter of his wife. The couple had been arguing as they walked home early one morning. He struck her, knocking her down unconscious. He then attempted to lift or drag the body away from the scene but she slipped from his grasp, hit her head on the pavement and subsequently died from a fractured skull. The trial judge directed the jury that they could convict of either murder or manslaughter (depending on his *mens rea* at the time of the initial assault) if Le Brun had accidentally dropped her while attempting to take her home against her wishes or whilst attempting to dispose of her body, or whilst covering up the initial assault in some other way. The court was of the opinion that if the act of unlawful force and the eventual act causing death were part of the 'same sequence of events', then the initial *mens rea* was sufficient to sustain the verdict of unlawful killing because the act which caused death and the necessary mental state did *not* have to coincide in point of time. Two separate points arise as a result of this decision.

The first is that this type of case can be analysed in the context of the principles of causation. As Lord Lane CJ put it:

> The original unlawful blow to the chin was a *causa sine qua non* of the later *actus reus*. It was the opening event in a series which was to culminate in death: the first link in the chain of causation, to use another metaphor. It cannot be said that the actions of the appellant in dragging the victim away with the intention of evading liability broke the chain which linked the initial blow to the death.

Do note that this suggests that the principle applies where the accused is seeking to 'evade liability' but not where he is acting in an attempt to redeem something from the situation, for example, trying to place the victim in a comfortable position or moving her inside a house in order to render assistance. However, given that there is only one question as far as causation is concerned: whether the act was a significant and operating cause of death, then whatever follows should not break the chain, unless it is a new cause wholly unrelated to the initial act.

The second point confirms that the 'transaction' or 'series of events' approach remains good law. Lord Lane explains it in this way:

> ... where the unlawful application of force and the eventual act causing death are part of the same sequence of events, the same transaction, the fact that there is an appreciable interval of time between the two does not serve to exonerate the defendant from liability. That is certainly so where the appellant's subsequent actions which caused death, after the initial unlawful blow, are designed to conceal his commission of the original unlawful assault ... in short, in circumstances such as the present ... the act which causes death and the necessary mental state to constitute manslaughter need not coincide in point of time.

This judgment is particularly interesting for two reasons. First, it confirms that the whole transaction or series of events cannot be split up and that together they constitute the *actus reus*. This approach admits that the *actus reus* and *mens rea* do not have to start or finish together but leaves intact the requirement that there must be a time (however fleeting) that the two coincide. Secondly, it suggests that the defendant must have been engaged upon a further unlawful activity. If he was acting for humanitarian purposes the outcome might well have been different.

3.8   Strict liability

For the majority of this chapter, it has been asserted that *mens rea*, usually intention or recklessness, must be proved in order to obtain a conviction. From this it may be assumed that the overwhelming majority of crimes are *mens rea* offences, and this is true in respect of the major offences. However, there are many minor regulatory offences, usually statutory, which do not require intention or recklessness or even negligence to be proved in respect of at least one element of the *actus reus*. These are known as *strict liability* offences. It is estimated that nearly half of the approximately 7,500 statutory crimes come within this description. Contrast strict liability with *absolute liability* offences. Here the prosecution are relieved of the duty of proving *mens rea* in relation to any element of the *actus reus* and it may be that access to general defences is denied. Additionally, it may not be necessary to prove that the *actus reus* was committed voluntarily. Such offences are rare (for two examples, see above, 2.2.4). The modern approach to offences of strict liability was enunciated by Lord Reid in *Sweet v Parsley* (1970) who spoke of the firmly established view that:

> Our first duty is to consider the words of the Act: if they show a clear intention to create an absolute offence that is the end of the matter. But such cases are very rare. Sometimes the words of the section which creates the particular offence make it clear that *mens rea* is required in one form or another. Such cases are quite frequent. But in a very large number of cases there is no clear indication either way.

He went on to say:

> In such cases, there has for centuries been a presumption that Parliament did not intend to make criminals of persons who were in no way blameworthy in what they did. That means that whenever a section is silent as to mens rea there is a presumption that, in order to give effect to the will of Parliament, we must read in words appropriate to require *mens rea* ... In the absence of a clear indication in the Act that an offence is intended to be an absolute offence, it is necessary to go outside the Act and examine all relevant circumstances in order to establish that this must have been the intention of Parliament. I say 'must have been' because it is a universal principle that if a penal provision is reasonably capable of two interpretations, that interpretation which is most favourable to the accused must be adopted.

Lord Scarman provides a valuable analysis of the modern approach to strict liability offences in the Privy Council case of *Gammon (Hong Kong) Ltd v AG for Hong Kong* (1984):

(1) there is a presumption of law that *mens rea* is required before a person can be guilty of a criminal offence;

(2) the presumption is particularly strong where the offence is 'truly criminal' in character;

(3) the presumption applies to statutory offences, and can be displaced only if this is clearly or by necessary implication the effect of the statute;

(4) the only situation in which the presumption can be displaced is where the statute is concerned with an issue of social concern; public safety is such an issue;

(5) even where the statute is concerned with such an issue, the presumption of *mens rea* stands unless it can be shown that the creation of strict liability will be effective to promote the objects of the statute by encouraging greater vigilance to prevent the commission of the prohibited act.

In *B v DPP* (2000), the most recent case in which the House of Lords has considered the issue of strict liability, their Lordships relied in particular upon the approach in *Sweet v Parsley* and also on that in *Gammon (Hong Kong)*.

It must not be assumed that strict liability can only be found in the context of statutory offences. There is limited recognition in certain areas of the common law. In one area, that of criminal contempt of court, the strict liability rule which applied to the common law was put onto a statutory basis by s 1 of the Contempt of Court Act 1981. This section provides that someone may be guilty of contempt *regardless of intent* where the publication in question creates a substantial risk of serious prejudice or impediment to particular proceedings *and* that proceedings are active. Public nuisance and criminal libel are two crimes which are exceptions to the common law rule in favour of *mens rea*. However neither of these offences would appear to be of relevance in modern law. Blasphemous libel is a common law offence which was resurrected in 1979 when the editor and publishers of *Gay News* were prosecuted. It was held by the House of Lords in *Lemon and Gay News Ltd* (1979) that to obtain a conviction it was sufficient for the prosecution to prove *mens rea* only so far as the intention to publish the materials was concerned and not that the defendants intended to blaspheme. It was denied by the majority that they were creating a strict liability offence although the minority were convinced that the opposite was true. Blasphemous libel occurs when material is published which outrages and insults a Christian's religious feelings. If, as the majority decided, the only *mens rea* relates to the intent to publish and not to whether it will outrage Christians then a strict liability offence would appear to have been created.

The courts appear to have blown hot and cold as regards the recognition of offences as being strict liability. *Sheppard* (1980) and *Gammon (Hong Kong)* seemed to herald a growing reticence towards the expansion of strict liability with Lord Diplock in the former case stating:

> The climate of both parliamentary and judicial opinion has been growing less favourable to the recognition of absolute offences over the last few decades, a trend to which s 1 of the Homicide Act 1957 and s 8 of the CJA 1967 bear witness in the case of Parliament, and in the case of the judiciary is illustrated by the speeches in this House in *Sweet v Parsley* (1969) ...

But in *Champ* (1981), for example, the Court of Appeal held that the crime of cultivating cannabis was a strict liability offence despite the fact that it is punishable by up to 14 years imprisonment. Indeed, in *Gammon (Hong Kong)*, a case concerned with Hong Kong's Building Regulations, the offence was punishable by up to three years imprisonment. Many people would view both crimes as 'truly criminal in character' but this did not prevent the courts classifying them as strict liability offences. Contrast this situation with s 6.02(4) of the US Model Penal Code, which proposes that the availability of imprisonment should be a conclusive reason against a finding of strict liability.

The House had no difficulty in *Pharmaceutical Society v Storkwain Ltd* (1986) in concluding that s 58(2)(a) of the Medicines Act 1968 created an offence of strict liability particularly as other sections in the Act expressly required *mens rea* to be proved. Thus, 'by omitting s 58 from those sections [of the Act] ... Parliament intended that there should be no implication of a requirement of *mens rea* in s 58(2)(a)'. The outcome was that a pharmacist who supplied prescription only drugs as a result of being given a false prescription was guilty of the offence albeit he was not at fault. Section 58(2)(a) provides:

> (a) no person shall sell by retail, or supply in circumstances corresponding to retail sale, a medicinal product of a description, or falling within a class, specified in an order under this section except in accordance with a prescription given by an appropriate practitioner ...

Another example of the courts' willingness to recognise strict liability is to be found in *Kirkland v Robinson* (1987). In this case, the appellant was convicted of possessing live wild birds contrary to s 1(2)(a) of the Wildlife and Countryside Act 1981 on the basis that as s 1(1) includes the word 'intentionally' but s 1(2) does not, Parliament must have intended it to be an offence of strict liability. Therefore the court held that his claim that he did not know that the bird in his possession was wild did not provide him with a defence. The Divisional Court thought the Wildlife and Countryside Act 1981 had been designed to help protect the environment which was viewed as 'an objective of outstanding social importance'.

How important is this point that Parliament by using a *mens rea* word in one section but omitting to use it in another can be taken by the courts as an indication that *mens rea* is not required in the latter section? It should be possible to provide a simple answer but in this area, as with so many aspects of strict liability the position is unclear as a result of inconsistencies between the cases. We saw above in the *Pharmaceutical Society* and *Kirkland* cases that it can be very important. Both cases followed the old Divisional Court case of *Cundy v Le Cocq* (1884). But, whilst it is an important factor, it is far from conclusive. In *Sherras v De Rutzen* (1895), where the circumstances were similar to *Cundy*, the Divisional Court did not find the provision created a strict liability offence. Day J held that the effect of the absence of the word 'knowingly' from the section was merely to shift the burden of proof onto the accused so that he had to demonstrate that he did *not* know of the prohibited circumstances. This approach has been followed subsequently on a number of occasions and it is thought to more accurately represent the current state of the law. This view is supported by Lord Reid's comment in *Sweet v Parsley* (1969) that:

> It is also firmly established that the fact that other sections of the Act expressly require *mens rea*, for example, because they contain the word 'knowingly', is not itself sufficient to justify a decision that a section which is silent as to *mens rea* creates an absolute offence [p 149].

In *B v DPP*, the victim, a girl aged 13 years, and the defendant, a 15 year old boy, were travelling on the same bus. The defendant sat next to the victim and asked her several times to perform oral sex with him. She repeatedly refused. He was charged with inciting a girl under 14 to commit an act of gross indecency contrary to s 1(1) of the Indecency with Children Act 1960. The primary facts were admitted at the trial, as was his honest belief that the victim was over 14 years. The defendant argued that he must be acquitted on the facts as admitted, but the prosecution submitted that the offence was one of strict liability. The justices ruled that the defendant's state of mind could not constitute a defence to the charge and he changed his plea to guilty. When the case found its way to the House of Lords, their Lordships were unanimous in quashing the defendant's conviction. They considered that the *actus reus* element as to age was no different from any other *actus reus* element and was subject to a presumption in favour of *mens rea*. This presumption was an expression of the principle of legality and could only be negatived by a compellingly clear implication, to be found in the language used, the nature of the offence, the mischief sought to be prevented and any other relevant circumstances. In this context, there were two very important factors in favour of the presumption and against strict liability:

- the offence is a serious offence with a severe punishment (10 years maximum imprisonment) and correspondingly high stigma for conviction;

- the offence is drawn broadly ('an act of gross indecency'), embracing conduct ranging from 'predatory approaches by a much older paedophile' to 'consensual sexual experimentation between precocious teenagers of whom the accused may be the younger of the two'. Thus, the conduct might be 'depraved by any acceptable standard', or 'relatively innocuous behaviour in private between two young people'.

They further considered that neither the aim of protecting young children, nor the alleged difficulty in proving knowledge of age if *mens rea* were required, were strong arguments against the presumption. Nor, in their view, did the statutory context compel the rejection of *mens rea* because 'the motley collection of offences, of diverse origins, gathered into the Sexual Offences Act 1956 displays no satisfactorily clear or coherent pattern', and so could give no compelling guidance. Their Lordships also rejected the option of requiring that the defendant's mistaken belief that the girl was 14 or over must be a reasonable belief.

The decision and reasoning in *B v DPP* is perhaps rather surprising for its rejection of strict liability and welcome for its approach to the issue of mistake in criminal law. However, it is doubtful whether it will have any major impact on the general approach to the imposition of strict liability. For example, we have already seen that the fact that a sentence of imprisonment is available for an offence is no guarantee that it will not be considered to impose strict liability. Is the strong reliance placed upon the availability of a maximum sentence of 10 years imprisonment by their Lordships in *B v DPP* likely to change this position? Probably not in view of Lord Steyn's assertion in that very same case that the offence under s 5 of the Sexual Offences Act 1956 (sexual intercourse with a girl under the age of 13) 'plainly creates an offence of strict liability', despite the fact that the offence carries a maximum sentence of life imprisonment and looks like a 'truly criminal' offence if ever there was one! It is true that his Lordship was considering s 5 along with s 6 (the offence of sexual intercourse with a girl under the age of 16), and derived his conclusion from his belief that they must be viewed as a pair, but this is unlikely to obscure the main message that a sentence of imprisonment, even one of life imprisonment, is not necessarily protection against imposition of strict liability.

Strict liability is by no means a relatively recent judicial creation. Its roots were firmly established in the 19th century and in a series of cases from 1846 onwards judges showed little reluctance towards the creation of strict liability offences. In the *Cundy v Le Cocq* (1884) case, C, a publican, sold alcohol to a drunken person, an action which contravened s 13 of the Licensing Act (LA) 1872. C claimed that he had no knowledge that the customer was drunk. The Divisional Court upheld his conviction and declared s 13 to be one of strict liability. Stephen J thought the words of the section amounted to 'an absolute prohibition' and that however genuine the publican's mistake regarding his customer's state of intoxication this would not provide him with a defence. As we have seen, the court was influenced by the fact that other sections of the LA 1872 contained the *mens rea* word knowingly, but significantly this word was absent in s 13.

In *Callow v Tillstone* (1900), a negligent examination of a carcass by a veterinary surgeon had resulted in a butcher selling meat which was unfit for human consumption. He, of course, had relied upon the veterinary surgeon's certificate that the meat was sound and would have no reason to assume that he was breaching the law. The butcher was convicted on the basis that the offence was one of strict liability. He had in fact sold meat which was unfit for human consumption. Just to compound his misery, the veterinary surgeon who was charged with aiding and abetting the offence had his conviction quashed on the basis that aiding and abetting required knowledge of the facts and an intention to encourage. Although he had been negligent in his examination of the animal, it could not be proved that *he knew* the meat was unsound.

Perhaps the best-known example of the judiciary's approach to strict liability in the 19th century is *Prince* (1875). The accused had been charged with s 55 of the OAPA 1861 (now, s 20 of the Sexual Offences Act 1956). The offence provided:

> Whosoever shall unlawfully take or cause to be taken any unmarried girl, being under the age of 16 years, out of the possession and against the will of her father or mother or of any other person having the lawful care or charge of her, shall be guilty of a misdemeanour ...

It will be noted that the section does not contain any of the conventional *mens rea* words – intention, recklessly, maliciously, knowingly, etc. The accused had enticed one Annie Phillips, aged 13, away from her parents. It was accepted that the young lady looked much older than her age would have led one to believe, and that she had informed the defendant that she was in fact 18. It was also accepted by the court that he believed her story *and* that it was not unreasonable for him to hold such a belief. In holding that the intention of the legislature was to create a strict liability offence, Blackburn J commented:

> ... the question, therefore, is reduced to whether the words of s 55 of the OAPA 1861, that whosoever shall unlawfully take 'any unmarried girl being under the age of 16, out of the possession of her father' are to be read as if they were 'being under the age of 16, and he *knowing* she was under that age'. No such words are contained in the statute, nor is there the word 'maliciously', 'knowingly', or any other words used that can be said to involve a similar meaning.

The defendant was accordingly convicted. *Prince* is a good illustration of a point previously made that strict liability simply means that the prosecution is relieved from the task of proving *mens rea* in relation to one or more elements of the *actus reus*. *Mens rea* may still need to be proved in respect of the other elements. In this case Prince possessed *mens rea* in relation to every element of the offence save that she was under 16 years of age.

However, it may well be that the decision in *Prince* is about to lose its force. At least three of their Lordships in *B v DPP* thought that the decision was not in line with the modern approach and was unsound. If this view prevails, other offences where age is an element of the *actus reus* and which have previously been regarded as imposing strict liability because of the decision in *Prince* will inevitably be subjected to scrutiny. Important examples are the offences of indecent assault on a female under 16 and on a male under 16 (ss 14 and 15 of the Sexual Offences Act 1956).

It will be apparent that it is not just minor regulatory crimes to which strict liability will apply, although it has been consistently stressed by the judiciary that the more serious the crime the less likely that the presumption in favour of *mens rea* will be displaced. This presumption was recognised in the 19th century and specifically alluded to in *Sherras v De Rutzen* (1895) by Wright J. The following words have been quoted and accepted as correct by the higher courts on numerous occasions (for example, see *Lim Chin Aik v The Queen* (1963) and *Sweet v Parsley* (1970):

> There is a presumption that *mens rea* is an essential ingredient in every offence; but that presumption is liable to be displaced either by the words of the statute creating the offence or by the subject matter with which it deals, and both must be considered.

In this case, a publican had been convicted of an offence contrary to s 16(2) of the LA 1872 in that he unlawfully supplied liquor to a police constable on duty.

Sherras reasonably believed the constable to be off duty. The Divisional Court in quashing his conviction believed that a strict approach to the construction of the section would place publicans in an invidious position because 'no care on the part of the publican could save him from a conviction', if it was unnecessary to prove knowledge as to whether a constable was or was not on duty.

Whilst it may be true that most of the regulatory offences will be viewed by the majority of people as minor this is by no means always the case. We have already seen in *Champ* and *Gammon (Hong Kong)* that the possibility of substantial terms of imprisonment for those who transgressed the legislation did not deter the judiciary from classifying it as strict liability.

Where there is an obvious danger to the community as a result of engaging in a particular activity, the courts are more likely to deny that the presumption in favour of *mens rea* should apply. In *Howells* (1977), the appellant had in his possession a firearm which he believed to be an antique, and he therefore concluded that he did not require a firearms certificate for the gun. In fact, the gun was a modern reproduction and did require a certificate. He was found guilty of contravening s 1(1)(a) of the Firearms Act 1968 which makes it an offence for a person:

> (a) to have in his possession, or to purchase or acquire, a firearm ... without holding a firearm certificate in force at that time ...

Howells argued that s 1 should not be construed so as to make it a strict liability offence and that an honest and mistaken belief should be recognised as a defence. The Court of Appeal had no doubts that the section should be construed strictly for the following reasons:

- that the wording of the section would appear to indicate such a conclusion;

- that the danger to the community from those possessing unlicensed firearms is so great as to warrant an absolute prohibition against their possession without proper authority;

- to allow a defence based upon an honest and reasonable belief that the firearm was antique and therefore didn't need a certificate would defeat 'the clear intention of the Act'.

In *Blake* (1997), the defendant was found guilty of an offence under s 1(1) of the Wireless Telegraphy Act 1949 of 'using any apparatus for wireless telegraphy without a licence'. Investigation officers were concerned that 'pirate' broadcasts were frequently interfering with emergency service radio communications. They raided the premises of Ragga FM and discovered DJ Casanova playing music. The Court of Appeal considered *Gammon (Hong Kong)* and concluded that the fact that offenders were potentially subject to imprisonment must indicate that Parliament viewed such broadcasts to be a matter of serious social concern which it wished to prevent in the interests of public safety. They concluded, therefore, that the offence was one of strict liability.

These cases would seem to emphasise the sort of public policy considerations which the judiciary take into account when construing legislation which lacks an obvious reference to *mens rea*.

It is possible to categorise strict liability offences by reference to the social context in which they operate although this is subject to the obvious comment that the cases display marked inconsistencies. For example, the courts have frequently construed legislation dealing with drugs and their misuse on a strict liability basis although there is a lack of clarity in at least one notable case. The House of Lords was given opportunity in *Warner v Metropolitan Police Commissioner* (1968) to consider whether s 1(1) of the Drugs (Prevention of Misuse) Act 1964 should be construed strictly. Warner had been found in possession of two boxes. One contained scent and the other 20,000 tablets of amphetamine sulphate. He was charged with possession of a prohibited drug contrary to s 1(1) of the Act. He claimed that while he was aware that he had the boxes in his possession he assumed they both contained scent. The House of Lords by a 4:1 majority dismissed his appeal, but it is defying logic to conclude that any consistent clarity of thinking was evidenced in this case. The dilemma facing the House was whether a person who possessed a package was deemed also to be in possession of its contents, even if he were to be mistaken as to their nature. Views ranged from possession of a package meant possession of its contents to the possibility of rebutting the presumption if the contents were of a wholly different nature from what it was thought the box contained, for example scent and dangerous drugs. One of the Law Lords thought that the 'innocent' possessor should not be guilty if for example, someone without the knowledge of the owner slipped prohibited drugs into her bag. Thankfully the Misuse of Drugs Act 1971 included a section which provided a defence if the accused could prove that he neither believed nor suspected nor had reason to suspect that the substance or product in question was a controlled drug (s 28(3)(b)).

In *McNamara* (1988), the Court of Appeal thought that the burden was on the prosecution to establish that the defendant 'had, and knew that he had, the box in his control *and* also that the box contained something'. This will be sufficient to establish possession (it is assumed that the prosecution proved that the package contained the particular drug alleged in the indictment). After that, the provisions of s 28(3)(b) come into play and the defendant is entitled to be acquitted if he can demonstrate that he 'neither believed nor suspected'. As will have been noted, this statutory defence, in line with many others, firmly places the burden of proof on the defendant.

Sweet v Parsley (1970) can be contrasted with *Warner* and reflects a more enlightened approach to strict liability. In *Sweet v Parsley*, the act in question was the Dangerous Drugs Act 1965 and Miss Sweet was charged with contravening s 5(b) in that she was 'concerned in the management of premises' which were used for the smoking of cannabis. She was a sub-tenant of a farm who let rooms to students. She did not live on the premises but kept a room for her occasional use. It was discovered that cannabis had been smoked at the farmhouse. Her conviction was quashed on the basis that the offence required that the presumption in favour of *mens rea* should apply. Their Lordships emphasised the importance of the effect of the strict liability in achieving some desirable purpose. Lord Reid observed:

> If this section means what the Divisional Court have held that it means, then hundreds of thousands of people who sublet part of the premises or take in lodgers or are concerned in the management of residential premises or institutions are daily incurring a risk of being convicted of a serious offence in circumstances where they are in no way to blame. For the greatest vigilance cannot prevent tenants, lodgers or inmates or guests whom they bring in from smoking cannabis cigarettes in their own rooms. It was suggested in argument that this appellant brought this conviction on herself because it is found as a fact that when the police searched the premises there were people there of the 'beatnik fraternity'. But surely it would be going a very long way to say that persons managing premises of any kind ought to safeguard themselves by refusing accommodation to all who are of slovenly or exotic appearance, or who bring in guests of that kind. And unfortunately drug taking is by no means confined to those of unusual appearance.

This point had been earlier addressed by the Privy Council in *Lim Chin Aik* (1963) where the defendant had entered Singapore in contravention of an order the existence of which he was unaware. His appeal against conviction was allowed. Lord Evershed expressed the opinion that:

> It is not enough ... merely to label the statute as one dealing with a grave social evil and from that to infer that strict liability was intended. It is pertinent also to inquire whether putting the defendant under strict liability will assist in the enforcement of the regulations. That means that there must be something he can do, directly or indirectly, by supervision or inspection, by improvement of his business methods or by exhorting those whom he may be expected to influence or control, which will promote the observance of the regulations. Unless this is so, there is no reason in penalising him, and it cannot be inferred that the legislature imposed strict liability merely in order to find a luckless victim ... Where it can be shown that the imposition of strict liability would result in the prosecution and conviction of a class of persons whose conduct could not in any way affect the observance of the law, their Lordships consider that, even where the statute is dealing with a grave social evil, strict liability is not likely to be intended.

Sweet v Parsley was welcomed because it avoided the great injustice that could result to all those who manage hotels, guest houses and lettings. Although it is true that they can choose their tenants it is unrealistic to assert that they can control what they do once they are behind the door of their hotel room. Hotels would attract few guests if they were to install spy cameras in each room in order that the management could observe whether or not anything illicit was taking place!

3.8.1 The justification for strict liability

Legal scholars are generally critical of the concept of strict liability. Arguments against its imposition include:

- that it is *unjust* to impose criminal liability upon a person who is not at fault. For example, what purpose is served by criminalising the acts of a butcher who unknowingly sells contaminated meat (with resulting damage to his reputation and livelihood) when he purchased the meat from a reputable supplier at market value and who had no reason to suspect that the quality of the meat was anything less than first class? The fact that the sentence imposed by the court is likely to be modest is irrelevant in this context;

- that it is unnecessary and does not lead to higher standards of protection for the public.

The arguments in favour of strict liability include:

- that it helps to prevent prohibited acts because it keeps people such as butchers 'on their toes' and in this way ensures higher standards than would otherwise prevail;

- that without it many of those charged with such offences would plead not guilty and the prosecuting authorities have neither the time or the personnel to litigate each case through the courts in the face of a large number of such pleas. This would lead to additional costs to the state and increased delays in the criminal justice system;

- those responsible for enforcement usually exercise their discretion and rarely prosecute in the complete absence of fault;

- the existence of specific statutory defences in some cases helps to alleviate possible injustice.

But does the certainty of conviction ensure higher standards for the public? No one would doubt that this is a laudable aim but whether imposing strict liability over a range of offences achieves these results is open to doubt. In *Alphacell Ltd v Woodward* (1972), the view was taken that contraventions of the Rivers (Prevention of Pollution) Act 1951 were 'not criminal in any real sense but acts which in the public interest were prohibited under a penalty'. Lord Salmon was of the opinion that to enforce strict liability would deter potential polluters. They would, he thought, 'not only ... take reasonable steps to prevent pollution but [would] do everything possible to ensure that they do not cause it'. That expectation was certainly not at the forefront of the defendant's mind in *FJH Wrothwell Ltd v Yorkshire Water Authority* (1984), when a director of the company deliberately poured 12 gallons of a poisonous herbicide into its drains. He assumed that the liquid would remain in a public sewer until it reached a public sewage works. Unfortunately, the drains from the company premises led into a nearby stream and enormous damage was caused to the stream and its fish population. The charge under s 2 of the Rivers (Prevention of Pollution) Act 1951 was that the company did cause to enter a stream 'poisonous noxious or polluting matter ...'. The magistrates', following *Alphacell v Woodward*, took the view that the offence was absolute and convicted. The company appealed. They did not seek to deny that the offence could be established without proof of *mens rea*, but rather that the company director's state of mind should have been taken into account particularly as he had no idea whatsoever that the actual consequence would flow from his actions. The Divisional Court dismissed the appeal on the basis that 'cause' was a simple English word which should be given its 'ordinary common sense' meaning. There was only one *cause* of the consequence that being the director's action in pouring the herbicide down the drain. The word *cause* does not appear to suggest that a mental element needs to be established and therefore the company had little chance of succeeding with its argument.

But what is it reasonable to expect from someone in the company director's position to do before he undertakes such an action? Must he check first with the water company, insist upon seeing the plans of the local sewage system or invest large amounts of money in order to ascertain the correct position if the other two courses of action are unproductive? Or take the risk? One suspects that many will adopt a standard of care which essentially balances the costs of prevention against the predicted likelihood of detection, conviction and the size of the penalty. Many companies will run the risk of being fined for their activities rather than invest time, effort and money in ensuring they stay within the law.

One suggestion is that liability should depend upon proof of negligence and that this would be a suitable compromise between the need to establish *mens rea* and strict liability. Would it not be preferable to impose penalties only on those who did not act reasonably? Someone who has no reason to suspect that his actions may breach the criminal law and who has acted reasonably in coming to that conclusion surely does not deserve to find himself in the same position as someone who deliberately flouts the law.

G Richardson has conducted research into those responsible for enforcing strict liability offences and the enforcement practices of the agencies they work for. She found that many enforcement personnel share the belief that many such offences are not 'real crimes' and see their primary duty as being not to enforce the law strictly but to ensure standards as high as possible. She found that they often viewed the sanctions imposed by the courts as derisory and were aware that in many cases their agencies' funds and resources were inadequate to enforce the law strictly. Despite this, however, she found many of the enforcers favoured the retention of strict liability because it made their job of routinely enforcing the law against the background of the criminal law and the implied threat of its invocation markedly easier (see 'Regulatory crime: the empirical research' [1987] Crim LR 295).

This does not of course mean that one has to agree with the views of the enforcement officials. Many people would consider it wrong that the determination of blame and the decision to prosecute is made by administrative bodies and their employees, in private, and with potential defendants denied the procedural safeguards normally available to those who face being charged with criminal offences.

3.8.2   Proposals for reform

The Law Commission's proposals are contained within the proposed codification of the criminal law (*A Criminal Code for England and Wales*, Law Com 177, 1989) and involve the provision of a standard definition of such key fault terms as 'intention', 'knowledge' and 'recklessness' (see cl 18). Clause 20(1) provides:

(1) Every offence requires a fault element of recklessness [that is, *Cunningham* style recklessness] with respect to each of its elements other than fault elements unless otherwise provided.

(2) [This] does not apply to pre-code offences ...

The Commission expressed the justification for such a clause to be:

An enactment creating an offence should ordinarily provide that the offence is one of strict liability in respect of one or more identified elements. It is necessary, however, to have a general rule for the interpretation of any offence the definition of which does not state, in respect of one or more elements, whether fault is required or what degree of fault is required. The absence of a consistent rule of interpretation has been a regrettable source of uncertainty in English law. Clause 20 provides such a rule ... The proposal to include this provision was well supported on consultation [para 8.25].

It is important to note that the proposal is expressed to apply in respect of *future* statutes only and that it would not, of course, fetter Parliament's right to pass future statutes imposing strict liability or liability for negligence. However, in order to do this, Parliament would have to make this clear in the legislation.

THE MENTAL ELEMENT – *MENS REA*

The prosecution must prove that the defendant brought about the *actus reus* with the state of mind prescribed by the definition of the particular crime. This state of mind is usually referred to as the *mens rea*.

Direct and oblique intention

Some crimes require proof that the defendant acted *intentionally*. Intention is not the same thing as motive. Where the prohibited consequence is wanted for its own sake this is referred to as *direct intention*. Where the defendant does not have an aim or purpose to cause a prohibited result but knows that his conduct is certain or almost certain to cause it, this is said to be *oblique intention*. This is true whether or not the defendant has some other aim or purpose in engaging in the conduct. Parliament has failed to define intention and the courts have experienced considerable difficulties in attempting to define the term. Though doubts still remain, the case law may have established that the defendant's foresight of a result as a certain or virtually certain consequence of his conduct is in itself intention, even in the absence of any aim or purpose to cause that result.

Recklessness

Defining *recklessness* has also proved problematic for the courts during recent years. Originally, it meant that the defendant undertook a deliberate and *conscious* unreasonable risk but in two landmark cases in 1981 the House of Lords added to this subjective test an objective element. These decisions are viewed by many legal scholars as flawed and wrong in principle because they lead not only to injustice in some cases but also because they have created serious uncertainty in the criminal law. Despite a ruling by the House in 1983 that the new definition applied throughout the law subsequent decisions have decided that the new objective element does not apply to particular offences. Indeed, currently the objective element now only applies, for most practical purposes, to offences under the CDA 1971.

Transferred malice

The doctrine of *transferred malice* is that the malice a defendant bears towards his intended victim may, in certain circumstances, be transferred to the actual victim. For example, if A intends to shoot B but misses and kills C, A's malice may be transferred from B to C and A can be convicted of murder.

Coincidence of *actus reus* and *mens rea*

The *actus reus* and *mens rea* must normally coincide in point of time. However, in some cases the courts have held the *actus reus* to be a continuing act and liability can be established if the defendant can be proven to have possessed *mens rea* at any point during the continuance of the act. Other cases have established that it is enough if the *mens rea* and *actus reus* can be said to have existed during a sequence of events.

Strict liability offences

Many crimes do not require the prosecution to prove that the defendant acted either intentionally or recklessly nor even negligently with respect to at least one element of the *actus reus*. These offences are usually, although not always, of a minor regulatory nature and are referred to as crimes of *strict liability*. Whether a particular crime will be found by the courts to require *mens rea* or to be a *strict liability* offence depends upon a variety of factors. The case law is inconsistent on this important point despite numerous attempts to clarify the matter. Whilst there are arguments both for and against strict liability legal scholars are, in general, hostile. Many would prefer an approach based upon negligence. The Law Commission favours a minimum liability threshold of (subjective) recklessness unless Parliament provides to the contrary.

CHAPTER 4

PARTICIPATION IN CRIME

4.1   Introduction

In this chapter, we consider the basis of liability for those who engage in criminal activity but who are not directly or immediately responsible for causing the *actus reus* of the particular crime. In broad terms the law distinguishes between principal (or joint principal) offenders and secondary parties who, to use the terminology of the relevant legislation, aid, abet, counsel or procure the commission of the offence. It may be that assistance has been given to a bank robber prior to his attempt to relieve the bank of £100,000. This assistance may take many forms. The bank manager (A) may have been involved to the extent of supplying the principal offender (D) with information about how to avoid the security systems installed at the premises. The bank manager may be out of the country on holiday with his family when the crime takes place, nevertheless it cannot and should not be denied that he has made an important contribution towards the perpetration of the offence. Another person (B) may have supplied the weapon used by the principal offender when the crime is attempted. Again it follows that the individual who is associated with the offence by prior involvement should bear some responsibility for the consequences which eventually ensue. A third person (C) may be waiting a couple of streets away ready to drive the principal offender from the scene of the crime. All these people are participating in the illegal enterprise and providing they do so with the requisite knowledge and, of course, voluntarily, there is every reason why the law should seek to ensure that criminal liability should follow.

The subject and the issues which arise can present difficulties because it is not just a matter of assessing the defendant's actions but also linking the actions with those of others. There must, of necessity, be an assessment of the mens rea not only of the perpetrator of the full offence but also those charged with aiding or encouraging the offence. For liability to result should those assisting or encouraging have to foresee the consequences of their involvement with the projected offence? Suppose that the robbery were to go wrong and a bank security guard is killed as he tries to prevent the principal offender from escaping. The bank manager (A) who supplied the information in return for cash may never have given a moments thought to the prospect of someone being killed as a result of the attempt to carry out the crime. He may have had no idea that D would carry a weapon. However, B who has supplied the weapon may know that D wishes to have a weapon with him yet seeks to distance himself from a murder charge on the basis that D assured him that it would be used only to frighten anyone who tried to hinder his progress. He may be willing to admit his participation in the robbery but not murder as he 'never thought it would come to that'. It will be evident that the *mens rea* for participation will be an important element in the analysis of the principles relating to 'secondary' party activity. Yet should the fact that those who encourage an offence or give assistance at an early stage but are not involved in carrying out the crime make them less culpable than the principal offender? The relevant legislative provision clearly suggests not. The Accessories and Abettors Act (AAA) 1861 as amended by the Criminal Law Act (CLwA) 1977 states:

> Whosoever shall aid, abet, counsel or procure the commission of any indictable offence whether the same be an offence at common law or by virtue of any act passed or to be passed, shall be liable to be tried, indicted and punished as a principal offender.

It follows that the liability of a secondary party flows from the prosecution establishing that a crime has in fact been committed although it should be noted at this stage that *Millward* (1994) held that on a charge of procuring an offence, in this case causing death by reckless driving, all that needed to be established was the *actus reus* of the main offence (see below, 4.2). Section 1 of the CLwA 1967 abolished the distinction between felonies and misdemeanours and therefore the s 8 of the AAA 1861 provision applies to all offences. Similar principles are applied to summary offences as a result of s 44 of the Magistrates' Courts Act 1980. As Lord Widgery CJ said in *AG's Reference (No 1 of 1975)* (1975):

> Thus in the past, when the distinction was still drawn between felony and misdemeanour, it was sufficient to make a person guilty of a misdemeanour if he aided, abetted, counselled or procured the offence of another. When the difference between felonies and misdemeanours was abolished in 1967, s 1 of the Criminal Law Act in effect provided that the same test should apply to make a secondary party guilty either of treason or felony.

Therefore, both principal and accessory face the same consequence if convicted. It is reasonable to assume that Parliament when choosing to use four words to describe the spheres of influence relating to an accessory meant those words to convey different meanings. Smith and Hogan (9th edn, 1999, London: Butterworths, p 122) suggest that 'All four expressions imply the commission of the offence' although Lord Widgery CJ observed in *AG's Reference (No 1 of 1975)*, if four words are employed:

> ... the probability is that there is a difference between each of those four words, and the other three, because, if there were no such difference, then Parliament would be wasting time in using four words where two or three would do, we approach the section on the footing that each word must be given its ordinary meaning.

To give the four words their 'ordinary meaning' as proposed by Lord Widgery does present some problems. For example, the word 'abet' is one which is by no stretch of the imagination to be found in everyday use. The House of Lords in *Lynch v DPP for Northern Ireland* (1975) suggested that the words 'aid and abet' are really a single concept in which 'aid' represents the *actus reus* and 'abet' the *mens rea* of the prohibited activity. However, as the Law Commission in its Consultation Paper, *Assisting and Encouraging Crime* (Law Com 131, 1993, para 2.12), points out 'it is difficult or impossible to lay hands on authority for that analysis nor is it clear to what legal results the analysis would lead'.

4.2 Procure

Lord Widgery, CJ in *AG's Reference (No 1 of 1975)* defined the word 'procure' but not the others. In this respect, to procure 'means to produce by endeavour'. One procures a consequence by 'setting out to see that it happens and taking the appropriate steps to produce that happening'. It must be emphasised that there need not be a conspiracy between the principal and secondary party and the principal offender may be acting in all innocence, even though it results in prohibited conduct. What there must be though is a causal connection between the act of the alleged procurer and the commission of the offence. The facts of the reference are instructive. The accused had surreptitiously laced his friend's drink. The friend had then driven his car whilst over the legal limit contravening s 6(1) of the Road Traffic Act 1972, thus becoming the principal offender to the road traffic offence. It was held that the accused was in fact guilty of procuring the absolute offence under s 6(1). It had to be shown that the person lacing the drink knew the other was going to drive and knew that the ordinary and natural result of lacing the drink would be to bring his blood alcohol concentration above the legal limit. The court also addressed the legal position of the 'generous host' who with their consent keeps topping up the glasses of his guests. If he knows that some or all are likely to drive home at the end of the dinner party, does this mean that his generosity will result in a conviction for procuring a 'drink/drive' offence? The court thought not. The first point to note is that his actions are not surreptitious. Secondly, there is dialogue between the parties. The host may well have enquired whether his guests wish to have more alcohol. Thirdly, it is the guests who will make the decision whether or not to drive having knowledge of all the circumstances. On balance the blame or fault rests with the drivers not the host. It could be argued that there is a parallel with someone who supplies a principal offender with equipment in order to carry out a crime. If A supplies a jemmy to D knowing that he intends to use it to gain entry to a property which he wishes to burgle then he is certainly aiding the commission of the offence even if he could not care less about how the implement is to be used. If the generous host supplies liquor knowing that his guests intend to drive home is he also culpable in the sense that he has supplied the means by which the offence is to be committed (see below, 4.6)?

The Court of Appeal in *Millward* (1994) decided that it is possible for a person to procure an offence even though the alleged principal offender is acquitted. In this case, the appellant had been convicted of procuring H, his employee, to cause death by reckless driving. On M's instructions, H had taken a tractor and trailer onto the highway. The tractor's hitch was in poor state of repair and during the journey it became detached and hit a car, causing the death of a passenger. H had no knowledge of the state of the hitch and was simply following his employer's instructions. M was convicted of procuring the offence. It is clear that the principal offender (H) lacked the *mens rea* of the offence although he caused the *actus reus* to occur by driving the tractor with the hitch of the trailer in a defective condition. Thus, there is an *actus reus* but the principal lacked the *mens rea*. There is in law no requirement for there to be any joint intention between accessory and principal in respect of procuring the offence. It follows that in such circumstances there is nothing to prevent the person with *mens rea*, that is, the procurer, from having his *mens rea* associated with the *actus reus* of the principal. Procuring means to 'produce by endeavour' and surely that is what M did in this case. He knew the risks involved, having the knowledge that the hitch was defective. He was prepared for the trailer to be pulled by the tractor on a public highway. He knew that there would be other road-users in the vicinity all the time the tractor and trailer were on the road.

One major criticism of this decision relates not so much to the principle that one can procure an *actus reus* but whether the accused did intend to procure the *actus reus* of this offence. It was never maintained by the prosecution that M was trying to kill anyone when giving the instruction to take the trailer on to the road in its defective condition and death is an integral part of the offence.

Secondary party liability is primarily derived from the existence of the completed offence and clearly this development is a substantial departure from that position. The principle was mooted as a possibility as long ago as 1975 in the case of *Cogan and Leak* (see below, 4.5.1). It is undoubtedly true in that case that Cogan intended to have intercourse with Mrs Leak. What was in doubt was whether he honestly believed that she was consenting. If he had such a belief then she was clearly not raped. However, the Law Commission is less than enthusiastic about the development, fearing that in order to meet the difficulties created by cases like *Cogan* the principle will 'reach too far'. It goes on to state:

> For that reason, we doubt whether it can be right to adopt a general rule for the abetting or counselling of a mere *actus reus*.

This could, of course, mean that the rule should be confined to procuring an *actus reus* and even then only where it is clearly the defendant's purpose to cause the *actus reus*. This view has been strengthened by the decision of the Divisional Court in *DPP v K and C* (1997). There two girls aged 14 and 11 ordered another girl, W, to remove her clothes and have sexual intercourse with a boy. The court stated:

> It would be singularly unattractive to find that because of the absence of a mental element on the part of the principal, the procurers could thereby escape conviction when they were found to have the requisite *mens rea* – the desire that rape should take place and the procuring of it.

4.3   Counsel

The word 'counsel' was given its 'natural meaning' in *Calhaem* (1985) which is to 'advise or solicit or something of that sort'. It was said to be unnecessary for the counselling to be the cause of the offence. Providing the principal offence is 'committed by the one counselled and providing the one counselled is acting within the scope of his authority' then the offence is made out. Therefore, counselling requires there to have been some agreement or consensus between the parties, but there is no necessity for a causal connection between the act of counselling and the offence. On the other hand, procuring does require a causal connection as in the example cited in *AG's Reference (No 1 of 1975)* but certainly no consensus between the parties as the act is unilateral.

4.4   Aid and abet

In practice, aiding and abetting is generally treated as a single concept. Lord Widgery CJ in *AG's Reference (No 1 of 1975)* thought that aiding and abetting 'almost invariably involves a situation in which the secondary party and the main offender are together at some stage discussing the plans which they may be making in respect of the alleged offence, and are in contact so that each knows what is passing through the mind of the other'. In other words, there needs to be a consensus but again without the causative link required in the act of procuring. Aiding, taking its ordinary dictionary definition, means to give help, assistance or support; and to abet means 'instigation, aid or encouragement' (*Compact Oxford English Dictionary*). 'Aiding and abetting' is, therefore, synonymous with the concepts of giving assistance and encouragement to the principal offender. This may take many forms as we have seen above, such as supplying weapons or driving a getaway car. However, there may be circumstances where there is no consensus or causation between the actions of the principal and secondary party, as for example where a person stumbles across another attacking a third party (P). If he then prevents passers-by or police from helping the victim because he desires P to be seriously injured, then it is clearly the case that he is giving aid to the principal offender even though they have never met or discussed the matter and should be found guilty of aiding and abetting the offence.

The range of activities which may be undertaken by an accessory are legion. It is probably unwise to attempt to categorise activities using the words of the AAA 1861. Far better to note the type of conduct which has been found to be capable of establishing 'secondary' participation in the crime of another. It is worth reminding ourselves that the law requires evidence of an *actus reus* otherwise there would be nothing of a criminal nature to which one could be an accessory. An examination of *Thornton v Mitchell* (1940) will illustrate the point. A bus driver acting on instructions from his conductor reversed his bus and in so doing injured two pedestrians. The driver was charged with careless driving and the conductor, who was offering assistance to the driver, with aiding and abetting. The outcome of this case reveals that the driver was found not to have been careless and therefore had not committed the *actus reus* of the offence. That being so the Divisional Court quashed the conductor's conviction for aiding and abetting for the obvious reason that 'a person cannot aid another in doing something which that other has not done'.

Nor, in these circumstances, could the secondary party be regarded as the principal offender acting through the innocent agency of the driver, because in the absence of an *actus reus* no crime had been committed.

4.5 Innocent agency

The concept of innocent agency has been employed with varying degrees of success and certainly in one case without an adequate legal foundation. In its simplest form, it illustrates the situation whereby the perpetrator of the *actus reus* does so innocently, that is, without the necessary *mens rea* (as in *Millward*, above). The person (D) who asks his friend (B) to offer a poisoned drink to his enemy will be guilty of murder as a principal offender on the assumption that the friend's action was one taken in all good faith. Quite clearly B does not possess the *mens rea* for murder having no intent to kill or cause grievous bodily harm. In this example, the *actus reus* of homicide is present with the *mens rea* for the offence being possessed by the person procuring the offence (D). The conclusion would be the same where B was acting as a result of duress by threats or labouring under an incapacity such as insanity.

4.5.1 'Principal' acquitted

An alleged principal offender may be acquitted for a number of reasons. The most obvious is where the accused lacks the *mens rea* for the crime. Secondly, the accused may have a defence such as duress and lastly as we have seen in *Thornton v Mitchell* (see above, 4.4) there may in law be no *actus reus* committed by the accused.

Let it be assumed that the secondary party possesses the *mens rea* and does an act which can be described as the *actus reus* of aiding, abetting, counselling or procuring, that is, something which is recognised as amounting to assistance or encouragement. In *Cogan and Leak* (1975), Leak was charged with aiding and abetting Cogan to commit rape on his (Leak's) wife. They were both found guilty at Crown Court and sentenced to two years (Cogan) and seven years (Leak). Cogan's conviction was quashed on appeal in light of the House of Lords' decision in *DPP v Morgan* (1975), which determined that a defendant to a rape charge should be acquitted if he was found to have an honest belief that the woman was consenting. In this case, it was clear that Leak had throughout intended that his wife should submit to intercourse with Cogan irrespective of whether she wished to permit the act. His role in the whole sequence of events is reflected in the heavy sentence as compared to that initially given to Cogan. Leak's conviction was however confirmed on the basis that he had procured the offence. The Court of Appeal had no doubt that the *actus reus* of rape was present and that *per* Lawton LJ:

> ... it had been procured by Leak who had the appropriate *mens rea*, namely his intention that Cogan should have sexual intercourse with her without her consent. Leak was using him as a means to procure a criminal purpose.

The tentative conclusion to emerge from this decision is that an accessory may be found guilty as a result of conduct which encourages the *actus reus* in circumstances where the principal offender is not liable. As we have seen above, *Millward* (1994) decides that an accessory who procures the *actus reus* may be found guilty of the offence. As we have seen, it does not seek to lay down any general principle in respect of liability for those abetting or counselling the offence and the Law Commission has grave doubts as to whether this development should ever occur.

The weakness of the *Cogan and Leak* decision lies in Lawton LJ's belief that Leak could have been indicted for rape as a principal offender *via* the innocent agency of Cogan. The Divisional Court in *DPP v K and C* clearly did not accept this statement and concluding that 'the appellants were procurers of the offence of rape and were in reality secondary parties not principals'. It must be remembered that in 1975 the legal principle was that a man could not be convicted of raping his own wife during cohabitation because 'the law presumes consent from the marriage ceremony' (*per* Lawton LJ, p 1062). However the presumption was held not to apply 'when a man procures a drunken friend to do the physical act for him'.

A further difficulty is that the indictment would not reflect the reality. Leak did not have sexual intercourse with his wife. A final problem occurs if the circumstances are modified so that a female procures a man to have intercourse with her friend. On this reasoning the female accessory could also be indicted as a principal to rape through the innocent agency of the perpetrator, which is plainly ludicrous as the offence can be committed only by a male. *Cogan and*

Leak must in this respect be treated with the utmost caution. The better view, it is submitted, relying on the recent authorities, is that in such circumstances a female can be successfully convicted of being a procurer even if the accused is acquitted for lack of *mens rea* but not a principal to the offence. This may, in practice, amount to procuring an *actus reus* but as we have shown there is authority to support this providing that it is the purpose of the procurer to bring about the *actus reus* (see *Millward*, above).

It is also necessary to make a critical appraisal of the decision in *Bourne* (1952). Bourne's conviction for aiding and abetting buggery, where he had forced his wife to have sexual connection with a dog, was upheld on the basis that the *actus reus* was present. It had been assumed by the court that if the wife had been charged she would have had a good defence based upon duress (coercion). The only difficulty with this is acceptance by the court that duress works on a confession and avoidance basis. As Lord Goddard CJ put it:

> Assuming that she could have set up duress, what does that mean? It means that she admits that she has committed the crime but prays to be excused from punishment for the consequences of the crime by reason of the duress.

Thus, in effect, admitting that the *mens rea* was present. However, it could be argued that her husband participated in her *mens rea* and therefore he has procured an offence or conversely could be the principal offender by merging his *mens rea* with the *actus reus* of his wife. It is less than satisfactory to convict people of offences which they cannot commit as principals in their own right. The 'device' of procuring an *actus reus* would seem better in principle although as we have said at the moment it is to be confined within very narrow limits.

4.6 *Actus reus*

Before a person can be convicted of secondary involvement in a crime, the normal principles of *actus reus* and *mens rea* have to be satisfied. Presence at the scene of the crime together with an act of assistance or encouragement will be strong evidence from which to conclude there is aiding and abetting but it is not necessarily conclusive. There must, according to *Clarkson* (1971), 'be an intention to encourage; and there must also be encouragement in fact' (Megaw LJ). In that case, a group of soldiers had stood by and watched while a woman was raped. They gave neither physical or verbal encouragement to the principals. Their appeals against conviction were allowed on the basis that the court-martial was not given the opportunity to consider whether the intention to encourage and actual encouragement were present. Similarly, in *Coney* (1882), the defendant's presence at a prize fight was not conclusive evidence of actual encouragement, although it would seem to indicate an intention to encourage the fighters to continue trading blows. Without the presence of the spectators the fight would be without purpose. Thus, *Coney* is authority for the proposition that voluntary presence at the scene of a crime may amount to encouragement but it is not conclusive.

The case of *Bland* (1988) has confirmed these principles and made it absolutely clear that those who share premises with others, being aware they are engaged in criminal activities, will not simply by their voluntary presence at the scene, be accessories to any offences. Bland lived with one Ratcliff who was engaged in drug-dealing from the premises. There was sufficient evidence from which a jury could have inferred knowledge on Bland's part that Ratcliff was dealing but no more. The court held that assistance, though passive, required more than simply knowledge. There should be evidence of encouragement or at least the right to control the person which had been 'entirely lacking' in this case. This is not meant to suggest that the *actus reus* is proved only if assistance and encouragement are proved. Evidence of either will be enough to establish the *actus reus*.

Presence by an accomplice at the scene of a crime may be categorised as encouragement in circumstances where the parties have agreed that a crime be committed, even though the accomplice does nothing by way of a positive act. In *Smith v Reynolds and Others* (1986), R and three others had been charged with wilfully obstructing a police constable in the execution of his duty. R was present in a van which was part of a 'peace convoy' seeking to get to Stonehenge. The driver of the vehicle drove it directly at a police constable. R's submission was that he was not assisting or encouraging the driver to steer at the police officer. He was clearly at the scene of the crime but claimed he was not giving assistance to the principal offender. The Divisional Court held that R could be guilty of aiding and abetting. He was part of a group of people who were prepared to confront the police in their endeavours to reach Stonehenge. There was clearly an agreement that they should act in this way. Therefore, there was no need to show any express words were spoken by way of encouragement to the driver. The mere fact they remained in the van was evidence enough that R and his colleagues were aiding and abetting the driver to commit the offence. The onus will be on the prosecution to prove that there was evidence of encouragement based upon mere presence together with an intention to encourage the principal offender.

If there is a duty to control the principal offender and that duty is relinquished, then in such circumstances, providing the requisite intention is present, the failure to control can amount to assistance or encouragement, by way of endorsement, of the principal's activities. In *Tuck v Robson* (1970), customers at a public house were found to be drinking after hours because the licensee failed to comply with his statutory duty to ensure all drinks were consumed by his customers within 10 minutes of closing time. It was held that simply by standing by and watching his customers continue to consume alcohol was evidence that he had encouraged them to breach the law. Here was a case of deliberate refraining from exercising the power and control that he undoubtedly possessed by virtue of being the licensee. Interestingly, the court was of the opinion that even if the publican had gone as far as to call 'time' or even switch off the lights, this still may not be enough to prevent a jury concluding that he had encouraged his patrons to continue drinking. This would appear to suggest that in such 'control' cases the licensee or agent may have to demonstrate positive action in order to show that the patrons' licence to drink had been revoked. This places an onerous duty on licensees to the extent that they may have to remove their customers' glasses at the appointed moment or at least show they have done everything reasonably possible to persuade their customers to comply with the law. Similar principles apply to those car owners who allow others to drive their vehicles and fail to prevent the drivers from breaching the speed limit or driving in a dangerous manner. In *Rubie v Faulkner* (1940), a learner driver was convicted of driving without due care and attention through overtaking on a dangerous bend. The defendant, who was a licence holder and whose job it was to supervise him, was convicted of aiding and abetting by failing to exercise control over his pupil.

A parent who fails to take action to prevent ill treatment of his or her child may also be an accessory. In these circumstances, there is no right to control the principal offender, but there is the duty to act in the best interests of the child. Failure to seek assistance or intervene on the child's behalf could be perceived by the principal as an encouragement to continue to ill treat the child providing always, of course, that there was evidence of an intention to aid the principal offender. It is worth noting Slade J's comments in *National Coal Board v Gamble* (1959):

> Mere passive assistance is sufficient only, I think, where the alleged aider and abettor has the power to control the offender and is actually present when the offence is committed.

This view is further supported by *JF Alford Transport Ltd; Alford; Payne* (1997), where the Court of Appeal held that a company and its managers could be guilty of aiding and abetting employees in the act of making false entries on tachograph records contrary to s 99(5) of the Transport Act 1968, provided there was evidence that they had known what the drivers were doing, they had had the right to intervene to prevent it, and that they had taken no steps to prevent the misconduct. The presence or absence of the defendants at the time of the misconduct was not seen as being critical.

Calhaem (1985) held that 'counselling' means to advise or solicit and, therefore, 'to counsel an offence' would suggest the proffering of advice and information with the purpose of encouraging the commission of the offence. It was suggested by Devlin J in *National Coal Board v Gamble* (1959) that:

> If voluntary presence is *prima facie* evidence of encouragement and therefore aiding and abetting, the intentional supply of an essential article must be *prima facie* evidence of aiding and abetting.

This is not meant to imply that counselling can only take place prior to the commission of the offence although in practice it probably will. The actions of a person at the scene of the crime giving the principal offender advice on how to bypass a bank security system may amount to both counselling and abetting. If that same person were a 100 miles away and communicating with the burglar by mobile phone giving instructions on how to enter the building without raising the alarm that would be an act of counselling. The action of counselling in this example is concurrent with the attempt by the principal to enter the building. It should not matter how the advice is given or from where it comes. The key question is whether there is something which amounts to assistance or encouragement and that it is done with the required *mens rea*. Other assistance prior to the event such as the supply of weapons or a motor car to be used as a get-away vehicle does not sit easily with the notion of counselling given that the natural meaning of the word is to 'advise' or 'solicit'. Nevertheless, always providing that the *mens rea* is evident, these are clear cases of assistance and should lead to liability irrespective of whether they are labelled abetting or counselling.

4.7   *Mens rea*

The mental element required by an accessory is a combination of intention and knowledge. The act must be intentional and the accused must possess the knowledge that leads to the conclusion that the act will encourage or assist the commission of the crime. However, there are certain points which deserve to be highlighted. The first is that the act of the accessory does not need to be undertaken with the intention that the crime be committed. Imagine that D supplies a weapon to someone that he knows wishes to kill his wife? The supplier (D) may be completely indifferent to the fate of the man's wife and have engaged in the transaction purely for financial reward. Devlin J in *National Coal Board v Gamble* (1959) thought that in such circumstances the supplier would still be an aider and abettor. This case decided that there had to be an intention to assist with knowledge of the relevant circumstances. An employee of the NCB allowed an overloaded coal lorry operated by a private company to leave a colliery, even though he was aware that it was overloaded and if driven on the highway would contravene the Motor Vehicles (Construction and Use) Regulations 1955. Although the driver was made aware of the overloading he said he would 'risk it' and the NCB employee thereupon issued the necessary document which allowed the lorry to leave the colliery. The NCB was charged with and convicted of aiding, abetting, counselling and procuring the carrier to commit the offence. It is clear that the employee had knowledge of the circumstances and then provided the document to the driver which in turn facilitated the crime. There was a clear intention to aid the commission of the crime although one does not doubt that the employee was totally indifferent as to whether or not the driver actually drove his lorry on the road. The focus on intention to do the act of assistance as opposed to intending the consequence of the principal's conduct is reinforced in *Gillick v West Norfolk Area Health Authority* (1985). Lord Scarman when considering any possible criminal liability for doctors supplying contraceptives to girls under 16 knowing that the girls may engage in unlawful sexual intercourse said:

> Clearly a doctor who gives a girl contraceptive advice or treatment not because in his clinical judgment the treatment is medically indicated for the maintenance or restoration of her health but with the intention of facilitating her having unlawful sexual intercourse may well be guilty of a criminal offence. It would depend ... on the doctor's intention.

4.8   Knowledge of the circumstances

Problems can arise in circumstances where the accessory is under a legal obligation to return property to the principal offender which he knows is going to be used to commit a crime. It would appear harsh to convict in such circumstances, it is argued, because the secondary party is legally obliged to return the property. Against this view, one can hardly envisage that he could be successfully sued for its return if the true purpose for which the item is to be used is known to a court. The distinction is untenable and it is suggested that, irrespective of the legal position vis a vis ownership, a conviction could follow if in returning, say, a gun, there clearly is an intention to aid with knowledge of the circumstances. *Lomas* (1913) is authority for the proposition that if when returning property there is simply an intention to comply with one's civil duty this cannot amount to aiding and abetting. This would appear to be correct as there would be no intention to aid the commission of a crime. But, if the person returning the item is aware of the purpose to which it will be put, then he should not be allowed to hide behind his civil law obligations and therefore avoid criminal liability. Support for this comes from the decision of the Court of Appeal in *Garrett v Arthur Churchill (Glass) Ltd* (1970). In this case, the court held that any duty to hand over goods to the owner takes second place to the public interest in preventing an unlawful act being perpetrated with the items.

A second general question relates to the quality of the knowledge possessed by the accessory in respect of the circumstances. Should, for example, the secondary party be fully aware of the precise details of the crime to be carried out by the principal offender before intention to aid is proved? Should one know for certain that the circumstances exist or is it sufficient that they are foreseen as probable, in other words, that he is reckless as to whether the circumstances do exist but is prepared to take the risk? And recklessness in which sense?

The answer to the first of these questions will very much depend on the facts. It may be that at the time of the act by the secondary party there are no precise details available in respect of the crime, only general information, for example, that a robbery is to be committed. In *Bainbridge* (1960), the Midland Bank at Stoke Newington had been broken into and access had been gained to the strongroom through the use of oxygen cutting equipment.

Eighteen thousand pounds had been stolen. The defendant did not dispute that he had purchased the equipment using false names and addresses but said that whilst aware that it would be used for a criminal purpose he had 'no knowledge that the equipment was going to be used for any such purpose as that for which it was used'. It was held that providing he knew the particular type of crime for which the equipment would be used then that was sufficient, but simply to have knowledge that it would be used for a criminal purpose was not. As Lord Parker CJ put it:

> The court fully appreciates that it is not enough that it should be shown that a person knew that some illegal venture was intended. To take this case, it would not be enough if the appellant knew – he says he only suspected – that the equipment was going to be used to dispose of stolen property. That would not be enough. Equally, this court is quite satisfied that it is unnecessary that knowledge of the intention to commit the particular crime which was in fact committed should be shown, and by 'particular crime' I am using the words in the same way as that in which counsel for the appellant used them, namely, on a particular date and particular premises.

The jury obviously disbelieved him and the Court of Criminal Appeal upheld his conviction. On this occasion, the equipment had been left behind in the bank but if we assume that the miscreants had taken it away and used it in raids on other banks would Bainbridge have been a secondary party to all activities of a similar type? Logically the answer must be yes.

In *Maxwell v DPP for Northern Ireland* (1979), the secondary party was uncertain as to which of a range of crimes might be committed by the principal offender. He had guided terrorists to a remote country public house unsure of the nature of the 'attack' to be carried out. He knew that violence was to be perpetrated and that premises could be damaged with life being endangered. The House of Lords held that a person could be convicted of aiding and abetting without proof of prior knowledge of the actual crime provided he contemplated the commission of one of a limited number of crimes by the principal and intentionally lent his assistance to the commission of such a crime. In this case, as he was a member of an illegal organisation (the Ulster Volunteer Force), he must have realised a bomb attack was an 'obvious possibility' among the offences likely to be committed. *Bainbridge* was approved and Lord Hailsham accepted that mere suspicion was not the test but knowledge of the type of crime. This approach does raise the question of which crimes fall within the definition of 'type of crime'. If D thinks that A is to enter a building in order to steal (burglary) by using a crowbar supplied by D for the purpose of gaining entry to X's house, will he still be an accomplice if it is actually used to commit criminal damage on a motor vehicle in order to steal its stereo cassette recorder? Or if the burglary took place but the principal offender was disturbed and used the crowbar to attack the occupier? Certainly, in this latter case, one could not imagine that he would be an accessory to grievous bodily harm unless of course this course of action was initially within the contemplation of the parties.

As to the second question, the Queen's Bench Divisional Court decided in *Blakely, Sutton v DPP* (1991), on a charge of procuring the commission by another of a drink-drive offence, that *Caldwell* recklessness was not enough. The court accepted that recklessness had two alternative versions:

(a) pursuing a course of conduct and giving no thought to the possibility of risk when there was an obvious risk (described as inadvertent recklessness); and

(b) recognising the conduct involved risk and going on nevertheless to run it (advertent), but that only the latter applied in these circumstances (see, also, Chapter 3).

The facts are similar to those in the *AG's Reference (No 1 of 1975)* case, except that the driver's drink was laced not in order that he might commit the offence but in order to prevent him from taking to the road. He was in the habit of occasionally staying the night with his mistress but on other evenings would return to his wife. On the evening in question, he had declared his intention to return home. He was careful never to consume more than two pints of beer if he was driving. Knowing this ,and in the hope of keeping him from returning home, his mistress and a friend laced his tonic water with vodka. They intended to tell him later in the evening that it was unwise to drive. Unfortunately, he left before they had a chance to tell him the truth. He was arrested and charged with a drink-drive offence. The others were charged with aiding and abetting the offence by procuring. It is clear that they did not intend the offence to be committed but were they reckless in the circumstances as to whether it would be committed? Can one, through recklessness, become an accessory? Relying on Lord Widgery's definition of procuring in *AG's Reference (No 1 of 1975)* of producing by endeavour the court stated:

> You procure a thing by setting out to see that it happens and to take the appropriate steps to produce that happening. That strongly suggested that the procurer must be shown to have intended to bring about the commission of the principal offence, and that mere awareness that it might result would not suffice. There was no hint that recklessness, let alone inadvertent recklessness, might suffice to convict the procurer.

The court held that the word recklessness was best avoided when considering the *mens rea* of a person accused of procuring the commission of a substantive offence. In this case the intention was to create the circumstances which would prevent him from driving. The conviction was quashed on the basis that the magistrates had applied the *Caldwell* test of recklessness in respect of whether he would drive or not, that is, she had given no thought to the obvious and serious risk that he would drive. Despite the strong opposition to the use of the word reckless there is just a suggestion that if the magistrates had applied the test of advertent recklessness the conviction may have been upheld.

Some support for this latter view can be found in *Carter v Richardson* (1974). In this case a learner driver was convicted of driving with excess alcohol. His supervisor was convicted of abetting. The supervisor quite clearly was aware that his pupil was over the limit and therefore there was sufficient evidence to conclude that he intended to encourage the offence. However, the court thought that it would have been sufficient if the supervisor had known that his pupil was 'probably' over the limit, that is, advertent recklessness.

The Law Commission (*Assisting and Encouraging Crime,* Law Com 131, 1993, para 2.55) takes the view that 'there is a substantial degree of agreement on the minimum requirements for accessory liability' and go on to cite this statement from McCullough J in *Blakely and Sutton* (1991):

> It must, at least, be shown that the accused contemplated that his act would or might bring about or assist the commission of the principal offence: he must have been prepared nevertheless to do his own act, and he must have done that act intentionally.

It may not be apparent from this statement that there is also a requirement that the accessory should be aware of 'all the elements which in law constitute that principal offence' (para 2.56). As stated above, this would appear to be a subjective awareness of those elements.

4.9   Joint enterprises

The preceding discussion has centred on a clear delineation between the perpetrator and secondary party in the sense that it has been implicit that for the most part the secondary party has played a supportive role. We now look at the situation where the parties embark upon a joint unlawful enterprise the essence of which is a common design. The general rule is that all the parties will be equally liable for the consequences which flow from implementing the agreement, and that includes any unforeseen consequences. The principle appears in *Anderson and Morris* (1966), where Lord Parker CJ stated:

> Where two persons embark on a joint enterprise, each is liable for the acts done in pursuance of that joint enterprise (including) liability for unusual consequences if they arise from the execution of the agreed joint enterprise.

In *Carberry* (1994), the court held that the trial judge might have been wise to have followed the traditional direction set out in *Anderson and Morris* to the effect:

... that a participant in a joint enterprise is liable for the acts done in pursuance of the joint enterprise. That includes liability for unusual consequences if they arise from the execution of the agreed joint enterprise. But if one participant goes beyond what has been tacitly agreed as part of the common enterprise, another participant is not liable for the consequences of the unauthorised act. It is a matter for the jury to decide whether there has been a departure from the agreed joint enterprise.

C was one of a group of four men who had been drinking heavily. As they left the public house one of the group kicked a passing car. The car stopped and its occupants engaged the men in a fight. D, one of the occupants of the car, was stabbed and died. All four were tried together on an indictment charging them with D's murder. C was acquitted of murder but found guilty of manslaughter. His appeal against conviction was allowed on the basis that the trial judge ought to have delivered the *Anderson and Morris* direction on joint enterprises. The ruling which the judge had given had been too favourable to the defendant.

It follows therefore that should any one or more parties to the agreement break ranks and go beyond the agreed joint enterprise then the others should not be liable for those consequences. This rule was established in *Davies v DPP* (1954), where Lord Simonds LC said:

I can see no reason why, if half a dozen boys fight another crowd and one of them produces a knife and stabs one of the opponents to death, all the rest of his group should be treated as accomplices in the use of a knife and the infliction of mortal injury by that means, unless there is evidence that there is intended or concerted or at least contemplated an attack with a knife by one of their number, as opposed to a common assault. If all that was designed or envisaged was in fact a common assault, and there was no evidence that (L), a party to that common assault, knew that any of his companions had a knife, then (L) was not an accomplice in the crime consisting in its felonious use.

The leading authority on joint enterprise is now the House of Lords' decision in *Powell and Daniels; English* (1997). The appeals arose out of two unrelated incidents but they were heard together because of the related points of law arising. In relation to both appeals, their Lordships had to consider the extent to which the definition of the *mens rea* for murder applicable to a principal offender applied in the case of an accomplice charged with murder. Previous cases, such as *Hyde* (1991) and *Chan Wing Sui v R* (1985), had held that it was sufficient for the accomplice to have foreseen the possibility of death or grievous bodily harm as a possible incident of the joint enterprise. The question certified for consideration by the House of Lords, therefore, was as follows:

Is it sufficient to found a conviction for murder for a secondary party to a killing to have realised that the primary party might kill with intent to do so or must the secondary party have held such intention himself?

The House of Lords, in giving an affirmative answer to the certified question, sought to rationalise the decision by way of reference to the dictates of public policy. Lord Hutton acknowledged that the disparity between the fault that had to be proved in respect of the principal charged with murder as compared with the accomplice was anomalous but went on to assert that:

> ... the rules of the common law are not based solely on logic but relate to practical concerns and, in relation to crimes committed in the course of joint enterprises, to the need to give effective protection to the public against criminals operating in gangs ... unlike the principal party who carries out the killing with a deadly weapon, the secondary party will not be placed in the situation in which he suddenly has to decide whether to shoot or stab the third person with intent to kill or cause really serious harm. There is, in my opinion, an argument of considerable force that the secondary party who takes part in a criminal enterprise (for example, the robbery of a bank), with foresight that a deadly weapon may be used, should not escape liability for murder because he, unlike the principal party, is not suddenly confronted by the security officer so that he has to decide whether to use the gun or knife or have the enterprise thwarted and face arrest ...

Lord Steyn acknowledged that application of the rule could result in a defendant being convicted of murder when, in truth, he could not have been said to have intended to kill or do grievous bodily harm, but he sought to refute the predictable criticism that the rule amounted to the imposition of constructive liability on accomplices. As he observed:

> ... liability is imposed because the secondary party is assisting in and encouraging a criminal enterprise which he is aware might result in the commission of a greater offence. The liability of an accessory is predicated on his culpability in respect of the greater offence as defined in law. It is undoubtedly a lesser form of *mens rea*. But it is unrealistic to say that the accessory principle as such imposes constructive criminal liability.

Lord Steyn went on to acknowledge that, if the prosecution had to prove that an accomplice to murder had foreseen the death of the victim, or at least the causing of grievous bodily harm, as virtually certain, there would be very few convictions for participation in murder. An accomplice would nearly always be able to provide evidence that his foresight fell short of this test, not least because the test would not be what he foresaw as the consequence of his actions, but what he foresaw as the consequence of the actions of another (the principal offender) – an altogether more difficult issue.

As Lord Steyn explained:

> ... it would in practice almost invariably be impossible for a jury to say that the secondary party wanted death to be caused or that he regarded it as virtually certain. In the real world, proof of an intention sufficient for murder would be well nigh impossible in the vast majority of joint enterprise cases.

The House of Lords was willing to accept that an accomplice might escape liability where he genuinely foresaw the risk of the principal killing or causing grievous bodily harm as merely negligible, but an accomplice would not escape liability where he had proceeded with the joint enterprise foreseeing the possibility of death or grievous bodily harm, but nevertheless maintaining a 'pious hope' that neither eventuality would transpire.

In *English,* a further certified question arose regarding the extent to which an accomplice would be held to be a party to the actions of the principal offender that deliberately exceed the scope of the agreed joint enterprise. E had agreed with W that they would attack police officers with a fencing post. During the course of the resultant disturbances, W pulled out a knife and stabbed a police officer to death. E had no knowledge that W had the knife.

The House of Lords considered the following certified question:

> Is it sufficient for murder that the secondary party intends or foresees that the primary party would or may act with intent to cause grievous bodily harm if the lethal act carried out by the primary party is fundamentally different from the acts foreseen or intended by the secondary party?

In broad terms, the House of Lords held that an accomplice would escape liability where the principal deliberately exceeded the scope of the joint enterprise, but, as will be seen below, such a summary barely does justice to the nuances of the ruling.

Suppose an accomplice (A) agrees to act as a look out whilst the principal (P) offender attacks V. Assume that A foresees the death of V, or at least grievous bodily harm, as a possible consequence of this attack. If V dies and P is proved to have intended death or grievous bodily harm P will be convicted of murder. Given the answer to the first certified question in *Powell and Daniels; English,* A can be convicted of murder as an accomplice. Suppose now that the agreement was that P would not use any weapon on V, but unknown to A, P arms himself with a knife that he uses to kill V. Assuming P is convicted of murder, does A escape liability for murder?

The House of Lords in *Powell and Daniels; English,* following previous authorities, such as *Davies v DPP* and *Anderson and Morris* (considered above), held that, even though, in the given example, A would have sufficient *mens rea,* he would not be an accomplice to the murder because of P's deliberate action in exceeding the scope of the joint enterprise. By choosing to use a weapon, P was acting on his own. A had ceased to be an accomplice to his actions. The only rider one might add to this, in the light of observations made subsequently by the Court of Appeal in *Uddin* (1998), is that, if P, having agreed not to use a weapon in an attack on V, suddenly produces a weapon and A, knowing that P is now thus armed, continues to participate in the attack on V, it could be argued that A has tacitly agreed to an altered common design and will incur liability for the consequences flowing from the use of the weapon.

In *English,* the accomplice had contemplated the use of a weapon by the principal offender, but the principal had deliberately and independently opted to use a more deadly weapon. The House of Lords held that this too amounted to a deliberate departure from the common design, thus relieving the accomplice of liability for the murder. This raises the difficult issue of how the courts determine that one type of weapon is more deadly than another. A fencing post is qualitatively different to a knife, but what is the difference between a broken bottle and a knife? The point was subsequently considered by Beldam LJ in *Uddin*, where he observed that:

> If the character of the weapon, for example, its propensity to cause death is different from any weapon used or contemplated by the others and if it is used with specific intent to kill, the others are not responsible for the death unless it is proved that they knew or foresaw the likelihood of the use of such a weapon.

In *Greatrex* (1998), the Court of Appeal appeared willing to accept that, if the common design envisaged P hitting V with an iron bar, there would be no deliberate departure from that plan by P if he opted to kick V with a shod foot instead.

It follows, therefore, that, if A contemplates the use of a deadly weapon by P to kill or do grievous bodily harm to V, and P kills V using a different, but equally deadly, weapon, A should be convicted as an accessory to murder. As Lord Hutton observed in *Powell and Daniels; English*:

> ... if the weapon used by the primary party is different to, but as dangerous as, the weapon which the secondary party contemplated he might use, the secondary party should not escape liability for murder because of the difference in the weapon, for example, if he foresaw that the primary party might use a gun to kill and the latter used a knife to kill, or vice versa.'

This will normally be the result, but care is still required as the courts might be prepared to distinguish between the way in which A contemplated the weapon would be used to cause grievous bodily harm, and the way in which P actually used a deadly weapon to kill. The case of *Gamble* (1989) illustrates the point well. G agreed to be an accomplice to what he thought would be the 'kneecapping' of V. The *modus operandi* contemplated was that the principal offender would use a gun to shoot the victim through the back of the knee. G, therefore, contemplated that V would suffer grievous bodily harm, caused by the use of a gun. Had V died from these wounds, G could clearly have been charged as an accomplice to the murder of V. He contemplated grievous bodily harm and the weapon used. Instead of 'kneecapping' V as expected, however, the principal offender slit V's throat with a knife, killing him. The court held that this act of the principal amounted to a deliberate departure from the common design that relieved G of liability as an accomplice. Contentious as the decision may seem, it was expressly approved by the House of Lords in *Powell and Daniels; English*. Hence, the principal offender, using the weapon contemplated by the accomplice, or an equally deadly weapon, but in a different way, can amount to a departure from the common design.

Note that, in the examples above, where P deliberately exceeds the scope of the common design, A escapes liability completely in relation to the death of V. There is no residual liability for manslaughter because, by the time the killing is carried out, P is effectively acting independently. A has ceased to be an accomplice. In what circumstances, therefore, might P be convicted of murder, and A convicted of manslaughter?

Suppose that A and P agree that they will burgle a house and during the course of the burglary P attacks and kills V, the householder. How is A's liability, if any, for the killing to be assessed? A is part of a joint enterprise and if A and P had not been inside the house V would still be alive. A will be guilty of burglary, but should he be liable for the homicide? The cases discussed above would suggest that an assessment should be made as to the purpose of the joint enterprise and what was within the contemplation of the parties at the time of the agreement. If A was aware that P was of violent disposition and thus contemplated death or grievous bodily harm (perhaps on the basis that he knew that P carried a weapon and was prepared to use it), then he, along with P, could well be found guilty of murder. If, however, A merely suspected that P might use it to threaten anyone who disturbed them, it would appear that A ought to be liable for manslaughter as opposed to murder. He would not have contemplated the possibility of death or grievous bodily harm occurring but would, on the basis of the *Newbury and Jones* (1976) test have foreseen some harm, albeit not serious harm.

Stewart and Schofield (1995) appears to confirm this result. The Court of Appeal held that a person who was a party to a joint enterprise which resulted in another's death could be guilty of manslaughter on the basis that the actions of the principal offender causing death were within the contemplation of the accomplice, even though the accomplice had not foreseen death or grievous bodily harm. Hobhouse LJ put it this way:

> ... where the allegation is joint enterprise, the allegation is that one defendant participated in the criminal act of another even though several defendants may, as a result of having engaged in a joint enterprise, be each criminally responsible for the criminal act of one of those defendants done in the course of carrying out the joint enterprise, their individual criminal responsibility will, in such a case, depend upon what individual state of mind or intention has been proved against them. Thus, each may be a party to an unlawful act which caused the victim's death. But one may have had the intent to kill him or to cause him serious harm and be guilty of murder, whereas another may not have had that intent and may be guilty only of manslaughter [p 165g].

The decision leaves open the question of whether a principal offender actually exceeds the scope of the common design where he acts in the way contemplated by the accomplice, but opts to do so with more *mens rea*. There are *dicta* in *Anderson and Morris* (1966) suggesting that an accomplice should cease to be regarded as a party to the principal's actions in such cases. To the extent that there is a conflict between the decision in *Anderson and Morris* and that in *Stewart and Schofield*, there is support for the former decision in *Lovesey and Peterson* (1969) and *Wan and Chan* (1995). Support for the *Stewart* line of reasoning comes from *Smith* (1963), *Betty* (1963), *Reid* (1975) and *Gilmour* (2000). In the latter case, G assisted in the petrol-bombing of a house. He foresaw damage being caused by fire. The principal offender had thrown the petrol bomb at the house intending to kill. The ensuing fire caused the death of three young boys who had been asleep in the house. The Court of Appeal of Northern Ireland held that G could be guilty of manslaughter because the principal had committed the very act contemplated by G, albeit with more *mens rea*.

As Professor Smith states in his commentary to the *Wan and Chan* case:

> ... it [is] clear that there is a conflict in the case law which should be resolved by the House of Lords as soon as possible [p 301].

The Law Commission in its Consultation Paper, *Assisting and Encouraging Crime* (Law Com 131, 1993) has gone as far as contemplating the abolition of aiding, abetting, counselling and procuring in favour of retaining the law of common design or joint enterprise. Professor Smith regards this last suggestion as heretical. The doctrine of joint enterprise, he believes, is not something distinct from the ordinary law of secondary participation but simply an aspect of it ([1995] Crim LR 298 and see, also, Smith, JC, 'Secondary participation in crime: can we do without it?' (1994) 144 NLJ 679, p 680). The law is clearly in urgent need of clarification.

4.10 Withdrawal from a joint enterprise

Where one party is actually aiding the other or has counselled the offence it is clear that certain other offences will already be complete irrespective of whether the accomplice seeks at a later stage to withdraw from the course of conduct which will eventually lead to the completed offence. If there is an agreement between the parties that satisfies the definition of conspiracy in s 1 of the CLwA 1977, then that crime is already complete. Similar considerations will apply to the other inchoate offences of incitement and attempt. In the latter case, it must be shown that the principal offender has done an act which is more than merely preparatory to the completed offence (see s 1 of the CAtA 1981).

This section therefore addresses the question of whether or not the law will allow a party to resile from the criminal enterprise, therefore indicating that any further action by other parties is done without the assistance or encouragement of the person intent upon withdrawal. In principle the law should, and in practice does, encourage a party to withdraw providing certain criteria are fulfilled. What is sought is clear evidence of a change of heart, that there is no wish to give assistance and certainly no intent so to do. The law's demands differ according to whether the act is one of counselling or aiding. In the former case, if D is simply advising A on how the crime may be committed then all that is required is for D to make it absolutely clear that he is withdrawing co-operation, will no longer give further information and that any action taken subsequently by A is without his approval. For example, in *Grundy* (1977), the accused had, some six weeks before a burglary, given information to the burglars relating to premises which were to be entered and the movements of the owners. Two weeks prior to the burglary he had been trying to stop them breaking in. It is to be noted that he directed his attempts at the others and did not take action to inform the police or warn those likely to have their premises invaded, which arguably would have been the most effective way of dissuading the other participants from embarking upon their criminal enterprise. It was held that he was entitled to have his defence of withdrawal left to the jury. The principle therefore appears to be that one can repent providing it is soon enough and the decision is communicated. In *Whitefield* (1984), D admitted to police that he had told two men who had broken into an adjoining flat that it was unoccupied and agreed they could break in by way of his own flat. However, he said that subsequently he decided not to take part and informed the others before the burglary took place. The trial judge withdrew his defence from the jury and he changed his plea to guilty. In allowing his appeal the Court of Appeal said that:

> ... it would have been sufficient for the appellant to communicate his withdrawal from the common enterprise by indicating that if the other person proceeded it would be without his aid and assistance.

It is argued by Allen (*Textbook on Criminal Law*, 5th edn, 1999, London: Blackstone, p 221) that this is unduly favourable to the accessory because the information given by both *Grundy* and *Whitefield* is of lasting use to the burglars and he suggests that withdrawal in such cases should be allowed only if the police have been informed or the owners of the premises warned. This of course is not always practicable or feasible and it is submitted that it be for the jury to decide on a case by case basis, whether there is sufficient evidence to indicate that he has done everything possible in the circumstances to withdraw and make it clear that he is no longer giving assistance or encouragement to the principal(s).

The Law Commission makes the point that once an accessory has encouraged or helped the principal then no change of mind will affect liability. Nevertheless it acknowledges that social policy considerations have lent credence to the counter-argument that if an accessory counters his assistance with equally obstructive measures, he should be acquitted because of his efforts to right the wrong. For that reason, the law has for centuries recognised that an accomplice, in at least some circumstances, may escape liability for the final offence by withdrawal before the crime is committed. It goes on to point out that repentance without action is insufficient (*Assisting and Encouraging Crime*, Law Com 131, 1993, paras 2.96 and 2.97).

In *Baker* (1994), the appellant together with another man attacked S with knives. B inflicted three stab wounds on S and then stated 'I'm not doing this'.

He did not touch S again although the attack was continued by others. B moved a short distance away and turned his back. S died as a result of receiving a total of 48 stab wounds. B accepted that at the outset he was part of a joint enterprise to cause serious harm to S. The Court of Appeal found no evidence from which to conclude that B had indeed withdrawn from the joint enterprise. The report puts it this way:

> The court was far from confident that B by his words and actions had effectively put an end to the joint enterprise so that he had no criminal responsibility for what happened after the three stab wounds which he inflicted. The words 'I'm not doing it' and the turning around and moving a few feet away were far from unequivocal notice that B was wholly disassociating himself from the entire enterprise. The words were quite capable of meaning no more than I will not myself strike any more blows. They were not an unequivocal indication that he did not intend to take any further part in any further assault on S and indeed he did no more than withdraw by a few feet [(1994) Crim LR 444, p 445].

Where the issue is one of aiding the principal offender, for example, being at the scene of the crime then simply to change one's mind once the situation has taken a turn for the worse will not absolve the defendant from liability. In *Becerra* (1975), the accused set out to commit burglary. B had given C a knife to use against anyone who might interrupt them. Once inside the property they heard someone approaching whereupon B said, 'Come on, let's go'. C stayed behind, stabbed and killed the approaching person. In B's defence to a murder charge, it was argued that he had withdrawn from the common design. The Court of Appeal in upholding his conviction concluded there was no evidence of an effective withdrawal. Something vastly different and more effective was required. The court contemplated the possibility that the only effective withdrawal in these circumstances would have been physical intervention so as to prevent use of the knife.

There is evidence that a less rigorous test is applied where violence erupts spontaneously and a participant seeks to indicate that he wants to disassociate himself from it. In *Mitchell* (1999), the Court of Appeal indicated that in such a case the defendant's act of distancing himself physically from the action might be enough. Only where violence was pre-planned did the court think there was a need for the accomplice to communicate his intention not to assist the enterprise any further.

In conclusion, it is probably true to say that an operative withdrawal can be more easily achieved at a preparatory stage than at the scene of the crime. The Law Commission's provisional conclusion is that for withdrawal to be effective the accessory should either:

- countermand his encouragement with a view to preventing the commission of the principal offence; or

- take all reasonable steps with a view to preventing its commission.

4.11 Liability for different offences

It has been stated that in the case of an unlawful killing the liability of the principal offender and secondary party may depend on their respective *mens rea*. Thus, if the principal offender (A) intends to cause at least grievous bodily harm to the victim of a joint enterprise between A and B and B has insisted from the outset that only a minor degree of force should be used, then in the event of death occurring A should be guilty of murder and B of manslaughter. Logically this principle should apply in order to convict the secondary party of a more serious offence than the principal. It was seen in *Cogan and Leak* that the secondary party's role was greater than the principal as was also the case in *Morgan*. Against this is the argument that there is a dependency relationship between the principal and secondary party, that is, the latter's liability depends upon the former's actions, and therefore the secondary party cannot have greater liability than the principal. This view had the support of the Court of Appeal in *Richards* (1974). She told two men that she wished to have her husband beaten up sufficiently badly for him to be hospitalised. At the appropriate time she signalled to the men who responded by attacking her husband. They caused lacerations to his scalp requiring two stitches but no serious injury resulted. All three were arraigned on an indictment containing two counts:

- wounding with intent contrary to s 18 of the Offences Against the Person Act 1861; and

- unlawful wounding contrary to s 20 of the same Act.

She was convicted of the s 18 offence and the two men of the s 20 offence. She appealed against conviction and sentence. The Court of Appeal held that in the circumstances, where she was not at the scene of the crime, she could not be found guilty of a greater crime than the principals, that is, her liability was limited or related to that of the principals. The court followed a passage from Hawkins's *Pleas of the Crown* (8th edn) to the effect:

> I take it to be an uncontroverted rule that (the offence of the accessory can never rise higher than that of the principal); it seeming incongruous and absurd that he who is punished only as a partaker of the guilt of another, should be adjudged guilty of a higher crime than the other.

Let it not be forgotten though that Mrs Richards actually commissioned the crime. She was hardly partaking of the guilt of another. The decision did not find favour with the House of Lords in *Howe* (1987) and was overruled. Lord Mackay endorsed what had been said by Lord Lane CJ in the Court of Appeal (1986). 'Suppose', he said:

> A hands a gun to D informing him that it is loaded with blank ammunition only and telling him to go and scare X by discharging it. The ammunition is in fact live (as A knows) and X is killed. D is convicted only of manslaughter as he

might be on those facts. It would seem absurd that A should thereby escape conviction for murder. We take the view that *R v Richards* was incorrectly decided.

4.12 Draft Criminal Code Bill

Part 9 of the Commentary on the Draft Criminal Code Bill relates to parties to offences and deals with cll 25–29. It distinguishes between principals and accessories and provides the following definitions:

Clause 26(1):

A person is guilty of an offence as a principal if:

(a) with the fault required for the offence he does the act or acts specified for the offence; or

(b) he does at least one such act and procures, assists or encourages any other such acts done by another; or

(c) he procures, assists or encourages such act or acts done by another who is not himself guilty of an offence because:

(i) he is under 10 years of age; or

(ii) he does the act or acts without the fault required for the offence; or

(iii) he has a defence.

Clause 27 must be examined in detail as it covers a whole range of activities associated with determining the liability of an accessory. The first part states that a person is guilty of an offence as an accessory if:

(a) he intentionally procures, assists or encourages the act which constitutes or results in the commission of the offence by the principal; and

(b) he knows of, or (where recklessness suffices in the case of the principal) is reckless with respect to, any circumstance that is an element of the offence; and

(c) he intends that the principal shall act, or is aware that he is or may be acting, or that he may act, with the fault (if any) required for the offence.

4.13 Vicarious liability

The law of torts recognises the principle that an employer may be liable for the tortious acts of his employee provided the employee is acting in the course of his employment. In *Pearks, Gunston and Tee v Ward* (1902), Channell J said:

By the general principles of the criminal law, if a matter is made a criminal offence, it is essential that there should be something in the nature of *mens rea*, and, therefore, in ordinary cases a corporation cannot be guilty of a criminal offence, nor can a master be liable criminally for an offence committed by his servant. But there are exceptions to this rule.

Viscount Reading CJ in *Mousell Brothers Ltd v London and North-Western Railway Company* (1917) confirmed the general principle but added:

> It may be the intention of the legislature, in order to guard against the happening of the forbidden thing, to impose a liability upon a principal even though he does not know of, and is not party to, the forbidden act done by his servant. Many statutes are passed with this object.

Atkin J in the same case commented:

> The legislature may prohibit an act or enforce a duty in such words as to make the prohibition or the duty absolute; in which case the principal is liable if the act is in fact done by his servants. To ascertain whether a particular Act of Parliament has that effect or not, regard must be had to the object of the statute, the words used, the nature of the duty laid down, the person upon whom it is imposed, the person by whom it would in ordinary circumstances be performed, and the person upon whom the penalty is imposed.

Judicial interpretation will be the determiner of whether a statute is deemed to impose vicarious liability as it is with strict liability offences. The offences in question are likely to be regulatory in nature as, for example, those imposing duties on licensees. It would be unreasonable to expect the licensee of a public house to carry out all the duties assigned to him under the terms of his licence. In practice he will delegate the majority of functions to his employees but this would not absolve him of responsibility should there be a breach of the law. The onus remains on the landlord to ensure that there is compliance with the duty. The delegation principle therefore imputes the *mens rea* of the employee upon whom the responsibility for complying with the duty has been delegated, to the employer making him liable for the breach of duty. In simple terms, the delegator will through his employee have brought about the *actus reus* with the requisite *mens rea*. This will only apply where the offence is one which requires *mens rea*. If it is an absolute liability offence then *mens rea* will be irrelevant and the delegation principle will be redundant. If it is a strict liability offence where *mens rea* to one or more aspects of the offence need be established, then providing the employee possesses the necessary guilty mind liability will rest with the delegator.

In *Somerset v Hart* (1884), Lord Coleridge CJ said that a man may put another in his position so as to represent him for the purpose of knowledge. This statement was cited with approval by Lord Hewart CJ in *Allen v Whitehead* (1930), where the licensee of a refreshment house was charged with an offence of allowing prostitutes to congregate on the premises. He had been warned by the police that it was an offence to harbour prostitutes at the said premises. The licensee had issued instructions to his manager not to allow women to enter the premises after midnight and had posted notices to this effect. He visited the property two or three times a week but there was no evidence of misconduct nor did he have any knowledge that his instructions were being ignored by his manager. Lord Hewart was of the opinion that the provision in the statute would be rendered nugatory if the licensee's contention that he had no knowledge of the events were allowed to prevail:

> This seems to me to be a case where the proprietor, the keeper of the house, had delegated his duty to a manager, so far as the conduct of the house was concerned. He had transferred to the manager the exercise of discretion in the conduct of the business, and it seems to me that the only reasonable conclusion is, regard being had to the purposes of this Act [s 44 of the Metropolitan Police Act 1839] that the knowledge of the manager was the knowledge of the keeper of the house.

The key question then is what in law amounts to delegation? *Vane v Yiannopoullos* (1965) determines that there must be a complete delegation of the licensee's duties and responsibilities and accordingly the licensee of a restaurant was not guilty of knowingly selling alcohol to those not partaking of a meal contrary to s 22(1)(a) of the Licensing Act 1961. He had informed the waitress not to serve alcohol to those not having a meal and then left the premises. She disobeyed his instructions. It is clear that he had in no way handed over the running of the restaurant to her and therefore her knowledge could not be imputed to him. The House of Lords indicated some unease with the delegation principle but nevertheless felt it to be too well-established to overturn. To convict a person who has no *mens rea* of an offence requiring knowledge is unfair and if Parliament wishes to impose liability it ought to draft legislation making it clear how this is to be achieved without recourse to what is in essence a legal fiction. This view is supported by the Law Commission in its draft Criminal Code:

> ... [the] delegation principle was regarded as anomalous by members of the House of Lords in *Vane v Yiannopoullos* and our Working Party proposed its abolition. Parliament will have to provide clearly for the attribution to one person of the fault of another if it wishes this to occur [*A Criminal Code for England and Wales*, Law Com 177, 1989, cl 29].

4.13.1 Defences

The statutes which are construed to create vicarious liability will occasionally make available defences to those who may be caught by the vicarious liability principle. For example, see s 24 of the Trade Descriptions Act 1968. A rather harsh ruling in *Tesco Stores Ltd v Brent London Borough Council* (1993) prevented the store from relying on the statutory defence created by s 11(2)(b) of the Video Recordings Act 1984. A cashier at one of the company's stores had sold an 18 classification film to a 14 year old boy. It was accepted that she had reasonable grounds for believing the boy to be under 18. The company was convicted of the offence, one assumes on the basis of the construction of the statute rather than an application of the delegation principle, as the management of the premises was certainly not delegated to the cashier. It is a defence if the defendant neither knows nor has reasonable grounds to believe that the person concerned has not reached the relevant age. The company clearly did not have this knowledge. Nevertheless, the Divisional Court drew no distinction between the company and the person supplying the video, that is, the cashier. The knowledge of the cashier was imputed to the company which in consequence lost its defence. The defence is rendered otiose by this decision in all cases where the employee has reasonable grounds for believing the purchaser to be under the relevant age. If the cashier has no grounds for believing the person is underage, then the company's defence will succeed. If the delegation principle were to apply then the defence would also be rendered redundant as the knowledge would establish the offence and not assist the defence.

4.13.2 Corporate liability

In Chapter 6, the Law Commission's recommendations and those of the Government are examined in the context of the review of the law on involuntary manslaughter regarding potential criminal liability of corporations for causing death. The Law Commission recommends the creation of a new offence of corporate killing. This section will therefore concentrate on possible corporate liability for offences other than those causing death.

Salomon v Salomon (1897) confirms a corporation is a separate legal person although it has no physical existence. As such it can only act through those who are employed by the company or acting as agents of the corporation. Criminal liability may therefore arise through the operation of the vicarious liability principle as we saw in the *Tesco* case above or the so called identification principle. This latter principle seeks to identify those who control the corporation and bestow upon them the privilege of being the embodiment of the corporation for the purposes of criminal liability. To put it simply, the acts and states of mind of these people are in law those of the corporation. Without either of these two principles applying, it follows that a corporation may not be guilty of a criminal offence. As Lord Hoffman said in *Meridian Global Funds Management Asia Ltd v The Securities Commission* (1995):

> To say that a company cannot do something means only that there is no one whose doing of that act would, under the rules of attribution, count as an act of the company [pp 506H–07A].

Examples of how the vicarious liability principle worked are *Director General of Fair Trading v Pioneer Concrete (UK) Ltd* (1994) and *British Steel plc* (1995). In the latter case, the company was prosecuted under s 3(1) of the Health and Safety at Work Act (HSWA) 1974. The company had employed subcontractors whose actions had resulted in two workers losing their lives. In upholding the conviction the Court of Appeal held that there was no due diligence defence in the HSWA 1974. Section 3 was deemed to create an absolute prohibition subject only to the words 'reasonably practicable' in the section. The section reads:

> (1) It shall be the duty of every employer to conduct his undertaking in such a way as to ensure, so far as is reasonably practicable, that persons not in his employment who may be affected thereby are not thereby exposed to risks to their health or safety.

As the court stated:

> It would drive a juggernaut through the legislative scheme if corporate employers could avoid criminal liability where the potentially harmful event is committed by someone who is not the directing mind of the company. Although there may be circumstances in which it might be regarded as absurd that an employer should even be technically guilty of a criminal offence, such cases are unlikely to be the subject of prosecution.

In the former case, the Director General had obtained an injunction restraining the company from acting in ways which breached the Restrictive Trade Practices Act 1976. The company gave explicit instructions to its staff, making it absolutely clear that the injunction was to be obeyed. Unknown to the management, a number of employees broke the terms of the injunction. The Director General succeeded in sequestrating the company's property on the basis that the company was liable for the acts of its employees carried out during the course of their employment. Lord Nolan explained that liability could only be avoided if the company had put into place completely foolproof preventive measures. See, further, on this point *Gateway Foodmarkets Ltd* (1997).

4.13.3 The principle of identification

The genesis of this rule dates back to 1944 and three cases decided that year, *viz*, *DPP v Kent and Sussex Contractors Ltd*; *ICR Haulage Ltd*; *Moore v Bresler Ltd*.

The principle is relatively straightforward. One seeks to identify those who manage or control the affairs of the company. These people are regarded as embodying the company itself (*Report on Involuntary Manslaughter*, Law Com 237, 1996, para 6.27). The result is that a corporation may face criminal liability for virtually any offence as the *mens rea* of those embodying the company will be determined by reference to the states of mind of these individuals. Lord Steyn in *Deutsche Genossenschaftsbank v Burnhope* (1995) put it this way:

> A company can be indicted for an offence of which *mens rea* is an ingredient. Indeed it is common ground that a company can be guilty of theft of property. If that is so, there can be no reason in principle why a company cannot be guilty of burglary. After all, the essence of burglary is simply theft while trespassing on the property of another. Thus, if the chairman of a company dishonestly instructs an innocent employee to enter the assured's warehouse and remove a bag containing valuables the company may be guilty of burglary [pp 724j–25a].

And in the same case Lord Keith of Kinkel said that in the circumstances the reason why the company was guilty of theft was that its directing mind and will, Mr Smith, was himself guilty of theft.

Explaining the ambit of the identification principle, Denning LJ in *HL Bolton (Engineering) Co Ltd v TJ Graham & Sons Ltd* (1957), observed:

> A company in may ways may be likened to a human body. It has a brain and a nerve centre which controls what it does. It also has hands which hold the tools and act in accordance with directions from the centre. Some of the people in the company are mere servants and agents who are nothing more than hands to do the work and cannot be said to represent the mind or will. Others are directors and managers who represent the directing mind and will of the company, and control what it does. The state of mind of these managers is the state of mind of the company and is treated by the law as such.

The leading authority on the identification principle is *Tesco Supermarkets Ltd v Nattrass* (1972). Washing powder advertised for sale at a reduced price in one of the company's stores was in fact sold at a higher price. Due to an oversight by an employee, the manager of the store was not informed that special packs of the product had all been sold leaving only the normal priced commodity. The company successfully pleaded the due diligence defence found at s 24(1) of the Trade Descriptions Act 1968. The fault was borne by the branch manager who had failed to supervise the assistant who had actually committed the offence. The act was therefore due to another person as specified in s 24(1). The branch manager was not part of the of the company.

It may not be absolutely clear who are the controlling officers of a company particularly if the company is large. Lord Reid in the *Tesco* case thought that a company could be criminally liable for the acts of its board of directors, the managing director and other superior officers who carry out the functions of management and speak and act as the company. Viscount Dilhorne thought that a company must identify the person or persons who are in actual control of the operations and who are not responsible to someone else in the company as to the manner in which those duties are carried out. Another way to identify the key people in the organisation is to look at the memorandum and articles of association and discover who is entrusted with the exercise of the powers of the company. The various ways of approaching the task may lead to slightly different results but what is clear is that there must be an attempt to discover who is the directing mind and will of the company and that is a matter of law not fact.

As discussed in Chapter 6, the Court of Appeal in *AG's Reference (No 2 of 1999)* (2000), has reaffirmed the adherence of the courts to the identification principle as regards corporate liability, notwithstanding the fact that the aggregation of the fault of various persons each of whom could be regarded as the controlling minds of the company could have made it easier to impose corporate liability for manslaughter arising out of the Southall train crash in 1997.

4.13.4 Distinction between vicarious liability and the identification principle

Although the eventual outcome may be the same, the process of establishing the necessary nexus between the company and the consequence is different. It is probably best summed up by the statement of Bingham LJ in *HM Coroner for East Kent ex p Spooner* (1989):

> It is important to bear in mind an important distinction. A company may be vicariously liable for the negligent acts and omissions of its servants and agents, but for a company to be criminally liable for manslaughter it is required that *mens rea* and *actus reus* should be established not against those who acted for or in the name of the company but against those who were to be identified as the embodiment of the company itself.

4.13.5 Conclusion

The larger the organisation, the more difficult it is to identify one or a small number of persons who are in reality the embodiment of the company making it easier for large organisations to escape criminal liability. It has been argued that the principle of aggregation should be used in this case where the *mens rea* of a number of people are aggregated to establish the required degree of fault necessary to achieve a conviction. For further discussion of this point in the context of corporate manslaughter, see Chapter 6.

PARTICIPATION IN CRIME

General principles

The law distinguishes between the contribution to a criminal enterprise by the principal offender(s) and any secondary parties. The liability for the completed offence remains the same, albeit their respective contributions to the offence varies from participant to participant.

The AAA 1861 as amended by the CLwA 1977 states:

> Whosoever shall aid, abet, counsel or procure the commission of any indictable offence whether the same be an offence at common law or by virtue of any act passed or to be passed, shall be liable to be tried, indicted and punished as a principal offender.

The words used in the AAA 1861 are an attempt to reflect the different modes of participation, either at the scene of the crime or beforehand. It must be remembered that secondary liability requires both an *actus reus* and a *mens rea* to be proved. The *actus reus* is established by proving that an act of assistance or encouragement has taken place. The *mens rea* is proved by establishing an intention to aid with knowledge of the circumstances. In the cases of aiding and abetting and counselling the law requires a consensus between the parties as well as a causal connection between the encouragement and the consequence. However procuring has been deemed to be a unilateral act therefore requiring no consensus between the parties. Nevertheless there will still need to be a causative element in respect of the act and the consequence. Those who assist the principal offender prior to the offence taking place do not need to know precise information about the crime to be attempted. The House of Lords and Court of Appeal have determined that knowledge of the type of crime to be carried out is all that is needed. So in *Bainbridge* the fact that the defendant knew the oxy-acetylene equipment was to be used for a bank robbery was sufficient to establish the mens rea for aiding and abetting robbery.

Joint enterprises

When parties act out their roles as a result of a common design the law refers to them being engaged in a joint enterprise. The general principle being that all parties to a joint enterprise will be liable for the consequences which ensue from the joint enterprise being carried out as agreed, irrespective of whether or not they are foreseen. Parties may be classed as joint principals in a situation were both or all have caused the *actus reus*. For example, A and B both stab C causing his death. In other cases, although there are two or more people engaged in carrying out the common design only one may cause the *actus reus* of the completed offence. In this case the other parties will have their liability determined by reference to the established principles of secondary participation. Where there is an intention to aid but one party states that he never believed for one moment that the principal offender would act as he did then liability will be determined by reference to the foresight of the secondary party. Thus, if D goes beyond the scope of the enterprise and kills someone, the secondary party may be guilty of murder if he realised that death or grievous bodily harm was a possible outcome. This will be proved by reference to all the evidence. So, if he knew that his fellow activist was carrying a gun or a knife, then it will be difficult to convince a jury that he did not realise that the weapon might be used to cause serious harm.

It is possible to extricate oneself from a joint enterprise but, as the case law illustrates, there has to be evidence of an effective withdrawal. This may mean doing everything possible to prevent the crime taking place or continuing. So, if A and B having broken into a warehouse are approached by the night watchman and A pulls a knife, it will not avail B if he simply tells A not to use it. If he tried to intervene and disarm A, that might well lead to a different outcome even though he failed to succeed and the watchman was killed.

Do not assume that the secondary party will always have played a minor role relative to that undertaken by the principal offender. So it will be recalled in *Cogan and Leak* the husband, although a secondary party, was deemed the more culpable having sought someone to have intercourse with his wife.

Vicarious liability

Judicial interpretation will determine whether or not a statute imposes vicarious liability. There are two recognised methods of determining vicarious liability:

* the delegation principle;
* the extended construction approach.

Corporate liability

This may be imposed through the use of the identification principle or through being vicariously responsible *via* the legal mechanisms outlined above. See Chapter 6 for discussion of the principles in the context of the law on involuntary manslaughter.

CHAPTER 5

PRELIMINARY OR INCHOATE OFFENCES

This chapter considers the three inchoate or preliminary offences recognised by the criminal law, incitement, conspiracy and attempt. All three were originally common law offences but conspiracy, in part, and attempt have been put on to a statutory footing. Incitement and the rest of the law on conspiracy are still subject to the common law. The conduct covered by these offences is necessarily preliminary to the completed crime and liability is not dependant upon whether or not the crime in question is actually committed. In broad terms, incitement relates to the activity whereby someone seeks to encourage another to commit an offence. Conspiracy has at its heart the striking of an agreement between two or more parties to commit a crime and an attempt is established, if with the requisite *mens rea* the party or parties have done something more than merely preparatory to the completed offence. In many cases, of course, the parties will go on to complete the offence and in practice any charges will relate to it, but it does not preclude the prosecution from deciding to proceed with the inchoate offence particularly if there is only circumstantial evidence to connect the accused with the completed offence.

It would be a mistake to treat these offences as being in some way inconsequential in comparison to the completed offences. The law seeks to discourage this type of conduct and severe penalties can follow conviction for any of these offences.

5.1 Incitement

In *Whitehouse* (1977), Scarman LJ referred to the case of *Higgins* (1801) which stated that incitement at common law consists of inciting another person to commit a crime. He also referred to the passage from *S v Nkosiyana* (1966) *per* Holmes J (cited in Smith, JC and Hogan, B, *Criminal Law*, 8th edn, 1996, London: Butterworths, p 273) to the effect that an inciter 'is one who reaches and seeks to influence the mind of another to the commission of a crime'. There are many differing opinions as to whether or not incitement should be regarded as an activity which should attract criminal liability. Wayne R LaFave and Austin W Scott (*Criminal Law*, 2nd edn, 1980, Belmont, CA: Wadsworth) consider that 'mere solicitation ... not accompanied by agreement or action by the person solicited, presents no significant social danger'. The opposing view is that this kind of activity is even more dangerous than a direct attempt at bringing about the crime because 'it may give rise to that cooperation among criminals which is a special hazard'.

5.1.1 Suggestion or encouragement

The *actus reus* can be anything from suggestion to actual encouragement of someone to commit a crime. In *Hendrickson and Tickner* (1977), the accused had admitted 'mentioning' to another (M) that a robbery was to take place and he had 'approached' M with a view to him taking part. Their appeal against conviction was dismissed on the basis that the jury had been entitled to draw the inference that there had been the necessary element of persuasion and encouragement. It is also instructive to consider the words of Lord Denning MR in *Race Relations Board v Applin* (1973) to the same effect, which emphasise the elements of encouragement or persuasion, but also includes inciting by 'threatening or by pressure, as well as by persuasion'.

5.1.2 General or particular

The incitement can be general or particular and need not be aimed at any particular person. Thus, one might commit the *actus reus* by advertising to the world at large in a newspaper or on television. A person seeking to incite may not wish to do so in a particularly overt way and, according to *Invicta Plastics Ltd v Clare* (1976), incitement may even be implied from the circumstances. In the event that the person solicited does not comprehend what is being communicated or the message fails to reach him, then the law admits of the possibility of a charge of attempted incitement providing something more than merely preparatory has been done (in order to comply with the requirements of the Criminal Attempts Act (CAtA) 1981 (see below, 5.9)). The old case of *Ransford* (1874) is authority for this proposition. A letter sent to a boy at school inviting him to commit gross indecency was intercepted and handed over to the school authorities. It was cited with approval in *Rowley* (1991) as an example of attempted incitement. In *Rowley,* the accused had left notes in public places offering money and presents to boys. There was nothing lewd, obscene or disgusting in the notes but the Crown claimed that they were designed to lure boys for immoral purposes. A conviction for attempted incitement was quashed on appeal simply because the notes went 'no further than to seek to engineer a preliminary meeting'. At the most he was 'preparing the ground for an attempt', but had not done anything which was more than mere preparation.

The Law Commission in its Consultation Paper, *Assisting and Encouraging Crime* (Law Com 131 , 1993), identifies as a main characteristic of incitement, as with conspiracy, the fact that a person may be guilty of the offence even when the offence incited is not in fact committed.

5.1.3   The act must amount to a crime

A further important point to note is that if the person incited commits the act, it must be proved that it amounts to a crime. In *Whitehouse* (1977), a man was charged with inciting his 15 year old daughter to aid and abet him to commit incest with her. He had invited her to have sexual intercourse with him but she had refused. Under s 11 of the Sexual Offences Act (SOA) 1956, a girl under 16 years of age could not be found guilty of incest as the law is designed to offer her protection from exploitation from those such as the defendant. Therefore, she could not be guilty of aiding and abetting a man to commit incest with her. The indictment did not disclose an offence known to the law as it charged the accused with inciting his daughter to commit a crime which in law she was incapable of committing. While this decision may seem harsh in that it allowed the defendant to escape liability, it is submitted it is entirely logical and the court is to be congratulated for not ignoring logic and reason in order to support a conviction simply because of his reprehensible conduct. Parliament, however, has created an offence under s 54 of the Criminal Law Act (CLwA) 1977, which makes it unlawful for a man to incite a girl under 16 years of age whom he knows to be his daughter, granddaughter, or sister, to have sexual intercourse with him. The result is that an accused would be charged as a principal offender to the statutory offence which avoids all complications with the inchoate offence of incitement. The principle is that a victim by reason of that status cannot be an accessory to an offence and cannot incite the offence.

5.1.4   Inciting incitement

There is also authority to support the proposition that one can incite incitement as where X persuades Y to encourage Z to take part in a crime. In *Sirat* (1986), the appellant was convicted of incitement to cause grievous bodily harm, by inciting B to cause grievous bodily harm to the appellant's wife. The prosecution's case was that S would have been content if he could have persuaded B to commit the offence or to have found someone else to do it for him. The case appears to decide that the common law offence of incitement to incite still exists. However, if A incites B to enter into an agreement with C to commit an offence, this would amount to inciting a conspiracy as agreement between B and C would be a necessary precondition to the final act. Section 5(7) of the CLwA 1977 abolished the offence of incitement to commit conspiracy. The crucial distinction is whether A is inviting B to conspire with C or whether he is asking him to persuade C to commit the offence. This latter situation can arise without there being any agreement between B and C and A may simply require B to give information to C in the hope that C will respond on his own initiative to bring about the result A desires. Support for this proposition is to be found in *Evans* (1986) where the charge was incitement to solicit to murder. The particulars of the offence were that the appellant unlawfully incited B to solicit, encourage, persuade, endeavour to persuade and propose to a person or persons unknown, to murder E. The Court of Appeal found that what she had done was not the equivalent of incitement to conspire because she had not wished B to enter into an agreement with a third party. B was 'being urged to procure an assassin and was not being urged to enter into a conspiracy with anyone'.

5.1.5   *Mens rea*

It is clear that in order to establish the *mens rea* for the offence, the prosecution must prove that the accused intended the offence which was incited to be committed and intended any consequences inherent in the *actus reus* of the crime. Additionally, there must be knowledge of or at least wilful blindness to the circumstances. In respect of the former point, incitement is similar to the crime of attempt in that the accused must intend the actual consequence. Thus, if the incitement or attempt relates to causing serious harm and not to killing the victim, then if the incitee does in fact kill, he will be liable for murder but the incitement or attempt will not relate to murder only grievous bodily harm. In *Curr* (1968), the Court of Appeal thought that the incitee should possess the *mens rea* for the offence incited, and as she did not the accused had his conviction quashed. This decision is surprising simply because with the law relating to preliminary offences, liability should not depend on the knowledge the person holds in relation to the final offence. The focus should be on the knowledge of the accused. Did he believe that the woman incited had the guilty knowledge? If so, then he should have been found guilty. This principle should apply even if they actually did have the requisite knowledge and the accused honestly believed they did not.

The argument that, as a general principle, there need be parity of *mens rea* between incitor and incitee was rejected by the Court of Appeal in *DPP v Armstrong* (2000). The accused had been put in touch with J on the basis that J would supply him with some child pornography. The accused spoke to J on the telephone and outlined what sort of material he wanted J to supply. Unknown to the accused, J was in fact an undercover police officer. When charged with incitement contrary to common law, the accused successfully argued that he could not be convicted because J had no intention of supplying the material. On appeal by way of case stated, the Divisional Court accepted the prosecution's argument that the offence of incitement was made out if, had the incitee done what was asked, he would have committed a criminal offence. *Curr* was distinguished on the basis that the offence under consideration in that case required proof that the women collecting the welfare benefits payments knew that they were not entitled to do so.

In *Invicta Plastics Ltd v Clare* (1976), the company had produced a device called 'Radatec' and advertised it in motoring magazines, inviting readers to send for further information. One implication to be drawn from the advertisement was that use of the device would ensure that drivers need never be caught out by police radar traps. The company was convicted of incitement to commit an offence contrary to the Wireless Telegraphy Act (WTA) 1949, that is, to operate the device without the appropriate licence. The company argued that there had to be evidence of an incitement to use the device and as this was not evident from the wording of the advertisement they should be found not guilty. Presumably, the company's purpose was to maximise its income from sales of the device. It was from the company's viewpoint irrelevant whether anyone would use the machine. Nevertheless, the company was found guilty on the basis that the word 'incite' was wide enough to encompass advertising in this particular way. But would any potential purchasers know or even suspect that they were in contravention of the WTA 1949 by using the device? In light of the decision in *Curr,* the assumption must be that the justices believed purchasers were intent upon committing the offence although very few if any would have been aware of which piece of legislation they were likely to contravene. Surely the better approach is to convict on the basis that the company intended purchasers to breach the WTA 1949. If they clearly did not produce the devices for this purpose, then it should be found not guilty. A better way to prevent proliferation of such devices is to enact legislation designed to ensure that the end users become principal offenders based upon their usage of such devices and publicise this fact as widely as possible. In *James and Ashford* (1985), the appellants had bought battery chargers for adaption to use in causing false readings on electricity meters, intending to sell them to another person, that is, a 'middleman' who presumably would seek to sell them, at a profit, to members of the public. These machines had one use only and therefore it was clear why they would be purchased. Nevertheless, there was no certainty that people would actually use them. The court quashed convictions for conspiracy to incite others to contravene s 13 of the Theft Act (TA) 1968 based upon s 1 of the CLwA 1977 (see below for discussion of statutory as opposed to common law conspiracy). However, the court was of the opinion that a common law conspiracy to incite might succeed in these circumstances. *Invicta Plastics* may be distinguished on the basis that supply to a wholesaler or 'middlemen' would not constitute incitement as there would be no 'advertisement or open persuasion to others to use these devices' (that is, the general public). In the *James and Ashford* situation, there is a conspiracy between the accused to incite the 'middleman' to purchase the machines but this does not prove that they sought to incite the end user to breach the law. In the *Invicta Plastics* case, the advertisements were designed to persuade the public to purchase and there could only be one purpose in mind, to avoid the police radar traps, given the thrust of the advertising.

In *Shaw* (1994), the defendant claimed he had only persuaded a fellow employee to accept false invoices and thus receive company cheques in order to expose the weaknesses inherent in the company's security system. His appeal was allowed but it is difficult to support the decision. It would appear that the court was not convinced that he had the *mens rea* for the completed offence, that is, dishonesty and the intention to permanently deprive. But this is irrelevant in respect of incitement. If D believed that the incitee would possess the *mens rea* for theft that is all that is required. As is pointed out in the commentary to the case ([1994] Crim LR 365, p 366), if the incitee had been charged with obtaining property by deception and Shaw as an accomplice then there would have been no need to show that Shaw possessed the *mens rea* of the completed offence. On this basis, the *mens rea* for incitement is more difficult to establish than that of counselling the offence!

5.1.6   Impossibility

Later in this chapter, consideration is given to the liability for conspiracy and attempt in circumstances where the completed offence is impossible to achieve even though it is assumed by the defendant that it is perfectly possible to bring it about. The act to be committed by the incitee must amount to an offence otherwise incitement of that event will not amount to a crime. D has made a mistake of law in that it is believed that the activity to be suggested to the incitee is a crime. In such circumstances, no harm will accrue as what has been done is perfectly lawful. But what if unknown to the inciter it is physically impossible for the incitee to achieve the ultimate goal? For example, D incites P to steal B's car. Unknown to D, P's car has been involved in a serious accident, consigned to the breakers yard and has been crushed. From D's point of view he believes that he is persuading P to commit a crime. If the car had been in existence the offence could have be committed. D has the necessary intent. Should he be absolved of responsibility because of a chance occurrence which unknown to him prevents the crime from taking place? One needs to examine the sections on impossibility in the context of attempt before analysing the law on inciting the impossible. Three possible situations may arise:

- at the time of the incitement, the act incited cannot be committed although D believes that it can, but subsequently it can. For example, the jewels to be stolen are lodged with the Bank of England but later the owner removes them so that his wife may wear them at a Royal Garden Party;

- at the time of the incitement, the act incited can be committed but at the time the completed offence is attempted it is impossible to achieve. For example, D incites P to steal a car which does exist at the time D speaks with P but is later involved in an accident before P can carry out the crime;

- at the time of the incitement, the act incited cannot be committed, nor can it ever be brought about although the inciter believes that it is possible.

The statutory provisions which apply to impossibility in the context of attempt and conspiracy do not apply to incitement which is still determined by the common law. *McDonough* (1962) determined, with regard to inciting butchers to receive stolen carcasses ,that the fact that at the time of the incitement they may not even have existed, let alone have been stolen, was irrelevant. It was clear what he intended should happen and he had tried to persuade the butchers to accept stolen goods. The court regarded the absence of stolen carcasses as having no bearing on his liability. However, in the context of attempt and conspiracy, the House of Lords had two opportunities to examine and reassess the common law on impossibility in the cases *of Haughton v Smith* (1975) and *DPP v Nock* (1978). In the event, it was determined that in cases of physical or factual impossibility, an agreement to engage in a course of conduct which could not in any circumstances have resulted in the offence could not amount to a conspiracy. Similarly, an attempt to produce a consequence which was impossible, for example, stealing money from a pocket which is empty, would not lead to a conviction for attempt. These decisions were at odds with the law stated in *McDonough* with regard to incitement.

The matter was further complicated by Lord Scarman's attempts in *DPP v Nock* to distinguish between general and specific instances of criminality. If the agreement or attempt should relate to a specific thing or person, then, if the person had, unknown to the conspirators, died or the specific item, for example, a gold ring, had been melted down, they could not be guilty of the inchoate offence. However, if the agreement or attempt related to something general, for example, to steal from anyone with £50 in their pocket, such a person may not be found immediately but would undoubtedly be found if the participants continued with their efforts.

These cases were applied to incitement by the Court of Appeal in *Fitzmaurice* (1983). The appellant had been asked by his father to find someone prepared to rob a woman on her way to a bank by snatching wages from her. He approached B and encouraged him to take part. In fact, the proposed robbery was a fiction thought up by the father in order, he hoped, to receive reward money from the police. The appellant genuinely believed the wages snatch was to take place. He was convicted of inciting B to commit robbery by robbing a woman near the bank.

The Court of Appeal held that the law relating to impossibility as stated by the House of Lords should equally apply to incitement. However, instead of quashing the appellant's conviction on the basis that no such robbery as planned would occur, the court adopted the 'general' and 'specific' distinction postulated by Lord Scarman in *Nock* and found these facts to fall into the 'general' category as undoubtedly they could, with patience, have found a woman carrying wages outside a bank in East London.

Neill J justified the conclusion in the following way:

> It is necessary in every case to decide on the evidence what was the course of conduct which was incited ... in some cases the evidence may establish that the persuasion by the inciter was in quite general terms whereas the subsequent agreement of the conspirators was directed to a specific crime and a specific target. In such cases where the committal of the specific offence is shown to be impossible, it may be quite logical for the inciter to be convicted even though the alleged conspirators (if not caught by s 5 of the CAtA 1981) may be acquitted.

Note that, in *DPP v Armstrong*, the Divisional Court rejected the accused's argument based on impossibility, holding that the incitee (the undercover police officer) could have supplied pornographic material from police stores had he been so minded.

The present position is anomalous in that, since attempt and conspiracy are both statutory offences and Parliament has addressed the issue of impossibility in the CAtA 1981, albeit without total clarity, the legal principles, with the exception of incitement, have been restated (see below, 5.7 and 5.12). The omission of incitement from the CAtA 1981 resulted from the recommendations of the Law Commission in its report on *Attempt and Impossibility in Relation to Attempt, Conspiracy and Incitement* (Law Com 102, 1980). The Law Commission accepted the view of the House of Lords in *DPP v Nock* and was prepared to distinguish the law relating to incitement from that of attempts.

5.2   Draft Criminal Code

The Law Commission now believes that, as far as possible, there should be consistency between the inchoate offences on the basis that they 'share a common rationale concerned with the prevention of substantive offences and they frequently overlap'. Sadly, no attempt has yet been made to put the code onto a statutory basis.

> Clause 47(1) of the Draft Criminal Code Bill relates to incitement and states:
>
> A person is guilty of incitement to commit an offence or offences if:
>
> (a) he incites another to do or cause to be done an act or acts which, if done, will involve the commission of the offences or offences by the other; and
>
> (b) he intends or believes that the other, if he acts as incited, shall or will do so with the fault required for the offence or offences.

5.3   Conspiracy

Although it is not possible to go into great detail, it is advisable to give some thought to the common law as it related to conspiracy prior to the CLwA 1977. This Act introduced the offence of statutory conspiracy but crucially preserves elements of common law conspiracy; notably conspiracy to defraud and to corrupt public morals. The common law recognised three other types of conspiracy; to effect a public mischief, to commit a tort and, of course, to commit a crime. A thorough review of the law was undertaken by the Law Commission in its report, *Conspiracy and Criminal Law Reform* (Law Com 76, 1976), and it recommended that the vast scope of common law conspiracy should be limited with the focus of the offence of statutory conspiracy being an agreement to commit one or more criminal offences.

The concern of the Law Commission can be illustrated by examining the House of Lords' decision in *Shaw v DPP* (1961). In this case, the defendant produced a contact magazine entitled *The Ladies Directory* in which prostitutes paid to advertise their services. He was convicted of three offences one of which was conspiracy to corrupt public morals despite one Law Lord seeming to accept that there may not be an exact precedent for such a conspiracy as this case reveals (Viscount Simonds, p 462). There was much discussion amongst the Law Lords as to whether or not there was a substantive offence of corrupting public morals, the prevailing view appearing to be that there was not. Thus, if this is a separate head of conspiracy, one is entitled to ponder on the extent of the offence. Exactly what conduct is deemed to be capable of corrupting public morals? Lord Simonds had suggested that the House of Lords possessed the 'residual power' to 'enforce the supreme and fundamental purpose of the law, to conserve not only the safety and order but also the moral welfare of the State', although this was later denied by Lord Simon in *Knuller v DPP* (1973). The real dilemma is how ordinary citizens are going to be aware in advance of whether any agreement which they propose to achieve will amount in law to a conspiracy although it is not a criminal offence. In other words, it appears to offend against a basic principle that the criminal law should be certain in its application (see above, 1.5, for further discussion of these cases).

The attempt at a full rationalisation failed because it was believed in 1977 that a comprehensive review of fraud offences and those offences relating to obscenity would be undertaken. The Law Commission has published its review of and recommendations for the law on conspiracy to defraud (*Conspiracy to Defraud*, Law Com 228, 1994). However, thus far, there has been no attempt to put the recommendations onto a statutory footing and therefore we are faced with examining both statutory and common law conspiracy in order to appreciate the extent and significance of this area of law. The basic requirements are common to both offences. At the heart of a conspiracy is evidence of an agreement between two or more persons. This suggests consensus between the parties, although perhaps not to each and every minute detail, together with evidence that the parties have decided to put into effect the unlawful purpose at the centre of their discussions or negotiations. In *Walker* (1962), the accused and colleagues were planning to steal. However, it was held that because he withdrew before the plans were finalised, he was not guilty of conspiracy. Lord Parker posed the question whether what had occurred had gone past the sphere of negotiation and become a matter of agreement. Evidence of the agreement may be expressed or implied from the circumstances and it must be communicated to the other party or parties. It appears that there are two types of conspiracy which recognise that communication, not face to face meeting, is the crux of an agreement. In a 'chain' conspiracy, A may only meet with B, who then communicates with C, who likewise contacts D. All are parties to the same conspiracy even though A may not even know D. A similar agreement may be reached *via* a 'wheel' conspiracy where one person at the centre communicates with all other parties. That person is known to each, yet the others may not know each other. In *Phillips* (1987), the accused along with four named persons and others unknown was charged with conspiracy to obtain by deception. The prosecution did not have to prove that everyone named was actually a party as long as it could be established that they each had conspired with at least one other person, whatever his identity. Card argues that ([1973] Crim LR 674, p 675):

> There are differing opinions on whether an agreement between two or more people to commit a crime should incur criminal liability. If, having reached the agreement, the parties put it into effect, at the point where they have gone beyond mere preparation the law of attempt will come into play. Few would argue against the principle that the function of the criminal law is to discourage individuals from attempting to commit crimes. But what of those who have not reached the stage at which the law on attempts kicks into play?

> ... if the further acts are insufficient to constitute an attempt, the punishment of the conspirators, both those who committed the overt acts and those who did no more than enter the agreement, can only be justified on the basis that it is the combination of persons which aggravates their conduct and produces liability.

He accepts that there is a compelling reason for retaining a law of conspiracy for those who have not fallen within the net of the law on attempts. If a large number of crimes have been committed at different times by different people, all acting pursuant to an agreement, it may be extremely difficult to obtain convictions for the substantive offences. However, it may be much easier to prove that they have been acting in concert and convict them of conspiracy.

Whatever the strength of the respective arguments, the fact is that a conspiracy is complete just as soon as the parties have reached agreement always assuming that they possess the intent required by the definition of the crime. (See, also, Dennis, I, 'The rationale of criminal conspiracy' (1977) 93 LQR 39.)

5.3.1   Limitations imposed by law

There are limitations imposed by the law as to with whom it may be possible to conspire (see s 2(2) of the CLwA 1977). For example, a person is not guilty of conspiracy if the only other party is his spouse or is a person under the age of criminal responsibility (10 years) or an intended victim of that offence or offences. In the first example, the parties must be married at the time the agreement is reached, that is, the *actus reus* completed. In *Chrastny (No 1)* (1992), the Court of Appeal held that a defendant can be convicted of conspiracy when the only other person with whom he or she agrees is a spouse, providing it is known by the defendant that there are other conspirators, notwithstanding that he or she has no detailed knowledge of them nor has come to any positive agreement with them. It was alleged that she had knowingly played a part in concealing part of a consignment of cocaine and laundering some of the proceeds of sale of the drug. There was no evidence that she knew any member of the gang which had imported the drugs other than her husband.

One cannot conspire with the intended victim of the conspiracy. It has been suggested by Professors Smith and Hogan (*Criminal Law,* 9th edn, 1999, London: Butterworths) that this can only apply where the offence exists for his or her protection. Thus, in circumstances such as those in *Brown and Others* (1993), where the appellants belonged to a group of sado-masochistic homosexuals who willingly participated in acts of violence against each other, a conspiracy charge would lie if the parties each agreed with one another to inflict violence. The fact that the 'victim' is consenting is, according to the decision, irrelevant and, in light of the view expounded by Smith and Hogan, the offence was certainly not one created for the victim's protection. The situation would, it is submitted, be different if D agreed to have intercourse with a girl under the age of 16. Here the law specifically seeks to prevent her exploitation and it can be maintained that the offence was therefore created for her protection.

It has been established that any person may be convicted as an accessory to a crime even though he or she is incapable of being a principal offender. Likewise with conspiracy, there is authority to support the principle confirming guilt as a conspirator when the defendant is incapable of being prosecuted as a principal. In *Burns* (1984), the father of a child was found guilty of conspiring with others to steal it from the mother, an offence contrary to s 56 of the Offences Against the Person Act 1861 (now repealed by the Child Abduction Act 1984). He could not be prosecuted for the full offence as he was the child's father. The Court of Appeal justified upholding his conviction on the basis that there was no authority which prevented the court from saying:

> ... that it is in any way wrong or unjust for a person who is exempt ... from prosecution for the substantive offence to be proceeded against for the crime of conspiracy. The dangers of permitting a father of children to collect a posse of men and suddenly launch a siege of the home of his estranged wife, to break in

and then snatch away sleeping children is surely self-evident. The criminal law does not in our view permit that sort of conduct.

It is also possible for there to be an acquittal of the other party to a conspiracy and for the conviction of the remaining conspirator to be upheld. Care must be taken to distinguish between two situations. It may be that the parties (X and Y) charged with conspiracy are alleged to have conspired with a third party who has not been apprehended or may simply be unknown to the police. If the jury having considered all the evidence concludes that the case against one conspirator (X) is proved, yet the case against the other (Y) is not, then according to *Anthony* (1965) there may still be a conviction against X. However, if X and Y are charged with conspiracy and there are no others involved, can a conviction against X be sustained if Y is acquitted? If yes, this would appear to offend against the principle that there should be two parties to a conspiracy. Section 5(8) of the CLwA 1977 provides:

> The fact that the person or persons who, so far as appears from the indictment on which any person has been convicted of conspiracy, were the only other parties to the agreement on which his conviction was based have been acquitted of conspiracy by reference to that agreement (whether after being tried with the person convicted or separately) shall not be a ground for quashing his conviction unless under all the circumstances of the case his conviction is inconsistent with the acquittal of the other person or persons in question.

There are various outcomes in such a situation which will primarily depend on the strength of the evidence in respect of each party. In *Longman and Cribben* (1980), the former was the proprietor of a garage and car sales business, The latter worked for Longman as a car salesman. They were charged with conspiring to defraud an insurance company of £3,323 by making a false claim in respect of the theft of a car. The evidence adduced by the prosecution was almost all circumstantial but the case against Cribben was much stronger than that against Longman. The Lord Chief Justice outlined the various circumstances and outcomes in this type of situation.

The trial judge must tell the jury to consider the case against each defendant separately. If the evidence against each is markedly different, for example, because X has confessed and Y has not, the judge should go on to tell the jury they may convict one and acquit the other. Therefore, it is proved that X conspired with Y but not that Y conspired with X. This is logical providing that the cases are considered separately. Where the evidence is of equal weight or 'nearly so', there may be a real risk of inconsistent verdicts and the judge should rule that both are to be found guilty or not guilty. If the jury is unsure about the guilt of one defendant in these circumstances, then both should be found not guilty. The final situation deals with the position at the end of the prosecution case where the evidence against one is such that it would be unsafe to ask a jury to convict. In this situation there is nothing to prevent the case from proceeding against the other if the evidence is stronger. The court put the test to be employed in these terms:

> Is the evidence such that a verdict of guilty in respect of (X) and not guilty in respect of (Y) would be, to all intents and purposes, inexplicable and therefore inconsistent? If so, it would be an occasion for the 'both guilty or both not guilty' direction. If not, then the separate verdict direction is required.

5.4   Statutory conspiracy

Section 1(1) of the CLwA 1977 as amended by s 5 of the CAtA 1981 provides:

(1) Subject to the following provisions of this Part of this Act, if a person agrees with any other person or persons that a course of conduct shall be pursued which, if the agreement is carried out in accordance with their intentions, either:

   (a) will necessarily amount to or involve the commission of any offence or offences by one or more parties to the agreement; or

   (b) would do so but for the existence of facts which render the commission of the offence or any offences impossible, he is guilty of conspiracy to commit the offence or offences in question.

It will be evident that it is difficult and unwise to seek to differentiate the *actus reus* and *mens rea* because an agreement invariably involves some form of consensus. We have already discussed the meaning of agreement, let us now focus on what the parties must agree, that is, to engage in a course of conduct which if carried out in accordance with their intentions will result in an offence being committed by one or more of the parties. The words 'course of conduct' must be taken to include reference to the intended consequences as far as result crimes are concerned. If X and Y have agreed to kill Z and they decide the way to do it is to place a bomb under his car wired to the ignition, then that 'course of conduct' will not in itself lead to Z's death. He (or someone else) will need to start the car for the bomb to be detonated. It would be rather odd if X and Y were not to face a conspiracy (or attempt) to murder charge, simply because the words 'course of conduct' were taken to exclude reference to the intended consequences. It becomes crucial that one is clear as to what the particular intended consequences are. It was accepted in *Siracusa and Others* (1989) that the *mens rea* sufficient to support the substantive offence will not necessarily suffice for a charge of conspiracy to commit the offence. For example, an intention to cause grievous bodily harm is sufficient to support a charge of murder but not a charge of conspiracy to murder. The appellants were convicted of conspiracy to be knowingly concerned in the fraudulent evasion of the prohibition on the importation of cannabis resin and a similar conspiracy to import heroin. O'Connor LJ stated the principle quite clearly:

> ... the prosecution must prove that the agreed course of conduct was the importation of heroin. This is because the essence of the crime of conspiracy is

the agreement and in simple terms, you do not prove an agreement to import heroin by proving an agreement to import cannabis ... The *mens rea* sufficient to support the commission of a substantive offence will not necessarily be sufficient to support a charge of conspiracy to commit that offence.

Consideration should also be given to s 1(2) of the CLwA 1977 which refers to circumstances, as opposed to consequences, relating to the course of conduct. For there to be liability for conspiracy, at least two parties to the agreement must intend or know that that fact or circumstance shall or will exist at the time when the conduct constituting the offence is to take place. For example, on a conspiracy to rape charge that they intend that the woman will not be consenting, or on a conspiracy to handle charge that the goods will be stolen. In practice, parties at the time of making the agreement will not know whether a particular circumstance will exist nor is it correct to say one intends a consequence over which one may have no influence. It would have been far better if Parliament had chosen to use the word 'believe'.

5.4.1 If the agreement is carried out in accordance with their intentions

The Law Commission in its report, *Conspiracy and Criminal Law Reform* (Law Com 76, 1976, para 7.2), was quite explicit on what it believed the requisite *mens rea* ought to be:

> Both must intend that any consequences specified in the definition of the offence will result and both must know of the existence of any state of affairs which it is necessary for them to know in order to be aware that the course of conduct agreed upon will amount to the offence.

The House of Lords in *Anderson* (1985) faced the question of whether it was implicit in s 1(1) that the conspirators must intend the substantive offence to be committed. This is an important consideration particularly for those who may enter an agreement for a myriad of reasons, none of which involve a commitment to take part in the course of conduct, let alone have any aspiration that the substantive offence should happen. Perhaps the person 'could not care less' or may even hope that, viewed from his own standpoint, the other parties to the agreement are all arrested before they can put their plan into action. In *Anderson*, the defendant met X in prison while on remand. The defendant expected to be released on bail and agreed with X to participate in a scheme effecting X's escape from prison, in which there were to be two other participants. He was to be paid £20,000 for his part in the scheme and actually received £2,000 on account on his release on bail. He was then injured in a road accident and took no further part in the scheme. He admitted that he had intended to acquire a diamond wire for cutting through metal bars and to give it to one of the other participants. He was charged with conspiracy to effect the escape of a prisoner lawfully detained at Her Majesty's Prison, Lewes, contrary to s 1(1) of the CLwA 1977. It was submitted for the defendant that he had never intended that the escape plan should be carried out nor had he believed that it could succeed, and thus he lacked the *mens rea*. The judge rejected the submission and he changed his plea to guilty. His appeal against conviction was dismissed by the Court of Appeal and eventually by the House of Lords. The House of Lords stated that the *mens rea* for statutory conspiracy is established 'if and only if' it is proved that when one enters into an agreement the defendant intended to play some part in the agreed course of conduct involving the commission of the offence. It was also confirmed that a person could be guilty of conspiracy even though 'he secretly intended to participate in only part of the course of conduct involving the commission of our offence'.

As Lord Bridge makes clear, it may:

> ... be a matter of complete indifference to him whether (the crime) is in fact committed or not. Parliament cannot have intended that such parties should escape conviction of conspiracy on the basis that it cannot be proved against them that they intended that the relevant offence or offences should be committed.

The difficulty, if indeed there is one, centres around the words 'if carried out in accordance with their intentions'. Clearly, a defendant such as Anderson could argue that it was never his intention that the substantive offence should be carried out. There is no 'collective' intention in such circumstances. However strong this argument, the House of Lords believed this would impose too onerous a burden on the prosecution if it had to be proved that all parties intended the substantive offence to be committed. It was also acknowledged that those such as law enforcement officers who infiltrate a criminal conspiracy in order frustrate the enterprise will not have the necessary *mens rea*. This point needs clarification given the decision of the Privy Council *in Yip Chiu-cheung v R* (1994). Lord Bridge said this in *Anderson*:

> There may be many situations in which perfectly respectable citizens, more particularly those concerned with law enforcement, may enter into agreements that a course of conduct shall be pursued which will involve commission of a crime without the least intention of playing any part in furtherance of the ostensibly agreed criminal objective, but rather with the purpose of exposing and frustrating the criminal purpose of the other parties to the agreement. The *mens rea* implicit in the offence of statutory conspiracy must clearly be such as to recognise the innocence of such a person, notwithstanding that he will, in literal terms, be obliged to agree that a course of conduct be pursued involving the commission of an offence.

Anderson was distinguished in *Yip*, where Lord Griffiths explained Lord Bridge's statement was meant to apply only to those situations were there was already a criminal conspiracy in existence. An undercover agent may be seeking to infiltrate an organisation in order to obtain information which will lead to the police being able to prevent a crime from taking place and to the arrest of the conspirators. In *Yip*, the defendant, a drugs dealer, met and agreed with N that they should together import drugs via Hong Kong into Australia. N was a drug enforcement officer from the US. The Hong Kong and Australian authorities were prepared to permit him to carry drugs in the hope of breaking up a drugs ring. The defendant argued that he could not be guilty of conspiracy because N did not possess the *mens rea* for the completed offence. This line of reasoning did not find favour with the Privy Council. Here was a situation where the 'respectable citizen' was involved from the outset and was therefore a party to the conspiracy. He intended to import drugs into Australia. The fact that this was being done with the tacit approval of the authorities was deemed to be irrelevant as it was held that the executive had no power to authorise a breach of the law and that it was no excuse for an offender to say he was acting under the orders of a superior officer. The fact that N intended to export the heroin to Australia was sufficient to ensure that he was to be regarded as a conspirator.

Taken to its logical conclusion, if all parties to a conspiracy are indifferent to whether the course of conduct leads to a substantive offence, despite giving the impression to each other that they do want it to happen, then there really is no conspiracy at all, but according to Lord Bridge a conspiracy conviction could still ensue. It is suggested in situations such as the example cited by Lord Bridge of the proprietor of a car hire business who agrees for a substantial payment to make available a hire car to a gang for use in a robbery, that there is clear evidence of aiding and abetting the conspiracy of the robbers who obviously do intend that the substantive offence be carried out. Reference should be made to *Siracusa* (1990), which sought to give meaning, if any be needed, to the clear words used by Lord Bridge in *Anderson*. He said, it will be recalled:

> ... [beyond the mere fact of agreement, the necessary *mens rea* of the crime is] established if, and only if, it is shown that the accused, when he entered into the agreement, intended to play some part in the agreed course of conduct in furtherance of the criminal purpose.

O'Connor LJ said in *Siracusa*:

> We think it obvious that Lord Bridge cannot have been intending that the organiser of a crime who recruited others to carry it out would not himself be guilty of conspiracy unless it could be proved that he intended to play some active part himself, thereafter.

> ... participation in conspiracy is infinitely variable, it can be active or passive ... consent, that is the agreement or adherence to the agreement can be inferred if it is proved that he knew what was going on and intention to participate in the furtherance of the criminal purpose is also established by his failure to stop the unlawful activity.

One final point on *Anderson* is that given that the whole *raison d'être* of conspiracy is the agreement made with the relevant *mens rea*, there appears to be no authority to support the contention that there must be an intention on the part of the accused to play some part in carrying out the agreed course of conduct.

5.4.2 The conditional intention argument

The courts have also had to deal with the so called conditional intention argument, as demonstrated by the cases of *Jackson* (1985), *Reed* (1982) and, most recently, *O'Hadhmaill* (1996). In *Jackson*, the appellants were convicted of conspiracy to pervert the course of public justice. They were aware of a plan that would result in W being shot in the leg should he be convicted of burglary for which he was on trial. The avowed purpose of this attack on W was to provide him with mitigation should he have been convicted. In the event, he was found guilty and the shooting, with his concurrence clearly took place. The appellants appealed against conviction on the ground that no offence had been committed since it depended on a contingency which might not have taken place – the conviction of W for burglary. The agreement, it was submitted, did not 'necessarily' involve the commission of an offence (see s 1(1)(a) of the CLwA 1977).

In dismissing their appeals, the court held that 'necessarily' in s 1 did not mean that there must inevitably be the carrying out of an offence. Rather, it meant that if the agreement were to be carried out in accordance with the plan, there must be the commission of the offence referred to in the conspiracy count. The rationale of this appears to be that there is a single agreement which is simply triggered by the occurrence of a particular event. The object of the agreement is a criminal offence, that is, to pervert the course of justice. See also the example cited in *Reed* where A and B agree to rob a bank, provided it is safe to do so, this being determined once they reach the bank. Without a doubt, there is an agreement to commit an offence, robbery, providing it is carried out in accordance with their intentions, that is, it is safe to do so.

But suppose the object of the agreement is a condition precedent to a further unlawful act. X and Y agree to rape Z and to kill anyone who might disturb them. Are they guilty of conspiracy to murder as well as a conspiracy to rape? This situation can be approached using the *Jackson* criteria or the two elements could be disaggregated into two separate conspiracies as there are after all two courses of conduct. If this is the case, then they could be guilty of conspiracy to murder on the basis they intend, subject to the condition precedent, to carry out a crime. The object of the agreement in each case is an offence. In *O'Hadhmaill* (1996), the appellant was a lecturer at Central Lancashire University. He was found with explosive devices in his possession and it was the prosecution's case that he was to have played a controlling part in an IRA bombing campaign throughout the United Kingdom. The defence argued that there was no settled intention to carry out explosions. This was based upon the fact that in December 1993 there had been a joint declaration issued by the Prime Ministers of Great Britain and Ireland and in consequence it was highly unlikely that the IRA would wish to engage in a bombing campaign. He was convicted and sentenced to 25 years imprisonment. His appeal was dismissed. The Court of Appeal accepted there was sufficient evidence for the *mens rea* of conspiracy to be proved. The joint declaration might have persuaded the IRA to refrain from planting bombs at that time but as events have all too graphically illustrated there would be no complete cessation of terrorist activity. In other words, there was clear an intention to engage in a course of conduct that would ultimately result in criminal activity. The conditional intention argument is therefore unlikely to succeed where there is clear evidence that the parties' objective is to commit a crime even though there is uncertainty as to when it might be achieved. There appears to be very little difference between this situation and the condition precedent case outlined above. There is an agreement to commit rape and an agreement to murder. They have clearly contemplated the act of killing and indicated that they are prepared to do it. There is a clear commitment to carry out the offence should they need to, a preparedness to act accordingly. Is this really so different in principle from the former case?

5.5 Common law conspiracy

Considered in 1977 to be residual offences likely to be abolished once a review of fraud and obscenity laws had been undertaken, the offences are still with us and there are no signs of them being consigned into obscurity. The offences are conspiracy to corrupt public morals or outrage public decency and conspiracy to defraud. They will be considered separately.

5.5.1 Conspiracy to corrupt public morals or outrage public decency

Section 5(3) of the CLwA 1977 seemingly preserves the common law offence of conspiracy to corrupt public morals or outrage public decency. Section 5(3) is not clearly worded and begs the question whether there is a substantive offence of corrupting public morals. (See the discussion in *Shaw v DPP* where the conclusion reached is that there is not.) It would appear that if there were to be recognised at common law substantive offences covering this area, then a conspiracy to achieve these consequences would be classed as a statutory conspiracy. However, the better view is that agreement between two or more persons to corrupt public morals is a common law conspiracy although this means that if an individual were to engage in this type of conduct apart from the conspiracy he or she would not commit a substantive offence. It is the conspiracy element only which is made criminal. The uncertainty surrounding the whole concept of public morality and public decency had led the Law Commission (*Conspiracy and Criminal Law Reform*, Law Com 76, 1976), to recommend abolition of common law conspiracy in this respect, but as we have seen, its views were ignored. There was conflict between the Court of Criminal Appeal and the House of Lords in *Shaw* over whether or not corrupting public morals was a substantive offence with the former holding it was and the latter concluding that it was not.

Further consideration was given in *Knuller v DPP* (1973). The accused had agreed to publish advertisements in the *International Times* in an attempt to facilitate the commission of homosexual acts in private between consenting adults. The SOA 1967 had decriminalised this type of behaviour provided the acts were done in private, the parties consented and had attained the age of 21. Knuller faced two separate counts of conspiracy. First, to corrupt public morals based upon the advertisements seeking to:

> ... induce readers to meet other persons for the purpose of sexual practices and to encourage readers to indulge in such practices, with intent thereby to debauch and corrupt the morals of youth.

The second count charged conspiracy to outrage public decency through the publication of 'lewd, disgusting and offensive', advertisements. The appellants were convicted on both counts and they appealed to the House of Lords. On the conspiracy to corrupt public morals count, the conviction was upheld but allowed on the public decency charge, although the majority held there is a common law offence of conspiracy to outrage public decency and significantly that there is a common law offence of outraging public decency. The House of Lords recognised three offences of 'general application' which involve indecency, indecent exposure of the person, keeping a disorderly house and exposure or exhibition in public of indecent things or acts. Lord Simon thought that outraging public decency 'goes considerably beyond offending the susceptibilities of, or even shocking, reasonable people'. He went on:

> Moreover, the offence is, in my view, concerned with recognising minimum standards of decency, which are likely to vary from time to time ... public decency must be viewed as a whole; and I think the jury should be invited, where appropriate, to remember that they live in a plural society, with a tradition of tolerance towards minorities, and that this atmosphere of toleration is itself part of public decency.

(Remember that *Knuller* was decided before the CLwA 1977 created the offence of statutory conspiracy.) Consideration was given to the meaning of the word 'corrupt'. Lord Reid thought 'corrupt' a strong word and was of the opinion that the words 'deprave' and 'corrupt' are synonymous. Lord Simon also held the opinion that 'corrupt' was a 'strong word' and went on to state 'the words "corrupt public morals" suggest conduct which a jury might find to be destructive of the very fabric of society'. It should also be noted that the House of Lords distanced itself from the proposition in *Shaw* that there was a residual power to create new offences, but that is not to say that the courts should not seek to apply established offences to new circumstances.

5.5.2 Conspiracy to outrage public decency

As a result of *Knuller* and more recent authorities, one can state quite categorically that there is a common law offence of outraging public decency. The conclusion with regard to conspiracy to outrage public decency is that it ought now to be removed from the realms of common law conspiracy and be recognised as a statutory conspiracy, that is, an agreement to commit a recognised criminal offence. Whatever the logic in favour of treating conspiracy to corrupt public morals in the same way, one cannot point to a line of authority recognising the offence at common law and any conspiracy must therefore continue to be treated as a common law conspiracy. In *Rowley* (1991), the appellant had left notes in public places, for example, public lavatories offering money and presents to boys who would make contact with him. It was alleged that the notes were designed to lure boys for immoral purposes, but there was nothing which would be classed as lewd or obscene in the notes. On appeal against conviction, the Court of Appeal recognised the common law offence of outraging public decency and determined that it consisted of the deliberate commission of an act which was in itself of a lewd, obscene or disgusting nature and outraging public decency. The crucial question for the jury to determine is whether a member of the public is outraged by the act. In *Gibson and Another* (1991), the defendants exhibited, at a commercial art gallery to which the public had access, a model's head to which were attached earrings made out of freeze dried human foetuses. They were charged with outraging public decency contrary to the common law. The Court of Appeal made it clear that outraging public decency was distinct from and did not depend on proof of a tendency to corrupt public morals. Counsel for the appellant did not seek to argue that no such offence existed. It concluded following Lord Simon in *Knuller* that the authorities 'establish that it is an indictable offence to say or do or exhibit anything in public, which outrages public decency, whether or not it tends to corrupt or deprave those who see or hear it'.

In *Knuller*, the House of Lords allowed the appeal on the count of conspiracy to outrage public decency on the grounds that the jury had been misdirected on the meaning of the word outrage. It should, however, be noted that while the House of Lords recognised the substantive offence, it was by a simple majority and one is well advised to consider the speeches of Lords Diplock and Reid on this point.

5.5.3 Conspiracy to defraud

Conspiracy to defraud is an offence which has attracted judicial attention on many occasions in the last 20 years. It is perhaps best explained by emphasising that while many fraudulent activities will be criminal and a conspiracy to bring about these consequences will inevitably be charged as a statutory conspiracy, some activities of a fraudulent type may not attract criminal sanctions. The agreement to bring about these consequences may well result in a conviction for common law conspiracy to defraud. This begs the question, however, as to what type of behaviour is encompassed by the word 'defraud'.

As a preliminary to this, it may be instructive to consider the facts of *DPP v Withers and Others* (1974). Care needs to be taken with this case as the charges relate not to conspiracy to defraud but to conspiracy to effect a public mischief, an offence which the House of Lords held was not one known to the law. It was, however, the opinion of the House of Lords that the facts were sufficient to have supported a charge of conspiracy to defraud. Withers and his partners ran an investigation agency and they used various ploys in order to obtain confidential information from financial institutions and governments when making reports on particular individuals for their clients. Deceit was practised on employees of the various organisations but this did not result in any substantive offence being committed. Lord Diplock said:

> It may be that the particulars of the offence which deals with deceiving officers charged with performing a public duty so as to induce them to act contrary to their duty would support a charge of conspiracy to defraud at common law.

More recently, the Privy Council in *Wai Yu Tsang v R* (1991) gave further consideration as to whether particular facts revealed a conspiracy to defraud. It was held that the matter would be determined by reference to what the parties had dishonestly agreed to do and 'in particular whether they have agreed to practise fraud on somebody'. What is clearly articulated is the principle that all that is required by way of proof is that 'the conspirators have dishonestly agreed to bring about a state of affairs which they realise will or may deceive the victim', that is, there is no need for anyone actually to be deceived. Nor is there any need to prove any actual loss had occurred as a result of the deception. It therefore appears that, as a result of this case, conspiracy to defraud is a crime which is not confined within narrow limits. Lord Goff said of 'intent to defraud' that it 'means simply an intention to practise a fraud on another, or an intention to act to the prejudice of another man's right'.

In *Scott* (1975), the appellant had agreed with employees of cinema owners that they should temporarily remove copyrighted films from the various cinemas at which they were employed in order that they might be copied, and then the copies sold on a commercial basis. The master copy of the film would be returned to the cinema from whence it had been abstracted. The appellant's appeal against conviction was based upon the fact that the conspiracy did not involve any deceit being practised on the companies and persons who owned the copyright and the distribution rights to the films. If there was no deceit, it was argued there could be no conspiracy to defraud. The House of Lords held that conspiracy to defraud did not necessarily involve deceit by the defendant of the person whom it was intended to defraud. In this case, there was an agreement to inflict economic loss and as this was to be achieved by dishonest means then there had been a conspiracy to defraud. If the films were to be distributed on a commercial basis, then it is reasonable to expect that fewer people would go to see the films at the cinema, thus reducing the owners' potential profit. In addition, Scott would not have paid royalties to the copyright owners, thus denying them something to which they were legally entitled. The House of Lords relied upon a long line of authorities dating back over two centuries to *Orbell* (1703). In the context of cases where the agreement is designed to lead to economic loss for the victim, Viscount Dilhorne defined the offence as follows:

> ... an agreement by two or more by dishonesty to deprive a person of something which is his or to which he is or would be or might be entitled and an agreement by two or more by dishonesty to injure some proprietary right [of the victim].

As the Law Commission points out on its report, *Conspiracy to Defraud* (Law Com 228, 1994):

> The risk of possible injury to another's right is sufficient prejudice. Where deception is involved, a person is treated as defrauded if induced to take an economic risk that he would not otherwise have taken or even, it seems, if there is a risk that he may be so induced; it is immaterial that in the event he suffers no loss. A similar principle applies to cases involving no deception [para 2.5].

One further point requires consideration. The cases mentioned make reference to the distinction between public officials and private individuals. We have seen that where the intended victim is a private individual the purpose of the conspirators must be to cause the victim economic loss by depriving him of some property or right. The public official, however, is simply performing public duties and the conspiracy to defraud need intend only to cause him to act contrary to his duty. The Privy Council in *Wai Yu Tsang* regarded this distinction as otiose. The general principle is that conspiracies to defraud are not restricted to cases of intention to cause economic loss to the intended victim. The Board relied on a statement by Lord Radcliffe in *Welham v DPP* (1961):

> The important thing about this definition is that it is not limited to the idea of economic loss, nor to the idea of depriving someone of something of value. It extends generally to the purpose of fraud and deceit. Put shortly, 'with intent

to defraud' means 'with intent to practise a fraud' on someone or other. It need not be anyone in particular. Someone in general will suffice. If anyone may be prejudiced in any way by the fraud, that is enough.

The Privy Council accepted that cases concerned with people performing public duties should not be regarded as a special category, but rather as exemplifying the general principle that conspiracies to defraud are not limited to cases where it is intended that the victim should suffer economic loss.

5.5.4 *Mens rea* for conspiracy to defraud

The *mens rea* for conspiracy to defraud appears to require proof of an intention to defraud and evidence of dishonesty. But what do conspirators actually intend in such cases? Do they intend to cause loss to another or is it more accurate to say they are intent only on creating gain or profit for themselves? If, as is suggested in *Wai Yu Tsang*, the *mens rea* is present if it is the conspirators purpose to cause prejudice to the victim by any fraudulent means, then what more is needed? However, the conspirators may not be at all concerned nor give any thought to the consequences of their agreement as it might affect the victim. They may be concerned only with the potential gain for themselves. In a complex fraud, they might not even comprehend how the victims may suffer loss. It is suggested by the authorities that an oblique intent may well be sufficient, that is, it is unnecessary to prove that the primary object of the conspiracy was to cause loss to another party. It is sufficient if the defendant has realised that loss would, nevertheless, be incurred. In *Cooke* (1986), the defendant was employed by British Rail as a member of a buffet car crew. He took on board his own food and refreshment, along with other members of the crew with the intention, it was alleged, of selling them to passengers and keeping the proceeds. Did he intend to defraud the passengers or British Rail or both? The House of Lords was not convinced that had they known the truth the passengers would have refused to purchase the refreshments offered by Cooke and his colleagues. Cooke's conviction was upheld on the basis that there was an intent to defraud his employers, British Rail. To make a profit by selling to passengers would inevitably deprive British Rail of profit as the passengers would not be purchasing from the carrier, assuming of course that the British Rail food had not run out! It would be incorrect to assert that his primary intention was to cause loss to British Rail, although it was an inevitable consequence of his main intention to create profit for himself. This is in line with *Welham* (1961) which established that an intent to defraud could be proved by showing an intention to act to the prejudice of another person's rights. This view is supported in *Wai Yu Tsang*, where Lord Goff sought to distinguish a 'conspirator's intention' (or immediate purpose) from his motive (or underlying purpose). *Wai Yu Tsang* thus decides that it is sufficient to prove that the conspirators had dishonestly agreed to bring about a state of affairs which they realised would or might deceive the victim thus causing him to

suffer loss or act in a manner prejudicial to his public duty. This also means that
the Court of Appeal's decision in *AG's Reference (No 1 of 1982)* (1983) should no
longer be treated as authoritative. Here, it was held that there was no
conspiracy to defraud a company if it would sustain damage only as a 'side
effect or incidental consequence' of the fraudulent scheme to unlawfully label
bottles of whiskey and sell them purporting to be a well known brand. There
would, said the court, be no conspiracy unless it was their 'true object' to inflict
such economic loss.

Dishonesty is also an ingredient of the offence and reference should be
made to the decision in *Ghosh* (1982), a case decided under the TA 1968. The
courts have consistently held that the legal approach to the meaning of
dishonesty should encompass both objective and subjective criteria and should
be the same irrespective of whether the offence is statutory or common law.
Ghosh decides that, in some cases, the judge should give the following direction
to the jury, *viz*: decide what is dishonest by applying the standards of ordinary
reasonable people. If, by this test, the actions of the accused appear to be
dishonest, then the jury must decide whether the defendant(s) realised that the
actions contemplated were dishonest by those standards.

5.6 Third parties

It would appear that common law conspiracy, unlike statutory conspiracy, may
be committed when neither or none of the conspirators actually intends to
perpetrate the offence. In *Hollinshead* (1985), the respondents had agreed to
make and sell to a third party 'black box' devices for altering electricity meters,
to the advantage of the user. It was the expectation of the parties to the
agreement that the third party would sell on the devices to others with the
avowed purposes of defrauding electricity boards. In the event, the third party
was a police officer and Hollinshead and his two colleagues were arrested.
They were charged, *inter alia*, with conspiracy to defraud contrary to common
law. The basis of their appeal against conviction was that the course of conduct
upon which they had agreed, that is, selling the devices to the third party, was
not unlawful even though, if carried through in accordance with their
expectations, a fraud would, in all probability, be perpetrated upon the
electricity boards. The Court of Appeal allowed their appeal and the Crown
appealed to the House of Lords. The House of Lords reinstated the convictions
on the basis that the agreement to manufacture and sell dishonest devices, the
sole purpose of which was to cause loss, amounted to a common law
conspiracy to defraud. The only use for these devices was a fraudulent one,
that is, to alter electricity meters and it must be taken to mean that the House
of Lords believed that in these circumstances the parties intended the fraud to
take place albeit by parties unknown to them.

As always in such circumstances it is not inevitable that the consequence will occur. The third party may not pass them on; the electricity boards knowing of their existence may alter their meters to counteract the threat thus making the devices obsolete. Once again it is arguably the case that their real intention is profit from the sale and they may be completely indifferent towards the end consequence. Neither can they be certain that fraud will occur. At best, to borrow from Lord Hailsham in *Hyam* and Lord Lane CJ in *Nedrick* they can only be morally or virtually certain the consequence will occur.

The Law Commission, in reviewing the current law, acknowledged at the outset that there is no general offence of fraud in English law, but that 'conspiracy to defraud comes close to being such an offence since its scope is extremely wide'. It cannot, of course, be committed by one person acting alone. It will be recalled that, as a result of the review of the law on inchoate offences in the 1970s, the assumption was that conspiracy should be restricted to those agreeing to commit a substantive offence. The implication being that an agreement to commit something that was not a substantive offence should no longer attract criminal liability.

However, the Law Commission thought that to abolish conspiracy to defraud without having put new statutory offences in place would 'have left an unacceptable gap in the law. Abolition would be possible only when suitable offences had been devised'.

As a result, there was an immediate difficulty once the CLwA 1977 became law. Could a common law conspiracy be charged if the facts revealed a statutory conspiracy? This was most likely to occur with offences involving dishonesty, most notably theft. The House of Lords in *Ayres* (1984) held that conspiracy to defraud should not be charged in such cases. Only where the dishonest conduct did not reveal a substantive offence would it be appropriate to charge conspiracy at common law. This, however, presented difficulties in cases of large scale fraud where the magnitude of what had been agreed encompassed conduct which both revealed substantive offences and fraudulent behaviour not amounting to an offence. The later House of Lords' decision in *Cooke* (1986) ameliorated the difficulty by permitting the use of conspiracy to defraud in such circumstances. Nevertheless, it was felt that the position needed statutory clarification and s 12 of the Criminal Justice Act 1987 reversed the *Ayres* decision. The section states:

(1) If a person agrees with any other person or persons that a course of conduct shall be pursued; and the course of conduct will necessarily amount to or involve the commission of any offence or offences by one or more of the parties to the agreement if the agreement is carried out in accordance with their intentions, the fact that it will do so shall not preclude a charge of conspiracy to defraud being brought against any of them in respect of the agreement.

The current position as a result of this section means that even though the facts would warrant a statutory conspiracy charge, this does not preclude a charge of conspiracy to defraud.

In November 1994, the Law Commission announced its intention to instigate a thorough review of the offences of dishonesty including those created by the TAs 1968 and 1978 and in consequence has concluded that conspiracy to defraud 'should remain intact pending our comprehensive review of the law. We have resolved that it would be inappropriate (to make piecemeal recommendations for reform of other aspects of the law of dishonesty' (*Conspiracy to Defraud* (Law Com 228, 1994, para 1.20)).

The report is therefore useful because the Law Commission reviews the working of the current law and identifies the major criticisms of conspiracy to defraud. Of particular interest is Pt IV which contains proposals as to which types of conduct would cease to be criminal if conspiracy to defraud were to be abolished. In consequence, the Law Commission is of the view that the following types of conduct should fall within the ambit of conspiracy to defraud, pending the outcome of the review of dishonesty offences:

- conduct which would amount to 'theft' if the property in question were capable of being stolen;

- some cases in which the owner of property is temporarily deprived of it;

- cases in which for the purposes of the Theft Act 1968 there is no property belonging to another;

- secret profits made by employees and fiduciaries;

- the obtaining without deception of benefits other than property;

- the evasion of liability without intent to make permanent default;

- the dishonest failure to pay for goods and services;

- gambling swindles;

- corruption not involving consideration;

- 'prejudice' without financial loss;

- assisting in fraud by third parties;

- cases in which a party is ignorant of the details of the fraud;

- deception of computers and other machines.

5.7 Impossibility

Section 5 of the CAtA 1981 amended s 1 of the CLwA 1977 by inserting s 1(1)(b) which deals with the situation where the existence of certain facts renders the commission of the substantive offence impossible:

> (1) ... if a person agrees with any other person or persons that a course of conduct shall be pursued which, if the agreement is carried out in accordance with their intentions, either:
>
> (a) will necessarily amount to or involve the commission of any offence or offences by one or more parties to the agreement; or
>
> (b) would do so but for the existence of facts which render the commission of the offence or any other offences impossible,
>
> he is guilty of conspiracy to commit the offence or offences in question.

Crucially, everything would now seem to depend on the parties intentions certainly as far as statutory conspiracy is concerned. Thus, if they agree to handle goods which they believe, wrongly, to be stolen, they may still be convicted of conspiracy to handle.

However, this provision relates only to statutory conspiracy and the common law would appear to be based upon the decision of the House of Lords *in Haughton v Smith* (1973) and *DPP v Nock* (1978). Therefore, in the case of common law conspiracy, impossibility will be a defence unless the failure is occasioned through inadequate means to effect the crime.

5.8 Jurisdiction

With the easing of restrictions on movement in the European Community and international travel so easily facilitated, it is likely that there will be an increase in the number of conspiracies which will have as their object a crime committed in another jurisdiction. Similarly, many agreements are likely to be concluded overseas with the crime taking place in England or Wales, or an agreement reached overseas for a crime to be effected in another overseas country but with some part of the plan being put into action in this jurisdiction (for example, an agreement in Kashmir to import heroin into England for onward transmission to the US).

5.8.1 Jurisdiction over conspiracies to commit offences outside the jurisdiction

Section 1(4) of the ClwA 1977 provides that, if parties make an agreement in England and Wales to commit an offence outside the jurisdiction they will only be guilty of conspiracy if the completed offence would be triable in England

and Wales. The most important example of such extraterritorial offences is murder; see, further, the speech of Lord Tucker in *Board of Trade v Owen* (1957).

Three significant legislative initiatives have, however, massively increased the jurisdiction of courts in England and Wales in respect of conspiracies to commit offences abroad. The Sexual Offences (Conspiracy and Incitement) Act 1996, enacted in the light of concerns about 'sex tourism', makes it possible to be with charged the offence of conspiracy even though the course of conduct agreed upon is to be performed outside the jurisdiction, provided a number of conditions are met:

- the agreement was that the conduct would occur wholly outside the jurisdiction; and

- the conduct in question would be illegal where performed; and

- were the conduct agreed upon to be carried out within the jurisdiction, it would constitute one of the offences specified in the Act (rape, indecency with children, indecent assault, etc); and

- some conduct occurred within the jurisdiction, performed either by a party to the agreement or an agent, this conduct either preliminary to or by the agreement being entered, or by action being taken in pursuance of the agreement within the jurisdiction.

Part 1 of the Criminal Justice Act 1993, which came into effect on 1 June 1999, extended the jurisdiction of courts in England and Wales to deal with two groups of 'cross frontier' offences. Group A includes offences such as theft, handling stolen goods, blackmail, obtaining goods and services by deception, and avoiding a liability by deception. Group B includes offences of inciting, conspiring or attempting to commit any Group A offence. Courts in England and Wales have jurisdiction over Group A offences provided a 'relevant event' occurs within the jurisdiction. A 'relevant event' is any act or omission proof of which is required in order to establish the commission of the offence. An offence within Group B can be charged (for example, conspiracy to commit theft in France) even though no 'relevant event' is scheduled to occur within the jurisdiction, provided:

- a party to the conspiracy or his agent has done anything in England and Wales in relation to it before its formation; or

- a party became a party to it in England and Wales; or

- a party to it did or omitted anything in England and Wales in pursuance of the agreement.

It must also be shown that the act or omission agreed upon would have constituted an offence in the jurisdiction where it was intended to occur. The precise description of the offence under the 'foreign' law is not significant – what matters is that the conduct would be punishable as a criminal offence. A charge of conspiracy to defraud can also be maintained, provided these conditions are met. If the provisions of the 1993 Act are invoked, an accused will be charged with conspiracy contrary to s 1 of the ClwA 1977.

A more general jurisdiction to try conspiracies to commit offences abroad is given to courts in England and Wales by virtue of ss 5–8 of the Criminal Justice (Terrorism and Conspiracy) Act 1998. The Act, which came into force on 4 September 1998, provides that it is an offence to conspire to carry out a course of conduct that would result in the commission of an offence in another jurisdiction, provided:

- the conduct would also amount to an offence in England and Wales; and

- a party to the conspiracy or his agent does something in England or Wales in relation to it before its formation; or

- a party became a party to the conspiracy in England or Wales; or

- a party to the conspiracy did or omitted to do something in England or Wales in pursuance of the agreement.

An accused charged with conspiracy under the 1998 Act is charged contrary to s1(A) of the ClwA 1977.

The provisions of the 1998 Act have been criticised on the grounds that they are obscurely worded, were hastily introduced in the wake of terrorist activity in Omagh, Dar es Salaam and Kenya, and go much further than is needed, effectively exporting the deficiencies and uncertainties of the domestic law of conspiracy to a wider world; see, further, the article by Colm Campbell ('Two steps backwards: the Criminal Justice (Terrorism and Conspiracy) Act 1998' [1999] Crim LR 941.)

5.8.2 Agreement abroad to commit an offence within the jurisdiction

An agreement abroad to commit an offence within the jurisdiction was ruled by the common law and not s 1(4) of the CLwA 1977. In *DPP v Doot* (1973), the respondents were American citizens who planned to import cannabis into that country by way of England. The cannabis was bought in Morocco, hidden in jars and brought to England. The respondents were charged with conspiracy to import dangerous drugs. It was contended that as the agreement had taken place outside England the court did not have jurisdiction to try the case. The House of Lords held that a conspiracy entered into abroad could be prosecuted in England if the parties acted in England in concert and in pursuance of the agreement.

As Viscount Dilhorne said:

Proof of acts done by the accused in this country may suffice to prove there was at the time of those acts a conspiracy in existence in this country to which they were parties and if that is proved, then the charge of conspiracy is within the jurisdiction of the English courts, even though the initial agreement is made outside the jurisdiction.

It is submitted that the House of Lords had to reach this conclusion to avoid the awful spectre of criminals taking a day trip to Calais in order to reach agreements to commit crimes in England and to escape liability for those agreements even though the object would be carried out within the jurisdiction.

Doot determines that some form of overt act is required within the jurisdiction but Lord Griffiths questioned this requirement in *Liangsiriprasert v US Government* (1990):

> But why should an overt act be necessary to found jurisdiction? In the case of conspiracy in England, the crime is complete once the agreement is made and no further overt act needs to be proved as an ingredient of the crime. The only purpose of looking for an overt act in England in the case of a conspiracy entered into abroad can be to establish the link between the conspiracy and England or possibly to show the conspiracy is continuing. Their Lordships can find nothing in precedent, comity or good sense that should inhibit the common law from regarding as justiciable in England inchoate crimes committed abroad which are intended, to result in the commission of criminal offences in England.

This conclusion was also reached with regard to statutory conspiracy in the case of *Sansom and Others* (1991). The defendants were arrested on board vessels which were stopped in the English Channel. It was alleged that a large amount of cannabis had been transported by ship from Morocco and was transferred to a second vessel in the Channel. It was submitted that as the agreement had been made outside the jurisdiction, no drugs had been imported into the jurisdiction, no unlawful act committed within the jurisdiction and no act in pursuance of the conspiracy had been carried out by the defendants in the jurisdiction, then the court did not have jurisdiction. The Court of Appeal held that, irrespective of whether the charge was statutory or common law conspiracy, it was triable in England even though no overt act had taken place within the jurisdiction. Taylor LJ justified the conclusion on three grounds:

- that it cannot have been Parliament's intention when enacting the CLwA 1977 to alter the common law rules as to extra territorial conspiracies without specific wording in the Act;

- the rules would apply to conspiracy to defraud but not to other conspiracies which would be an 'absurdity';

- the Privy Council in *Liangsiriprasert*, being aware that most conspiracies are statutory, would have specifically made clear that it was limiting its thinking to common law conspiracies if that indeed had been the case.

The CJA 1993 now confirms the position in respect of a conspiracy abroad to commit a Group A offence or a conspiracy to defraud in this country even though nothing occurs in this country. The crucial thing is to establish that a relevant event was planned to occur in this jurisdiction. A 'relevant event' in relation to any Group A offence is defined in s 2 of the CJA 1993 to mean: 'Any act or omission or other event (including any result of one or more acts or omissions) proof of which is required for the conviction of the offence.'

Thus, if X and Y agree in Germany that they will travel to England to receive a car stolen the previous day in Brighton and a few hours later they change their minds, the offence, assuming there is evidence of the agreement, would be complete and any subsequent change of mind irrelevant. Other offences not covered by the CJA 1993 will still be covered by the common law as outlined above.

5.9   Attempt

The law on attempts is to be found in the CAtA 1981, having until then been ruled by the common law. As an aid to appreciating some of the principles applicable to the modern law an understanding, in outline at least, of the difficulties encountered by the common law will be of value. This may be achieved by examining the Law Commission report on *Attempt and Impossibility in Relation to Attempt, Conspiracy and Incitement* (Law Com 102, 1980) or the article by Ian Dennis ('The Criminal Attempts Act 1981' [1982] Crim LR 5). For the avoidance of doubt, the common law relating to attempt was repealed by the Act (see s 6(1)).

The law on attempts primarily addresses the issue of failure, that is, the inability to make a success of the proposed criminal enterprise. It acknowledges that the accused has failed to bring about the actus reus of the particular crime he or she has in mind. The failure may take many forms. The poisoner who mistakenly uses a harmless substance or the hired assassin who misses his victim and thus fails in his attempt to kill certainly intend to bring about the actus reus of the crime in question. However, this is not meant to suggest that if the accused goes on to complete the offence its completion will provide a defence to a charge of attempt. Section 6(4) of the CLwA 1967 states:

> ... where a person is charged on an indictment with attempting to commit an offence or with any assault or other act preliminary to an offence, but not the completed offence, then – he may be convicted of the offence charged notwithstanding that he is shown to be guilty of the completed offence.

At common law, an attempt to commit a felony was a misdemeanour and according to the doctrine of 'merger' if the felony was completed the misdemeanour disappeared having 'merged' with the completed offence. The CLwA 1967 abolished felonies and s 6(4) applies to indictable offences. But what of summary trials? In *Webley v Buxton* (1977), the appellant was charged before justices with attempting to take away a motor cycle without the owner's consent. It was conceded by the prosecution that the full offence had in fact been committed. The defence contended that because of the doctrine of merger the defendant could not be guilty of an attempt. The court held that as a result of the abolition of the distinction between felonies and misdemeanours by s 1(2) of the CLwA 1967 the attempt did not merge with the completed offence and the justices were entitled to convict.

On this basis, it would appear possible to convict the defendant of both the attempt and completed offence at the same time but in practise this is unlikely to happen.

While we should heave a collective sigh of relief when defendants fail to achieve their objectives, the one factor which should not be ignored is that a guilty mind is present and the moral culpability the same, irrespective of whether the desired consequence is achieved or even achievable! Schiemann J. expressed the rationale underpinning the law on attempt in *AG's Reference (No 3 of 1992)* (1994):

> One way of analysing the situation is to say that a defendant, in order to be guilty of attempt, must be in one of the states of mind required for the commission of the full offence, and did his best, as far as he could, to supply what was missing from the completion of the offence. It is the policy of the law that such people should be punished notwithstanding that in fact the intentions of such a defendant have not been fulfilled [p 126(c)].

Perhaps unsurprisingly, it is the mental element required for an attempt rather than the *actus reus* which has proved the more problematic. That Parliament views an attempt to commit a crime as a serious action cannot be doubted and is reflected in the heavy sentences which may be imposed, for example, life imprisonment for attempted murder, and for indictable offences the same maximum penalty which may be imposed for the completed offence.

The offence is stated thus (s 1(1)):

> If, with intent to commit an offence to which this section applies, a person does an act which is more than merely preparatory to the commission of the offence, he is guilty of attempting to commit the offence.

5.10   *Actus reus*

The *actus reus* is clearly stated in the section as doing 'an act which is more than merely preparatory' to the completed offence. (For an appraisal of the Law Commission proposals which underpinned the CAtA 1981, see Dennis, I, 'The elements of attempt' [1980] Crim LR 758.) Dennis argued that the Law Commission tried to preserve a balance between the interests of the individual and the interests of society so that 'not all acts towards the commission of an offence should be punishable ...'.

This definition requires there to be an act and by implication it is impossible to be found guilty of an attempt in respect of an omission. The parents who, as in *Gibbins and Proctor*, deliberately starve their child with the intent to kill will be guilty of murder if the child dies. Should they be guilty of attempted murder if the child survives? Yet what is the act or series of acts they have carried out? The *Concise Oxford Dictionary* defines 'act' to mean 'something done' 'the process of doing something.' Could it not be maintained that they are doing something in letting their child die? Clearly, though, it would be difficult to imagine that a failure to act sits easily in the context of s 1 of the CAtA 1981.

One should clearly discern which *actus reus* and therefore which crime is being attempted and this may be achieved by not only considering the activities in which the defendant was engaged but any other evidence available to the jury, for example, a confession. Section 4(3) makes it clear that this is a matter of fact and accordingly is for the jury to determine. As may well be imagined, a substantial body of case law had evolved under the common law but this is now, at best, simply of illustrative value. Taylor LJ in *Kenneth Jones* (1990), commenting on whether common law authority had any relevance, believed the approach of construing the s 1 words by reference to previous case law was 'misconceived' and went on to make the point that:

> The 1981 Act is a codifying statute. It amends and sets out completely the law relating to attempts and conspiracies. In those circumstances the correct approach is to look first at the natural meaning of the statutory words, not to turn back to earlier case law and seek to fit some previous test to the words of the section.

This approach has been endorsed by the Court of Appeal in *AG's Reference (No 1 of 1992)* (1993):

> In *R v Kenneth Jones*, and again in *R v Campbell* (1990), this court made it clear that the words of the Act were to be applied in their plain and natural meaning. The words are not to be interpreted so as to reintroduce either of the earlier common law tests. Indeed, one of the objects of the Act was to resolve the uncertainty those tests created.

In *Kenneth Jones* (1990), it fell to be determined whether on a charge of attempted murder the accused had done a more than merely preparatory act in pointing a sawn off shotgun at his intended victim, when the safety catch was still in place and the victim was unable to confirm that the defendant's finger was on the trigger. The defendant therefore had three things to do before he could achieve his objective:

- take off the catch;
- put his finger on the trigger;
- pull the trigger.

It was held that the defendant's acts in obtaining a weapon, shortening the barrel and going to the place where he knew the victim would be, amounted only to mere preparation. However, to enter the victim's car, take out a loaded gun and point it at the victim were acts which were more than merely preparatory, even though there was more to do before the final act could be accomplished. Williams has argued that it is not 'an abuse of language to say that Kenneth Jones started his attempt as soon as he set out with his firearm, his disguise and his Spanish money, or even when he acquired his firearm and his disguise with the firm purpose of using it in the offence ...' (Williams, G, 'Wrong turnings in the law of attempt' [1991] Crim LR 417, p 419).

In the *AG's Reference (No 1 of 1992)* (1993), the Court of Appeal confirmed that a man could commit the *actus reus* of attempted rape even though he had not attempted to penetrate the victim's vagina, providing there was sufficient evidence available to show he had done acts which were more than merely preparatory to the completed offence. Lord Taylor CJ suggested that such evidence might be the woman's distress, the state of her clothing, the position in which she was seen, the man lowering his trousers and any interference with the woman's private parts.

The two common law tests referred to by the Lord Chief Justice *in AG's Reference (No 1 of 1992)* are the last act and the 'series of acts' tests. In the former, the defendant should have committed his intended last act before it could be said he was proximate (the former common law test) enough to the completed offence. The major authorities supporting this test were *Eagleton* (1855) and *DPP v Stonehouse* (1977) in which in the latter case Lord Diplock asked whether the accused had 'crossed the Rubicon and burnt his boat', that is, passed the point of no return. In the latter, the process of turning preparation into attempt involves the defendant in a series of acts, some of which are merely preparatory, others illustrating his clear desire to bring about the completed offence and would if not interrupted have resulted in the actual commission of the offence (see *Stephen's Digest of the Criminal Law*, 9th edn, 1950).

The practical difficulty with the wording of the statute is that whilst all actions apart from the last act are 'preparatory' the use of the word 'merely' suggests that a distinction should be drawn between those acts of preparation which indicate the accused has embarked upon the crime, and those that do not send out this signal.

The dilemma is where the distinction is to be drawn and as this is a matter for the jury there is always going to be some uncertainty. The judge, of course, still has to rule on whether there is sufficient evidence to go to the jury. In *Campbell* (1990), the Court of Appeal ruled that it was inevitable that matters had to be decided on a case by case basis. The defendant had been seen reconnoitring a post office and had in his possession an imitation gun, sunglasses and a threatening note. His appeal against conviction on a charge of attempted robbery was allowed. It was accepted that he might have still been of a mind to rob the post office, but many things remained to be done including the crucial incident of entering the premises at which the alleged robbery was to take place.

Griffin (1993) makes it clear that the judge must decide if there is sufficient evidence to put to the jury but that it is for the jury to conclude whether or not the defendant's act falls within the provisions of s 1(1) of the CAtA 1981. In this case, the accused was charged with attempting to take her children, who were in the care of the local authority, out of the jurisdiction. To this end, she bought single tickets to the Republic of Ireland for herself and the children and made preparations for travel. She then sought permission to withdraw them from school on the pretext that she was to take them to the dentist. When challenged by the head teacher, she left the school without the children and was subsequently arrested. She was convicted and appealed on the basis that there was insufficient evidence of something more than merely preparatory to the completed offence, which would have occurred once the children were actually out of the jurisdiction. The Court of Appeal thought that the judge had been correct in putting the matter before the jury. It was accepted that most of her actions amounted only to mere preparation but once she approached the head teacher with the request to remove the children from school then attempted abduction was underway. It is worth comparing these facts with those in *Campbell* (1991) where it was held that his actions did not in law constitute anything more than mere preparation, despite the fact that he was within a few feet of the post office which had been targeted for the 'crime'. It could hardly be said that the accused in Griffin came anywhere close to succeeding in her attempt to abduct the children and remove them from the jurisdiction.

The recent cases reflect an approach advocated by the Court of Appeal in *Gullefer*, a 1986 case reported in 1990. There the appellant had wagered £18 at a greyhound racing meeting and was facing the loss of his stake as the dogs rounded the final bend with his chosen greyhound nowhere in the running. He therefore jumped onto the track and waved his arms in an attempt to distract the dogs. If he had been successful in his endeavours, the race would have been declared void and his stake money returned to him. In the event he failed. He was charged with attempted theft. His appeal against conviction was allowed on the basis that his actions were merely preparatory to his attempt to steal. If the race had in fact been declared void, then that alone would not have indicated that theft was to be committed. Gullefer would still have had to go back to the bookmaker and then demand that his £18 be returned. Consider whether the acts of the defendant in *Rowley* (1991) were more than mere preparatory acts and thus whether he could be convicted of attempting to outrage public decency (see above, 5.5.2).

It might be worth considering whether some of the pre-1981 Act cases would still be decided in the same way under the legislation. For example, in *Robinson* (1915), a jeweller having insured his stock for £1,200 staged a burglary so that he might make a claim against the insurance company. He was convicted of attempting to obtain money by false pretences. His appeal against conviction was allowed on the basis that R's actions were only remotely connected with the commission of the full offence. Would the result be different today? By analogy with *Campbell* (1990) and *Gullefer* (1990), the answer would be no. The staging of the fake burglary would in all probability amount to an act of mere preparation. Robinson would need to acquire the appropriate forms, complete and forward them to the insurance company before it could be said that he was attempting to obtain property by deception. This view is also supported by the decision in *Geddes* (1996). The appellant was seen by a teacher in the boys' lavatory block of a school. He had no right to be there. He had with him a rucksack which contained a large kitchen knife, some lengths of rope and a roll of masking tape. He was charged with attempted false imprisonment. His appeal against conviction was allowed. The Court of Appeal acknowledged that the demarcation line between acts which were merely preparatory and those which might amount to an attempt was not always clear or easy to recognise. It is legitimate to pose the question 'has he actually tried to commit the offence?'. Conversely, if an accused had only 'got ready or put himself in a position or equipped himself to do so', then this would not satisfy the statutory test. In this case, the appellant had not had contact with any pupils nor communicated with nor confronted anyone and therefore had not gone beyond mere preparation. This decision and that in *Campbell* gives rise to feelings of unease. Does it now mean that the police cannot intervene in such circumstances until such time as the accused actually confronts or communicates with the intended victim? In cases of armed robbery or abduction, any potential intervention must wait until there is an increased chance that the intended victim will be injured. It may be said that other offences could be used rather than attempt for example the offence of going equipped at s 25 of the TA 1968 but here the police would need to know that the perpetrators were armed. The report indicates that the court in *Geddes* was 'filled with the greatest unease' and yet nevertheless felt bound to reach the decision it did. These are decisions which are difficult to explain to the general public particularly when viewed in light of the tragedies involving firearms resulting in death and injury to members of the public which have occurred in the UK and elsewhere in the last decade. Also bear in mind that the s 25 offence will apply only where the accused was going equipped to carry out burglary, theft or to cheat.

5.11 *Mens rea*

There is only one state of mind acknowledged in the definition of the crime and that is intention. The accused must act with the 'intent to commit an offence'. This is one area where the pre-existing common law has seemingly influenced the post-1981 Act case law. In *Mohan* (1975), the Court of Appeal had concluded that attempt was a crime of specific intent and had defined that to mean a:

... decision by the accused to bring about, so far as it lay within his power, the commission of the offence which it was alleged that he had attempted to commit, no matter whether the accused desired that consequence of his act or not.

There does appear to be a contradiction in that it is difficult to imagine someone doing everything in his power to bring about a consequence and yet not desiring that consequence. In *Pearman* (below), it was said that the court was trying to:

... deal with a case where the accused has, as a primary purpose, some other object, for example, a man who plants a bomb in an aeroplane, which he knows is going to take off, it being his primary intention that he should claim the insurance on the aeroplane when the freight goes down into the sea. The jury would not be put off from saying that he intended to murder the crew simply by saying that he did not want or desire to kill the crew, but that was something that he inevitably intended to do ...

A reckless state of mind will not suffice, nor will evidence which will establish that the accused knew or foresaw that the consequences of the act will 'be likely' to lead to the commission of the completed offence.

In the first post-Act case to consider the issue, the Court of Appeal could find 'no reason' why *Mohan* should not be binding. Therefore, a direction by the trial judge in *Pearman* (1984) to the effect that foresight of the probable consequences should be equated with intention was deemed to amount to a misdirection and the conviction for attempting to cause grievous bodily harm with intent was quashed.

It is incumbent upon those analysing this area of the law to be aware that whatever the mens rea for the completed offence only intention will suffice for a charge of attempt, as evidenced in *O'Toole* (1987), where reference in the indictment to recklessness on a charge of attempted criminal damage meant that the conviction had to be quashed. The accused must be doing everything in his power to bring about the completed offence and this is inconsistent with the concept of recklessness.

A relatively recent case raised the interesting point of how relevant, if at all, the *Moloney/Hancock/Nedrick* line of cases is with respect to the definition of intent. In *Walker and Hayles* (1990), the appellants had attacked the victim, saying they would kill him, and then threw him over the balcony of a third floor flat. He survived his ordeal. They were charged with attempted murder. Their appeals were based on the use, by the trial judge, of the concept of a high degree of probability in directing the jury on the issue of intent, that is, in throwing someone from a third floor balcony is death highly probable? The appeals were dismissed because the judge had at an early stage in his direction told the jury that they must be sure that the accused were 'trying to kill' and this was synonymous with 'purpose'. The problem with a charge of attempted murder as distinct from murder is that a person could intend serious injury to be occasioned by his action but not intend death. On a murder charge, the intent to cause serious injury would be enough to convict if death occurred, but not for an attempt where according to *Mohan* one must be doing everything in one's power to bring about the consequence. The court in *Walker and Hayles* confirms that a 'simple direction' indicating that the defendant must be trying to achieve death (the consequence) will almost always suffice. But what of the case where the jury believes the accused intended to cause serious harm but not to occasion death, but that death was a 'highly probable' consequence of the action deliberately performed by the accused? *Walker and Hayles* suggests that providing the jury are convinced that death was a 'virtually certain' consequence of the deliberate activity then it may convict of attempted murder, based upon the guidance given in *Nedrick*. The Court of Appeal preferred the use of 'virtual certainty' to 'high degree of probability' (see above, 3.3.2, for a full analysis of oblique intention).

The difficulties discussed in *Walker and Hayles* surfaced again in *Fallon* (1994). The defendant was charged with attempting to murder a police officer. The trial judge had directed the jury on the meaning of intent and at one stage had invited the jury to consider whether, if the officer had died, 'would his death as a matter of virtual certainty have been a natural consequence of the act ...?' There can be no doubt that his direction was influenced by the decision in *Moloney* (1985). The Court of Appeal substituted a conviction on the alternative count of causing grievous bodily harm with intent and went on to observe that:

> ... the case was yet another example of the confusion that may be sown in the minds of a jury by unnecessary and elaborate analysis of the meaning of intent and by the failure to follow guidance given in *Hancock and Shankland* (1986).

The preceding discussion has considered the mental element in respect of the consequence. The definitions of some crimes, of course, make reference to circumstances as well as consequences. If such a crime figures in an attempt charge, for example, rape, where reference needs to be made to the issue of consent, will it be a requirement of such a charge that intent is required for both consequences and circumstance? Thus, on a charge of attempted rape, is it necessary to prove both an intent to have unlawful sexual intercourse and an intent that the woman should not consent? The substantive offence demands either intent or recklessness in respect of the circumstance of consent. The issue was addressed in *Khan* (1990), where the Court of Appeal concluded that it was enough if D intended to have intercourse and was reckless as to whether the woman was consenting. As Russell LJ put it:

> ... the intent of the defendant is precisely the same in rape and in attempted rape and the *mens rea* is identical, namely an intention to have intercourse plus knowledge or recklessness as to the woman's absence of consent. No question of attempting to achieve a reckless state of mind arises; the attempt relates to the physical activity; the mental state of the defendant is the same. A man does not recklessly have sexual intercourse, nor does he recklessly attempt it.

> Recklessness in rape and attempted rape arises not in relation to the physical act of the accused but only in his state of mind when engaged in the activity of having or attempting to have sexual intercourse.

This view differs from that expressed by the Law Commission in its report on *Attempt and Impossibility in Relation to Attempt, Conspiracy and Incitement* (Law Com 102, 1980), which was in favour of requiring intent towards both consequences and circumstances. However, the 1989 proposed draft Criminal Code (cl 49(2)) is in accord with the view expressed in *Khan*, so providing that, if recklessness as to circumstances is an essential element of the substantive offence, then it will suffice for the attempt to commit that offence.

The approach adopted in *Khan* was applied in *AG's Reference (No 3 of 1992)* (1994). The charge was one of attempted aggravated arson contrary to s 1(2) of the Criminal Damage Act (CDA) 1971. In the early hours of the morning, the appellants threw a petrol bomb from their vehicle in the direction of another car containing four people. There were two others standing on the pavement chatting to the occupants of the car. The bomb missed and smashed against a nearby wall. The respondents were arrested and inside their car was found a milk crate containing a number of petrol bombs.

Section 1(2) of the CDA 1971 requires either intent or recklessness in respect of whether life will be endangered as a result of the damage to property. The defendants were acquitted on the direction of the judge. She ruled there was no evidence to show that the defendants intended by the destruction of the car to endanger the lives of the occupants or the bystanders. Furthermore, acknowledging that intention towards damaging or destroying the property was a requirement for an attempt, she concluded that it was impossible to intend to be reckless as to whether the life of another would be endangered.

The Attorney General referred the matter to the Court of Appeal under s 36 of the CJA 1972. The court held that it was sufficient for the Crown to establish a specific intent to cause damage and that the defendant acted recklessly in respect of the threat to life. The court accepted that the mental state of a defendant in such circumstances 'contained everything which was required to render him guilty of the full offence'. There clearly was an intent to cause damage to property, that is, the car, and presumably, at least 'Caldwell style' recklessness towards endangering life (see above, 3.4) The court noted:

> ... that at one time it was proposed that intention should be required as to all the elements for an offence, thus making it impossible to secure a conviction for attempt in circumstances such as the present. However, this proposal has not prevailed and has been overtaken by *R v Khan*, and the formulation of the Draft Code which does not incorporate the proposal.

There are two major issues to consider as a result of this case. The first is that of recklessness. The draft code would have the foresight of the accused in respect of the likelihood of endangering life assessed on a 'subjective' basis and not by reference to *Caldwell*. This decision means that a defendant must intend to damage or destroy property, that is, must realise the consequence of his action is virtually certain to result, yet at the same time need give no thought to the aggravated element of the offence, providing ordinary people in his situation would be inclined to do so. This would seem to be extremely favourable to the prosecution. Secondly, it is argued by Smith ([1994] Crim LR 350) that, in respect of offences that do not require *mens rea* in respect of all elements of the *actus reus*, strict liability will be introduced into the law of attempts. If correct, this is a significant step, particularly as the offence is regarded as one of specific intent. Taking as his example the facts of *Prince* (1875), Smith invites us to consider the case of a 25 year old man who is intent upon having sexual intercourse with a girl who is in fact 15, but whom he reasonably believes to be 16. D attempts sexual intercourse but fails. He is charged with attempting to have intercourse with a girl under 16 contrary to s 6 of the SOA 1956. No *mens rea* needs to be proved in respect of the completed offence other than the intent to have intercourse which clearly he has. The girl is under 16. The man being over 24 has no defence based upon a reasonable belief that she is 16 or over. The conclusion is that strict liability is brought into the law on attempt. No intent needs to be established in respect of a circumstance, that is, her age.

There is, of course, no reason why the law should not follow this path but such a development should not result from one reference to the Court of Appeal, particularly, as Professor Smith says, 'one suspects that the issue was not fully appreciated or debated on the reference'.

5.12 Impossibility

The common law on impossibility as it applied to attempted crimes was thoroughly and controversially reviewed in *Haughton v Smith* (1973). A brief look at this case should prove helpful in understanding the problems created by the decision of the House of Lords in *Anderton v Ryan* (1985). In *Haughton v Smith,* the House of Lords concluded that where the substantive offence could not be achieved either because it was factually or legally impossible then no charge of attempt would lie. An example of factual impossibility is where the object of the crime is absent even though the accused believes otherwise, as in the case of someone seeking to steal a valuable ring from a locked drawer, when in fact the drawer is empty. An example of the latter is to be found in the facts of the actual case where Smith thought he was handling stolen goods which in fact did not possess that quality, having been returned to lawful custody prior to Smith receiving them (see s 24(3) of the TA 1968).

However, a person could be guilty of an attempt where the failure was occasioned by inadequacy as to the means employed to commit the substantive offence. One might be correct in assuming that it is possible to break into the Bank of England using a hairpin, although in practice one would believe it to be 'impossible'. If our locksmith was found with his hairpin inserted into the lock on the main door of the bank, one could quite logically conclude that he was attempting to steal, however remote in reality his chances might in fact be.

The decision was subject to intense debate and Parliament purported to change the effect of *Haughton v Smith* in s 1(2) and (3) of the CAtA 1981 which reads:

(2) A person may be guilty of attempting to commit an offence to which this section applies even though the facts are such that the commission of the offence is impossible.

(3) In any case where:

(a) apart from this sub-section a person's intention would not be regarded as having amounted to an intent to commit an offence; but

(b) if the facts of the case had been as he believed them to be, his intention would be so regarded,

then, for the purposes of sub-s (1) above, he shall be regarded as having had an intent to commit that offence.

Section 1(2) seeks to ensure that liability will result even though the existence of certain facts makes it impossible to bring about the intended consequence. Section 1(3) which is strictly not needed as the state of the law is a 'fact' just as much as a non-existent ring is a 'fact', deals with legal impossibility and demands that attention is focused upon the accused's state of mind. Did Roger Smith intend to handle stolen goods? The answer to which is quite clearly yes. He believed them to be stolen and acted accordingly.

What appears to be a reasonably clear piece of drafting was called into question in *Anderton v Ryan* (1985) when the defendant's conviction for attempting to handle stolen goods was quashed on the basis that she had carried out an 'objectively innocent' act when purchasing a video recorder. She believed it to be stolen, and in all probability it was stolen, but the prosecution could not prove it. The decision would obviously be regarded as correct if *Haughton v Smith* still represented the law, as a case of legal impossibility, but s 1(2) and (3) had, according to the majority, not affected legal impossibility situations. You are advised to read the minority speech of Lord Edmund Davies which is an accurate appraisal of what Parliament actually intended to achieve. The law on this topic is now to be found in the decision of the House of Lords in *Shivpuri* (1986), which overruled *Anderton v Ryan* and Lord Bridge's speech, in particular, is worth reading if only for its humility. Lord Bridge 'confessed' to reaching the wrong conclusion in *Anderton*, that it could not in any way be distinguished from the *Shivpuri* case and felt there was no other option available except to overrule the decision. 'If a serious error embodied in a decision of this House has distorted the law, the sooner it is corrected the better.'

Shivpuri had been caught in possession of a substance which he believed to be a prohibited drug. In fact the powder was snuff and it is not unlawful to possess or deal in the substance. He intended to deal in heroin or cannabis. His actions were on the face of it morally reprehensible and his conviction for attempting to be knowingly concerned in dealing with and harbouring a prohibited drug was upheld. He clearly had the requisite intent to satisfy s 1 of the CAtA 1981 and the *actus reus* was complete with regard to the intended offence.

The provisions of the CJA 1993 (discussed above) in respect of jurisdictional issues affecting the law of conspiracy apply equally to the law of attempt, that is, attempting to commit a Group A offence. A person can be guilty of an attempt to commit a Group A offence irrespective of whether the attempt was made in England and Wales or it had an effect in England and Wales (see s 3(3)).

The Law Commission in its draft Criminal Code proposed no change in respect of the law relating to impossibility other than to bring the law on incitement into line with that relating to attempt and conspiracy. Clause 50 treats the three preliminary offences together. Therefore, a person would be guilty of incitement, attempt or conspiracy although the commission of the completed offence is impossible: '... if it would be possible in the circumstances which he believes or hopes exist or will exist at the relevant time.'

PRELIMINARY OR INCHOATE OFFENCES

This chapter has discussed the inchoate or preliminary offences of incitement, conspiracy and attempt. These offences give recognition to the fact that society seeks to discourage its members from contemplating as well as participating in criminal activity. Incitement unlike the other two crimes remains a common law offence and aims to deter those who seek to persuade or encourage others to commit crimes. The usual way to commit such an offence will be to make a direct approach, although as we have seen it is possible to influence a number of people, for example, by advertising in a newspaper inviting readers to commit a crime, for example, to murder the Prime Minister.

Incitement

Incitement may be either express or implied as seen in the *Invicta Plastics* (1976) case. A further important point is that the offence is only established once it has come to the other party's notice although the law does recognise an offence of attempting to incite when the communication fails. *Whitehouse* (1977) decides that, if the act to be done by the person incited would not amount to a crime, then there is no liability for incitement. The *mens rea* for the offence is intention that the offence incited be committed.

Care should be taken to remember that in 'impossibility' situations the common law still governs incitement, even though the CAtA 1981 has put the law onto a statutory basis in respect of conspiracy and attempt.

Conspiracy

Conspiracy is largely a statutory offence under s 1 of the CLwA 1977 but elements still remain part of the common law. Conspiracy to corrupt public morals and public decency and to defraud have not been incorporated into the statutory framework. The *actus reus* of conspiracy is proof of an agreement between two or more persons to commit an offence. So agreement is at the heart of the offence whether it be statutory or common law conspiracy. There are various limitations imposed by law as to who may be parties to a conspiracy. For example, a person is not guilty of conspiracy if the only other party is his spouse or is a person under the age of criminal responsibility. Nor can one conspire with the intended victim of the conspiracy. The strength of evidence against those accused of conspiracy may result in only one of a number of people charged being found guilty. Reference to the judgment of the Lord Chief Justice in *Longman and Cribben* (1980) is important. Close analysis of s 1 of the CLwA 1977 is crucial in respect of statutory conspiracy the important elements being:

- agreement;

- course of conduct;

- in accordance with their intentions;

- will necessarily amount to or involve the commission of an offence.

It is worth recalling that a conditional intention is sufficient *mens rea* for conspiracy.

Common law conspiracy requires a study of two discrete areas of law. Important cases involving conspiracy to corrupt public morals are *Shaw* (1962) and *Knuller* (1972), the latter recognising that there is a substantive offence at common law of outraging public decency. Conspiracy to defraud has attracted considerable judicial attention over the years as well as review by the Law Commission in 1994. The major rule appears to be that statutory conspiracy should be charged where the object of the conspiracy would amount to a substantive offence, for example, theft. Conspiracy to defraud will be available where the object of the agreement involves fraud, dishonesty or deceit but does not amount to a substantive offence. Good examples are *Scott* (1975) and *Cooke* (1986). *The mens rea* for the offence is proof of an intention to defraud and evidence of dishonesty. Dishonesty is to be assessed using the *Ghosh* (1982) test.

If parties conspire to commit the impossible, then the outcome will be different depending on whether statutory or common law conspiracy is charged. In the former case, s 5 of the CAtA 1981 will apply but in the latter the common law as laid down in *Haughton v Smith* (1973) and *DPP v Nock* (1978) will apply.

There are jurisdictional issues which need to be assessed and attention should be paid to the provisions of the CJA 1993, the Criminal Justice (Terrorism and Conspiracy) Act 1998 as well as the important cases of *Doot* (1973), *Sansom* (1991) and *Liangsiriprasert* (1990).

Attempts

The law on attempt is to be found in s 1 of the CAtA 1981. The *actus reus* requires proof that the accused did an act which is more than merely preparatory to the completed offence. This is not easy to establish as numerous cases have illustrated, for example, *Gullefer* (1990), *Griffin* (1993) and *Campbell* (1990). There is no absolute test to determine when mere preparation becomes preparation. The *mens rea* required is an intention to commit the offence. The pre-Act law has influenced the post-Act case law and reference should be made to *Mohan* (1975) and *Pearman* (1984). Also influencing this area of the law have been the decisions in *Hancock and Shankland* (1985), *Moloney* (1985) and *Nedrick* (1986) and has led to calls for the meaning of the word intention to be put onto a statutory basis. Intent is the only state of mind needed to establish an attempt;

the mens rea for the full offence being irrelevant. Thus, for attempted murder only an intent to kill will suffice while for murder an intent to cause grievous bodily harm is enough to establish the *mens rea*. Note, however, the decision in *Khan* (1990) to the effect that recklessness to a circumstance may be sufficient providing there is intent towards the consequence. So, on a charge of attempted rape, an intent to have intercourse being reckless as to whether the woman is consenting is enough to ensure a conviction. Impossibility in attempt is covered by the statutory provisions and not the common law.

CHAPTER 6

HOMICIDE

This chapter focuses upon the major crimes of murder and manslaughter which are analysed together with the statutory 'special' defences of provocation and diminished responsibility recognised under the Homicide Act 1957. Reference will also be made to offences in which death is the major feature but which are not classified, for particular reasons, as either murder or manslaughter, as in the case of child destruction contrary to s 1 of the Infant Life Preservation Act 1929 or infanticide under s 1 of the Infanticide Act 1938. Attention is also drawn to the significant House of Lords' decision in *AG's Reference (No 3 of 1994)* (1997) which established the principle that manslaughter but not murder can be committed if a child *in utero* is injured and dies as a result of an attack on the mother providing:

- the child has been born and enjoyed an existence separate from its mother;

- the injuries caused or contributed substantially to the death;

- the requisite *mens rea* against the mother is established.

A number of high profile transport disasters over recent years, such as the sinking of the Zeebrugge ferry and the Paddington, Southall and Clapham rail crashes, have fuelled a public debate concerning the criminal liability of corporations for manslaughter. Proposals to reform the law relating to both corporate and individual manslaughter, first put forward by the Law Commission in 1996 (*Legislating the Criminal Code: Involuntary Manslaughter,* Law Com 237, 1996), have been largely adopted by the Government in a Consultation Paper published in May 2000.

6.1   Murder

> Murder is when a man of sound memory, and the age of discretion, unlawfully killeth within any county of the realm any reasonable creature in *rerum natura* under the King's peace, with malice aforethought, either expressed by the party, or implied by law, so that the party wounded, or hurt, and die of the wound, or hurt, and within a year and a day after the same [Coke, 3 Co Inst 47].

This classic definition of murder has been modified by statute and there is no longer a requirement that death should occur within a year and a day of the occurrence which in law is deemed to have caused death. The rule can be traced back to the 13th century and, as the Law Commission stated in its Consultation Paper, *The Year and a Day Rule in Homicide* (Law Com 136, 1994):

> The rule is a legacy of a time when medical science was so rudimentary that if there was a substantial lapse of time between injury and death, it was unsafe to pronounce on the question whether the defendant's conduct or some other event caused death.

Cases were few and far between and the most usually cited example was *Dyson* (1908). This was a manslaughter case where the defendant had inflicted injuries upon his child in November 1906 and again in December 1907. The child died on 5 March 1908. The judge had left it to the jury to convict if they believed that death could have been caused by the injuries inflicted in 1906. The Court of Appeal accepted that this amounted to a misdirection and quashed the conviction.

The Law Commission favoured abolition and was clearly influenced by the fact that the rule did not command support in other jurisdictions. It was not part of the law in Scotland or South Africa, had been abolished in all Australian States except Queensland and law reform bodies in Canada and New Zealand had recommended abolition. The Model Penal Code in the US did not contain the rule. The reasons for advocating abolition are given in the Consultation Paper on *The Year and a Day Rule in Homicide* (Law Com 136, 1994, para 6.19). With advances in medical science, it is now much easier to ascertain the cause of death and the rule had prevented prosecutions where it was incontrovertible that the initial incident caused death albeit more than a year and a day after the incident. It is also clear that the rule led to convictions for lesser crimes than were appropriate in the circumstances merely because the victim lived for more than a year and a day.

Parliament has now accepted the Commission's favoured option and the rule has been abolished as a result of the Law Reform (Year and a Day) Act 1996 which came into force in August 1996. This measure, a Private Members' Bill, passed through the Commons without opposition and brought to an end a rule which was traceable to the Statute of Gloucester in 1278. If it is alleged that the cause of death occurred more than three years before the victim died, then the consent of the Attorney General is required before a prosecution can be brought. Otherwise, the normal rules of causation will apply. However, if the person who it is intended should be prosecuted has been convicted of another offence referable to the death, then the Attorney General's consent will also be required.

6.1.1   Who may be killed?

Coke's definition requires a human being ('reasonable creature') as the victim of the crime of murder. It follows that a foetus cannot be the victim of a homicide but this point requires some elucidation. It is still correct in circumstances where the foetus dies whilst still in the womb. If there is evidence, however, which proves that after the birth the child enjoyed an existence independent of the mother then he or she may be a manslaughter victim subject to the rules on causation and *mens rea*. The House of Lords so confirmed in the case of *AG's Reference (No 3 of 1994)* (1997) (see, also, Chapter 3). The Attorney General, acting under powers conferred by s 36(1) of the Criminal Justice Act 1972, referred the following questions to the Court of Appeal and subsequently to the House of Lords:

- whether, subject to proof of requisite intent, the crimes of murder or manslaughter could be committed where unlawful injury was deliberately inflicted to a child *in utero* or to a mother carrying a child *in utero* where the child was subsequently born alive, existed independently of the mother and then died, the injuries *in utero* either having caused or made a substantial contribution to the death; and

- whether the fact that the child's death was caused solely as a consequence of injury to the mother rather than as a consequence of direct injury to the foetus could remove any liability for murder or manslaughter in those circumstances.

The respondent had stabbed his girlfriend who, to his knowledge, was pregnant. As a direct consequence of the attack, the woman's uterus was penetrated as was the abdomen of the foetus. The gestation period was estimated to be approximately 22–26 weeks. An operation was performed but the surgeon was of the opinion that the foetus had not sustained any injury and the pregnancy proceeded for some three weeks before the woman went into labour. The child was grossly premature and survived only four months. The defendant was charged with murder of the child. At his trial, the judge ruled there was sufficient evidence upon which the jury could conclude that the causal connection between the stabbing and death was established. However, as a matter of law, he ruled that there could in the circumstances be no conviction for either murder or manslaughter. In reaching its conclusion, the House of Lords stressed the importance to the prosecution of establishing that the child had an 'existence independent of its mother'. This suggests that the child must have taken a breath and have an independent circulation. However, in *Brain* (1834), Park J thought that it was not essential that the child should have taken its first breath prior to the act which caused its demise, reasoning that many children are born alive, 'yet do not breathe for some time after their birth'.

Senior (1832) would suggest that an attack on a child in the process of being born even before it has breathed will 'if the child is afterwards born alive, and dies thereof, and there is malice, be murder'.

The law prior to the HA 1957 was based upon the felony/murder rule which meant that an act carried out in the process of committing a felony could lead to a murder conviction if death were to be caused as a result of the act. Therefore, the statement in *West* (1848) to the effect that:

If a person, intending to procure abortion, does an act which causes a child to be born so much earlier than the natural time, that it is born in a state much less capable of living, and afterwards dies, in consequence of its exposure to the external world, the person who, by this misconduct, so brings the child into the world, and puts it thereby in a situation in which it cannot live, is guilty of murder,

must be considered in the context of this rule. Therefore, proof of an intent to commit a felony sufficed to establish the *mens rea* for murder.

A killing must be unlawful if a conviction for homicide is to result. Lord Hope in the House of Lords accepted that the fact that a child is not yet born did not prevent the requirements for the *actus reus* from being satisfied for both murder and manslaughter. This was because 'for the foetus life lay in the future. It could carry with it the effects of things done to it before birth which, after birth, might prove to be harmful'. From this it follows that it is necessary only for the child to be 'in being, at the time of death' (*Senior*).

It must be remembered that the conclusion that manslaughter and not murder is committed in these circumstances relates only to the situation where the attack is carried out against the mother, death being an indirect outcome of the act. In cases of unlawful act manslaughter (see below, 6.8.1), the requirements are:

• an unlawful and dangerous act;

• the unlawful and dangerous act had been done intentionally;

• all sober and reasonable people would have recognised the risk that some harm would result.

It is unnecessary to prove that the assailant had known that his act was likely to injure the person who had died as a result of the attack.

The unlawful and dangerous act had been the stabbing of the mother. The assailant had intended to attack the mother. The foetus/child came within the 'scope of the *mens rea* which the assailant had when he stabbed the mother' (*per* Lord Hope). All the necessary ingredients of the offence of manslaughter were present and providing the assailant's conduct satisfied the principles of causation then the crime was complete.

This welcome clarification of the law in respect of an attack on the mother ultimately resulting in death to her new born child does not provide answers to other questions. It says nothing about the legal position of the neglectful mother. Let us assume that her foetus is born alive but dies a short time later as a direct result of the impact of the mother's behaviour over the period of her pregnancy. In our example, the mother may be a drug addict and in addition have a severe alcohol problem. Despite advice to the contrary, she persists in consuming large quantities of drink and drugs. The combination does irreparable damage to the internal organs of the foetus and the child succumbs to its injuries within minutes of its birth. If the mother has deliberately embarked upon this course of conduct intending that the foetus suffer serious injury then there would appear to be a strong case against her for the murder of her child. What, however, if as a result of her addiction she fails to take reasonable care of herself with similar consequences ensuing? She may in her more lucid moments be aware of the likely consequences of her behaviour yet nevertheless fail to take remedial action. It follows from the *Reference* that a manslaughter verdict ought to be possible based upon her grossly negligent behaviour but that was not confirmed (or even addressed) by the Court of Appeal or House of Lords. It is well-established in civil law that there may be liability for post-natal damage caused by pre-natal acts. This proposition is not simply dependant upon the Congenital Disabilities (Civil Liability) Act 1976 for its authority but draws support from the Court of Appeal's decision in *Burton v Islington Health Authority* (1992). In that case, it was held that the health authority owed a duty of care to an unborn child and could be sued for medical negligence once the child had been born. There would appear to be little need to rely on the doctrine of transferred malice to establish liability in this type of case which appears to fall neatly into the ambit of the current law on gross negligence manslaughter. So the current decision is limited to those cases where there is an attack, an act, against the mother and says nothing about omissions which may result in death. This may be eventually resolved when the Law Commission fulfils its stated intention to review the law on omissions.

Over the last decade, much has been written about various religious sects or cults whose beliefs often lead members to consider taking their own lives. Suppose that a pregnant member of such an organisation decided to take her own life by inflicting a serious stab wound to herself. This she does by plunging the knife into her lower abdomen causing serious injury to her child as well as herself. Luckily she is able to receive immediate and sophisticated medical treatment. She survives and her baby is delivered by caesarean section. Sadly the child survives for only 15 minutes, death being attributed to the wounds perpetrated by the mother on herself. Section 1 of the Suicide Act 1961 abrogated the rule that it was a crime for a person to commit suicide. Does this mean that the mother's attack upon herself is not unlawful? If so then she could not be convicted of homicide in respect of her child. It will be said that in such circumstances a compassionate rather than a legalistic approach ought to be adopted and perhaps rightly so, but it nevertheless remains uncertain whether or not there is sufficient *mens rea* to support a prosecution for causing death to the child. It could be argued that as the mother has failed to take her own life then an attempted murder charge would be possible and thus provide the prosecution with the appropriate *mens rea* in respect of the child.

Nor does the case decide whether *murder* is committed if there is a direct attack on the foetus intending to kill or cause it grievous bodily harm. Lord Hope's acknowledgment that an attack on the mother can satisfy the *actus reus* of both murder and manslaughter would seem to present no problems in that respect. But what of the *mens rea*? Is there an intent to kill or cause grievous bodily harm to a 'reasonable creature'? There would appear no reason in principle why the assailant should not face a murder charge if the child is born alive and then dies as a result of the attack. The defendant intended to kill the human being who has just passed away as a direct consequence of the attack incurred whilst in the womb. Unfortunately, the House of Lords declined to deal with this question on the basis that the issue did not arise from the facts before the court.

6.1.2   When does death occur?

The guidelines laid down by the Royal Medical Colleges emphasise brain death as the major criterion for establishing death and although the Court of Appeal in *Malcherek and Steel* (1981) drew back from endorsing them as the legal test for death, it was plainly impressed with the approach. Lord Lane CJ put it this way:

> There is, it seems, a body of opinion in the medical profession that there is only one true test of death and that is irreversible death of the brain stem, which controls the basic functions of the body such as breathing.

Thus, if this test represents the law, someone who is on a ventilator or a life support machine, being brain dead, cannot be a murder victim, although a charge of attempt may lie providing the necessary intent can be proved. In *Airedale NHS Trust v Bland* (1993), a young man had been crushed at the Hillsborough football ground tragedy in 1989. He was in a 'persistent vegetative state' for some three and a half years due to 'catastrophic and irreversible damage to the higher functions of the brain'. It was accepted in law that he was still alive. Lord Goff said:

> It is true that his condition is such that it can be described as a living death; but he is nevertheless still alive. This is because, as a result of developments in modern medical technology, doctors no longer associate death exclusively with breathing and heart beat, and it has come to be accepted that death occurs when the brain, and in particular the brain stem, has been destroyed ... the evidence is that Anthony's brain stem is still alive and functioning and it follows that, in the present state of medical science, he is still alive and should be so regarded as a matter of law [p 865(g)].

6.2   Causation

It will be recalled that most of the major authorities which focus on the issue of causation relate to the offence of murder or manslaughter. Difficult ethical problems may arise as well as complex legal questions over the apparently simple question of who has caused the victim's death. It will be recalled that Nicola Padfield, in her article 'Clean water and muddy causation' ([1995] Crim LR 683), suggested that there three elements which were vital when considering causation in homicide cases. The first is to establish that death would not have resulted 'but for' the accused's conduct. Secondly, the defendant's act must be more than a minimal cause of death and finally, there must be no *novus actus interveniens* which breaks the chain of causation. The terminally ill patient constantly in pain who begs a merciful and quick release from suffering will not absolve the doctor from legal responsibility for that death if the final injection is administered with the specific aim of bringing about the patient's demise. The doctor has accelerated death possibly by only a few hours or even minutes but it is clear in law who has caused the death. The potential ramifications for the medical practitioner who adopts this course of conduct, having taken the view that it is not only in the patient's best interests but also in accordance with the patient's (and possibly immediate family's) wishes, are enormous. In *Cox* (1992), the doctor injected his patient with potassium chloride death resulting very shortly afterwards. He had done so in accordance with the patient's wishes and with the full knowledge and concurrence of her immediate family. She was terminally ill and in great pain. He was convicted of attempted murder on the basis that his act was intended to bring about her death. The attempted killing was therefore unlawful. The impact on Dr Cox is powerfully spelt out by Hazel Biggs in her article, entitled 'Euthanasia and death with dignity' ([1996] Crim LR 878):

> Here the doctor exercised absolute respect for his patient's autonomy by responding to her appeals that he curtail her suffering by killing her. He was then subjected to the indignity of a criminal trial, where he was convicted of attempted murder, and a professional disciplinary hearing which questioned his professional and moral integrity. Cox received a suspended jail sentence and may now practise medicine only under the close supervision of other physicians. His dignity was jeopardised because he acceded to his patient's request for a dignified death [p 885].

The issue of causation was discussed in some detail in Chapter 2 (see above, 2.4) and readers are urged to revisit that discussion prior to proceeding with the rest of this chapter.

6.3   *Actus reus* of murder

The *actus reus* of murder may be broken down into the following components:

- the defendant did the act (or omitted to comply with a legally recognised duty);
- the act was deliberate;
- the act was unlawful as distinct from a lawful homicide for example, killing in self-defence;
- the act (or omission) was a significant cause of death;
- the death was of a person 'in being'.

6.4   *Mens rea* of murder

Lord Browne-Wilkinson in *Airedale NHS Trust v Bland* (1993) describes the *mens rea* for murder in one, apparently straightforward, sentence: 'Murder consists of causing the death of another with intent to do so.'

It is now well established that either an intention to kill or an intention to cause grievous bodily harm will satisfy the 'intent' requirement. It is this 'intent' which differentiates murder from manslaughter. Practitioners will often refer to the *mens rea* for murder by resorting to the term malice aforethought. Lord Goddard CJ in *Vickers* (1957) described the term 'malice aforethought' as a term of art. This is perhaps an overstatement in that in practice it is simply taken to mean the *mens rea* required by law. It does not imply that the action must be premeditated, desired or that any sort of ill will must be borne by the defendant towards the victim.

Attention ought to be paid in the first instance to Chapter 3 and the discussion of the meaning of intention in criminal law and its application via cases such as *Moloney, Hancock and Shankland, Nedrick and Woollin*. It will be recalled that these cases represent the culmination of the protracted debate on whether or not an acceptable definition of the word intention could be formulated for trial judges to put to juries. The debacle of *Hyam v DPP* (1975) proved, if proof be needed, that a consensus was almost impossible to achieve and this obviously influenced the approach approved by Lord Bridge in *Moloney* (1985). Judges should refrain from helping juries other than to say that intention is a simple English word, invite juries to assess the evidence and then reach a conclusion. However, as Professor Smith points out in his commentary to the case of *Scalley* (1995), 'intention is an ordinary word of the English language [and] as an ordinary word, it usually implies that the result is an aim or objective, a desired result, which is narrower than the legal meaning' (p 506). In the light of the House of Lords decision in *Woollin* (1998), therefore, the model direction to the jury in a murder case (where some direction on the meaning of intent was required) would be to the effect that they are not entitled to find the necessary intention unless they feel sure that death or serious bodily harm was a virtual certainty (barring some unforeseen intervention) as a result of the defendant's actions and that the defendant appreciated that such was the case. The jury would also have to be reminded that the decision is one for them to reach on a consideration of all the evidence.

6.4.1   Intention to cause grievous bodily harm

Grievous bodily harm must be taken to mean really serious harm. So decreed the House of Lords in *DPP v Smith* (1961). Lord Hailsham in *Cunningham* (1981) was adamant that: 'The definition of grievous bodily harm means "really serious bodily harm" in current English usage ...' The Court of Appeal in

Saunders (1985) concluded that a broken nose was, on any view, serious bodily injury. It confirmed that a trial judge would not be misdirecting a jury if the word 'really' were to be omitted from the summing up. The *Compact Oxford English Dictionary* states that the word is 'commonly placed immediately in front of the word or phrase on which emphasis is laid' and as such is used to 'emphasise the truth or correctness of an epithet or statement ...'. The Law Commission in its report, *Offences Against the Person and General Principles* (Law Com 218, 1993), refers to the 'outdated language of "grievous bodily harm"'. However, despite the criticisms these words still form part of the *mens rea* of murder.

Intention to cause grievous bodily harm was confirmed as part of the common law in *Cunningham* (1981). The appellant had attacked the deceased in a public house and hit him repeatedly with a chair. It was claimed that the appellant had not intended to kill the victim but there was no doubt that his actions had resulted in the victim receiving serious injuries from which he died. The trial judge told the jury that if they found that Cunningham intended to cause really serious injury then he would be guilty of murder. He was convicted and appealed on the basis that the jury ought to have been directed to consider whether or not he intended to endanger life and it did not follow that to cause serious injury meant that death was the inevitable result. His appeal was dismissed by the House of Lords and Lord Hailsham cited with approval the statement of Lord Goddard CJ in *Vickers* (1957):

> Murder ... has always been defined in English law as either an express intention to kill such as could be inferred when a person, having uttered threats against another, produced a lethal weapon and used it on him, or an implied intention to kill, as where the prisoner inflicted grievous bodily harm, that is to say, harmed the victim by a voluntary act intended to harm him and the victim died as the result of that grievous bodily harm. If a person does an act on another which amounts to the infliction of grievous bodily harm he cannot say that he did not intend to go so far ... he must take the consequences. If he intends to inflict grievous bodily harm and that person dies, that has always been held in English law, and was at the time when the Act of 1957 was passed, sufficient to imply the malice aforethought which is a necessary constituent of murder [p 868h].

Lord Edmund Davies in *Cunningham*, whilst favouring the view that the *mens rea* of murder should be limited to an intention to kill, believed that any change to the law as expressed in *Vickers* must result from parliamentary, not judicial, intervention:

> It is a task for none other than Parliament, as the constitutional organ best fitted to weigh the relevant and opposing factors. Its solution has already been attempted extra judicially on many occasions, but with no real success ...

The HA of 1957 retained the concepts of express and implied malice whilst abolishing constructive malice. Constructive malice applied to those who killed in the furtherance of committing a felony or while seeking to evade lawful arrest or effecting or assisting an escape or rescue from legal custody. Subject to any defence being available, a murder conviction would be the result. This despite the fact that there may have been no evidence of an intention to kill or cause grievous bodily harm. Indeed, the facts of *Vickers* illustrates the point. He had been disturbed by the 73 year old owner of the premises which he had unlawfully entered. His purpose in being there was to steal and he well knew that the old lady was somewhat deaf and presumed that in the circumstances she was unlikely to be aware of his presence. Unfortunately, he was disturbed and attacked the owner with his fists. Her death was caused by shock occasioned by the general injuries she had received. Section 1 of the HA 1957 had already become law and therefore the question for the jury was whether he had an intention to kill or to cause grievous bodily harm, that is, express or implied malice. However, Lord Goddard CJ in the Court of Criminal Appeal had no doubt that the facts indicated that the killing had been done in the furtherance of the burglary and if this case had arisen some time before the passing of the HA 1957 then it would have been a straightforward application of the constructive malice doctrine. However, since the HA 1957 had become law, the question was whether, ignoring the burglary, the appellant had the intention to cause grievous bodily harm. His conviction for murder was upheld. Another example of the constructive malice doctrine is to be found in *Beard* (1920), where, it will be recalled, the appellant had killed in the furtherance of rape.

In the course of his speech in *Powell and Daniels; English* (1997), Lord Steyn conceded that:

> In English law a defendant may be convicted of murder who is in no ordinary sense a murderer ... This rule [by which he meant the fact that intention to do grievous bodily harm would suffice for murder] turns murder into a constructive crime.

What then is the argument in favour of retaining this form of constructive liability enshrined in the current *mens rea* for murder? The conventional wisdom is based on a theory of 'just deserts' – an attacker bent on causing grievous bodily harm cannot guarantee that death will not follow, given the unpredictability, whether a serious injury will result in death. In effect, the law regards such a defendant as being willing to take the risk that the victim will die. The obvious riposte to this is that murder should be reserved for those who intend to kill. The offence of manslaughter exists to cater for those willing to risk the death of their victims, where the risk materialises. The shortcomings of the current law are, of course, compounded by the fact that that the penalty for murder is a mandatory life sentence.

Clause 54 of the draft Criminal Code declares that the *mens rea* for murder ought to be:

(a) intending to cause death; or

(b) intending to cause serious personal harm and being aware that it may cause death.

In addition to considering the draft Criminal Code in respect of the proposed *mens rea* for murder, it is advisable to cross-refer the proposals of the Law Commission contained in the draft Criminal Code Bill to be found in the Commission's report *Offences Against the Person and General Principles* (Law Com 218, 1993). The Law Commission proposes the new offence of intentional serious injury and 'intentionally' is defined this way:

1   For the purposes of this Part a person acts:

(a) 'intentionally' with respect to a result when:

(i) it is his purpose to cause it; or

(ii) although it is not his purpose to cause it, he knows that it would occur in the ordinary course of events if he were to succeed in his purpose of causing some other result ...

If the law on non-fatal offences were to be reformed without any change to the law on murder, then it can be expected that this formula would form the basis for the definition of implied malice. However, if the draft Criminal Code formulation of the *mens rea* for murder were to become law, there would need to be at least an awareness on the part of the defendant that his conduct might result in death.

6.5   Manslaughter

Manslaughter, for the purposes of this discussion, is divided into two types, voluntary and involuntary. The former category relates directly to various provisions of the HA 1957 which deal with cases where there is an intent to cause serious harm or death but because of provocation, diminished responsibility or acting in pursuance of a suicide pact, any conviction is for manslaughter, thus giving a discretion to the judge at the time of passing sentence. That discretion is currently denied in the case of murder where the mandatory sentence is one of life imprisonment. The latter category covers unlawful killing in circumstances where the defendant has committed an unlawful act, or being under a legal duty has carried out an activity in such a grossly negligent manner that death has resulted.

6.6   Voluntary manslaughter

It should be remembered throughout the discussion on voluntary manslaughter that the accused must have been charged with murder otherwise the relevant provisions of the HA 1957 will not be applicable.

6.6.1 Provocation

Section 3 of the HA 1957 states:

> Where on a charge of murder there is evidence on which the jury can find that the person charged was provoked (whether by things done or by things said or by both together) to lose his self-control, the question whether the provocation was enough to make a reasonable man do as he did shall be left to be determined by the jury; and in determining that question the jury shall take into account everything both done and said according to the effect which, in their opinion, it would have on a reasonable man.

It will be evident that this section requires careful scrutiny. The points to be considered are:

- it applies only to a charge of murder whether a principle or accomplice (see *Marks* (1998)), and if successfully pleaded the conviction will be for manslaughter;

- there must be evidence capable of amounting to provocation and this will be determined by the judge. The judge's role is extremely limited since the success or failure of the defence is left to be determined by the jury;

- provocation may result from things said, done, or a combination of both;

- the effect of the provocation must have caused the defendant to lose his self-control often referred to as the subjective condition *per* Lord Steyn in *Acott* (1996);

- it must be determined by the jury whether or not in the circumstances the reasonable man would have lost his self-control;

- who is the reasonable man? What are his characteristics and which, if any, of these, is the jury entitled to consider in its deliberations? The analysis of this section is based upon subjective and objective factors, did the defendant lose his self-control (subjective) and would the reasonable man also succumb (objective)?

The classic definition of provocation was given by Devlin J in *Duffy* (1949):

> Provocation is some act, or series of acts, done (or words spoken) which would cause in any reasonable person, and actually causes in the accused, a sudden and temporary loss of self-control, rendering the accused so subject to passion as to make him or her for the moment not the master of his mind.

This common law definition was modified by the HA 1957. The historical context which underpinned the development of provocation at common law was outlined by Lord Diplock in *DPP v Camplin* (1978). The overriding requirement was for there to have been violence perpetrated by the deceased against the accused except in two situations. First, the discovery by a husband of his wife committing adultery and secondly a father alighting upon a man in the act of sodomising his son. Words alone were incapable of amounting to provocation. The reference in s 3 to the 'reasonable man' has its origins in the common law. As a result of the decision in *Lesbini* (1914), a dual test was accepted in which reference was to be made to whether or not the reasonable man might react as the accused had done, that is, lose his self-control. Lord Goff in *Morhall* (1995) considered that this development appeared to have been:

> ... an act of policy designed to set a standard of self-control which must be complied with before the accused is able to rely on the defence of provocation [p 664d].

It was argued in *Thornton* (1992) and *Ahluwalia* (1992) that as this definition was given prior to the HA 1957, it was open to a court to redefine the common law basis of provocation, as a result of the comment by Lord Diplock in *Camplin* (1978) that the section had abolished 'all previous rules of law as to what can or cannot amount to provocation'.

At the centre of the submission was the desire to persuade the court that it should no longer be a requirement for there to have been a 'sudden and temporary loss of self-control'. The Lord Chief Justice, ever mindful of the policy considerations underpinning the rule, thought that such a well recognised principle should not be overturned without parliamentary intervention. The law on provocation ought to be humane in application whilst at the same time not encouraging self-help or retribution.

6.6.2 The judge rules on the evidence

The judge has to rule on the evidence and no more. Occasionally, the suggestion of provocation may arise as a result of a plea of some other defence which, if successful would result in acquittal for the accused, for example, self-defence. If such a defence were to fail, the accused may seek to appeal on the basis that provocation should have been considered by the jury. In the case of *Wellington* (1993), the trial judge had concluded there was no evidence of loss of self-control and as such refused to refer the issue of provocation to the jury. The Crown accepted that if there had been any evidence of the loss of self-control then the judge was under a duty to leave the defence to the jury. However, no such foundation had been laid and this interpretation was supported by the Court of Appeal. The requirement to establish a proper foundation is not a particularly arduous one to fulfil providing there is some evidence of specific provoking conduct. In this case, the appellant had not claimed that he had lost his self-control, although he maintained that he had been acting 'instinctively' when trying to fend off the victim, while he had a knife in his hand. The evidence of a pathologist might prove important if, for example, the injuries to the deceased showed a frenzied or savage attack had taken place which might be consistent with the attacker having lost his self-control. In *Rossiter* (1994), the Court of Appeal held that whenever there was evidence which supported the contention that the accused had lost his or her self-control, however tenuous it might be, then the judge should refer the issue of provocation to the jury. The Court of Appeal went further in *Cambridge* (1994), holding that a trial judge is 'required' to leave provocation to the jury even though counsel had chosen not to rely on the defence. Lord Taylor CJ considered what type of evidence gave rise to the duty to pass the matter to the jury. It was not, he said, for the judge to 'conjure up a speculative possibility of a defence that is not relied on and is unrealistic' (p 765b). He was, however, of the opinion that the reference by Russell LJ in *Rossiter* to 'material capable of amounting to provocation, however tenuous it may be', described the provocative acts and words, 'and not the evidence of their existence'.

A further example of judicial proactivity is to be found in *Stewart* (1995) where the Court of Appeal held that the trial judge had been correct to refer the matter of provocation to the jury even though counsel had not raised the issue. The trial judge had concluded that the evidence was consistent with the possibility of a 'frenzied attack' which ought to be put to the jury as a counterbalance to the element of premeditation relied upon by the prosecution. A judge has to assess whether, on all the evidence, there is a reasonable possibility that a jury might conclude that the defendant had been provoked to lose his self-control, even though the judge may hold the belief that no reasonable person would have reacted in that way (see *Cambridge*, above).

In *Cocker* (1989), the applicant's wife suffered from an incurable disease and repeatedly begged her husband to kill her, requests to which he eventually acceded. The judge ruled that there was no evidence of the accused being actuated by provocation whereupon he changed his plea to guilty. In *Singh* (1992), the defendant had strangled his wife in order to stop her 'incessant nagging'. He had endured her 'sharp and persistent tongue' for over 15 years. The jury accepted his defence of provocation. In the majority of cases, the judge will conclude that sufficient evidence exists and will leave the matter to the jury. The clearest example is where the defendant has been subjected to violence or abuse at the hands of a partner or spouse. In *Line* (1992), defence counsel said: 'She would wait for him to come to bed at three or four in the morning to be assaulted, to be buggered, to be raped. She was pushed over the limit.' Line had stabbed her husband 17 times with a kitchen knife after enduring months of violence and sexual abuse. She was found not guilty of murder and sentenced to 18 months' imprisonment, suspended for two years, for manslaughter.

Further consideration has been given to this issue in recent decisions of the House of Lords and Court of Appeal. In *Acott* (1996), the appellant who lived with his mother had been charged with her murder after she was found dead from multiple injuries. The appellant claimed that his mother had sustained the injuries as a result of a fall although two pathologists called by the Crown testified that the deceased had endured a sustained attack before she died. A pathologist called by the defence thought that there was a possibility that she could have died in the way described by her son. Counsel for the prosecution had throughout cross-examination repeatedly put to the appellant the suggestion that he might have lost his self-control. This was, unsurprisingly, denied, as it would have been tantamount to admitting that his mother did not come by her injuries as a result of an accident. There was evidence that his mother used to berate him, treat him like a child and belittle him because he was financially dependant upon her. The defendant was aged 48. The trial judge did not put any issue of provocation to the jury and he was convicted of murder. His appeal to the Court of Appeal was on the basis that once the prosecution had raised the possibility of provocation it should have been put to the jury. The appeal was dismissed both in the Court of Appeal and in the House of Lords on the ground that there had to be some evidence either direct or inferential of what was done or said in order to provoke the accused and that was absent in this case. The House of Lords ruled that there had to be:

> ... some evidence of the nature of the provocation ... if there was no evidence of a specific act or words of provocation resulting in a loss of self-control, but merely the speculative possibility that there had been an act of provocation, it would be wrong for the judge to direct the jury to consider provocation.

The bottom line of course is that in such circumstances there is no triable issue of provocation. For counsel to raise the possibility by way of cross-examination without more direct evidence of provoking conduct would in part detract from the real issues in the case under trial. It is virtually impossible for a jury to determine either the subjective and objective condition without some evidence as to the nature of the provocation.

The burden of proof rests with the prosecution. As Lord Devlin said in *Lee Chun-Chuen v R*:

> It is not of course for the defence to make out a *prima facie* case of provocation. It is for the prosecution to prove that the killing was unprovoked. All that the defence need do is to point to material which could induce a reasonable doubt [p 229].

A similar situation arose in *Dhillon* (1997), where, as a result of an altercation between a group of market traders, D drove his van at a group of men, hitting the deceased and causing him to fall to the ground. The van then passed over his body killing him. The defence argued that it was an accident but the judge was of the opinion that as a result of the evidence adduced provocation could be pleaded. Having discussed his thoughts with counsel, it was agreed that the judge would not direct the jury on the issue of provocation. D was convicted of murder. His appeal was allowed and a verdict of manslaughter substituted. The court recognised the dilemma faced by the judge but felt the judge to have been wrong in not following his inclination and:

> ... acknowledge that the evidence of loss of temper and of being assaulted was sufficient to have imposed upon him a duty of leaving this issue to the jury ...

A judge must not be tempted to second guess the outcome of the jury's deliberations on the issue of provocation. Even if the judge is utterly convinced that the jury will reject the defence, he is still legally obliged to put the issue in front of them. The possibility of a perverse verdict being delivered may be extremely slight but nevertheless the defendant is entitled to be given that chance providing there is the slightest shred of evidence indicating that the accused lost his self-control and some evidence of the nature of the provocation.

Prior to reading the next two sections the following passage by Professor Ashworth, taken from his article, 'The doctrine of provocation' ([1976] CLJ 292, pp 317–18), ought to be considered. It was cited with approval by the House of Lords in *Acott* and describes the 'core features of the modern law of provocation':

> Provocation mitigates moral culpability to the extent that a person acted in a less-than-fully-controlled manner in circumstances in which there was reasonable justification for him to feel aggrieved at the conduct of another. The law's subjective condition operates to ensure that it was not a revenge killing, but rather a sudden and uncontrolled reaction to perceived injustice. The objective condition looks at the element of partial justification and, inevitably, to the conduct of the provoking party. It requires of the jury an assessment of the seriousness of the provocation, and a judgment as to whether the provocation was grave enough to warrant a reduction of the crime from murder to manslaughter. The question of sufficiency is one of degree, and the legal rules, although they can take the court so far, cannot determine this ultimate question. Of course there will be clear cases-as, for example, where the teenage son loses control and attacks his bullying father – and there will be doubtful cases – as, for example, where the husband kills his wife during a quarrel over infidelity, which the parties had more or less accepted for a considerable time. Each case is for the decision of the jury, properly directed as to the law [p 712b].

6.6.3   Sudden and temporary loss of self-control

For the defence of provocation to be made out, there must be evidence that the defendant suffered a sudden and temporary loss of self-control. The Court of Appeal has reaffirmed the principle in decisions such as *Thornton (No 2) (1995)*, where the Lord Chief Justice, dealing with the issue of battered woman syndrome, stated:

> A defendant, even if suffering from that syndrome, cannot succeed in relying on provocation unless the jury considered she suffered or may have suffered a sudden and temporary loss of self-control at the time of the killing.

This does not mean, however, that evidence of cumulative provocation has no relevance to the defence of provocation. If one uses battered woman syndrome as an example, it is clear that the severity of the syndrome and the extent to which it has affected the defendant may influence a jury in favour of accepting that there was a sudden loss of self-control. So, a minor incident which would not cause the majority of people to lose their self-control may be more readily explained if the defendant is a victim of a course of persistently violent conduct.

Lord Taylor CJ accepted in *Dryden* (1995) that, in the context of the accused's obsession with his property and his long running dispute with the local planning authority, the threatened demolition of his bungalow by the authority could have been seen as the 'last straw' in the build-up of stress upon the accused. Similarly, in *Humphreys* (1995), Hirst LJ emphasised that, in considering the evidence of provocation, the jury should have been directed to consider the history of the 'tempestuous relationship' between the accused and the deceased, and the fact that the 'cumulative strands of potentially provocative conduct' could be seen as 'building up until the final encounter'.

In *Ahluwalia* (1992), the appellant, an unwilling partner to an arranged marriage, had suffered many years of severe violence and abuse at the hands of her husband. There was evidence to show that on one occasion he had tried to run her down and on others had threatened to kill her. He also taunted his wife about affairs he had with other women. On the evening in question, the couple had argued and the husband threatened to beat up his wife the following morning. During the night, she entered his bedroom where he was sleeping, poured petrol on the floor and then, having retreated, set it alight. Her husband died as a result of the burns he received in the ensuing fire. The appellant was convicted of murder and sentenced to life imprisonment. She appealed contending, *inter alia*, that the violence and humiliation she suffered at the hands of her husband over a period of some 10 years amounted to provocation. The court confirmed that the longer the delay and 'the stronger the evidence of deliberation on the part of the defendant the more likely it would be that the prosecution would be able to negative provocation'. (The appellant's appeal was allowed in light of new medical evidence which raised the possibility that, at the time of the killing, she was suffering from diminished responsibility and a rehearing was ordered.) The response to the provocative behaviour therefore does not need to be immediate. The time lapse is something for the jury to take into account. The longer the time lapse between the last act and the response the more likely it is that the jury will reject the defence. If the severely abused wife says to herself, 'If he hits me again I will kill him' and in the event does so, then this is inconsistent with the requirement for a sudden and temporary loss of self-control. If, however, she responds to the last act of violence by picking up a knife and stabbing her husband, then the evidence ought to be put before the jury. As Lord Morris put it in *Camplin* (1978):

> It will be for the court to decide whether, on a charge of murder, there is evidence on which a jury can find that the person charged was provoked to lose his self-control; thereafter all questions are for the jury.

Similarly, in *Thornton* (1992), the Court of Appeal held that, while provocative acts over a period of time which did not result in a sudden and temporary loss of self-control could not amount to provocation, they could provide the 'context or background against which the accused's reaction to provocative conduct had to be judged'. In *Burke* (1987), the issue of provocation was left to the jury where the accused, who had been involved in an argument at a nightclub, left the dance floor, fetched a knife, returned to the dancers and there stabbed the victim. The jury rejected her plea of provocation. *Baillie* (1995) would tend to suggest that a substantial delay between the acts relied upon as constituting provocation combined with a strong element of revenge underpinning the behaviour which led to the killing of the victim is not necessarily fatal to a plea of provocation. A father distraught at the fact that M had been pressurising one of his son's to purchase drugs from him had been informed by the son that M had threatened him. The defendant (B), who had been drinking heavily, armed himself with a sawn off shotgun and a cut throat razor and went looking for M. M received substantial injuries from the razor and as he fled B fired the gun twice. M died as a result of being hit by flying particles from a wire fence which had taken the brunt of the shotgun blasts. The judge did not direct the jury on the issue of provocation as 'any sudden and temporary loss of self-control must have ceased by the time of the fatal act'. Nevertheless the court allowed the appeal. While recognising the 'many and obvious difficulties' with the evidence, the court felt constrained by precedent and accepted that the jury should have had the opportunity to consider the evidence of provocation. If the words 'sudden and temporary loss of self-control' are meant to be synonymous with there being an absence of premeditation, it is difficult to see how a case such as *Baillie* can have been correctly decided. It is hard to avoid the conclusion that conscious control on the part of the accused during the build-up to the fatal event will not of itself lead to a plea of provocation being withdrawn from the jury.

6.6.4 Provocative behaviour of a third party

It is worth noting that the provocative behaviour does not necessarily have to emanate from the victim. In *Davies* (1975), the Court of Appeal held that words or behaviour from a third party were not excluded under the HA 1957 from consideration by the jury. In this case, the appellant claimed to have been provoked as a result of seeing his wife's lover on his way to meet her. He had with him a shotgun which he fired at his wife, killing her instantly. Conduct directed by the victim towards a third party may also be relevant as the section invites the jury to take account of 'everything' both done and said according to the effect which, in their opinion, it would have on a reasonable man.

6.6.5 The objective factor

The HA 1957 demands that, once the subjective element has been established, the objective factor must be considered. Would the reasonable man have lost his self-control? At common law, the reasonable man was not to be attributed any of the characteristics of the accused. So, in *Bedder* (1954), the House of Lords held that the jury should ignore the effects of taunts (about his impotency) on an impotent defendant and focus simply on what effect they would have on the reasonable man; see, further, *Mancini v DPP* (1941) and *Holmes v DPP* (1946). In *Camplin*, the House of Lords made it clear that, given the impact of s 3 of the HA on the common law, the objective test could not be applied fairly without taking into account certain characteristics of the accused. Camplin was a 15 year old who had been buggered by a man in his 50s. Camplin's response was to hit his assailant over the head with a large metal frying pan, killing him. He put forward a defence of provocation based upon the act of buggery, the fact that afterwards he was overwhelmed with shame and that he had lost his self-control when he heard the man laughing in response to his sexual triumph. Camplin was convicted of murder, the jury having been directed that they had to assess the response to the provocation by reference to a reasonable man of full age. The House of Lords, allowing Camplin's appeal, acknowledged that the degree of self-control to be expected of a boy of 15 was much less than that expected of an adult and thus the age and sex of the accused should have been attributed to the 'reasonable man' for the purposes of assessing the degree of self-control to be expected of the accused. As Lord Diplock explained, a trial judge would, in future, have to explain to the jury that:

> ... the reasonable man referred to is a person having the power of self-control to be expected of an ordinary person of the sex and age of the accused, but in other respects sharing such of the accused's characteristics as they think would affect the gravity of the provocation to him, and that the question is not merely whether such a person would in like circumstances be provoked to lose his self-control but also would react to the provocation as the accused did.

In the period between the decision in *Camplin*, in 1978, and what is now the leading authority on the objective element in the defence of provocation, the House of Lords' decision in *Smith (Morgan)* (2000), the courts struggled with two linked questions. The first was whether or not characteristics other than the age and gender of the accused could be attributed to the reasonable person for the purposes of the objective test. If the answer to the first question was in the affirmative, the second question was whether these additional characteristics were relevant only to explain the gravity of the provocation, or whether they could be taken into account in assessing what degree of self-control it was reasonable to expect in the circumstances.

In *Camplin*, for example, we know that that House of Lords ruled that age and gender could be taken into account, so that the test (in that case) became one of how the reasonable 15 year old boy would have reacted. It is clear, however, that the circumstance of having been sexually assaulted also had to be taken into account to explain the gravity of the provocation – it explains why the taunts were so provocative. The more difficult question was whether or not the fact that Camplin had been sexually assaulted could be taken into account in assessing the degree of self-control to be expected.

To understand the background to the debate, it is necessary to examine the two conflicting lines of authority that culminated in the House of Lords' ruling in *Smith (Morgan)*.

The Court of Appeal

In *Newell* (1980), the Court of Appeal, following *obiter* statements found in the New Zealand case of *McGregor* (1962), adopted the position that characteristics of the accused, including mental peculiarities, could be taken into account when assessing how the reasonable person would have responded to the provocation in question. Although not applied to the appellant's advantage in *Newell*, this argument was developed in later cases such as *Thornton (No 2)*, where it was held that battered woman syndrome could be important background information in relation to whatever had driven the accused to fatally stab her husband. Additionally, it was the court's view that it could also have had an impact on the defendant's personality, thus making it a significant characteristic. The court effectively adopted the objective test so that it became a question of whether or not the hypothetical reasonable woman would have reacted to the provocation in the same way as the defendant given the personality disorder.

The problem was also considered at length in *Humphreys* (1995). The appellant had, during her adolescence, turned to drugs and prostitution. At the age of 17, she commenced a relationship with a man aged 33. The relationship was described as 'tempestuous'. He was a jealous and possessive man who, on a number of occasions, had beaten the appellant. One night the appellant cut her wrists, fearing that on his return he would beat her and force her to have sex with him and possibly others against her will. The victim taunted her saying that she had not made a very good job of slashing her wrists. She responded by stabbing him with a kitchen knife. She raised provocation as a defence, citing the cumulative violent behaviour to which she had been subjected. Evidence was given which showed that she was of abnormal mentality, with 'immature, explosive and attention seeking traits'. The judge refused to allow the jury to consider these factors, reasoning that the reasonable young woman would not possess such characteristics. The Court of Appeal held that this amounted to a misdirection. The characteristics should have been taken into account provided 'they were permanent characteristics which set the accused apart from the ordinary person in the community and were specifically relevant to the provocative words or actions relied on to constitute the defence'. The court thought that attention seeking behaviour could be regarded as a psychological illness or disorder which was not inconsistent with the concept of the reasonable person. The court followed the reasoning in *Dryden* (1995), to the effect that juries were entitled to consider:

> ... those permanent characteristics or traits which served to distinguish the accused from the ordinary person in the community and were specifically relevant to the events relied on as constituting the provocation.

See, also, *Parker* (1997), where the Court of Appeal held that the defendant's chronic alcoholism, because it had caused damaged to the left temporal lobe of his brain, ought to have been taken into account when assessing his defence of provocation.

The House of Lords and the Privy Council

Decisions such as *Camplin*, *Morhall* (1995) and *Luc Thiet Thuan v R* (1996) all observed (to varying degrees) a dichotomy between characteristics of the accused (other than age and gender) that could be attributed to the reasonable person for the purposes of assessing the gravity of the provocation, and characteristics of the accused that could not be attributed to the reasonable person when assessing the degree of self-control to be expected, because such characteristics were seen as being inimical to the concept of reasonable self-control. At the heart of these decisions was a desire to preserve a clear distinction between the defences of diminished responsibility and provocation, and a desire to uphold an objective standard of reasonable behaviour in the face of provocation.

In *Camplin*, Lords Morris and Simon gave example 'characteristics' that might be influential in persuading a jury to accept the defence of provocation. Lord Simon drew attention to a statement such as: '"Your character is as crooked as your back". This would have a different connotation to a hunchback on the one hand and to a man with a back like a ramrod on the other.' In a similar vein, Lord Morris gave this example: 'If the accused is of a particular colour or particular ethnic origin and things are said to him which are grossly insulting, it would be utterly unreal if the jury had to consider whether the words would have provoked a man of different colour or ethnic origin, or to consider how such a man would have acted or reacted.' Their Lordships were quick to point out, however, that those who were exceptionally excitable, pugnacious, ill tempered or drunk would be denied the defence based upon these characteristics.

In *Morhall*, the House of Lords held that addiction to glue-sniffing, although reprehensible and undesirable, was a characteristic that could be taken into account when assessing the gravity of the provocation, where that provocation consisted of taunts about the addiction. An addiction to glue-sniffing, however, was not seen as a characteristic that could be invoked to argue for any relaxation of the objective test for self-control. The jury would have been expected to conjure with the rather surreal concept of the reasonable glue-sniffer, exhibiting the self-control to be expected from the reasonable person.

On this basis, as indicated above, ethnic origin could be taken into account to explain the gravity of the provocation, where the provocation comprised racist taunts directed at the accused's ethnic origin. Belonging to a particular ethnic group would not, however, excuse a loss of self-control – the objective standard would be imposed.

In *Luc Thiet Thuan* (1996), the Privy Council held that mental infirmity, which had the effect of reducing the appellant's self-control, was not to be attributed to the reasonable person for the purposes of the objective element of the test in provocation. There was evidence that, following a fall, the appellant was prone to 'hot flushes' which caused him to suffer explosive outbursts temporarily rendering him incapable of controlling his temper. The expert diagnosis was that he suffered from 'episodic dyscontrol condition'. Lord Goff refused to accept that this was a mental peculiarity that should be attributed to the reasonable person for the purposes of determining the objective self-control dimension of provocation. He dismissed decisions such as *Newell*, *Ahluwalia* and *Humphreys* as having exercised an 'unhappy influence' over the development of this branch of the law, adding that:

> [T]heir Lordships wish to add that they do not find it possible to segregate certain psychological illness or disorders as being 'in no way repugnant to or wholly inconsistent with the concept of the reasonable person' ... and so attributable to the reasonable person for the purposes of the objective test in provocation, notwithstanding that the effect of such an illness or disorder is to deprive the person so afflicted of the ordinary person's power of self-control.

Mental infirmity was, of course, seen as being relevant to the defence of diminished responsibility and, if successful, could lead to the same conclusion (as to which see below, 6.7.2).

The ruling in *Smith (Morgan)*

On the one hand, therefore, there was the Court of Appeal taking the view that characteristics of the accused, including those amounting to 'mental peculiarities', could be attributed to the reasonable person in assessing the degree of self-control to be expected of the accused. On the other hand, the House of Lords and Privy Council (albeit principally Lord Goff) insisted that, whilst virtually any characteristic would be taken into account if it went to the gravity of the provocation, no characteristics beyond age and gender would be attributed to the reasonable person if they might be seen as undermining the objective nature of the self-control test.

A resolution of this conflict by the House of Lords was urgently required and was in due course supplied by the ruling in *Smith (Morgan)*. The accused had stabbed the victim to death and sought to rely on his severe depression as a characteristic to be taken in to account in assessing how the reasonable person would have reacted to the provocation. The trial judge ruled that the characteristic could only be relevant in assessing the gravity of the provocation and the jury found the accused guilty of murder. Allowing the appeal, Potts J rejected the notion that the House of Lords' decision in *Camplin* necessitated any distinction between attributing such characteristics to the reasonable man in terms of their relevance to the gravity of the provocation, and their relevance to his reaction to it. He brushed aside the significance of *Morhall* on the basis that the House of Lords in that case had been: '... concerned with a different problem altogether – the characteristic supplying the sting of provocative conduct. There is nothing in Lord Goff's speech in that case inconsistent with Lord Taylor CJ's reasoning in *Thornton (No 2)* or of this court in the other decisions cited.'

The Crown appealed to the House of Lords, where the following certified question was considered:

> Are characteristics other than age and sex, attributable to a reasonable man, for the purpose of s 3 of the Homicide Act 1957, relevant not only to the gravity of the provocation to him but also to the standard of control to be expected?

The House of Lords held (by a majority of 3:2, Lords Hobhouse and Millett dissenting) that, whilst the test for provocation still comprised a subjective element and an objective element, it was no longer appropriate to direct a jury to consider the objective stage by reference to how a reasonable person (with or without attributes of the defendant) would have reacted. Assuming the subjective element was satisfied, the correct approach was now to direct a jury to consider what degree of self-control it was fair and just to expect from a defendant. In effect, the distinction between characteristics having a bearing on the gravity of the provocation, and those having a bearing on the ability to exercise a reasonable degree of self-control has been swept aside. It is now simply a question of what it was reasonable to expect from the defendant, given his characteristics and circumstances. The decision vindicates the stance taken by the Court of Appeal.

Lord Slynn rejected the argument that Lord Diplock in *Camplin* had sought to lay down a purely objective test for self-control (age and gender notwithstanding). As he explained:

> ... it does not seem to me that Lord Diplock is saying that the question as to the reaction to provocation is wholly objective: on the contrary, he appears to me to be indicating that personal characteristics may be something the jury could take into account. He is certainly not limiting the characteristic which can be taken into account to age (or sex) ... in *Camplin* it was asked in effect what could reasonably be expected of a 15 year old boy. In my view the section requires that the jury should ask what could reasonably be expected of a person with the accused's characteristics. This does not mean that the objective standard of what 'everyone is entitled to expect that his fellow citizens will

exercise in society as it is today' is eliminated. It does enable the jury to decide whether in all the circumstances people with his characteristics would reasonably be expected to exercise more self-control than he did or, put another way, that he did exercise the standard of self-control which such persons would have exercised. It is thus not enough for the accused to say 'I am a depressive, therefore I cannot be expected to exercise control'. The jury must ask whether he has exercised the degree of self-control to be expected of someone in his situation.

Lord Hoffman considered the impact of s 3 of the HA 1957 and observed:

> ... in my opinion ... it would not be consistent with s 3 for the judge to tell the jury as a matter of law that they should ignore any factor or characteristic of the accused in deciding whether the objective element of provocation had been satisfied ... In a case in which the jury might consider that only by virtue of that characteristic was the act in question sufficiently provocative, the effect of such a direction would be to withdraw the issue of provocation altogether and this would be contrary to the terms of s 3 ... It meant, as I have said, that he could no longer tell them that they were obliged as a matter of law to exclude 'factors personal to the prisoner' from their consideration ... It seems to me clear, however, that Lord Diplock was framing a suitable direction for a case like *Camplin* ... and not a one-size-fits-all direction for every case of provocation ... The jury is entitled to act upon its own opinion of whether the objective element of provocation has been satisfied and the judge is not entitled to tell them that for this purpose the law requires them to exclude from consideration any of the circumstances or characteristics of the accused.

The effect of the decision is that, whilst the jury should be directed to the effect that the same standard of behaviour was to be expected from every person regardless of their individual psychological make-up, the jury should be left sufficient discretion to do justice. This might involve the jury in taking the view that there was some characteristic of the accused (temporary or permanent) which had affected the degree of control that could reasonably be expected of him, and the characteristic was of such a nature that it would be unfair not to take it into account.

Lord Clyde adverted to the balancing act involved in the application of this more subjective and flexible approach. The challenge as he saw it was for the jury to arrive at a verdict that could be said to: '... fairly meet any peculiarities of the particular case consistently with the recognition of the importance of curbing temper and passion in the interest of civil order.' He saw the critical question as being that of the proportionality between the provocation and the response. As he put it: 'The gravity of the provocation, which prompts the loss of self-control, and the reasonableness of the response may both be aspects of the same question ...' He did not believe that the tension between the need to protect society from those unable to control their emotions and the desire of the law to show compassion to human frailty could be solved by recourse to the concept of the reasonable man. He concluded:

When what is at issue is the scale of punishment which should be awarded for his conduct, it seems to me unjust that the determination should be governed not by the actual facts relating to the particular accused but by the blind application of an objective standard of good conduct.

If the test has become essentially one of 'what was it reasonable to expect from the accused?', the question inevitably arises as to whether there are conditions that are still nevertheless excluded when the jury comes to consider the reasonableness of the accused's reaction.

Lord Hoffman, in the course of his speech, observed that an accused who flies into a rage and kills simply because he has been crossed or thwarted, or because he is unusually possessive or jealous, should not be allowed to rely on his anti-social propensities as the basis for the defence of provocation. He added that a direction that the jury should ignore characteristics such as jealousy and obsession 'was the best way to ensure that the defence was not brought into disrepute'. Further, in his speech, he sought to distinguish between characteristics and what he described as 'defects in character', such as a tendency to violent rages or childish tantrums. Lord Clyde similarly ruled out 'a quarrelsome or choleric temperament' or 'exceptional pugnacity or excitability' as characteristics that could render the accused's loss of self-control reasonable.

The accused's bad temper always was excluded as a characteristic as regards the objective test in provocation, for obvious reasons. There will doubtless be difficulties, however, in drawing the line between mental peculiarities that count as characteristics, and those that are merely seen as defects of character. Was the accused's obsession with his property in *Dryden* a characteristic or a character defect?

The difficulties that are likely to lie ahead in this post-'reasonable person' era were succinctly summarised by Lord Hobhouse in his dissenting speech, where he observed:

> It is not acceptable to leave the jury without definitive guidance as to the objective criterion to be applied. The function of the criminal law is to identify and define the relevant legal criteria. It is not proper to leave the decision to the essentially subjective judgment of the individual jurors who happen to be deciding the case. Such an approach is apt to lead to idiosyncratic and inconsistent decisions. The law must inform the accused, and the judge must direct the jury, what is the objective criterion which the jury are to apply in any exercise of judgment in deciding upon the guilt or innocence of the accused. Non-specific criteria also create difficulties for the conduct of criminal trials since they do not set the necessary parameters for the admission of evidence or the relevance of arguments.

6.6.6   Self-induced provocation

It may be that the defendant has, by his or her own behaviour, prompted a response from the deceased which resulted in a retaliatory act which caused death. May the defendant raise provocation when it appears that it has been induced by his or her own conduct or behaviour? The Privy Council addressed the issue in *Edwards* (1973) and concluded that, in principle, a 'blackmailer cannot rely on the predictable results of his own blackmailing conduct as constituting provocation sufficient to reduce his killing of the victim from murder to manslaughter'.

However, it has already been stated that s 3 of the HA 1957 requires everything to be taken into account by the jury and that ought to include consideration of whether there was an element of self-induced provocation. The Court of Appeal took the opportunity in *Johnson* (1989) to explain *Edwards*. Self-induced provocation was stated to be a 'reaction by another caused by the defendant's conduct which in turn led him to lose his own self-control'. If there was evidence of provocation, whether or not it was self-induced, it should be left to the jury. The court thought that the words used by Lord Pearson in *Edwards* were not capable of being interpreted so as to exclude provocation from the jury.

6.6.7   Degree of retaliation

A final point is that the jury must consider the degree of retaliation by asking whether the reasonable man would have lost his self-control and retaliated in the same way as the accused.

In *Phillips* (1969) Lord Diplock stated:

> ... the learned judge made it clear to the jury that it was their responsibility, not his, to decide whether a reasonable man would have reacted to the provocation in the way that the appellant did. In their Lordship's view, this was an impeccable direction'.

Brown (1972) is further authority for the proposition that there need not be a reasonable relationship between the degree of provocation and the extent of the retaliation in order for the defence to succeed. Talbot J held that it was:

> ... relevant for the jury to compare the words or acts or both of these things which are put forward as provocation with the nature of the acts committed by the accused ... It may be for instance that a jury might find that the accused's acts were so disproportionate to the provocation alleged that no reasonable man would have so acted. We think therefore that a jury should be instructed to consider the relationship of the accused's acts to the provocation when asking themselves the question 'Was it enough to make a reasonable man to do as he did?

6.6.8 Draft Criminal Code

Attention is drawn to cl 58 of the draft Criminal Code, which omits any reference to the 'reasonable man'. It states:

> A person who, but for this section, would be guilty of murder is not guilty of murder if:
>
> (a) he acts when provoked (whether by things done or by things said or by both and whether by the deceased person or by another) to lose his self-control; and
>
> (b) the provocation is, in all the circumstances (including any of his personal characteristics that affect its gravity), sufficient ground for the loss of self-control.

The commentary accompanying the draft code makes it clear that the defendant should be judged on the facts as he believed them to be. It is made absolutely clear that personal characteristics may be highly relevant to the success or failure of the defence (providing the provocation relates to those characteristics). So, as is pointed out at p 251 of the commentary, if the defendant is sexually impotent it would be irrelevant if the alleged provocation consisted in an assault with intent to rob. However, if it consisted of taunts as to the impotence, 'that personal characteristic would be highly relevant'.

6.7 Diminished responsibility

Section 2(1) of the HA 1957 states:

> Where a person kills or is party to the killing of another, he shall not be convicted of murder if he was suffering from such abnormality of mind (whether arising from a condition of arrested or retarded development of mind or any inherent causes or induced by disease or injury) as substantially impaired his mental responsibility for his acts and omissions in doing or being a party to the killing.

The effect of this section, like the defence of provocation, is to reduce murder to manslaughter. The defence is only available where death actually occurs; hence, it is not a defence to a charge of attempted murder (see Campbell (1997)). In *Chambers* (1983), Leonard J outlined the sentencing options open to a judge in cases of diminished responsibility:

> His choice of the right course will depend on the state of the evidence and the material before him. If the psychiatric reports recommend and justify it, and there are no contrary indications, he will make a hospital order ... [if] the defendant constitutes a danger to the public for an unpredictable period of time, the right sentence will, in all probabilities, be one of life imprisonment ... In cases where the evidence indicates that the accused's responsibility for his acts was so grossly impaired that his degree of responsibility for them was

minimal, then a lenient course will be open to the judge. Providing there is no danger of repetition of violence, it will usually be possible to make such order as will give the accused his freedom, possibly with some supervision ... There will however be cases in which there is no proper basis for a hospital order; but in which the accused's degree of responsibility is not minimal. In such cases the judge should pass a determinate sentence of imprisonment ...

Section 2(2) of the HA 1957 places the burden of proof upon the defence. *Dunbar* (1958) decides that the appropriate test is that of the balance of probabilities. At the centre of the defence is the concept of abnormality of mind which was commented upon by Lord Parker CJ in *Byrne* (1960) in the following terms:

> [An abnormality of the mind is] a state of mind so different from that of ordinary human beings that the reasonable man would term it abnormal. It appears to be wide enough to cover the mind's activities in all its aspects, not only the perception of physical acts and matters, and the ability to form rational judgment as to whether an act is right or wrong, but also the ability to exercise will power to control physical acts in accordance with that rational judgment.

Lord Parker went on to point out that once the jury considers it more likely than not that the accused is suffering from an abnormality of mind, the crucial question is whether the abnormality was such as to substantially impair his mental responsibility for his acts. That is going to be a question of degree and for the jury to determine. Byrne was a sexual psychopath who had killed a young woman at the YWCA in Birmingham and then mutilated her body. It was not disputed by the medical witnesses that he suffered from an abnormality of mind the manifestation of which was that he suffered from violent perverted sexual desires which had proved impossible to control. The trial judge was held to have been wrong to withdraw the issue of diminished responsibility from the jury.

Without adequate direction, juries may be somewhat confused as to the distinction between an abnormality of mind and a disease of the mind, a vital ingredient in relation to the *M'Naghten* Rules and the defence of insanity. It must, however, be stressed that the defence of diminished responsibility has largely replaced the defence of insanity in cases of murder. The Court of Appeal held in *Brown* (1993) that it was 'generally desirable' for judges to supplement the statutory definition and refer to aspects of the 'mind' such as perception, understanding, judgment and will. It will be recalled that in *Sullivan* (1983) the House of Lords ruled that the word 'mind' should be used in the 'ordinary' sense of 'reason, memory and understanding'. There would appear to be no reason why this 'definition' should not suffice for a plea of diminished responsibility. As with insanity, the final decision is not a medical but a legal one and there is no specific requirement that medical evidence needs to be adduced as it does with the insanity defence. However, it is unlikely that juries would wish to agree that the accused is suffering from an abnormality of mind without some medical evidence to support their conclusions.

6.7.1 Intoxication and diminished responsibility

Section 2 of the HA 1957 requires that the diminished responsibility must result from one or more of the following:

- arrested or retarded development of mind;

- any inherent causes;

- induced by disease or injury.

The Court of Appeal has considered the interrelationship between intoxication and the special defence in two cases, *Tandy* (1989) and *Egan* (1992). In *Tandy*, the appellant had killed her daughter. She was an alcoholic and the Court of Appeal confirmed that for drink to produce an abnormality of mind, the:

> ... alcoholism had to have reached such a level that the accused's brain was damaged so that there was gross impairment of his judgment and emotional responses or the craving had to be such as to render the accused's use of drink involuntary because he was no longer able to resist the impulse to drink.

If, as in this case, the accused had simply not resisted an impulse to drink she could not rely on the defence of diminished responsibility. The taking of her first drink on that fateful day was not an involuntary action. In a case such as this, there are three elements which need to be established. First, of course, the accused must be suffering from an abnormality of mind at the time of the act which resulted in death, that is, in this case the strangulation; secondly, that the abnormality was induced by disease, namely alcoholism; and, thirdly, that the abnormality of mind induced by the alcoholism was such as substantially impaired her mental responsibility for her act of strangling her daughter. The evidence had to prove that she was a chronic alcoholic if the second element was to be established. This means that there would need to be gross impairment of judgment and emotional responses and some evidence of brain damage. However, if brain damage could not be shown then providing that 'the appellant's drinking had become involuntary ... she was no longer able to resist the impulse to drink', then the defence would still be available to a defendant. It follows that, if the act of drinking is involuntary, then, in the absence of any other reason, the alcoholism must be the cause of the abnormality of mind. The evidence of the accused clearly indicated that she was capable of exercising some degree of control over her actions even after she had consumed her first drink.

In *Egan*, the defendant admitted that he had drunk 15 pints of beer and several gin and tonics before killing a 79 year old widow. Medical evidence showed that he suffered from an abnormality of mind by reason of arrested or retarded development of mind and intellectual impairment with possibly a psychopathic disorder. His psychological problem was permanent, the intoxication relevant only to the night in question; he was not an alcoholic. The questions for the jury, ignoring the intoxication, were whether he would have killed as he did and whether he would have done so as a result of diminished responsibility. He was convicted of murder and his conviction was upheld by the Court of Appeal. The jury presumably decided that he was not under diminished responsibility to an extent that substantially impaired his responsibility for the killing. 'Substantial' was to be approached in a 'broad common sense way' and 'substantial' meant more than:

> ... some trivial degree of impairment which does not make any appreciable difference to a person's ability to control himself, but it means less than total impairment.

These directions were taken from *Lloyd* (1966) and were specifically approved by the Court of Appeal in *Egan*.

The court referred to the 'troublesome' subject of diminished responsibility where drink was a factor. The cases of *Gittens* (1984) and *Atkinson* (1985) were cited as 'high authority' on the subject. In *Gittens*, the appellant suffered from depression for which he received medical treatment. His wife 'preferred the company of another man to that of her husband' and no doubt this factor contributed to his depression. On the night in question, he drank to excess and also took some tablets which had been prescribed for him. In the early hours of the morning a violent argument ensued which resulted in him clubbing his wife to death. He then attacked, raped and strangled his stepdaughter. He was convicted of murder and appealed on the basis of a misdirection as to diminished responsibility. In allowing his appeal, the court referred to the fact that an abnormality of mind induced by alcohol or drugs is not generally speaking due to inherent causes and therefore does not fall to be considered within the terms of the section. The jury had been invited to consider whether the substantial cause of his behaviour was inherent causes or the alcohol or drugs. It was conceivable that if properly directed the jury would have reached the conclusion that drink, drugs and inherent causes all contributed to the abnormality of mind. In *Atkinson* (1985), the court adopted Professor Smith's analysis of *Gittens* contained in his commentary to the Criminal Law Review report ([1984] Crim LR 553) to the effect that, if a defendant had not taken drink:

- would he have killed as he in fact did?; and

- would he have been under diminished responsibility when he did so?

Egan also approved of this direction. Read together with *Tandy* this appears to suggest that if a defendant acted as he did because of drink then intoxication would be the appropriate defence to a murder charge. If the drink had been consumed involuntarily because the defendant is an alcoholic, then the jury is entitled to conclude that the defendant acted under diminished responsibility.

6.7.2 Provocation and diminished responsibility

It has long been recognised that an accused charged with murder might seek to raise the defences of provocation and diminished responsibility in tandem. Either defence, if made out, would have the effect of reducing the accused's liability to manslaughter. For many years, it was thought that the defences might, to some extent, be seen as mutually exclusive, in so much as diminished responsibility was based on a mental abnormality that resulted in an impairment of the accused's self-control, whereas in provocation, the question was whether a sane reasonable person would have been provoked to kill as the accuse did.

In his seminal article, 'The doctrine of provocation' ([1976] CLJ 292), Professor Andrew Ashworth, observed that, although the conventional wisdom supported the 'mutually exclusive' view, it was nevertheless 'difficult to shed all one's misgivings about whether the law actually operates in this way'.

As outlined above, 6.6.5, however, during the latter years of the 20th century, the Court of Appeal began to recognise that evidence of mental peculiarities could be relevant for both defences. Hence, in *Thornton (No 2)*, evidence that the accused had been suffering from battered woman syndrome at the time she killed was seen as a factor to be taken into account in assessing the reasonableness of her actions. In *Ahluwalia*, the appeal was allowed and a retrial ordered because diminished responsibility had not been raised at the defendant's trial despite medical evidence available at the time which indicated that she suffered from endogenous depression when the act was committed. In *Hobson* (1998), the Court of Appeal accepted that battered woman syndrome could provide a basis for the defence of diminished responsibility not least because it had, since 1994, been included in the British classification of mental diseases recognised by the psychiatric profession.

Both *Humphreys* (1995) (accused suffering from 'abnormal mentality, with immature, explosive and attention seeking traits [such as] ...her tendency to slash her wrists') and *Dryden* (1995) ('eccentric and obsessional personality traits, a depressive illness and paranoid thinking') are cases where the evidence of mental abnormality could clearly have formed the basis of a plea of diminished responsibility, yet they are both cases where the Court of Appeal accepted that provocation could be put forward.

Lord Goff, in *Luc Thiet Thuan*, was fiercely critical of this development, observing that it cannot have been the intention of Parliament, in creating a new defence of diminished responsibility in s 2 of the HA 1957, that there should be such an overlap between the statutory defence and provocation. As he argued:

> If diminished responsibility was held to form part of the law of provocation, the extraordinary result would follow that a defendant who failed to establish diminished responsibility on the burden of proof placed upon him by [s 2 of the HA] might nevertheless be able to succeed on the defence of provocation ... on the basis that, on precisely the same evidence, the prosecution had failed to negative, on the criminal burden, that he was suffering from a mental infirmity affecting his self-control which must be attributed to the reasonable man for the purposes of the objective test.

As has been seen from the subsequent House of Lords' decision in *Smith (Morgan)*, the reasonable man test has now effectively been abandoned, in favour of an inquiry into whether the accused displayed what was (for him) a reasonable degree of self-control. This is likely to have the effect of blurring still further the distinction between the two defences. Lord Hoffman appeared to admit as much when, in the course of his speech in *Smith (Morgan)*, he observed that:

> The boundary between the normal and abnormal is very often a matter of opinion. Some people are entirely normal in most respects and behave unusually in others. There are people (such as battered wives) who would reject any suggestion that they were 'different from ordinary human beings' but have undergone experiences which, without any fault or defect of character on their part, have affected their powers of self-control. In such cases the law now recognises that the emotions which may cause loss of self-control are not confined to anger but may include fear and despair ...

His view that, for example, abused wives should not have to plead that they are mentally abnormal in order to gain the protective shield of a defence in criminal law may be welcomed in many quarters, but it has to be asked whether, as Lord Millett put it in *Smith (Morgan)*, the objective element of provocation has been 'eroded and its moral basis subverted' in order to provide a defence of diminished responsibility wider than that intended by Parliament. It is significant to note that the accused in *Smith (Morgan)* only sought to rely on provocation because the jury, having heard the evidence and having been properly directed upon the requirements under s 2 of the HA, rejected the defence.

6.7.3 Draft Criminal Code

Consideration should also be given to the draft Criminal Code. Clause 56 covers diminished responsibility:

(1) A person who, but for this section, would be guilty of murder is not guilty of murder if, at the time of his act, he is suffering from such mental abnormality as is a substantial enough reason to reduce his offence to manslaughter.

(2) Mental abnormality means mental illness, arrested or incomplete development of mind, psychopathic disorder, and any other disorder or disability of mind, except intoxication.

(3) Where a person suffering from mental abnormality is also intoxicated, this section applies only where it would apply if he were not intoxicated.

The definition of mental abnormality proposed by the Law Commission follows word for word the definition of mental disorder to be found in s 1(2) of the Mental Health Act 1983. It will be noted that intoxication is excluded. The clause also makes it clear to a jury that the relevant time to consider diminished responsibility is at the time of the act and not the time of the trial.

6.7.4   Suicide pacts

Section 4(1) of the HA 1957 provides:

It shall be manslaughter and shall not be murder for a person acting in pursuance of a suicide pact between him and another to kill the other or be party to the other being killed by a third person.

A suicide pact is defined by s 4(3) as a 'common agreement between two or more persons having for its object the death of all of them, whether or not each is to take his own life'.

It follows that for there to be an 'agreement' or 'pact' the parties must have a 'settled intention of dying in pursuance of the pact'. Section 4(2) places the onus on the defence to prove that the killing was carried out in pursuance of a suicide pact.

6.8   Involuntary manslaughter

If death has occurred but the defendant did not possess an intent to kill or an intent to cause grievous bodily harm, that is, without malice aforethought, then providing the action or omission was not totally accidental and therefore blameless, any ensuing prosecution will be for manslaughter. The law appears to recognise the following categories:

- unlawful act (or constructive) manslaughter;

- reckless (subjective) manslaughter;

- gross negligence, the subject of detailed analysis in *Adomako* (1994).

6.8.1   Unlawful act manslaughter

The reliance on the requirement for the act to be unlawful begged the question whether or not a civil wrong would be a sufficient peg upon which to hang a manslaughter charge. *Franklin* (1883) decided that criminal liability should not flow from the 'mere fact of a civil wrong'. In that case, the defendant was standing on West Pier at Brighton and threw a large box which he had removed from a refreshment stall over the side. It struck the victim who was swimming near the pier causing his death. The court regarded a civil wrong, trespass, against the stall holder as immaterial and the case was put to the jury on the broad ground of negligence.

The modern definition was expressed by the House of Lords in *Newbury and Jones* (1976). In this case, the appellants were standing on the parapet of a bridge which straddled a railway line. Seeing a train approaching, they pushed a piece of paving stone over the parapet onto the front of the train. It crashed into the driver's cab striking, killing the guard who happened to be there. Lord Salmon said an accused was guilty of manslaughter if it was proved that he intentionally did an act which was unlawful and dangerous and that the act inadvertently caused death. In deciding whether or not the act was dangerous the test is would 'all sober and reasonable people' recognise that it was dangerous, not whether the accused recognised it as such. This definition is based upon two authorities, *Larkin* (1943) and *Church* (1966). In the former case, the accused threatened a man with a 'naked razor'. In evidence, he said he had only intended to frighten the victim's lover, but she, he claimed, was drunk and this caused her to sway against the razor and her throat was cut by accident.

Humphries J, giving the decision of the Court of Criminal Appeal, commented:

> Where the act which a person is engaged in performing is unlawful, then, if at the same time it is a dangerous act, that is, an act which is likely to injure another person, and quite inadvertently he causes the death of that other person by that act, then he is guilty of manslaughter.

Lord Salmon spoke of this as 'an admirably clear statement of the law which has been applied many times'. He goes on to say:

> It makes it plain:
>
> (a) that an accused is guilty of manslaughter if it is proved that he intentionally did an act which was unlawful and dangerous and that that act inadvertently caused death; and
>
> (b) that it is unnecessary to prove that the accused knew that the act was unlawful or dangerous. This is one of the reasons why cases of manslaughter vary so infinitely in their gravity. They may amount to little more than pure inadvertence and sometimes to little less than murder [p 367c].

Edmund Davies J in *Church* thought that it was not enough to tell a jury that whenever any unlawful act is committed which results in death a manslaughter verdict must inexorably follow. For such a verdict to result, the 'unlawful act must be such as all sober and reasonable people would inevitably recognise must subject the other person to, at least, the risk of some harm resulting therefrom, albeit not serious harm'.

If one analyses the facts of *Newbury and Jones*, it is not immediately apparent what it is that constituted the unlawful act. Workmen had left the paving stone on the parapet of a railway bridge. There can be no doubt that the defendants, who were aged 15, pushed it over the parapet, as a train was passing underneath. The case proceeded on the basis that they had committed an unlawful act but it is not obvious exactly what it was, unless it was the act of dropping the stone. But, if this act is viewed as a property offence, then one must question whether or not that should be sufficient foundation for the result: an offence against the person. The House of Lords certainly proceeded on the basis that an unlawful act had occurred, a point taken up by Beldam LJ in *Scarlett* (1993):

> As in *DPP v Newbury*, in *Church* the accused's intentional conduct was plainly unlawful; no question arose whether his actions were or were not unlawful [p 635c].

One might engage in an analysis of *Lamb* (1967) in order to illustrate the approach to determining whether, and if so on what basis, there is liability. Here two young men were playing with a revolver. They knew there were two bullets in the chambers and that neither was opposite the barrel. As a joke one pointed the gun at the other who also treated the incident as a joke. The gun detonated and the friend was killed. The first question to ask is whether there is an unlawful and dangerous act. One does not doubt that it is potentially dangerous especially if unaware of the likely rotation of the chambers. However, if the case is viewed on the basis that the defendant believed there to be no risk, then all sober and reasonable people might conclude there was no danger.

But is it unlawful? If so what is the crime? A 'technical' assault is putting someone in fear of harm being inflicted upon them. The friend treated it as a joke, he was not frightened. It would suggest that the *actus reus* of a 'technical' assault was absent. The court proceeded on the basis that the *mens rea* was absent. However, the courts consistently refer to assault when in fact they mean a battery and undoubtedly the *actus reus* of battery was present. What of the possession of the gun? In *Jennings* (1990), the victim tried to restrain his brother who was carrying a sheath knife and in so doing was stabbed. Jennings was charged with manslaughter by unlawful act. The Crown argued that the offence of carrying an offensive weapon contrary to s 1 of the Prevention of Crime Act 1953 was such an unlawful act. It was held that the knife was not an offensive weapon *per se*. Therefore, to walk down a street with a knife in hand was not a criminal offence unless he had the intention of using it to inflict injury. Therefore, there was nothing which could constitute an unlawful act for the purposes of manslaughter. The Court of Appeal in *Scarlett* (1993) confirmed that the mental element required to be proved before an assault can be established is an intent to apply unlawful force to the victim.

It was perhaps inevitable that in *Lamb* the Court of Appeal would conclude the judge's direction, to the effect his action was an unlawful and dangerous act, was fatally flawed. This same question was raised in *Cato* (1976), where death resulted from the appellant's act of injecting the deceased with a mixture of heroin and water albeit with the deceased's approval. The jury convicted on two counts; manslaughter and under s 23 of the Offences Against the Person Act (OAPA) 1861, of 'unlawfully and maliciously administering a noxious thing so as to endanger the life of another person'. Lord Widgery CJ, in dealing with the issue of what conduct amounted to an unlawful act, thought that it was possible to 'rely on the charge under s 23 of the OAPA 1861'. Nevertheless he went on to comment that if one ignored s 23:

> ... we think there would have been an unlawful act here, and we think the unlawful act would be described as injecting the deceased Farmer with a mixture of heroin and water which at the time of the injection and for the purposes of the injection Cato had unlawfully taken into his possession.

It suggests that the possession of heroin supplies the necessary quality of unlawfulness whilst the administration of the heroin is the act. The combination of the two factors lead to the conclusion an unlawful act has been committed. It is submitted that the word unlawful qualifies the act and that possession alone does not establish that the act was unlawful for the purposes of the crime of manslaughter.

In *Arobieke* (1988), the accused had gone to a railway station looking for P. There had been animosity between A and P, and the latter, having seen A at the station, assumed that he was under potential threat of harm, left his train and was electrocuted trying to cross the tracks. There was no evidence that A had issued any threats or that as a result of his demeanour P could have naturally assumed that he was at risk. The court in allowing his appeal against conviction for manslaughter thought there was insufficient evidence for the jury to conclude that an assault had been committed. One might conclude that A's presence at the station together with the knowledge that P was also present is only a preparatory act and as such insufficient conduct to establish the *actus reus* for an attempted assault or battery.

The confusion in respect of what amounts to an unlawful act for the purposes of manslaughter results from comments by Lords Salmon and Edmund Davies in *Newbury and Jones* (1976). Lord Salmon was of the opinion that it was unnecessary to prove that the accused knew that the act was unlawful or dangerous, that is, as long as there was an intention to commit the act then looked at subjectively nothing more needed to be proved. The uncertainty generated as a result of this decision has led to calls for the reform of the law as illustrated by the comments of Beldam LJ in *Scarlett* (1993). Clearly of the opinion that a miscarriage of justice had occurred, the judge went on to state:

> ... the Criminal Law Revision Committee's 14th Report, *Offences Against the Person* (Cmnd 7844, 1980), recommended abolition of the antiquated relic of involuntary manslaughter based on the commission of an unlawful act and the adoption of the more rational and systematic approach to the offence of manslaughter. The present law is in urgent need of reform in spite of recent judicial attempts to make the law more compatible with a modern system of criminal justice [p 631f].

This case was concerned with the attempts of a publican to exclude a customer who was the worse for drink. The prosecution's case was that excessive force was used to eject the deceased from the premises and as a result he fell and hit his head, thus sustaining the injury from which he died. The appellant had undoubtedly used some force and intended to do so but there was little from which the jury could conclude that he intended or was reckless as to whether excessive force was used. The court in allowing the appeal stressed that a defendant should be guilty of an assault only if it is proved that he had acted with the mental element necessary to constitute his action as an assault, that is, 'that the defendant intentionally or recklessly applied force to the person of another' (p 636e).

6.8.2   Omissions

The above discussion has focused on acts but that also raises the question of whether or not an omission can be classed as an unlawful act. The decision of the Court of Appeal in *Lowe* (1973) would suggest not. The accused had neglected his child and as a result caused death. He had clearly committed an offence under the Children and Young Persons Act (CYPA) 1933 but this was held not to be sufficient to establish a basis for a manslaughter conviction. Although *Sheppard* (1980) overruled *Lowe*, which had treated the offence under the CYPA 1933 as one of strict liability, the wider principle appears to have survived unscathed. It is difficult to comprehend why a deliberate failure to act should be treated differently from an act of commission if the consequences are exactly the same. The failure to feed a child is clearly an unlawful act and if persisted in over a period of time can be every bit as devastating to the child as a positive course of conduct. However, if the conduct of a parent amounts to gross negligence, then a manslaughter charge will lie *via* that route rather than constructive manslaughter.

In *Khan (Rungzabe)* (1998), the Court of Appeal allowed an appeal against a conviction for manslaughter where the appellant had supplied heroin to a 15 year old who subsequently died of an overdose. The court noted that it viewed the case as one of causing death by omission (effectively failing to supervise the deceased), and thus only liability for killing by gross negligence could arise. As the trial judge, had not directed the jury on this issue the conviction could not stand (see, further, below, 6.8.4).

6.8.3   Dangerous character

The unlawful act must be of a dangerous character. In *Church* (1966), Edmund Davies J stated that:

> ... the unlawful act must be such as all sober and reasonable people would inevitably recognise must subject the other person to, at least, the risk of some harm resulting therefrom, albeit not serious harm.

The test is clearly based upon an objective assessment of the circumstances. For example, what conclusions might a reasonable person be expected to reach about the impact of a burglary, late at night, where the occupant of the property is not far short of his 90th birthday? If it is to be reasonably expected that he has a weak heart, or in poor health, then the act of burglary immediately becomes a dangerous act. If, however, the reasonable person would not suspect that the householder might react in such a way as to put his life at risk, then a manslaughter conviction is unlikely to be secured, on the basis that the act is not a dangerous one. If one sets this against the *dictum* of Edmund Davies J it would certainly be possible to sustain an argument that all burglaries are inherently dangerous in the sense that some harm albeit not serious harm could result to anyone who happens to be in the property at the time of the entry. Should the assessment include reference to the knowledge possessed by the accused before entering the property? If the house was thought to be empty and that was a reasonable conclusion to reach, then in such the circumstances the act of burglary is not dangerous as there is no risk of harm to the person.

Lord Salmon in *Newbury* (1976) had no doubt that the test remained objective: '... the test is not did the accused recognise that it was dangerous but would all sober and reasonable people recognise its danger.'

These issues were vividly illustrated in *Watson* (1989) and *Dawson* (1985). In the former case the 87 year old occupier was confronted by two men, late at night, who had thrown a brick through the window of his property, entered, confronted him and then escaped without taking anything. Unknown to the accused, the victim suffered from a serious heart condition and died some 90 minutes later from a heart attack. The Crown maintained this was a direct consequence of his property being invaded. The Court of Appeal treated the burglary as an ongoing event during which the accused were gathering knowledge and information about the victim. During the course of the burglary, they and therefore the reasonable person would have become aware of his frailty, albeit they may not have possessed such knowledge at the outset of the venture. In *Dawson,* the defendant and accomplices had attempted to rob the victim who was an attendant at a petrol filling station. He suffered from a diseased heart, a fact unknown to the men. They had pointed a replica gun at him, banged a pickaxe handle on the counter and demanded money. One man wore a balaclava. The victim died within an hour of the attempted robbery. The Court of Appeal allowed their appeals against conviction for manslaughter. All sober and reasonable people might realise that such an attack would cause some fear or apprehension, perhaps even terror, to be felt by the victim but would surely not foresee some harm being occasioned without knowledge of the victim's vulnerability. It is suggested, as a result of *Dawson*, that the reasonable person in such circumstances must foresee that the shock or terror would result in physical injury before the act is classed as 'dangerous'. It is perhaps worth emphasising that the unlawful act must be a significant cause of death. In this case, one answer might be the fact that his medical condition was poor and that a heart attack might be brought on at any moment. Conversely, the victim might still be alive today if he had not been confronted by a gang of thugs intent upon robbery. What happened to the doctrine of taking your victim as you find him?

6.8.4 Reckless and gross negligence manslaughter

As a result of the House of Lords' decision in *Adomako* (1994), it is possible to state that gross negligence manslaughter has survived the decisions in *Caldwell* (1982) and *Lawrence* (1982) and will be applicable in circumstances where death occurs as a result of a breach of duty owed by one person to another. Reckless manslaughter would therefore appear applicable to situations not involving a breach of duty or in cases where the act is not unlawful, although this now plays only a limited role in the law on manslaughter. Attention should be paid to the decision of the House of Lords in *Seymour* (1983), but do note that *Seymour* has now been overruled by *Adomako*.

Seymour faced a charge of manslaughter even though he could have been charged with the statutory offence of causing death by reckless driving contrary to the Road Traffic Act 1972. The trial judge had directed the jury along the lines of *Lawrence* when dealing with the meaning of reckless. The 'objective' element, the failure to foresee an obvious and serious risk of death, was applicable to motor manslaughter, said Lord Roskill. In *Kong Cheuk Kwan* (1985), a collision occurred between two hydrofoils in waters between Hong Kong and Macau. There was no obvious reason for the collision; the weather was fine, the skies clear, the water calm. The defendant was master of one of the vessels and he and others were charged with the manslaughter of four people. In assessing his navigational skills that day, the jury should have been directed along the lines of *Lawrence*, that is, had he created an obvious and serious risk of causing physical damage to some other ship and thus to other persons who might have been travelling in the area at the time? If so, had he given any thought to the possibility of that risk or, while acknowledging the risk had none the less gone on to take it? However if such circumstances were to be repeated today, the case would undoubtedly be treated as one of breach of duty, that is, gross negligence manslaughter.

In *Adomako* (1994), the House of Lords declined to follow *Lawrence* with the result that so called 'motor manslaughter' is no longer a recognised species of manslaughter. A motorist may still commit manslaughter, for example, driving in such a grossly negligent way that he loses control killing a pedestrian or perhaps a passenger in the car. Reckless manslaughter would appear to operate within narrow limits and in practice will be confined to cases of deliberate or advertent risk taking. Someone who causes death by an act which he or she foresees will make death a highly probable event, should be guilty of reckless manslaughter and may even be guilty of murder if the jury is convinced that the accused realised that death was a virtually certain occurrence to flow from the act (see Chapter 3). It should be noted, however, that *Adomako* did not even recognise reckless manslaughter as a species of manslaughter separate from gross negligence manslaughter. What is yet to be conclusively determined is whether someone in such circumstances who foresees death as only a possibility will be guilty of manslaughter. It must be remembered that an unlawful act is not a requirement for either reckless or gross negligence manslaughter.

The uncertainty created by the emergence of recklessness in its *Caldwell/Lawrence* form was well illustrated in *Goodfellow* (1986), where the appellant had caused three deaths as a result of arson. The Court of Appeal recognised that the case could fall into either category of unlawful act or reckless manslaughter. (Note that this decision is pre-*Adomako*.)

The questions for the jury were:

• was the act committed intentionally?;

• was it unlawful?;

• would reasonable people recognise it would cause some physical harm albeit not necessarily serious harm?;

• did the act cause death?

Deliberately torching a property knowing there are people inside inevitably leads to positive answers to all these questions and the conclusion that a clear case of unlawful act manslaughter has been established.

As far as reckless manslaughter is concerned, the jury could have been persuaded that *Goodfellow* acted in a manner likely to create an obvious and serious risk of causing physical injury and, having recognised the risk gone on to take it. By way of criticism, it could equally be said that he assessed the situation and concluded there was no risk, particularly as prior to the act, he had carried out experiments in order to assess the likely consequences of the conduct. The existence of two closely related types of involuntary manslaughter was bound to create confusion and there was and still is a clear need for rationalisation to occur. As Professor Smith said in his commentary on *Goodfellow* in the *Criminal Law Review* ([1986] Crim LR 468):

> The law is in a discreditable state of uncertainty and it is high time the government looked again at the recommendations made by the Criminal Law Revision Committee in their 14th report (to the effect that involuntary manslaughter be replaced with the new offence of causing death recklessly).

However, it is better to proceed on the basis that the overwhelming majority of manslaughter cases will fall into either the unlawful act or gross negligence categories although it should be borne in mind that the Law Commission has recommended the abolition of unlawful act manslaughter and its replacement by the new offence of reckless killing (*Legislating the Criminal Code: Involuntary Manslaughter*, Law Com 237, 1996, para 5.6).

Lord Hewart CJ in *Bateman* (1925) said:

> ... in order to establish criminal liability the facts must be such that, in the opinion of the jury, the negligence or incompetence of the accused went beyond a mere matter of compensation between subjects and showed such disregard for the life and safety of others as to amount to a crime against the State and conduct deserving punishment.

This statement, although it has been criticised on the basis that it leaves matters of law to the jury, does emphasise that conduct sufficient to establish negligence in civil law will never suffice in criminal law. The leading case was *Andrews v DPP* (1937). Andrews was driving a van at a speed in excess of the limit in the centre of Leeds late one evening. He collided with a man who was crossing the road. He failed to stop after the collision. Lord Atkin referred to the distinction between civil and criminal negligence:

> Simple lack of care such as will constitute civil liability is not enough. For the purposes of the criminal law there are degrees of negligence, and a very high degree of negligence is required to be proved before the felony is established. Probably of all the epithets that can be applied 'reckless' most nearly covers the case but it is probably not all embracing, for 'reckless' suggests an indifference to risk, whereas the accused may have appreciated the risk, and intended to avoid it, and yet shown in the means adopted to avoid the risk such a degree of negligence as would justify a conviction.

Lane LJ in *Stone* (1977), having cited the above passage from *Andrews*, said:

> It is clear from that passage that indifference to an obvious risk and appreciation of such risk, coupled with a determination nevertheless to run it, are both examples of recklessness.

The House of Lords' decision in *Adomako* (1994) is of great significance in helping to clarify the ambit of gross negligence manslaughter and whether or not recklessness is a relevant concept within this species of manslaughter. Attention is also drawn to the Lord Chief Justice's enjoinder in the Court of Appeal urging the Law Commission not to delay in its examination of the law relating to manslaughter. The appellant was the anaesthetist at an operation when he failed to notice that an endotracheal tube had become disconnected from the ventilator supplying oxygen to the patient. As a result, the patient suffered a cardiac arrest and subsequently died. The time period between the disconnection occurring and the appellant noticing that this was the cause of the problem was some six minutes. He was charged with manslaughter and convicted. It was not denied by the appellant that he had been negligent but it was his contention that his conduct was not criminal. The Court of Appeal treated the issue as one of breach of duty and stated the ingredients of involuntary manslaughter by breach of duty to be:

- the existence of a duty;

- the breach of the duty causing death; and

- gross negligence on the part of the accused which the jury considered justified a criminal conviction.

In respect of the *mens rea*, the Court of Appeal was of the opinion that proof of any of the following states of mind might convince a jury that a defendant had been grossly negligent:

- indifference to an obvious risk of injury to health;

- actual foresight of the risk coupled with the determination to run it;

- an appreciation of the risk coupled with an intention to avoid it but also coupled with such a high degree of negligence in the attempted avoidance as the jury considered justified the conviction; and

- inattention or failure to advert to a serious risk which went beyond 'mere inadvertence' in respect of an obvious and important matter which the defendant's duty demanded he should address.

The House of Lords dismissed *Adomako*'s appeal. In so doing, the then Lord Chancellor, Lord Mackay, was of the opinion that in determining whether a defendant's conduct amounted to gross negligence regard should be had to the seriousness of the breach taking into account all of the circumstances. Of crucial importance would be a consideration of the likelihood of death resulting from the act or omission and as Lord Mackay stressed:

> The essence of the matter, which is supremely a jury question, is whether, having regard to the risk of death involved, the conduct of the defendant was so bad in all the circumstances as to amount in their judgment to a criminal act or omission [p 87c].

It was made absolutely clear that it is unnecessary to refer to the definition of recklessness in *Lawrence* (1981), although reckless may be given its ordinary meaning if a trial judge deemed it to be appropriate. Lord Mackay acknowledged that the interests of justice would not be served by an 'over-elaboration of definition of the word "reckless"'. The term may, therefore, be used to indicate to juries the extent to which 'a defendant's conduct must deviate from that of a proper standard of care'.

It is suggested that in assessing the conduct of the accused, the four situations recognised by the Court of Appeal (outlined above) will inform trial judges when directing juries. If the risk to which the defendant is indifferent, or which he foresees but nevertheless goes ahead, is death rather than some injury to health, then a jury should conclude that a case of gross negligence has been established. It is assumed that a duty has been established and 'on the ordinary principles of the law of negligence the defendant has been in breach of a duty of care towards the victim who has died' (p 86j). Lord Mackay's speech emphasises that regard should be had to the risk of death occurring whereas the Court of Appeal was of the opinion that a finding of gross negligence would result if there was an indifference to an obvious risk of injury to health. The *Newbury and Jones* (1976) definition of unlawful act manslaughter demands an unlawful act of a dangerous character which all sober and reasonable people would recognise would cause some harm, albeit not serious harm. This may help to explain the attention paid by the Court of Appeal to the risk of something other than death. Yet why should someone be convicted of homicide without the law requiring proof that he either foresaw the risk of death occurring or was indifferent as to whether death occurred when it would be obvious to most people that the risk was present?

The Lord Chancellor is to be applauded for seeking to emphasise the importance of foresight of the risk of death as opposed to harm as a key concept when assessing liability for manslaughter. The avoidance of the word 'reckless' in its technical sense is also to be welcomed. However, there are some criticisms which may be levelled at the decision. The first is that civil law principles appear to be called in aid as a prerequisite to an assessment of criminal liability. Whether there is a duty of care and whether there has been a breach will depend on the law of negligence, according to Lord Mackay. Whether or not a duty of care arises should be viewed as a matter of law. In cases such as *Singh* (1999), there is little difficulty in establishing the necessary duty of care. The accused's father was the landlord of premises in multiple occupation. One of his tenants died of carbon monoxide poisoning, the result of an incorrectly installed gas appliance. Although the accused had not personally installed the appliance, the court found that, as a result of his close involvement in the running of the properties owned by his father, that he was aware of the need to ensure that gas fires were properly installed. On this basis, it was held that there was sufficient proximity for a duty of care to arise. The gas fitter concerned was also convicted of killing by gross negligence. By contrast, in *Khan (Rungzabe)* (above), Swinton Thomas LJ left open the question of whether a supplier of heroin owed any duty of care to the 15 year old recipient of the drug. Sybil Sharpe, in her article 'Grossly negligent manslaughter after

Adomako' ((1994) 158 JP 725), maintains that 'the tortious and criminal duty of care may not necessarily be co extensive'.

This point was taken up by the Law Commission in its Consultation Paper, *Involuntary Manslaughter* (Law Com 135, 1994), where the point is made that 'negligence' in the manslaughter context means nothing more than 'carelessness'. The Law Commission report, *Legislating the Criminal Code: Involuntary Manslaughter* (Law Com 237, 1996, para 3.11), was of the view that 'it does not carry the technical meaning that it has in the law of tort, where it depends on the existence of a duty of care owed and a breach of that duty'.

In the majority of situations, this should not create many problems because the conduct of the accused would be deemed to be 'bad' irrespective of which test was applied. However, the position in respect of omissions could be more problematic. In Chapter 2, it was stated that in criminal law there is no general rule which imposes upon any citizen a duty to act (see, for example, Ashworth, A, 'The scope of criminal liability for omissions' (1989) 105 LQR 424). Yet certain cases have outlined circumstances when it would appear there is a duty to act; the most controversial being that of *Stone and Dobinson* (1977). If, having voluntarily assumed responsibility for the welfare of an elderly mentally incapacitated relative, the care provided is inadequate and as a result that person dies, a conviction for manslaughter is a distinct possibility. Examined from a tortious viewpoint, it is by no means certain that liability would ensue unless death had arisen through the carer's incompetence (see above, 2.5.1).

The question is: has the decision in *Adomako* (1994) changed the criminal law in respect of omissions and brought it into line with tortious principles? If the answer is yes, then it is possible that *Stone and Dobinson* no longer represents the law on manslaughter by omission. The Law Commission is clear in its conclusions:

> The law on this subject is so unclear that it is difficult to tell whether the effect of Lord Mackay's speech was indeed to change the law, and, if so, what the implications of this change might be. It is, however, clear that the terminology of 'negligence' and 'duty of care' is best avoided within the criminal law, because of the uncertainty and confusion that surround it' [para 3.13].

The second criticism is that the test for gross negligence manslaughter offered by Lord Mackay invites juries to consider questions of law. The test is 'circular'. Juries are to be directed to convict if they believe the defendant's conduct 'criminal'. It will be recalled that Lord Mackay used the following words:

> The jury will have to consider whether the extent to which the defendant's conduct *departed from the proper standard of care incumbent upon him involving as it must have done a risk of death to the patient, was such that it should be judged criminal* [emphasis added].

As juries do not give reasons for their decisions, it will be impossible to ascertain upon what criteria the conduct has been judged. It is suggested that this will lead to uncertainty in the law and thus go against a fundamental principle of the criminal law that it must be certain in its application.

6.8.5 The Law Commission's report on involuntary manslaughter (1996)

In March 1996 the Law Commission published its long awaited report, *Legislating the Criminal Code: Involuntary Manslaughter* (Law Com 237, 1996). We have already dealt in this chapter with many of the criticisms levelled against the crime of involuntary manslaughter. The Commission also draws attention to the difficulties connected with the law on manslaughter by omission. The major problem centres around the uncertainty as to the circumstances which must exist before a positive duty to act is recognised by the law. The most problematic being the so called 'voluntarily accepted duty' as exemplified by the case of *Stone and Dobinson* (1977).

The Law Commission acknowledged that 'there is one further way in which manslaughter may now be committed in the absence of an intention to kill or cause serious injury' (para 2.26). This is a reference to (subjective) reckless manslaughter where the accused had recognised that his conduct involved the risk of causing death or serious harm but nevertheless goes ahead and unreasonably takes the risk. This category of manslaughter has, however, not developed to any significant extent primarily because most cases of this type will be prosecuted as unlawful act manslaughter. The Law Commission is clear as to the deficiencies of the current law. The first is the breadth of the offence. This is a reference to the different types of conduct which may be categorised as involuntary manslaughter. This creates problems for the sentencer, a point, confirmed by Lord Lane CJ in *Walker* (1992), where he remarked: '... manslaughter ranges in its gravity from the borders of murder right down to those of accidental death.'

In practice, this means that the same label is applied to vastly differing types of conduct and therefore degrees of culpability. The Law Commission believes that this 'devalues' the conduct of those seriously at fault by linking their act or omission within a crime which encompasses less heinous conduct.

A further major criticism is summed up by the Law Commission in this way:

> Unlawful act manslaughter is therefore ... unprincipled because it requires only that a foreseeable risk of causing some harm should have been inherent in the accused's conduct, whereas he is convicted of actually causing death, and also to some extent punished for doing so [para 3.6].

The difficulties relating to gross negligence manslaughter and liability for omissions have been outlined above.

Having highlighted the criticisms of the current law, the Law Commission went on to consider the moral basis of criminal liability for unintentionally causing death. It concludes that a person ought to be criminally liable only in the following circumstances:

- when the defendant unreasonably and inadvertently takes a risk of causing death or serious injury; or

- when the defendant unreasonably and inadvertently takes a risk of causing death or serious injury, fails to advert to the risk and is therefore culpable because:

  (a) the risk was foreseeable; and

  (b) the defendant has the capacity to advert to the risk.

The condemnation of the current offence because of the breadth of conduct encompassed within it led the Law Commission to recommend the creation of 'two offences of unintentional killing, based upon differing fault elements, rather than one single broad offence'. The first offence is that of reckless killing. Clause 1 of the draft Involuntary Homicide Bill defines the offence in this way:

> A person who by his conduct causes the death of another is guilty of reckless killing if:
>
> (a) he is aware of a risk that his conduct will cause death or serious injury; and
>
> (b) it is unreasonable for him to take that risk having regard to the circumstances as he knows or believes them to be.

The second new offence is that of killing by gross carelessness. The Commission rejected an argument that there was little distinction between subjective recklessness and gross carelessness, favouring the view that there was a clear moral distinction between the two. A person who knowingly takes a risk is surely more culpable than one who carelessly fails to advert to a risk. The semantic argument is not in doubt; it remains to be seen how effectively the distinction is to be drawn in practice.

Clause 2 of the draft Bill defines the proposed offence in the following way:

> 2(1) A person who by his conduct causes the death of another is guilty of killing by gross carelessness if:
>
> (a) a risk that his conduct will cause death or serious injury would be obvious to a reasonable person in his position;
>
> (b) he is capable of appreciating that risk at the material time; and
>
> (c) either:
>
>   (i) his conduct falls far below what can reasonably be expected of him in the circumstances; or
>
>   (ii) he intends by his conduct to cause some injury or is aware of, and unreasonably takes, the risk that it may do so.
>
> (2) There shall be attributed to the person referred to in sub-s (1)(a) above:

(a) knowledge of any relevant facts which the accused is shown to have at the material time; and

(b) any skill or experience professed by him.

(3) In determining for the purposes of sub-s (1)(c)(i) above what can reasonably be expected of the accused regard shall be had to the circumstances of which he can be expected to be aware, to any circumstances shown to be within his knowledge and to any other matter relevant for assessing his conduct at the material time.

(4) Sub-section (1)(c)(ii) above applies only if the conduct causing, or intended to cause, the injury constitutes an offence.

The formulation of this offence suggests that there is a minimum standard of behaviour below which a person must not fall in order to avoid criminal liability. The Law Commission, however, suggests that a person will have to fall far below that standard for criminal liability inexorably to follow. Out go the terms 'negligence' and 'duty of care', thereby avoiding any unnecessary overlap with the civil law.

The risk of death or serious injury must be one which is obvious to the reasonable person in the accused's position. The Law Commission proposes that obvious should mean 'immediately apparent', 'striking' or 'glaring' making it absolutely clear that the failure to recognise a risk will not make the defendant culpable unless it would have been obvious to a reasonable person in his position. Attention is drawn to paras 5.36 and 5.37, which are examples of how it is proposed the new offence will operate.

The Government has confirmed its commitment to legislate in this area and in May 2000 published its own Consultation Paper, *Reforming the Law on Involuntary Manslaughter: The Government's Proposals*, largely building upon the work of the Law Commission. In one respect, the Government's proposals go further than those of the Law Commission, in that they propose the introduction of a third form of involuntary manslaughter arising where the defendant kills intending to cause only a minor injury, but where death nevertheless results because of some unforeseeable event. This third head of involuntary manslaughter would carry a maximum penalty of between five and 10 years imprisonment. An example of this type of liability might arise where the defendant blackmails his victim, causing his victim to die of a heart attack. The harm envisaged might be minor psychological distress, but the unforeseeable event causing death is the victim's pre-existing heart condition.

The Law Commission, somewhat reluctantly, has decided that there should be no change to the present law in respect of omissions. This aspect of the criminal law, the ambit of which is very uncertain, should, believes the Law Commission be examined in respect of the whole of the criminal law and not just with reference to the law on manslaughter. When and in what circumstances the law should impose liability for an omission is described as a 'very controversial' issue and should at some future point form the basis for a discrete law reform project. The recommendation in respect of manslaughter by omission is that it should, for the time being, continue to be governed by the common law. Clause 3 states:

> A person is not guilty of an offence under ss 1 or 2 (of the draft Involuntary Homicide Bill) by reason of omission unless the omission is in breach of a duty at common law.

The law at present provides for those who kill as a result of bad driving to be charged either with the statutory offence of causing death by dangerous driving contrary to s 2 of the Road Traffic Act 1991 or the common law offence of gross negligence manslaughter. As a result of *Adomako* (1994), which ruled that *Seymour* (1983) was no longer good law, there is only one test for gross negligence in the context of the law of manslaughter. The Law Commission recommends that there should be no change to the statutory offence and that where appropriate the two new offences should be available to the Crown Prosecution Service.

6.8.6 Corporate killing

In addition to its review of the current law relating to involuntary manslaughter and recommendations for reform, the Law Commission took the opportunity to recommend the introduction of a new offence of corporate killing. This is designed to appease those who believe that companies, acting through their boards of directors, ought to face liability where it can be proved that a decision or decisions of the board has resulted in death, for example, the failure to commit the necessary finance in order to remedy known deficiencies in an aircraft or ferry. Such a decision inevitably compromises safety, increases the likelihood of disaster and therefore puts passengers at risk of death. Of importance in this context is the extent of the knowledge possessed by the board as to the likely impact of a decision not to invest. If the board has commissioned a report from a safety expert which gives clear advice that the failure to invest will not compromise safety, then it is going to be extremely difficult for the prosecution to establish that the board was culpable in the circumstances.

The *Herald of Free Enterprise* disaster in 1987 and, soon afterwards, the deaths of nearly 40 people in the King's Cross Underground fire raised the question of whether a company and members of its management ought to be able to face manslaughter charges if a causal link could be established between inadequate management decision taking and disasters such as those mentioned above. The Law Commission has looked closely at the issues and concluded that a new offence of corporate killing should be included in the draft Involuntary Homicide Bill. In essence, a corporation could become liable for the offence of corporate killing as defined by the Law Commission if:

- a management failure by the corporation is the cause or one of the causes of a person's death; and

- that failure constitutes conduct falling far below what can reasonably be expected of the corporation in the circumstances.

There is a management failure by a corporation if:

- the way in which its activities are managed or organised fails to ensure the health and safety of persons employed in or affected by those activities; and

- such a failure may be regarded as a cause of a person's death notwithstanding that the immediate cause is the act or omission of an individual.

It should be noted that the existence of such an offence does not preclude a corporation being found guilty of either of the two major offences in the Bill, that is, reckless killing and gross carelessness (cl 4(5)).

Reference should be made to Chapter 4 for further information on the vicarious liability principle in respect of corporate crime generally, an area of law which is not without its problems. In this context, reference should be made, in particular, to the case of *P & O European Ferries (Dover) Ltd* (1990) (the *Herald of Free Enterprise* case). The trial judge had no doubts that as a matter of principle a company could be found guilty of manslaughter. For this to occur, there had to be identified a person or persons who represented the company and who possessed the necessary *mens rea* for the crime of manslaughter. This is a relatively straightforward task if the company is small and the decision makers are easily identified, as in the successful prosecution of Kite and OLL Ltd in 1994. In that case, four schoolchildren lost their lives when taking canoeing lessons at a leisure activities centre run by the company. The managing director had on two occasions been made aware that safety at the centre was substandard and had failed to respond to the warnings given by qualified and experienced instructors. Both the managing director and the company were found guilty of the crime. If such circumstances were to occur again then it would appear that either of the two major offences could apply. There is clearly a duty placed upon the company to take care of its customers and by failing to provide adequate supervision there is a breach of that duty and a direct causal connection between the lack of supervision and the consequence. Similarly, given that the managing director was aware that there were serious safety deficiencies, yet nevertheless went ahead with the venture, there would seem to be little to prevent a finding of reckless killing being reached.

In the *P & O* case, none of the defendants, ruled the judge, could on the evidence be found guilty of manslaughter in his own right and therefore the prosecution failed. It had been argued, without success that the court should recognise the 'principle of aggregation' which would have permitted the individual faults, albeit minor, to be accumulated in order to reach the required degree of fault to underpin a manslaughter prosecution.

A similar argument in favour of aggregation of liability was also rejected in *AG's Reference (No 2 of 1999)* (2000), the prosecution arising from the Southall train crash in West London. The Court of Appeal held that, in the absence of any statutory intention to impose corporate liability on the basis of aggregation, the correct approach was still to identify the state of mind of the company with the state of mind of the person who could be regarded as the 'directing mind and will' of the company. JC Smith, in his commentary on this decision ([2000] Crim LR 478), was deeply critical of the approach taken by the Court of Appeal on this point. Whilst accepting that the aggregation principle could not be used where an offence required proof of subjective fault, he argued that there was no objection to using it where, as the Court of Appeal had confirmed in the case, an offence such as killing by gross negligence involved proof of that a specific standard of care had not been maintained. A finding of gross negligence was confirmation that the way in which an enterprise had operated fell way below acceptable minimum standards. Such a situation could arise where the combined effects of three separate but factually related failures by senior officers to maintain a safe system of working combined to produce a fatality.

How might the *P & O* case be dealt with in the context of the new offence of corporate killing? If one analyses the basic information, it will be seen that individual employees were found to be wanting in the way they carried out their duties. The ferry had sailed from Zeebrugge harbour and had capsized four minutes later. The ship had sailed with its inner and outer bow doors open. The doors should have been closed by an assistant bosun but he was asleep in his cabin at the moment the ferry set sail. The Chief Officer had responsibility to ensure that the bow doors were closed but the practice had emerged whereby he interpreted his duty as being to ensure that the assistant bosun was at the controls. The Sheen Report (Department of Transport, Report of the Court No 8074, 1987) into the disaster found the Chief Officer's failure to check on the doors to have been the immediate cause of the incident. Ultimate responsibility for the overall safety of the vessel lay with the Master. He apparently simply followed the system approved by the Senior Master and there was no reference in the 'Ship's Standing Orders' to the fact that it should not sail with the bow doors open. The Senior Master had overall responsibility for co-ordination between all the Masters and crews who worked on the *Herald of Free Enterprise*. The Sheen Report concluded that he should have introduced a 'fail safe system', designed to ensure that the ship and its passengers were not subjected to unnecessary dangers. It is worth quoting certain passages from the report in order to identify where the inquiry concluded the blame lay:

Full investigation into the circumstances of the disaster leads inexorably to the conclusion that the underlying or cardinal faults lay higher up in the Company. The board of directors did not appreciate their responsibility for the safe management of their ships. They did not apply their minds to the question: What orders should be given for the safety of our ships? The directors did not have any proper comprehension of what their duties were ... All concerned in the management, from the members of the board of directors down to junior superintendents, were guilty of fault in that all must be regarded as sharing responsibility for the failure of management. From the top to bottom the body corporate was infected with the disease of sloppiness. The failure on the part of the shore management to give proper and clear directions was a contributory cause of the disaster [para 14.1].

The Law Commission is of the view that if such circumstances were to arise again and assuming the new offence of corporate killing is on the statute book, the company could be convicted of the new offence. The company had failed to ensure that a safe system operated which would ensure the safety of the ferries and passengers. It is reasonable to expect that the board of a company operating ferries would never wish to compromise standards.

The Law Commission views the new offence as 'broadly corresponding' to the individual offence of killing by gross carelessness. Although the new offences of reckless killing and gross carelessness are referred to as 'individual' crimes, there is no reason in principle why a company should not face prosecution for either of these offences. It is suggested that this is likely to occur when it is possible to identify an individual as the 'controlling mind' of the company and the individual failure is synonymous with being a management failure (see *Kite and OLL Ltd*, above).

There is, of course, a fundamental question which needs to be addressed – that of causation. It is difficult to imagine that the accepted test of causation formulated nearly 40 years ago would be apposite in circumstances similar to those of the *P & O* case. The immediate cause of death was the failure of members of the crew to close the bow doors. This was also the operating cause and substantial cause of death. In circumstances where there has been a management failure, it would not be just to absolve the company from criminal responsibility simply because the immediate cause of death is the action of an employee of that company. Therefore, the Law Commission proposes that for purposes of the corporate offence a management failure may be regarded as the cause of death even though the immediate cause is the act or omission of an individual. (An individual is not to be subject to a prosecution for the corporate offence.)

The Law Commission's report recognises that the current law on manslaughter is totally inadequate and is in urgent need of reform. The proposals are well thought out and, on the face of it, workable. The Government's own Consultation Paper (*Reforming the Law on Involuntary Manslaughter: The Government's Proposals*, see above, 6.8.5) on reforming involuntary manslaughter endorses the Law Commission's proposals, but suggests that the new offence of corporate killing should apply to 'any trade or business undertakings not just incorporated organisations'. It also proposes that other organisations such as the Health and Safety Executive and Civil Aviation Authority should be empowered to investigate and prosecute the new offences. The Law Commission has rightly shied away from making recommendations in respect of the law relating to omissions purely in the context of manslaughter in favour of an overall review of the current position in criminal law. The law on omissions has evolved piecemeal over the last 100 years and would certainly benefit from a thorough reappraisal.

6.9   Infanticide

Section 1 of the Infanticide Act (IA) 1938 makes it an offence for a woman:

> ... by any wilful act or omission (to cause) the death of her child being a child under the age of 12 months ...

The section goes on to indicate that, if, at the time of the act or omission, the balance of her mind was disturbed by reason of her not having fully recovered from the effect of giving birth or by reason of lactation consequent upon the birth, then what would appear at first sight to be murder will be treated as infanticide and, if convicted, she will be punished as though found guilty of manslaughter. The limitations established by s 1 of the IA 1938 are:

- the benefit of the section is applicable only to the mother;

- it applies only if she causes the death of her child – if it is caused by anyone else then the charge will be murder or manslaughter depending on the intent although diminished responsibility might be an appropriate defence in such circumstances. The section is so phrased to suggest that it is the child to whom the mother has given birth which must be the victim. If she kills another child of her family then infanticide would appear not to be a defence;

- the child in question must be under 12 months old;

- the balance of the mother's mind must be disturbed by reason of the effect of giving birth or by reason of lactation consequent upon giving birth;

- if the balance of her mind is not disturbed and she kills, the charge will be murder;

- if the child is killed by someone other than the mother the IA 1938 will not apply.

The Butler Committee on Mentally Abnormal Offenders recognised that, in 1938, the defence of diminished responsibility had not been created and expressed the view that this would now cover killing in such circumstances as described in s 1. However, the Law Commission's draft Criminal Code recommends retention of the defence, albeit in a modified form.

Clause 64(1) states:

A woman who, but for this section, would be guilty of murder or manslaughter of her child is not guilty of murder or manslaughter, but is guilty of infanticide, if her act is done when the child is under the age of 12 months and when the balance of her mind is disturbed by reason of the effect of giving birth or of circumstances consequent upon birth.

The scope of the defence is thus broadened and can include circumstances, other than lactation, which caused the mother to kill. It has been suggested that social conditions, poverty or family pressures will be covered by the reference to circumstances but this may prove unacceptable to many people.

Support for this approach comes from RD Mackay in his research study, 'The consequences of killing very young children' ([1993] Crim LR 21). He concludes by stating:

... [the study] ... lends no support to the fact that diminished responsibility is either being widely used in cases which might otherwise be infanticide or that as it stands the HA 1957 would safely cover all the cases which presently fall within the IA 1938 ... if the lenient sentences which women receive when convicted under the IA 1938 are to be ensured then there appears to be a continued need for a separate offence of infanticide and cl 64 of the draft Criminal Code Bill seems an appropriate vehicle to secure this.

6.10 Child destruction

Section 1(1) of the Infant Life (Preservation) Act (IL(P)A) 1929 creates the offence of child destruction and imposes criminal sanctions upon those who intentionally kill any child capable of being born alive. The section makes it clear that an offence will not be committed if the killing is done in good faith for the purpose of preserving the life of the mother. (This statutory provision should be read together with an earlier statutory offence that of attempting to procure a miscarriage contrary to s 58 of the OAPA 1861.)

It will be apparent that one needs to determine at what point in the gestation process the law will accept that a child in the womb is capable of being born alive. This is a question of law for the judge not an issue of fact for the jury. The Act, creates a rebuttable presumption that a woman who has been pregnant for a minimum period of 28 weeks is carrying a child who is capable of being born alive. The 28 week criteria was imposed by Parliament over 60 years ago and with advances in medical technology this requirement does not now accord with reality. The case of C v S (1987) addressed the issue in the context of a pregnancy of between 18 and 21 weeks. The mother wished to have an abortion and the father, who was not married to the mother, sought to prevent her by maintaining that a termination would breach the provisions of the IL(P)A 1929. His contention was that a foetus of between 18 and 21 weeks was capable of being born alive because, to quote Sir John Donaldson's judgment:

> At that stage the cardiac muscle is contracting and a primitive circulation is developing. Thus the foetus could be said to demonstrate real and discernible signs of life.

The Court of Appeal concluded that a foetus at this stage of development 'would be incapable ever of breathing either naturally or with the aid of a ventilator', as the lungs would not be fully developed. Therefore, to abort at this stage would not amount to an offence under the IL(P)A 1929.

In *Rance v Mid Downs Health Authority* (1991), Brooke J was of the opinion:

> The anencephalic child (who lacks all or most of the cerebral hemispheres but is capable of using its lungs) and the spina bifida child ... is each born alive, if, after birth, it exists as a live child, that is to say breathing and living by reason of its breathing through its own lungs alone, without deriving any of its living or power of living by or through any connection with its mother. Once a foetus has reached that stage of development in the womb that it is capable, if born, of possessing those attributes, it is capable of being born alive within the meaning of the IL(P)A 1929.

It was held that a child of 26–27 weeks' gestation, who could have breathed unaided for up to three hours, was, in law, capable of being born alive.

The Abortion Act (AA) 1967 permits abortion provided that the pregnancy has not extended beyond 24 weeks and for the purposes of calculating the period the AA 1967 offers no legal guidance as to when a pregnancy is deemed to have begun. For the purposes of the IL(P)A 1929, a foetus which is between the 24th and 28th week of gestation may still be regarded as being capable of being born alive by reference to the criteria outlined in *C v S* and *Rance*.

It will be apparent that the offence of child destruction is closely bound up with two other pieces of legislation. The OAPA 1861 makes it an offence to attempt to procure a miscarriage (s 58), and the AA 1967 establishes that doctors carrying out abortions will not fall foul of s 58 providing they are complying with the terms of the AA 1967. The AA 1967 was amended by the Human Fertilisation and Embryology Act (HFEA) 1990 to the effect that an offence under the IL(P)A 1929 will not be committed providing the registered medical practitioner is terminating the pregnancy in accordance with the provisions of the AA 1967. Thus, if acting lawfully under the terms of the AA 1967, a doctor causes the death of a child capable of being born alive, then the IL(P)A 1929 will not be breached. A jury may return a verdict of guilty of the s 58 of the OAPA 1861 offence on an indictment for child destruction.

It is not an offence under s 1 of the IL(P)A 1929 if the act which caused the death was done in good faith and with the purpose only of preserving the life of the mother. Authority as to the meaning of the words 'preserving the life of the mother' is difficult to discover. In *Bourne* (1939), the defendant performed an operation terminating the pregnancy of a 14 year old girl who had become pregnant as a result of a terrifying rape. The operation was performed with the consent of the child's parents. Evidence was given by the doctor that he genuinely believed that the continuance of the pregnancy would probably cause serious injury to the girl and that he was acting to save the life of the mother. M'Naghten J took the view that the jury was entitled to conclude that the offence had not been committed if the defendant believed 'that the probable consequence of the continuance of the pregnancy will be to make the woman a physical or mental wreck'. Ashworth J, in *Newton and Stungo* (1958), also concluded that, when considering whether the act was done for the purpose of preserving the life of the mother, the impact on either physical or mental health or both could be taken into account. Preserving life has therefore been given a wider meaning that of preserving the health, physical or mental, of the mother.

Note that the offence under s 58 is complete once there is an attempt to procure a miscarriage. The offence of child destruction requires the death of the child capable of being born alive.

Reference should be had to the terms of the AA 1967, as amended by s 37 of the HFEA 1990.

6.10.1 Draft Criminal Code

The draft Criminal Code endorses the current legislative position regarding child destruction and proposes cl 69:

(1) A person is guilty of child destruction if he intentionally causes the death of a child capable of being born alive before the child has an existence independent of his mother, unless the act which causes death is done in good faith for the purpose only of preserving the life of the mother.

(2) The fact that a woman had at any material time been pregnant for 28 weeks or more is *prima facie* proof that she was at that time pregnant of a child capable of being born alive.

HOMICIDE

This chapter has discussed the law relating to the offences of murder and manslaughter, infanticide, child destruction. It has also drawn attention to the role of the special defences of provocation and diminished responsibility and makes passing reference to the legal position of those who fail to carry through the agreement at the centre of a suicide pact.

Murder

Murder requires malice aforethought which is simply the intention to kill or the intention to cause grievous bodily harm. The killing of a human being with the requisite intent will result in a conviction for murder assuming that the prosecution is able to establish that the accused caused the *actus reus*. There is no longer any need to prove that death occurred within a year and a day of the incident relied upon as establishing the *actus reus*.

Note that, providing a child has been born alive and taken at least one breath independently from its mother, it is in law a human being and can therefore be the victim in respect of a homicide, even though the injuries which resulted in death were sustained while still in the womb.

Voluntary manslaughter

Voluntary manslaughter refers to the special defences in ss 2, 3 and 4 of the HA 1957, that is, diminished responsibility, provocation and suicide pacts. These defences apply only on a charge of murder and if successful reduce any conviction to one of manslaughter.

Provocation

Provocation is currently a controversial defence and has come under scrutiny for two major reasons. The first is the requirement that provocation should require evidence of an immediate loss of self-control. The second is the requirement that the effect of the provocation should be assessed by reference to how the reasonable man would respond. The courts allow a number of characteristics of an accused to be bestowed on the reasonable man arguably making the assessment increasingly subjective. The relationship between provocation and diminished responsibility has recently come under scrutiny in the context of whether a defendant suffering from an abnormality of mind should rely on s 2 or s 3 for a defence.

Diminished responsibility

Diminished responsibility should be considered along with other defences relating to the mind, that is, insanity and automatism. The abnormality of mind must have substantially impaired the defendant's responsibility for this actions.

Involuntary manslaughter

Involuntary manslaughter refers to unlawful act manslaughter and manslaughter caused by recklessness or gross negligence. The Law Commission report, *Legislating the Criminal Code: Involuntary Manslaughter* (Law Com 237, 1996), outlines the reasons why radical reform is needed and proposes new offences including one of corporate killing. In broad terms, this category of homicide will cover all those situations which result in death but the accused does not possess malice aforethought (excluding, of course, pure accidents where there is no culpability).

Infanticide and child destruction

Infanticide and child destruction are statutory offences. The former offence is a recognition that society should seek to be compassionate when a mother kills her child within a year of birth while suffering from post-natal depression or some other form of illness which causes the balance of her mind to be disturbed. The latter seeks to protect foetuses capable of being born alive. Note the rebuttable presumption that a child is only capable of being born alive after the 28th week of gestation.

Remember to cross-refer to various clauses in the draft Criminal Code.

CHAPTER 7

GENERAL DEFENCES

In the last chapter, certain special defences such as provocation and diminished responsibility were examined. In this chapter attention is focused on the defences which do not relate to specific crimes such as homicide but have a relevance to crimes in general. Most academic commentators and the Law Commission's draft Criminal Code emphasise the twin themes of justification and excuse as a basis for the existence of most defences. In the former case, it is argued that although the accused possessed the *mens rea* for the offence and caused the *actus reus* there is a justification which should preclude a conviction. A good illustration is where the accused pleads self-defence. Imagine the case of a defendant (D), who, returning home after an enjoyable evening at the theatre, finds himself confronted with a gang of would be robbers who have entered his property and are holding his wife hostage. He is threatened that unless he reveals the whereabouts of the key to his safe his wife will have her throat cut. He refuses and one of the men moves menacingly towards his wife and as he does so pulls a knife from his pocket. D picks up a poker from the hearth and hits one of the robbers over the head killing him instantly. The second robber seeks to escape but is pursued and caught. It transpires that both men were carrying knives. Is it really accurate to say that D has engaged in wrongful conduct? Would ordinary people regard with abhorrence the action that D took upon himself? Should he not be applauded for seeking to protect his wife from a potentially murderous attack? His conduct should not be regarded as unlawful. He was justified in taking the action he did.

Where excuse is pleaded by way of defence, the accused does not deny causing either the *actus reus* or possessing the requisite *mens rea*, but seeks to deny culpability and thus be excused from the consequences, because, for example, he was intoxicated at the time of the act. The consequence of raising a successful defence, upon whichever basis, is an acquittal. This may lead one to conclude that it is unnecessary to perpetuate the distinction between excuse and justification if the outcome is the same. However, there are reasons why the distinction should be preserved. One key issue centres on the crime of aiding and abetting. Assume in our example above that D and a friend (A) had returned from the theatre and found D's wife held hostage. D attacks the robbers and calls upon his friend to assist. Providing D's actions were deemed appropriate in the circumstances the friend would not become liable for aiding and abetting the killing. D's action is lawful and it is not a crime to abet a lawful activity! Let us now assume that A visits D's house and discovers D attacking his wife. D calls on A to assist him. A who has never liked D's wife does so and she is severely injured. It transpires that D is, unknown to A, suffering from a mental disorder and successfully pleads the defence of insanity. There is no reason why A should not be convicted of aiding and abetting or, for that matter, convicted in his own right of causing grievous bodily harm, subject to the rules of causation (see Chapter 4 and the decision in *Cogan and Leak* (1975)).

7.1   Insanity

The point in contention at a limited number of trials is whether an accused acted as he did because he was suffering from a mental disorder or acting as an automaton where the mind does not control the body. Automatism was considered in Chapter 2, and insanity will be discussed in this chapter. By pleading insanity, one is seeking to deny responsibility for the crime by reference to one's mental condition at the time of committing the *actus reus*, that is, one is seeking to be excused the consequences of one's actions. Additionally, doubts may be cast over a defendant's mental capacity at the time of the trial leading to a finding that he is unfit to plead.

7.1.1   Prior to the trial

As indicated above, insanity may be an issue at the outset of the trial, in that the accused may seek to establish that he is unfit to plead to the charge. The relevant law is to be found in s 4 of the Criminal Procedure (Insanity) Act (CP(I)A) 1964, as substituted by s 2 of the Criminal Procedure (Insanity and Unfitness to Plead) Act (CP(IUP)A) 1991. The question of fitness to be tried is determined by the jury. If the trial proceeds, that is, the jury finds that the accused is fit to plead and stand trial, then another jury has to be empanelled. Section 4(2) makes it clear that the judge may defer a decision on the mental disability of the accused 'until any time up to the opening of the case for the defence'. The issue of fitness to be tried must be determined as soon as it arises. The jury is not entitled to make a determination except on the written or oral evidence of two or more registered medical practitioners and at least one must have been approved by the Secretary of State as having special expertise in the field of mental disorders.

In *Podola* (1960), the accused had been indicted for murder. He claimed that he was unfit to plead owing to loss of memory of events prior to and at the time of the alleged homicide. The jury found that his memory loss was not genuine and he was eventually found guilty of murder. The Home Secretary referred the issue of fitness to plead to the Court of Criminal Appeal. It will be apparent that this case was judged not by reference to the CP(I)A 1964 but its predecessor the Criminal Lunatics Act (CLA) 1800. The relevant words were:

... if any person indicted for any offence shall be insane, and shall upon arraignment be found so to be by a jury lawfully empanelled for that purpose, so that such person cannot be tried upon such indictment ...

The appellant was perfectly capable of pleading to the charge, was able to follow the evidence and could exercise his right to challenge jurors. The crux of the matter was 'where there was the partial obliteration of memory ... a prisoner could not make a proper defence and could not "comprehend" the details of the evidence ...'. The court held that the appeal should be dismissed. The accused's amnesia in respect of the period when the alleged offence took place would not necessarily prevent the accused receiving a fair trial providing he was thereafter of normal mental capacity. The CLA 1800 was superseded by the CP(I)A 1964 which does not refer to the word 'insane' but the decision in *Podola* would appear to remain good law.

Even if an accused is found unfit to plead, the court must determine whether or not he has actually committed the *actus reus* of the offence charged. To do otherwise would run the risk of incarcerating a defendant who was wholly innocent of the charge alleged. Any doubt as to the correctness of this approach was dispelled by the House of Lords in *Antoine* (2000). The accused had been found unfit to plead in respect of charges of murder and manslaughter and a second jury was empanelled, under the terms of s 4 of the CP(I)A 1964, as amended by the CP(IUP)A 1991, to assess whether or not the accused had committed the acts alleged. The question arose as to whether or not, in the course of this hearing, he could put forward the defence of diminished responsibility. Confirming that this was not possible, the decision of the House of Lords stresses that such a hearing is concerned with whether or not the prohibited act has been caused by the accused. Diminished responsibility, relating as it does to *mens rea*, is therefore not in issue. To the extent that it appeared to suggest a contrary conclusion, the earlier decision of the Court of Appeal in *Egan* (1996), was to be disregarded.

Similar issues will arise where the accused, although fit to plead, claims that he was suffering from insanity at the time of the offence. The Court of Appeal's ruling in *AG's Reference (No 3 of 1998)* (1999), expressly affirmed by the House of Lords in *Antoine*, was to the effect that a special verdict could be returned provided there was evidence that D had committed the *actus reus* of the offence charged (see the Trial of Lunatics Act 1883).

If the accused is found unfit to plead and the jury concludes that the accused did the act or omission which forms the basis of the charge, then the court may deal with the accused by making an admission order to a suitable hospital, a guardianship order under the Mental Health Act (MHA) 1983, a supervision or treatment order or an absolute discharge.

7.1.2   At the trial

An examination of some of the case law cited in Chapter 2 indicates that defendants often go to great lengths to avoid pleading insanity and risking committal to a special hospital. The consequence of the trial judge's ruling in *Quick and Padisson* (1973) that insanity not automatism was the appropriate defence, was a change of plea from not guilty to guilty in order to avoid the stigma or consequences of being found not guilty by reason of insanity. The CP(IUP)A 1991, now gives the court a wider range of powers of disposal except where the penalty is fixed by law, as in murder, when a hospital order must be made. However, the insanity plea is not widely used, as RD Mackay pointed out in his article, 'Fact and fiction about the insanity defence' ([1990] Crim LR 247). If the insanity defence proves successful, a special verdict is returned that the accused is not guilty by reason of insanity. The court possesses the following powers:

- to order that the accused be admitted to a hospital;

- to make a guardianship order within the meaning of the MHA 1983;

- to make a supervision and treatment order within the meaning of Sched 2 to the CP(IUP)A 1991;

- to order an absolute discharge.

7.1.3   *M'Naghten* Rules

The legal rules relating to an insanity plea are to be found in the *M'Naghten* Rules of 1843. Daniel M'Naghten was in that year acquitted because of his mental condition at the time he shot Sir Robert Peel's secretary. This generated extensive debate in the legislative chamber of the House of Lords, culminating in the House of Lords inviting judges of the common law courts to answer five questions on the topic of insanity as a defence to a criminal charge. The result was the *M'Naghten* Rules:

> ... the jurors ought to be told in all cases that every man is presumed to be sane, and to possess a sufficient degree of reason to be responsible for his crimes, until the contrary be proved to their satisfaction; and that to establish a defence on the ground of insanity, it must be clearly proved that, at the time of the committing of the act, the party was labouring under a defect of reason, from disease of the mind, as not to know the nature and quality of the act he was doing; or, if he did know it, that he did not know he was doing what was wrong.

The advent of the special defence of diminished responsibility which is available only to those charged with murder (see above, Chapter 6) and the abolition of the death penalty has resulted in little use being made of the Rules but this does not mean to suggest that they are redundant.

Despite their antiquity, the Rules received endorsement from Lord Diplock in *Sullivan* (1983) when he said: 'The *M'Naghten* Rules have been used as a comprehensive definition for this purpose by the courts for the last 140 years.'

Sullivan is a significant case which highlighted once again the dilemma faced by a defendant whose attempt to establish a defence of automatism fails. Sullivan suffered from epilepsy. There had been a period in his life when he was subject to major seizures but medication had lessened their intensity and at the time of the relevant conduct he was proved to suffer minor seizures known as *petit mal*, perhaps once or twice each week. On the day in question, he was chatting to elderly neighbours when he was suddenly overcome by a seizure. One of the neighbours, a Mr Payne, aged 80, was kicked by the appellant and required hospital treatment. The prosecution accepted that the defendant had no recollection of the events but the trial judge ruled that his defence was one of insanity and not automatism, which Sullivan's counsel had wished to establish. As a consequence of that ruling, the defendant pleaded guilty to assault occasioning actual bodily harm. He appealed against the judge's ruling. Lord Diplock, in giving the decision of the House of Lords, considered that the word 'mind' in the Rules 'is used in the ordinary sense of the mental faculties of reason, memory and understanding'. Therefore:

> If the effect of a disease is to impair these faculties so severely as to have either of the consequences referred to in the latter part of the Rules, it matters not whether the aetiology of the impairment is organic, as in epilepsy, or functional, or where the impairment itself is permanent or transient and intermittent, provided that it subsisted at the time of the commission of the act.

Lord Diplock ended his speech by saying: 'Sympathise though I do with the appellant, I see no other course open to your Lordships than to dismiss this appeal.'

7.1.4 The nature and quality of the act

The second part of the *M'Naghten* Rules refers to the nature and quality of the act. In *Codere* (1916), it was held that these words refer to the physical, as opposed to the moral or legal quality of the act. The remaining element applies in circumstances where the defendant knows the nature and quality of his act but does not know that it is wrong to act in such a manner. In *Codere*, it was suggested that the test should be based upon the 'ordinary standard adopted by a reasonable man', in circumstances where he was unaware that his act was contrary to the law of the land. In *Windle* (1952), the accused had killed his wife by giving her a fatal dose of aspirin tablets. The report indicates that his wife was some 18 years older than her husband and that she was probably certifiably insane and constantly talked about committing suicide. Her husband endured a miserable existence until he decided to kill her. After the event he apparently told police that 'he supposed he would be hanged for it'.

This statement indicated that he knew his actions were contrary to law. He had raised insanity as a defence but Devlin J at Birmingham Assizes had withdrawn it from the jury. The Court of Criminal Appeal held that he was correct to do so. Lord Goddard CJ put it this way:

> The question ... in all cases is one of responsibility. A man may be suffering from a defect of reason, but, if he knows that what he is doing is wrong – and by 'wrong' I mean contrary to law – he is responsible.

He went on to reject the notion that 'wrong' had some qualified meaning such as 'morally' wrong.

The case for a review of the defence, given that it is now over 150 years since the questions posed to the judges were answered, is strong albeit few defendants resort to using it. The Butler Committee on Mentally Abnormal Offenders (Cmnd 6244, 1975) suggested that the word 'insanity' should be dropped in favour of 'mental disorder'. It recommended that a verdict of 'not guilty by reason of mental disorder' should be introduced where the mental disorder prevented the defendant from forming the requisite *mens rea* for the offence and secondly where the defendant was aware of what he was doing but it was medically proved he was suffering from a mental disorder.

7.1.5 Draft Criminal Code

The draft Criminal Code pursues the idea of the defence being based upon proof of a mental disorder. Clause 34 defines 'mental disorder' in these terms:

(a) severe mental illness; or

(b) a state of arrested or incomplete development of mind; or

(c) a state of automatism (not resulting only from intoxication) which is a feature of a disorder whether organic or functional and whether continuing or recurring, that may cause a similar state on another occasion.

Clause 35 establishes the basis of the proposed defence:

> A mental disorder verdict shall be returned if the defendant is proved to have committed an offence but it is proved on the balance of probabilities (whether by the prosecution or by the defendant) that he was at the time suffering from severe mental illness or severe mental handicap ...
>
> (2) Sub-section (1) does not apply if the court or jury is satisfied beyond reasonable doubt that the offence was not attributable to the severe mental illness or severe mental handicap.
>
> (3) A court or jury shall not, for the purposes of the verdict under sub-s (1) find that the defendant was suffering from severe mental illness or severe mental handicap unless two medical practitioners approved for the purposes of s 12 of the MHA 1983 as having special experience in the diagnosis or treatment of mental disorder have given evidence that he was so suffering.

Severe mental illness is defined in Clause 34 as including one or more of the following:

(i) lasting impairment of intellectual functions shown by failure of memory, orientation, comprehension and learning capacity;

(ii) lasting alteration of mood of such degree as to give rise to delusional appraisal of the defendant's situation, his past or his future or that of others, or lack of any approval;

(iii) delusional beliefs, persecutory, jealous or grandiose;

(iv) abnormal perceptions associated with delusional misinterpretation of events;

(v) thinking so disordered as to prevent reasonable appraisal of the defendant's situation or reasonable communication with others.

'Severe mental handicap' means a state of arrested or incomplete development of mind which includes severe impairment of intelligence and social functioning.

Clause 35 is designed to cover the second limb of the *M'Naghten* Rules, that is, the defendant who knows the nature and quality of his act but does not know that it is wrong. Clause 36 covers the nature and quality 'limb'. This clause makes it clear that it is the fault element which is lacking and if this is proved on the balance of probabilities to be a result of the defendant suffering from mental disorder at the time of the act then he would be entitled to the 'special' verdict.

7.1.6   The burden of proof in respect of insanity

The burden of proof is upon the accused based upon the balance of probabilities. Normally, it is for the prosecution to prove its case beyond all reasonable doubt but the *M'Naghten* Rules state that in the case of insanity the burden of proof is on the defence. As Viscount Kilmuir LC said in *Bratty v AG for Northern Ireland*:

> To establish the defence of insanity within the *M'Naghten* Rules the accused must prove on the preponderance of probabilities first a defect of reason from a disease of the mind, and, secondly, as a consequence of such a defect, ignorance of the nature and quality (or the wrongfulness) of the acts.

In respect of the first limb of the Rules, it is a moot point whether the common law presumption placing the burden of proof on the defence is strictly necessary. The burden of proof in criminal cases is on the prosecution. If it fails to establish beyond all reasonable doubt that the accused had the requisite *mens rea* for the crime, then the case fails. It would appear unnecessary for the defence to have to disprove a fact which clearly falls, in the overwhelming majority of cases, within the ambit of the prosecution.

Yet, if one considers the second limb of the Rules, there is a clear case for placing the obligation on the defence to establish that the accused did not know that the nature and quality of the act or that it was wrong. This is because it is not part of the prosecution's role in criminal law to prove that the accused knew, for example, that the act was wrong. The obligation is to prove that the accused intended or was reckless to the consequence or circumstance as defined by the requirements of the offence. It is also open to either the judge or the prosecution to raise the defence of insanity. On the evidence, the prosecution may wish to allege that the accused is insane as an alternative to the accused raising the defence of automatism. In this situation, both defences may be left to the jury and the burden of proof in respect of insanity falls upon the prosecution.

It is worth adding that insanity will not be a defence unless a guilty intent is an essential element of the offence. If the offence, for example, driving with excess alcohol, is one of strict liability, there being no requirement for *mens rea*, then insanity is not available as a defence. In *DPP v H* (1997), the defendant suffered from manic depressive psychosis an illness which involved symptoms of distorted judgment and impaired sense of time and morals. On the day of the offence, the accused had been behaving irrationally. The court held that he was not entitled to plead insanity as the offence under s 59(1)(a) of the Road Traffic Act (RTA) 1988 was one of strict liability.

7.2   Infancy

Harper J, in *R (A Child) v Whitty* (1993) began his judgment with these words:

> 'No civilised society,' says Professor Colin Howard 'regards children as accountable for their actions to the same extent as adults'. The wisdom of protecting young children against the full rigour of the criminal law is beyond argument. The difficulty lies in determining when and under what circumstances that protection should be removed.

Do children have the capacity to appreciate fully the consequences of their actions and that they may lead to the committing of a criminal offence? Age is a relevant factor in other areas of law, for example a person under the age of 16 does not have the legal capacity to contract a valid marriage. The answer to the question is obviously yes, depending one suspects, on the age of the child. The levels of understanding of seven and 17 year olds differ enormously and the criminal law seeks to reflect this in its approach to criminal responsibility and fault for those who have not reached the age of majority.

7.2.1   Terminology and trial

The various statutes which make provision for young people use different terminology for example, 'juvenile', 'young person', 'child', 'young offender'.

In the criminal law context, the great majority of juveniles are now tried in youth courts, formerly known as juvenile courts (s 70 of the Criminal Justice Act (CJA) 1991). These are courts of summary jurisdiction. However, if the juvenile is charged with a serious offence, the magistrates may decline jurisdiction and the case will be remitted to the Crown Court for trial. The limited circumstances where a juvenile may be tried on indictment are to be found in s 24 of the Magistrates' Courts Act 1980 (as amended by the Criminal Justice and Public Order Act 1994):

(1) Where a person under the age of 18 appears or is brought before a magistrates' court on an information charging him with an indictable offence other than homicide, he shall be tried summarily unless:

(a) he has attained the age of 14 and the offence is such as is mentioned in sub-s (2) of s 53 of the Children and Young Persons Act 1933 (under which young persons convicted on indictment of certain grave crimes may be sentenced to be detained for long periods) and the court considers that if he is found guilty of the offence it ought to be possible to sentence him in pursuance of that sub-section; or

(b) he is jointly charged with a person who has attained the age of 18 and the court considers it necessary in the interests of justice to commit them both for trial; and accordingly in a case falling within para (a) or (b) of this sub-section the court shall commit the accused for trial if either it is of the opinion that there is sufficient evidence to put him on trial or it has power under s 6(2) above so to commit him without consideration of the evidence.

(2) Where, in a case falling within sub-s (1)(b) above, a magistrates' court commits a person under the age of 18 for trial for an offence with which he is charged jointly with a person who has attained that age, the court may also commit him for trial for any other indictable offence with which he is charged at the same time (whether jointly with the person who has attained that age or not) if the charges for both offences could be joined in the same indictment.

In *T v UK; V v UK* (1999), the European Court of Human Rights held that the practice of trying juveniles in adult courts could involve, and had done so in these particular cases, violations of the defendants' rights under the European Convention on Human Rights, notably, the right to a fair trial guaranteed by Art 6. The Court found that the defendants had not been able to communicate effectively with their legal advisers due to the trauma of the proceedings and that some measures taken to help the defendants', such as providing a raised dock area, simply exacerbated their sense of being on show to the public. The response to this ruling has taken the form of a Practice Direction (*Practice Direction (Crown Court: Trial of Children and Young Persons)* (2000)). This provides that all efforts should be made to ensure that attendance at such trials is strictly limited; that a timetable is agreed to ensure that young defendants can concentrate on events at the trial and follow what is happening; and that the trial should be conducted with the minimum level of formality consistent with a fair procedure. Whether these measure satisfy the requirement of the European Convention on Human Rights in practice remains to be seen.

7.2.2 Under 10 years of age

A child under the age of 10 is irrebuttably presumed incapable of criminal fault, irrespective of whether or not the *actus reus* was committed with the relevant *mens rea*. The child is said to be *doli incapax*. A child under 10 will be absolved of all criminal responsibility for his actions but civil proceedings may be commenced by the local authority under s 31 of the Children Act (CA) 1989 if, as a result of his behaviour, the relevant sections of the CA 1989 are satisfied. It should, however, be noted that simply because a child has committed a 'crime' does not mean the child will automatically be taken into care. The CA 1989 makes the welfare of the child the paramount consideration and it will have to be shown that the child is suffering, or is likely to suffer, significant harm and the harm or likelihood of harm is attributable to lack of parental care or control. Evidence, therefore, that a child is engaged in criminal activities may be used to establish that harm is being suffered through the inattention or indifference of the parents.

The minimum age for attracting criminal responsibility has been fixed at seven, eight and 10 during this century and it may be that, in light of well publicised cases involving young children, the age of responsibility should be reviewed again. It must be emphasised that, whatever the consequences, however serious they may be, in law no crime has occurred if the actions were carried out by someone who, at the time of the act, was under 10 years of age.

This is in stark contrast to the law in Scotland. Normal criminal responsibility operates from the age of eight and in the opinion of Lord Jauncey of Tullichettle, 'I do not understand that injustice is considered to have resulted from this situation' (*C v DPP* (1995) (p 45j)).

. In *Walters v Lunt* (1951), a seven year old boy passed on to his parents a tricycle which he had 'stolen'. They were aware of this fact. They were found not guilty of handling stolen goods as the goods could not in law be regarded as being stolen. It would, of course, have been different if they had persuaded or forced their son to take the tricycle. In those circumstances, they would have been acting through an innocent agent and would have become principals to the act of theft.

7.2.3 Over 10 years of age

Following the enactment of s 34 of the Crime and Disorder Act 1998, the law in England and Wales imposes criminal liability (in the sense of culpability) on children aged 10 and above in the same way as it imposes liability on adults.

This major change was achieved with the following words: 'The rebuttable presumption of criminal law that a child aged 10 or over is incapable of committing an offence is hereby abolished.'

As the provision hints, prior to the enactment of s 34 special rules applied to juvenile defendants between the ages of 10 and 14. In essence, no defendant falling within that age range could be convicted of an offence unless the prosecution had been able to prove, in addition to establishing whatever *mens rea* was required by the definition of the offence, that the defendant had acted with what was known as 'mischievous discretion'. According to *Corrie* (1919), this involved proof that the defendant had known that what he was doing was gravely or seriously wrong.

The change to the law brought about by s 34 was heralded by *Codification of the Criminal Law: A Report to the Law Commission* (Law Com 143, 1985), which stated:

> The law at present is that such a child [over 10 but under 14] can be guilty of an offence but only if, in addition to doing the prohibited act with such fault as is required in the case of an adult, he knows that what he is doing is 'seriously wrong'. It is presumed at his trial that he did not have such knowledge, and the prosecution must rebut this presumption by proof beyond reasonable doubt. The presumption, it has been said, 'reflects an outworn mode of thought' and 'is steeped in absurdity'; and it has long been recognised as operating capriciously. Its abolition was proposed in 1960 by the Ingleby Committee on Children and Young Persons. We believe there is no case for its survival in the Code.

Indeed, the move towards the criminalisation of younger defendants can also be found in earlier provisions, such as s 1 of the CJA 1993, which abolished the longstanding presumption that a boy under 14 years of age could not be convicted of the serious offence of rape. There have been a number of convictions since the law was changed.

The House of Lords was presented with the opportunity to alter the law in the way that the 1998 Act now has, in *C v DPP* (1995), but declined to so on the grounds that such a radical change in the law should result not from judicial decision making, but rather from parliamentary intervention, should it be accepted that such a change of policy was desirable.

Notwithstanding that the special provision for defendants between the ages of 10 and 14 has now been removed by the 1998 Act, debate continues as to whether it is fair and appropriate to impose criminal liability at such a young age. Laws J, when *C v DPP* was before the Divisional Court, cited the following reasons for abolishing the doctrine of 'mischievous discretion':

- children grow up more quickly now than at any time in our history;

- the presumption was out of step with the general law;

- the phrase 'seriously wrong' was conceptually obscure;

- the rule is illogical because the rule can be rebutted by proof that the child was of normal mental capacity for his age;

- the need for the prosecutor to rebut the presumption may give rise to injustice where the rebuttal involves proving previous convictions.

Blackstone (4 BI Corn, 22nd edn, pp 23–24) said 'the capacity of doing ill, or contracting guilt, is not so much measured by years and days, as by the strength of the delinquent's understanding and judgment'. It may, therefore, be worthwhile giving consideration to the points raised by B Lloyd-Morris and H Mahendra in their article, '*Doli incapax* and mental age' ((1996) 146 NLJ 1622). They argue that in 'normal' children 'mental development keeps pace with physical growth and the passing of years'. They go on:

> However, in children with what are now called learning difficulties or disabilities ... there may be substantial discrepancies between such mental functions as intellectual aptitude or educational attainment and physical attributes as chronological age.

They conclude that mental age is a more reliable index of a child's understanding than chronological age. Whilst the law still regards chronological age as the foundation of the *doli incapax* rule, perhaps it is time for more research to be undertaken on this particular issue.

It is perhaps worth noting that, in *T v UK; V v UK* (1999), the applicants sought, *inter alia*, to argue that the imposition of liability for murder on defendants as young as 10 or 11 amounted to a violation of Art 3 of the European Convention on Human Rights. In rejecting the argument, the Court noted the absence of any common standard amongst other Signatory States. In effect, the rule in England and Wales was regarded as being within the margin of appreciation afforded to each Signatory State.

It should be borne in mind that s 34 places juvenile defendants in the same position as adults only as regards establishing fault. Special procedures and safeguards apply as regards the trial process and the giving of evidence.

7.3   Intoxication

The issue of intoxication may be relevant when seeking to determine the question of whether the accused possessed the *mens rea* necessary for the crime with which he is charged. Evidence of intoxication either from drink or drugs may show quite clearly that the defendant was incapable of forming the *mens rea* or, even though capable, because of intoxication, did not. Intoxication may also lead a person to engage in conduct which he believes, because of his condition, to be lawful when in fact it is not. The inebriated student staggering home from the Union and coming across a group of fellow revellers may believe they are about to attack him. He therefore 'gets in his retaliation first' and assaults one of them believing he is acting in self-defence. Should he be exonerated?

The Court of Appeal in *Bowden* (1993) made it clear that the fundamental question was whether or not the accused possessed the necessary intent for the specific intent crime in question. Hence, in *McKnight* (2000), the fact that the accused had consumed large quantities of alcohol so that he could not remember what he had been doing at the time of the alleged offence was held not to be conclusive proof that he had been 'intoxicated' in the sense that word is used to denote the defence at common law at the time. The degree of intoxication was the key issue. There had to be evidence that he had been prevented from having the required degree of foresight in respect of his actions – in particular, that he had been prevented by the intoxication from foreseeing or knowing what he would have foreseen or known had he been sober.

The fact that an accused has been, without his knowledge, supplied with intoxicants that subsequently lower his inhibitions and lead him to perform criminal acts that he might not have performed had he been sober is again no defence if there is evidence that the accused nevertheless acted with sufficient *mens rea*. The House of Lords in *Kingston* (1994) expressly rejected any suggestions (accepted by the Court of Appeal) that the law should recognise a new defence of 'disinhibition', even though the accused was able to plausibly argue that it was not his 'fault' that he had had the *mens rea*.

Intoxication may also form part of the *actus reus* of an offence, for example, s 3A of the RTA 1988 of causing death by careless driving when under the influence of drink or drugs.

The Law Commission in its Consultation Paper, *Intoxication and Criminal Liability* (Law Com 127, 1993), puts it this way:

> The person who commits criminal acts while he is intoxicated, at least when he is voluntarily so intoxicated, does not therefore appeal to excuse; but rather raises the prior question of whether, because of his intoxicated state, he can be proved to have been in the (subjective) state of mind necessary for liability. Issues of intoxication are, thus, intimately bound up with the prosecution's task of proving primary guilt of the defendant: that he did indeed do the act prohibited by the definition of the offence with the relevant state of mind [para 1.12].

The law has developed, albeit on a piecemeal basis, around two concepts, each of which is difficult to define. The first is specific intent and the second basic intent. As a result, all crimes have to be allocated to one or other of these categories for the purposes of the law on intoxication. The outcome is that defendants relying on voluntary intoxication as a defence to a basic intent crime may be convicted 'notwithstanding that the prosecution has not proved any intention or foresight, or indeed any voluntary act' (Criminal Law Revision Committee, 14th Report, *Offences Against the Person*, Cmnd 7844, 1980, para 257).

The Law Commission in its report, *Legislating the Criminal Code: Offences Against the Person and General Defences* (Law Com 218, 1993), recognised the difficulty:

> There is, however, no agreement as to the criteria by which offences are divided between crimes of basic and of specific intent; and that fact alone makes it impossible to formulate this approach as a general legislative test [para 44.3].

7.3.1 Specific and basic intent crimes

In *DPP v Morgan* (1975), Lord Simon gave the following definition of basic intent crimes:

> By 'crimes of basic intent' I mean those crimes whose definition expresses (or more often, implies) a *mens rea* which does not go beyond the *actus reus* ... I take assault as an example of a basic intent crime where the consequence is very closely connected to the act.

Unfortunately, there is no clear principle which applies to specific intent crimes. Lord Simon in *DPP v Morgan* referred to ulterior intent crimes where the *mens rea* goes beyond the *actus reus* and gave s 18 of the Offences Against the Persons Act (OAPA) 1861 as an example, that is, wounding with intent to cause grievous bodily harm. The *actus reus* is wounding and there must be *mens rea* towards this, but the prosecution must also prove a mental element going beyond the wounding, as Lord Simon puts it, 'it must show that the accused foresaw that serious physical injury would probably be a consequence of his act'. Burglary, contrary to s 9 of the Theft Act 1968, is another example of an ulterior intent crime. The difficulty occurs because, certainly as far as the law on intoxication is concerned, certain crimes which do not accord with this definition have been designated as specific intent crimes. The most obvious example is murder where the *mens rea* does not go beyond the *actus reus*, in which case on Lord Simon's definition it should be categorised as a basic intent crime.

In *Caldwell* (1981), the House of Lords had to decide whether criminal damage was a crime of basic intent and therefore whether or not drunkenness was available as a defence. The majority decided that if the charge was worded so as to clearly indicate that the prosecution sought to prove the defendant intended to destroy or damage property belonging to another, evidence of self-induced intoxication was admissible in his defence. Conversely, if the charge was so framed as to include reference to reckless behaviour, then it would be classed as a basic intent crime and evidence of self-induced intoxication would be inadmissible.

Thus, the law appears to have developed on the strength of that decision although that is to pay little heed to the dissenting voice of Lord Edmund Davies in *Caldwell*. He referred to Professor Glanville Williams's conclusion in his *Textbook of Criminal Law* (1978, London: Stevens, p 431) to the effect that all crimes of recklessness, however serious, will be held to be crimes of basic intent. He concludes, 'It is a very long time since we had so harsh a law in this country' (p 972j). Crimes which include recklessness as part of the definition will be considered to be basic intent crimes and those requiring proof of intent, specific intent crimes. It is suggested that one simply examines the case law on intoxication and attempts to categorise on that basis instead of seeking some overarching principle which differentiates the two types of crime.

The so called specific intent rule emanates from the decision of the House of Lords in *DPP v Beard* (1920). Lord Birkenhead LC, after considering the case law, concluded:

> ... that where a specific intent is an essential element in the offence, evidence of a state of drunkenness rendering the accused incapable of forming such an intent should be taken into consideration in order to determine whether he had in fact formed the intent necessary to constitute the particular crime. If he was so drunk that he was incapable of forming the intent required, he could not be convicted of a crime which was committed only if the intent was proved ...

Lord Birkenhead described the proposition as 'plain beyond question' and, since the unanimous decision of seven Law Lords in *DPP v Majewski* (1976), the specific intent rule is part of our law until Parliament decrees otherwise. However, as Lord Elwyn-Jones LC pointed out in *Majewski*, the position 'becomes less plain in the later passage of his speech'. Lord Birkenhead concluded that what he had previously stated was:

> ... only in accordance with the ordinary law applicable to crime, for, speaking generally (and apart from certain special offences), a person cannot be convicted of a crime unless there was *mens rea*. Drunkenness, rendering a person incapable of the intent, would be an answer, as it is for example in a charge of attempted suicide.

The current position, as a result of *Majewski*, is not in doubt, but the above passage indicates the shaky foundation upon which the specific intent rule is based. *Caldwell* determined that, subject to how the charge is laid, criminal damage may be viewed as a basic or specific intent crime and *Majewski* confirms that assault is a basic intent crime for the purposes of the defence of intoxication.

In *Majewski*, the defendant had attacked the landlord of a public house and after the arrival of a number of police officers at the property had assaulted some of them. Later at the police station he had struck two others. The following morning he attacked a police inspector who had gone into his cell. He was charged with a total of seven counts of assault. At his trial he testified that over the 48 hours culminating on the attack on the publican he had consumed a considerable quantity of drugs and alcohol and that at the time of the attacks he had no idea what he was doing. He claimed to have no recollection of the incidents that had occurred. The trial judge directed the jury to ignore the fact that the defendant had been intoxicated at the time of the disturbances. He was convicted on all seven counts.

Clearly, the defendant had been incapable of forming the *mens rea* for assault which is a crime requiring either intention or recklessness in respect of the *actus reus*. On the basis of the definition offered by Lord Simon in *Morgan* (above), assault is to be regarded as a basic intent crime. He appealed on the basis that, in informing the jury to disregard his intoxicated state, the trial judge had contravened s 8 of the CJA 1967. It will be recalled that s 8 states that a court or jury in determining whether a person has committed an offence:

   (a) shall not be bound in law to infer that he intended or foresaw a result of his actions by reason only of its being a natural and probable consequence of those actions; but

   (b) shall decide whether he did intend or foresee that result by reference to all the evidence, drawing such inferences from the evidence as appears proper in the circumstances.

The appellant's contention was that his state of intoxication was part of 'all the evidence' and should, therefore, have been taken into account. However, as the law stood prior to *Majewski,* assault not being a specific intention crime, it had to be regarded as one of basic intent. Recklessness is part of the *mens rea* of the crime. Thus, to become intoxicated to such a degree should be regarded as evidence of recklessness which should help to convict, rather than exonerate him from the consequences of his actions.

The House of Lords held that s 8 was irrelevant as it dealt only with matters of evidence and the specific and basic intent rules were matters of the substantive law. All seven Law Lords agreed that the specific intent rule should be confirmed and that in crimes of basic intent of which assault was one, the intoxication 'supplies the evidence of *mens rea*', *per* Lord Elwyn Jones LC. He posed the vital question in these terms:

> If a man consciously and deliberately takes alcohol and drugs not on medical prescription, but in order to escape from reality, to go 'on a trip', to become hallucinated, whatever the description may be, and thereby disables himself from taking the care he might otherwise take and as a result by his subsequent actions causes injury to another – does our criminal law enable him to say that because he did not know what he was doing he lacked both intention and recklessness and accordingly is entitled to an acquittal?

Lord Elwyn-Jones having reviewed the major authorities (*Beard* (1920); *AG for Northern Ireland v Gallagher* (1963); and *Bratty* (1963)) concluded that intoxication was relevant only to specific intent crimes. He cited Lord Denning's statement in *Bratty*:

> If the drunken man is so drunk that he does not know what he is doing, he has a defence to any charge, such as murder or wounding with intent, in which a specific intent is essential, but he is still liable to be convicted of manslaughter or unlawful wounding for which no specific intent is necessary ...

... I do not for my part regard that general principle as either unethical or contrary to the principles of natural justice. If a man of his own volition takes a substance which causes him to cast off the restraints of reason and conscience, no wrong is done to him by holding him answerable criminally for any injury he may do while in that condition. His course of conduct in reducing himself by drugs and drink to that condition in my view supplies the evidence of *mens rea*, of guilty mind certainly sufficient for crimes of basic intent. It is a reckless course of conduct and recklessness is enough to constitute the necessary *mens rea* in assault cases: see *Venna* (1975) *per* James LJ. The drunkenness is itself an intrinsic, an integral part of the crime, the other part being the evidence of the unlawful use of force against the victim. Together they add up to criminal recklessness.

Support for this view was found in the US Model Penal Code:

When recklessness establishes an element of the offence, if the actor, due to self-induced intoxication, is unaware of a risk of which he would have been aware had he been sober, such unawareness is immaterial.

The outcome as Lord Salmon said in *Majewski* may 'not comply with strict logic' (because after all these are *mens rea* crimes) but 'this rule accords with justice, ethics and common sense, and I would leave it alone' (p 159c).

Further support for this distinction in approach to specific and basic intent crimes comes from Lord Mustill in *Kingston* (1994):

As to proof of intent, it appears that at least in some instances self-induced intoxication can be taken into account as part of the evidence from which the jury draws its conclusions; but that in others it cannot. I express the matter in this guarded way because it has not yet been decisively established whether for this purpose there is a line to be drawn between offences of 'specific' intent. That in at least some cases a defendant cannot say that he was so drunk that he could not form the required intent is however clear enough. Why is this so? The answer must, I believe, be the same as that given in other common law jurisdictions; namely that such evidence is excluded as a matter of policy' [p 364c].

There would appear to be two reasons underpinning this policy. The first is to regard intentional drunkenness as a substitute for the mental element ordinarily required by the offence. The second supports the view that a person should not be able to rely on the absence of a mental element when that has occurred as a result of his own voluntary actions.

The impact of this rule is that the voluntary consumption of alcohol or dangerous drugs to an excessive degree will be presumed to be reckless behaviour and as a result relieve from the prosecution the burden of proving recklessness. As we have seen the law recognises two types of recklessness, *Caldwell* and *Cunningham*. In the former, a person can be deemed to have been reckless as a result of failing to consider the risk or risks associated with the particular course of conduct. Intoxication in such circumstances is totally irrelevant. There is little point trying to establish lack of foresight when none needs to be proved. However, what if the accused does give thought to the element of risk but because of his intoxicated state concludes wrongly there is nothing which ought to prevent him from proceeding? The answer would appear to be that he would have no defence. *Majewski* is absolutely clear on the point. Under consideration is a basic intent crime and evidence of intoxication is irrelevant to the issue of *mens rea*.

What should be borne in mind, however, is the proposition that (assuming an offence requires proof of *Cunningham* recklessness) D should not be convicted of a basic intent crime, even where his intoxication is voluntary, if there is evidence that he would not have been aware of the risk in question even if he had been sober. This proposition was cited with approval by the Court of Appeal in *Richardson and Irwin* (1999), and is recited in cl 22 of the draft Criminal Code Bill (see below, 7.3.6) and the US Model Penal Code (see above).

7.3.2 Dangerous and non-dangerous drugs

As a consequence of two decisions in the early 1980s it is necessary to consider drugs as falling into two categories; those which are 'dangerous' and those which are not, that is, do not lead to aggressive or unpredictable behavioural patterns. In *Hardie* (1984), the accused was in a distressed state because his domestic arrangements had broken down and he had been asked by the woman with whom he had cohabited for nearly a decade to leave their home. He admitted taking a limited number of valium tablets which had been prescribed for his former partner. He expected that the tablets would have calmed him down. In fact it resulted in him displaying signs of intoxication and eventually setting fire to a wardrobe at their flat. He claimed to have no memory of the event. He was charged with criminal damage. The trial judge had ruled that because the defendant had voluntarily taken the drug then he could not use intoxication as a defence. He was convicted. The Court of Appeal took a different view. It confirmed that the 'basic intent rule would apply in circumstances where the intoxication resulted from the introduction into the body of alcohol or dangerous drugs'. However, the court recognised that 'intoxication or similar symptoms may arise in other circumstances' from those which would conclusively indicate reckless behaviour on the part of the accused. It was suggested that the taking of a sedative or soporific drug would therefore not automatically rule out the availability of a defence in the case of basic intent crimes, because their consumption alone without more would not indicate a defendant was reckless. The court was adamant, however, that the consumption of any drugs prior to driving would never be a defence to a charge of reckless driving (now, of course, dangerous driving).

In *Bailey* (1983), a diabetic had failed to take sufficient food after taking a normal dose of insulin and had struck his victim over the head with an iron bar. He was charged with offences contrary to ss 18 and 20 of the OAPA 1861. The trial judge ruled that his defence of automatism based upon hypoglycaemia was not available on either count because it was self-induced. This was clearly incorrect in respect of the s 18 offence which is regarded as a specific intent crime. The accused had failed to take food after drinking a mixture of sugar and water. In respect of the s 20 offence (a crime of basic intent), the Court of Appeal also found for the appellant. Self-induced automatism could be a defence in circumstances where the condition had arisen other than from intoxication due to alcohol or drugs. To consume alcohol or dangerous drugs would be regarded as reckless conduct, whereas in this case it could not be presumed to be reckless conduct to fail to take food after a dose of insulin. As Griffiths LJ put it:

> The question in each case will be whether the prosecution has proved the necessary element of recklessness. If the accused knows that his actions or inaction are likely to make him aggressive, unpredictable or uncontrolled with the result that he may cause some injury to the others and he persists in the action or takes no remedial action when he knows it is required, it will be open to the jury to find that he was reckless.

In essence, what is being said is that the defendant became involuntarily intoxicated and therefore the vital evidence of culpability is absent. It should not matter whether this involuntary intoxication results from another's actions or where the defendant, as in *Hardie*, makes an 'innocent' (or non-reckless?) mistake as to the consequences of his actions. One might query whether *Hardie* should not be regarded as *Caldwell* reckless, as that case was one of criminal damage. Was it not the case that he failed to give thought to the consequences of taking drugs prescribed for someone else? If so, then he was *Caldwell* reckless if ordinary people in a similar position would have given thought to the possible outcome of taking the drugs. Conversely, it could be regarded as a lacuna case, where he addressed the issue and concluded that, given the nature of the drugs, they would not have any adverse effect on him.

The law on involuntary intoxication was reviewed by the House of Lords in *Kingston* (1994). It was not prepared to recognise a defence of exculpatory excuse since the absence of moral fault was not sufficient to negative the *mens rea* of an offence. In circumstances were a person unwittingly became intoxicated as a result of another's actions, the only question was whether at the time of committing the offence the defendant possessed the necessary *mens rea*. The reasons for getting into that condition would be for mitigation not liability. So, involuntary intoxication is not a defence to a criminal charge where there is evidence of *mens rea*. Conversely, if, as a result of the involuntary intoxication, the defendant was incapable of forming the necessary intent and therefore did not possess the *mens rea*, then the offence could not be made out. Arguably, this should apply to both basic and specific intent crimes. In the former case, the recklessness required for the offence is established as a result of the voluntary intoxication of the accused. That provides the necessary fault and is according to Lord Mustill 'substituted' for actual evidence of recklessness. However, if the defendant is completely unaware that his lemonade, for example, has been 'spiked' and as a result becomes intoxicated there is no element of fault present and he deserves to have his defence of lack of *mens rea* recognised as a defence to a basic intent crime. It would be anomalous to do otherwise particularly as *Hardie* permits a jury to consider the behaviour of the defendant in cases of voluntary consumption of non-dangerous drugs. In the latter case, the specific intent rule will apply and the only question will be did the accused possess the *mens rea* for the offence?

7.3.3   Application of the law

The basic strategy is to attempt to negative the *mens rea* required for specific intent crimes. As we have seen (above) and, as was pointed out in *Cole* (1993), the true question for the jury is whether the accused actually formed the intent, not whether he or she was capable of forming the intent. Proof that a defendant was capable of forming the *mens rea* does not mean that he or she actually did form the required intent.

The decision when to consume alcohol or to take drugs is also a relevant consideration in respect of the defence of intoxication. Therefore, if there is evidence that the intent was formed prior to the consumption of alcohol or dangerous drugs, then there are *dicta* to suggest that the defendant cannot rely on his drunken state in order to establish a defence. In *AG for Northern Ireland v Gallagher* (1963), Lord Denning referred to what has become known as the 'Dutch courage situation'. The accused had made up his mind to kill his wife. He bought a knife and a bottle of whisky – either to give himself Dutch courage to do the deed or to drown his conscience after it or perhaps both! He did in fact carry out his intention: '... the wickedness of his mind before he got drunk is enough to condemn him, coupled with the act which he intended to do and did do.'

He went on:

> I think the law on this point should take a clear stand. If a man, whilst sane and sober, forms an intention to kill and makes preparation for it knowing it is a wrong thing to do, and then gets himself drunk so as to give himself Dutch courage to do the killing, and whilst drunk carries out his intention, he cannot rely on self-induced drunkenness as a defence to a charge of murder, nor even as reducing it to manslaughter. He cannot say he got himself into such a stupid state that he was incapable of an intent to kill [p 382].

The difficulty with this view is that it does not appear to recognise that the *mens rea* needs to coincide with the *actus reus* and that the basic principle for the defence of intoxication is whether or not the accused actually did have the intent when the *actus reus* was committed. It requires one to accept the principle of the *actus reus* commencing at the time the intent was formed, that is, buying the alcohol and getting drunk is all part of the *actus reus* of the killing. It is part of a premeditated plan which ultimately will result in the death of a human being.

It will be recalled that s 8 of the CJA 1967 establishes that a court or jury in determining whether a person has committed an offence 'shall decide whether he did intend or foresee that result by reference to all the evidence'.

The House of Lords in *Majewski* responded by confirming that s 8 was inapplicable in this context because the section was evidential only whereas the intoxication rule was one of substantive law.

For an application of this principle, however illogical it may appear in the context of a *mens rea* crime, one ought to examine the decision in *Lipman* (1969). Lipman, after taking the hallucinatory drug LSD, had killed his girlfriend. She was found by her landlord having suffered two blows to the head and with some eight inches of sheeting crammed into her mouth. He claimed that he had been on an 'LSD trip' and believed that he was fighting serpents at the centre of the earth. He had awoken to find his companion dead. He was found guilty of manslaughter, a basic intent crime, even though it was not seriously disputed that he had no knowledge of what he was doing. In the light of subsequent decisions, one could argue that he was reckless in putting himself in the position whereby he lost control of his actions. Conversely, he could maintain that he had no prior knowledge or reason to believe that such a consequence would occur and a jury, properly directed might well be disposed to believe him. In light of the *Hardie* decision, if a court were to find LSD not to be a dangerous drug, however unlikely that may be, for the purposes of the intoxication defence, then the jury would be entitled to consider whether he was reckless in taking the drug.

This case and the House of Lords' decisions remind us that public policy considerations are likely to underpin the legal principles in this area of law. As Lord Denning acknowledged in *AG for Northern Ireland v Gallagher* (1963): '... the general principle of English law (is) that, subject to very limited exceptions, drunkenness is no defence to a criminal charge.'

7.3.4 Intoxication and mistake

The law at present distinguishes between different kinds of mistake made by someone who is voluntarily drunk. If the offence is one of specific intent then the drunken mistake is a relevant consideration for the jury. If the drunken mistake is to self-defence, or the amount of force needed for self-defence, then it is not a relevant mistake irrespective of whether the accused is charged with a basic or specific intent crime. As will be seen below, 7.4, a mistake as to circumstances may provide a defence provided that belief is honestly held. The *Gladstone Williams* (1987) case establishes that belief does not need to be reasonable. What, then, is the situation if that mistaken belief is engendered because of intoxication? If the offence is one of specific intent, then intoxication is a factor in considering whether or not the accused had the necessary intent as where the defendant is charged with murder but claims he acted in self-defence.

The interrelationship between intoxication and mistake has been explored in a number of cases. In *O'Grady* (1987), the Court of Appeal held that a defendant was precluded from relying on self-defence if, as a result of voluntary intoxication, he had used excessive force when defending himself. This would apply irrespective of whether the charge was one relating to a basic or specific intent crime. The reason for this finding is to be found in a statement of McCullough J, who gave the defendant leave to appeal to the Court of Appeal, which was cited by Lord Lane CJ:

> Given that a man who mistakenly believes he is under attack is entitled to use reasonable force to defend himself, it would seem to follow that, if he is under attack and mistakenly believes the attack to be more serious that it is, he is entitled to use reasonable force to defend himself against an attack of the severity he believed it to have. If one allows a mistaken belief induced by drink to bring this principle into operation, an act of gross negligence (viewed objectively) may become lawful even though it results in the death of the innocent victim. The drunken man would be guilty of neither murder nor manslaughter.'

This decision has been supported by *O'Connor* (1991), where the defendant who had been drinking heavily had killed another man, but maintained that he believed himself to be under attack and was therefore acting in self-defence. The Court of Appeal held that *O'Grady* was binding upon it and therefore the fact that the trial judge had failed to direct the jury on the issue of drunkenness and self-defence was irrelevant. *O'Grady* has been savagely criticised because it can lead to illogical results and at best must be seen as a policy decision. The Law Commission has found it impossible to support the decision. From a self-defence viewpoint the jury is not entitled to recognise the defendant's intoxication in deciding whether or not he intended to act in self-defence, but when considering whether he had sufficient intent to kill or cause grievous bodily harm, it is entitled to consider intoxication, *via* the specific intent rule.

The common law rule as regards self-defence would therefore appear to be that, where a mistake arises as a result of voluntary intoxication, the defendant cannot rely on his mistake. The problem with the *O'Grady* decision is that it divorces the issue of proof of intent from that of mistake. *Richardson and Irwin* (1999), on the other hand, suggests that voluntary intoxication should be taken into account if it leads D to mistakenly believe that P is consenting to harm (in this case, rough horseplay) in circumstances where P's consent could afford a defence. How this is to be reconciled with earlier cases, such as *Woods* (1981), where D's drunken mistake as to P's consent was held to provide no defence to a charge of rape, is not at all clear. Logic and policy decisions do not sit easily together in this area of law!

7.3.5 Statutory as opposed to a common law defence

The issue has also arisen with respect to a statutory as opposed to a common law defence. *Jaggard v Dickinson* (1980) concerned a charge of criminal damage arising from an attempt by the defendant to gain entry into what she believed was a friend's property but which in fact belonged to a neighbour, although it was identical in appearance. She broke two windows and damaged a curtain. It transpired that she was drunk. Criminal damage was treated as a basic intent crime and therefore voluntary consumption of alcohol is to be regarded as a reckless act and intoxication would therefore not succeed as a defence. However, s 5(2) and (3) of the Criminal Damage Act 1971 allows a defendant to plead an honest belief that there is a lawful excuse why one should be permitted to damage or destroy another's property. The court accepted that an honest belief induced by intoxication was a factor which would be taken into account in determining whether a defence within the terms of s 5 had been set up. She claimed that as she knew the occupant of the house she wished to break into and thought that he would consent if he had known the circumstances she should be allowed the benefit of s 5(3). The Divisional Court allowed her appeal.

This decision further illustrates the inconsistency and illogicality of this area of law. In this statutory context, a mistaken belief induced by drink can be taken into account in deciding whether a defendant actually held that belief, but in respect of the common law of self-defence, drunkenness which makes the defendant mistakenly believe he is under attack cannot help to justify his response.

7.3.6 The Law Commission

Clause 22 of the draft Criminal Code Bill deals with intoxication. If the fault element of the crime requires recklessness to be proved it is proposed that someone who is voluntarily intoxicated shall be treated:

(a) as having been aware of any risk of which he would have been aware had he been sober;

(b) as not having believed in the existence of an exempting circumstance (where the existence of such a belief is in issue) if he would not have so believed had he been sober.

Intoxicant is defined to mean 'alcohol or any other thing which, when taken into the body, may impair awareness or control'.

Voluntary intoxication means 'the intoxication of a person by an intoxicant which he takes, other than properly for a medical purpose, knowing that it is or may be an intoxicant'.

The Law Commission was extremely active in this area of the law in the 1990s and considered the role of intoxication in the criminal law on no less than three occasions. In 1993, it published its Consultation Paper *Intoxication and Criminal Liability* (Law Com 127) and, later in the same year, its report *Legislating the Criminal Code: Offences Against the Person and General Defences* (Law Com 218) makes reference to the effect of intoxication. In 1995, its report, *Legislating the Criminal Code: Intoxication and Criminal Liability* (Law Com 229), was published. It is worthwhile consulting both the Consultation Paper and the final report as the Law Commission's views demonstrate an amazing *volte face*. The 1993 paper contained two major proposals: first, that the *Majewski* rule be abolished; and, secondly, that a new offence of criminal intoxication be created. The Law Commission had no doubt that what was required was a 'thorough going replacement of the common law rule, rather than any attempt at marginal reform' (para 4.19).

In its report it expresses the view that 'the *Majewski* approach operates fairly, on the whole, and without undue difficulty, but it is both desirable and necessary to set out the relevant principles clearly in codified form' (para 1.32). Apparently the Law Commission accepted the views of the senior judiciary that the public would find abolition of the *Majewski* rule objectionable. The Law Commission, therefore, proposes that the bulk of the present law should be put onto a statutory footing. This means that, when addressing primary considerations such as intention, knowledge, purpose, belief, fraud or dishonesty, intoxication should be a factor to take into account. However, in respect of other aspects of *mens rea*, most notably recklessness, a defendant will be treated as having been aware of anything which he would have been aware of, if not for his intoxication. The focus will be upon the actual *mens rea* for each offence and the terminology of basic and specific intent will disappear. In effect, this will introduce a rebuttable presumption in respect of recklessness, allowing the court to take into account factors that might have affected an awareness of risk. This might include the physical and mental problems of the accused.

The Law Commission seeks to reverse the effect of the decisions in *O'Grady* and *O'Connor* although the wording employed to describe this change is tortuous in the extreme (see para 7.12). In essence, it is proposed that, if the accused is charged with a specific intent offence, his 'intoxicated' mistake may be taken into account to determine liability, but not in cases of basic intent. (It should be noted that these terms will become redundant if the recommendations are implemented.)

Someone taking drugs in circumstances like those in *Hardie* will be able to benefit from the law only if it the drugs were consumed for medicinal purposes, in which case it will be treated as a case of involuntary intoxication. Other 'involuntary' situations are where the intoxication resulted from duress or the intoxicant was taken without knowledge or awareness on the part of the accused.

A person is to be regarded as intoxicated if 'awareness, understanding or control is impaired'. 'Intoxicants' are alcohol, drugs and any other substance which once in the body has the capacity to impair awareness, understanding or control.

In February 1998, the Home Office published its White Paper, *Violence: Reforming the Offences Against the Person Act 1861*, accompanied by a draft Bill. Clause 19 of that Bill proposes reforms to the law relating to intoxication in so far as that defence relates to non-fatal offences against the person. In essence, the Home Office proposals endorse the approach taken by the Law Commission in *Legislating the Criminal Code: Offences Against the Person and General Defences* (Law Com 218, 1993) (and, indeed, the draft Criminal Code Bill, cited above). Under this formulation, a defendant who becomes intoxicated of his own volition would be treated as having been aware of any risk of which he would have been aware had he not been intoxicated, and as having known or believed in any circumstances which he would have known or believed in had he not been intoxicated.

7.4   Mistake

A defendant may allege that he did not possess the *mens rea* for the crime with which he is charged because he was labouring under a mistake of fact and thus did not intend or was not reckless to the particular consequences or circumstances required by the definition of the crime. The leading cases of *DPP v Morgan* (1975) and *B v DPP* (2000) make it clear that, where such a mistake prevents the accused from possessing the requisite mental element, then, providing it is an honest albeit unreasonable mistake, the defence will succeed. In effect, providing the mistake is honest it will succeed. If the crime in question is one of strict liability, then absence of *mens rea* for whatever reason will not provide a defence. In the *Morgan* case, the defendant invited three colleagues to have intercourse with his wife telling them that she would be a willing participant. His wife alleged that she was raped and that there was no evidence that she was consenting to the intercourse. The judge directed the jury that, if the men reasonably believed that she was consenting, then the prosecution would not have established the *mens rea*. All four men were convicted and appealed on the basis that the judge had misdirected the jury as to the basis of the defence of mistaken belief. The House of Lords, by a 3:2 majority, held that, if they honestly believed the woman to be consenting, even if there were no reasonable grounds for such a belief, they could not be guilty of rape. The proviso found at s 2(1) of the Criminal Appeal Act (CApA) 1968 was applied to uphold their convictions even though there had been a misdirection by the trial judge. (For further information on the working of the proviso and amendments brought about by the CApA 1995, see Chapter 1.)

Section 1(2) of the Sexual Offences (Amendment) Act 1976 put the *Morgan* decision onto a statutory footing. The trend towards subjectivity in respect of *mens rea* was further supported in *Gladstone Williams* (1987) where the Lord Chief Justice, Lord Lane, stated the principle in this way:

> The jury should be directed ... that the prosecution have the burden or duty of proving the unlawfulness of the defendant's actions, second, that if the defendant may have been labouring under a mistake as to the facts he must be judged according to his mistaken view of the facts and, third, that that is so whether the mistake was, on an objective view, a reasonable mistake or not.

He went on to apply this reasoning to self-defence. Williams had claimed that his assault on the victim was motivated by the mistaken belief that the victim was attacking someone else (when, in fact, he was trying to apprehend the person who had attempted to rob a woman). His conviction was quashed by the Court of Appeal. If the jury concludes that a defendant believed or may have believed that the use of force was necessary to protect himself or prevent a crime from taking place, then the prosecution has not proved its case. A jury will, of course, be directed to take account of all the circumstances, and give consideration as to whether they believe the mistake was unreasonable. If they believe it was unreasonable, they are entitled to conclude, but do not have to, that the belief was not honestly held.

As Lord Griffiths said in *Beckford v R* (1987):

> Where there are no reasonable grounds to hold a belief it will surely only be in exceptional circumstances that a jury will conclude that such a belief was or might have been held [p 432d].

Prior to the *Morgan* decision, the law on mistake had been developed using an objective standard in helping juries to decide whether an 'acceptable' mistake had taken place. The major authority was *Tolson* (1889). Having been deserted by her husband in 1881, she heard nothing of him for some six years and, presuming herself to be widowed, she went through a ceremony of marriage to another man. Her husband reappeared some 10 months later. Her conviction for bigamy was quashed on the basis that she believed and had reasonable grounds for believing her husband to be dead, his elder brother having informed her that her husband been lost at sea as he made his way to the US. *Tolson* was distinguished in *Morgan* on the basis that the House of Lords in *Morgan* was dealing with a *mens rea* offence, whereas in *Tolson* the court was having to decide what requirement of *mens rea* to read into a statutory offence which contained no such express requirement. Section 57 of the OAPA 1861 defines bigamy in these terms: 'Whosoever, being married, shall marry any other person during the life of the former husband or wife ... shall be guilty of an offence.'

It will be seen that there is no reference to any particular mental element and, indeed, the minority in *Tolson* actually regarded bigamy as a strict liability offence. Lord Cross in *Morgan* dealt with the bigamy issue in stating:

> I would not have thought it right for us to call it (the element of reasonableness as part of a defence) in question in this case. In fact, however, I can see no objection to the inclusion of the element of reasonableness in what I may call a '*Tolson*' case ... if the definition of the offence is on the face of it 'absolute' and

the defendant is seeking to escape his *prima facie* liability by a defence of mistaken belief, I can see no hardship to him in requiring the mistake – if it is to afford him a defence – to be based on reasonable grounds ... there is nothing unreasonable in the law requiring a citizen to take reasonable care to ascertain the facts relevant to his avoiding doing a prohibited act.

However, the development of the law since *Morgan* has diminished the importance of reasonableness, whilst championing the necessity for an honest belief in order to prevent the prosecution from proving the presence of the necessary *mens rea*. Lord Nicholls, in the course of his speech in *B v DPP* (2000), indicated that the requirement of reasonable belief should be abandoned altogether save where expressly required by statute. As he observed, when *mens rea* is ousted by a mistaken belief, it is ousted. It matters not that the belief is an unreasonable belief. He added:

Considered as a matter of principle, the honest belief approach must be preferable. By definition, the mental element in a crime is concerned with a subjective state of mind, such as intent or belief.

He added that, where an overriding objective limit such as a requirement that a belief was held on reasonable grounds was added, it had the effect of displacing the subjective element, so that a conviction could follow a failure to achieve an objective standard, not for having a particular culpable state of mind.

7.5   Duress by threats

Lord Hailsham LC in *Howe* (1987) states that the defence of duress is of 'venerable antiquity and wide extent'. Lord Morris in *Lynch v DPP* (1975) posed the fundamental questions which go to the heart of the defence:

If someone acts under duress – does he intend what he does? Does he lack what in our criminal law is called *mens rea*? If what he does amounts to a criminal offence ought he to be convicted but be allowed in mercy and in mitigation to be absolved or relieved from some or all of the possible consequences.

He later rejected the view that duress could act only mitigate the consequences of a conviction or absolve from punishment. The accepted approach was put by Lord Wilberforce in *Lynch* to the effect that 'the element of duress prevents the law from treating what was done as a crime'. In other words, the victim of the duress commits the *actus reus* and additionally knows what he is doing, but, if proved, duress will prevent the law from treating the enterprise as criminal. The defendant may argue that, given the circumstances, he or she had no choice but to act as he or she did. Is this correct? The defendant could have chosen not to commit the act and face the consequences of the threats. Those may be very severe and may not have been, of course, referable only to the defendant. A man's family may have been held hostage. The defendant may, prior to making his decision, receive conclusive evidence that his son's life is at risk if he does not do as the captors desire. However hard the decision making process, it still remains true that he has a choice and does not have to commit the offence with which he is now charged. Is his action involuntary? He certainly does not act as an automaton and remember that the courts have limited that defence to a narrow band of circumstances. He does not act involuntarily in the same way as someone who is forced to commit the *actus reus* of the offence as in *Larsonneur* (1933) (see above, 2.2.4).

Lord Morris is clear as to why duress should be allowed as a defence:

> If then someone is really threatened with death or serious injury unless he does what he is told to do is the law to pay no heed to the miserable, agonising plight of such a person? For the law to understand not only how the timid but also the stalwart may in a moment of crisis behave is not to make the law weak but to make it just. In the calm of the courtroom measures of fortitude or of heroic behaviour are surely not to be demanded when they could not in moments for decision reasonably have been expected even of the resolute and the well disposed.

Ponder for a moment the facts of *Steane* (1947). In 1940, Steane had entered the service of the German Broadcasting Service and taken part in disseminating German propaganda at a time when Britain was standing alone against the might of the German armed forces. He claimed, and it was not disputed, that threats of physical violence and internment in a concentration camp had been made against him and his family. In these circumstances, he acted as he did only to save his wife and children and not with intent to assist the enemy. What would you have done in such circumstances? Would one's will not have been overborne by the prospect of never again seeing one's family? Should the law be compassionate and exonerate such a person from criminal responsibility? (It should be noted that duress was not an issue in the case as the court found that in law he did not possess the intention to assist the enemy, intent unusually being equated with desire or purpose.)

7.5.1 The extent of the defence

Lord Griffiths in *Howe* (1987) saw the defence of duress as a 'merciful concession to human frailty', but it is a defence which, as the law currently stands, does not apply to the crimes of treason, murder and attempted murder. This has raised questions as to the proper extent of the defence and persuaded Lord Keith in *Gotts* (1992) to comment:

> The complexities and anomalies involved in the whole matter of the defence of duress seem to me to be such that the issue is much better left to Parliament to deal with in the light of broad considerations of policy.

In *Gotts*, the House of Lords was asked to determine whether or not the defence was available to someone charged with attempted murder, the question having been left open by the House of Lords in *Howe* (1987). The appellant who at the time of the offence was aged 16 seriously injured his mother with a knife. He was charged with attempted murder and pleaded not guilty. At his trial, he raised the defence of duress, stating that his father had threatened to shoot him unless he killed his mother. The trial judge ruled that such evidence was inadmissible since duress was not, as a matter of law, a defence to a charge of attempted murder. He changed his plea to guilty and appealed against the judge's ruling. On a 3:2 majority, it was decided that, as a matter of public policy, the defence was unavailable to someone charged with attempted murder. This would appear to be a logical conclusion, given that duress is not a defence to a charge of murder. Attempted murder requires an intent to kill, yet the *mens rea* for murder can be satisfied by proving an intent to cause serious bodily harm. There is often no certainty that, in carrying out the act, the accused will achieve his purpose in bringing about death. If he should be successful, duress is not available as a defence. If, by sheer good fortune, the victim survives the attack and the charge is one of attempted murder, he would, in the absence of the decision in *Gotts*, be able to introduce duress. As a result of this decision, there is one anomaly still to be resolved. It would appear that duress may be a defence to a charge of causing grievous bodily harm with intent (s 18 of the OAPA 1861). Thus, if a person causes death, having an intent to kill, duress is not available. However, if he has the intent to cause grievous bodily harm, which is after all part of the *mens rea* for murder, and again through good fortune the person survives, then duress is available. It is a 'nice question', as Lord Keith, one of the minority in *Gotts*, points out, why the defence should not be available on an attempted murder charge but is available to a s 18 charge:

> It is unsatisfactory that the defence of duress should be available in the latter case but not in the former [p 834e].

7.5.2 The extent of the duress

The test for duress has been developed by the common law over many years. An individual's response to the threat must be judged against the likely reaction of the ordinary person in a similar situation. In *Graham* (1982), it was stated that as a matter of public policy it was essential 'to limit the defence of duress by means of an objective criterion formulated in terms of reasonableness'.

Lord Lane CJ drew parallels between provocation and duress. In the former, words or conduct must be such as to make the reasonable person lose self-control, in the latter the words or actions must break the will of another. He went on to establish that:

> The law requires a defendant to have the self-control reasonably to be expected of the ordinary citizen in his situation. It should likewise require him to have the steadfastness reasonably to be expected of the ordinary citizen in his situation.

The test for duress contains both subjective and objective elements. The subjective element was put this way by Lord Lane in *Graham*:

(1) was the defendant, or may he have been impelled to act as he did because, as a result of what he reasonably believed [the person making the threat] had said or done, he had good cause to fear that if he did not so act [the person] would kill him or cause him serious physical injury?

(2) if so, have the prosecution made the jury sure that a sober person of reasonable firmness, sharing the characteristics of the defendant, would not have responded to whatever he reasonably believed [the person] said or did by taking part in the killing. The fact that a defendant's will to resist has been eroded by the voluntary consumption of drink or drugs or both is not relevant to this test.

If the defendant has made an honest mistake as to the threat, it would appear that he will not be able to rely on the defence unless it is also reasonable for him to have made the mistake. This is confirmed by the Court of Appeal's decision in *Cairns* (1999) and is in marked contrast to what Lord Lane CJ said in *Williams* (1987), from which one concludes that an honest mistake as to the facts is sufficient to set up self-defence or prevention of crime.

As Lord Lane has pointed out, the defendant is expected to have the steadfastness reasonably to be expected of the ordinary citizen. He also referred to the parallels between the law on provocation and duress in respect of the effect of words or conduct on the reasonable person and, in the case of duress, whether that person would lose his self-control or succumb to threats. In *Bowen* (1996), the defendant had an IQ of 68 and at his trial on a charge of obtaining services by deception contrary to s 1 of the Theft Act 1978 raised the issue of duress. He claimed that his actions in obtaining electrical equipment on credit, failing to make any payments and then selling them was motivated by his desire to avoid having his house petrol-bombed. Two men, he said, had threatened to carry out the attack if he did not obtain the goods for them. The Court of Appeal referred to the 'classic statement' of the law in *Graham*, which alludes in the second limb to a sober person of reasonable firmness, 'sharing the characteristics of the defendant'.

The question for the court was which were the relevant characteristics of the accused to which the jury should have regard in considering the second objective test? In the earlier case of *Hegarty* (1994), the court had acknowledged that age, sex and physical health were all characteristics which could be taken into account but doubted whether a personality disorder of the type possessed by the accused was relevant. Medical evidence could be assessed in connection with the subjective part of the equation and this would include mental abnormality but would only be relevant in the objective part of the test if connected to the ability to resist the threats.

In *Horne* (1994), the Court of Appeal held that 'characteristics' should be interpreted narrowly in respect of the objective test, otherwise that element of the two-limb test would be completely undermined, that is, if virtually all of the characteristics of the accused were to be taken into account then the test would in effect be wholly subjective. The appellant had sought to adduce psychiatric evidence to the effect that he was unusually pliable and vulnerable to pressure. The judge refused to admit the evidence, saying that mental characteristics such as inherent weakness, vulnerability and susceptibility to threats were inconsistent with the requirements of the objective test. The Court of Appeal affirmed this view.

The court in *Bowen* agreed that age, sex and physical health or disability may be relevant characteristics but: '... beyond that it is not altogether easy to determine from the authorities what others may be relevant.'

The court considered that the following principles were to be derived from the authorities:

- if the accused is more 'pliable, vulnerable, timid or susceptible to threats than the normal person ... these are not characteristics with which the reasonable/ordinary man is to be invested';

- the defendant may be in a category of persons that the jury would recognise as being less able to resist pressure, for example, as a result of pregnancy or serious physical disability;

- some characteristics relevant to provocation may not be relevant to duress, for example, a person's homosexuality may be the subject of taunts and therefore going to the heart of provocation, but homosexuality could not be relevant to duress. There is no reason to assume that a homosexual is any less or more robust in resisting the type of threats relevant to duress;

- characteristics due to self-induced abuse, for example, alcohol or glue sniffing cannot be relevant;

- psychiatric evidence is admissible to show the accused is suffering from some recognised mental illness or psychiatric condition providing persons suffering from such conditions may be more susceptible to pressure or threats. This may help the jury to decide whether a reasonable person suffering from such an illness might have been impelled to act as the accused did.

Having reviewed the principles, the court concluded that a low IQ short of mental impairment is not a characteristic that makes those who have it less courageous and less able to withstand threats and pressure. Professor Smith (Smith, JC and Hogan, B, *Criminal Law*, 9th edn, 1999, p 240), having reviewed the case law, suggests that the 'objective test has broken down and that we are moving closer to the test proposed by the Law Commission: "the threat is one which in all the circumstances (including any of [the defendant's] characteristics that affects its gravity) he cannot reasonably be expected to resist".'

7.5.3   Threats of death or serious bodily harm

The threat must be of death or serious bodily harm. Murnagham J in *AG v Whelan* (1934) in a passage approved by the House of Lords in *Lynch* (1975) commented:

> It seems to us that threats of immediate death or serious person violence so great as to overbear the ordinary power of human resistance should be accepted as justification for acts which would otherwise be criminal.

A similar comment can also be found in *Hudson and Taylor* (1971). The law will not place threats to property on a par with threats of death or serious physical injury. Lord Simon's 'working definition' as expounded in *Lynch* was put in these terms:

> ... such [well grounded] fear, produced by threats, of death or grievous bodily harm [or unjustified imprisonment] if a certain act is not done, as overbears the actor's wish not to perform the act, and is effective, at the time of the act, in constraining him to perform it.

Where so little is clear, this at least seems to be established:

> ... that the type of threat which affords a defence must be one of human physical harm (including, possibly, imprisonment), so that threat of injury to property is not enough.

Lord Simon does go on to acknowledge that a threat in certain circumstances, 'may be as potent in overbearing the actor's wish not to perform the prohibited act as a threat of physical harm' but 'the law must draw a line somewhere; and as a result of experience and human valuation, the law draws it between threats to property and threats to the person'. The threat of physical harm or death cannot be from D himself (that is, D escapes from prison to stop himself committing suicide) (see *Roger* (1997)).

The threat of death or serious harm may not be the only factor influencing the defendant to act as he did. In *Valderrama-Vega* (1985), the defendant had received death threats from a Colombian Mafia-style organisation and had as a result tried to import cocaine into England. He was also in financial difficulty and additionally feared that the organisation would disclose his homosexual inclinations to his family. Duress was available said the trial judge if the defendant had acted solely on the basis of the death threats. This was potentially misleading because the jury might have believed the defence should have been rejected if other factors affected his decision. The correct approach was to ask whether he would have acted differently but for the death threats. It was stated in *Hudson and Taylor* that the threats must be effective on the mind of the accused at the time the *actus reus* is perpetrated. Two girls aged 19 and 17 were charged with perjury but claimed that when they gave false evidence they had done so only because of threats which had been made against them. They had actually seen one of those who had threatened them sitting in the public gallery, as they were about to give evidence. The defence failed presumably on the basis that the girls had failed to seek protection when it was readily available to them. The Court of Appeal, in allowing the appeal against conviction, thought the threat no less effective simply because it would not be carried out at the time the crime was committed, it was certainly a possibility that the threats could have been carried out later that night 'in the streets of Salford'. Of course, a threat of future violence may be so remote as to have little impact on the will of the defendant, but that was not the position in this case.

In *Abdul-Hussain and Others* (1999), the defendants sought to raise the defence of duress in respect of charges of hijacking a plane. They feared that, as Shiite Muslims from southern Iraq, if they were deported to Iraq, they would be tortured and or killed by the authorities there. The trial judge had refused to leave the defence of duress to jury on the basis that the threat of death or grievous bodily harm had been insufficiently imminent at the time of the hijacking. Allowing their appeals, the Court of Appeal accepted the contention that the threat of death or grievous bodily harm need not actually be immediate. What mattered was that the defendant's will to resist the threats was overborne by the prospect of imminent peril of death or grievous bodily harm. The court usefully illustrated this point by giving the example of Anne Frank not having to wait for the Gestapo to knock on her door before being able to rely on the defence of necessity in relation to fleeing in a stolen car.

In *Cole* (1994), C claimed that he had 'no choice' as to whether he robbed two building societies. He owed cash to moneylenders who he claimed had threatened him, hit him with a baseball bat and threatened his girlfriend and child because of his inability to repay. The judge ruled that duress was only available where the threats were directed to the commission of the particular offence charged. Here, the threat related to the inability or unwillingness to repay the loan. He was not threatened with the unpleasant consequences if he failed to rob a building society. There had to be a direct link between the threat and the offence.

This decision would appear to limit the scope of the defence to those situations where the duressor is very specific in terms of what he or she requires the defendant to do. If A says to D, 'You owe me £1,000 and if you don't rob the Pontypridd Building Society I'll seriously injure you and your child' that would appear to be adequate to comply with the test. However, if D is told 'You owe me £1,000 and if I don't have it by Friday I'll seriously injure you and your child and – oh! – by the way all building society offices in Pontypridd lack proper security' that may not be enough. Or suppose he simply says 'Get the £1,000 to me by Friday or else ... I don't care what you do but I want my money'. Only in the first of these examples had the threatener nominated the crime. But, in terms of impact on the defendant, are the other examples really so different in character as to deny him the opportunity to have his plea considered by the jury?

The defence is likely to be denied if the accused has voluntarily joined a criminal organisation, because he has put himself into a position where he may expect others to use force to exert their will over him, particularly if he should try to resile from their operations. The leading case is *Sharp* (1987), where Lord Lane CJ stated the principle thus:

> Where a person has voluntarily, and with knowledge of its nature, joined a criminal organisation or gang which he knew might bring pressure on him to commit an offence and was an active member when he was put under such pressure, he cannot avail himself of the defence of duress.

In *Ali* (1995), the Court of Appeal applied *Sharp* (1987) and stated the rule thus:

> The crux of the matter was knowledge in the defendant of either a violent nature to the gang or the enterprise which he had joined, or a violent disposition in the person or persons involved with him in the criminal activity he voluntarily joined. If a defendant voluntarily participated in criminal offences with a man 'X' whom he knows to be of violent disposition and likely to require him to perform other criminal acts, he could not rely on duress if 'X' does so.

These cases may usefully be contrasted with *Shepherd* (1987). The appellant was convicted of five counts of burglary. A number of men would enter the shop, some would distract the shopkeeper while the others took the goods. S claimed that after the first expedition he wanted to withdraw but was threatened by other gang members with violence to him and his family and so he felt compelled to carry on. The trial judge ruled that duress was not available. The appeal was allowed and the convictions quashed. This case can be distinguished from the others on the basis that the defendant was not at the outset joining a gang with a known propensity for violence and who could anticipate what might happen if his nerve failed. This might apply, for example, to those joining paramilitary groups or gangs of armed robbers. In this case, there would be no immediate assumption that, should he wish to withdraw, then he might be faced with serious violence. As the court said:

> ... there are certain kinds of criminal enterprises the joining of which, in the absence of any knowledge of propensity to violence on the part of one member, would not lead another to suspect that a decision to think better of the whole affair might lead him into serious trouble. In such cases, if trouble materialises unexpectedly and puts the defendant into a dilemma in which a reasonable man might have chosen to act as he did, the concession of human frailty is available to the defendant.

The defence of duress may also be denied to a defendant who can be regarded as having brought about the situation whereby he is subjected to threats forcing him to commit offences. In *Heath* (1999), D had incurred debts with a drugs dealer and relied upon this as the explanation as to why the dealer had forced him into committing offences in order to 'repay' the debt. Again, the court thought it sufficient that D had placed himself in a situation where he was aware of the risk that he might be compelled to commit offences.

7.5.4 Limitations to the defence

As stated above, it has been a consistently upheld principle that duress should not be available to a principal to murder and this was confirmed by the House of Lords in *Howe* (1987) and had previously been accepted by the Privy Council in *Abbott v The Queen* (1976). The reason generally given for this is that the law cannot be seen to place a greater value on the life of one person as opposed to another. Is it forgivable to save one's own life at the expense of another person or group of people? Equally, is the person who kills 40 people by planting a bomb in a busy shopping centre in order to save the life of his wife and daughter to be regarded as a hero? One suspects not, at least by the relatives and friends of those killed. Yet is it reasonable to expect a person to sacrifice his own life and that of his family in order to save the lives of those engaged upon a shopping expedition? One suspects most people would plant the bomb in the hope that it might be discovered and life not placed in jeopardy, particularly if he or his family faced certain death for disobeying. In many of the cases in which duress has been considered, the judges have made reference to the threat of terrorism and the potential exploitation of the defence by those who force others to commit atrocities on their behalf (see, for example, Lord Hailsham LC in *Howe* (1987)) as a reason for not extending the defence to one charged with murder as a principal offender. *Howe* also confirmed that duress is not a defence to a secondary party to murder. *Gotts* has now determined that the defence is not available to someone charged with attempted murder. However, it is worth noting that all the Law Lords in this case with the exception of Lord Lowry thought that Parliament ought to give consideration as to whether the defence should be denied to those who have committed extremely serious offences and also whether the rationale for the defence should be based upon mitigation or exculpation.

The Law Commission in its 1993 report, *Offences Against the Person and General Defences* (Law Com 218), recommends that duress of threats should be a complete defence to all crimes and, to reduce concern at this extension of the law in respect of murder and attempted murder, the Law Commission proposes that the burden of proof would move to the defence. At the moment, the obligation of disproving duress rests upon the Crown. Therefore, the accused would have to prove that he knew or believed:

- that a threat has been made to cause death or serious injury to himself or another if the act is not done; and

- that the threat will be carried out immediately if he does not do the act or, if not immediately, before he or that other can obtain effective official protection; and

- that there is no other way of preventing the threat being carried out; and

- the threat is one which in all the circumstances (including any of his personal characteristics that affect its gravity) he cannot reasonably be expected to resist (cl 25 of the draft Criminal Law Bill).

7.6   Duress of circumstances

The emergence of this defence has occurred on a piecemeal basis over the last decade and was originally part of the uncertain law on necessity. It is now firmly seen as part of the law on duress. *Cole* (1994) referred to the development of two distinct defences although confusingly expressed them in these words: '... duress by threats and duress of circumstances (necessity).' The former occurs when the threatener nominates the crime, the latter where the accused acts to avoid an imminent danger of death or serious injury to himself or another, if in the circumstances he could not reasonably be expected to act otherwise.

The Law Commission (*Offences Against the Person and General Defences*, Law Com 218, 1993, paras 35.4 and 35.5) draws a distinction between duress and necessity:

> By contrast with the defences of duress ... there appear to be some cases, more properly called cases of 'necessity' where the actor does not rely on any allegation that circumstances placed an irresistible pressure on him. Rather he claims that his conduct, although falling within the definition of an offence, was not harmful because it was, in the circumstances, justified.

In *Willer* (1986), the Court of Appeal in allowing his appeal rejected a defence of necessity but nevertheless believed the jury ought to have been given the opportunity to consider whether he drove under a form of compulsion. There had been no direct threat aimed at Willer and therefore this could not be treated as a straightforward case of duress by threat, hence the development of this sub-species of duress. The charge was one of reckless driving. He had driven on onto a pavement in order to endeavour to escape form a group of youths who were going to seriously assault him and his passengers. In the circumstances he felt compelled to break the law. The headnote in the *All England Law Reports* in the case of *Conway* (1988) is confusing. It states:

> Necessity can only be a defence to a charge of reckless driving where, objectively, the facts establish duress of circumstances, that is, that the defendant was constrained by circumstances to drive as he did to avoid the threat of death or serious injury to himself or some other person.

The court stressed that duress of circumstances was available only if from an objective standpoint it can be said the defendant was acting to avoid the threat of death or serious injury.

These strands were brought together in *Martin* (1989). The defendant claimed that his wife had suicidal tendencies and on a number of occasions had attempted to take her own life. Her son, Martin's stepson, had on the day in question overslept and risked losing his job if he arrived late for work. His mother apparently distraught, urged Martin to drive him to his place of employment. She threatened to commit suicide if he did not accede to her requests. Martin had been disqualified from driving and was naturally reluctant to take his car onto the highway. Eventually, he relented because he said 'he genuinely and ... reasonably believed that his wife would carry out her threat unless he did as she demanded'. He was apprehended by the police. Simon Brown J, delivering the judgment of the Court of Appeal, summarised the principles applicable to what was in effect a plea of necessity (the defence had adduced medical evidence to the effect that in her mental condition Mrs Martin would have attempted suicide if her husband had not done what she demanded):

(1) English law does, in extreme circumstances, recognise a defence of necessity. Most commonly this defence arises as duress, that is pressure on the accused's will from the wrongful threats of violence of another. Equally however, it can arise from objective dangers threatening the accused or others. Arising thus it is conveniently called 'duress of circumstances'.

(2) ... the defence is available only if, from an objective standpoint, the accused can be said to be acting reasonably and proportionately in order to avoid a threat of death or serious injury.

The judge should invite the jury to consider two questions when duress of circumstances is raised as a defence: first, whether or not the accused acted as he did because he had reason to fear that death or serious injury would result; and, secondly, whether 'a sober person of reasonable firmness, sharing the characteristics of the accused' would have responded by acting in the same way as the accused. If a positive answer is given to both these questions, the defence of duress of circumstances is established and the accused must be acquitted.

These developments have prompted a reappraisal of one of the most famous cases in English criminal law.

On Saturday 1 November 1884, the trial of Tom Dudley and Edwin Stephens commenced at Exeter Assizes. Cast adrift in an open boat, they had killed a young member of their crew who admittedly was near to death, in order that they might feast on his flesh. A few days later, they were rescued and, following that, amid intense publicity, stood their trial for murder. They claimed that it was necessary for them to act as they did in order to stay alive. Baron Huddleston, the trial judge, told the jury:

There was no more necessity that they should kill the boy than that they should kill one of themselves. All they required was something to eat: but the necessity of something to eat does not create the necessity of taking and excuse the taking of the boy.

These men were faced with a choice and hardly a palatable one at that! To take life in self-defence is justified, but the law has steadfastly refused to extend justification to these circumstances. This case should now be considered an example of duress by circumstances and not one of necessity or justification. If the situation were to occur today, the outcome would be no different even though the case would in all probability be viewed as duress of circumstances. The current law prevents either form of duress being pleaded as a defence to murder or attempted murder. But the situation might well be different if the recommendations of the Law Commission are implemented. However, they might now be able to benefit from the defence of diminished responsibility under s 2 of the Homicide Act 1957, in that they suffered from an abnormality of mind due to the extreme circumstances in which they found themselves. Is it not permissible to sacrifice one life in order to save more? The famous example of the climbers roped together, when one slips and is saved from death only because he is roped to his colleagues, helps to illustrate the point. His colleagues, realising they too will perish unless the weight of their friend is released, sever the rope and send him to his death. In such circumstances, where there is no realistic prospect of survival for the person who had slipped, is it really to be expected that the other climbers should also perish?

The Law Commission has proposed the following clause as the basis for a statutory defence of duress of circumstances:

(1) No act of a person constitutes an offence if the act is done under duress of circumstances.

(2) A person does an act under duress of circumstances if:

(a) he does it because he knows or believes that it is immediately necessary to avoid death or serious injury to himself or another; and

(b) the danger that he knows or believes to exist is such that in all the circumstances (including any of his personal characteristics that affect its gravity) he cannot reasonably be expected to act otherwise.

It is for the defendant to show that the reason for his act was such knowledge or belief as is mentioned in para (a).

Note that the clause will not apply to a person who has knowingly and without reasonable excuse exposed himself to the danger known or believed to exist.

7.6.1 Necessity

English law has over the centuries paid lip service to a defence of necessity but has held back from giving a full-blown commitment. The argument runs that faced with the choice of two evils, the defendant is justified in adopting the particular course of action which breaches the criminal law. The defence, it is suggested, was at the heart of the decision in *Bourne* (1938), where a surgeon performed an abortion on a 14 year old girl who had been raped. He was charged under s 58 of the OAPA 1861 with unlawfully using an instrument with intent to procure a miscarriage. In his direction to the jury, the judge asked them to consider whether the surgeon had acted in good faith, and, if so, he could not be said to be acting unlawfully. To save the life of the mother, it was necessary to destroy the foetus, thus the jury's acquittal of Bourne was a clear signal that they viewed the act as justified, that is, necessary. One can point to the Abortion Act 1967 as a statutory recognition of the defence of necessity, that is, two doctors acting in good faith for the benefit of the mother.

7.6.2 Civil cases

It is also worth considering two civil cases, *Gillick v West Norfolk and Wisbech Area Health Authority* (1986) and *Re F (Mental Patient: Sterilisation)* (1989), in which aspects of necessity are raised. In the former case, the question arose whether or not a doctor prescribing contraceptives to a girl under 16 would be guilty of aiding and abetting unlawful sexual intercourse. The House of Lords believed he would not, providing he was acting in the best interests of the young person in the sense that he held an honest belief that the girl's health – mental, physical or emotional – would be protected by his actions. In simple terms, he helps her to bring about the offence because he believes it is necessary for her well being that she should be protected against an unwanted pregnancy. In the latter case, the House of Lords recognised that a 36 year old woman with a mental capacity of a four or five year-old could be sterilised, even though she had no comprehension of what was happening and could not give her consent. Despite her mental age, the woman either was or was likely to become sexually active or vulnerable to sexual activity, hence the intervention of the authorities. Lord Goff viewed the situation as one of necessity. It is accepted that one can act on behalf of another without that person's consent in emergency circumstances but this could not be said to be covered by that doctrine. As Lord Goff put it: 'The principle is one of necessity, not of emergency.' In *Re A (Children)* (2000), Brooke LJ, ruling that it would be lawful for surgeons to operate to separate conjoined twins J and M, where not to do so would inevitably result in the otherwise avoidable death of J, held that the preconditions for necessity would be made out if: (a) the operation was needed to avoid 'inevitable and irreparable evil'; (b) the operation was no more than had reasonably to be done for the purpose to be achieved; (c) the evil inflicted was not 'disproportionate to the evil avoided'.

7.6.3 Types of necessity

Lord Goff in *Re F (Mental Patient: Sterilisation)* (1989) went further in expounding the circumstances when necessity can act to render lawful that which would otherwise be unlawful. He said:

> That there exists in the common law a principle of necessity which may justify action which would otherwise be unlawful is not in doubt. But historically the principle has been seen to be restricted to two groups of cases, which have been called cases of public necessity and cases of private necessity.

As an example of the former, he cites destroying another man's property in order to prevent a catastrophic fire as in the Great Fire of London in 1666. In the latter case, the unlawful act is done by an individual in order that his own person or property might be saved from imminent danger. He then goes on to recognise a third group of cases:

> ... which is also properly described as founded on the principle of necessity. These cases are concerned with action taken as a matter of necessity to assist another person without his consent. To give a simple example, a man who seizes another and forcibly drags him from the path of an oncoming vehicle, thereby saving him from injury or even death, commits no wrong.

The third group of cases to which Lord Goff alludes are brought within the doctrine of necessity only if two requirements are satisfied:

(1) it is not practicable to communicate with the assisted person; and

(2) the action taken must be such as a reasonable person would in all the circumstances take, acting in the best interests of the assisted person.

These principles are of course expounded in the context of a civil case and do not go so far as to establish a 'wide ranging' doctrine of necessity within the confines of the criminal law.

Is it not in the public interest for the law to finally give recognition to the defence of necessity? The acceptance of justification as a basis for any defence of necessity is to acknowledge that the public interest will ultimately determine whether the action was justified. Lord Griffiths in *F v West Berkshire Health Authority* (1989) thought the two 'to be inextricably interrelated conceptual justifications for the humane development of the common law. Why is it necessary that the mentally incompetent should be given treatment to which they lack the capacity to consent? The answer must surely be because it is in the public interest that it should be so'.

More recent case law would confirm that the judiciary is not prepared to permit an expansion of such a defence. In *Cichon* (1994), the defendant was charged with allowing a pit bull terrier to be in a public place without being muzzled, contrary to s 1(2)(d) of the Dangerous Dogs Act 1991. He claimed that he removed the muzzle because the dog suffered from kennel cough and that it was, in the circumstances, cruel to keep it muzzled. Was the defendant's conduct justified? The court thought not. The Act had as its aim the security of the public. It was said that neither the Act nor the common law allowed a person to make a value judgment as between what was good for the dog and what was good for the public. The court regarded the statutory provision as imposing absolute liability and Parliament could not have intended necessity to apply although there appears to be no reason in principle why necessity should not apply to absolute or strict liability offences. Assuming the dog to have been well secured and not placed in a position where it could cause any danger to the public, why should a person acting to relieve the suffering of an animal not be able to rely on the defence?

In *Harris* (1995), the court would not permit necessity as a defence to a charge of careless driving although it has been recognised as a defence to the more serious charge of reckless driving. A police car had crossed a red traffic signal while pursuing a vehicle suspected of carrying armed robbers. It collided with another vehicle. Regulation 34 of the Traffic Signs Regulations 1981 permits a vehicle being used for police purposes to avoid compliance with traffic signals providing in crossing a stop line it does not cause danger to the drivers of other vehicles. In this case, the defence of necessity would not have applied because the police driver had not acted reasonably and proportionately in seeking to avoid a threat of death or serious injury. The decision for the defendant was to balance the likelihood of the armed robbers seriously injuring someone against the possibility of a serious collision occurring to the road junction. However, Curtis J thought that in other circumstances necessity might well act as a defence. It would appear illogical to recognise the defence in respect of the lesser offence of careless driving but not in respect of the more serious, reckless driving.

Since necessity is a common law defence, its effect can always be abrogated by statute. The defence has been recognised but, as Professor Smith states in his commentary to *Cichon*, 'its nature and extent remains shadowy' ([1994] Crim LR 918).

In *Harris* (1995), the court referred to 'the defence of necessity (not duress) of circumstance'. In other cases, the courts have preferred to refer to duress of circumstance. Other courts simply speak of the defence of necessity. Duress of threats is a defence founded upon action taken because the defendant is under threat of death or serious injury. The test contains both objective and subjective elements. It seems totally inappropriate to use this sort of terminology when assessing whether, as in *Re F* (1989), a mentally incompetent person should be sterilised. Similarly, there is no 'threat' to the police officer who decides that his public duty demands that he crosses a road junction when the lights are against him. His will is not overborne in the accepted sense. The officer has made a decision in light of the circumstances known at the time and presumably would seek to maintain that it was his honest belief that the public interest demanded such a course of action. If, looked at objectively, the decision was a reasonable one, then the defence of necessity ought to be established. There appears to be no overriding reason why this matter should be looked at in the context of the defence of duress of circumstance. There is every reason therefore for recognising only two elements of the defence, namely the defence of duress and the defence of necessity.

The Law Commission wishes the defence to be retained:

> We therefore consider that, as part of the policy of retaining common law defences ... this specific defence of necessity should be kept open as something

potentially separate from duress. That is provided for by cl 36(2) of the Criminal Law Bill, which expressly saves 'any distinct defence of necessity' when abrogating the common law defences of duress by threats and of circumstances [para 35.7].

However, the question which still needs to be asked is why any special recognition needs to be given to a defence based upon duress of circumstance even though the Criminal Law Bill proposes to retain it (cl 26).

7.7 Self-defence and prevention of crime

Self-defence has long been part of the common law and allows individuals to use reasonable force in order to defend themselves should they come under attack. Lord Parker CJ approved this statement of the law in *Chisam* (1963):

> ... where a forcible and violent felony is attempted upon the person of another, the party assaulted, or his servant, or any other person present, is entitled to repel force by force, and, if necessary, to kill the aggressor.

In *Whyte* (1987), Lord Lane CJ endorsed the following propositions:

- a man who is attacked may defend himself but may only do what is reasonably necessary to effect such a defence;

- what is reasonable will depend on the nature of the attack;

- the response must not be out of all proportion to the demands of the situation;

- if someone is in imminent danger, it may be necessary to take instant action in order to avert that danger.

In *Oatridge* (1992), the Court of Appeal thought that the following questions were to be asked when self-defence was raised by the defendant:

- was the defendant under actual or threatened attack by the victim?;

- if yes, did the defendant act to defend himself against this attack?;

- if yes, was his response commensurate with the degree of danger created by the attack?

It should also be noted that, in addition to the common law of self-defence, s 3(1) of the Criminal Law Act 1967 provides:

> A person may use such force as is reasonable in the circumstances in the prevention of crime, or in effecting or assisting in the lawful arrest of offenders or suspected offenders or of persons unlawfully at large.

7.7.1 Mistake and self-defence

The basic rules on self-defence are relatively unambiguous, but before they are examined further one other point needs to be made. A person may believe that he is under attack when in fact he has made a mistake. It will be recalled that the case of *Gladstone Williams* (1987) confirmed that, providing the person honestly believed the situation was as he thought, then the case must proceed on the basis that the honest belief was fact, irrespective of whether it was a reasonable belief. As the Lord Chief Justice put it in the context of self-defence:

> In a case of self-defence, where self-defence or the prevention of crime is concerned, if the jury come to the conclusion that the defendant believed, or may have believed, that he was being attacked or that a crime was being committed, and that force was necessary to protect himself or to prevent the crime, then the prosecution have not proved their case.

This has been endorsed by the Court of Appeal in *Oatridge*. If the defendant honestly believed that he or she was under attack, even though that was in fact not the case, then the jury is to be invited to consider whether the response was 'commensurate with the degree of risk which the defendant believed to be created by the attack under which he believed himself to be'.

The Privy Council endorsed *Gladstone Williams* in *Beckford* (1987). Lord Griffiths was of the view that the honestly held, although mistaken, belief negatives the intent to act unlawfully.

In *Scarlett* (1993), Beldam LJ said:

> [The jury] ought not to convict him unless they are satisfied that the degree of force used was plainly more than was called for by the circumstances as he believed them to be and, provided he believed the circumstances called for the degree of force used, he is not to be convicted even if his belief is unreasonable.

This should not be interpreted to mean that a defendant can use any degree of force which he believes to be reasonable, however ill-founded that belief. The force used must be objectively reasonable in the circumstances that the defendant believes them to be. In *Owino* (1995), the appellant was convicted of two counts of assaulting his wife occasioning her actual bodily harm. He claimed that the injuries were sustained while he was using reasonable force to restrain her from assaulting him. The jury convicted and his appeal was dismissed. The court held that a person is not entitled to use any degree of force that is believed to be reasonable, however ill founded that belief. The degree of force used will be assessed objectively and the circumstances subjectively, that is, as the defendant honestly believed them to be.

7.7.2 What is reasonable force ?

What amounts to reasonable force will depend upon the facts and circumstances of each particular case. In *Whyte*, for example, the defendant had used a lock-knife with a six inch blade, which he had already opened against an unarmed man whom it appeared had not made any sort of threatening gesture towards him. His conviction for wounding with intent contrary to s 18 of the OAPA 1861 was upheld by the Appeal Court.

In *Palmer* (1971), Lord Morris of Borth-y-Gest thought that, in some situations, it would be possible to take 'simple avoiding action'. Yet some attacks may be very serious and certainly dangerous:

> If there is some relatively minor attack, it would not be common sense to permit some action of retaliation which is wholly out of proportion to the necessities of the situation. If an attack is serious so that it puts someone in immediate peril then immediate defensive action may be necessary. If the moment is one of crisis for someone in imminent danger, he may have to avert the danger by some instant reaction. If the attack is all over and no sort of peril remains then the employment of force may be by way of revenge or punishment or by way of paying off an old score or may be pure aggression. There may no longer be any link with a necessity of defence.

Lord Morris accepted that a person under attack cannot weigh to a nicety the exact measure of his necessary defensive action. If a jury thought that, in a moment of unexpected anguish, a person attacked had only done what he honestly and instinctively thought was necessary, that would be the 'most potent evidence that only reasonable defensive action had been taken'.

In order not to appear to be the aggressor in such circumstances, it is obviously going to support the defendant's case for self-defence if it can be shown that he retreated from the attacker before seeking to defend himself. It must be emphasised that there is no rule of law to the effect that one must retreat, before the defence can be set up. *Bird* (1985) decided that the jury should weigh up all the evidence. A failure to clearly indicate an unwillingness to get involved is one factor to be taken into account. As Lord Lane CJ said:

> Evidence that the defendant tried to retreat or tried to call off the fight may be a cast-iron method of casting doubt on the suggestion that he was the attacker or retaliator or the person trying to revenge himself. But is not by any means the only method of doing that.

Edmund Davies LJ in *McInnes* (1971) reflected on a defendant's willingness to 'disengage and temporise' to be seen to be acting as the peacemaker rather than aggressor.

The House of Lords examined certain aspects of the law on self-defence in *Clegg* (1995), albeit that, strictly speaking, self-defence did not arise from the facts of the case. The appellant was a soldier serving in Belfast. A vehicle had been stopped by another patrol when it suddenly accelerated away. A member of that patrol shouted to Private Clegg's group, inviting them to stop the car. The car with its headlights full on approached the patrol and shots were fired at the car. Private Clegg fired four shots. It was accepted by the court that three shots had been discharged in self-defence, Private Clegg believing that he or a colleague in his patrol were potential targets for terrorists. However, the fourth shot was fired when the car was some 50 yards past the soldiers. This bullet hit a passenger in the car, causing her death. The car had been stolen by 'joyriders' who had no terrorist connections.

The House of Lords, recognising that the danger for Private Clegg had passed, accepted that there could be 'no question of self-defence, and therefore no question of excessive force in self-defence'. The House of Lords considered the following question: does the existing law allow a verdict of manslaughter instead of murder where the force used in self-defence is excessive?

The High Court in Australia had decided in *Howe* (1958) that it was reasonable in principle to regard homicide as reduced to manslaughter in circumstances where the plea of self-defence failed because of excessive force being used. That decision did not find favour with the Privy Council in *Palmer* (1971). The outcome, to use Lord Lloyd's phrase in *Clegg*, is that there is no 'halfway house'. If the prosecution can show that what was done does not amount in law to self-defence, then the killing is unlawful and the accused will be guilty of murder, providing he intended to kill or cause grievous bodily harm, unless of course he has other defences available such as provocation or diminished responsibility. If self-defence succeeds, then the killing was lawful and there is no liability. The position in Australia has since been reversed as a result of the decision in *Zecevic* (1987). The House of Lords concluded:

> In my opinion the law of England must now be taken to be settled in accordance with the decision of the Privy Council in that case (*Palmer*). Thus the consequence of the use of excessive force in self-defence will be the same in the law of England, Scotland, Australia, Canada and the West Indies [that is, the defence either succeeds or it fails. If it succeeds, the defendant is acquitted. If it fails, he is guilty of murder].

Whether there should be a change in the law will be a matter for Parliament to consider, as it is bound up with the issue of whether there should be a mandatory life sentence for murder. If a judge had a discretion in sentencing, the issue raised in *Clegg* would not be so acute. At worst, Clegg shot intending to kill or seriously injure an occupant of the vehicle knowing that he was not under any threat: a clear case of murder. At best, he was responding instinctively to a potential terrorist attack. He had little time to assess all the relevant factors before making a decision. In other words, this was a misjudgment on his part which was understandable given the prevailing environment in Belfast at the time.

7.7.3 The Human Rights Act 1998 and self-defence

Article 2(2) of the European Convention on Human Rights, as incorporated by the Human Rights Act 1998, provides that:

> Deprivation of life shall not be regarded as inflicted in contravention of this Article when it results from the use of force which is no more than absolutely necessary ...:
>
> (a) in defence of any person from unlawful violence ...

In *McCann v UK* (1996), the European Court of Human Rights held that, where agents of the State use force in reliance on one of the exceptions listed in Art 2(2), and it transpires that the action was based on a mistake of fact (that is, a *Gladstone Williams* scenario), there will be no violation of Art 2, provided the honest belief of those acting in self-defence is based on good reasons. This creates the possibility that the law relating to mistakenly acting in self-defence in England and Wales may be in contravention of the requirements of the Convention, as the former simply requires evidence that D honestly believed it was necessary to act in self- defence, even where lethal force is used. There is no need for D to additionally establish that his belief was based on 'good reason'. See, further, *Andronicou v Cyprus* (1998), and Andrew Ashworth's commentary on the case at [1998] Crim LR 823 .

7.8 Draft Criminal Law Bill

The Law Commission in its its report, *Legislating the Criminal Code: Offences Against the Person and General Defences* (Law Com 218, 1993), recommends that an offence will not be committed if there is justifiable use of force:

27(1) The use of force by a person for any of the following purposes, if only such as is reasonable in the circumstances as he believes them to be, does not constitute an offence:

(a) to protect himself or another from injury, assault or detention caused by a criminal act;

(b) to protect himself or (with the authority of that other) another from trespass to the person;

(c) to protect his property from appropriation, destruction or damage caused by a criminal act or from trespass or infringement;

(d) to protect property belonging to another from appropriation, destruction or damage caused by a criminal act or (with the authority of the other) from trespass or infringement; or

(e) to prevent crime or a breach of the peace.

The above relates to the protection of person, property or the prevention of crime. A further clause, cl 28, deals with the justifiable use of force in effecting or assisting an arrest and states:

(1) The use of force by a person in effecting or assisting in a lawful arrest, if only such as is reasonable in the circumstances as he believes them to be, does not constitute an offence.

A person is to be taken as using force when applying force to or causing impact on the body of another. Additionally, if he threatens to use force or detains another without using force, he shall still be treated as using force (see cl 29).

GENERAL DEFENCES

This chapter covers a range of defences recognised by the law which if successful will result in the acquittal of the defendant or in the case of insanity possible hospitalisation. Justification and excuse are the bedrocks upon which the defences are built.

Insanity

Insanity may be relevant before the trial or at the time of the trial. Is the defendant fit to plead? Is he mentally capable of understanding the charges laid against him? The relevant law is to be found in the CP(I)A 1964 as amended by the CP(IUP)A 1991. If the defence of insanity is raised at the trial, then it is covered by the *M'Naghten* Rules. These presume every person to be sane unless proved otherwise. The defence is likely to succeed if it can be shown that at the time of the act the accused was suffering from a defect of reason caused by a disease of the mind so as not to know the nature and quality of the act or if he did that he did not know it was wrong. The burden of proof is on the defence on the balance of probabilities.

Infancy

Children under the age of 10 incur no criminal liability. Children over the age of 10 are treated as adults for the purposes of establishing *mens rea*. Section 34 of the Crime and Disorder Act 1998 has abolished the concept of mischievous discretion as that applied to defendants between the ages of 10 and 14.

Intoxication

A person intoxicated when he or she commits the crime may seek to maintain they had no *mens rea* for the crime. That may be true but it will not necessarily lead to an acquittal. A defendant may be intoxicated as a result of drink or drug consumption or both. The result may be an inability to form the *mens rea* or an ability but because of intoxication did not form the *mens rea* for the crime. The law recognises specific and basic intent crimes and decrees that intoxication may be admitted in evidence on as a defence to specific intent crimes (see *Majewski* (1975)). Basic intent crimes require recklessness and the excessive consumption of alcohol or drugs is likely to be deemed to be a reckless act. A distinction also needs to be drawn between dangerous and non-dangerous drugs. It will not be automatically presumed to be reckless to consume non-dangerous drugs (see *Hardie* (1983)). Where a defendant is mistaken as a result of intoxication and acts in light of that mistake, he will not be allowed to rely on mistake as a defence.

Mistake

A person may allege that he did not possess the *mens rea* for the offence because of labouring under a mistake of fact. Mistake will provide a defence providing the belief was honestly held. The reasonableness of the grounds for holding that belief will undoubtedly influence a jury in deciding whether the defendant honestly held the belief.

Duress

Evidence of duress prevents the law from treating what was done as a crime. It has been said that the defence is a 'merciful concession to human frailty'. It does not however apply to murder, attempted murder or treason. There has to be evidence of a threat to kill or cause serious injury to the defendant or a near relative. The test for duress contains both subjective and objective factors as outlined by Lord Lane CJ in *Graham* (1982). A defendant is expected to have the steadfastness to be expected of the ordinary citizen. The characteristics of the defendant will be pertinent in assessing whether a person's will has been overborne. Those who voluntarily join criminal or terrorist organisations are unlikely to be able to rely on duress if 'forced' to commit crimes. The last decade has seen the emergence of the defence of duress of circumstances. The defence appears to work where the defendant acts to avoid an imminent danger of death or serious injury to himself or another, if in the circumstances he could not reasonably be expected to act otherwise.

Necessity

Never wholeheartedly embraced by the judiciary as a defence. The idea is that faced with a choice of two evils the defendant is justified in adopting a course of action which breaches the criminal law. For example, breaking the speed limit in order to deliver someone in need of emergency medical treatment to hospital. Examine Lord Goff's examples of necessity in *Re F* (1989).

Self-defence

Long part of the common law this defence allows persons to use reasonable force in order to defend themselves. What amounts to reasonable force will depend on all the circumstances. If excessive force is used, then the defence is lost.

CHAPTER 8

OFFENCES AGAINST PROPERTY: THEFT

The next two chapters are concerned with offences against property which are detailed in the Theft Act (TA) 1968 and TA 1978 and the Theft (Amendment) Act 1996. There will also be an examination of the offence of criminal damage contrary to the Criminal Damage Act 1971.

8.1   Introduction

The TA 1968 is the result of the work of the Criminal Law Revision Committee (Eighth Report, *Theft and Related Offences*, Cmnd 2977, 1966). The Larceny Act 1916 had created innumerable problems of interpretation for the courts resulting in over complexity because of the integration of many civil law concepts, particularly in respect of the crime of larceny. The TA 1968 therefore set out to create a new order which it was hoped would be intelligible to the ordinary person. In many respects, the TA 1968 achieved this objective, but now, over 30 years on, and many cases later, the ordinary person would have some real difficulty in understanding much of the law. As will be seen later the House of Lords has hardly helped to create the certainty one expects from the criminal law.

The basic definition of theft is contained in s 1 of the TA 1968 and reads:

> A person is guilty of theft if he dishonestly appropriates property belonging to another with the intention of permanently depriving the other of it; and 'thief' and 'steal' shall be construed accordingly.

The offence carries a maximum sentence of seven years' imprisonment. It will be immediately apparent that the *actus reus* and *mens rea* concepts can be easily distinguished. The *actus reus* is described by the words 'appropriates property belonging to another', and the *mens rea* includes proof of dishonesty and an intention permanently to deprive the other of the property.

Sections 2 to 6 of the TA 1968 give help and assistance as to how these key words are to be interpreted and therefore require careful consideration. Perhaps the starting point ought to be s 4 which deals with property because this determines what can actually be stolen.

8.2   Property

Section 4(1) of the TA 1968 states that property includes 'money and all other property, real or personal, including things in action and other intangible property'. There are limitations imposed by other sub-sections but undoubtedly s 4(1) is a very wide provision. However, it is worth emphasising particular issues at this point. Property includes both tangible and intangible property and s 4(1) identifies a particular kind of intangible property, a *thing in action*. A 'thing in action' is a right which may be enforced against another person by an action in law. This very right itself is property under the 1968 Act and so can be stolen. A simple example of a thing in action is a right possessed by one party to a contract against the other party to the contract. In the case of *Marshall and Others* (1998), the defendants obtained unexpired Underground tickets and Travelcards from members of the public and then sold them to other travellers. The tickets were marked as not transferable and the convictions for theft of the tickets as *pieces of paper* were upheld. However, the Court of Appeal suggested that not only did a customer have a thing in action against London Underground (the right to travel) but also London Underground had a thing in action against the customer (the right to prevent transfer). The Court's conclusion that the defendants might also have appropriated that right, the thing in action, by selling the tickets is much more questionable. Perhaps the most important example of a thing in action in the context of theft is the right possessed by the holder of an account with a bank against the bank. Despite popular usage, the account holder does not have 'money in the bank', only the bank has money in the bank. Each account holder has a thing in action against the bank, the right to compel the bank to pay an amount of money equivalent to the credit in the account. Suppose the account holder to have a credit of £5,000. That is £5,000's worth of right which, as property, can be stolen in whole or in part. It is important to be clear that it is not the money which is being stolen but the right to it (should a rogue subsequently get the money from the bank, he will steal the money itself from the bank). So, in *Kohn* (1979), a company accountant authorised to draw cheques on the company's behalf drew cheques to meet his own debts and was convicted of theft of the company's thing in action against the bank. In that case, the account was sometimes in debit but within the limits of an agreed overdraft. An agreed overdraft also gives the account holder a thing in action which can be stolen (compare also the credit limit associated with credit cards, store cards and the like). If the account is in debit beyond any agreed overdraft, then the account holder has no thing in action against the bank and so nothing to steal.

It is more difficult to determine what will count as intangible property apart from a thing in action. One possibility is confidential information (by contrast with the medium in which the information is conveyed, such as on a piece of paper). It was held in *Oxford v Moss* (1979) that a student who had seen a proof copy of a university examination paper he was due to sit was not guilty of theft of the information because information was not 'property' and therefore was incapable of being stolen. Of course, if he had dishonestly appropriated the piece of paper on which the examination was printed, then he could have been found guilty of theft of the paper, providing there was evidence of an intention to permanently deprive the university of the paper. If a student and a member of the administration conspired together to obtain the information, they could be found guilty of a conspiracy to defraud, suggesting that the law recognises there is something worth protecting. The meaning of defraud has been discussed extensively in a range of cases over the last 30 years. *Scott* (1975) accepted that to cause economic loss was one consequence of fraudulent behaviour. If the university became aware that its security had been breached, then it would be put to the expense of producing new examination papers. The fraud would have resulted in economic loss to the university. *Welham* (1961) held that the term 'defraud' is not confined to causing or taking the risk of causing pecuniary loss to another. So, for example, it is fraud to deceive a public official into doing something he would not have done but for the deceit. One example might be the forging of a doctor's prescription in order to obtain drugs. Of course, the drugs are tangible whereas the information is intangible, but s 4(1) makes it clear that property can include intangible property. If both would fall within the scope of interests worthy of protection under the law of conspiracy, is there not a case for treating not only the drugs but also the information as property and so within the scope of the offence of theft? (For further information on the law on conspiracy, see Chapter 5.)

Though land is property within the definition in s 4(1), s 4(2) provides that land or things forming part of land and severed from it by the defendant cannot be stolen except when:

- he is a trustee or personal representative, or is authorised by power of attorney, or as liquidator of a company, or otherwise, to sell or dispose of land belonging to another, and he appropriates the land or anything forming part of it by dealing with it in breach of the confidence reposed in him; or

- he is not in possession of the land and appropriates anything forming part of the land by severing it or causing it to be severed, or after it has been severed; or

- being in possession of the land under a tenancy, he appropriates the whole or part of any fixture or structure let to be used with the land.

In the case of a person who is not in possession of the land, there is a further limitation, for s 4(3) states:

> A person who picks mushrooms growing wild on any land, or who picks flowers, fruit or foliage from a plant growing wild on any land, does not (although not in possession of the land) steal what he picks, unless he does it for reward or for sale or other commercial purpose.

So, even if a person who is not in possession of the land severs mushrooms, flowers, fruit or foliage, he will not be guilty of theft unless either he has not 'picked' it (for instance, he has uprooted a whole bush rather than picked fruit from the bush) or he has done it for reward or for sale or for some other commercial purpose. Thus, the provisions are designed to deter those who would ravage the countryside for commercial benefit. To remove flowers growing wild in order to enhance the appearance of one's office will not amount to an offence. To do so with intent to sell the flowers at the local market would bring one inside the ambit of the legislation.

There are also limitations on the theft of wild creatures. Section 4(4) states:

> Wild creatures, tamed or untamed, shall be regarded as property; but a person cannot steal a wild creature not tamed nor ordinarily kept in captivity, or the carcass of any such creature, unless either it has been reduced into possession by or on behalf of another person and possession of it has not since been lost or abandoned, or another person is in course of reducing it into possession.

It will be seen that such creatures must have been reduced into someone's possession before they can be stolen or be in the course of being so reduced. To take animals from a zoo, whether tamed or untamed, would amount to theft providing there was the necessary *mens rea* of an intention permanently to deprive the zoo of the animals.

Conversely, if a fox were to come into a private garden on a regular basis in search of food one could hardly say that it had been reduced into the possession of the landowner and therefore if someone were to capture the fox that would not amount to theft.

8.3   Appropriation

For theft to occur, the property has to be appropriated and this is a concept which has created many difficulties of interpretation over the last 30 years. The basic definition is contained in s 3 of the TA 1968:

> (1) Any assumption by a person of the rights of an owner amounts to an appropriation, and this includes, where he has come by the property (innocently or not) without stealing it, any later assumption of a right to it by keeping or dealing with it as owner.
>
> (2) Where property or a right or interest in property is or purports to be transferred for value to a person acting in good faith, no later assumption by him of rights which he believed himself to be acquiring shall, by reason of any defect in the transferor's title, amount to theft of the property.

In his dissenting speech in *Gomez* (1993), Lord Lowry suggested that the:

> ordinary and natural meaning of 'appropriate' is to take for oneself, or to treat as one's own, property which belongs to someone else. The primary dictionary meaning is 'take possession of, take to oneself, especially without authority' and that is in my opinion the meaning which the word bears in s 1(1).

Later in his speech, Lord Lowry refers to the primary meaning of 'assumption' as 'taking on oneself which is a unilateral act'. In *Morris* (1983), Lord Roskill's view of appropriation was put in these terms:

> ... not an act expressly or impliedly authorised by the owner but an act by way
> of adverse interference with or usurpation of those rights.

For the avoidance of doubt, it must be emphasised that Lord Roskill thought that an adverse interference with *any* right of the owner was sufficient; there being no need for the prosecution to prove that *all* the rights of the owner had been usurped.

The suggestion therefore appeared to be that an appropriation was an unauthorised act, because the removal of goods from a supermarket shelf was done with the implied authority of the owners of the shop. That implied authority continued with the honest shopper as he or she wheeled a trolley around the store until arrival at the checkout when on payment of the appropriate amount of money the goods would pass to the shopper. Even a dishonest shopper would have implied authority from the owner as long as he had not acted in such a way as to exceed the limits of the authority. Putting goods into a trolley or basket would be within the apparent authority. Hiding them by putting them into a pocket or a bag, or taking them beyond the checkout without having paid would be outside the authorisation. However, as will be seen later, *Gomez* (1993) decided that 'consent to or authorisation by the owner of the taking by the rogue is irrelevant' (*per* Lord Keith) and the above comments should be read in light of this clear statement of principle. In *Morris*, the appellants had taken goods from the shelves of a supermarket and removed the price labels, substituting lower priced labels, which had been taken from other goods on offer within the store. Both appellants were convicted of theft, one having been apprehended having paid the lower price and the other as he was at the checkout. The appeals were based on the argument that their acts were inconsistent with the true meaning of appropriation in that switching price labels did not amount to an assumption of the rights of the owner. The House of Lords dismissed their appeals.

It will be apparent that the switching of price labels in a supermarket may give rise to speculation as to whether any other offences have been committed. Is the defendant attempting to obtain property by deception? These actions must surely be regarded as mere preparation given the more recent authorities dealing with s 1 of the Criminal Attempts Act (CAtA) 1981. There is still much more to do before the deception is practised. The goods will have to be taken to the checkout, removed from the trolley and placed onto the conveyor belt. To change labels at the very outset of the plan would not appear to bring the accused within the terms of the CAtA 1981. Nor will the facts support a conviction under s 15 of the TA 1968 if they are insufficient to even bring the accused within the meaning of the attempts legislation. Yet the House of Lords is prepared to accept that theft has been committed in these circumstances. Presumably, when the accused is reaching for the goods, then an attempted theft is taking place, always accepting that the necessary *mens rea* can be proved. One can only speculate as to how many people engaged upon this type of activity will intend to commit theft as opposed to preparing the ground for an attempt to deceive the cashier.

8.3.1   Consent or authorisation by the owner

Section 3 makes no reference to the absence of consent as a vital ingredient in determining whether or not, in law, an appropriation has occurred. We have seen above that in Lord Roskill's opinion an appropriation cannot have occurred unless there has been an 'adverse interference with or usurpation of any of the rights of an individual'. This would appear to suggest that where there is evidence that any interference with the property was with the consent of the owner the element of adverse interference is not proved. Prior to the TA 1968 coming into force, the law was regulated by the Larceny Act 1916 and under this legislation it had been necessary to prove that the property alleged to have been stolen was taken 'without the consent of the owner'. Lord Lane CJ had neatly summed up the perceived difficulty in the Court of Appeal in *Morris* (1983) when he said:

> As to the meaning of the word 'appropriation' there are two schools of thought. The first contends that the word 'appropriate' has built into it a connotation that it is some action inconsistent with the owner's rights, something hostile to the interests of the owner or contrary to his wishes and intention or without his authority. The second school of thought contends that the word in this context means no more than to take possession of an article and that there is no requirement that the taking or appropriation should in any way be antagonistic to the rights of the owner.

In *Eddy v Niman* (1981), it was held that to take goods from a supermarket shelf intending to steal but to think better of it before approaching the cash desk would not amount to theft, illustrating the 'first school of thought'. Here, he was simply doing what all shoppers are permitted, if not encouraged to do, that is, placing goods in a trolley or basket.

Lord Roskill in *Morris* considered the crucial House of Lords' authority, *Lawrence v Commissioner of Police for the Metropolis* (1971). This case dealt with the important question of whether, in law, an appropriation must be without the consent of the owner and is an example of the second 'school of thought'. In that case the appellant was a taxi driver who had collected a passenger from Victoria Station and transported him to Ladbroke Grove in London. The passenger was an Italian student who spoke little English and had his destination address written on a piece of paper. Lawrence tried to indicate that it was a long journey and therefore very expensive (which was untrue). The passenger offered him £1 from his wallet but the appellant, noticing the wallet was still open removed a further £6. The correct fare should have been just over 50 p in today's currency. He was charged with theft and convicted of stealing £6. The House of Lords in *Lawrence* rejected the argument that there could not be theft if the owner of the property had authorised the acts which were done by the defendant. Viscount Dilhorne with whom the other Law Lords agreed said:

> I see no ground for concluding that the omission of the words 'without the consent of the owner' was inadvertent and not deliberate, and to read the sub-section as if they were included is, in my opinion, wholly unwarranted. Parliament by the omission of these words has relieved the prosecution of the burden of establishing that the taking was without the owner's consent. That is no longer an ingredient of the offence.

Lord Roskill's support for *Lawrence* appears to be contradicted by his own speech in *Morris*, where he refers to appropriation as something which has not been 'expressly or impliedly authorised by the owner'. It could be said that this statement by Lord Roskill was strictly *obiter* because the House of Lords agreed that the appropriation only took place once the goods were taken from the shelves and the labels had been switched. This flatly contradicts the Court of Appeal's view to the effect that the appropriation took place when the goods were removed but before the label switching. The reasoning behind the Court of Appeal's decision is that even though the taking was authorised, it was taken not for any lawful purpose but for the defendant's own use. There is always the possibility that the labels on goods could be switched without the goods being removed from the shelf. According to Lord Roskill, this would not amount to an appropriation but the later removal of the goods, for example, to place into the shopper's own basket, would create the required adverse interference to amount to an appropriation.

If consent is to be relevant to the issue of theft, as distinct from appropriation, then there is a strong case for it to be viewed in the context of s 2(1) of the TA 1968. This provides that a person's appropriation of property is not to be regarded as dishonest if the property was appropriated in the belief that the other person would have consented if he had known of the circumstances.

8.3.2 Outline of the *Gomez* case

The issues raised by the cases of *Lawrence* and *Morris* were considered by the House of Lords in *Gomez* (1993).

In this case, Gomez was employed as an assistant manager at an electrical goods shop. Along with two acquaintances, a plan was agreed whereby goods to the value of £17,200 would be supplied by the shop in return for two building society cheques, which the parties knew to be stolen. Gomez, as assistant manager, was to seek authorisation and therefore clearance for the goods to be supplied in return for the cheques. The manager, to whom the request was put, instructed Gomez to make enquiries of the bank in order to ascertain whether the cheques were acceptable. Gomez later dishonestly told the manager they were 'as good as cash'. The cheques were eventually returned with the order not to pay because they had been stolen. Gomez was charged with two counts of theft. The Court of Appeal (1991) was of the view that there was a voidable contract between the owners of the shop and the receiver of the electrical goods and therefore the transfer of goods was 'with the consent and express authority of the owner and that accordingly there was no lack of authorisation and no appropriation'. This approach by the Court of Appeal was based upon the *Morris* decision. The House of Lords by a 4:1 majority restored the conviction. Expressed in its narrow form, the *ratio* of the case is that an appropriation, for the purposes of s 1, is complete, even though it is expressly or impliedly authorised and was therefore with the owner's consent, if it was induced by fraud, deception or false representation. The House of Lords concluded that the fraud, deception or false representation practised on the owner made the appropriation dishonest. *Lawrence* together with the case of *Dobson v General Accident Fire and Life Assurance Corporation* (1989) was approved, the *dictum* of Lord Roskill in *Morris* disapproved and two other decisions, *Skipp* (1975) and *Fritschy* (1985), were overruled.

8.3.3 The deep division of opinion on the consent/authorisation issue

A cursory look at these cases before giving further consideration to *Gomez* will illustrate the deep division of opinion on this issue of consent/authorisation and appropriation. Consideration will also be given to three post-*Gomez* decisions, *Mazo* (1996), *Hopkins and Kendrick* (1997) and *Hinks* (2000), which show that the decision in *Gomez* does not represent the last word on this issue (see below, 8.3.5).

    Dobson was heard by the Court of Appeal, Civil Division and concerned a plaintiff who was insured by the defendants under a home insurance policy. This policy provided cover against all the usual contingencies including theft. The plaintiff had advertised for sale a gold watch and diamond ring at a total price of £5,950. He was telephoned by a man who claimed to be interested in purchasing the items and a sale was agreed with payment to be by building society cheque. The transaction was completed but, a few days later, the plaintiff was informed that the cheque had been stolen and was consequently worthless. Dobson then made a claim on his insurers under the theft clause of his policy. The insurers denied liability on the basis that the watch and ring had not been stolen within the meaning of s 1 of the TA 1968. The county court in which he commenced the action found for him and the insurers appealed on the basis, *inter alia*, that, as the owner consented to the taking, there could in law be no appropriation. The Court of Appeal preferred *Lawrence* to *Morris* and concluded there was sufficient authority in Viscount Dilhorne's speech in *Lawrence* to conclude that there would be an appropriation, even where there was evidence of consent to the taking. Parker LJ recognised the inconsistency between *Lawrence* and *Morris* and chose not to follow the latter of the two decisions of the House of Lords. Nor did he, perhaps wisely, attempt to reconcile the two cases. He put it this way:

> I am fully conscious of the fact that in so concluding I may be said not to be applying *R v Morris*. This may be so, but in the light of the difficulties inherent in the decision, the very clear decision in *Lawrence*'s case and the equally clear statement in *R v Morris* that the question whether a contract is void or only voidable is irrelevant, I have been unable to reach any other conclusion.

Bingham LJ while admitting it was difficult to find a basis upon which to reconcile *Lawrence* and *Morris* nevertheless suggested that, in the former case, the Italian student had simply permitted the taxi driver to take the money and this was not consistent with the concept of consent. Applying this to the case in point, the plaintiff had allowed or permitted the rogue to take the items, but because he lacked vital information had not consented to the taking.

In *Skipp*, the defendant had posed as a genuine haulage contractor and had been given a job to deliver three loads of oranges and onions from London to Leicester. The goods were duly loaded onto his lorry and he went on his way. Before reaching Leicester, he drove off with the goods. The question arose as to when he had appropriated the loads. The Court of Appeal held that Skipp was guilty of theft of the loads only when he did an act inconsistent with his authorisation, in other words, at the point where he departed from the chosen route to Leicester. The original taking had been with consent. *Skipp* was reconciled with *Lawrence* in *Dobson* on the basis that, as Parker LJ put it:

> ... there was much more than mere consent of the owner. There was express authority, indeed instruction to collect the goods. It could not therefore be said that the defendant was assuming any rights. Whatever his secret intentions he was, until he diverted the goods, exercising the owner's right on his instructions and on his behalf.

In *Fritschy*, the defendant was convicted of the theft of a number of krugerrands. Fritschy was the agent of a Dutch company which dealt in the coins and he was asked to come to England to collect a consignment on behalf of a customer and to take them to Switzerland. He collected them, went to Switzerland and then made off with them. His conviction for theft was quashed on the basis that there was no evidence of any act within the jurisdiction which was inconsistent with what he was expressly authorised to do. Parker LJ in *Dobson* treats *Fritschy* in the same way as *Skipp*, and points out the clear authority from his employers. This was completely different from *Lawrence* where there was evidence only that he allowed or permitted the act to take place.

8.3.4   The decision in *Gomez*

Gomez decides that consent or authorisation by the owner to the act in question is irrelevant in deciding if there has in law been an appropriation. On one reading of the decision in *Gomez* it can be maintained that the *ratio* applies only to cases where the consent has been induced by fraud, deception or false representation. If this were so, then the supermarket cases such as *Eddy v Niman* would probably still follow the *Morris* approach. The point of law of general public importance related only to where consent had been obtained by false representation. Therefore, anything considered by the Law Lords not involving false representations could be said to be *obiter dicta*. However, there is no indication that the decision has been applied in its 'narrow' context. It will be noted that *Gomez* was a case where fraud was perpetrated on the manager through the false representation made by the appellant that he had checked with the bank and that the building society cheque was 'as good as cash'. The authorisation was then given for the transaction to proceed. The decision does not appear to differentiate between consent freely given and consent induced by a fraudulent representation. It will be apparent that Gomez could have been charged under s 15 of the TA 1968 with obtaining property belonging to another by deception and one may only speculate as to why this course of action was not adopted, as there would appear to be no obstacle to a conviction, given the clear deception practised on the manager.

Approval was given to Lord Roskill's statement in *Morris* that the assumption by the defendant of any of the rights of an owner was sufficient to satisfy s 3(1) of the TA 1968. Lord Keith's opinion was that any interference with any property belonging to another would amount to an appropriation, although whether or not it amounted to theft would depend on other factors, such as proof of dishonesty and an intention to deprive the other permanently of the item. Two examples were given by Lord Keith, using the supermarket context:

> It seems to me that the switching of price labels on the article is in itself an assumption of one of the rights of the owner, whether or not it is accompanied by some other act such as removing the article from the shelf and placing it in a basket or trolley. No one but the owner has the right to remove a price label from an article or to place a price label upon it. If anyone else does so, he does an act, as Lord Roskill put it, by way of adverse interference with or usurpation of that right.

He then dealt with the example of the practical joker mentioned by Lord Roskill in *Morris*:

> The practical joker (who has switched labels) ... is not guilty of theft because he has not acted dishonestly and does not intend to deprive the owner permanently of the article. So the label switching in itself constitutes an appropriation ...

One of the consequences of this approach is that an act which would probably not even amount to the *actus reus* of an *attempt* to obtain by deception is sufficient to amount to the *actus reus* of the full offence of theft.

The minority view was put forward by Lord Lowry. He acknowledged that 'any attempt to reconcile the statements of principle in *Lawrence* and *Morris* is a complete waste of time'. He advocates the simple approach of prosecuting under s 15 of the TA 1968 all offences involving obtaining by deception and prosecute 'theft in general under s 1'. In that way, some thefts will come under s 15, but no 'false pretences will come under s 1'.

Whatever one's stance is on the consent/authorisation issue, the law would appear to be clear if somewhat controversial. Professor Smith in his commentary on *Gomez* ((1993) Crim LR 304, p 309) states: 'Better to accept that we now have this extraordinary wide law of theft, unless and until it has to be reconsidered by the House of Lords.' A little earlier in the same case commentary, he had suggested that the 'ordinary meaning of "appropriation" has gone out of the window' (p 307).

8.3.5 Further developments

The Court of Appeal has had occasion to deal with the issue since the decision of the House of Lords in *Gomez*. In *Gallasso* (1993), the appellant was a nurse in a home for severely mentally handicapped adults and part of her duties involved looking after the patients' finances. Each patient had a trust account at a building society and any monies were paid into these accounts. Gallasso was the sole signatory and regularly drew money out for the patients' day to day needs. J, a patient, received a cheque for £4,000 and Gallasso opened a second trust account for him into which she paid the cheque. Later, she transferred £3,000 into his first account and the remainder into her own account. A few months later, another cheque for £1,800 was received and she opened, on his behalf, a new cashcard account at the same building society branch. She faced three counts of theft relating to three transactions: count 1 relating to the opening of a second account; count 2, the payment of £1,000 into her own account; and count 3, the opening of the cashcard account. The judge rejected a submission of no case to answer on counts 1 and 3. Counsel had argued that, as the cheques had been properly paid by Gallasso, there was no evidence of appropriation. The jury acquitted on count 1 and she did not challenge her conviction on count 2. She appealed against her conviction on count 3. In allowing her appeal, the court acknowledged that, since *Gomez*, it was 'now clear that a taking of property with the owner's consent could amount to appropriation'. The court thought that paying the cheque into the patient's account could not be regarded as an appropriation, since it was 'evidence of Gallasso affirming J's rights rather than assuming them for herself'. The court seems to have been swayed by the argument that there must be a taking even though it may be with consent and here the paying in 'was not a taking at all'. But *Gomez* did not say that there had to be a taking in order for there to be, in law, an appropriation. The label switching example given by Lord Roskill in *Morris* (1983) surely does not involve any taking but was held to be an appropriation and endorsed by the House of Lords in *Gomez*. It is difficult to see how *Gallasso* can stand as an authority on the meaning of appropriation given the clear statement of principle which emanated from *Gomez*. Lloyd LJ thought that: 'Lord Keith did not mean to say that every handling is an appropriation.' With respect, what Lord Keith may have meant to say is not important. That is what he did say but, of course, in practice, no criminal consequences will ensue without the other elements of the offence being present.

In *Mazo* (1996), it was difficult to identify any act of deception and the Court of Appeal had to decide whether to give effect to the decision in *Gomez*. M was a maid to Lady S and, claimed the prosecution, took dishonest advantage of S's mental incapacity by accepting cheques totalling £37,000 from S. S's bank was suspicious and the chief cashier telephoned S but was simply told to go ahead and cash the cheques. M claimed that the cheques were gifts from a grateful employer and the Crown accepted that if this were true then there could be no theft. Her appeal against conviction for theft was allowed. Clearly it is important to focus on the mental capacity of the donor and donee. If S had made the transfers having the mental capacity to make a valid gift, then it is difficult to see why, in the absence of fraud or undue influence, the donee should be guilty of theft. If, in applying civil law principles, there is a clear indefeasible transfer of ownership from the donor to the donee then it would be untenable for the criminal law to conclude that the recipient is guilty of theft. If one analyses the facts by reference to s 1 of the TA 1968 and applying *Gomez* it does appear that M should be guilty of theft. She has assumed all the rights of the owner over the £37,000. This money has been obtained with the approval of the former owner. Clearly, there is consent but as we have seen that is irrelevant as to whether or not there is an appropriation. There is little prospect of M returning the money to S and therefore there would appear to be an intention to deprive S permanently of her money and that leaves only the question of dishonesty. In circumstances such as these, it is not unusual for an elderly person to bestow gifts upon a devoted carer but not of this magnitude. That may be done by way of will but rarely before the death of the donor. If this is indeed the case, the jury, applying the *Ghosh* principles (see below, 8.6), would have to decide whether or not she was acting honestly in accepting such gifts. In *Mazo*, the jury in returning a guilty verdict seems to have concluded that she was acting dishonestly. However, an application of civil law principles draws us to the conclusion that a valid gift has been made given that S had the mental capacity required to make such a gift. In *Re Beaney (Deceased)* (1978), it was held that the degree of understanding required for the making of a valid *inter vivos* gift was relative to the transaction to be effected. If the subject matter and value of the gift were trivial in relation to the donor's other assets, a low degree of understanding was sufficient but:

> ... if the effect of the gift was to dispose of the owner's only asset of value and to pre-empt the devolution of his estate under his will or on his intestacy, the degree of understanding required was as high as that required for a will and the donor had to understand the claims of all potential donees and the extent of the property to be disposed of.

If, therefore, the donee is legally entitled to keep the gift, it would be untenable for the criminal law to conclude that a case of theft had been made out.

This issue was revisited in *Kendrick and Hopkins* (1997). H and K were convicted of conspiracy to steal. They ran a residential home and the Crown maintained that they had taken over the running of the affairs of a resident aged 99 who was virtually blind and incapable of managing her affairs. Over a period, they cashed her investments, obtained enduring power of attorney and effected a new will signed by her making them her beneficiaries. Their defence was that at all times they were acting with her authorisation and in her interests. The jury convicted and the Court of Appeal dismissed their appeal. The court distinguished *Mazo* on the basis that here the 'donor' did not have the mental capacity to understand the consequences of her actions. In such circumstances such dispositions are invalid and the property in law continues to belong to the 'donor'. Where the recipients are aware of the donor's incapacity, it is more likely than not that the jury will conclude that they were acting dishonestly in seeking to benefit from the donor's misfortune.

In *Kendrick and Hopkins*, the court expressed doubts about whether the concession had been properly made in *Mazo* that a valid indefeasible gift inevitably meant that no theft could be committed. By the time of the decision in *Hinks* (2000) (actually decided in 1998), these doubts had flowered into outright rejection of the proposition. *Hinks* was yet another case involving a barely competent and gullible victim being induced to part with large amounts of money in an exploitative relationship dominated by the defendant. Rejecting the defendant's attempt to rely on the argument that she could not be guilty of theft for receiving valid gifts, and upholding her conviction, the Court of Appeal asserted:

> In our judgment, in relation to theft, one of the ingredients for a jury to consider is not whether there has been a gift, valid or otherwise, but whether there has been appropriation. A gift may be clear evidence of appropriation. But a jury should not, in our view, be asked to consider whether a gift has been validly made because, first, that is not what s 1 of the Theft Act requires; secondly, such an approach is inconsistent with *Lawrence* and *Gomez*; and, thirdly, the state of mind of a donor is irrelevant to appropriation.

The court in *Mazo* did not specifically say why there can be no theft when there is a valid indefeasible gift. The argument advanced above is that it would be inconceivable that the civil law should acknowledge that the defendant has obtained rights of ownership over the property which cannot be taken away at the same time as the criminal law should declare the defendant to be a thief because of the very acquisition of the gift. The simple way of explaining this with regard to the elements of theft would be to say that there has been no appropriation but this explanation appears to be unavailable so long as the *Gomez* interpretation of appropriation prevails. This is the message of *Hinks*. Unless that interpretation is modified, those charged with theft in such circumstances will have to rely on absence of dishonesty or try to persuade the court that there is simply an overriding principle that the criminal law cannot be seen to be in conflict with the civil law in this area. There are other areas of law in which conflicts between civil and criminal law occur, and S Gardner has argued that the two need not necessarily be congruent and that either criminal law should reflect moral perceptions which may not be applicable in the civil law or, more tentatively, that a conviction for theft where the civil law has bestowed an indefeasible title should render that title no longer indefeasible ('Property and theft' [1998] Crim LR 35). Not surprisingly, Gardner's interesting arguments have provoked considerable opposition, most notably from Professor JC Smith, though the Court of Appeal in *Hinks* derived 'some comfort' from them and rejected Professor Smith's powerful arguments that the civil law of property is an essential foundation for the law of theft and that retrospective adjustment of property rights turning on a jury's perceptions of dishonesty is inconceivable ([1997] Crim LR 359; [1998] Crim LR 80).

It is also worth noting that the Court of Appeal in *Mazo*, albeit *obiter*, appeared to treat the *ratio* of *Gomez* as confined to consent obtained by fraud, deception or false representation. The decisions in *Kendrick and Hopkins* and, especially, *Hinks* give no support to this view.

8.3.6 The 'company cases'

The *Gomez* decision also encompasses what were referred to as the 'company cases'. A company may own property and, as such, may be the victim of theft. The problem in this context is that of an owner or those in *de facto* control of the company who give consent to what is being done, for example, the removal of company property, thereby apparently preventing the act amounting in law to an appropriation. The decision in *Gomez* means that this is now a matter of academic interest as consent is irrelevant. Lord Browne-Wilkinson put it this way:

> Whether or not those controlling the company consented or purported to consent to the abstraction of the company's property by the accused, he will have appropriated the property of the company. The question will be whether the other necessary elements are present, viz was such appropriation dishonest and was it done with the intention of permanently depriving the company of such property?

Authorities such as *Roffel* (1985) and *McHugh* (1988) were not, in Lord Browne-Wilkinson's opinion, 'correct in law' and therefore should not be followed. In the latter case, the court had endorsed the proposition that an act which was done with the authority of a company cannot in general amount to an appropriation, although Mustill LJ was somewhat sceptical as to its correctness but acknowledged that the facts of the case did not require him to look at the issue more closely. In *Roffel*, the sole director and shareholder was not guilty of theft simply because the company had consented to his actions.

Specifically endorsed were the decisions of the Court of Appeal in *AG's Reference (No 2 of 1982)* (1984) and *Philippou* (1989). In the former case, the two defendants were the shareholders and directors of various companies engaged in property development and money lending. It was alleged that they had, with each other's consent, appropriated company funds for their own private use by drawing cheques on the companies' bank accounts. At their trial, the judge ruled that, as they were the only shareholders and directors of the companies, their consent to the appropriation had to be taken as the consent of the companies and, therefore, they had not acted dishonestly. It was accepted that there had been an appropriation within the meaning of s 3 of the TA 1968 and that the only issue was one of dishonesty.

In the latter case, the appellant and his colleague were directors of three companies and used the assets of one to buy property in Spain in the name of another company which they owned. Sums totalling £369,000 had been withdrawn from the account of one of their companies and the Court of Appeal held that this act amounted to an appropriation of company property. The act was clearly an adverse interference with the assets of the company as the company would receive no benefit from the transaction. The fact that the directors gave 'consent' was irrelevant to the matter of appropriation.

8.3.7 Appropriation where no possession or control is acquired

A thief will usually take possession or control of the property which he steals and so an appropriation will usually involve a taking of possession or control and some touching of the property. Yet it is clear that an assumption of the rights of an owner does not necessarily require that any of these things shall have taken place. In the case of intangible property, by definition no touching is possible. The consequence is that some acts which look like mere preparation (and so not even an attempt) may actually be sufficient for the full *actus reus* of theft.

In *Pitham and Hehl* (1977), a man, knowing that his friend was in prison, took the two appellants to the friend's house and sold them some furniture. Crucial to deciding the question of whether they were guilty of handling was whether or not the goods had been stolen, that is, had the man appropriated his friend's property? Lawton LJ accepted that the man, one Millman, had assumed the rights of the owner. He had acted as the owner by showing them the property and inviting them to buy what they wanted. He was at that point assuming the rights of the owner. It is, of course, the owner's right to invite offers for his property and this right had been assumed by Millman. As the court put it: '... the moment he did that he appropriated McGregor's goods to himself. The appropriation was complete.' It might be unwise to assume that courts will feel bound to interpret all offers to sell property as amounting to an appropriation. The Court of Appeal was struggling to uphold the defendants' convictions for handling and may have been led into error in striving to do so.

As explained earlier, a thing in action is intangible property, an important form of which is the credit in a bank account. How can such a credit be appropriated? The simple answer might seem to be by any action which appears to result in the diminution of the balance. So, in *Kohn,* the defendant drew cheques which, when presented and acted upon by the paying bank, resulted in the company's account being debited. This might suggest that the appropriation takes place when the bank acts upon an instruction and records the debit to its customer's account. This was the approach taken in *Tomsett* (1985), in which a telex message sent by the defendant from London fraudulently diverted money from a New York bank to a bank in Geneva. It was held that the appropriation did not take place in London, but where the message was received and acted upon.

However, a contrary view was taken in the case of *Governor of Pentonville Prison ex p Osman* (1989). Osman was chairman of a company, Bumiputra Malaysia Finance Ltd, a wholly owned subsidiary of a major Malaysian bank, Bank Bumiputra Malaysia Bhd. He had transmitted telex messages to a correspondent bank in New York with instructions to transfer funds from one account to another. It was clear that this had been done without authorisation. The only property capable of being stolen as a result of the transaction was the thing in action. The important question was, if there was an appropriation of the thing in action, within which jurisdiction had it occurred? Counsel for Osman argued that the moment of appropriation was when the account in the US was debited. Counsel for the respondents argued that there was an appropriation when the telex was sent and the appropriation therefore took place in Hong Kong from whence the telex originated. The Court of Appeal accepted the latter argument.

Lloyd LJ put it this way:

> ... we regard ourselves bound, or as good as bound, by the meaning attributed to the word 'appropriation' by the unanimous decision of the House of Lords in *R v Morris.* Applying that meaning to the facts, a defendant 'usurps' the customer's rights when he, without the customer's authority, dishonestly issues the cheque drawn upon the customer's account. If adverse interference adds anything to usurpation, then he also thereby adversely interferes with the customer's rights. The theft is complete in law, even though it may be said that it is not complete in fact until the account is debited.

Therefore, the Court of Appeal is confirming the fact that appropriation takes place at the moment the telex is sent and from wherever the telex is dispatched, in this case Hong Kong.

The issue was examined again in *Ngan* (1998). The defendant had opened a bank account in England and was assigned an account number which had formerly been the account number of a debt collection agency. Consequently, in addition to modest credits from her work, her account was credited with sums totalling £77,767 which were intended for the agency. The defendant then signed blank cheques and sent them to her sister in Scotland, who knew of the circumstances. Two cheques were presented in Scotland and one in England for sums totalling £55,000 before the mistake was discovered by the Bank. The Court of Appeal quashed the defendant's conviction for theft of the thing in action (the credit balance to the amount of each cheque which properly belonged to the agency – of course, the credit balance in the account was a credit balance in the defendant's favour! The court held that it belonged to the agency by virtue of the operation of s 5(4), on which see below) in respect of the two instances of presentation in Scotland, but upheld her conviction in respect of the presentation in England. The court applied the principle in *Osman* that the act of theft was the *presentation* of the cheque. So, the Scottish instances took place outside the jurisdiction, but the English one was within the jurisdiction. All the other acts done by the defendant, including the drawing of the cheque and the sending of it to her sister, were preparatory and did not amount to an assumption of the rights of the owner. Note that the court interpreted *Osman* as holding that the assumption takes place when a cheque is *presented*. In *Osman*, the argument was about whether the appropriation took place on the sending of a telex instruction or only when the bank acted on that instruction and made adjustments to the client's account. If presenting a cheque is equated with issuing a telex instruction, then, clearly, the point of presentation would *suffice*. However, what the court in *Osman* actually said was that the appropriation takes place when the defendant 'dishonestly *issues* the cheque'. Where the defendant herself presents the cheque for payment, this will be when she *issues* it. When she sends it to another to present (making that other the payee), does she not issue it when she sends it, when she does the last act that she can do?

Osman was distinguished by the court in *Governor of Brixton Prison ex p Levin* (1997), in which the defendant operated a computer in Russia to gain access to the computer of a bank in the US and to effect transfers of money from that bank to accounts held at other banks. The court held that the defendant could not send any instructions until he had first gained access to the computer in the US. The appropriation of the account holder's right to give instructions took place in the computer, which was in the US. More realistically, it was argued, it took place in both places virtually simultaneously but, in the absence of a dual location theory, it made more sense to regard the appropriation as taking place in the US, because the defendant's physical location in Russia was of far less significance than the fact that he was looking at, and operating on, magnetic disks located in the US.

8.3.8 'Innocent' appropriation

The latter part of s 3(1) refers to someone who may have come by the property without stealing it. Any later assumption of a right by 'keeping or dealing with it as owner' will satisfy the section. In *Broome v Crowther* (1984), the accused offered to sell for £5 a stolen theodolite worth approximately £200. He thought it might be stolen but accepted assurances that it was not. Several months later, he was informed that the theodolite was indeed stolen. A few days later the police recovered the theodolite from his house. In the intervening period, he had been trying to make up his mind what, if anything, he should do. He was charged with handling and theft. The Divisional Court accepted his argument on the theft charge that appropriation needs conduct and that as there had been nothing positive once he had acquired the knowledge then there was no appropriation.

The TA 1968, however, is clear in that an appropriation can occur if there is 'any later assumption of a right to it by keeping' and surely this covers the situation in the *Broome v Crowther* case. Lord Roskill in *Morris* also refers to the possibility of appropriation by an act which need not necessarily be 'overt' but this does emphasise the requirement of an act as opposed to an omission or just doing nothing.

8.3.9 Continuing appropriation?

The Court of Appeal considered the question of whether property is capable of being appropriated more than once in *Atakpu and Abrahams* (1993). The issue arose in connection with expensive motor vehicles hired by the defendants on the continent, brought into this country, and then sold on to unsuspecting buyers. Could these cars, stolen abroad, be stolen again and again within the jurisdiction each time a transaction occurred? Having reviewed the case law including *Hale* (1978), the Court of Appeal concluded:

- theft can occur as a result of a simple appropriation but the transaction may not be complete until several appropriations later;

- 'theft is a finite act – it has a beginning and an end';

- there is no case law which suggests, let alone decides, that 'successive thefts of the same property' can amount to separate appropriations.

The court was content, *per* Stuart Smith LJ, to: '... see the logic that if there are appropriations each one can constitute a separate theft, [but] we flinch from reaching that conclusion.'

An analysis of s 3(1) provides the answer, so that if a person has come by property through stealing it (as in this case), any later dealing with it is, by implication, not included among the assumptions of the right of an owner which amount to an appropriation within the meaning of s 3(1):

> ... it follows in our judgment that if goods have once been stolen, they cannot be stolen again by the same thief exercising the same or other rights of ownership over the property.

Gomez decides that any dishonest assumption of the rights of an owner made with the necessary intention is theft and this implies that there can be no such thing as a continuous appropriation. However, the court did not wish the law to become that rigid as it would lead to injustices occurring. It decided, therefore, that it should be left to the 'common sense' of the jury to decide that the appropriation can continue as long as the thief 'can sensibly be regarded as in the act of stealing', or is 'on the job'. Therefore, as the theft of the vehicles took place abroad, the defendants could not be charged with theft in England. Further consideration ought to be given to the facts of this case in trying to decide where the appropriation took place. The cars were obtained as a result of deception at the point of hiring. According to *Gomez*, the appropriation is complete at that point, that is, in Belgium or Germany. However, if the cars had been obtained as a result of a legitimate hiring agreement which confined the use of the vehicles to, say, Germany, as long as the driver was within that country, has he really appropriated the vehicle? He is simply doing what he is authorised to do and has in fact contracted and paid to do. Once he leaves Germany in order to bring the vehicle to the UK, then at that point he has clearly exceeded his authority and, but for *Gomez*, the appropriation would take place at that point. *Morris* required evidence of adverse interference with the rights of the owner and that does not occur until the German border is crossed, but of course the court in *Gomez* chose to follow *Lawrence* and not *Morris*. The situation in *Atakpu and Abrahams* was considered by Glanville Williams as long ago as 1978. In his article, 'Appropriation: a single or continuous act' ([1978] Crim LR 69), he concluded that any argument in favour of a continuous appropriation rule would turn on policy rather than authority. Taken to its logical conclusion, if there was in law a continuous appropriation rule then, as Williams says: 'This might enable handling, with all its complexities, to be abolished.'

8.3.10 Property belonging to the defendant

It is clear that, at the time an appropriation takes place, the property must belong to another within the meaning attributed to these words in s 5 of the TA 1968. In the overwhelming majority of cases, this will present no problems whatsoever, but occasionally property will actually belong to the defendant at the time of the alleged appropriation and, therefore, theft cannot be committed.

Greenberg (1972) was a case in point, where the defendant, having filled his car with petrol, then decided not to pay and drove away from a self-service petrol station. It was decided that as the property in the petrol had passed to the defendant when it flowed from the pump into his tank, when he later decided not to pay for it, the petrol belonged to him, in that he had ownership, possession and control within the meaning in s 5. He had therefore not dishonestly appropriated property belonging to another and his conviction for theft was overturned. Similar reasoning underpins the decision in *Edwards v Ddin* (1976). In this case, the defendant had driven into a petrol station and instructed the attendant to fill the tank with petrol. On completion of the refuelling, he drove away without paying. He was charged with theft. It was held that he had not appropriated property belonging to another, as, at the time of the alleged dishonest appropriation (driving away) the petrol was, for the purposes of s 5 of the TA 1968, deemed to belong to him. Of course, if the defendants in each case had, prior to initiating the transactions, determined not to pay, then a more appropriate charge would be under s 15 of the TA 1968 of dishonestly obtaining property by deception. Because of the decision in *Gomez*, a charge of theft could also be brought if the defendant was dishonest from the outset.

8.3.11 Conclusion

It will be apparent that *Gomez* has failed to bring into this area of the criminal law the certainty which is demanded. The House of Lords in *Gomez* chose to ignore the recommendations of the Criminal Law Revision Committee in its Eighth Report, *Theft and Related Offences* (Cmnd 2977, 1966). Of course, in seeking the intention of Parliament, a court is not bound to take such reports into account but, in this case, it was Parliament's avowed intention to give effect to the Committee's recommendations. The Committee clearly intended that the word 'appropriates' should encompass the tort of 'conversion' and, therefore, the concept of usurpation of another's rights. An analysis of the report would, in all probability, lead the reader to conclude that the *Morris* decision more closely matches the intent of the Committee than does that in *Gomez*. Why was it not taken into account? Lord Keith offers the following reason:

> In my opinion, it serves no useful purpose at the present time to seek to construe the relevant provisions of the Theft Act by reference to the report which preceded it, namely the Eighth Report of the Criminal Law Revision Committee, *Theft and Related Offences* ... The decision in *Lawrence*'s case was a clear decision of this House upon the construction of the word 'appropriates' in s 1(1) of the TA 1968, which had stood for 12 years when doubt was thrown upon it by *obiter dicta* in *R v Morris*. *Lawrence*'s case must be regarded as authoritative and correct, and there is no question of it now being right to depart from it.

That decision by Lord Keith has not passed without critical comment. Professor Smith in commenting on the case ([1993] Crim LR 304, p 306) opines:

> The only reason for not doing so offered by Lord Keith was that the point of law was the subject of a decision in *Lawrence* while the flatly contradictory observations of the whole House in *Morris* were *obiter dicta*. If that was sufficient to settle the matter, the appeal was a waste of time and a great deal of public money. The decision shows scant respect for the five Law Lords in *Morris* who concurred in an opinion now held to be untenable and fails to have regard to the many doubts that have been expressed about the decision in *Lawrence*.

If that were not enough he introduces his commentary on *Mazo* ([1996] Crim LR 435, p 436) with these words:

> On the long roll of disastrous decisions by the House of Lords on criminal matters, *Gomez* must rank pretty high ... The initial reaction of the Court of Appeal to *Gomez* seems to have been one of incredulity.

We have obviously not heard the last of this debate!

8.4   Belonging to another

Section 5(1) provides the basic definition of when property belongs to another:

> Property shall be regarded as belonging to any person having possession or control of it, or having in it any proprietary right or interest (not being an equitable interest arising only from an agreement to transfer or grant an interest).

It will be obvious from this that property may belong to another for the purposes of theft even though that person has no proprietary interest in it, merely having possession and/or control.

This raises an interesting question of whether the owner of property can be guilty of stealing his own property. The typical example of theft involves a person who is not the owner of the property appropriating it from someone who is. However, the definition of 'belonging to another' encompasses lesser interests than ownership and it may be that the owner can steal his own property from a person who has one of those lesser interests. The sensible answer to this question might seem to be that the owner could only steal his own property from a person with a lesser interest if that person would be entitled to resist the owner's claim for the *immediate* return of the property – say, because there is a contractual hiring of the property or because there is a lien, a right to retain the property until money is paid (as in the case of an unpaid repairer of goods). This was not the view taken by the Court of Appeal in *Turner (No 2)* (1971). In that case, the appellant had taken his car to a garage for repair. The repairs were completed and the car left outside the garage overnight awaiting collection by its owner. Unknown to the garage owner, Mr Brown, the appellant had a spare set of keys, one set having been handed to Mr Brown when the car was deposited with him. The appellant, without Mr Brown's consent, removed the car and omitted to pay for the repairs which had been carried out. The jury by a majority found Turner guilty of stealing his own car; this conclusion being possible as a result of the wording of s 5(1) of the TA 1968. The decision was upheld by the Court of Appeal on the grounds that, at the time when the defendant dishonestly took his car away, it belonged to the garage proprietor in the simple sense that he had possession and control of it. Of course, as an unpaid repairer he also had a lien over the car and so could have resisted the defendant's claim for its return, yet the court disregarded the lien and rested its decision purely on the fact of possession and control. The implication is that any owner of property who lends it to another could be guilty of theft if he were then dishonestly to take it back (say, secretly, in order to cause the other to fear that he had lost it) even though he could openly demand the return of the property and the other would have no claim to resist the demand. *Turner (No 2)* is to be compared with *Meredith* (1973), where the defendant removed his car from a police car pound, it having been placed there during the course of a soccer match at which he was a spectator, because it had been causing an obstruction. It was held that he could not be guilty of stealing his own property. The police had no legal right to retain the car as against the owner and, therefore, whatever his intent, he was not guilty of taking property belonging to another. If one disregards the lien in the *Turner* case, it is difficult to find a distinction between them. The car was undoubtedly in the possession and control of the police, it was on their property and had a police steering lock attached to it.

8.4.1 Control

The word 'control' was subject to judicial scrutiny in *Woodman* (1974). The owners of a disused factory had agreed to sell all the scrap metal on the site. The purchasers entered the premises and removed the vast majority of the metal, apart from a small amount which proved too inaccessible to warrant removal. The metal remained there, unknown to the owners of the site, for a couple of years until removed by Woodman and an accomplice. His defence to a charge of theft of the metal was that the property did not belong to another because the owners of the land had sold their proprietary interest in the metal (to a person who had abandoned their rights in the residue) and, being unaware of its presence on their land, had neither possession nor control of the scrap metal. The Court of Appeal had no doubt that as the company controlled the site then they controlled the articles left on the site. As the company had erected fences around the property in order to exclude trespassers, there was sufficient evidence from which to conclude they controlled the site. Woodman had therefore appropriated property belonging to another. The court suggested that, if a third party had deposited explosives or drugs on the land, then the owner's lack of knowledge would 'produce a different result from that which arises under the general presumption to which we have referred'.

8.4.2 Abandoned property

Property may of course be abandoned, in which case it may not be the subject of a theft charge simply because it belongs to no one. However, the courts will be slow to conclude that property has been abandoned and, it is submitted, will require evidence that the owner could not care less what happened to the property. Discarding property in a council litter bin will not amount to abandonment, as the title to that property is being passed to the council. In *Hancock* (1990), D was charged with theft of gold and silver coins approximately 2,000 years old which he had discovered while using a metal detector on land near Guildford which had been the site of a Roman-Celtic temple. He claimed that, when he found the coins, they were not altogether in one place but scattered about. If this were untrue, it would have led to the inference that the coins had been hidden by someone who intended to return and recover them and could be viewed as treasure trove belonging to the Crown. Conversely, if they had been scattered over a wide area, the conclusion could be reached that they were dropped there at different times as sacrifices or votive offerings and there would be no intention that they should be recovered at a later stage. The legal position appears to be that the Crown has a prerogative right to all treasure trove, which was hidden by the owner with a view to later recovery. However, if the owner deliberately abandoned the property or it was accidentally lost it is not to be regarded as treasure trove. The Court of Appeal decided that it was for the jury to determine whether the coins were in fact treasure trove and therefore the property of the Crown. In doing so, they must apply the ordinary criminal burden and standard of proof. The jury had to be sure that the coins were deposited by someone intending to retrieve them at a later date before they could be regarded as belonging to the Crown. The Crown, therefore, has a proprietary interest not possession or control unless of course the treasure trove is discovered on Crown property. In *Waverley Borough Council v Fletcher* (1995), the defendant while using a metal detector in a public park discovered a valuable medieval gold brooch some nine inches below the surface. A coroner's inquisition subsequently determined that it was not treasure trove, that is, the Crown had no proprietary interest in the brooch. The local authority sought a declaration that the brooch was its property. The Court of Appeal agreed with the authority. It applied the principle that the owner or lawful possessor of land owned all that was in or attached to it. The court viewed the digging up and removal of property from the park as a trespass and was quite clear that the local authority had a better title to the brooch than the finder.

The Treasure Act 1996 abolishes the law on treasure trove. Treasure still vests in the Crown and therefore any appropriation of treasure will be from the Crown. In light of the *Waverley* decision and the new Act, it is possible that theft may be committed against both a landowner and the Crown, as each will have a proprietary interest in the property. The former because in owning the land he has a proprietary interest in anything buried on the land and the latter because of the terms of the Act.

8.4.3 Trust property

Section 5(2) of the TA 1968 deals with property held on trust and provides that:

> ... where property is subject to a trust, the persons to whom it belongs shall be regarded as including any person having a right to enforce the trust, and an intention to defeat the trust shall be regarded accordingly as an intention to deprive of the property any person having that right.

In the majority of cases, if a trustee steals from a trust, then the situation will be covered by applying s 5(1), because any beneficiaries of the trust will have an equitable interest, which amounts to a proprietary interest within the terms of s 5(1). The purpose of s 5(2) is to ensure that, where a trust does not have recognised beneficiaries, then any property appropriated by the trustee will still be regarded as belonging to another. An example of this would be a charitable trust.

8.4.4 Obligation to retain and deal

Section 5(3) of the TA 1968 states:

> ... where a person receives property from or on account of another, and is under an obligation to the other to retain and deal with that property or its proceeds in a particular way, the property or proceeds shall be regarded (as against him) as belonging to the other.

In some circumstances, property may be received by a person who is then expected to deal with it on behalf of the giver, but in circumstances where the legal title to the property passes to the recipient. If the property is then misappropriated, in the sense that the person acts in a way inconsistent with his obligation, a theft charge would, but for the existence of s 5(3), not lie against the wrongdoer simply because he owned the property, which was also in his possession and control. This is because the property would not belong to another. Let us assume that all members of the academic registrar's department of a university decide to operate a Christmas club, with each member contributing £2 each week throughout the year, to be collected by one of their number. The total each week is to be deposited in an interest bearing building society account and the total amount plus interest returned to the members of the syndicate to spend prior to the Christmas vacation. Each time a member gives £2 to the collector, he is in law making the collector the owner of the two £1 coins. That individual would, presumably, have no qualms if he saw the collector immediately use those coins in order to give change to another member who tendered a £5 note. However, although he has become the owner he is not free to deal with the money in any way he wishes. Each member expects him to place a sum equivalent to the total amount collected into a particular building society account. Were he to refrain from so doing, then, as a result of s 5(3), he could be found guilty of theft of the money. He has received property from another, he is under an obligation to the other to deal with the property in a particular way, and therefore the money is to be regarded as belonging to the other. The Criminal Law Revision Committee in its Eighth Report, *Theft and Related Offences* (Cmnd 2977, 1966) cites a similar example:

> Sub-section (3) ... provides for the special case where property is transferred to a person to retain and deal with for a particular purpose and he misapplies it or its proceeds. An example would be the treasurer of a holiday fund. The person in question is in law the owner of the property; but the sub-section treats the property, as against him, as belonging to the persons to whom he owes the duty to retain and deal with the property as agreed. He will therefore be guilty of stealing from them if he misapplies the property or proceeds.

The starting point for the examination of this sub-section is the case of *Hall* (1973). The defendant ran a travel agency and clients paid him money as deposits for holidays and flights. The tickets failed to materialise and many people lost their money. It transpired that, when he had received money, it was paid into the firm's general trading account and not into any specially created client or flight account. His defence was based on the assertion that he could not be convicted of theft simply because the business had not prospered. He was convicted of theft of the monies and appealed on the basis that the monies paid to him by clients belonged to him and he could not be said to have appropriated property belonging to another. The Court of Appeal allowed the appeal, despite criticising his 'scandalous conduct'. The court recognised that a contractual obligation was created between the clients and Hall, but that of itself did not prove that the clients expected him to retain and deal with that property or its proceeds in a particular way and, as such, no 'obligation' within the meaning of s 5(3) could be imposed upon him. As Edmund Davies LJ said:

> ... what was not here established was that these clients expected them 'to retain and deal with that property or its proceeds in a particular way', and that an 'obligation' to do so was undertaken by the appellant ... each case turns on its own facts. Cases could, we suppose, conceivably arise where by some special arrangement (preferably evidenced by documents), the client could impose on the travel agent an 'obligation' falling within s 5(3). But no such special arrangement was made in any of the seven cases here being considered.

The Court of Appeal in *Rader* (1992) distinguished *Hall* in a case which involved R receiving sums totalling nearly £10,000 from the victim which he said 'would be put to good use' and returned to him on a fixed date with some sort of profit. None of the money was repaid, nor did any profit or interest accrue. It appeared that R had transferred the money to an acquaintance in the US who had failed to repay the funds. He was convicted of theft and his appeal dismissed. The Court of Appeal was left in no doubt that R had been under an obligation to invest the money in such a way (presumably non-speculative) as to produce a profit for the victim. Do note the overlap with s 15, as if it could have been proved that R had obtained the money by deception, for example, by R telling the victim he would use it in one way when his intention was to the contrary, then he would have obtained the property by deception.

It will be apparent that business would grind to a halt if customers were to be allowed to insist that the actual money paid to travel agents or insurance agents were to be used in a particular way. *Lewis v Lethbridge* (1987) decided that the accused 'need not be under an obligation to retain particular monies. It is sufficient that he is under an obligation to keep in existence a fund equivalent to that which he has received'. Yet it is emphasised by the Divisional Court that there must be evidence of an obligation to do so. If the accused is permitted to do what he likes with the property, his only obligation being to account in due course for an equivalent sum, s 5(3) does not apply. The court cited with approval the summary by Professor Smith in *The Law of Theft* (5th edn, 1984, London: Butterworths) to the effect that 'the obligation is to deal with that property or its proceeds in a particular way'. The appellant had obtained sponsorship for a friend who was running in the London Marathon. He received £54 but did not hand it over to the relevant charity. The question was whether or not he was under an obligation to hand over the notes and coins he had been given or equivalent sum. The court allowed his appeal because the justices had wrongly concluded that the debt owed to the charity could be described as 'proceeds' of the money he had received. This decision would have surprised the many charities in this country and donors also would be wary of handing over sponsorship money if they were aware that the collector was under no obligation to deal with the particular money in a particular way. It would be different if money was placed directly into a collecting box provided by the charity, as the representative would not normally have access to the cash and would have an obligation to hand over the particular money in the box to the charity. If he destroyed the box in gaining access to the money then s 5(3) would be unnecessary as there would be sufficient evidence to show theft of the box which presumably belonged to the charity, and also of the contents. However, *Lethbridge* was disapproved in *Wain* (1995). The defendant had raised money for charity by organising various events. The money raised was paid into a special bank account. The money was to be distributed to various charities by another company and one of its representative consented to Wain paying the money into his own account. He used the money for his own purposes. The Court of Appeal concluded that what he had done amounted to theft as he was under an obligation to retain the proceeds of the money collected and deal with them in a particular way. The approach in *Lethbridge* was criticised as being too 'narrow'.

In *Huskinson* (1988), the respondent was charged with theft of £279 from the Housing Services Department. He was a tenant who fell into arrears with his rent. He was sent a cheque for £479 but gave only £200 to his landlord, spending the rest on himself. It was held by the Divisional Court that the case could not be brought within s 5(3). Was he under an obligation to the Housing Services Department to deal with the cheque or its proceeds in a particular way? The relevant legislation and regulations did not impose an express obligation on a tenant to pay the sum received directly to the landlord and it was held to be impossible to imply such an obligation. The court suggested that, had the defendant been able to pay his landlord from other funds prior to receiving the cheque, he would have been quite entitled to use the cheque or its proceeds for his own purposes. This decision can be criticised on the basis that the money was paid to him to meet a specific need and, in such circumstances, surely he should be obliged to use it for that purpose? The obligation must be legal and not moral or social, according to the decision in *Gilks* (1972). It would appear from *Mainwaring* (1981) that a jury should be directed that whether or not there is an obligation is a matter of law. The Court of Appeal proposed that:

> What ... a judge ought to do is this: if the facts relied upon by the prosecution are in dispute he should direct the jury to make their findings on the facts, and then say to them: 'If you find the facts to be such and such, then I direct you as a matter of law that a legal obligation arose to which s 5(3) applies.

This direction of Lawton LJ in *Mainwaring* (1981) was followed in *Dubar* (1995). The appellant had received £1,800 from S with which to buy a car. In S's view, the money was given in the expectation that D would purchase a D-registration Ford Orion 1.4. D's version of events was that he was given the money in order to find a car of appropriate value whether it be a Ford, Vauxhall or any other make. He claimed that he had therefore not been placed under an obligation to deal with the money in a particular way as required by s 5(3). Needless to say, a car was never purchased and D used the cash in order to settle debts and on general spending.

The Courts-Martial Appeal Court held that the correct approach was to invite the jury to reach a conclusion on the facts. In light of their conclusion, the judge would then direct them as to whether a legal obligation had or had not arisen. It was not for the jury to determine whether an obligation under s 5(3) had arisen. The judge had directed the jury in this way:

> If you are sure that S and D agreed and intended that D was to use the money for no other purpose than to, buy a specific Ford Orion motor car for S or otherwise return the money to S ... if you are sure of those facts, then I tell you, as a matter of law, that D was under a legal obligation to deal with the money in a particular way.

That, said the Courts-Martial Appeal Court, was a 'correct following of the classic division of function between judge and jury ...'. The appellant's appeal against conviction was allowed but on other grounds.

Clients investing money via a financial intermediary will also be pleased to discover that such agencies are not to be equated with travel agents for the purposes of establishing an obligation under s 5(3) of the TA 1968. This was stated by the Court of Appeal in *Hallam and Blackburn* (1995). Monies were received from clients for investment on their behalf or from insurance companies to be passed to clients, but instead paid into their own or their company accounts. Clients, it was said, retained an equitable interest in such monies and therefore in any cheques drawn and the proceeds resulting from the investment. The court was of the view that it was immaterial whether the property was regarded as belonging to the clients under s 5(1), (2) or (3). They had therefore appropriated property belonging to another.

Wills (1991) determines that:

> ... whether a person is under an obligation to deal with property in a particular way can only be established by proving that he had knowledge of the obligation. Proof that property was not dealt with in conformity with the obligation is not sufficient in itself ...

8.4.5   Mistake and obligation to make restoration

Section 5(4) of the TA 1968 deals with the situation where property is obtained as a result of another's mistake:

> Where a person gets property by another's mistake, and is under an obligation to make restoration (in whole or in part) or the property or its proceeds or of the value thereof, then to the extent of that obligation the property or proceeds shall be regarded (as against him) as belonging to the person entitled to restoration, and an intention not to make restoration shall be regarded accordingly as an intention to deprive that person of the property or proceeds.

This sub-section deals with the acquisition of property as a result of another's mistake, not, it may be noted, where any form of deceit or deception is practised. A pre-TA case will illustrate what the sub-section is attempting to cover. In *Moynes v Coopper* (1956), the defendant was paid his full entitlement to wages even though he had received an advance. His strict entitlement was to 3 s 9 d not the £7 3 s 4 d which had been paid. He was acquitted of stealing the excess, but it would appear that he would now be caught by the provisions in s 5(4), as he would be under a legal obligation to make restitution of the difference. There have been, as may be expected, a number of cases of overpayment in the context of employment.

In *AG's Reference (No 1 of 1983)* (1984), a woman police officer had by mistake received £74 for overtime and wages and this amount together with her salary was paid by giro into her bank account. She was not, initially, aware of the error but did at some later stage make the discovery and decided against making restitution to her employer, the Metropolitan Police. At her trial for theft, the judge stopped the case and directed the jury to acquit. The Attorney

General referred the issue to the Court of Appeal, asking whether someone who receives overpayment of a debt due to him, for example, salary, may be guilty of theft if he intentionally fails to repay the amount of overpayment. In concluding that theft would be committed in such circumstances the court held that once the person's account had been credited, the bank owed him a debt, and, as we have seen, that is to be regarded as a thing in action and property within the meaning of s 4(1) of the TA 1968. There is clearly a mistake on the part of the employer and, applying the general principles of restitution, there is an obligation to repay the benefit received. Although the thing in action belonged to her, it was the value of the thing which she was obliged to restore to the Metropolitan Police. Accordingly, provided that the other elements of s 1 were present, there would be no obstacle to a conviction for theft.

In *Davis* (1988), a mistake by the London Borough of Richmond resulted in the defendant receiving housing benefit each week for some weeks by way of two identical cheques instead of just one. Even when he was no longer entitled to any benefit, one cheque each week continued to be sent. He endorsed the cheques to shopkeepers for cash or to his landlord to pay for his accommodation. He was charged with theft of cash rather than of the cheques. Applying s 5(4), his convictions were upheld where he had obtained cash but were quashed where he had merely endorsed the cheques for accommodation. The cash represented the proceeds of the cheques and the defendant was under an obligation to make restoration.

However, s 5(4) may not be necessary to achieve a conviction in such cases. In *Chase Manhattan Bank NA v Israel-British Bank* (1979), it was held that, where money is paid to another under a mistake of fact, the person who pays that money retains an equitable interest in it. In Theft Act terms, this could amount to a sufficient interest under s 5(1) for the property still to 'belong to' the original owner. Indeed, in *Shadrokh-Cigari* (1988), where the defendant had withdrawn money which he knew had been credited to a bank account by mistake, the Court of Appeal held that his conviction for theft could be supported by virtue of s 5(1) or s 5(4).

Finally, in this section one ought to consider the decision of the Court of Appeal in *Gilks* (1972). It establishes that the only obligation which will be recognised for s 5(4) is a legal one. Cairns LJ put it this way:

> In a criminal statute, where a person's criminal liability is made dependent on his having an obligation, it would be quite wrong to construe that word so as to cover a moral or social obligation as distinct from a legal one.

Gilks had placed a bet on the outcome of a horse race and as a result of a mistake by the assistant manager of the betting shop, was given over £100 more than he was entitled to receive. He was, from the moment he was being paid, aware of the overpayment and afterwards refused to consider repayment on the basis that Ladbroke's (a well known chain of bookmakers) could afford the loss! He was convicted of theft, but not, it should be noted, as a result of applying s 5(4). A gaming transaction is legally unenforceable and therefore there is no legal obligation to make restoration. The court managed to find other reasons to uphold the conviction. It held that ownership in the property had not passed to Gilks because of the mistake. When Gilks decided to keep the money, it still belonged to another, that is, the betting shop, the court relying on the old authority of *Middleton* (1873), where the mistake had been as to the identity of the recipient. In this case, the assistant manager did not make any mistake as to identity nor as to the amount. He intended to, and did, give *Gilks* £117.25. *Gilks*, it is submitted, should be regarded as wrongly decided. Given the *ratio* in *Shadrokh-Cigari*, the betting shop retained an equitable interest in the money and a conviction would now be sustainable applying this principle. Of course, since the House of Lords decided in *Gomez* that the consent of the owner to the transfer of ownership has no bearing on whether or not the defendant appropriates the property, it would now be possible to convict Gilks simply on the grounds that he appropriated the money when the bookmaker paid it to him and he was dishonest in taking it. This is yet another reason why the scope of application of s 5(4) may be much narrower than originally intended.

The final point to note is that the property must belong to another at the time of the appropriation. It is important to determine at what point in a transaction ownership does actually pass. This issue was confronted in *Greenberg* (1972) where the court emphasised that the decision would depend on the intention of the parties. It will be recalled that the court held that ownership was transferred when the petrol flowed from the petrol pump into the car's petrol tank, and not when the customer tendered payment.

In *Dobson* (1989), Parker LJ accepted Lord Roskill's view in *Morris* that it is:

> ... wrong to introduce into this branch of the criminal law questions whether particular contracts are void or voidable on the ground of mistake or fraud or whether any mistake is sufficiently fundamental to vitiate a contract.

Providing that the property belongs to someone other than the defendant at the time of the act of appropriation, then s 5 is satisfied and whether title passes under a voidable contract is unimportant.

8.5   *Mens rea*: dishonesty

The TA 1968 does not provide a definition of what amounts to dishonesty and, given that society's views of what is or is not dishonest are ever changing, it was probably wise for Parliament not to attempt so to do. The Criminal Law Revision Committee (Eighth Report, *Theft and Related Offences*, Cmnd 2977, 1966) preferred the word 'dishonestly' as opposed to 'fraudulently' on the basis that it would be easier for jurors to understand:

'Dishonesty' [is] something which laymen can easily recognise when they see it, whereas 'fraud' may seem to involve technicalities which have to be explained by a lawyer.

What, however, the TA 1968 does is to highlight some circumstances where a person's appropriation of property belonging to another is not to be regarded as dishonest. These are:

(a) if he appropriates the property in the belief that he has in law the right to deprive the other of it, on behalf of himself or of a third person; or

(b) if he appropriates the property in the belief that he would have the other's consent if the other knew of the appropriation and the circumstances of it; or

(c) (except where the property came to him as trustee or personal representative) if he appropriates the property in the belief that the person to whom the property belongs cannot be discovered by taking reasonable steps.

Section 2(2) confirms that 'a person's appropriation of property belonging to another may be dishonest notwithstanding that he is willing to pay for the property'.

8.5.1 The approach to the assessment of dishonesty

The assessment of dishonesty involves both judge and jury. The leading case is *Ghosh* (1982). The charge was in fact under s 15(1) of the TA 1968, that of obtaining property by deception, a section which requires evidence of dishonesty before a conviction can be obtained. The test of dishonesty should be the same as for s 1 of the TA 1968, given the significant overlap between the two offences. The court rejected an assertion that the approach should be 'purely objective, however attractive from the practical point of view that solution may be'. The court showed extreme reluctance to adopt a purely subjectivist approach because that would be to abandon 'all standards but that of the accused himself, and to bring about a state of affairs in which Robin Hood would be no robber'. There had been instances where a court had prior to *Ghosh* proceeded on a subjective basis as in *Boggeln v Williams* (1978). Having had his electricity supply disconnected because of his failure to settle a debt owed to the East Midlands Electricity Board, he informed the board that he proposed to reconnect the supply. He did not, however, bypass the meter and it was, therefore, possible for the board to ascertain how much power had been consumed. He was charged with the offence of dishonestly using electricity without due authority, contrary to s 13 of the TA 1968. The Queen's Bench Divisional Court accepted that, in circumstances where a defendant genuinely believed he was not acting dishonestly and also genuinely and reasonably believed that he would have the ability to pay for the electricity consumed, then his state of mind could not be classed as dishonest. There are obvious disadvantages in leaving it to the jury to decide dishonesty by simply determining whether or not the accused held the belief that he was acting honestly or that he had no idea that his conduct could be viewed as dishonest by the majority of people in the jurisdiction. In an area of law where certainty and consistency of approach should be paramount in order that individuals can determine their behaviour patterns, the 'subjectivist' approach would appear to be undesirable.

8.5.2   The twofold test

Ghosh determines that the test for dishonesty should encompass objective and subjective strands. The first question to answer is the objective one of whether the jury would conclude by reference to the 'ordinary standards of reasonable and honest people', that the defendant's act is dishonest. If the answer is yes, then the jury must focus on whether the defendant himself 'must have realised that what he was doing was by those standards dishonest'. If the answer to the first question is no, then the defendant must be acquitted. Lord Lane CJ went on to add that:

> It is dishonest for a defendant to act in a way which he knows ordinary people consider to be dishonest, even if he asserts or genuinely believes that he is morally justified in acting as he did.

8.5.3   Criticisms of the twofold test

It will be apparent that this 'twofold' test does not eradicate the potential for inconsistency between juries, although the chances are much reduced because of the presence of the objective element. However, the first part of the test requires juries to apply the 'current standards of ordinary decent people' as Lawton LJ put it in *Feely* (1973), and views are bound to differ as to the appropriate standard. *Feely* is a case in point. The accused was the manager of a betting shop who along with other managers received a communication from his company that the practice of 'borrowing' from tills was prohibited. In spite of this warning he 'borrowed' £30 intending to repay the money at a later date. There was evidence to prove that he was owed more than double this amount by his employers and he also left an IOU once the shortfall had been discovered. Looked at objectively would a jury applying the current standards of ordinary decent people be at one in concluding his actions were dishonest? Members of the jury may well be those 'upright citizens as the ordinary run of British Rail passengers may be presumed to be', but Lord Bridge in *Cooke* (1986) was 'not prepared to assume that they would necessarily refuse to take and pay for refreshments even if they knew perfectly well that the buffet staff were practising the kind of "fiddle" here involved'. Surely the type of conduct engaged in by *Cooke* or *Rashid* (1977) (see Chapter 9) lays a fair claim to be considered as 'objectively' dishonest? The second part of the test also raises some queries. The jury has to assess whether the accused realised what he was doing was dishonest, but what of the person whom the jury accepts believed was acting honestly but who because of his lifestyle or beliefs does not subscribe to the standards of ordinary people? Lord Lane CJ in *Ghosh* gave the following example in order to illustrate the point:

> Robin Hood or those ardent anti-vivisectionists who remove animals from vivisection laboratories are acting dishonestly, even though they may consider themselves to be morally justified in doing what they do ...

It is certainly arguable that an accused who did not realise that his conduct would not receive the assent of ordinary people should be entitled to be acquitted although it is likely that a jury which has found the conduct objectively dishonest will take a great deal of convincing that the accused did not so realise. Lord Lane CJ cites the example of a man who has come to this country from one where public transport is free. He alights from a bus without paying. The action would appear to be objectively dishonest but the defendant would, according to Lord Lane, be found not to be dishonest as a result of applying the second limb of the 'test'. Apart from the fact that one is unsure exactly which Theft Act offence Lord Lane CJ had in mind, this could be treated as a simple case of mistake. Based on his knowledge of the circumstances, he honestly believed that he was entitled to travel for free. (Presumably, he could face prosecution under s 3 of the TA 1978. He has certainly made off without paying, but a conviction would depend on whether or not he knew payment on the spot was required.)

However strong the criticisms levelled against *Ghosh*, there can be no doubt that the decision does represent the law on the matter. The direction was approved in *Lightfoot* (1993), where the Court of Appeal emphasised that there was a clear distinction between a person's knowledge of the law and his 'appreciation that he was doing something which, by ordinary standards of reasonable and honest people, was regarded as dishonest'. An individual may be unaware of the legal provisions which make his conduct an offence, but be well aware that his actions would be regarded as dishonest by his fellow citizens. It was pointed out in *Squire* (1990) that a *Ghosh* direction need not be given on each and every occasion where dishonesty is an issue. It was further stated in *Roberts* (1987) and *Price* (1990) that it could be potentially misleading in some cases to give a *Ghosh* direction. In *Price*, it was said that the *Ghosh* direction was necessary only where the defendant might have believed that what he was alleged to have done 'was in accordance with the ordinary person's idea of honesty'.

8.5.4   Section 2(1)(a) of the TA 1968

If the defendant believes that he has the legal right to deprive the other of his property then he is not to be regarded as dishonest. The sub-section appears to rule out any objective assessment as it is centred on the defendant's belief as to his right to deprive the other of the property. Thus, in *Small* (1987), where the defendant claimed that he genuinely thought a car he was accused of stealing had been abandoned, a reference by the trial judge to whether or not he reasonably believed the car had been dumped or abandoned was held to be a misdirection.

8.5.5   Section 2(1)(b) of the TA 1968

This sub-section deals with a defendant who believes he would have had consent if the other had known of the appropriation. Again, as with s 2(1)(a), the sub-section is written from a subjectivist viewpoint. The defendant, who by reference to past conduct, can establish that he believed the owner would have consented on this occasion if he had known of the actual appropriation will be entitled to benefit from the section and not be regarded as dishonest.

8.5.6   Section 2(1)(c) of the TA 1968

This sub-section deals with property which has been lost and as such ownership rights remain with the loser, unlike the situation where property has been abandoned. The focus is, as with the other sub-sections, on the defendant's belief. What constitutes reasonable steps will vary with the circumstances. If a defendant finds a £5 note in the street, then it is reasonable to assume that the owner has not reported its loss to the police and a failure to hand it in would not be evidence of dishonesty. Conversely, if it is £5,000, then the opposite conclusion is likely to be reached.

8.5.7   Section 2(2) of the TA 1968

A person may be willing to pay for property and even to pay over the odds, but, as a result of s 2(2) that would not prevent a finding of dishonesty if he were aware that the owner had no wish to dispose of his property. If, however, he has no reason to assume that the owner would not willingly accept a cash sum equivalent to the value of the article, then a jury may be inclined to the view that he is not dishonest. It is submitted that individuals should not receive encouragement to deal with other people's property as they would wish simply because they have the means to give value.

8.5.8 Conclusion

The *Ghosh* decision has been the subject of much critical comment. The decision was a compromise to avoid applying either a purely objective or subjective approach to the assessment of dishonesty. The difficulty, of course, as Andrew Halpin ('The test for dishonesty' [1996] Crim LR 283) maintains, 'is the absence of a moral consensus within modern society over dishonesty'. He argues that the *Ghosh* test should be abandoned in favour of one of two options. The first is a purely subjective approach to the issue of dishonesty, which allows the 'individual defendant to limit his criminal liability by his own moral standards'. The second is for Parliament to create a legal definition of dishonesty. The first he rejects because the protection of a person's property is made dependent upon the 'the moral outlook of the person seeking to interfere with it'. The second option he believes should be given serious consideration. In his article, 'Dishonesty: objections to *Feely* and *Ghosh*' ([1985] Crim LR 341), Edward Griew argued that whether a defendant is dishonest is clearly for the jury to decide but they should be able 'to turn to the law for clear guidance'. In other words, what is dishonest should be a matter of law.

The current position is that *Ghosh* has 'technical authority' but there are quite clearly situations which the courts regard as being dishonest thus permitting 'objective standards to be imposed by the courts' (see Halpin, p 289).

8.6 Intention to deprive permanently

The TA 1968 requires that before theft can be committed there is evidence of the intention permanently to deprive the other of his or her property. There is no requirement that he or she should actually be deprived. The shoplifter who leaves the shop without paying will have some difficulty in refuting the allegation that he or she intended permanently to deprive the owner of the goods. The person who snatches a chocolate eclair from a confectionery stall and consumes it on the spot leaves no one in any doubt that he or she has not only the intention to, but actually did, permanently deprive the owner of his or her property. In discussing the *actus reus* of theft, above, reference was made to the fact that theft may be complete when a person takes items from a supermarket shelf and places them into his or her pocket rather than a basket. Or, in switching price labels, there is the assumption that having removed the goods from the shelf and switched the labels theft may be established. Yet the most difficult element for the prosecution is likely to be establishing proof of the intention permanently to deprive. In theory, if the customer changes his or her mind and replaces the goods on the shelf then it is too late, the theft is complete. Yet how strong is the evidence likely to be to prove that at the moment of appropriation the defendant had the intention permanently to deprive the store of the items, if a few minutes later the goods are returned to the shelf?

8.6.1 Section 6(1) of the TA 1968

Section 6(1) provides:

> A person appropriating property belonging to another without meaning the other permanently to lose the thing itself is nevertheless to be regarded as having the intention of permanently depriving the other of it if his intention is to treat the thing as his own to dispose of regardless of the other's rights; and a borrowing or lending of it may amount to so treating it if, but only if, the borrowing or lending is for a period and in circumstances making it equivalent to an outright taking or disposal.

A particularly important word is 'dispose'. To intend simply to use someone else's property should not satisfy the section. The meaning of 'dispose of' in s 6(1) was considered in two cases. In *Cahill* (1993), the court found Professor Smith's comments in *The Law of Theft* (6th edn, 1989, London: Butterworths, p 73) 'helpful'. He stated:

> It is submitted, however, that an intention merely to use the thing as one's own is not enough and that 'dispose of' is not used in the sense in which a general might 'dispose of' his forces but rather in the meaning given by the *Shorter Oxford Dictionary*: 'To deal with definitely: to get rid of; to get done with, finish. To make over by way of sale or bargain, sell.'

However, the Divisional Court in *DPP v Lavender* (1994) thought the dictionary definition 'too narrow'. A disposal, it was said, could also include dealing with the property. To treat goods as one's own was also deemed to be within the definition of 'dispose of'. *Cahill* was not cited to the court and it is submitted that this latter interpretation unjustifiably extends the ambit of the offence and should not be relied upon. In *Lloyd* (1985), it was held that in a case of 'borrowing or lending' the intention to permanently deprive would be proved only if the goods were returned in a fundamentally changed state, so that any utility value would have been lost. In this case, Lloyd had removed from the cinema, where he was employed, films which were intended to be shown commercially. They were copied by two accomplices and then returned to the cinema. His conviction for conspiracy to commit theft was questioned on the basis that:

> ... the goodness, the virtue, the practical value of the films to the owners has not gone out of the article. The film could still be projected to paying audiences, and ... audiences ... would have paid for their seats.

Thus, the borrowing was deemed not to be the equivalent of an outright taking or disposal.

Lord Lane CJ in *Lloyd* pointed out that s 6(1) covers the situation where a defendant takes something and then offers it back to the owner for him to purchase if so minded. The defendant could claim that he has no desire to hold onto the property for one second more than is necessary. The court felt that in such circumstances this would be the equivalent to an outright taking. The authority for the proposition is stated to be *Hall* (1848) and an example given by Lord Lane CJ is:

> I have taken your valuable painting. You can have it back on payment to me of £X,000. If you are not prepared to make that payment, then you are not going to get your painting back.

It may be that in such 'ransom' cases the latter element is implicit in the former part of the statement. If the property which is appropriated is money, it is made clear by s 6(1) that even if the defendant has the intention to repay, there is still an outright taking because it is most unlikely that he will return the actual currency which he removed. This was illustrated in *Velumyl* (1989), where the appellant had taken over £1,000 from his company's safe in breach of his authority and company rules. He claimed to have given the money to a friend and expected to be able to return the equivalent amount two days later. The Court of Appeal had no doubt that Velumyl had the requisite intention to permanently deprive because he had no intention to return 'the objects which he had taken'.

If someone takes property belonging to another, intending to decide at a later stage whether he will retain the articles if they appear valuable or negotiable, is this to be regarded as a sufficient intention? The issue of 'conditional intention' was considered by the courts in the 1970s in cases such as *Easom* (1971), *Husseyn* (1977) and *Walkington* (1979), culminating in the decision of the Court of Appeal in *AG's References (Nos 1 and 2 of 1979)* (1979). It was held in this case that a person charged with burglary and who had entered a building intending to steal anything of value, that is, conditional upon there being anything of value in the building, did have the necessary intent under s 9(1)(a) of the TA 1968 because it is not necessary to prove that he intended to steal any specific item. Similarly, if one takes a handbag intending to steal and upon examination discovers it to be empty, there is nothing to prevent a charge of attempted theft being preferred. In the case of the full offence of theft, however, the prosecution have to be able to prove that the defendant intended permanent deprivation in relation to a specific item of property. So, if the defendant has not made up his mind whether he wishes to keep a particular item of property and rejects it after inspection, he has not demonstrated any such intention in relation to that item and cannot be guilty of stealing it. In essence, these were the facts of *Easom* in which the defendant fell into a trap set for him by the police who were trying to catch a thief operating in a cinema. Posing as an ordinary member of the public, a police woman put her bag on the floor by her seat in the cinema. The defendant sat close to her, picked up her bag and looked through it. However, he did not find anything worth taking and he returned the bag and all its contents. His conviction for theft of the handbag and its contents was quashed. Note that he could not have been convicted of attempted theft of the handbag and its contents either, but that he could have been convicted of attempted theft more generally (as indicated above, 5.12, impossibility – the absence of anything worth taking – is no barrier to a conviction for attempt).

8.6.2 Section 6(2) of the TA 1968

Section 6(2) states:

> Without prejudice to the generality of sub-section (1) above, where a person, having possession or control (lawfully or not) of property belonging to another, parts with the property under a condition as to its return which he may not be able to perform, this (if done for purposes of his own and without the other's authority) amounts to treating the property as his own to dispose of regardless of the other's rights.

This sub-section covers the situations where a defendant who may have come by the property lawfully, for example, as a bailee, or unlawfully, pledges the property, intending to fulfil the necessary conditions in order to redeem the pledge at a later date and then return it to the owner. The sub-section emphasises that if the condition imposed is one which he may not be able to perform then the action may be treated as the equivalent of an intention permanently to deprive, that is, treating the property as his own to dispose of, regardless of the other's rights.

8.7   Conclusion

In *Hallam and Blackburn* (1995), the Court of Appeal once again referred to the complexity of the law relating to theft. Beldam LJ said:

> Once again the law of theft was in urgent need of simplification and modernisation, so that a jury did not have to grapple with concepts couched in the antiquated 'Franglais' of 'chose in action', and scarce public resources were not devoted to hours of semantic argument divorced from the true merits of the case. It was hoped that those responsible for considering law reform would produce a simplified law which juries could more readily understand.

The Law Commission has accepted the challenge. In November 1994, the Law Commission announced its intention to embark on a comprehensive review of offences of dishonesty, including those created by the TA 1968 and TA 1978. The Law Commission acknowledges that there have been 'radical and multifarious advances in the use of modern technology [and], in consequence, it is likely that certain acts of dishonesty might not be effectively covered by the present legislation' (*Conspiracy to Defraud,* Law Com 228, 1994, para 1.16)). This project has now reached the stage of a Consultation Paper on *Fraud and Deception* (Law Com 155, 1999) (see below, 9.12).

OFFENCES AGAINST PROPERTY: THEFT

The starting point of any consideration of the law relating to theft should be the Criminal Law Revision Committee's Eighth Report on *Theft and Related Offences* (Cmnd 2977, 1966). The TA 1968 was based upon the Committee's recommendations and although we have seen that there has been a reluctance on the part of the House of Lords to use the report as an aid to construction it does provide the foundation knowledge needed for a study of this branch of the criminal law. We have seen that, over the past three and half decades, the law has become increasingly complex and, in some cases, fraught with uncertainty (see the whole issue of appropriation and consent), which has lead judges such as Beldam LJ to call for urgent reform.

It has to be noted that the prosecution must prove all elements of the offence, that is, that there has been a dishonest appropriation of property belonging to another with the intention to permanently deprive the other of it. If the defence can establish that one of the five elements is absent then the accused is entitled to be acquitted.

Actus reus

The *actus reus* of theft is proved by showing beyond all reasonable doubt that there has been an appropriation of property belonging to another. The *mens rea* requires proof that the appropriation was done dishonestly and with the intention to permanently deprive the other of that property.

It has been seen that whether or not an appropriation has occurred may be difficult to establish. As a result of *Gomez*, it is possible to maintain that any action may in law amount to an appropriation however innocent it may appear. Taking my elderly neighbour's pension book to the Post Office to collect her pension would appear to be an appropriation. I am exercising one of her rights in that I am using the book and therefore denying her the right to do the same. My actions though would not amount to theft because I am doing so with her permission and for her benefit and therefore I do not act dishonestly. If *Morris* were to represent the law, then, in such circumstances, there would be no appropriation because there would be no adverse interference with her property. The whole issue of consent and appropriation needs to be studied carefully, particularly in light of recent cases such as *Mazo*, *Kendrick and Hopkins* and *Hinks*. At the heart of appropriation is whether or not there is an assumption of any of the rights of the owner.

The property must belong to another and s 5 aids the prosecution by deeming that property shall for the purposes of theft belong to anyone having ownership, possession or control. Therefore, if A lends her portable colour television to B who takes it home, B has possession and control but A still retains ownership. If D were to steal the set from B's house he would commit theft against both A and B.

Property may belong to someone for the purposes of the TA 1968 even though that person is unaware of its existence as, for example, where he owns land but is unaware of all the items on the land.

Sections 5(3) and (4) deem that, in certain circumstances, property which in civil law will belong to the defendant may be regarded as belonging to another. It will be recalled that there is some uncertainty over s 5(3) when a person has been put under an obligation to deal with property or proceeds in a particular way. Remember also that s 5(4) may be redundant if it is accepted by the court that the person who transfers property under a mistake retains an equitable interest in the property. More generally, the decision in *Gomez* has significantly increased the scope of the offence of theft and may also have reduced the need for use of s 5(4).

Mens rea

The *mens rea* word of dishonesty is proved by applying a twofold test based upon a jury's assessment of both objective and subjective criteria. Would ordinary people conclude that the act done by the accused is dishonest? If the answer is yes, the jury must then proceed to listen to the accused's version of events and may conclude that in the circumstances he should not be regarded as dishonest. Having reached a conclusion that the act is objectively dishonest, it is more than likely that the jury will then go on to reject the individual's explanation although this is not inevitable.

The accused must also be shown to have intended to permanently deprive the other of the property within the meaning of s 6. It will be recalled that a borrowing can be the equivalent of an outright taking.

Finally, remember that there is an significant overlap between ss 1 and 15 of the TA 1968. Where fraud or deception are used in order to obtain property belonging to another, then s 15 will be the most appropriate charge. On the face of it, *Gomez* was a straightforward obtaining by deception rather than a s 1 offence.

OFFENCES AGAINST PROPERTY: OTHER OFFENCES UNDER THE THEFT ACTS 1968 AND 1978 AND CRIMINAL DAMAGE

9.1   Robbery (s 8 of the TA 1968)

It will be apparent that theft is at the heart of the offence of robbery. The purpose of engaging in a robbery is to steal and it is differentiated from the primary offence by the additional, aggravating element of force. Section 8(1) of the Theft Act (TA) 1968 provides:

> A person is guilty of robbery if he steals, and immediately before or at the time of doing so, and in order to do so, he uses force on any person or puts or seeks to put any person in fear of being then and there subjected to force.

Section 8(2) states:

> A person guilty of robbery, or of an assault with intent to rob, shall on conviction on indictment be liable to life imprisonment.

As the first part of this definition emphasises, to be guilty of robbery one must first steal, and all elements of s 1 of the TA 1968 will have to be established. So, even though force may be used, if the accused is not acting dishonestly or the intention to permanently deprive is lacking then a robbery charge will be inappropriate. In *Robinson* (1977), the appellant's conviction for robbery was quashed on the basis that he honestly believed he was entitled to the money which was owed by the victim to him. If force was used to enforce such an obligation, then an assault charge or a more serious offence might lie depending on the nature of the physical attack. If the theft has been completed with the necessary force being applied then robbery is established as soon as the theft is complete. In *Corcoran v Anderton* (1980), the defendants wrestled with the owner for possession of her handbag and the theft was complete as soon as she lost possession, although in the event one of the assailants dropped it as they ran off, without having succeeded in their objective of permanently depriving her of the bag.

9.1.1   Force

The TA 1968 requires proof of either the use or the threat of force against the person. It appears that it is to be left to the jury to determine whether or not force has been used or threatened. The Act does not provide a definition. In *Coulden* (1987), the Court of Appeal, following *Dawson and James* (1976), confirmed that the old distinction between force on the person and force on property had not survived the Act. The matter should be left to the jury. C had followed a woman who was carrying a shopping basket. He approached her from behind and wrenched the basket from her grasp and ran away. He was charged with robbery and theft and convicted of the former offence. In his appeal against conviction, he argued that as there had been little resistance to his actions, in law it could not be established that he had used 'force'. The court rejected the submission, holding that it was for the jury to decide, taking into account all the circumstances. The Criminal Law Revision Committee (Eighth Report, *Theft and Related Offences*, Cmnd 2977, 1966, para 65) had doubts as to whether or not this type of situation should amount to anything more than theft. It stated:

> We should not regard mere snatching of property such as a handbag, from an unresisting owner as using force for the purpose of the definition, though it might be so if the owner resisted.

The use or threat of force may be against any person, and it is clear from the wording that the threat of the application of force at some stage in the future is not covered by s 8 ('then and there subjected to force').

In the overwhelming majority of cases, the force will be applied against the victim who is in possession and control of the property. However the section refers to force on 'any person' so long as it is used or threatened in order to steal. Therefore to threaten or use force on a security guard, in order to facilitate access to a strongroom containing gold bars, would be enough, even though he had no proprietary interest whatsoever in the property.

9.1.2 Immediately before or at the time of stealing

A literal interpretation of these words would have a limiting effect on the scope of the section and draw attention to those aspects of the conduct which are closely related in time to the act of appropriation. It would, for example, rule out the gang who hold a bank manager captive in his house overnight before escaping with his keys which they use hours later to gain access to his bank. It is submitted that all the circumstances should be considered and, if the force used has a direct bearing on facilitating the theft, then one should view it as part of the same transaction. The force in the above example has been used with one purpose in mind: to commit theft. Similarly, the use of or threat of force seconds after the appropriation has taken place would seem to rule out a robbery conviction. However, the Court of Appeal in *Hale* (1978) held that the act of appropriation was a continuous act and that it should be left to the jury to decide when it has finished. In this case, Hale and his accomplice entered the victim's house and Hale put his hand over her mouth to stop her from screaming, while the other went upstairs and took her jewellery box. They then tied her up and made their escape. The jury could have convicted of robbery on the basis of the force used against the victim in order to prevent her from raising the alarm, but the court also considered whether a robbery conviction could be sustained on the basis that the tying up was the act of 'force', an act which apparently took place when the jewellery box was already in their possession. Eveleigh LJ said:

> We also think that they were also entitled to rely upon the act of tying her up provided they were satisfied (and it is difficult to see how they could not be satisfied) that the force so used was to enable them to steal. If they were still engaged in the act of stealing the force was clearly used to enable them to continue to assume the rights of the owner and permanently to deprive Mrs Carrett of her box, which is what they began to do when they first seized it.

This approach was confirmed by the Court of Appeal in *Lockley* (1995). The appellant and two others took cans of beer from an off licence and, when challenged by the shopkeeper, used violence against him. It was submitted on their behalf that the theft was complete before any force was used and, therefore, the robbery issue should not have been left to the jury. In confirming that *Hale* was still good law, the court held that an appropriation was an act that continued until the transaction was complete and, thus, force was used in order to steal.

9.1.3 *Mens rea*

Clearly, there must be evidence of an intent to steal and the defendant must be shown to have acted dishonestly and with intent to permanently deprive. It is suggested that there should also be proved an intent in respect of the force used. If the accused intends to steal, yet has no intention to subject the victim to the use of force or cause that person to apprehend that force may be used against him, the crime should amount to theft but not to robbery.

9.2 Burglary (s 9 of the TA 1968)

Section 9 of the TA 1968 creates two offences, one where a person enters a building as a trespasser with intent to commit a range of ulterior offences and a second where a person has entered as a trespasser and then commits one or more of a more limited range of offences:

(1) A person is guilty of burglary if:

    (a) he enters any building or part of a building as a trespasser and with intent to commit any such offence as is mentioned in sub-s (2) below; or

    (b) having entered into any building or part of a building as a trespasser he steals or attempts to steal anything in the building or that part of it or inflicts or attempts to inflict on any person therein any grievous bodily harm.

(2) The offences referred to in sub-s (1)(a) above are offences of stealing anything in the building or part of a building in question, of inflicting on

> any person therein any grievous bodily harm or raping any woman therein, and of doing unlawful damage to the building or anything therein.

There are numerous elements of these offences to which consideration must be given. The *actus reus* of the crimes centre on the entry into any building or part of a building as a trespasser.

9.2.1 Building

Sub-section 4 makes it clear that the word 'building' includes an 'inhabited vehicle or vessel, and shall apply to any such vehicle or vessel at times when the person having a habitation in it is not there as well as at times when he is'. Nevertheless, despite this limited guidance, there is no all embracing definition included in the TA 1968. In the old case of *Stevens v Gourley* (1859), Byles J considered that a building comprised 'a structure of considerable size and intended to be permanent or at least to endure for a considerable time'. In *Norfolk Constabulary v Seekings and Gould* (1986), the appellants had tried to gain entry to two articulated lorry trailers being used by a supermarket as temporary storage space while building redevelopment was taking place. Each was supported by its own wheels and struts and an electric cable ran from the supermarket to supply the lighting. Access was gained via steps which had been placed against each trailer. It was held that the character of the structure had not changed from that of a vehicle and therefore was not a building for the purposes of an attempted burglary charge. This case is distinguishable from *B and S v Leathley* (1979), where a freezer container was classed as a building because it did not have any wheels and was immobile.

Given its literal meaning, the word 'building' covers structures which house many smaller units, for example, a large block of flats or suites of offices belonging to or leased by different companies. This means that an entry into the building with intent to steal from any of the smaller units would amount to burglary even though the defendant is arrested before reaching the particular unit from which he proposes to steal. If, indeed, the culprit is apprehended at the moment entry is effected into a block of flats and it is clear that the proposed theft is to occur from the penthouse flat, the TA 1968 would allow a conviction for burglary to follow. If not, the charge would have to be attempted burglary or theft and whether or not the accused is convicted is likely to depend on whether or nor a jury would regard the acts as being more than merely preparatory. In practice, the judge will have to decide that there is sufficient evidence from which to conclude that a building within the meaning of the TA 1968 is in existence.

Walkington (1979) considered the meaning of the words 'part of a building'. The appellant had entered an Oxford Street store as, he claimed, a *bona fide* customer. He had noticed a cash register behind a three-sided movable counter with the drawer partially open. He placed himself behind the counter, opened the drawer and, on realising it was empty, slammed it shut. He was arrested and charged with burglary. The Court of Appeal held that, as the store's management had 'impliedly prohibited customers' from entering that area, there was 'ample evidence' from which it could be concluded by the jury that the counter area amounted to 'part of a building' for the purposes of s 9(1)(a). The court also confirmed that, if the accused entered that part of the building as a trespasser with the intent to steal, it was 'immaterial' that there was nothing worth stealing or nothing to steal. On the assumption that he entered the store lawfully, the trespass occurred only in relation to the part of the building to which he was not entitled to go.

In *Laing* (1995), the defendant was found in a department store some time after it had closed for the day. He was apprehended in a stock area not open to the public. Surprisingly, the prosecution did not suggest that he might be guilty of burglary having entered the store lawfully and then moved to a part of the building to which the public were denied access at which point he would have become a trespasser. The judge directed the jury to consider whether he was a trespasser when found.

In allowing the appeal, the court confirmed that there was no evidence to prove that he was a trespasser when he entered the store and it was not suggested that he became a trespasser by moving from one part of the building to another. There is only one question to be answered, whether the charge is under s 9(1)(a) or (b). Did the defendant enter the building or part of the building as a trespasser?

9.2.2 Entry

The section requires that the defendant 'enters' or 'entered' as a trespasser. Prior to the TA 1968 the common law regarded the insertion of any part of the body into the building as sufficient to constitute an entry. After a serious flirtation with a different approach, the courts seemed to have settled upon an interpretation of the requirements of the 1968 Act as to entry which is indistinguishable from the original common law approach. An apparent decision to begin afresh was initially signalled in the leading case of *Collins* (1972), which was described by Edmund Davies LJ as:

> ... about as extraordinary a case as my brethren and I have ever heard either on the Bench or while at the Bar – were [the facts] put into a novel or portrayed on the stage, they would be regarded as being so improbable as to be unworthy of serious consideration and as verging at times on farce.

Collins was charged with burglary with intent to commit rape. Naked, apart from his socks, he was balancing on the window sill of the victim's bedroom when she, mistaking him for her boyfriend, invited him into her bed and full sexual intercourse took place. It was only later that she suspected things were not quite right, switched on the bedside light and discovered that her visitor was not the person she believed she had been inviting into her bed. Collins' defence was that he had not entered the building before she gave her consent and therefore had not entered the building as a trespasser. The Court of Appeal considered that it was imperative that an 'effective and substantial entry' must have taken place before consent was given in order for an entry to be complete.

This ruling was reassessed in *Brown* (1985). The appellant had been seen by a witness with the top half of his body inside a shattered shop window and he appeared to be rummaging about inside the window. His feet were on the ground outside. He appealed against his conviction for burglary on the ground that he had not entered the building, since his body was not entirely within it. The court held that it was not required for the whole of a person's body to be inside the building. The crucial word of the Edmund Davies test in *Collins* was 'effective' and '"substantially"' did not materially assist in the matter'. It was hardly surprising that the court upheld the conviction as it was obvious that he could give effect to his purpose with only half his body inside the shop. In this case, there was an effective entry because Brown was able to reach the articles he wished to steal. But this is not always going to be the case, even if the whole body is in the building. If Collins had entered the house through the front door without any consent having been given, he would, given that his physical condition and state of undress indicated his purpose in being there, be guilty of burglary. Yet it could hardly be claimed that his entry was 'effective', if this word is meant to refer to the ulterior offence, as he may have been apprehended straightaway, or the girl's bedroom door may have been bolted so that he would be unable to gain entry or she may not have been in the house. The better view is that 'effective' must refer to the entry and the crucial question is whether or not the defendant is better able to carry out the ulterior offence.

The importance of *Collins* as an authority has undoubtedly diminished and this was confirmed by the Court of Appeal in *Ryan* (1996). At approximately 2:30 am, an elderly householder found R stuck in a downstairs window of his house. His neck and right arm were inside the window the rest of his body was outside. He claimed that he was trying to reach a baseball bat that a friend had put through the window. He was convicted of burglary. His appeal was based on the proposition that in law there had been no entry as, given his predicament, he was unable to steal anything from the premises. The court dismissed his appeal holding that it was totally irrelevant whether a defendant was or was not capable of stealing anything from the premises. This decision appears to suggest that for there to be an entry in law there does not need to be either an 'effective' or 'substantial' entry. It would appear that we are back to the common law position stated above.

If an instrument is used only in order to facilitate an entry, then the common law view was that this did not in law constitute an entry on the part of the person using the instrument. However, if the instrument was used in order to bring about the ulterior offence then this was an entry. Thus, if a fishing rod is pushed through an open window in order to 'hook' jewellery lying on a bedside cabinet, this would be sufficient to constitute an entry on the part of the person manipulating the rod. There is no authority which challenges the view that the common law has survived the TA 1968.

9.2.3 Trespasser

A person must enter a building as a trespasser before the *actus reus* of burglary is complete. The civil law recognises that a person is a trespasser if without permission or any legal right he enters a building intentionally, recklessly or negligently. The requirements of the civil law need to be satisfied before a person can be convicted of burglary. The criminal law requirements were stated by Edmund Davies LJ in *Collins* to be:

> ... there cannot be a conviction for entering premises 'as a trespasser', unless the person entering does so knowing that he is a trespasser and nevertheless deliberately enters, or, at the very least, is reckless whether or not he is entering the premises of another without the other party's consent.

A question raised in *Collins* was whether he had entered the building as a trespasser before the young lady purported to give authorisation. There can be no doubt that, from the outset, he was intent upon entering the property as a trespasser. If permission to enter was granted before there had been an effective and substantial entry, then he could not be guilty of burglary as he would not have entered as a trespasser. Conversely, if he was inside the room before she invited him into her bed, then the offence would already be complete.

Attention should be paid to the position or status of the person who purports to give authority to enter a building. In *Collins*, it was argued that the girl's mother was the occupier and, therefore, the daughter did not have the authority to give consent to his entry. This was dismissed by Edmund Davies LJ with these words: 'Whatever be the position in the law of tort, to regard such a proposition as acceptable in the criminal law would be unthinkable.'

Much will depend upon the knowledge of the defendant prior to or at the time of entry. If he knows that the girl's mother has specifically instructed her not to allow anyone into the house, then he would be a trespasser. Conversely, if he had no such knowledge nor reason to believe such a prohibition exists, then his entry with 'permission' would appear lawful. If he is given apparent authority to enter by a mature young lady who, from his point of view, could be the occupier, or he has no reason to suspect anyone else may be the occupier, again he ought to be found not to be a trespasser. Parents may impliedly give consent to their children to invite their friends into the house but one suspects that implied authority will be subject in many cases to the proviso that it is for a purpose which they would endorse, and intercourse with their daughter at 3 am is unlikely to feature on an 'approved' list of activities!

The Court of Appeal has given consideration as to whether or not a person is a trespasser if he enters intending to exceed the permission granted or to act in a way which is inconsistent with that permission. In *Jones and Smith* (1977), the appellants had been charged under s 9(1)(b) of the TA 1968 as they entered a house belonging to Smith's father and stole two television sets. Smith's defence was that his father had given him a 'general licence' to go into his house whenever he wanted to, and consequently his entry together with Jones into the house was lawful. It was argued on Smith's behalf that in these circumstances the fact that Smith had already made up his mind to take the television sets before entering the property would not make him a trespasser.

James LJ, citing *Collins* and *Hillen and Pettigrew v ICI (Alkali) Ltd* (1936), held that a person is a trespasser for the purposes of s 9(1)(b) if:

> ... he enters premises of another knowing that he is entering in excess of the permission that has been given to him, or being reckless whether he is entering in excess of the permission that has been given to him to enter, providing the facts are known to the accused which enable him to realise that he is acting in excess of the permission given or that he is acting recklessly as to whether he exceeds that permission ...

In *Jones and Smith*, the Court of Appeal dismissed their appeal on the basis that they had entered the premises with knowledge that they were exceeding the permission granted by Smith's father. In *Collins*, the court allowed the appeal because of the uncertainty over whether or not he had entered the bedroom before the permission was granted.

General permission to enter premises implies that someone entering can never be classed as a trespasser whatever the purpose. This idea was, however, rejected by the court in *Jones and Smith*, where James LJ applied the reasoning of Lord Atkin in *Hillen and Pettigrew v ICI (Alkali) Ltd* (1936) that the general permission to an invitee:

> ... only extends so long as and so far as the invitee is making what can reasonably be contemplated as an ordinary and reasonable use of the premises (he is not invited to use any part of the premises for purposes which he knows are wrongfully dangerous and constitute an improper use).

9.2.4   The ulterior offences

Under s 9(1)(a) of the TA 1968, four offences are specified – theft, rape, grievous bodily harm and criminal damage – and it must be established that the defendant had the necessary intent at the time of entry to the building or part of a building. A conditional intention to steal will be sufficient to prove intent for these purposes. It was held in *AG's References (Nos 1 and 2 of 1979)* (1979) that, providing the indictment does not aver specifically to a specific item to be stolen, then all that is required is proof that the accused intended to steal. It may be that the intent is simply to steal 'anything of value' found on the premises but, in law, it does not matter that those premises may not contain anything of value.

Under s 9(1)(b), only two offences are specified: those of theft and inflicting grievous bodily harm, or the attempt to do either. The major point of contention centres around the meaning of the words 'inflicting upon any person therein any grievous bodily harm'. The decision in *Jenkins* (1983) means that the infliction of grievous bodily harm need not amount to an offence. Section 9(1)(a) requires an 'offence' to be committed but that word is absent from s 9(1)(b). Purchas LJ gave the following example:

> An intruder gains access to the house without breaking in (where there is an open window, for instance). He is on the premises as a trespasser, and his intrusion is observed by someone in the house of whom he may not even be aware, and as a result that person suffers severe shock, with a resulting stroke. In such a case it would be difficult to see how an assault could be alleged; but nevertheless his presence would have been a direct cause of the stroke, which must amount to grievous bodily harm. Should such an event fall outside the provisions of s 9, when causing some damage to the property falls fairly within it?

The problem with this example is that the trespasser does not appear to possess the intent to cause grievous bodily harm and, if the section is read as a whole, then it would appear that, for a conviction to result under s 9(1)(b), the infliction of grievous bodily harm must amount to an offence. The Draft Criminal Code (cl 147) seeks to remedy this apparent deficiency of the TA 1968:

> This clause takes the opportunity to correct a plain and unintended error in s 9 of the Theft Act 1968. Taken literally, burglary (contrary to s 9(1)(b)) could be committed accidentally by someone in a building as a trespasser.

It reads:

> (b) having entered a building or part of a building as a trespasser he commits in the building or part of a building in question an offence of theft or attempted theft; or causing, or attempting to cause, serious personal harm.

9.3 Aggravated burglary (s 10 of the TA 1968)

This is a serious offence punishable by a maximum of life imprisonment. The 'aggravated' element of the offence relates to the possession of firearms, imitation firearms, offensive weapons or explosives at the time the burglary is committed.

Section 10(1) of the TA 1968 makes it an offence for:

> A person (to commit) any burglary and at the time has with him any firearm or imitation firearm, any weapon of offence, or any explosive; and for this purpose:

(a) 'firearm' includes an airgun or air pistol and 'imitation firearm' means anything which has the appearance of being a firearm, whether capable of being discharged or not; and

(b) 'weapon of offence' means any article made or adapted for use for causing injury to or incapacitating a person, or intended by the person having it with him for such use; and

(c) 'explosive' means any article manufactured for the purpose of producing a practical effect by explosion, or intended by the person having it with him for that purpose.

'Weapon of offence' is to be given a wider meaning than 'offensive weapon' in s 1(4) of the Prevention of Crime Act 1953. First, the definition goes beyond that of 'offensive weapon' by including not only any article made or adapted for use for or carried with an intention of causing *injury* to a person but also of *incapacitating* a person. Secondly, a weapon is not an offensive weapon merely by virtue of its use as such. So, if a person is lawfully carrying an article without any intention of using it for causing injury but he uses it spontaneously to do so, he does not thereby commit the offence under the Prevention of Crime Act 1953. Nor does he do so by spontaneously seizing some article and using it. But the courts have taken the view that use is sufficient for aggravated burglary. So, in *Kelly* (1992) the defendant was held to have been properly convicted of aggravated burglary when he used a screwdriver (which he had with him to gain entry) to prod the victim in the stomach.

The article must be with him at the time of committing the burglary. In *Francis* (1982), the defendants armed with sticks demanded entry to a house by kicking and banging on the door. They were allowed to enter. It was unclear whether it was just before entering or just after when they discarded their sticks, and proceeded to steal items from the house. They were charged with aggravated burglary. Their convictions for the offence were quashed because the judge's direction to the jury had not made it clear that either the defendants had to have committed burglary under s 9(1)(a) whilst having the weapons with them or burglary under s 9(1)(b) whilst having the weapons with them. The judge had stated that the prosecution were required to prove only that the defendants were armed when they entered the house as trespassers. However, they might not have committed burglary under s 9(1)(a) (which would inevitably rule out aggravated burglary), because they might have entered with the sticks, but without intending any further offence. Conversely, though they had committed burglary under s 9(1)(b), they might not have committed aggravated burglary because they might already have discarded the sticks before they committed theft in the house. By contrast, the conviction in *O'Leary* (1986) was easy to affirm. The defendant had entered a house as a trespasser and had then picked up a kitchen knife before going upstairs, where he used it to threaten the victim into handing over property. Here, he had armed himself with the knife before committing burglary under s 9(1)(b) and so had the knife with him at the time of committing burglary. It is possible that, where two or more are engaged in committing burglary, the one who enters the building will enter without any weapon and will leave outside accomplices who do have weapons. This is not sufficient to convert the burglary into aggravated burglary. A burglar must have the weapon with him in the building. In *Klass* (1998), the defendant and two others went to a caravan, wrenched open the door and demanded money from the victim. When he said that he had none, one of the other men hit him with a pole and pursued him as he ran away, hitting him repeatedly. There was evidence that the defendant had entered the caravan and he was convicted of aggravated burglary. His conviction was quashed and one for burglary was substituted. Aggravated burglary could only be committed if the burglar (or one of them, if there were two or more) had the weapon with him in the building.

To comply with the requirement that a person 'has with him' an article included in s 10 it has been held that the accused must know that he has the article, that is, that he was aware that the article had the qualities enumerated in s 10(a), (b) or (c). It was no defence to the accused in *Stones* (1989) to claim that he carried a knife only as a defensive measure in case of attack. He knew he had the weapon, was aware that it would cause injury or incapacitate a person, and could resort to using it in the course of a burglary should the circumstances demand it.

9.4 Taking a motor vehicle or other conveyance without authority (s 12 of the TA 1968)

The taking of a conveyance without authority does not require proof of an intention to permanently deprive, in order to obtain a conviction. It is this element which differentiates the offence from that under s 1 of the TA 1968 of theft of a conveyance. The basic offence is contained in s 12(1) of the TA 1968:

> Subject to sub-ss (5) and (6) below, a person shall be guilty of an offence if, without having the consent of the owner or other lawful authority, he takes any conveyance for his own or another's use or knowing that any conveyance has been taken without such authority, drives it or allows himself to be carried in or on it.

The sub-sections referred to, that is, (5) and (6), make it clear that sub-s (1) does not apply to pedal cycles, (but these are subject to summary proceedings) and that a person does not commit an offence:

> ... by anything done in the belief that he has lawful authority to do it or that he would have the owner's consent if the owner knew of his doing it and the circumstances of it.

A conveyance is defined as 'any conveyance constructed or adapted for the carriage of a person or persons whether by land, water or air, except that it does not include a conveyance constructed or adapted for use only under the control of a person not carried in or on it, and 'drive' shall be construed accordingly'. *Bogacki* (1973) decided that the words 'use' and 'take' were not synonymous and that, before a person can be convicted of the offence, it must:

> ... be shown that he took the vehicle, that is to say, that there was an unauthorised taking possession or control of the vehicle by him adverse to the rights of the true owner or person otherwise entitled to such possession or control, coupled with some movement, however small ... of that vehicle following such unauthorised taking [Roskill LJ, p 837].

In this case, Bogacki had boarded a bus in a depot and attempted to start the engine. He failed to get it to move before he was apprehended. His conviction was quashed on appeal.

The taking must be for his own or another's use and this means that it must be used as a conveyance. Any taking which involves using the conveyance as a conveyance will inevitably qualify – most obviously, driving away a vehicle or sailing off in a boat – but it is also possible to commit the offence by taking the conveyance for later use as a conveyance. For example, taking away a boat on a trailer with the intention of subsequently sailing in it, as happened in *Pearce* (1973).

In *Bow* (1976), the defendant together with his brother and father had driven to a country estate. They had with them air rifles and the assumption was that they were on a poaching expedition. The men, when challenged by a gamekeeper refused to identify themselves and the police were summoned. The gamekeeper blocked their exit from the estate with his Land Rover. Bow got into the vehicle, released the handbrake and allowed it to coast for some 200 yards so that their own car, driven by his brother could proceed from the estate. He was charged and convicted of the s 12 offence. His appeal was dismissed. The court accepted he was using the vehicle as a conveyance. Presumably if he had released the handbrake and pushed the vehicle in order to increase momentum that would not amount to an offence under s 12. But to sit in it and be transported led to the conclusion that it was being used as a conveyance. It is submitted that the defendant must intend to use the conveyance as a means of transport and not for some other purpose. So, in *Dunn and Derby* (1984), following *Pearce*, the court accepted a submission of no case to answer when the prosecution could not prove that the defendants had intended to use the motorbike as opposed to simply admire it. The two men had admitted pushing the motorcycle some 40 yards in order, they claimed, to look at it by a porch light. There can be no doubt that they had unauthorised possession of the cycle but it had not been used as a means of transport nor could it be established that it was their intention to use it as a conveyance. If what they claimed was the truth, then they were clearly not guilty. However, if they took it to the spot in order to discover how to start it, intending to drive away, then they should be guilty. If they were walking away with the cycle, intending to sell it to the first person who would offer them £1,000, then once again the offence would not be established. A charge under s 1 of the TA 1968 would be appropriate in such circumstances as they clearly intended to permanently deprive the owner of the property.

If the conveyance is already lawfully in the defendant's possession, he may still commit the offence if his use of the vehicle does not comply with the terms of the authorisation. In *McGill* (1970), the defendant borrowed the vehicle under strict instruction to return it once he had driven a friend to a railway station. He retained the vehicle and continued to use it for his own purposes for a few more days. His claim that as long as the original taking was with consent it did not matter that he didn't fulfil the conditions, was rejected by the Court of Appeal. The car had been borrowed for a particular purpose and once that purpose had been achieved it was clear that he had taken the car for his own use.

The taking of the conveyance must be without the 'consent of the owner or other lawful authority'. In a case such as *McGill*, where the authorisation was given in very specific terms, there are few problems, but what is the position if the consent is obtained as a result of deception and without the owner being in full possession of all the facts including the use to which the defendant intended to put the conveyance, information which, of course, is likely to influence his judgment? In *Peart* (1970), P had induced B to lend him his car, falsely stating that he intended to drive to Alnwick, when in fact he wished to drive to Burnley. It was agreed that the car should be returned by 7.30 pm and P was still in possession of the vehicle at 9 pm. He had known that B would not have consented if he had revealed the true destination. His conviction was quashed on the basis that the misrepresentation did not vitiate consent. The taking had been with consent, the mistake had been towards the purpose for which the car was to be used. In *Whittaker v Campbell* (1983), where the appellant had used a driving licence which he had found to hire a van, the conviction was quashed on the basis that fraud did not vitiate consent. The fraud related only to the acquisition of the vehicle and not to the purpose for which it was to be used. Contrasting the decision in *McGill*, with that in *Peart*, one can easily identify the similarities in each case. In *McGill* the consent was exceeded once he retained the vehicle after delivering his friend to the station. In *Peart*, one may argue that the consent was exceeded once he was still in possession of the vehicle beyond 7.30 pm, irrespective of whether he was in Alnwick or Burnley or any point between the two towns. Further evidence to sustain an argument to the effect that *Peart* should regarded as being on all fours with *McGill* relates to the moment Peart departed from the route to Alnwick in order to take the road to Burnley. At that point, he was exceeding his authority and there was no consent for that particular journey.

9.4.1 *Mens rea*

Section 12(6) of the TA 1968 provides that, if the accused can show he believed that he had lawful authority or would have had the owner's consent if the owner knew of his doing it and the circumstances of it, the prosecution will not be able to establish the *mens rea*.

It was held by the Court of Appeal in *Clotworthy* (1981) that a subjective assessment of belief was appropriate. It was irrelevant whether or not he actually had authority or would have had consent, it is simply a matter of proving to a jury's satisfaction that he honestly held that belief. In line with the law on mistake, the more unreasonable the belief the more likely it is that the prosecution case will succeed.

It was decided by the Divisional Court, in *DPP v Spriggs* (1993), that, once a vehicle which has been unlawfully taken is abandoned, any further taking without authority by someone other than the original offender amounts to a new offence. There would appear to be no reason in principle why the original offender who has returned the vehicle or abandoned it and who subsequently decides to retake it should not also be convicted of the offence. *MacPherson* (1973) is authority for the proposition that s 12 is a basic intent crime and therefore intoxication will be irrelevant in deciding whether or not the accused had the requisite *mens rea* for the offence.

9.5 Aggravated vehicle-taking

The Aggravated Vehicle-Taking Act (AVTA) 1992 came into force on 1 April 1992 and inserted a new s 12A into the TA 1968. As a result,. a person commits the offence of aggravated vehicle-taking in relation to a mechanically propelled vehicle (note that this is a narrower category that 'conveyance') when he commits an offence under s 12(1) of the TA 1968 referred to as the basic offence and (s 12A):

(1)(b) it is proved that, at any time after the vehicle was unlawfully taken (whether by him or another) and before it was recovered, the vehicle was driven, or injury or damage caused, in one or more of the circumstances set out in paragraphs (a) to (d) of sub-s (2) [they being]:

(2)(a) that the vehicle was driven dangerously on a road or other public place;

(b) that, owing to the driving of the vehicle, an accident occurred by which injury was caused to any person;

(c) that, owing to the driving of the vehicle, an accident occurred by which damage was caused to any property, other than the vehicle;

(d) that damage was caused to the vehicle.

It is a defence under s 12A(3)(a) to show that the driving, accident or damage occurred before the person charged committed the basic offence. The fact that he was 'neither in nor on nor in the immediate vicinity of the vehicle' when that driving, accident or damage occurred also provides a defence (s 12(A)(3)(b)).

This Act is Parliament's response to the increasing and justified concern over the number of vehicles being taken and used for 'joyriding' and other dangerous activities. The AVTA 1992 seeks to impose punishment in circumstances where, if other Road Traffic Act offences were charged, it would be difficult to secure the proof of who caused the damage. For example, where four or five people are in the vehicle, their stories may be at variance, one with another, or where the vehicle is stripped of its saleable components and then left abandoned, there could be difficulty in proving those who took the car actually caused the criminal damage without the provisions of this Act. It would appear that, as regards s 12A(2)(b), (c) and (d), no fault element needs to be established. In *Marsh* (1996), the appellant was charged with aggravated vehicle taking, the aggravating circumstance being that under sub-s (2)(b), that is, owing to the driving of the vehicle, an accident occurred by which injury was caused to any person. In this case, the car had been unlawfully taken but was not being driven in a negligent or careless manner. A woman had run into the road and was knocked down by the car. She was not seriously injured. Nevertheless, the Court of Appeal upheld the conviction despite the lack of any culpability on the part of the appellant. The only question said the court, given the wording of the Act, was whether the driving of the vehicle was the cause of the accident. On this very strict interpretation, if there is no culpability whatsoever, the mere fact that the basic s 12 offence has taken place will be enough to convert the offence into one of aggravated vehicle-taking. The child who is knocked down having rushed into the road in pursuit of her ball without paying any attention to the road conditions will unwittingly establish the offence if the car she runs into has been unlawfully taken from its owner. If the car, which is being driven well within the speed limit and with the driver taking all due precaution is owned by the driver, then there would appear to be no offence nor would the facts establish civil liability for negligence. It would be difficult to conclude in either situation that the driving of the vehicle was the 'cause of the accident'. Nevertheless, as a result of this case, the provision is to be subject to a strict interpretation and 'simply by being there' the defendant will in all probability be convicted. The court justified its decision on the basis that heavier sentences should be imposed on those who take vehicles and then cause an accident, irrespective of any fault in the driving. In other words, there would have been no risk to the person crossing the road if the defendant had not acted unlawfully in removing the vehicle.

Whatever the merits of this offence as an attempt to deal with the problems of 'joyriding', it is evident that the provisions of s 12A(2)(b)–(d) are highly unusual in not requiring any fault at all on the part of the defendant beyond his initial fault in taking the vehicle. Nor can the defendant easily determine what he must do to divest himself of responsibility, for the section refers in the vaguest terms imaginable to proof that he was not 'in nor on nor *in the immediate vicinity* of the vehicle' when the incident occurred. For the person who has committed the basic offence by 'allowing himself to be carried in or on' the vehicle, the liability is potentially even harsher, since he will not be able to escape responsibility even by protesting to the driver and urging him to stop. It will be interesting to see whether anyone seeks to challenge the offence of aggravated vehicle-taking in its present form by way of the Human Rights Act 1998.

9.6 Blackmail (s 21 of the TA 1968)

The *Compact Oxford English Dictionary* gives the following information about the origins of the word blackmail:

> A tribute formerly exacted from farmers and small owners in the border counties of England and Scotland and along the Highland Border, by freebooting chiefs, in return for protection or immunity from plunder.

The word is defined in these terms:

> Any payment extorted by intimidation or pressure, or levied by unprincipled officials, critics, journalists etc upon those whom they have it in their power to help or injure. Now usually a payment extorted by threats or pressure, especially by threatening to reveal a discreditable secret; the action of extorting such a payment.

Section 21(1) of the TA 1968 expresses it this way:

> (1) A person is guilty of blackmail if, with a view to gain for himself or another or with intent to cause loss to another, he makes any unwarranted demand with menaces.

9.6.1 The demand

The *actus reus* of the offence is to make a demand with menaces. Section 21(2) of the TA 1968 refers to acts or omissions and the demand may take either of these forms in addition to a spoken demand. It is not necessary for the demand to be explicit as seen in *Collister and Warhurst* (1955). The defendant heard two police officers discussing the chances of them dropping a charge against him in return for payment. It was their intention that the defendant should overhear this conversation and a direct demand was never actually made to him. Nor does the section imply that the demand must actually be received by the victim. If the victim is actually outside the jurisdiction the offence may be committed provided the demand is issued within the jurisdiction. In *Treacy v DPP* (1971), a letter containing the unwarranted demand with menaces was posted in this country, the intended recipient residing in Germany. The House of Lords held that the offence had been committed. Lord Diplock considered that if the letter had been posted in Germany to a victim in this country it would still amount to an offence on the basis that the demand continues as the letter continues its journey and it is not straining the wording of the Act to say the demand is 'made' in this country. The demand must be made 'with a view to gain for himself or another or with intent to cause loss to another'. Section 34(2) of the TA 1968 indicates that '"gain" and "loss" are to be construed as extending only to gain or loss in money or other property'.

In *Bevans* (1988), the appellant, who was crippled with osteoarthritis, pointed a handgun at his doctor and demanded a morphine injection to ease his pain, threatening to shoot the doctor if he failed to comply with his demand. He was charged with blackmail and his conviction was upheld by the Court of Appeal. The court had no doubt that the substance injected into him was 'property' and the demand involved gain to Bevans. The reasons why he wanted the drug were deemed irrelevant. Property had been given to him as a result of the demand. The limitation imposed by the TA 1968 means that someone who obtains services as distinct from money or other property will not be guilty of blackmail even if those services have resulted from an unwarranted demand with menaces, unless these services can be viewed as having a monetary value.

9.6.2   Menaces

Lord Wright in *Thorne v Motor Trade Association* (1937) offered the following opinion on the meaning of the word menaces:

> I think the word 'menace' is to be liberally construed and not as limited to threats of violence but as including threats of any action detrimental to or unpleasant to the person addressed. It may also include a warning that in certain events such action is intended.

And Cairns LJ in *Lawrence* (1971) thought that 'menaces' was an ordinary English word which needed no elaboration from trial judges. This was confirmed by the Court of Appeal in *Garwood* (1987). The use of the word 'menace' as opposed to 'threat' results in greater flexibility and for a more common sense approach to be adopted if required. An example is *Harry* (1974), where the accused, the treasurer of a college rag committee, was charged with blackmail after having sent letters to 115 shopkeepers inviting them to contribute to rag funds and thus avoid 'any rag activity which could in any way cause you inconvenience'. The judge ruled, applying the test in *Clear* (1968), that there were no menaces. *Clear* required that 'the mind of an ordinary person of normal stability and courage might be influenced or made apprehensive so as to accede unwillingly to the demand'; and the shopkeepers who had received letters were as a group unconcerned about the 'threat'. The Court of Appeal in *Garwood* (1987) concluded that there were two occasions when a further direction on the meaning of menaces might be required.

The first is: 'Where the threats might have affected the mind of an ordinary person of normal stability but did not affect the person actually addressed.' The court thought that in such circumstances there would be sufficient menace. The second situation is where the threats 'in fact affected the mind of the victim, although they would not have affected the mind of a person of normal stability'. In this case, the menaces are again proved, always assuming that the accused is 'aware of the likely effect of his actions on the victim'.

The *mens rea* for the offence is determined by proof that the defendant's demand must be with a view to gain for himself or another, or with intent to cause loss to another, and s 34(2)(a) makes it clear that it is irrelevant whether or not any such gain or loss is temporary or permanent. The 'gain' and 'loss' elements are expressed disjunctively although in practice a demand upon the victim will usually cause him loss and as a consequence the blackmailer will gain. A further aspect of *mens rea* is contained within the requirement that the demand with menaces must be 'unwarranted'.

9.6.3 Unwarranted

Whether or not the demand is unwarranted should be determined by reference to the defendant's belief in whether he has:

- reasonable grounds for making the demand; and

- that the use of menaces is a proper means of reinforcing the demand.

The approach is subjective. In the first case, the crucial issue is whether the defendant believed there were reasonable grounds for making the demand, not whether reasonable grounds existed. It was put this way by Bingham J in *Harvey* (1981):

> It matters not what the reasonable man, or any man other than the defendant, would believe save in so far as that may throw light on what the defendant in fact believed. Thus the factual question of the defendant's belief should be left to the jury ...

The second limb requires that the defendant believes that his use of menaces is a 'proper' means of reinforcing the demand. Bingham J thought it to be a word of:

> ... wide meaning, certainly wider than (for example) 'lawful'. The test is not what he regards as justified, but what he believes to be proper. And where the threats were to do acts which any sane man knows to be against the laws of every civilised country no jury would hesitate long before dismissing the contention that the defendant genuinely believed the threats to be a proper means of reinforcing even a legitimate demand.

Harvey also makes it clear that the matter is not to be resolved by reference to the defendant's own moral beliefs:

... no assistance is given to any defendant, even a fanatic or a deranged idealist, who knows or suspects that his threat, or the act threatened, is criminal, but believes it to be justified by his end or peculiar circumstances.

9.7 Handling stolen goods (s 22 of the TA 1968)

Handling is a crime which attracts a substantially higher maximum sentence than theft, on the basis that without those who are prepared to deal in stolen property there would be fewer thefts. Deter the handlers, reduce the amount of theft seems to be the message! The maximum sentence for theft is seven years while the maximum for handling is 14.

Section 22(1) of the TA 1968 provides:

A person handles stolen goods if (otherwise than in the course of stealing) knowing or believing them to be stolen goods he dishonestly receives the goods, or dishonestly undertakes or assists in their retention, removal, disposal or realisation by or for the benefit of another person, or if he arranges to do so.

9.7.1 Stolen goods

Section 34(2)(b) of the TA 1968 informs us that 'goods' includes money and every other description of property except land, and includes things severed from the land by stealing.

Section 24(4) of the TA 1968 provides that:

Goods obtained in England or Wales or elsewhere either by blackmail or in the circumstances described in s 15(1) of this Act shall be regarded as 'stolen'; and 'steal', 'theft', and 'thief' shall be construed accordingly.

This definition is extended by s 24A(8) to include money derived from a wrongful credit made to an account. This means that the proceeds of a money transfer obtained by deception under s 15A of the TA 1968, when withdrawn, are stolen goods for the purposes of handling (for a discussion of s 15A, see below, 9.8.6).

Section 24(2) of the TA 1968 provides:

For the purposes of these provisions references to stolen goods shall include, in addition to the goods originally stolen and parts of them (whether in their original state or not):

(a) any other goods which directly or indirectly represent or have at any time represented the stolen goods in the hands of the thief as being the proceeds of any disposal or realisation of the whole or part of the goods stolen or of goods so representing the stolen goods; and

(b) any other goods which directly or indirectly represent or have at any time represented the stolen goods in the hands of a handler of the stolen goods or any part of them as being the proceeds of any disposal or realisation of the whole or part of the stolen goods handled by him or of goods so representing them.

For example, if the original stolen goods are sold for cash, either by the thief or the initial handler, then the proceeds will also be regarded as 'stolen' and may be the subject of a charge of handling. Similarly, if the stolen goods are exchanged for other property, this will be regarded as stolen for the purposes of s 22 of the TA 1968. Therefore, if A steals a Roman coin from the British Museum and sells it for £15,000 to B, an antiques dealer, who knows of its origins, the sum represents the original stolen goods, being the proceeds of the disposal or realisation.

If A then gave £5,000 to his wife in order for her to go on holiday, assuming she is aware of its origins, then she would be guilty of handling. If A were to bank the £10,000 and subsequently write cheques against that account, anyone receiving a cheque knowing of the origins of the account would also be guilty of handling. The thing in action 'represents' the original stolen goods. The Court of Appeal in *AG's Reference (No 4 of 1979)* (1981) accepted that:

> ... a balance in a bank account, being a debt, is itself a thing in action which falls within the definition of goods and may therefore be goods which directly or indirectly represent stolen goods for the purposes of s 24(2)(a).

The court added:

> ... where ... a person obtains cheques by deception and pays them into her bank account, the balance in that account may, to the value of the tainted cheque, be goods which 'directly ... represent ... the stolen goods in the hands of the thief as being the proceeds of any disposal or realisation of the ... goods stolen ...' within the meaning of s 24(2)(a).

Reference should also be made to s 24(3) of the TA 1968, a little known provision which played a significant role in helping to shape the common law on attempted crime in the case of *Haughton v Smith* (1973). In that case, the police had stopped a lorry containing stolen corned beef and had eventually allowed it to proceed to its destination in the hope of apprehending those waiting to receive and distribute the stolen goods. A charge of handling stolen goods was not proceeded with against Smith, who had received the goods, because s 24(3) provides that goods cease to be regarded as possessing the quality of being stolen if they have been 'restored to the person from whom they were stolen or to other lawful possession or custody'. In this case, they were in the possession and custody of the police, although Lords Hailsham and Dilhorne doubted whether this point should have been conceded by the prosecution, as the goods were not in the physical custody of the police once the lorry was allowed to proceed.

Whether or not goods are in the possession of the police or 'other lawful possession or custody' will depend to a large extent on the intention of the person seeking to take possession. In *AG's Reference (No 1 of 1974)* (1974), a constable came across an unattended vehicle in which he saw packages of new clothes. He suspected that they were stolen, so he immobilised the vehicle by removing the rotor arm and kept watch. A few minutes later the accused appeared and was arrested and charged with handling. The question arose as to whether the goods had been restored to lawful possession or custody before the accused appeared and endeavoured to start the car.

The Court of Appeal held that in the circumstances everything would depend upon the constable's intention. It should be left to the jury to decide whether a decision had been reached to take possession of the items so that they could not be removed. If the jury concluded that the officer had not yet made up his mind, then the goods would not have been reduced to lawful possession and the s 24(3) 'defence' would not be applicable, that is, the goods would possess the characteristic of being stolen.

9.7.2   Otherwise than in the course of stealing

Handling can only occur once the 'course of stealing' is over, and this to a certain degree differentiates the activity of theft from that of handling. A thief can become a handler once the course of stealing is over, for example, by assisting in the retention of the property by or for the benefit of another person. As a consequence of this provision D would not be guilty of handling a moment after the dishonest appropriation, even though it was his intention to retain the goods on another person's behalf.

The crucial question therefore is when exactly does stealing finish, thus allowing handling to occur? If two accomplices, X and Y, break into A's warehouse, one (X) going inside, while the other (Y) remains outside, placing goods into their van which have been passed to him by his friend, does this make Y a handler or is he to be more appropriately considered a joint principal to theft?

In *Pitham and Hehl* (1977), the Court of Appeal favoured the view that an appropriation is an instantaneous act. Therefore, when the defendants handled the furniture offered to them, the theft was already complete and they were guilty of handling stolen goods. If it is correct that theft is an instantaneous act, then there would appear to be no need for Parliament to use the words, 'otherwise than in the course of stealing' in s 22 of the TA 1968. *Hale* (1978) supports this contention by holding that an appropriation may be a continuing act. This view is also endorsed in *Atakpu and Abrahams* (1993), where Ward J, giving the judgment of the court, said:

> We would prefer to leave it for the common sense of the jury to decide that the appropriation can continue for so long as the thief can sensibly be regarded as in the act of stealing ... so long as he is 'on the job'.

The conclusion must be that *Pitham and Hehl* is of doubtful authority on this point.

9.7.3   The forms of handling

The section is quite specific on the ways in which handling can occur. There are four different types of activity:

(a) receiving stolen goods;

(b) undertaking the retention, removal, disposal or realisation of the goods by or for the benefit of another person;

(c) assisting in the activities mentioned in (b);

(d) arranging to do any activities in (a), (b) or (c).

9.7.4   Receiving

This mode of handling, together with arranging to receive does not require that it should be carried out for the benefit of another person. The TA 1968 offers no guidance on the meaning of 'receiving' and therefore recourse should be had to the existing authorities, even though many predate the Act. In the majority of instances, the person receiving the stolen goods will gain immediate possession or control of the property. This will mean that the thief divests himself of possession or control. The thief who retains total control of the stolen goods prevents handling from occurring. The old case of *Miller* (1854) determines that the goods do not need to be in the physical possession of the handler. It will be sufficient to establish receiving if D has authorised a friend or colleague to take possession on his behalf. Possession or control must be distinguished from inspection as the latter activity will not result in handling until such time as a decision has been reached on whether D will retain the goods or take possession or control. If that occurs at a date different to that of the inspection, then handling by receiving will occur once the goods are taken into his possession or control. However, he may be guilty of arranging to receive once the agreement has been struck.

The crucial point is that whatever the actual circumstances the prosecution will have to show that D had possession or exercised control over the stolen property albeit that it may only be for a limited period.

One may only arrange to receive goods which are actually stolen. The argument advanced on behalf of the prosecution in *Park* (1988), to the effect that one could arrange to handle goods which were yet to be stolen, was decisively rejected by the Court of Appeal. Any arrangement with a person who is aware of the nature of the goods is additionally likely to amount to a conspiracy to handle that is, a statutory conspiracy contrary to s 1 of the Criminal Law Act 1977.

9.7.5   Undertaking or assisting

These two activities must be directly connected to the retention, realisation, removal or disposal of the stolen goods. In *Sanders* (1982), it was held that mere use of stolen goods with the knowledge that they were stolen did not amount to assisting in their retention. In that case, the defendant's conviction for handling was quashed where it was proved only that he had used a stolen battery charger and heater in his father's garage. Adopting this view, Cantley J in the Court of Appeal in *Kanwar* (1982) stated:

> ... something must be done by the offender, and done intentionally and dishonestly, for the purpose of enabling the goods to be retained. Examples of such conduct are concealing or helping to conceal the goods, or doing something to make them more difficult to find or identify.

He went on to stress that physical acts were not essential and that verbal representations, oral or written, would suffice if designed to conceal the identity of the stolen goods. In this case, the defendant had told lies to the police when they executed a search warrant for stolen goods at her house. She knew that her husband had brought the stolen goods to the house, but tried to persuade the police that she had bought the goods. Though the judge misdirected the jury by suggesting that it was enough that she was willing to have the goods in the house and to use them, her conviction for handling was upheld because of the clear evidence that she had tried to mislead the police.

In *Coleman* (1986), the appellant had been convicted of handling by assisting in the disposal of money stolen by his wife. Large sums had been siphoned off from her employers and some £650 had been used to pay solicitors' fees relating to a property purchase which was in their joint names. A direction by the trial judge that 'assisting' was proved by the prosecution establishing that he had benefited from the property purchase was held to be wrong. The *actus reus* is assisting in the disposal and obtaining a benefit was not evidence that he had assisted in the disposal. If he had taken an active part in advising his wife on which property to choose, that would lead to a different conclusion. To do nothing other than receive a benefit from another's disposal of money does not amount to handling.

In *Pitchley* (1972), the word 'retention' was held to mean 'keep possession of, not lose, continue to have'. In this case, the appellant was given £150 by his son and requested to take care of it for him. He placed it into his Post Office savings account. The money had been stolen but the appellant only became aware of this two days later and then left it in his account. He was questioned by police four days later. He was convicted of handling on the basis that permitting the money to remain under his control was sufficient to amount to a retention on behalf of another person.

'Removal' is defined as the 'act of conveying or shifting to another place; the fact of being so transferred' (*Compact Oxford English Dictionary*). Therefore, if D takes stolen goods from A's abode to an agreed hiding place, this would be enough, even though D may be getting absolutely no benefit whatsoever from the transaction and it may even cost him money if he were to use his own vehicle and petrol. 'Realisation' relates to the selling of stolen property or if the goods are exchanged for something else whether that has value or not. 'Disposal' is defined as 'putting away, getting rid of, settling or definitely dealing with' (*Compact Oxford English Dictionary*).

These activities must be carried out by or for the benefit of another person. In *Bloxham* (1982), the appellant had purchased a car which unknown to him had been stolen. He later suspected that the car had been stolen and sold it on to a third party. He was charged with handling by undertaking in its disposal for the benefit of another person. He submitted that he had disposed of the car for his own benefit, not that of the purchaser and therefore the purchaser was not 'another person' within the meaning of the term. The House of Lords held that he had been wrongly convicted. It was the purchase not the sale, that is, disposal which was for the purchaser's benefit, and by no stretch of the imagination could a purchase be described as a disposal or realisation of the goods 'by' the purchaser.

9.7.6 *Mens rea*

There are two elements to the *mens rea* for handling. First, proof of dishonesty which will be judged by reference to the test in *Ghosh* and the approach adopted with respect to theft. Secondly, the section requires knowledge or belief that the goods are indeed stolen. Prior to the TA 1968, the law required proof of actual knowledge that the goods were stolen. The Criminal Law Revision Committee recognised that this could present real difficulties for the prosecution:

> Often the prosecution cannot prove (actual knowledge). In many cases guilty knowledge does not exist, although the circumstances of the transaction are such that the receiver ought to be guilty of an offence. The man who buys goods at a ridiculously low price from an unknown seller whom he meets in a public house may not know that the goods are stolen, and he may take the precaution of asking no questions. Yet it may be clear on the evidence that he believes that the goods were stolen [Eighth Report, *Theft and Related Offences*, Cmnd 2977, 1966, para 64].

Lawton LJ in *Harris* (1987) thought the words 'knowledge or belief' to be 'words of ordinary usage' and that trial judges should not in the majority of cases attempt any elaboration. In *Grainge* (1974), Eveleigh J held that suspicion alone was insufficient to establish either knowledge or belief. However, if a defendant was suspicious and then intentionally closed his eyes to the consequences, a jury might conclude that he held the requisite belief although it is improbable that jurors would conclude that he knew the goods to be stolen.

The test is a subjective one: did this defendant know or believe the goods to be stolen? In *Atwal v Massey* (1971), magistrates had found that the accused ought to have known from the circumstances that the goods were stolen. The Court of Appeal, in allowing his appeal against conviction, held that the test was did this defendant realise the theft has occurred, or did he suspect the goods to be stolen and deliberately shut his eyes? *Brook* (1993) confirms this subjective approach. A direction by the trial judge that the jury could be assisted in determining the accused's belief by deciding 'if there could be no other reasonable conclusion but that the goods were stolen' was flawed and led to the appeal being allowed. As the court put it, 'what was relevant was B's state of mind at the time of receipt, not an independent view as to whether there could be any other reasonable conclusion than that the goods were stolen'. The court approved of the test laid down in *Hall* (1985) that belief was something short of knowledge:

> It might be said to be the state of mind of a person who said to himself, 'I cannot say I know for certain that those goods are stolen', but there can be no other reasonable conclusion in the light of all the circumstances, in the light of all that I have heard and seen.

The court also considered that a person would be said to know goods to be stolen if told by someone with first hand knowledge, such as the thief or burglar. However, it is evident that the Court of Appeal has not yet settled on a way of interpreting the 'belief' aspect which can be properly and confidently explained to a jury by the trial judge. In *Forsyth* (1997), the trial judge had based his direction on *Hall*, but the conviction was quashed because that direction was considered to be potentially confusing. The problem is that 'suspicion', whether weak or strong, is neither knowledge nor belief but the *Hall* approach comes close to accepting that strong suspicion is enough. In these circumstances, it may be that the judge simply has to leave the jury to determine the issue for themselves because, whatever he says, there is a good chance that it will be considered to be incorrect!

Occasionally, the prosecution may wish to prove knowledge or belief by reference to the common law doctrine of 'recent possession' or by using s 27(3) of the TA 1968. The 'recent possession' doctrine applies in circumstances where the defendant is found in possession of stolen property and declines to offer any explanation. The judge may direct the jury that they may infer knowledge or belief. The doctrine also applies where the defendant offers an explanation but the jury is satisfied beyond all reasonable doubt that it is false.

9.8 Deception offences

Deception offences are to be found in the TA 1968 and the TA 1978, as amended. There are various offences of dishonestly obtaining 'something' by deception. These are:

- property;

- money transfers;

- pecuniary advantage;

- services;

- evasion of liability.

Deception is defined in s 15(4) of the TA 1968 and means:

> ... any deception (whether deliberate or reckless) by words or conduct as to fact or as to law, including a deception as to the present intentions of the person using the deception or any other person.

Section 5(1) of the TA 1978 incorporates this definition into the offences under ss 1 and 2 of the Act. The s 15(4) definition refers to 'any deception (whether deliberate or reckless)'. Therefore, if the defendant has knowingly made a false statement or representation, then he will be liable to conviction, as he will if he believes it may not be true. In *Goldman* (1997), the Court of Appeal held that the recklessness required in the offence of obtaining property by deception is subjective since an objective interpretation would be inconsistent with the requirement for dishonesty. The same must be true for all the deception offences.

The deception may result from words or conduct, and be either express or implied. If D expressly represents to P a shopkeeper that he is a famous film actor and produces documentary evidence which purports to support his claim, thereby obtaining goods from the shop as a direct consequence of the representation, he will be guilty of the s 15 of the TA 1968 offence. In *Gilmartin* (1983), the Court of Appeal held that a person who issues a post-dated cheque is impliedly representing that at the due date the cheque would be met. Goff LJ stated the general presumption in these terms:

> For the sake of clarity, we consider that in the generality of cases under ss 15 and 16 of the 1968 Act the courts should proceed on the basis that by the simple giving of a cheque, whether post-dated or not, the drawer impliedly represents that the state of facts existing at the date of delivery of the cheque is such that in the ordinary course the cheque will on presentation for payment on or after the date specified in the cheque, be met.

The implied representation here is that, when he issues the cheque, he knows of no reason why there will not be sufficient funds in his account when the cheque is presented for payment. An implied representation is something that 'goes without saying'. The customer in a restaurant or the driver pulling into a petrol station are impliedly representing that they are honest customers who will pay for what they receive at the end of the transaction. In *Hamilton* (1990), the defendant had forged the authorising signature on stolen company cheques, paid them into his own account and then withdrawn cash. It was held that, in presenting a withdrawal slip, he was representing that the credit balance in the account was genuine and that he was legally entitled to demand the money:

> By identifying the account, he represented that he was the person to whom the bank was indebted in respect of the account, and by demanding withdrawal of a stated sum he necessarily represented that the bank owed him that amount.

If, at the time of making the representation, the defendant genuinely believes there are sufficient funds in his account or believes there will be prior to the post-dated cheque being presented, then the question is simply whether or not the jury accepts that the defendant acted dishonestly. If so, the defendant will be convicted, if not, acquitted. However, the person to whom the statement is made will still be deceived, that is, a deception has been practised albeit that the defendant genuinely believed that he had sufficient credit in his account to meet his liabilities. However, if he does not have the 'present intention' which is referred to in s 15(4) of the TA 1968, the representation will be false. Comparison between these cases and *Greenstein* (1976) is instructive because the appellants believed there would be sufficient funds in the account when cheques sent to a company in order to purchase shares were presented for payment. The convictions were upheld seemingly on the basis that they had given assurances there would be funds in the account when the cheques were first presented but were reckless in the sense that they could not be sure in the circumstances that sufficient funds would be available.

Statements of a price at which a job can be done or a service can be provided ('quotations' or 'estimates') raise an interesting issue. Such statements usually imply only that the maker intends to perform the service for that sum (subject to any reasonably understood margins of error) which, clearly, will involve some profit to himself. If the recipient believes that the estimate does not represent good value, he is free to look elsewhere. If he chooses to engage a workman at a price far higher than he could have negotiated, he usually can blame no one but himself. But, in limited circumstances where a relationship of *trust and confidence* exists between the maker and the recipient, it may further imply that the price is reasonable by reference to what would usually be charged. This relationship of trust and confidence was established and a conviction upheld in *Silverman* (1987), where a tradesman fitted central heating for an excessively high price for two old ladies, for whom he had previously done satisfactory, reasonably priced work.

9.8.1 Implied representations

The person who enters a restaurant and consumes a meal, or the motorist filling up his car with petrol, imply that they have the ability to pay for the service or property. They are 'honest' customers in the eyes of those delivering the goods or services although in practice the waiter in the restaurant or the petrol pump attendant probably gives no thought at all to the honesty or credit worthiness of the person in front of them. It follows though that they would not wish to deal with the potential customer if they were aware that the person was impecunious. In *DPP v Ray* (1973), the defendant had ordered a meal and at that stage intended to pay for it. Having then consumed the meal he decided not to pay. The customer is making an implied representation throughout the meal that he intends to pay. At the moment he changes his mind, yet nevertheless continues to act as a honest customer, the deception is perpetrated. The consequence is that the law recognises that deception can occur as a result of silence.

In *Rai* (2000), the defendant applied to the local council for a grant towards providing a downstairs bathroom for his elderly and infirm mother. Two days after a grant of £9,500 had been approved, his mother died. He did not inform the local council and the work on the bathroom went ahead. He was subsequently charged with obtaining services by deception. The prosecution sought to argue that his silence in failing to notify the council of his mother's death itself constituted conduct within s 15(4) of the 1968 Act. He accepted that he had remained silent, and had not told the council of his mother's death at any time until after the building works were completed, but the contention on his behalf was that he had no legal or contractual duty to inform the council and that mere silence or inactivity could not constitute the required conduct. Thus, there had been no deception. The judge ruled that there was evidence that the defendant had committed a deception, basing his decision principally on an analogy with *DPP v Ray*. The Court of Appeal dismissed the appeal against conviction, holding that:

> ... on a common sense and purposive construction of the word 'conduct', it does, in our judgment, cover positive acquiescence in knowingly letting this work proceed as the appellant did in the present case.

In essence, this was a simple case in which silence amounted to a deception because the defendant made a statement which was initially true but later became untrue before acted upon (even though approval of the grant preceded the death of his mother) and he did not correct it. It certainly did not require the rather artificial search for a deception in which the court in *DPP v Ray* was forced to engage.

In the case of *Firth* (1990), the failure by a consultant obstetrician to comply with his duty to declare whether patients referred by him to a National Health Service hospital were private patients was held to be a deception, as a result of which he avoided charges which would otherwise have been levied against him. The Court of Appeal thought 'it mattered not whether it was an act of commission or omission'. The *Compact Oxford English Dictionary* would support this, offering two definitions of the word 'deception' viz:

(a) the action of deceiving or cheating;

(b) that which deceives; a piece of trickery; a cheat; sham.

The words or conduct must relate to 'fact or as to law or present intentions', although in practice the overwhelming majority of deceptions will be of fact.

9.8.2 Guarantee and credit cards

Problems have arisen in circumstances where a cheque is supported with a bank guarantee card and where credit cards are used. The effect of using a guarantee card is that the cheque must be honoured by the bank providing certain conditions as to the use of the card are fulfilled. This is the case even if there are insufficient monies in the account or an overdraft facility has not been arranged. The issue was examined by the House of Lords in the case of *Metropolitan Police Commissioner v Charles* (1976). Having opened a current account, his bank manager granted an overdraft facility of £100 and issued Charles with a cheque card. This allowed him to write cheques of up to £30 in the knowledge that they would be honoured by the bank. He proceeded to use 25 cheques each for £30 backed by the cheque card to fund his gambling activities. He did not have enough money in his account to cover the cheques when presented at his bank and had quite clearly exceeded his overdraft limit. The bank was obliged to pay the total of £750 as the cheques were backed by a guarantee card. He was charged under s 16(1) of the TA 1968 with obtaining a pecuniary advantage by deception. It will be evident that there is no misrepresentation regarding the honouring of the cheques. The conditions of use were complied with and the defendant therefore knew the cheques would be honoured. However, the House of Lords held that there was a false representation in the sense that he was holding himself out as having the bank's authority to use the card, when he knew that conditions as to the use of cheques had been imposed. His bank manager had told him that he should not cash more than one cheque a day for £30.

Where the giving of a cheque is supported by a guarantee card the representee need not be concerned about the 'ordinary' representations. The correct use of the card will result in payment being made by the bank.

In *Lambie* (1981), the House of Lords applied similar reasoning in concluding that a person who pays by the use of a credit card represents that she has the authority of the bank (the credit card company) to bind the bank to the transaction. So, the defendant was guilty of obtaining a pecuniary advantage from a store by deception when she obtained goods by using her credit card despite knowing that she had so far exceeded her credit limit that she was no longer permitted to use the card. Note that the particular form of pecuniary advantage in question was contained in a provision since repealed by the Theft Act 1978 (and replaced by s 2 of that Act) but that the principle in relation to the deception remains valid. Contrast this case with *Nabina* (2000), where the defendant had dishonestly obtained credit cards from various companies by giving false information about his personal details. The cards would not have been issued to him had the companies known the truth, but his authority to use them had not been revoked. He then used the cards to obtain goods from stores and was convicted under s 15 of the 1968 Act of obtaining those goods by deceiving the stores as to his authority to use the cards. Here, the convictions were quashed because there was no evidence from any of the issuers of the cards that any of the transactions had not been, or would not be, honoured, nor that, in the circumstances, they regarded the defendant as acting outside the authority which they had respectively conferred on him. Note that the difficulties about proving a deception might have been circumvented here by charging the defendant with theft. After *Gomez*, the fact that the owners of the goods willingly handed them over to him is irrelevant when the question of appropriation is being examined. The defendant appropriated all the goods when he obtained them. The only stumbling block is dishonesty. If it could be proved that because of his fraud in *acquiring the cards* he was dishonest when he *used the cards to obtain the goods*, then all the elements of theft were present. Would a jury conclude that he was dishonest? The jury in *Nabina* itself obviously did. The argument for theft in the *Lambie* kind of case, where the defendant's dishonesty at the time of the transaction was undeniable, is all the stronger.

9.8.3   Deception must cause the obtaining

It is the deception which must be the cause of the obtaining. Therefore, if the intended victim does not believe the representation which has been made or cannot understand what is being said, then it cannot be proved that the deception is the cause of the obtaining. In *Laverty* (1970), the defendant had practised a deception regarding the age of a motor vehicle but the purchaser gave evidence that he had not relied on the false information as an inducement to buy. The Court of Appeal quashed his conviction for obtaining property, that is, the price of the vehicle, by deception, as this had not resulted in him obtaining the money.

The Court of Appeal in *King* (1987) held that it was a matter of fact to be decided by the jury whether or not the deception was 'an operative cause of the obtaining of property'. In *Miller* (1992), the applicant was convicted of three counts of obtaining property by deception. He had operated from time to time as a unlicensed taxi driver working between Heathrow and Gatwick airports. The amount charged to those foreign visitors inveigled into travelling with him was some 10 times in excess of the normal fare. The accused sought leave to appeal against his convictions on the grounds that at the time the money changed hands the victims realised to some extent that he had been lying. In other words, they did not hand over the money because they believed he was entitled to that amount as representing the correct fare, but because they felt under some pressure or obligation to do so. The court refused leave to appeal. This case has been criticised (see Smith, JC [1992] Crim LR 745) on the basis that it was not the deception which caused the passengers to part with their money.

They did so because they felt intimidated. In such a situation, the appropriate charge would appear to be theft and not the s 15 offence. As Professor Smith says:

> If D gains entry to P's house by pretending to be the rent collector and then demands 10 times the rent from P, who now knows that D is not the rent collector but pays because she is frightened, this is surely not obtaining by deception.

In *Coady* (1996), the accused was convicted on two counts of obtaining petrol by deception. He had informed the garage attendant that he should charge the amount to the company account of a former employer. His convictions were quashed on the basis that the prosecution had not established that the representations were made before the petrol flowed into his tank. It is clear that the representation must have been made prior to the obtaining and must have operated on the mind of the other. The Court was sceptical about the wider representation for which the prosecution also contended, namely, that, when the accused drove onto the forecourt, he represented an intention to pay which he did not in fact possess. It is arguable that, if the defendant intends to pay by a method which he knows he should not use but which he also knows will secure payment (for example, unauthorised use of a credit card), then he intends to pay. Can the same truly be said of a person who uses a method which he knows will not secure payment? Presumably, in *Coady*, it was impossible for the defendant to bind his former employer to the transaction. Why then should he not have been guilty of obtaining the petrol by the deception that he intended to pay unless there was genuine doubt about when he decided that he would not pay himself but, instead, would 'pay' by charging it to his former employer's account? In any case, if he was acting dishonestly at the time when he put the petrol into his tank, he must have stolen it.

It was held in *Rozeik* (1996) that, if a deception is practised on a company, the deception must be upon a person in the company who is responsible for the transaction in question unless he was a party to the fraud.

It is worth examining these cases and asking exactly what amounted to the causal connection between the deception and the obtaining. For example, in the cheque and credit card cases (*Charles* and *Lambie*), it was evident that the casino and the shop were guaranteed to receive the money, providing they complied with certain procedures which were not connected to the question of authorisation to use the cheques or the credit worthiness of the person tendering the credit card. The cases proceed on the basis that if the parties had known the truth regarding lack of authorisation they would not have conducted business with the accused, but, as they did transact with him, there was an operative deception. It was pointed out by Lord Ackner in *Kassim* (1991) that:

> ... the whole object of the card (cheque guarantee) is to relieve the tradesman from concerning himself with the relationship between the customer and his

own bank, the tradesman may well not care whether or not the customer was exceeding authority accorded to him by his own bank. All he will be concerned with is that the conditions on the card are satisfied. Such cases obviously give rise to the difficulty of establishing an operative deception.

In *Lambie*, the shop assistant gave evidence to the effect that neither she nor her shop were in the least bit concerned about the relationship between the customer and her bank. Providing the conditions were met, then the credit card would be honoured irrespective of whether the bank had authorised their customer to use the card. It is therefore difficult to see how the assistant was deceived into accepting the card *as a result of the false representation*. Nevertheless, that is what the House of Lords concluded.

In *DPP v Ray* (1973), the House of Lords held that the waiter had been deceived by Ray into leaving the room, so enabling him to attempt to leave the restaurant without having first settled the bill. Applying the same reasoning as above, if the waiter had known of R's change of mind, then it is extremely unlikely that he would have left him alone, and the House of Lords was prepared to accept that this was evidence of an operative deception. Whether the deception would have worked on the mind of the representee is not always easy to determine. It is worth revisiting the discussion in *Cooke* (1986), where Lord Bridge ponders the likely response of the British Rail passenger faced with the prospect of deciding whether or not to purchase the sandwich prepared by the steward as opposed to the variety provided by the company. The approach appears to be to leave the matter to the jury as to whether the evidence will support the conclusion that the deception, express or implied, is the effective cause of the obtaining. In *Doukas*, it was necessary to decide whether a waiter could have been guilty of obtaining money by deception from customers of the hotel in which he worked. His plan had been to substitute his own wine for carafe wine ordered by the customers and to keep the payment for himself. The Court of Appeal accepted that the judge had been correct in leaving the issue of deception to the jury because customers must be considered to be honest and not willing to participate in a fraud on the hotel, so that they would have rejected the wine had they known the truth. The court also suggested that a customer would reject the waiter's wine because, whether or not it was inferior to the hotel's carafe wine, he would not know exactly what he was getting or be able easily to take action if something was wrong with it.

9.8.4 Dishonesty

Dishonesty is a common factor in all five offences. *Ghosh* (1982) was a s 15 case and its approach to the assessment of dishonesty should apply to all offences. In *Woolven* (1983), it was held on a charge of attempting to obtain property by deception that a direction based on *Ghosh* seemed likely to cover all occasions. It must be made clear that, even though the deception may be dishonest, it does not automatically follow that the obtaining will be dishonest, for example, where the defendant believes he has a legal right to claim the property in question. In other words, the issue of dishonesty is a separate issue from the other *mens rea* requirement, whether or not the deception was either deliberate or reckless. Consequently, in *Clarke* (1996), the defendant's conviction for obtaining a pecuniary advantage by deception had to be quashed because he had changed his plea to guilty when the judge indicated that he considered that the defendant had committed the offence if he made the representations alleged, they were false and that the victim had engaged him as a result of those representations. This wrongly implied that it was necessarily dishonest to tell lies to obtain employment, no matter what the defendant's explanation for the lies or more general explanation for his conduct. In *Buzalek and Schiffer* (1991), the Court of Appeal accepted that, in the majority of cases, a *Ghosh* direction was unnecessary and should only be given where D was saying 'I thought that what I was doing was honest but other people, and the majority of people, might think it not ...' (following *Price* (1990)).

9.8.5 Obtaining property by deception

Section 15(1) of the TA 1968 provides:

> A person who by any deception dishonestly obtains property belonging to another, with the intention of permanently depriving the other of it, shall ... be liable ...

For these purposes, 'property' has the same meaning as in s 4(1) but the limitations specified in s 4(2)–(4) on what property can be stolen do not apply to the deception offence. For instance, land can be obtained by a deception, such as moving boundary markers where theft could only be committed if it were first severed.

It follows that a thing in action can be obtained by deception just as much as any tangible item of property. However, a particular problem has arisen in connection with the thing in action associated with a bank account. It will be recalled from the discussion of theft that the credit balance in a bank account can be appropriated by some act which amounts to an assumption of rights over that credit, such as presenting a forged cheque designed to result in the payment of cash or the transfer of the credit. It is sufficient for theft that the defendant assumes the rights over the credit balance. He does not have to acquire the thing in action itself. By contrast, the offence of obtaining property by deception requires proof that the property which the defendant obtains is the very property which the victim owned or possessed. This is unproblematic with most kinds of property. The defendant purports to buy a car for cash but the notes are forgeries. The property which he obtains, the car, is the very property which the victim both owned and possessed. But, if the defendant

369

induces the victim to transfer a credit from the victim's bank account to the defendant's bank account, even though the debit to the victim's account exactly matches the credit to the defendant's account, does the defendant now own the property which belonged to the victim? It took the courts a very long time to heed the warnings of commentators and to declare that there are two different things in action, so that the defendant does not obtain property *belonging to another*. The pronouncement was finally made by the House of Lords in *Preddy* (1996).

The accused had been charged under s 15(1) of the TA 1968 with obtaining property by deception. The defendants had applied to building societies or other lending institutions for advances which were to be secured by mortgages on properties to be purchased by the applicant. The mortgage documentation or other accompanying documentation contained one or more false statements. The appellants accepted that the applications were supported by false representations, but claimed that at the time the advances were to be repaid there would be sufficient funds because the houses could be resold at a higher price than the purchase price. The basis of the decision by the House of Lords to allow the appeal was that the borrowers, the alleged mortgage fraudsters, had not obtained property belonging to another as required by s 15. In crediting the bank accounts of the appellants, there was no property belonging to the lending institutions. The lending institution's credit balance was a chose in action which as a result of the transfer was extinguished. The asset, that is, the debt owed to the appellant by his bank, was an:

> ... asset created for him and had therefore never belonged to anybody else. Thus, the prosecution could not show that the borrower defendant had obtained property belonging to another ... [Law Commission, *Offences of Dishonesty: Money Transfers*, Law Com 243, 1996, para 1.5].

This decision caused considerable consternation and provoked a number of appeals. Parliament acted very rapidly to plug the gap now at last revealed and passed the Theft (Amendment) Act 1996. This inserted s 15A into the 1968 Act, creating a new offence of obtaining a money transfer by deception (see below, 9.8.6).

To obtain ownership without possession or control of the property will be sufficient to satisfy s 15. In *Wheeler* (1990), it was agreed that Wheeler, a market stall holder, would sell a medal to a customer for £150, possession being retained by Wheeler until the customer returned with the payment. The contract was therefore concluded and the customer became the owner even though he did not take possession. Wheeler, subsequent to the customer's return, discovered the medal was stolen, but when at a later stage the customer returned and enquired about the status of the medal, Wheeler said that he was the owner. He was charged with obtaining property by deception, that is, the £150. His conviction was quashed because, at the time of the deception as to ownership, the medal already belonged to the customer. Wheeler therefore could not give any assurances or representations that he was the owner because the customer knew that he, not Wheeler, was the owner. (Title passed from Wheeler to the customer as this was a sale in market overt, whereby a person without title can give good title to the purchaser (see s 22 of the Sale of Goods Act 1979).)

Earlier discussion has made it clear that the decision in *Gomez* means that almost all cases of obtaining property by deception will also be cases of theft. However, proving the former will often be more difficult than proving the latter. Consequently, the prosecution may well be able to avoid the complications of the deception offence by opting instead to prosecute for theft.

A good example of where theft rather than s 15 would have been a more appropriate charge is *Talbott* (1995). The defendant was charged with six counts of obtaining property by deception. She was in receipt of income support and made an application for housing benefit in which she made certain untrue statements. It was not contended that she was not entitled to the benefit. What was at issue was whether the payment officer at the local authority would have made payment if it had been known that the statements were untrue. They gave evidence to say they would not and had therefore been deceived by the representations made on the application form. She was convicted and her appeal dismissed.

However, it is arguable that theft would have been a more appropriate charge. Since the decision in *Gomez,* it cannot be maintained that an appropriation has not taken place simply because cheques were received with the consent of, in this case, the local authority. She appropriated property belonging to the local authority with the intention to permanently deprive each time she paid a cheque into her bank account. The issue of dishonesty is the same whether or not the charge is under s 15 or s 1 of the TA 1968. A person obtains property if he obtains 'ownership, possession or control ... and "obtain" means obtaining for another or enabling another to obtain or to retain' (s 15(2)).

The mental element, in addition to dishonesty, is the intention to permanently deprive the other of the property. Section 15(3) states that s 6 shall apply for the purposes of s 15 with, of course the reference to 'appropriating' changed to that of 'obtaining'.

9.8.6 Obtaining a money transfer

Section 15A of the 1968 Act provides:

(1) A person is guilty of an offence if by any deception he dishonestly obtains a money transfer for himself or another.

(2) A money transfer occurs when:

(a) a debit is made to one account;

(b) a credit is made to another; and

(c) the credit results from the debit or the debit results from the credit.

(3) References to a credit and to a debit are to a credit of an amount of money and to a debit of an amount of money.

(4) It is immaterial:
   (a) whether the amount credited is the same as the amount debited;
   (b) whether the money transfer is effected on presentation of a cheque or by another method;
   (c) whether any delay occurs in the process by which the money transfer is effected;
   (d) whether any intermediate credits or debits are made in the course of the money transfer;
   (e) whether either of the accounts is overdrawn before or after the money transfer is effected.

'Deception' is to carry the same meaning as contained in s 15 of the TA 1968.

Section 15A(1) and (2) makes it an offence to act as did *Preddy* and his colleagues. It is important to note that sub-s (3) limits the offence to 'money'. If D induces P to give him a cheque, D will be guilty of the new offence when he presents the cheque at his bank and it is honoured. It is not strictly true to say that the deception has induced the transfer of the money, but s 15A(4)(b) would imply that this is the case. If, having received a cheque, D decides not to cash it, then he will in all probability not be guilty of an attempt to commit the offence, as he has not done something which is more than merely preparatory. On presenting the cheque, he will be guilty of an attempt and when it is honoured the full offence will be committed.

9.8.7 Obtaining a pecuniary advantage by deception

By s 16(2) of the TA 1968, pecuniary advantage is obtained in cases where a person:

   (b) is allowed to borrow by way of overdraft, or to take out any policy of insurance or annuity contract, or obtains an improvement of the terms on which he is allowed to do so; or

   (c) he is given the opportunity to earn remuneration or greater remuneration in an office or employment, or to win money by betting.

Section 16(1) provides that:

> A person who by any deception dishonestly obtains for himself or another any pecuniary advantage shall be liable to imprisonment for a term not exceeding five years.

Under s 16(2)(b) it had been held that a pecuniary advantage is gained when an overdraft facility is obtained and there is no need to prove the facility was used (*Watkins* (1976)). Emphasis was placed on the words 'allowed to borrow', which of course do not suggest that he actually borrowed money. If the cheque card cases are considered, it will be apparent that, in a case such as *Charles*, the writing of cheques to the total of £750 increased his indebtedness to the bank, that is, increased his overdraft beyond the limit which the bank imposed. At first sight, this appears to amount to a s 16(2)(b) offence, but on further consideration it is difficult to accept that the bank has allowed him to borrow by way of overdraft by deception. The bank is in full possession of the relevant information and agrees to honour the cheques, it is hardly deceived into this 'act of will' as it was described in *Bevan* (1987). Whatever the weakness in the reasoning, the authorities support the view that 'a bank card transaction is a borrowing by way of overdraft'. Professor Smith in his commentary on *Bevan* ([1987] Crim LR 129) makes the point that:

> The notion that [an] appellant was allowed to borrow money on overdraft when his bank reimbursed the paying bank is, with respect, a curious one.

The court in *Bevan* had cited Professor Smith's own commentary to the case of *Waites* (1982) where it was said in considering the words 'allowed to borrow by way of overdraft':

> The effect of the decision is this: if the bank, on issuing a card, tells the customer, 'You may use this card to back your cheque but in no circumstances may you overdraw your account', and the customer does overdraw, the bank has allowed him to borrow by way of overdraft. Views differ as to the ordinary meaning of the words: but to say that the bank has allowed conduct which it has expressly forbidden seems hard to justify.

Section 16(2)(c) covers those who as a result of making false claims as to their qualifications or experience gain the opportunity to earn remuneration or greater remuneration in an 'office or employment', or win money by betting. *Callander* (1992) will serve as an illustration of some of the key elements. The appellant had falsely represented that he was a member of the Chartered Institute of Management Accountants and that he also held qualifications from the Institute of Marketing. He was as a result employed by two businessman to prepare accounts and submit tax returns. He collected fees but did not do the work. He was charged under s 16(1) on the basis that he had dishonestly obtained the opportunity to earn remuneration in an office or employment by the deception that he possessed the necessary qualifications to do the job. He appealed against conviction on the grounds that he offered to provide services as an independent contractor and thus he had not gained remuneration 'in an office or employment'. The Court of Appeal held that despite being an independent contractor he had been 'employed' by the businessmen.

The *Shorter Oxford English Dictionary* defines 'employ' as 'to find work or occupation for', and 'employment' as 'that on which [one] is employed; business; occupation; a commission'. The court accepted that the word 'employment' was wide enough to describe this particular relationship.

However, in *McNiff* (1986), the appellant was granted the tenancy of a public house after having made false statements regarding previous convictions, his date of birth and his forenames. He was granted a tenancy to take effect once the appropriate justices' licence had been obtained. He appealed, claiming that a tenancy was not an 'office' or 'employment' within s 16(2)(c). The court allowed his appeal against conviction, seeing what he had done as gaining the opportunity to apply for an office in which remuneration would be earned as distinct from the opportunity to earn remuneration.

9.8.8 Obtaining services by deception

Section 1 of the Theft Act 1978 provides:

> (1) A person who by any deception dishonestly obtains services from another shall be guilty of an offence.

> (2) It is an obtaining of services where the other is induced to confer a benefit by doing some act, or causing or permitting some act to be done, on the understanding that the benefit has been or will be paid for.

Though the original intention was that the offence should be based on deceptions as to the intention to pay for the services, it seems that, as actually expressed, any deception will suffice. Thus, a person may be guilty, even though he intends to pay, if he tells lies which enable him to get services that he would not otherwise have got.

'Services' are defined in s 1(2) to include any case where:

(a) the victim is *induced to do an act* – this is the most obviously recognisable kind of service in everyday terms. For example, V repairs D's car, cuts D's hair, or cleans D's house;

(b) the victim *causes an act to be done* – for example, D contracts with V for the repair of his car but V does not do the work himself, rather he instructs his employees to do it;

(c) the victim *permits an act to be done* – for example, D goes to the swimming baths and is allowed to swim there on payment of money, or D enters a petrol filling station where he is allowed to put petrol into the petrol tank of his car.

The obtaining of the services must confer a benefit. It is probable that *benefit* is interpreted liberally, so that it does not necessarily have to appear as such to others as long as it appears so to the defendant. At any rate, anything which would be regarded as *consideration* in contract will surely be regarded as a benefit for these purposes.

There must be an *understanding that the benefit has been or will be paid for*. It follows that a service performed without expectation of payment will not fall within the offence even if only performed because of the deception. If D induces V, her neighbour, to look after her baby by telling V that she needs to attend hospital when in reality she wants to go out for a drink, the offence will not be committed because there was never any expectation that the service would be paid for. On the other hand, there seems to be no requirement for a contractually enforceable obligation. Thus, where D obtains services from, say, a prostitute with no intention of paying, he commits the offence even though the prostitute could not enforce payment in civil law because it would be an illegal contract. It is possible that 'paid for' can extend beyond cash or its equivalent to encompass, say, reciprocal services (in a way that would constitute consideration in contract). If V repairs D's plumbing on the understanding that D will repair one of V's windows, that may be sufficient but the point remains open for argument. Finally, the understanding does not necessarily require a belief that that specific service has been or will be paid for. D may mislead V into believing that he is entitled to services of that nature by virtue, for instance, of his membership of a club or similar organisation. Thus, D will be guilty of the offence where he uses his friend's membership card to obtain roadside repairs to his car from a vehicle breakdown and recovery organisation.

In *Halai* (1983), the defendant (who had only £28 in the bank) was convicted of obtaining services by deception from C, the agent of a building society, when he induced C to instruct a surveyor to prepare a report on a house by paying with a postdated cheque for £40 which was dishonoured. However, it was held that he was not guilty of obtaining services from the building society either in being allowed to open a savings account on the basis that he could pay in a valid cheque for £500 or in getting a mortgage advance on the (false) basis that he had been in a particular job for 18 months. In the first case, it was suggested, there was no understanding about payment (this would surely depend on whether any charges would be made); in the second case, it was said that a mortgage is not a service but, rather, 'a lending of money for the purchase of property' (the two do not seem to be mutually exclusive!). By contrast, in *Widdowson* (1986), the Court of Appeal asserted that the defendant could be guilty of this offence where, by deception, he managed to enter into a hire purchase agreement for the purchase of a car. This, too, seems to be 'a lending of money for the purchase of property' but the Court of Appeal said: 'The finance company confers a benefit by delivering possession of the vehicle to the hirer, or by causing or permitting the garage to do so, on the understanding that the hirer has paid, or will pay, a deposit and subsequent instalments.'

The decision in *Halai*, that obtaining a loan by way of a mortgage does not amount to a service, was persistently criticised and was eventually overturned by s 4 of the Theft (Amendment) Act 1996. This section inserts a new s 1(3) into the Theft Act 1978. The new sub-section reads:

> ... it is an obtaining of services where the other is induced to make a loan, or to cause or permit a loan to be made, on the understanding that any payment

(whether by way of interest or otherwise) will be or has been made in respect of the loan.

The decision in *Halai* was in any case revisited in two Court of Appeal cases in 1997. In *Graham* (1997), the Court purported to overrule *Halai* on the mortgage point but uncertainty persisted because this was not part of the *ratio decidendi*. Subsequently, the Court in *Cooke*, as part of the *ratio decidendi* of the decision, held that *Graham* was correct. Consequently, the *Halai* approach is no longer valid law. The main, and temporary, significance of the subsequent overruling of the case by *Cooke* is that its effect is completely retrospective. By contrast, s 1(3) of the Theft Act 1978 took effect only from December 1996.

9.8.9 Evasion of liability by deception

Section 2 of the TA 1978 replaced s 16(2)(a) of the TA 1968 which had proved unworkable, having been described by Edmund Davies LJ in *Royle* (1971) as a 'judicial nightmare'. The new offence is stated in these terms:

... where a person by any deception:

(a) dishonestly secures the remission of the whole or part of any existing liability to make payments, whether his own liability or another's; or

(b) with intent to make permanent default in whole or in part on any existing liability to make a payment, or with intent to let another do so, dishonestly induces the creditor or any person claiming payment on behalf of the creditor to wait for payment (whether or not the due date for repayment is deferred) or to forgo payment; or

(c) dishonestly obtains any exemption from or abatement of liability to make a payment (shall be guilty of an offence).

The liability referred to must be an existing one with the exception of s 2(1)(c) which simply refers to 'liability'. However, the liability which must exist for the purposes of s 2(1)(a) and (b) is one which may have been created only moments before the evasion takes place. For example, if the defendant takes goods to a cashier and then pays by credit card, the liability to pay will have come into existence shortly before the card is used. Section 2(2) makes it clear that liability means 'legally' enforceable liability, thus, gaming debts would not be covered.

'Remission' means release from a payment or debt (*Compact Oxford English Dictionary*). It follows from this that the creditor must be aware of the debt and respond to the deception by reducing the amount or cancelling it altogether. So, in *Jackson* (1983), a stolen credit card had been presented to pay for petrol and other goods. The Court of Appeal upheld the conviction on the basis that the garage would have received full payment from the credit card company and the appellant had therefore secured full remission of the debt.

Inducing a creditor to wait for or forgo payment is an offence, providing it is done with the intent to make permanent default. Assume X owes Y £1,000, the payment of which is due at the end of the month. If X spins Y a hard luck story designed to get Y to agree to the date for payment being put back, and in which period X knows he will leave the jurisdiction, then, assuming X intends never to pay, the offence will be committed. However, if X is simply stalling for time and does intend to pay at a later stage, an offence is not committed.

A creditor may be induced to forgo payment where the deception simply causes him to stop expecting or seeking payment even though he does not give up the right to the payment. A creditor may also forgo payment where the deception results in the creditor believing that he has already been paid, for example, where D tells P, falsely, that he has already settled the debt with P's wife or agent. Section 2(1)(b) also covers deceit on behalf of a third party which results in payment being delayed, providing the third party intends to make permanent default. *Attewell-Hughes* (1991) is authority for the proposition that s 2(1)(b) envisages an offence being committed in two ways: first, where a defendant wishes to make permanent default in respect of his own liability; and, secondly, where a defendant 'intends to make permanent default in whole or in part on behalf of another' (*per* Bingham LJ). It is, of course, important to recognise in the latter case that the third party must be the one who makes permanent default of his own liability. The liability does not attach to the person uttering the deception.

Section 2(1)(c) does not refer specifically to existing liability and the Criminal Law Revision Committee's example (13th Report, *Section 16 of the Theft Act 1968*, Cmnd 6733, 1977, para 15) quite clearly illustrates this. It envisaged a ratepayer (now, council tax payer) making a false statement in order to obtain a rebate to which he is not entitled. He acquires an abatement of his liability to pay. In *Firth* (1990), the consultant obtained an exemption from his liability to pay NHS charges by not declaring his referrals were private and not NHS patients. In consequence, the hospital was unaware that charges should have been levied.

9.9 Making off without payment (s 3 of the TA 1978)

Section 3 of the TA 1978 provides:

> ... a person who, knowing that payment on the spot for any goods supplied or services done is required or expected of him, dishonestly makes off without having paid as required or expected and with intent to avoid payment of the amount due shall be guilty of an offence.

This offence 'fills the gap' created by decisions such as *Greenberg* (1972). Greenberg, it will be recalled, made off from a self-service petrol station after having filled up his car with petrol. He was not guilty of theft because at the moment of appropriating the petrol it belonged to him and he was not charged with obtaining property by deception because he had entered the garage as an honest customer, only making up his mind not to pay once he had the petrol in his tank. Greenberg would now be found guilty of this offence. He would know that payment on the spot was required; in fact, many garages post notices on the petrol pumps informing customers of this expectation and possible liability under s 3 if they should fail to pay. Goods, that is, petrol, have been supplied and he has no good reason for making off without payment. There is clearly an intent to avoid payment.

As a result of this section the prosecution is spared the experience of trying to prove theft or obtaining property by deception.

9.9.1   *Actus reus*

The *actus reus* centres on the supply of goods or service provided. Consider *Troughton v Metropolitan Police* (1987) in which a taxi driver was in breach of contract for failing to take the defendant to his destination. Under s 3(3), the offence is not made out if the supply of goods or the doing of the service is contrary to law, or where the service done is such that payment is not legally enforceable. The driver could not therefore lawfully demand the fare and the appellant was 'never in a situation in which he was bound to pay or even tender money for the journey'. As a result, he had not made off without payment. For the offence to be complete, the defendant must have made off! In *McDavitt* (1981), it was said that in restaurant cases the defendant must have left the premises, although a literal interpretation of the section would suggest this is unnecessary. This reasoning is akin to that under s 6 of the TA 1968, which *prima facie* indicates an intention to permanently deprive if the alleged thief has left a supermarket, or bookshop without making payment. In this case, if the defendant has left the premises, that is, the spot where payment is required to be made, then it is difficult to refute the allegation that he has made off. Where there is more than one spot for making payment, then it would be for the judge to rule where exactly payment was required and then up to the jury to decide on the evidence if the defendant has made off. The Court of Appeal in *Brooks and Brooks* (1983) considered that the words 'dishonestly makes off' were easily understandable by any jury. In *Aziz* (1993), the defendant and a friend had requested a taxi in order to take them to a club some 13 miles away. They refused to pay the fare, whereupon the driver started to take them back to their hotel. He then decided to take them to a police station, whereupon D's colleague damaged the vehicle and they both ran away. D was caught and charged with the s 3 offence. It was argued in his defence that he had not made off from the spot where payment was required, that is, the end of the journey. The Court of Appeal held that the TA 1968 did not require that payment should be made at any particular spot. Payment in this case could have been made at any number of places and the obligation to pay certainly continued even when the driver was taking the man back to the hotel. According to the Court of Appeal, one normally 'makes off' when departing from the place where payment would normally be made.

9.9.2 Consent

The issue of consent is relevant to this offence. Can it be said that D has made off if he has consent to go? Or suppose the consent is induced by deception as where D tells P he cannot pay for his meal but he will leave his name and address and will return later in order to pay? If this is false information, then the departure by D in such circumstances will undoubtedly amount to making off. In *Hammond* (1982), the trial judge ruled that tendering a worthless cheque and thereby leaving with 'consent' meant the offence was not committed. Section 3(1) expects 'payment on the spot ... [as] required or expected' and certainly the passing of a worthless cheque is neither 'required or expected'. *Hammond* may have been wrongly decided.

The position is not so clear where D gives P his correct name and address and is allowed to leave. Unknown to P, D does not intend to pay. This form of departure does not sit easily with the term 'makes off' which seems to imply without consent. In the final analysis, everything may depend on the honesty or otherwise of the person departing. Dishonesty is required and this will be assessed using the *Ghosh* direction in the light of whether the defendant knew that payment on the spot was expected or required. If he had an honest belief that it was not, then he should be acquitted. The House of Lords in *Allen* (1985) held that the words 'intent to avoid payment' meant the defendant intended to avoid payment *permanently*. Therefore, if the defendant's intention was simply to avoid or put off payment for a few hours or days, then the offence would not be complete. In this case, the defendant had left a hotel where he had been staying without settling his account which amounted to £1,286. His defence was that he genuinely expected to be able to pay the bill, expecting to receive sufficient funds from which to pay the account at some point in the near future. The House of Lords held that an intention to defer or delay payment did not suffice to establish the offence. It could be argued that, if Parliament had intended this outcome, then the word 'permanently' could have been included in the offence. The decision encourages those who make off to run bogus defences based upon the argument that they expected to return to pay at a later stage. However, the point has never seriously been challenged since the decision in *Allen* and, therefore, for all practical purposes, the point was concluded by the House of Lord's ruling.

9.10 Going equipped to burgle, steal or cheat (s 25 of the TA 1968)

This offence is aimed at deterring those who, being away from their place of abode, carry with them articles which may be used in connection with burglary, theft or cheating.

Section 25 of the TA 1968 states:

A person shall be guilty of an offence if, when not at his place of abode, he has with him any article for use in the course of or in connection with any burglary, theft or cheat.

'Theft' includes the offence of taking and driving away a conveyance contrary to s 12 of the TA 1968 and cheating is defined by reference to s 15 of the TA 1968 (see above, 9.8, on deception offences).

9.10.1 Away from his place of abode

In order to be guilty of the offence, a defendant must be away from his place of abode. An unusual argument was advanced by the defendant in *Bundy* (1977) that his car was his place of abode as he was at the relevant time 'sleeping rough'. It was held that, while it was not disputed that a car might constitute a 'place of abode' in the circumstances, it was being used as a vehicle and the point where he was arrested was not the site where the vehicle was being used as a place of abode. Lawton LJ thought there were two elements in the meaning of the phrase 'place of abode':

... the element of site and the element of intention. When the appellant took the motor car to a site with the intention of abiding there, then his motor car on that site could be said to be his 'place of abode', but when he took it from that site to move it to another site where he intended to abide, the motor car could not be said to be his 'place of abode' during transit.

9.10.2 Any article

Being away from his place of abode the defendant must be proved to have with him or her any article for use in the course of or in connection with burglary, theft or cheating. The use of the words 'any article' means that literally anything could come within the scope of the Act. In *Rashid* (1977), bread and tomatoes which were to be used by a British Rail steward in order to make sandwiches to sell to travellers came within the words 'any article'. The Court of Appeal in *Doukas* (1978) had no difficulty concluding that the defendant had 'articles' when he was arrested carrying two bottles of cheap wine which he intended to sell to diners at the hotel where he was a wine waiter. In *Corboz* (1984), a small quantity of coffee was the subject matter of the s 25 charge in circumstances reminiscent of those in *Rashid*.

In the matter of *McAngus* (1994), the defendant sought to sell counterfeit clothing and had taken potential purchasers to a warehouse to show them what appeared to be branded goods. It was held that he had with him items to be used in connection with cheating, even though it was not his intention to sell the items directly to the public. Indeed, it may have been of no concern to him at all what the purchasers told their clients.

9.10.3 With him

The fact that the article must be 'with him' does not mean it has necessarily to be on his or her person. Notions of possession and control spring to mind so that if the articles are in the defendant's car, which is parked a short distance away from the scene of the burglary or theft, then that will be sufficient if the defendant drove the car with the articles to the scene of the crime.

The decision in *Minor v DPP* (1988) would, however, suggest that, providing the 'theft was to follow the acquisition of possession of the articles', then it would not matter if they had been found only minutes before the theft was attempted. In this case, the articles were two petrol cans and a siphoning tube and the appellant was seen with another man preparing to siphon petrol from the tanks of two cars. There was no evidence before the court to suggest that they had taken the articles with them to the cars, although there was no other reasonable explanation of how the cans and tubing came to be where they were.

It would seem to follow from this decision that, if one is walking late at night down the local high street and notices a piece of wood in the gutter which is then used to smash a shop window in order to steal a range of designer clothes displayed in the window, a s 25 offence is committed. The section is aimed at those who go equipped and this type of conduct ought not to be covered by it. There are many other offences with which this person could be charged, particularly criminal damage and theft. However, if, on taking the piece of wood into his or her possession, he or she places it in his or her car and drives around with it for a few days while seeking to locate appropriate premises to burgle, s 25 would be the appropriate offence.

9.10.4 Cheating

The crime of cheating within s 25 of the TA 1968 has caused difficulty for the courts. (See, for example, the discussion in *Cooke* (1986).) In *Doukas* (1978), the court had no doubts that the hypothetical customer should be viewed as reasonably honest and reasonably intelligent and, if aware that wine not supplied by the hotel was being offered to him, would have refused to participate in the transaction. The House of Lords in *Cooke* and the Court of Appeal in *Rashid* (1977) declined to adopt the same reasoning in respect of British Rail passengers:

> The immediate reaction of all three members of this court was that in the ordinary case it would be a matter of complete indifference to a railway passenger whether the materials used in making a sandwich were materials belonging to British Rail or materials belonging to the steward employed by British Rail, so long as the sandwich was palatably fresh and sold at a reasonable price. Who knows but that the steward's sandwiches might have been fresher than British Rail's? Why should the passenger concern himself with the source of the materials? [Bridge LJ in *Rashid*, p 239(d).]

'Cheat' is defined by s 25(5) of the TA 1968 to mean an offence under s 15 of the Act, obtaining property by deception. It is therefore important to consider the response of the hypothetical railway passenger in order to determine whether if offered such items the response would be an outright and possibly indignant refusal or acceptance without question. Under s 15, the deception must be the cause of the obtaining of the property, that is, money and, therefore, if the passenger knowing the truth would have handed over his money then that could not have been obtained as a result of the deception.

It would appear that the issue is one for the jury taking account of all the circumstances. In *Whitehouse and Antoniou* (1989), the appellants were charged with going equipped to cheat in that they had with them counterfeit cassette tapes which they were seeking to sell to passers-by outside an underground station. However, they stated they never claimed the tapes were genuine, and if asked told potential customers that they were good quality copies. The Court of Appeal thought that it was open to the jury to conclude from the evidence that 'any purchaser was relying upon a representation that they were genuine', even though they were sold for much less than the retail selling price. Did the defendants intend to deceive? If the tapes were 'genuine', in the sense that they contained all the music on the original recording, then they would not appear to intend to deceive the purchasers as to content. Quality is another matter, but, if they were convinced there was no difference between the copies and the masters, in what way do they intend to deceive the potential customers? Would the buyers have been deceived? Would they have refused to buy if they had known the truth? One suspects not, if the price was acceptable to them.

9.10.5 Knowledge

For a conviction to be obtained, the prosecution must prove knowledge on the part of the defendant that he has with him the relevant articles. If they have, unknown to him, been placed into his car or suitcase by a third party then he should be found not guilty, because he is unaware he has the articles and cannot intend to use them to carry out one of the listed offences. *Ellames* (1974) decides that there is no need for the defendant to have a specific crime in mind, any theft or burglary will be sufficient. This reasoning was taken one step further in *Hargreaves* (1985) where the Court of Appeal held that if a defendant had the intention to use an article in order to steal, given a suitable opportunity, that would be sufficient to establish the *mens rea*. It would not, however, reach the same conclusion where a defendant had yet to decide whether he should use an article should the opportunity arise. Section 25(3) places the evidential burden on the accused. It states:

> Where a person is charged with an offence under this section, proof that he had with him any article made or adapted for use in committing a burglary, theft or cheat shall be evidence that he had it with him for such use.

This puts pressure on the accused to give evidence as to why he had such equipment in his possession. If he does not do so, the jury may be invited to conclude that he had the necessary intent.

9.11 Criminal damage

Section 1(1) of the Criminal Damage Act (CDA) 1971 provides:

> A person who without lawful excuse destroys or damages any property belonging to another intending to destroy or damage any such property or being reckless as to whether any such property would be destroyed or damaged shall be guilty of an offence.

If the criminal damage is caused by fire then the offence is charged as arson, with the maximum punishment being life imprisonment as opposed to the 10 year maximum for the s 1(1) of the CDA 1971 offence.

9.11.1 Property need not be destroyed

One fundamental feature of the offence is that it may be committed without the property being destroyed. The *actus reus* requirement is for property belonging to another to be either damaged or destroyed. It is difficult to give precise meaning to these two words, but case law would indicate that factors to be taken into account include whether the value or usefulness of the property has been affected, whether there has been any physical harm of a permanent or temporary nature, the nature of the property and whether there has been any expenditure incurred to remedy the damage. In *Cox v Riley* (1986), the erasure by the defendant of the programmes on a plastic circuit card was held to amount to damage as the card required reprogramming in order to reinstate its utility value. The machine, a computerised saw, depended on the card being programmed in order to be operable and, as a consequence of the defendant's actions, its usefulness was impaired and cost was incurred in order to restore it to its former state. In *Hardman and Others v Chief Constable of Avon and Somerset Constabulary* (1986), members of CND had used water soluble 'paint' to paint human silhouettes on a pavement to mark the 40th anniversary of the Hiroshima bombing. Their expectation was that rainwater and pedestrian traffic use would result in the paintings being erased. However, before this occurred, the local authority employed a group of people to clean the pavements. It was held that there had been damage because the local authority had been put to expense and inconvenience. The court approved the approach of Walters J in *Samuels v Stubbs* (1972) to the effect that:

> ... it is difficult to lay down any very general and, at the same time, precise and absolute rule as to what constitutes 'damage'. One must be guided in a great degree by the circumstances of each case, the nature of the article, and the

mode in which it is affected or treated. Moreover, the meaning of the word 'damage' must be controlled by its context.

In *Blake v DPP* (1993), the use of a marker pen to write a biblical quotation on a concrete pillar amounted to criminal damage (see below, 9.11.5). However, in *A (A Juvenile) v R* (1978), a young football supporter who had spat on a policeman's coat was found not to have committed criminal damage because the coat did not require to be dry cleaned nor was the officer put to any expense. In *Morphitis v Salmon* (1990), a scaffold bar had been scratched but its value or usefulness was not impaired in any way and therefore M's conviction for criminal damage was quashed. Placing a clamp on a car which is unlawfully parked will not amount to damage according to the Queen's Bench Divisional Court in *Lloyd* (1992).

In *Whiteley* (1991), a computer 'hacker' was convicted of criminal damage having gained unauthorised entry to JANET, the Joint Academic Network, and altered passwords and changed and deleted files. His appeal against conviction was based upon the submission that it was only intangible information on the computer disks and not the disks which had been damaged and, as criminal damage was limited to acts against tangible property (see s 10(1) of the CDA 1971), then he had been wrongly convicted. Lord Lane CJ thought that argument flawed. There was no need to show that any damage was tangible, only that tangible property had been damaged. The authorities (such as those quoted above) indicated that, if the usefulness of the disks had been impaired, then that amounted to damage for these purposes. However, the Computer Misuse Act (CMA) 1990 now deals with the types of occurrences found in *Whiteley* and *Cox v Riley* which should now be charged under s 3 of the CMA 1990 and not the CDA 1971. But similar types of activity not involving computers could still attract liability under the CDA 1971, for example, activity involving audio cassette tapes or compact discs.

It is obviously difficult to establish a general rule as to what amounts to damage and much will depend on all the circumstances of the case. It appears unnecessary for there to be damage in the conventional sense that the property is harmed or its appearance changed. To remove the rotor arm from a car causes damage in the sense that the vehicle cannot be used but this does not necessarily involve damage to any of the car's components or bodywork. If property cannot be used for its normal purpose, then that should be sufficient evidence to prove that the property has been damaged.

9.11.2 Definition of property

Property is defined in s 10(1) of the CDA 1971 and in many ways is similar to the s 4 provision in the TA 1968. It deals only with tangible property, whether real or personal and includes money and:

(a) including wild creatures which have been tamed or are ordinarily kept in captivity, and any other wild creatures or their carcasses if, but only if, they have been reduced into possession which has not been lost or abandoned or are in the course of being reduced into possession; but

(b) not including mushrooms growing wild on any land or flowers, fruit or foliage of a plant growing wild on any land.

For the purpose of this sub-section, 'mushroom' includes any fungus and 'plant' includes any shrub or tree.

9.11.3 The damaged property must belong to another

The property damaged or destroyed must belong to another, that is:

- any person having the custody or control of it;

- any person having in it any proprietary right or interest (not being an equitable interest arising only from an agreement to transfer or grant an interest); or

- any person having a charge on it;

- where property is subject to a trust, the person to whom it belongs shall be treated as including any person having a right to enforce the trust;

- property of a corporation sole shall be treated as belonging to the corporation notwithstanding a vacancy in the corporation.

Strangely, in s 10(2) of the CDA 1971, the words 'custody or control' are used rather than the more familiar 'possession or control' found in s 5 of the TA 1968. The concept of possession has caused difficulties particularly with regard to drug offences, but it has caused few problems for the courts in interpreting the TA 1968 and therefore would have been unlikely to produce problems if it had been included in this Act.

9.11.4 Intention or recklessness as to causing damage

The defendant must be shown to have caused the damage or destruction intentionally or recklessly and without lawful excuse. It has to be proved that D intentionally damaged or destroyed property belonging to another or was reckless as to whether it would be. Thus, he cannot be guilty of the offence if he honestly believes that the property he is damaging or destroying is his own.

This was confirmed by the Court of Appeal in *Smith (David Raymond)* (1974). Providing the belief of law or fact is honestly held, then there will be no offence. In this case, the appellant, a tenant, had damaged floorboards in order to remove wiring attached to his stereo equipment. He had actually laid the floorboards months earlier with permission from the landlord. He believed the floorboards were his and that he was entitled to damage them, when in fact in law they became part of the landlord's property. His conviction was quashed. Recklessness was defined in *Caldwell*, which was, it will be recalled, a criminal damage case (see Chapter 3). If the prosecution charges the defendant with either intentionally or recklessly causing damage, then intoxication can be excluded as a defence in the latter case, as criminal damage would not be viewed as a specific intent crime. (See the discussion of *Merrick* (1995), above, 3.4.1.)

The role of transferred malice in criminal damage cases needs to be explored. If D, intending to damage or destroy P's property, fails but causes damage to X's house, then there is no reason why his *mens rea* against P's property should not be transferred to X's property. However, there may be no need to rely on the doctrine of transferred malice providing it can be shown that D in carrying out his plan was reckless as to whether X's property would be damaged. For example, it may be quite foreseeable that there was a real risk that X's property would suffer in consequence of the attack against P's property. This helps to resolve the problem highlighted in *Pembliton* (1874), where the *mens rea* is directed against the person but in the event property is damaged. D throws a brick at P who is standing in front of a shop window. His purpose is to harm P. If the brick misses and shatters the window, then liability for criminal damage is likely to follow on the basis of D's recklessness in respect of the property.

9.11.5 Lawful excuse

What does or does not amount to a lawful excuse has generated much discussion. Section 5 of the TA 1968 provides that a person will have a lawful excuse:

(2)(a) if at the time of the act or acts alleged to constitute the offence he believed that the person or persons whom he believed to be entitled to consent to the destruction of or damage to the property in question had so consented, or would have so consented to it if he or they had known of the destruction or damage and its circumstances; or

(b) if he destroyed or damaged or threatened to destroy or damage the property in question or, in the case of a charge of an offence under s 3 above, intended to use or cause or permit the use of something to destroy or damage it, in order to protect property belonging to himself or another or a right or interest in property which was or which he believed to be vested in himself or another, and at the time of the act or acts alleged to constitute the offence he believed:

(i) that the property, right or interest was in immediate need of protection; and

(ii) that the means of protection adopted or proposed to be adopted were or would be reasonable having regard to all the circumstances.

(3) For the purposes of this it is immaterial whether a belief is justified or not if
    it is honestly held.

The section is additional to any defences recognised by law as a defence to
criminal charges.

Section 5 was considered in *Blake v DPP* (1993). Blake, a vicar, was convicted
of criminal damage. He had been one of a group of people protesting against
the military action against Iraq in what became known as the Gulf War. He had
used a marker pen with which to write a biblical quotation on a concrete pillar
close to the Houses of Parliament. He claimed to be simply carrying out God's
instructions and as he believed God to be the person entitled to consent to the
damage of property he had a defence within s 5(2)(a). He also sought to invoke
s 5(2)(b) in that he damaged the pillar in order to protect the property of others,
that is, those likely to be affected by military action.

The Divisional Court dismissed his appeal against conviction. While
accepting that he genuinely and honestly believed he had the consent of God,
the court could find no legal authority which would recognise this as a lawful
excuse under English law. Was his action taken to protect or was it capable of
protecting property? The court made an objective assessment of the facts and
found the act incapable of offering any protection to property in the Gulf States.
Nor could he rely upon duress of circumstances or necessity as there was no
immediate danger to himself or others who were with him at the
demonstration.

One difficulty with this reference to objectivity is that s 5(2)(b) is written in
subjective terms. *Hunt* (1977) and *Ashford and Smith* (1988) had concluded that
an objective assessment had to be made of whether an act had been done 'in
order to protect property'. *Hall* (1989), a decision of the Court of Appeal, holds
that the first step is to establish the accused's purpose in acting as he did. This
depends on the accused's own view and employs a subjective test. Once the
accused's purpose has been established, the second step is to determine
whether he acted in order to protect property. Here, an *objective* test is used,
even though this seems to be plainly contrary to the words of s 5(2)(b). Thus, in
Hall itself, it was held that cutting the perimeter fence of RAF bases as part of
a protest designed to get the bases closed down so that they would no longer
be targets for a Soviet nuclear strike and thus, ultimately, to protect
surrounding houses, was not within the defence of lawful excuse. The
possibility of protecting property by this method was far too remote from the
damage. A further ground for the decision in *Hall* was that there was no
evidence that the accused believed that the property was in *immediate* need of
protection. Compare *Johnson v DPP* (1994), where the accused was a squatter
who had changed locks on the doors of the house. The court did not accept that
he had genuinely believed that he was doing so to protect his property, but held
that, even if he had, there was no evidence that he believed that it was in any
immediate need of protection rather than that there was some vague,

unspecified future danger. Once again, the application of an objective approach is evident.

Section 5(2)(a) was subject to judicial scrutiny in *Denton* (1982). An employee acting on his employer's instructions had set fire to some machinery at a cotton mill, causing damage in the amount of £40,000. The fire had been started in the hope of collecting insurance monies in order to prop up what was a faltering business enterprise. The trial judge had ruled that there could be no lawful consent given by the owner to Denton when the whole venture had been undertaken for fraudulent purposes. This meant that the defendant could not rely on s 5(2)(a). He appealed against conviction. In allowing the appeal the court acknowledged that the owner had a right to destroy his own property and could therefore authorise someone else to do it on his behalf. To this extent, the defendant perhaps had no need to rely on s 5(2)(a) for a defence because s 1 requires the act to be done without lawful excuse and in these circumstances there was a lawful excuse. It is clear the defendant honestly believed he had his employer's consent and therefore the judge's ruling was incorrect.

An honest belief, including one which results from an excessive consumption of alcohol, even though it might not be held if the person was sober, is what is required, as illustrated by *Jaggard v Dickinson* (1980). In this case, the appellant went to a house late one night. She was drunk and mistakenly thought the house to belong to her friend who she believed would not be averse to her breaking in. She appealed against her conviction on the ground of lawful excuse, despite having reached her conclusions while intoxicated. The court allowed her appeal.

9.11.6 Destroying or damaging property with intent to endanger life

Section 1(2) of the CDA 1971 states:

> A person who without lawful excuse destroys or damages any property, whether belonging to himself or another:
>
> (a) intending to destroy or damage any property or being reckless as to whether any property would be destroyed or damaged; and
>
> (b) intending by the destruction or damage to endanger the life of another or being reckless as to whether the life of another would be thereby endangered shall be guilty of an offence.

The section does not require that life actually be endangered, only that the accused intended to endanger life or was reckless as to whether life would be endangered.

In *Dudley* (1989), the defendant threw a firebomb at a house. The fire was extinguished, having caused only minor damage, and the occupants were not harmed or their lives actually endangered. He was convicted of the s 1(2) offence even though there was no evidence that life was endangered, or was likely to be so. The Court of Appeal, in dismissing his appeal, held that the words 'destruction or damage' referred to that which was intended or as to which there was recklessness.

In *Sangha* (1988), the appellant had set fire to furniture which resulted in the premises in question being burnt out. When he started the fire, there was no one else in the flat and apparently there was little or no danger of the fire spreading to nearby properties. He submitted that there was no case to answer under s 1(2)(b) as his act did not create a danger to the life of another and consequently he could not be reckless in that respect. It was held by the Court of Appeal, applying the *Caldwell* test of recklessness, that, *per* Tucker J:

> ... the question was whether the ordinary prudent bystander would have perceived an obvious risk that property would be damaged and that life would thereby be endangered? ... The time at which his perception is material is the time when the fire is started.

The appeal was dismissed. Section 1(2)(a) does not provide that the property to be destroyed or damaged must belong to another, so to damage one's own property with the intent to endanger the life of another would be sufficient.

The House of Lords has held that with regard to endangering life a defendant's mental element must go beyond the initial damage to the consequence of that damage.

In *Steer* (1987), the defendant had fired shots with an automatic rifle at the house of a former business partner. Windows were shattered but the occupants of the house were unhurt. There was no evidence to show that the shots had been aimed at the occupants. He was convicted of causing criminal damage, being reckless as to whether life would be endangered. He appealed on the basis that the only danger to his former partner and his wife had come from the firing of the gun, and not from the damage, that is, shattered windows, caused by firing the gun. The House of Lords upheld this submission, finding that the damage to life must result from the damage to or destruction of property. Therefore, a defendant must intend the damage to endanger life or be reckless as to whether it does. Thus, if D severs the brake pipes on his wife's car, intending that her life should be endangered as soon as she drives the vehicle, he would be guilty of the offence if the car failed to respond to the brake pedal being depressed. The ordinary prudent bystander would presumably conclude that this type of activity has really only one purpose and on that basis the offence would be complete even if she did not drive the vehicle. Another and possibly more appropriate charge would be attempted murder. In *Webster and Warwick* (1995), each case had concerned acts which damaged property and caused individuals to be showered with glass and roofing material. In neither case did anyone receive any injuries. The appellants submitted that the actual damage created had to endanger life not the means by which the damage had been caused. It was held, applying *Steer*, that the prosecution had to prove that the danger to life resulted from the destruction of or damage to property and it was not sufficient for the prosecution to prove that the danger to life resulted from the defendant's acts which caused the destruction or damage. The words 'destruction or damage' in s 1(2)(b) referred to the consequence of what the defendant intended to cause or to the risk of which he was reckless, not that which in fact occurred. The key questions were whether there was an obvious risk of life being endangered (reckless), and how the defendant intended that life should be endangered. If the intended consequence and the actual consequence resulting from the damage are the same, there is absolutely no problem. However, if the intended consequence or the consequence to the risk of which he was reckless and the actual consequence are different, then the Court of Appeal is firmly of the view that it is the intended consequence which is important in determining whether there was intention or recklessness as to endangering life.

It should be noted that s 5 of the TA 1968, which deals with lawful excuse, does not apply to s 1(2) of the CDA 1971. However, s 1(2) of the CDA 1971 does refer to lawful excuse and this is to be read in conjunction with any excuse which is recognised by law, for example, where D causes criminal damage while acting in self-defence to save the life of someone receiving a vicious beating. If D damages property and as a result puts the assailant's life at risk, then he would not commit the offence under s 1(2) of the CDA 1971.

9.11.7 Other sections

Section 2 of the CDA 1971 provides:

> A person who without lawful excuse makes to another a threat, intending that that other would fear it would be carried out:
>
> (a) to destroy or damage any property belonging to that other or a third person; or
>
> (b) to destroy or damage his own property in a way which he knows is likely to endanger the life of that other or a third person; shall be guilty of an offence.

Section 3 of the CDA 1971 provides:

> A person who has anything in his custody or under his control intending without lawful excuse to use it or cause or permit another to use it:
>
> (a) to destroy or damage any property belonging to some other person; or
>
> (b) to destroy or damage his own property in a way which he knows is likely to endanger life of some other person shall be guilty of an offence.

9.12 Reform of Theft Act offences

The discussion of theft and related offences in this and the previous chapter has revealed that, though the Theft Act 1968 significantly clarified and improved the law, deficiencies have continued to emerge in the 32 years since its enactment. Some of these deficiencies have been met by amendments to the 1968 Act and the creation of new offences (as, for example, in the Theft Act 1978) but there is a case for a more broad ranging review of the property offences. The discussion of conspiracy to defraud in Chapter 5 has explained that the unfulfilled aspiration to complete a general review of fraud in criminal law has sometimes impeded the enactment of a comprehensive and coherent set of offences in certain areas. However, progress is being made on various fronts. As mentioned in Chapter 8, in 1994 the Law Commission announced an intention to engage in a thorough review of the offences of dishonesty. As part of this review, it has published a Consultation Paper, *Fraud and Deception* (Law Com 155, 1999).

In that Paper, the Law Commission considered and rejected arguments for a general fraud offence based either on dishonesty or on deception. Their objections to the first possibility were that far too much would rest on the uncertain characterisation of conduct as criminal by fact finders (most obviously, juries) and that the consequent uncertainty in the definition of the offence might result in a serious conflict with the requirements of the European Convention on Human Rights. Their objections to the second were that such an offence would extend the law too far, and in such an indeterminate way that it could not be justifiable in principle. They considered that any gaps in the current law could be closed by extensions to existing offences.

Their proposals for reform of deception offences include:

- that the offence of obtaining property by deception (s 15 of the TA 1968) should be amended to provide simply that the owner of the property be deprived of it, irrespective of whether anyone else obtains it (dealing with the *Preddy* problem);

- that the requirement in the s 15 offence for an intention permanently to deprive should be abolished;

- that the offence of obtaining services by deception (s 1 of the Theft Act 1978) should encompass a service for which no payment was expected, provided that, but for the deception, payment would have been expected;

- that, in view of the fact that the use of a deception is generally wrongful and that an additional dishonesty requirement in the deception offences unduly favours those who should be found guilty, the dishonesty requirement should be abandoned. This would be subject to a defence that the defendant genuinely believed him or herself to be legally entitled to the property, service, etc;

- that a new offence involving misuse of payment cards (credit, debit and cheque cards and the like) should be created so that the current law of deception need no longer be used. This offence would involve causing a legal liability to pay money to be imposed on another without the other's consent.

The Law Commission hopes to publish a final report in 2001.

OFFENCES AGAINST PROPERTY: OTHER OFFENCES UNDER THE THEFT ACTS 1968 AND 1978 AND CRIMINAL DAMAGE

Robbery

Robbery is an offence under s 8 of the TA 1968. In essence, it requires the use of force in order to commit theft. The force or threat of force must be used 'immediately before or at the time of' the stealing and 'in order to' steal.

Burglary

Burglary is a fairly complex offence, which requires a defendant to enter a building or part of a building as a trespasser with the intent to commit one or more of a range of ulterior offences. Difficulties centre around the concept of trespass, particularly at what point a person is deemed to have entered a building as a trespasser. The aggravated element relates to the possession of weapons or imitation firearms at the time the burglary is committed.

Taking a conveyance/aggravated vehicle-taking

Taking a conveyance and aggravated vehicle-taking are the 'old' and 'new' together in one offence. The key element for a basic offence is absence of authority/consent for the taking.

Blackmail

The *actus reus* of the offence of blackmail is to make an unwarranted demand with menaces. Section 21 of the TA 1968 specifies when a demand is warranted.

Handling

The offence of handling has the potential for complexity particularly over the *mens rea* requirements of knowledge or belief. Handling can result from a wide range of conduct. A thief can be a handler in certain circumstances, just as a handler can be a thief.

Deception offences

These offences are found in the TA 1968 and TA 1978, as amended. The TA 1968 deals with obtaining property by deception and the TA 1978 obtaining services by deception. To obtain a pecuniary advantage by deception is covered by s 16 of the TA 1968, the evasion of liability by s 2 of the TA 1978. Section 15A of the TA 1968 makes it an offence to obtain a money transfer by deception.

Going equipped

To be away from one's place of abode having articles which may be used for the theft, burglary or cheating will mean that the offence of going equipped under s 25 of the TA 1968 is likely to have been committed. 'Articles' is given a wide construction by the courts.

Criminal damage

Destroying or damaging property belonging to another without lawful excuse either intending or being reckless to the consequence amounts to criminal damage.

CHAPTER 10

NON-FATAL OFFENCES AGAINST THE PERSON

10.1 Introduction

The focus of this chapter is what might be called the 'mainstream' non-fatal offences against the person, such as causing grievous bodily harm, malicious wounding, actual bodily harm, assault and battery. The most significant sexual offences are also considered. Certain aggravated forms of assault, such as assault upon a police officer in the execution of his duty contrary to s 89(1) of the Police Act 1996, fall more appropriately within the ambit of constitutional law and are thus beyond the scope of this text. It will be recalled that, for murder or manslaughter to be committed, the victim must be a 'reasonable creature in *rerum natura*', that being interpreted to mean a human being having taken one breath independently from his mother (see Chapter 6). The *ratio* of *AG's Reference (No 3 of 1994)* (1996), to the effect that a foetus or child capable of being born is to be regarded as part of the mother until it had a separate existence of its own, has implications for this area of law. The foetus not being regarded as a 'person' in law cannot therefore be the subject victim of an assault or battery. However, if the foetus is to be treated as part of the mother, then any attack directed at the foetus is, *ipso facto*, to be regarded as an attack against her and should be charged accordingly depending on the severity of the consequences and the *mens rea* of the accused.

10.2 Assault and battery

Section 39 of the Criminal Justice Act (CJA) 1988 states that: 'Common assault and battery shall be summary offences ...'

Much confusion surrounded the law on assault and battery for the following reasons. First, it had been assumed that common assault and battery were common law crimes, given that there is no statutory definition of the offences. However, the Divisional Court in *DPP v Little* (1992) held that the offences had, since the Offences Against the Person Act (OAPA) 1861, been separate statutory offences, on the basis that the OAPA 1861 had put pre-existing common law offences into statutory form.

Secondly, there are terminological difficulties, since judges have used the word assault to include what amounts to a battery. Assault was defined in *Venna* (1975) and in *Fagan v Metropolitan Police Commissioner* (1968), and the definition was adopted by the Law Commission in its Consultation Paper,

Legislating the Criminal Code: Offences Against the Person and General Principles (Law Com 122, 1992, para 9.1), in the following terms:

> ... an assault is an act by which a person intentionally or recklessly causes another to apprehend immediate and unlawful personal violence and a battery is an act by which a person intentionally or recklessly inflicts personal violence upon another.

The Law Commission goes on to state that 'the term 'assault' is now in both ordinary legal usage and in statutes, regularly used to cover both assault and battery'.

Thirdly, as demonstrated in *DPP v Little*, since there are two separate offences a count alleging assault and battery is bad for duplicity. Section 47 of the OAPA 1861 created the offence of assault occasioning actual bodily harm and if this is now deemed to contain two offences, assault occasioning actual bodily harm and a battery occasioning actual bodily harm, then the utmost care should be taken by prosecutors to charge either assault or battery occasioning actual bodily harm. As we have stated above, assault and battery are summary offences but become indictable offences in the context of s 47 of the OAPA 1861, that is, if they occasion actual bodily harm.

Section 39 of the CJA 1988 is clear. Unfortunately, the very next section refers only to 'common assault'. Section 40 permits the drafter of an indictment to include counts for certain summary offences in addition to those for which the accused has been committed for trial. Common assault is one of those summary offences. If, therefore, 'common assault' in s 40 is to be given the same meaning, the narrow meaning, as is attributed to assault in s 39, then battery would not be embraced. As Henry LJ said in *Lynsey* (1995), when dealing with the correct interpretation of s 40 of the CJA 1988: 'At this point angels prepare to dance on needles and legal pedants sharpen their quill pens.'

The Court of Appeal resolved the issue in favour of the 'wider' meaning thus 'common assault' in s 40 includes both assault and battery. No one doubts that the law needs to be overhauled. The Law Commission produced its final report on *Offences Against the Person* in November 1993 (Law Com 228). It explains that:

> ... in the general terminology of the criminal law 'assault' is sometimes used to mean (physical) battery; sometimes to mean ('psychic') assault by causing another to expect such battery; and sometimes the word 'assault' is used without distinguishing between its meaning as psychic assault and its meaning as battery [para 12.16].

It concluded that:

> The only safe course is to assume that assault in s 47 of the OAPA 1861 is to be interpreted as including not only psychic assault, but also battery, in the sense of any intentional or reckless physical contact with another.

The conclusion is that both battery and psychic assault should be included in a new statutory definition of assault. Clause 6 of the proposed Criminal Law Bill reads:

(1) A person is guilty of the offence of assault if:

    (a) he intentionally or recklessly applies force to or causes an impact on the body of another:

        (i) without the consent of the other; or

        (ii) where the act is intended or likely to cause injury, with or without the consent of the other; or

    (b) he intentionally or recklessly, without the consent of the other, causes the other to believe that any such force or impact is imminent.

(2) No such offence is committed if the force or impact, not being intended or likely to cause injury, is in the circumstances such as is generally acceptable in the ordinary conduct of daily life and the defendant does not know or believe that it is in fact unacceptable to the other person.

10.2.1 Assault

Assault, as opposed to battery relates only to causing someone to apprehend '... immediate and unlawful violence' being inflicted upon them. Unfortunately, judges often speak of assault when in fact they are referring to battery. Lord Lane CJ in *Mansfield Justices ex p Sharkey* (1985) makes it clear that an assault can occur without physical contact:

> There is no need for it to proceed to physical contact. If it does; it is an assault and battery. Assault is a crime independent of battery and it is important to remember that fact.

It follows that the intended victim must apprehend some personal violence although it is unnecessary to prove that he was actually frightened. The reference to 'violence' is something of an overstatement because all that is required is 'any intentional touching of another person without the consent of that person and without lawful excuse. It need not necessarily be hostile or rude or aggressive' (Lord Lane CJ in *Faulkner v Talbot* (1981)). However, in *Brown* (1993), the majority seemed to accept that hostility is an element in assault. Lord Jauncey said: 'If the appellant's activities in relation to the receivers were unlawful they were also hostile and a necessary ingredient of assault was present.' Lord Lowry was glad 'to adopt everything which has been said by my noble and learned friend Lord Jauncey' (on the issue of hostility). However, Lord Mustill, one of the minority, was not convinced. He states:

> Hostility cannot, as it seems to me, be a crucial factor which in itself determines guilt or innocence, although its presence or absence may be relevant when the court has to decide as a matter of policy how to react to a new situation.

The six appellants had, over a 10 year period, willingly engaged in sado-masochistic acts for their own sexual gratification. The activities took place in private and all participants consented to the acts being committed upon them including genital torture, branding and beatings with a cat-o'-nine tails. There were various charges of assault occasioning actual bodily harm (s 47 of the OAPA 1861) and unlawful wounding contrary to s 20 of the OAPA 1861. It is difficult to comprehend how the six appellants could have been found to be acting in a hostile way towards each other. They were all consenting and presumably they did so for enjoyment and personal satisfaction. The reasoning appears to depend upon the assumption that what was deemed unlawful was also hostile. Yet the acts indulged in by the appellants only became unlawful acts if they were found to be assaults. It is submitted that the better view is that there is no requirement for hostility before an act can become an assault.

The criminal law has, until relatively recently, been reluctant to acknowledge that words alone can constitute an assault, however much terror they may strike in the heart of the victim. The authority for this proposition dates back to 1823 and the case of *Meade and Belt* (1823), when Holroyd J held that 'no words or singing could ever constitute an assault'.

However, Goddard CJ in *Wilson* (1955) thought that the defendant's words 'get out the knives' would amount to an assault. If words are accompanied by an appropriate gesture which indicates that what is said is likely to happen, then an assault would have taken place. It is difficult to comprehend why words alone should not amount in law to an assault if it is clear the victim is immediately concerned that some form of physical harm will occur, for example, if the words are spoken in the middle of the night, with the consequence being that the victim cannot see who is there and is extremely frightened.

In *Ireland* (1997), the House of Lords had to decide whether or not silence could amount to an assault. The appellant had been convicted of assault occasioning actual bodily harm contrary to s 47 of the OAPA 1861. Over a four month period, he had made numerous telephone calls to three women. One of the complainants received 14 telephone calls within an hour. The making of each call was followed by silence. The impact of this behaviour on each of the women was severe. All suffered significant psychological symptoms such as stress, inability to sleep, nervousness and anxiety. The appellant argued that his acts did not cause the victims to apprehend 'immediate and unlawful violence'.

The House of Lords expressly rejected the contention, based on *Meade and Belt*, that words alone could not constitute an assault. Lord Steyn in particular saw no reason why 'something said should be incapable of causing an apprehension of immediate personal violence'. The House of Lords also endorsed the ruling in *Chan-Fook* (1996), to the effect that actual bodily harm, for the purposes of s 47 of the 1861 Act, could encompass psychiatric injury, supported by medical evidence, going beyond mere panic, distress and fear.

The decision goes further, however, in recognising the possibility that silent telephone calls might actually cause the assault, provided the caller causes his victim to apprehend immediate personal violence, or the possibility of it.

Care must be taken not to fall into the trap of concluding that verbal abuse or threats will necessarily constitute an assault. Evidence will be required of the effect on the victim. The fact that the victim immediately feels threatened does not necessarily mean that the victim apprehends immediate physical violence. Much will depend on the circumstances of the case. Were D communicates his threats or warnings by means of some instantaneous form of communication, it is unlikely that an offence will be made out unless the victim and accused are in close proximity. If a secretary receives an email communication five minutes before she is about to close the office which tells her 'not to walk home alone tonight', she may be extremely concerned. If it is from the office practical joker, she may do nothing more than send a forthright response. If it is from someone within the organisation of whom she is unaware, then she may with some justification feel threatened. If the night is dark and she does indeed walk a fair distance to catch her train, she may then conclude that she is being watched. If she is aware that a serial rapist is at large in the vicinity, she may apprehend immediate and unlawful personal violence. Conversely, if the communication is by email from New Zealand, she may wonder what is going on but is unlikely to expect that she will suffer 'immediate and unlawful personal violence'.

The famous case of *Tuberville v Savage* (1669) illustrates the point that words may negative an assault. The defendant in that case uttered the immortal words, 'If it were not Assize time I would not take such language from you'. D had spoken the words simultaneously with the action of putting his hand on the sword, the words thus giving P the impression that he was not at risk. If the action precedes the words, in all probability, it will be too late to rely upon any statement to negative an assault as P will already have apprehended that a battery would occur. So, for example, in *Read v Coker* (1853), a group of men indicated quite forcefully to P that unless he left their premises they would break his neck. This was held to amount to an assault. They would have been entitled to use reasonable force to eject P on the basis that he was a trespasser and therefore such action would have been lawful. To amount to an assault their actions would have needed to be regarded as excessive force.

To frighten someone even though the victim is apparently safe from attack was held in *Smith v Superintendent of Woking Police Station* (1983) to amount to an assault. Late one evening, the defendant had entered private property and looked through the windows of a bed-sitting room. The occupier saw him, was terrified and screamed, whereupon he ran away. His conviction was upheld on the basis that she had been frightened that personal violence could have resulted although there was no immediate prospect that he could have entered the premises and inflicted harm on her. This decision has been criticised because it was obvious to P that D could not have entered the property and inflicted violence. Nevertheless, that does not take into account the fact that the victim may well be frightened of the unknown. She may know that all the doors and windows are locked, but what she may not know is what D intends to do next. He may have with him a large hammer which he intends to use to smash the window and gain entry. Shaking a fist at his intended victim may cause alarm but not fear of immediate harm, shaking a fist containing a hammer would surely cause the victim to apprehend violence even though she is locked in the house.

10.2.2 *Mens rea* for assault

The mental element requires proof of intention or recklessness towards the victim causing him to apprehend immediate physical violence. Despite some uncertainty in the case law, it appears that recklessness will be given its *Cunningham* rather than *Caldwell* meaning. *DPP v K* (1990) applied *Caldwell* on a charge of assault occasioning actual bodily harm but this case was not followed by the Court of Appeal in *Spratt* (1991), which applied *Cunningham*. *Parmenter* (1991) followed *Spratt* and the House of Lords in the consolidated appeals in *Parmenter and Savage* (1991) confirmed the applicability of the *Cunningham* approach to recklessness.

10.3 Battery

A battery is the actual infliction of unlawful personal violence. It will be apparent that not every battery includes an assault. If D hits P, who is asleep, then that will be a battery even though P has no immediate apprehension that unlawful violence is to be inflicted upon him. The law recognises an implied consent in some circumstances where there is physical contact between people. If D jostles P as they stand together in a crowded underground train, then P is taken to have impliedly consented to the contact. In *Collins v Wilcock* (1984), Goff LJ said:

> Generally speaking, consent is a defence to a battery; and most of the physical contacts of ordinary life are not actionable because they are impliedly consented to by all who move in society and so expose themselves to the risk of bodily contact. So nobody can complain of the jostling which is inevitable ... in ... an underground station or a busy street; nor can a person who attends a party complain if his hand is seized in friendship, or even if his back is (within reason) slapped.

He went on to say that these examples are regarded as instances of implied consent but suggests that it would be better to 'treat them as falling within a general exception embracing all physical contact which is generally acceptable in the ordinary conduct of daily life'. This is probably a better way to rationalise the situations particularly as those who are very young or who have mental disabilities cannot give consent. It is also worth revisiting *Fagan v Metropolitan Police Commissioner* (1968) and noting that the Court of Appeal accepted that a battery could be a continuing act, the offence being complete once there was evidence of *mens rea* (see above, Chapter 2).

There is no requirement that any force must be directly applied to the person, so, as in *DPP v K*, if D places acid into an electric hand-dryer, thus causing the next user to be sprayed with the liquid, then that will be a battery, even though D did not spray the acid himself. In *Haystead v DPP* (2000), the defendant punched W whilst she was holding her child. The force of the blow caused W to drop the child, the child falling to the floor sustaining an injury to his head. Upholding the conviction for the offence of assault against the child by beating, the Divisional Court held that the battery to the child could be caused by the defendant without his having used force directly to the child's person. The act of W in dropping the child could not be regarded as a 'fully voluntary' intervening act breaking the chain of causation. It appears that touching a person's clothing will be regarded as the equivalent of touching the person. In *Thomas* (1985), the appellant was a school caretaker whose conviction for indecently assaulting two schoolgirls was quashed by the Court of Appeal. In one instance, he had touched and rubbed a girl's skirt. When she objected, he walked away. The court accepted that the touching of a person's clothing was the equivalent of touching the person who was wearing the clothes. The conviction was quashed on the basis that the circumstances were not inherently 'indecent'.

10.3.1 *Mens rea* for battery

In *Venna* (1975), the appellant was involved in a struggle with police officers who were attempting to arrest him. He fell to the ground and lashed out with his feet and in so doing kicked the hand of one of the police officers, fracturing a bone. He was charged with assault occasioning actual bodily harm contrary to s 47 of the OAPA 1861 although this was a case of battery. The court held that either intention or recklessness (*Cunningham*) was sufficient to establish the *mens rea* for the offence. Therefore, an accused will have the requisite *mens rea* for battery if there is an intention to apply force to the body or being reckless whether force is applied.

It is worth noting that assault and battery are regarded as basic intent offences for the purposes of the law relating to intoxication seemingly on the basis that either may be established by proof of recklessness.

10.3.2 Consent

The role of consent in the criminal law has been the subject of much debate and critical comment over the last few years. Enormous interest was aroused by the decision of the House of Lords in *Brown* (1993) and the Law Commission has published two Consultation Papers on the subject, in 1993 and 1995. The former was entitled *Consent and Offences Against the Person* (Law Com 134) and the latter, *Consent in the Criminal Law* (Law Com 139).

The Law Commission in *Consent in the Criminal Law* emphasises the importance of four cases in the last 120 years which help to trace the development of the law from Victorian times to the present day. Those cases are:

- *Coney* (1882);

- *Donovan* (1934);

- *AG's Reference (No 6 of 1980)* (1981); and

- *Brown* (1993).

In summarising the law, the Law Commission stated:

> In short, the consent of the injured person does not normally provide a defence to charges of assault occasioning actual bodily harm or more serious injury. On to this basic principle the common law has grafted a number of exceptions to legitimise the infliction of such injury in the course of properly conducted sports and games, lawful correction, surgery, rough and undisciplined horseplay, dangerous exhibitions, male circumcision, religious flagellation, tattooing and ear piercing [*Consent in the Criminal Law,* Law Com 139, 1995, para 1.11].

The general principle is to be found in *AG's Reference (No 6 of 1980)* (1981). Lord Lane CJ stated:

> ... it can be taken as a starting point that it is an essential element of an assault that the act is done contrary to the will and without the consent of the victim ... Ordinarily, then, if the victim consents, the assailant is not guilty.

It is up to the prosecution to negative consent. The conventional wisdom is that, if D deceives P into consenting to his performing a particular act that would otherwise amount to an assault, battery, or indecent assault upon P, such consent is nullified where the deception relates to the identity of P or the nature of the act: see *Williams* (1987) (considered below, 10.7.3). The law is less clear where D exercises a deception as to his attributes. This question has recently arisen in two cases concerning medical qualifications. In *Richardson* (1998), the defendant was a dentist who continued to treat patients despite having been suspended from practice by the General Dental Council. She was convicted on six counts alleging offences contrary to s 47 of the OAPA 1861, the trial judge having ruled that the apparent consent of the patients to receiving treatment had been vitiated by the fraud as being qualified to continue with the work. The Court of Appeal, allowing the appeal, held that what was in issues was the nature of the mistake made. As there had been no mistake on the part of the victim regarding the identity of the appellant or the nature of the act she was to perform, the consent was not vitiated by the appellant's silence as to her having been suspended. Compare this with *Tabassum* (2000), where the appellant was convicted of indecent assault where he had persuaded women to undergo breast examinations on the basis that they were participating in trials of software to be used by doctors. The Court of Appeal, confirming the conviction, held that there was clear evidence that the women concerned had only consented to being examined by the appellant because they believed he was medically qualified – which was not the case. Both *Clarence* (1888) and *Linekar* (1995) were distinguished on the basis that, in both cases, the women concerned consented to sexual intercourse and sexual intercourse resulted, albeit with unforeseen consequences: in *Clarence*, the contraction of a venereal disease; in *Linekar*, the non-payment for sex. *Richardson* was distinguished as a case where the prosecution had (wrongly) proceeded on the basis that there had been a mistake as to identity. The court then concluded that the women examined by the appellant had consented to the nature of the acts performed (having their breasts examined) but not the quality of the act (a bogus medical examination) and therefore there had been no true consent. The decision seems questionable in the light of earlier cases. It suggests that deception as to the quality of the act can vitiate consent. It also suggests that there is a doctrine of informed consent in criminal law, a notion denied by the Court of Appeal in *Richardson*. Duress, that is, threats of death or serious physical violence will also negative consent providing the will has been overborne by the threats. Looked at from the defendant's point of view, if he genuinely and honestly believes the other person is consenting, then he is entitled to be found not guilty even though his belief is a mistaken one (as determined by *Morgan* (1976) and *Gladstone Williams* (1984)). There is no requirement that any belief must be based upon reasonable grounds.

10.3.3 Public interest

At the heart of the consent defence is the question: to what can P consent? The answer to this question involves giving consideration to what is deemed to be in the public interest. In *AG's Reference (No 6 of 1980)*, it was acknowledged that the public interest will create exceptions to the general principle that, if the victim consents, then an assault or battery has not in law happened. In *Coney* (1882), the consent of the prize-fighters was deemed irrelevant as the fight was illegal. In *Donovan* (1934), the defendant had caned a girl for the purpose of sexual gratification. His defence was that the girl had consented. The court deemed consent to be irrelevant if the act complained of was unlawful, which it would be if it involved the infliction of bodily harm. Swift J in *Donovan* defined 'bodily harm' to include:

> ... any hurt or injury calculated to interfere with health or comfort of the prosecutor. Such hurt or injury need not be permanent, but must, no doubt, be more than merely transient and trifling.

The court acknowledged that there were exceptions to this principle. The first relates to lawful sporting activity where the participants are bound by rules and regulations, for example, rugby, soccer, boxing. This exception is justified on the ground that the law wishes to encourage 'manly diversions'. The consent, however, relates only to force which can be reasonably expected in the course of a game. If, as all too frequently happens, a rugby player hits an opponent in an 'off the ball' incident then that clearly goes beyond the rules of the game and consent cannot be presumed. Boxing, of all these 'sports' presents the greatest difficulty. Here both fighters are intending to inflict harm on their opponent and there have been numerous instances where fighters have died as a result of the injuries received in the ring. Yet the activity was recognised as a lawful by the House of Lords in *Brown*. The Law Commission in its Consultation Paper, *Consent in the Criminal Law* (Law Com 139, 1995), takes the view that participating in an activity which is widely regarded as beneficial should not be regarded as being against a person's interests. The State though must be satisfied that the risks involved are properly controllable and containable (para 13.19 and p 182, fn 23).

The second relates to surgery performed with the consent of the patient. If there is a benefit to the patient (and this might include psychological benefit as in the case of cosmetic surgery), then this would not normally amount to a criminal offence.

A further exception was recognised in *Jones* (1987). Two schoolboys aged 14 and 15 had been injured after being tossed into the air by the appellants. The appellants regarded the whole incident of horseplay as a joke and apparently this view was shared by the victims. The Court of Appeal held that 'consent to rough and undisciplined play where there is no intention to cause injury is a defence, in this case, to inflicting grievous bodily harm'. A similar line of reasoning was adopted in *Atkin and Others* (1992), where convictions contrary to s 20 of the OAPA 1861 were quashed on the basis that the victim had willingly taken part in horseplay or 'mess-games' being indulged in by RAF officers. The victim had white spirit poured over him and set alight, although he was wearing a fire resistant suit. The old adage 'boys will be boys' seems to be at the heart of these cases.

In *Brown*, the House of Lords by a 3:2 majority held that sado-masochistic acts which resulted in actual bodily harm or wounding were offences irrespective of whether or not the victim gave consent. Of the majority, Lord Templeman thought:

> Society is entitled and bound to protect itself against a cult of violence. Pleasure derived from the infliction of pain is an evil thing ... such violence is injurious to the participants and unpredictably dangerous. I am not prepared to invent a defence of consent for sado-masochistic encounters which breed and glorify cruelty.

The majority further decided that it was in the public interest to protect society from the danger of corrupting young people or seeking to influence them to participate, given the potential for serious physical injury.

What is clear from the Law Commission's Consultation Paper, *Consent in the Criminal Law* (Law Com 139, 1995), is that there are many people who are engaged in sado-masochistic activities who would disagree with Lords Templeman and Lowry that their wish is simply to satisfy 'a perverted and depraved sexual desire' *per* Lord Lowry or that 'sado-masochistic encounters involve the indulgence of cruelty by sadists and the degradation of victims', *per* Lord Templeman. The Law Commission quotes from various respondents, 'a wealth of evidence on consultation from people of both sexes who engaged in sado-masochistic activities to enhance sexual power', in order to show that such acts are carried out by large numbers of people. The Law Commission goes on to propose that 'the intentional causing of any injury to another person other than a serious disabling injury should not be criminal if, at the time of the act or omission causing the injury, the other person consented to injury of the type caused'.

What exactly does *Brown* decide? There seemed to be agreement that consent may be a defence to a common assault and indecent assault but not to either the s 47 or s 20 of the OAPA 1861 offences. However, the House of Lords was prepared to recognise that there were certain lawful activities where consent to engage in the activity knowing of the risk of injury is present and provides a defence should bodily harm be caused. (Obvious examples are the sports of boxing and rugby.) The case also demonstrates the fundamentally different approach to the particular issue adopted by the majority and minority. The majority appeared to regard the problem as one of violence and cruelty whereas the minority regarded it as an issue about private sexual relations and the response of the criminal law (see Lord Mustill's speech).

On the basis of the foregoing, it can be stated that those who perpetrate actual bodily harm, or worse, will not be able to avail themselves of the defence of consent unless the injury is caused during an activity falling within one of the public policy exceptions outlined above. The difficulty is in determining the contours of those public policy exceptions. This issue is usefully illustrated by the decision of the Court of Appeal in *Wilson* (1996). The defendant, using a hot knife, branded his initials on his wife's buttocks. His wife had not made any complaint to the police and the marks were only discovered when she was being medically examined. He was charged with the s 47 of the OAPA 1861 offence of assault occasioning actual bodily harm. He admitted responsibility but claimed that the act was not only done with her consent but at her instigation. It had apparently been done as a tangible manifestation of their love for each other. The judge ruled that, in light of the decision in *Brown*, he was bound to rule that the wife's consent did not provide the defendant with a defence. The defendant was convicted. The Court of Appeal allowed his appeal, holding that '*Brown* was not authority for the proposition that consent was no defence to a charge under s 47 ... in all circumstances where actual bodily harm was deliberately inflicted'. The court thought there was no logical difference between this act of branding and that of tattooing which is a lawful activity. It was also deemed not to be in the public interest that such consensual activity between husband and wife in the privacy of their own home 'should be visited by the sanctions of the criminal law where there was no aggressive intent ...'. This decision is difficult to reconcile with the clear statement of Lord Jauncey in *Brown*:

> ... consent of the victim is no answer to anyone charged with the latter offence (s 47) or with contravention of s 20 unless the circumstances fall within one of the well-known exceptions such as organised sporting contests and games, parental chastisement or reasonable surgery. There is nothing in ss 20 and 47 of the OAPA 1861 to suggest that consent is either an essential ingredient of the offence or a defence thereto [p 90h].

Are we now to draw the conclusion that marital branding is to be added to the list of 'well known' exceptions and does this only apply to the bottom and not other areas of the body? Lord Templeman in *Brown* refers to one of the accused branding another on the thigh: 'In one case a victim was branded twice on the thigh and there was some doubt as to whether he consented to or protested against the second branding.' The clear implication is that the first branding was consensual. Is there any real distinction between the two cases sufficient to justify the conclusion reached in *Wilson*? The report in the *Criminal Law Review* says that the branding was at the wife's instigation. All the participants in *Brown* were willingly involved in the activities. In that sense, they were all instigators of what took place. In *Wilson*, the husband did not have any 'aggressive intent' towards his wife. There is no evidence in *Brown* that any of the individuals had aggressive intent against any of the others. This was a single occurrence between a man and his wife in private. Does this mean that, if the parties had been long term cohabitees, rather than husband and wife, then the prosecution would have been successful? Or, what if the Wilsons had been male homosexuals living together in a stable relationship? Therefore, the approach could apply to other relationships which might include those based upon friendship rather than those actually living together. *Brown*, though, involved group sado-masochistic activities of the 'grossest kind' and this is where the distinction might lie. Assume that, as a result of the publicity surrounding this case, Mr and Mrs Wilson are approached by some of their married friends asking if they will show them how it is done. The Wilsons invite three couples to their house, demonstrate the branding technique and then observe whilst the other couples engage in the activity. Are the three couples to be found guilty under s 47 on the basis that a group activity is unlawful, whereas a couple alone would not commit an offence? Common sense would say no. There is a clear need for basic principles to be developed.

Otherwise, the case by case approach will only create further uncertainty. Certain activities are, from a public policy perspective, deemed lawful, but there appears to be no public policy dimension which will lead to the endorsement of sado-masochistic activities and therefore consent is irrelevant in these situations. The difficulty lies in trying to establish which activities are deemed to be sado-masochistic and, in light of *Wilson*, bottom branding in private between married couples is not to be labelled sado-masochistic. The current domestic law on the availability of consent as a defence to the infliction of harm, even amongst adults with a predilection for sado-masochistic activities, appears to be consistent with the requirements of the European Convention on Human Rights, as incorporated by the Human Rights Act 1998. The appellants in *Brown* took their case to the European Court of Human Rights – see *Laskey, Jaggard and Brown v United Kingdom* (1997) – where it was unanimously held that the House of Lords' ruling was consistent with Art 8 of the Convention to the extent that the limitations on the defence of consent could be viewed as necessary in a democratic society for the preservation of health or morals.

10.4 Assault occasioning actual bodily harm (s 47 of the OAPA 1861): further thoughts

Reference has already been made to what in law constitutes the *actus reus* of the s 47 of the OAPA 1861 offence. There, has however, been extensive discussion as to the precise ambit of the *mens rea* of the offence. Intention or recklessness is required to be proved towards the assault or battery, but what was not clear was whether intention or recklessness need be established towards causing actual bodily harm. The authority of *Roberts* (1971) indicated there was no need to establish intention to cause actual bodily harm or recklessness as to whether it was caused so long as it flowed naturally from the 'technical' assault or battery. Bodily harm, it will be recalled, means 'any hurt or injury calculated to interfere with the health or comfort of the prosecutor'.

In *Roberts*, the accused had instructed P, a passenger in his car, to remove her clothing. In an endeavour to escape his attentions, she jumped from the moving car and suffered minor injuries. The Court of Appeal required *mens rea* only towards the assault or battery and providing the bodily harm was 'the natural result of what the alleged assailant said and did' then that was sufficient. This latter issue had to be considered objectively, for example, could it reasonably have been foreseen as a consequence of what he was saying or doing? This clear statement of principle was thrown into doubt as a result of the cases of *Spratt* (1991) and *Parmenter* (1991), which held that *mens rea* was required to be proved in relation to causing actual bodily harm and at the very least this should be subjective recklessness. As a result, Spratt, who had fired an air pistol through a window in his flat, hitting two young girls with pellets, had his conviction quashed as he had been unaware that there were children playing outside, that is, he did not have the *mens rea* for either assault or battery.

However, *Savage* (1991) followed *Roberts* and therefore, given the conflicting authorities, there was a need for the House of Lords to resolve the issue. In *Savage and Parmenter* (1991), the House of Lords approved *Roberts* and disapproved *Spratt* on this point. On a s 47 charge, it must be established that D committed an assault and consequently actual bodily harm resulted, but there was no obligation on the Crown to prove either intention or recklessness on the part of the defendant towards the actual bodily harm. The reasoning is that the word 'occasioning' relates only to the issue of causation and is assessed objectively. The House of Lords also overruled the Court of Appeal's decision in *Parmenter* on this point.

10.5 Wounding and grievous bodily harm

Section 18 of the OAPA 1861 states:

> Whosoever shall unlawfully and maliciously by any means whatsoever wound or cause any grievous bodily harm to any person with intent to do some grievous bodily harm to any person or with intent to resist or prevent the lawful apprehension or detainer of any person, shall be guilty of ... an offence.

The maximum penalty is life imprisonment. There are numerous elements to this offence which deserve attention. There is a distinct overlap in terminology with s 20 of the OAPA 1861 and some of this discussion will relate to both offences.

Section 20 provides:

> Whosoever shall unlawfully and maliciously wound or inflict any grievous bodily harm upon any other person, either with or without any weapon or instrument, shall be guilty of a misdemeanour and shall be liable ... to imprisonment for not more than five years.

10.5.1 Wound

Each offence contains a reference to wounding although it is not a requirement for a successful prosecution. In law, for there to be a wounding the continuity of the whole skin must be broken. In *JCC v Eisenhower* (1983), the appellants had been charged under s 20 of the OAPA 1861 with wounding a young man by firing an air pistol, a pellet from which hit him in the eye. It was found as fact by the magistrates that the victim had bruising just below his eyebrow and internal rupturing of blood vessels in the eye. The Divisional Court quashed their convictions under s 20, on the basis there had not, in law, been a wounding. Goff LJ, after examining authorities as far back as 1831, concluded:

There must be a break in the continuity of the skin. It must be a break in the continuity of the whole skin, but the skin may include not merely the outer skin of the body but the skin of an internal cavity ... where the skin of the cavity is continuous with the outer skin of the body.

There is authority which suggests that any wound must be a result of a battery having occurred. Glidewell LJ in *Savage* (1991) stated: '... does the allegation of wounding import or include an allegation of assault? In our view, in the ordinary way, unless there are some quite extraordinary facts it inevitably does.'

A battery, it will be recalled, is the actual infliction of unlawful personal violence but it is not clear why if D digs a pit and lines the bottom with broken glass he should not be said to have caused a wound simply because he was not there to push P into it. D's actions have caused P's wound even though he was not around to apply force to P. *Wilson* (1983) would suggest that providing the wound is directly inflicted there is no need to establish that a battery has been committed.

10.5.2 Grievous bodily harm

It was decided in *DPP v Smith* (1961) that grievous bodily harm means 'really serious harm'. It follows that there can be grievous bodily harm inflicted without any wounds being caused to the victim. The decision in *Ireland* (above) raises the possibility of really serious psychological injury amounting in law to grievous bodily harm. Whether or not harm amounts to grievous bodily harm is to be determined objectively. It is a misdirection to tell a jury that harm amounts to grievous bodily harm simply because they would regard the particular harm caused in the case before them to be 'grievous' (see *Brown and Stratton* (1998)).

10.5.3 Inflict and cause

Section 18 of the OAPA 1861 includes the word *cause* in relation to grievous bodily harm, whereas s 20 of the OAPA 1861 contains the requirement that the accused should *inflict* grievous bodily harm. According to *Wilson* (1983), the word 'cause' in s 18 has a wider meaning than 'inflict' in s 20. In *Mandair* (1994), Lord Mackay LC said:

> In my view, 'cause' in s 18 is certainly sufficiently wide to embrace any method by which grievous bodily harm could be inflicted under s 20 and since causing grievous bodily harm in s 18 is an alternative to wounding I regard it as clear that the word 'cause' in s 18 is wide enough to include any action that could amount to inflicting grievous bodily harm under s 20 where the word 'inflicts' appears as an alternative to 'wound' ... the word 'cause' is wider or at least not narrower than the word 'inflict' [p 719f and h].

In *Burstow* (1997), the House of Lords considered again the meaning of the two verbs. The appellant was convicted of inflicting grievous bodily harm contrary to s 20 of the OAPA 1861. He had become obsessed by a female colleague and had persecuted her by making nuisance telephone calls, damaging her car and breaking into her house. He served a term of imprisonment but on release continued with his behaviour. In consequence, the victim suffered psychological illness described as 'grievous harm of a psychiatric nature'. The prosecution accepted that grievous bodily harm included psychiatric injury. Counsel for the appellant submitted that 'inflict' in s 20 necessarily required the application of physical force directly or indirectly to the body of the victim and that that had not happened in this case.

Whilst accepting that the words 'inflict' and 'cause' were not entirely synonymous, the House of Lords' decision recognised that, for all practical purposes, the two expressions were largely interchangeable. As Lord Steyn observed, the problem is one of construction.

> What I am saying is that in the context of the Act of 1861 one can nowadays quite naturally speak of inflicting psychiatric injury. Moreover, there is internal contextual support in the statute for this view. It would be absurd to differentiate between ss 18 and 20 in the way argued on behalf of Burstow. As the Lord Chief Justice observed [in the Court of Appeal] this should be a very practical area of the law. The interpretation and approach should so far as possible be adopted which treats the ladder of offences as a coherent body of law.

The fact that *Burstow* was the third occasion that the House of Lords has considered ss 18 and 20 of the OAPA 1861 within the space of 10 years lends support to the view that new legislation is urgently needed to put this area of law onto a modern footing.

In *Clarence*, the defendant was charged under both s 20 and s 47 of the OAPA 1861. He was suffering from venereal disease, yet nevertheless engaged in sexual intercourse with his wife. She would not have consented to the intercourse had she known of his medical condition. He was convicted on both counts but his appeal was allowed by a majority of 9:4 on the basis that an assault was needed for both crimes. However, if D did not inflict harm on his wife when there was direct physical contact of the most intimate type how can it be maintained that Burstow inflicted harm on his victim? The distinction lies in the fact that Clarence's wife was deemed to have consented to the intercourse whereas Burstow's victim certainly did not consent to his heinous conduct which ultimately led to her suffering serious psychiatric injury. For authorities taking the opposite approach, that an assault is not a prerequisite to a conviction under s 20, see *Lewis* (1970) and *Martin* (1881). In the latter case D, shortly before the end of a theatre performance, switched out the lights and placed an iron bar across a doorway. Panic ensued and numerous people were injured as a result of being unable to gain access to the exit stairs. He was convicted of inflicting grievous bodily harm. Section 18, for example, would appear appropriate for the person who knows he is HIV positive and who deliberately engages in sexual intercourse intending that his partner should contract the illness. Section 20 should apply where the defendant, knowing he is HIV positive, engages in intercourse realising he might infect his partner.

The House of Lords considered the conflicting case law in *Wilson* (1983). Lord Roskill stated:

> I am content to accept, as did the full court, that there can be an infliction of grievous bodily harm contrary to s 20 without an assault being committed. [Although in many, if not the majority of cases, there will be an assault.]

The House of Lords relied upon the Australian decision of *Salisbury* (1976). In this case, it was said that grievous bodily harm can be inflicted either by direct application or 'though it [the act] is not itself a direct application of force to the body of the victim, does directly result in force being applied violently to the body of the victim, so that he suffers grievous bodily harm'.

This means that one can inflict grievous bodily harm without actually assaulting the victim even though force is not applied *directly* to the body. Of course, every direct application of force to the body will amount to a battery and therefore every time grievous bodily harm is inflicted there must in law be a battery,

However, where there is an *act or omission* which 'does directly result in force being applied violently to the body' this does *not necessarily* amount to an assault in the sense of putting someone in fear of harm being inflicted as where the victim is struck from behind, but it can amount to inflicting grievous bodily harm. If D intended to *cause* grievous bodily harm by this method, he is guilty of the s 18 offence.

Given the decisions of the House of Lords in *Ireland* and *Burstow* dealing with those who suffer psychological injury as a result of 'stalking' and related behaviour it the fact that the application of harm has been 'indirect' will not prevent convictions under either s 20 or s 47.

10.5.4 Maliciously

It is beyond doubt that in this context 'maliciously' must be given its *Cunningham* (1957) meaning. A person acts maliciously if he acts intentionally or recklessly in its subjective sense. In *Farrell* (1989), the judge had directed the jury in objective terms on a s 20 of the OAPA 1861 charge. The Court of Appeal in quashing the conviction relied on *Cunningham* and *Morrison* (1989), to the effect that, where the word maliciously appeared in a section, the jury should be directed in subjective terms, that is, recklessness as to whether the particular harm envisaged by the section should occur, the accused foreseeing that it might, yet still going on to take the risk.

The House of Lords in *Savage* and *Parmenter* (1991) confirmed that the defendant need not foresee the physical harm of the gravity caused but need only have foreseen some physical harm albeit of a minor character. In *Mowatt* (1968), Diplock LJ said in respect of s 20: 'It is enough that he should have foreseen that some physical harm to some person, albeit of a minor character, might occur.' (More recent decisions of the Court of Appeal have stressed that the defendant must have foreseen bodily harm not 'should' have foreseen it.)

Section 18 of the OAPA 1861 requires the ulterior intent to cause grievous bodily harm. Where the charge is maliciously causing grievous bodily harm with intent to cause grievous bodily harm, malicious can mean only intentionally. One cannot recklessly and intentionally cause grievous bodily harm at the same time. However, if the charge is one of malicious wounding with intent to cause grievous bodily harm, then it is perfectly feasible that one can act recklessly in respect of the wounding while intending to cause grievous bodily harm. Similarly, where the charge is wounding with intent to resist lawful arrest, the presence of an intent to resist arrest should not lead to the conclusion that the defendant foresaw the possibility of wounding resulting from his conduct. 'Recklessly' must, according to *Morrison*, be applied subjectively. 'Intention' carries the same meaning as for murder (see Chapters 3 and 6) and an intention to cause grievous bodily harm is sufficient *mens rea* for murder.

10.5.5 Ancillary offences

The problems highlighted by the *Burstow* case have, to some extent, been addressed by the enactment of the Protection from Harassment Act (PHA) 1997. The Act creates two new criminal offences, as well as introducing civil remedies for those who suffer harassment. Section 1 of the PHA 1997 makes it an offence to pursue a course of conduct which:

- amounts to harassment of another; and

- which the defendant knows or ought to know amounts to harassment of the other.

A person is deemed to know that conduct will amount to harassment if 'a reasonable person in possession of the same information would think the course of conduct amounted to harassment of the other'. A person who commits an offence under s 1 is liable on summary conviction to imprisonment for a term not exceeding six months or a fine not exceeding level 5 on the standard scale or both. Section 4 of the PHA 1997 creates the offence of 'putting people in fear of violence'. It states:

> 4(1) A person whose course of conduct causes another to fear, on at least two occasions, that violence will be used against him is guilty of an offence if he knows or ought to know that his course of conduct will cause the other so to fear on each of those occasions.

(2) For the purposes of this section, the person whose course of conduct is in question ought to know that it will cause another to fear that violence will be used against him on any occasion if a reasonable person in possession of the same information would think the course of conduct would cause the other so to fear on that occasion.

(3) It is a defence for a person charged with an offence under this section to show that:

- his course of conduct was pursued for the purpose of preventing or detecting crime;

- his course of conduct was pursued under any enactment or rule of law or to comply with any condition or requirement imposed by any person under any enactment; or

- the pursuit of his course of conduct was reasonable for the protection of himself or another or for the protection of his or another's property.

A person convicted on indictment is liable to a term of imprisonment not exceeding five years, a fine or both. References to harassment include alarming the person or causing the person distress and conduct is deemed to include 'speech' (s 7 of the PHA 1997).

The problem of racially motivated violence has been specifically addressed in measures enacted as part of the Crime and Disorder Act 1998. For these purposes, s 28 of the Act provides that an assault is racially motivated if:

(a) at the time of committing the offence or immediately before or after doing so, the offender demonstrates towards the victim of the offence hostility based on the victim's membership (or presumed [by the offender] membership) of a racial group; or

(b) the offence is motivated (wholly or partly) by hostility towards members of a racial group based on their membership of that group. For the purposes of s 28 'racial group' means 'a group of persons defined by reference to race, colour, nationality (including citizenship) or ethnic or national origins.

The fact that an assault is racially motivated is regarded under the Act as an aggravating factor, providing the court, following conviction, with the power to impose longer sentences than would otherwise be the case. The 1998 Act creates racially aggravated forms of common assault: ss 47 and s 20 of the OAPA; ss 2 and 4 of the Protection from Harassment Act 1997; criminal damage; and certain public order offences.

10.6 Reform of non-sexual assaults

Decisions of the House of Lords and the Court of Appeal handed down during the last 10 years are replete with *obiter dicta* highlighting the need for a wholesale reform of the archaic laws relating to non-fatal, non-sexual offences against the person.

The Law Commission, in its report, *Legislating the Criminal Code: Offences Against the Person and General Principles* (Law Com 218, 1993), put forward a scheme for the rationalisation of the common law and statutory offences outlined above, and these proposals were adopted by the government as the basis for its Consultation Paper, *Violence: Reforming the Offences Against the Person Act 1861*, published in March 1998. The Consultation Paper included a draft Bill providing details of what the proposed new offences would look like.

Clause 1 seeks to replace s 18 of the 1861 Act with an offence of intentionally causing serious injury to another. As with the current offence, it would carry the possibility of life imprisonment. Clause 2 envisages an offence of recklessly causing serious injury to another. This would effectively replace s 20, at least as regards the infliction of grievous bodily harm. The maximum penalty envisaged following conviction on indictment is seven years. Section 47 of the 1861 Act would be replaced by the offence provided for in cl 3, which states that: 'A person is guilty of an offence if he intentionally or recklessly causes injury to another.' The offence would carry the possibility of five years' imprisonment following conviction on indictment.

The offences of common assault and battery would be replaced by new offences set out in cl 4. They comprise the offence of intentionally or recklessly applying force to or causing an impact on the body of another, or intentionally or recklessly causing another to believe that any such force or impact is imminent. The offences would be summary only.

The problem of the implied consent that is assumed to exist in respect of the physical contact with others that arises as a normal part of everyday life (for example, squeezing into an already crowded train carriage) is adverted to in cl 4(2), which provides that:

> ... no such offence is committed if the force or impact, not being intended or likely to cause injury, is in the circumstances such as is generally acceptable in the ordinary conduct of daily life and the defendant does not know or believe that it is in fact unacceptable to the other person.

Injury for the purposes of the more serious assault offences is defined to encompass both physical and mental injury (cl 15) but, for the purposes of the offences proposed under cll 2 and 3, injury excludes harm that is caused by the transmission of disease. The aim here is that the deliberate transmission of the HIV virus could be an offence under cl 1, but there could be no liability for reckless transmission under cll 2 and 3.

The Government's Consultation Paper outlines the rationale for adopting this position:

> The Law Commission's original proposal, which included illness and disease in the definition of injury, would have resulted in the intentional or reckless transmission of disease being open to prosecution. They argued that the width of their proposal would be balanced by the fact that prosecution would only be appropriate in the most serious cases. The Government has considered their

views ... but is not persuaded that it would be right ... to criminalise the reckless transmission of normally minor illnesses such as measles or mumps, even though they could have potentially serious consequences for those vulnerable to infection ... [This is an issue of importance that] ... has ramifications beyond the criminal law, into the wider considerations of social and public health policy. The Government is particularly concerned that the law should not seem to discriminate against those who are HIV positive, have AIDS or viral hepatitis or who carry any kind of disease. Nor do we want to discourage people from coming forward for diagnostic tests and treatment, in the interests of their own health and that of others, because of an unfounded fear of criminal prosecution ... The Government therefore proposes that the criminal law should apply only to those whom it can be proved beyond reasonable doubt had deliberately transmitted a disease intending to cause a serious illness ... This proposal will clarify the present law which, because it is largely untested is unclear; by doing so the effect of the law will be confined to the most serious and culpable behaviour ... It is very difficult to prove both the causal linkage of the transmission and also to prove that it was done intentionally. To do so beyond reasonable doubt is even more difficult. The Government does not expect that the proposed offence will be used very often, but considers that it is important that it should exist to provide a safeguard against the worst behaviour [paras 3.12–3.19].

The draft Bill proposes the adoption of standard fault terms for the new offences. Clause 14 provides as follows:

14(1) A person acts intentionally with respect to a result if:

   (a) it is his purpose to cause it; or

   (b) although it is not his purpose to cause it, he knows that it would occur in the ordinary course of events if he were to succeed in his purpose of causing some other result.

(2) A person acts recklessly with respect to a result if he is aware of a risk that it will occur and it is unreasonable to take that risk having regard to the circumstances as he knows or believes them to be.

(3) A person intends an omission to have a result if:

   (a) it is his purpose that the result will occur; or

   (b) although it is not his purpose that the result will occur, he knows that it would occur in the ordinary course of events if he were to succeed in his purpose that some other result will occur.

(4) A person is reckless whether an omission will have a result if he is aware of a risk that the result will occur and it is unreasonable to take that risk having regard to the circumstances as he knows or believes them to be.

(5) Related expressions must be construed accordingly.

(6) This section has effect for the purposes of this Act.

10.7 Sexual offences

Although the term 'sexual offences' suggests a discrete body of offences that should be seen as standing apart from other categories of crime, most sexual offences are, in fact, aggravated forms of assault. This is most obviously the case with offences such as indecent assault, but it is equally true in respect of more serious offences such as rape. Given its sub-text of sexual politics, the topic of sexual offences, perhaps more than other areas of criminal law, tends to be the subject of heated debate regarding issues such as relations between men and women, criminalisation and decriminalisation of homosexual activities, and the age at which young persons should be granted full bodily autonomy.

Certain offences, such as rape, raise unique issues, such as the risk of pregnancy. Sexual offences involving penetrative intercourse carry with them the possibility of infection with serious, or even deadly consequences, such as the case where the victim becomes HIV positive following intercourse.

As a backdrop to all of these issues are the evidential problems peculiar to sexual offences. In many cases, there will be no third party witnesses to the event, given the very nature of the acts concerned, resulting in a contest between the plausibility of the evidence given by the accused as against that given by the complainant. In rape cases, there is the additional factor of the 'lifestyle' of the complainant and its impact on the jury's view of whether or not he or she might have consented to the physical contact (that is, the sexual intercourse) – a debate that rarely if ever arises in cases of assault or wounding.

10.7.1 Rape

Until 1994, rape was a crime which could be committed only by a man against a woman. The Sexual Offences Act (SOA) 1956 stated that it was an offence for a man to rape a woman. The definition of rape had been developed by the common law until the Sexual Offences (Amendment) Act (SO(A)A) 1976 came into force. This Act codified the common law as determined by the House of Lords in *Morgan* (1975) which resulted in the following definition:

(1) a man commits rape if:

he has unlawful sexual intercourse with a woman who at the time of the intercourse does not consent to it; and at the time he knows that she does not consent to the intercourse or is reckless as to whether she consents to it
…

(2) It is hereby declared that if at a trial for a rape offence the jury has to consider whether a man believed that a woman was consenting to sexual intercourse, the presence or absence of reasonable grounds for such a belief is a matter to which the jury is to have regard, in conjunction with any other matters, in considering whether he so believed.

The Criminal Justice and Public Order Act (CJPOA) 1994 has now amended the definition of rape and substituted the following s 1 into the SOA 1956:

1(1) It is an offence for a man to rape a woman or another man.

(2) A man commits rape if:

    (a) he has sexual intercourse with a person (whether vaginal or anal) who at the time of the intercourse does not consent to it; and

    (b) at the time he knows that the person does not consent to the intercourse or is reckless as to whether that person consents to it.

(3) A man commits rape if he induces a married woman to have sexual intercourse with him by impersonating her husband.

Section 1(2) of the SOA 1956 is retained in a slightly amended form now that rape may be committed against either a woman or a man. Therefore, for 'woman' read 'woman or man'. The maximum sentence is life imprisonment.

10.7.2 *Actus reus*

It follows from this that the *actus reus* is complete if the following are satisfied:

- there is intercourse, whether vaginal or anal; and
- there is an absence of consent.

Intercourse is deemed complete upon proof of penetration only (s 44 of the SOA 1956 as amended by the CJPOA 1994). If the man continues to penetrate the person after consent is withdrawn, then the *actus reus* of rape is complete even though the initial penetration was with consent. In *Kaitamaki* (1985), the accused claimed that he became aware that she was not consenting after the initial penetration had taken place. He admitted that he did not desist from intercourse. He was convicted of rape. It follows, therefore, that in such circumstances rape becomes a crime of omission. Few people would view rape as a crime of omission and it would therefore be better if the definition of rape contained the words 'or continues to have sexual intercourse when he knows that consent has been withdrawn'. A defendant in the position of Kaitamaki would still be guilty of rape but at least his liability would be founded upon an 'act' rather than an 'omission' in the sense of a failure to withdraw.

The former definition of rape in the SO(A)A 1976 included a requirement that the sexual intercourse should be 'unlawful'. That is no longer a requirement under the new definition of rape. This was taken to mean that the intercourse had to be outside the bonds of matrimony which was the premise upon which the rule that a man could not rape his wife was built. Despite the fact that the rule was some 300 years old, the House of Lords in *R* (1991) dispensed with it holding that the word 'unlawful' was 'mere surplusage'.

Lord Keith went on to say:

> The fact is that it is clearly unlawful to have sexual intercourse with any woman without her consent, and that the use of the word in the sub-section adds nothing.

Prior to the passing of the SOA 1993, a boy under the age of 14 was to be conclusively presumed to be incapable of causing the *actus reus* of rape. That presumption was abolished by s 1 of the SOA 1993. In theory, a defendant as young as 10 can now be charged with rape.

10.7.3 Consent

The prosecution must prove the absence of consent on the part of the victim in order to establish the *actus reus* of rape. The key question is did the person consent to the intercourse? That appears to be the only issue. In *Larter and Castleton* (1995), the 14 year old victim of the alleged rape was said to be asleep at the time of the intercourse and said she remembered nothing of what happened. Accepting this as fact, it is clear that she did not consent to the intercourse and the appeals against conviction were dismissed. Consent, of course, may be 'manufactured' by the defendant in the sense that it was obtained as a result of fraud, threats, force or fear. There are old authorities which decide that consent is vitiated, that is, nullified if it is obtained in such circumstances (for example, *Day* (1841) and *Wright* (1866)).

The SOA 1956 makes no reference to the effect of fraud, force or fear on the issue of consent. *Olugboja* (1981) held that the SO(A)A 1976 (see, now, SOA 1956 as amended) was declaratory of the common law, and that the only issue was whether or not at the time of the intercourse the woman was consenting. The case discusses the distinction, if any, between consent and consent by submission, an example of the latter being the actress who 'submits' to the film director's request for sexual intercourse in the hope of gaining a part in his next film. If he has offered her a role, a promise which he knows he will not keep, then again it could be alleged she has 'submitted' because if she had known the truth she would have chosen not to participate. Dunn LJ put it this way:

> [The jury] should be directed that consent, or the absence of it, is to be given its ordinary meaning and if need be, by way of example, that there is a difference between consent and submission; every consent involves a submission, but it is by no means follows that a mere submission involves consent.

This raises one major difficulty. Is it incorrect to say that every consent involves a submission? The word is defined in the *Compact Oxford English Dictionary*: 'The action of submitting to an authority, a conquering or ruling power; the act of yielding to the claims of another, or surrendering to his will ...' The nymphomaniac cannot surely be alleged to have 'submitted' to the will of her partner. The woman who persuades her partner to engage in sexual intercourse is 'not yielding to the claims of another'. However, the Court of Appeal in

Larter and Castleton continued to repeat the opinion that every consent involves a submission but not every submission involves consent.

Although the courts continue to peddle this distinction, it is really a 'red herring'. The only question, as the Court of Appeal emphasised in *Malone* (1998), is *did he or she consent*? In *Linekar* (1995), the complainant was a prostitute and agreed to have intercourse with the appellant for £25. After intercourse, he left without paying. The jury found that he had never had any intention of paying. The court held, allowing his appeal against conviction, that the absence of consent, not the existence of fraud, was necessary to make the conduct rape. In this case, the prostitute had consented to sexual intercourse with the appellant. The reality of consent was not destroyed because she thought that he would pay her £25. In *Elbekkay* (1995), the complainant thought that the person who had entered her bed early in the morning was her boyfriend. She permitted intercourse to begin and then realised that something was not quite right. She opened her eyes and discovered that it was a friend who was staying with the couple. The Court of Appeal upheld the conviction on the basis that she was not consenting to intercourse with this man. There had been a mistake as to identity and that is one of the grounds sufficient to negative the apparent consent to intercourse, the other being a mistake to the nature of the act. In *Williams*, a singing master had sexual intercourse with one of his pupils aged 16 by pretending that the act of intercourse was a method of training her voice. The girl showed no resistance as she believed what he said and was, apparently, unaware that he was having sexual intercourse with her. He was convicted of rape and his appeal was dismissed. The court approved the summing up of Branson J to the effect that:

> ... where she is persuaded that what is being done to her is not the ordinary act of sexual intercourse but is some medical or surgical operation in order to give her relief from some disability from which she is suffering, then it is rape although the actual thing that was done was done with her consent, because she never consented to the act of sexual intercourse. She was persuaded to consent to what he did because she thought it was not sexual intercourse and because she thought it was a surgical operation.

In this more enlightened age, it is difficult to comprehend that a 16 year old girl would believe that she was engaging in a 'surgical operation'! Perhaps in 1920 it could have been conceivable but it was never actually proved that she was unaware of the facts of life, in which case she would not have consented to an operation but to the act of intercourse and Williams should have had his conviction quashed.

Fraudulent behaviour covers a wide spectrum of activity. To impersonate a woman's husband and thereby to be permitted to have sexual intercourse is specifically covered by s 1(3) of the SOA 1956, as substituted by the CJPOA 1994. Clause 89 of the *Draft Criminal Code* (Law Com 177, 1989), recommended that any fraud as to the nature of the act, impersonation of the husband or any other man should continue to amount to rape. Other frauds, for example, as to status or wealth as opposed to identity should not affect consent. If a woman knows that it is X she wishes to have intercourse with and she is not mistaken as to the nature of the act, then it is difficult to accept that other misapprehensions, for example, as to his marital status, wealth or position, should have any effect whatsoever on the issue of consent.

10.7.4 *Mens rea*

The accused must intend to have intercourse and have knowledge that the victim does not consent to sexual intercourse or be reckless whether or not she is consenting. The authorities hold that it is *Cunningham* not *Caldwell* recklessness that is required. This is also in line with the decision in *Morgan* that the accused is entitled to be acquitted if he honestly believed that the person was consenting. As we saw in Chapter 3, there had been an attempt by Lord Lane in *Pigg* (1982) to extend the *Caldwell* definition of recklessness to rape but that had produced only uncertainty. Lord Lane had considered that a man might be reckless if he were indifferent *and* gave no thought to the possibility that the woman was not consenting. It is difficult to envisage someone simultaneously being both indifferent *and* giving *no thought* to the issue of consent. Bristow J in *Satnam and Kewel* (1983) concluded that:

> Any direction as to the definition of rape should therefore be based on s 1 of the SO(A)A 1976 and upon *DPP v Morgan*, without regard to *R v Caldwell* or *R v Lawrence*, which were concerned with recklessness in a different context and under a different statute ... In [criminal damage cases] the foreseeability, or possible foreseeability, is as to the consequences of the criminal act. In the case of rape the foreseeability is to the state of mind of the victim.

A person who gives no thought as to whether the other party is consenting might be deemed reckless if *Caldwell* were the appropriate authority. But it is not; so what of the defendant who claims that he never gave any thought to the issue of consent? On a purely subjective analysis, he neither intended nor was reckless to consent. If it transpires that there was no consent, then that would need to be communicated and therefore it is difficult to envisage a situation where a jury would accept that no thought at all had been given to the matter of consent. Always remembering, of course, that *Morgan* requires an honest belief that the victim was consenting in order to refute the prosecution's case and this can only be achieved if the defendant addressed the point. Rape is a crime of basic intent and therefore voluntary intoxication is no defence.

10.8   Indecent assault

Section 14 of the SOA 1956 creates the offence of indecent assault on a woman and s 15 of the SOA 1956 indecent assault on a man. The sections make clear that girls or boys under the age of 16 cannot in law give any consent which would prevent the act from being an assault.

Lord Ackner in *Court* (1989) stated that the prosecution had to prove three things in order to establish an indecent assault:

(1) that the accused intentionally assaulted the victim;

(2) that the assault or the circumstances accompanying it were capable of being considered by right minded persons as indecent; and

(3) that the accused intended to commit such an assault as is referred to in (2).

So, in *Sargeant* (1997), a conviction under s 15(1) was upheld where the appellant had grabbed the victim, aged 16 and forced him to masturbate into a condom. The boy had not been touched in a sexual manner but an assault had taken place when the appellant had grabbed him and the court had no doubt that this was done in circumstances of indecency.

The sections require evidence of a 'technical' assault or a battery. Assault means to put someone in fear of harm being inflicted upon them. A battery requires actual contact with the victim. It follows that where the case proceeds on the basis of a 'technical' assault, D must have intended that it will be associated with circumstances of indecency. For an assault to amount to an indecent assault, it must take place in circumstances of indecency. The test according to the decision in *Court* (1989) is whether 'right-minded people' would think the assault indecent. A doctor may obtain sexual satisfaction or gratification from an intimate examination of a female patient, but if the examination was clinically necessary, then there is no indecent assault. The result would be different if the examination was unnecessary. In *George* (1956), the defendant tried to remove a shoe from his victim, an act from which he obtained some sort of sexual thrill. His conviction was quashed because, looked at objectively, the circumstances were not indecent. Therefore, if the circumstances do not include any perceived element of indecency, then whatever the motive of the accused this will not amount to an indecent assault. Right-minded individuals observing what was taking place would not conclude they were watching an indecent event unfolding before their eyes. However, some circumstances will lead to only one conclusion, that is, there was an indecent assault. Thus, Lord Ackner in *Court* gives the example of a man ripping off a woman's clothes against her wishes. In *Court*, a 26 year old man 'spanked' a 12 year old girl against her wishes. He claimed he suffered from a buttock fetish and could offer no further explanation for his conduct. It is hard to imagine in the circumstances, what conclusion other than a finding of guilty could have been reached. In *Beal v Kelley* (1951), the defendant had indecently exposed himself to a young boy and when the boy refused to handle him indecently, he got hold of the boy's arm and pulled him towards himself. Here the assault in itself was not indecent but the combination of an assault together with circumstances of indecency was enough to establish the offence.

Other cases could be more marginal, in that the circumstances may lead to the conclusion that the activity was indecent but yet again may not. In such circumstances, evidence of motive may well be the most important factor. Lord Ackner states:

> ... any evidence which tends to explain the reason for the defendant's conduct, be it his own admission or otherwise, would be relevant to establish whether or not he intended to commit, not only an assault, but an indecent one.

A person charged with an indecent assault may raise the defence of consent, although *Donovan* (1934), *Boyea* (1992) and *Brown* (1993) decide that, subject to recognised exceptions, one cannot consent to an assault where actual bodily harm has been caused. As indicated above, 10.3.2, consent can be vitiated by the defendant's deceit as to his identity or the nature of the act he proposes to perform. *Tabassum* is evidence of the difficulty in distinguishing between nature and quality and the law is in need of clarification on this point.

An indecent assault can be committed by one female on another female, since s 14(1) of the SOA 1956 makes it an offence for a person to commit an indecent assault on a woman. A woman may, of course, commit an indecent assault on a man or boy. In *Faulkner v Talbot* (1981), the court held that it was not an offence for a woman to permit a 14 year old boy to have intercourse with her. However, where the woman touched the boy in an indecent way as a preliminary to sexual intercourse, then she committed an indecent assault. This was held to be the case irrespective of whether the boy was consenting or not. This leads to the rather strange conclusion that it is an offence to do something on the way to intercourse but the act of intercourse is not. The conclusion though is justifiable on the basis of the wording of s 15(1) of the SOA 1956.

An indecent assault can occur even though there is no hostility towards the victim. As Lane CJ said in *Faulkner v Talbot*, an assault 'need not be hostile or rude or aggressive, as some of the earlier cases seem to indicate', but presumably P still needs to apprehend that force will be applied to him.

10.9 Other offences

There are, of course, a whole range of sexual offences which are outside the scope of this book because they will rarely, if ever, form part of the core element of a criminal law syllabus. However, the following offences need to be noted and may sometimes form an alternative to a charge of rape:

- s 2 of the SOA 1956 makes it an offence to procure a woman, by threats or intimidation, to have sexual intercourse in any part of the world;

- s 3 of the SOA 1956 creates the offence of procuring a woman, by false pretences or false representations, to have sexual intercourse in any part of the world.

It will be seen that these offences may be appropriate where there has been fraud or threats to persuade the woman to consent to intercourse but there are doubts about whether a conviction for rape will be obtained because of the uncertainty over the consent issue:

- s 5 of the SOA 1956 makes it an offence for a man to have unlawful sexual intercourse with a girl under the age of 13;

- s 6 of the SOA 1956 makes it an offence for a man to have unlawful sexual intercourse with a girl under 16.

    Section 6(3) should be noted as it provides that it will be a defence for a man under the age of 24, who has not been previously charged with a like offence, to show that he believed the girl to be over 16 and had reasonable cause for the belief. Parliament has expressly stated that the belief as to the girl's age must be based on reasonable grounds;

- ss 10 and 11 of the SOA 1956 deal with the crime of incest. Section 10 makes it an offence for a man to have sexual intercourse with a woman 'whom he knows to be his grand-daughter, daughter, sister or mother'. Under s 11, a woman will be guilty of incest if she permits a man she knows to be her grandfather, father, brother or son to have sexual intercourse with her 'by her consent'.

    It is clear that knowledge is an important ingredient of the offence and therefore the prosecution will be unable to establish its case if the accused can show that he or she honestly believed that his or her partner did not belong to either consanguinity grouping listed in ss 10 and 11. To counteract the effect of the decision in *Whitehouse* (1977) (see above, 4.8), s 54 of the Criminal Law Act 1977 makes it an offence for a man or boy to incite to have sexual intercourse with him a girl under the age of 16 whom he knows to be his sister, half-sister, daughter or granddaughter.

The Indecency with Children Act 1960 makes it an offence for any person to commit an act of gross indecency with or towards a child under the age of 14, or to incite a child under that age to such an act with him or another. The offence carries the possibility of 10 years' imprisonment. The offence has, in some respects, been interpreted broadly by the courts, with a view to maximising the protection than can be afforded to children in respect of the actions of sexual predators. In *Speck* (1977), it was held that inactivity could amount to an 'act' for these purposes – the appellant had allowed a young girl to touch his penis and leave her hand there whilst he had an erection. It had been assumed that the offence was one of strict liability as regards the element of the *actus reus* relating to the age of the victim, but the House of Lords, in *B v DPP* (2000), has held that a defendant can be acquitted if he honestly believes the child in question to be above the age of 14. The ruling is an emphatic statement of support for the subjectivist approach to criminal liability, the House of Lords noting that the offence in question was a serious one, carrying with it considerable social stigma in the event of a conviction. Their Lordships were also mindful of the breadth of the offence, covering as it did the activities of paedophiles preying on children at one extreme, to the activities of sexually precocious teenagers engaged in consensual sexual activity at the other. On that basis, it was felt that the imposition of strict liability could not be supported on the grounds of seeking to obtain a clear and focused statutory objective.

10.10 Reform of sexual offences

The Sexual Offences (Amendment) Bill currently before Parliament seeks to make a number of significant changes to the law relating to sexual offences. The first is to reduce the age of consent in cases of buggery to 16. The second is to reform the law so that a person under the age of consent engaging in the act of buggery will not be committing an offence by so doing. Finally, the Bill proposes a new offence to be charged where a person over the age of 18 has sexual intercourse or engages in any other sexual activity with or directed towards a person under 18, where the accused is in a position of trust in relation to the younger person. A position of trust could arise where, in a number of situations, including where the person over the age of 18 is responsible for the training or supervision or care of others under the age of 18 who are detainees, residents in accommodation provided by statutory or voluntary bodies, or in full time education.

NON-FATAL OFFENCES AGAINST THE PERSON

Assault

Assault and battery are separate offences and are to be regarded as summary offences except when charged under s 47 of the OAPA 1861. Much confusion had resulted from the fact that judges used the word assault to mean battery. Assault is causing someone to apprehend immediate and unlawful violence will be inflicted upon them. Therefore, assault occurs without any physical contact. There is no need to prove that the victim was actually frightened. It is enough to show that he or she apprehended that some personal violence is likely to occur. It is not necessary for there to be any hostility or aggressive or rude behaviour. Words alone may amount to an assault and may of course negative an assault. The decision in *Ireland* (1997) holds that silence can amount to an assault but that will very much depend on the circumstances of the case. The House of Lords also held that the apprehension of psychological injury is sufficient but that may depend on a previous course of conduct having be established as in *Burstow* (1997).

The *mens rea* for assault is either intention or recklessness. Recklessness is to be given its *Cunningham* meaning.

Battery

Battery is the actual infliction of unlawful personal violence. Every battery does not include an assault as in the case of a victim who is asleep. There are many everyday situations were the law presumes consent to the application of 'force' as when people are crowded together at a football match or crammed into the carriage of an underground train. Force does not need to be directly applied as in the *Ireland* case. *Venna* establishes that the *mens rea* for the offence is either intention or recklessness.

Assault and battery are regarded as basic intent crimes for the purposes of the law relating to intoxication.

Consent

Interest in the role of consent as a defence to a charge of battery was generated as a result of *Brown* (1993). The Law Lords held by a three to two majority that consent could be no defence to a s 47 of the OAPA 1861 charge. Or at least that is what they appeared to decide. This ruling has now been called into question as a result of the decision in *Wilson* (1996), which concluded that a wife's

425

consent to having her buttocks 'branded' prevented an offence occurring under s 47. The court regarded the act as a private one between a married couple in the privacy of their own home and was the equivalent of tattooing which is lawful. The court also recognised certain activities as being lawful which otherwise would clearly amount to battery, for example, sporting occasions such as a boxing bout. What amounts to the public interest in this context is extremely hard to define. The House of Lords in *Brown* seemed to be saying that group sado masochistic acts were contrary to the public interest.

The *mens rea* of s 47 requires intent or recklessness towards the assault or battery but no *mens rea* towards causing actual bodily harm.

Sections 18 and 20 of the OAPA 1861

Sections 18 and 20 of the OAPA 1861 offences should be viewed together as there is considerable overlap between the offences. Section 18, a specific intent crime, requires an intent to wound or cause grievous bodily harm. Section 20 requires the defendant to have acted maliciously in wounding or inflicting grievous bodily harm. 'To wound' means that the continuity of the skin must be broken. *Burstow* (1997) suggests that there is little difference in the way one may cause or inflict grievous bodily harm. There is House of Lord's authority in *Mandair* (1994), which acknowledges that 'cause' is wide enough to cover anything subsumed under the word 'inflict'.

The *mens rea* for s 18 is intent and, for s 20, malice which is interpreted to mean acting intentionally or recklessly in the *Cunningham* sense.

Sexual offences

Statutory changes occurred to the law on rape in 1956, 1976 and 1994. Rape may only be committed by a man but, since the CJPOA 1994, a man may now commit rape against another man. The *actus reus* of rape is to have sexual intercourse with a man or woman without his or her consent. The *mens rea* is either an intention to have intercourse without consent or being reckless as to consent. Reckless is taken in its *Cunningham* sense to mean that the defendant was aware that there was a possibility that the woman was not consenting. Intercourse is deemed complete upon proof of penetration only. There is no longer a requirement that the sexual intercourse should be unlawful. The House of Lords in *R* (1991) held that the word was 'mere surplusage'. No special rules apply to the matrimonial relationship. A man can therefore rape his wife if all the requirements of the legislation are met.

The issue of consent has troubled the courts over a number of years. The key issue is whether or not the woman was consenting. So a woman who is sleeping at the time of penetration cannot be consenting. Consent may be 'manufactured' through fear, force or fraud and, although older cases hold that, when obtained in such circumstances, consent is vitiated, there is really only one question for the jury: was this victim consenting to intercourse with the accused? If there has been a mistake as to identity, then consent will be vitiated. *Collins* (1972) is a good example, where the woman's boyfriend was expected to pay her a nocturnal visit and she believing Collins to be her boyfriend permitted intercourse to take place only discovering her mistake once the light was switched on.

It is an offence for a person to commit an indecent assault (ss 14 and 15 of the SOA 1956). Three things need to be established in order for the prosecution to succeed on a charge of indecent assault:

- the accused must intentionally assault the victim;

- the assault or circumstances accompanying it must be capable of being considered by right minded people as indecent;

- that the accused intended to commit an assault in circumstances of indecency.

It will not always be obvious to right minded people that an indecent event is unfolding before their eyes as in *George*, where the defendant tried to remove the victim's shoe as he obtained some sort of sexual thrill from this activity. Other cases will be more straightforward, as in *Court*, where the defendant slapped a young girl on the buttocks. A person charged with indecent assault may raise the defence of consent but case law decides that consent will be irrelevant where actual bodily harm has been caused.

An indecent assault can be committed by one female on another or a female on a male. There is no need for the indecent assault to be accompanied by any sort of hostility or aggressive behaviour.

Other offences involving sexual intercourse are to be found at ss 2, 3, 5, 6, 10 and 11 of the SOA 1956.

FURTHER READING

Chapter 1, An Introduction to the Study of Criminal Law

Ashworth, A and Blake, M, 'The presumption of innocence in English criminal law' [1996] Crim LR 306

Brooke, Sir H, 'The Law Commission and criminal law reform' [1995] Crim LR 911

Buxton, R, 'The Human Rights Act and the substantive criminal law' [2000] Crim LR 331

Devlin, P, *The Enforcement of Morals*, 1965, Oxford: OUP

Farmer, L, 'The obsession with definition: the nature of crime and critical legal theory' (1996) 5 SLS 57

Hart, HLA, *Law, Liberty and Morality*, 1963, Oxford: OUP

James, A, Taylor, N and Walker, C, 'Criminal Cases Review Commission: economy, effectiveness and justice' [2000] Crim LR 140

Lacey, N, 'Contingency and criminalisation', in Loveland, I (ed), *Frontiers of Criminality*, 1995, London: Sweet & Maxwell

Lacey, N *et al*, *Reconstructing Criminal Law*, 1990, London: Weidenfeld & Nicolson

Law Commission, *Legislating the Criminal Code: Offences Against the Person and General Principles*, Law Com 218, 1993, London: HMSO

Law Commission, *A Criminal Code for England and Wales*, Law Com 177, 1989, London: HMSO, Vols I and II

Norrie, A, 'After *Woollin*' [1999] Crim LR 532

Roberts, P, 'Taking the burden of proof seriously' [1995] Crim LR 783

Smith, ATH, '*Legislating the Criminal Code*: the Law Commission proposals' [1992] Crim LR 396

Smith, ATH, 'Judicial law making in the criminal law' (1984) 100 LQR 46

Spencer, JR, 'The case for a code of criminal procedure' [2000] Crim LR 519

Williams, G, 'The definition of crime' (1955) CLP 107

Wolfenden Committee, *Report of the Committee on Homosexual Offences and Prostitution*, Cmnd 247, 1957, London: HMSO

Chapter 2, *Actus Reus*

Ashworth, A, 'The scope of criminal liability for omissions' (1989) 105 LQR 424

Butler Committee on Mentally Abnormal Offenders, Cmnd 6244, 1975, London: HMSO

Hart, HLA and Honoré, T, *Causation in the Law*, 2nd edn, 1985, Oxford: OUP

Hogan, B, 'Omissions and a duty myth', in Smith, P (ed), *Criminal Law: Essays in Honour of JC Smith*, 1986, London: Butterworths

Hogan, B, 'The *Dadson* principle' [1989] Crim LR 684

Norrie, A, 'A critique of criminal causation' (1991) 54 MLR 685

Padfield, N, 'Clean water and muddy causation' [1995] Crim LR 683

Padfield, N, 'Casenote on *Hennessy*' [1989] CLJ 354

Smith, JC, 'Casenote on *Cheshire*' [1991] Crim LR 709

Williams, G, 'Criminal omissions – the conventional view' (1991) 107 LQR 86

Williams, G, '*Finus* for *novus actus*' [1989] CLJ 391

Chapter 3, The Mental Element – *Mens Rea*

Lacey, N, 'A clear concept of intention: elusive or illusory' (1993) 56 MLR 621

Leigh, LH, *Strict and Vicarious Liability*, 1982, London: Sweet & Maxwell

Norrie, A, 'After *Woollin*' [1999] Crim LR 532

Norrie, A, *Crime, Reason and History*, 1993, London: Weidenfeld & Nicolson

Norrie, A, 'Subjectivism, objectivism and the limits of criminal recklessness' (1992) 12 OJLS 45

Richardson, G, 'Regulatory crime: the empirical research' [1987] Crim LR 295

Rowan-Robinson, J, 'Crime and regulation' [1988] Crim LR 211

Smith, JC, 'Casenote on *Reid*' [1992] Crim LR 821

Smith, JC, 'A note on intention' [1990] Crim LR 85

Williams, G, 'Unresolved problems of recklessness' (1988) 8 LS 74

Wilson, W, 'Doctrinal rationality after *Woollin'* (1999) 62 MLR 448

Wootton, B, *Crime and the Criminal Law,* 2nd edn, 1981, London: Sweet & Maxwell

Chapter 4, Participation in Crime

Beynon, H 'Causation, omissions and complicity' [1987] Crim LR 539

Gobert, J, 'Corporate criminality: new crimes for the times' [1994] Crim LR 722

Lanham, D 'Accomplices and withdrawal' (1981) 97 LQR 575

Law Commission, *Assisting and Encouraging Crime*, Law Com 131, 1993, London: HMSO

Smith, JC, 'Secondary participation in crime can we do without it?' (1994) 144 NLJ 679

Smith, KJM, 'The Law Commission Consultation Paper on complicity' [1994] Crim LR 239

Smith, KJM, 'Complicity and causation' [1986] Crim LR 663

Sullivan, GR, 'Intent, purpose and complicity' [1988] Crim LR 641

Williams, G, 'Letting offences happen' [1990] Crim LR 780

Chapter 5, Preliminary or Inchoate Offences

Aldridge, P, 'The Sexual Offences (Conspiracy and Incitement) Act 1996' [1997] Crim LR 30

Orchard, GL, 'Agreement in criminal conspiracy' [1974] Crim LR 297

Silber, S, 'The Law Commission, *Conspiracy to Defraud* and the dishonesty project' [1995] Crim LR 461

Smith, JC, 'Some thoughts on the Law Commission's report: *Conspiracy to Defraud'* [1995] Crim LR 209

Smith, JC, 'Conspiracy under the Criminal Law Act 1977' [1977] 598

Smith, KJM, 'Proximity in attempt: Lord Lane's midway course' [1991] Crim LR 576

Williams, G, 'Wrong turnings in the law of attempt' [1991] Crim LR 417

Williams, G, 'The Lords and impossible attempts' [1986] CLJ 33

Chapter 6, Homicide

Ashworth, A, 'Reforming the law of murder' [1990] Crim LR 75

Biggs, H, 'Euthanasia and death with dignity: still poised on the fulcrum of homicide' [1996] Crim LR 878

Keating, H, 'Law Commission report on involuntary manslaughter: the restoration of a serious crime' [1996] Crim LR 535

Mackay, RD, 'The consequences of killing very young children' [1993] Crim LR 21

Nicolson, D and Sanghvi, R, 'Battered women and provocation: the implication of *R v Ahluwalia*' [1993] Crim LR 728

Padfield, N, 'Clean water and muddy causation: is causation a question of law or fact, or just a way of allocating blame?' [1995] Crim LR 683

Wells, C, 'Law Commission report on involuntary manslaughter: the corporate manslaughter proposals: pragmatism, paradox and peninsularity' [1996] Crim LR 545

Williams, G, '*Mens rea* for murder: leave it alone' (1989) 105 LQR 387

Chapter 7, General Defences

Glazebrook, P, 'The necessity plea in English criminal law' [1972] CLJ 87

Lynch, ACE, 'The scope of intoxication' [1982] Crim LR 139

Orchard,G, 'Surviving without *Majewski*-a view from down under' [1993] Crim LR 426

Parish, S, 'Self defence: the wrong direction?' [1997] Crim LR 201

Paton, E, 'Reformulating the intoxication rules: the Law Commission's report' [1995] Crim LR 382

Smith, JC and Hogan, B, *Criminal Law*, 9th edn, 1999, London: Butterworths

Williams, G, 'The theory of excuses' [1982] Crim LR 732

Chapter 8, Offences Against Property: Theft

Beatson, A and Simester, A, 'Stealing one's own property' (1999) 115 LQR 372

Elliott, DW, 'Directors' thefts and dishonesty' [1991] Crim LR 732

Gardner, S, 'Property and theft' [1998] Crim LR 35

Griew, E, 'Dishonesty: the objections to *Feely* and *Ghosh*' [1985] Crim LR 341

Halpin, A, 'The test for dishonesty' [1996] Crim LR 283

Smith, JC, 'Stealing tickets' [1998] Crim LR 723

Spencer, JR, 'The metamorphosis of section 6 of the Theft Act' [1977] Crim LR 653

Sullivan, GR and Warbrick, C, 'Territoriality, theft and *Atakpu*' [1994] Crim LR 650

Williams, G, 'Theft and voidable title' [1981] Crim LR 666

Williams, G, 'Temporary appropriation should be theft' [1981] Crim LR 129

Williams, G, 'Appropriation: a single or continuous act?' [1978] Crim LR 69

Chapter 9, Offences Against Property: Other Offences under the Theft Acts 1968 and 1978 and Criminal Damage

Law Commission, *Offences of Dishonesty: Money Transfers*, Law Com 243, 1996, London: HMSO

Smith, JC, 'Obtaining cheques by deception or fraud' [1997] Crim LR 397

Spencer, JR, 'Handling, theft and the *mala fide* purchaser' [1985] Crim LR 92

Spencer, JR, 'The mishandling of handling' [1981] Crim LR 682

Chapter 10, Non-Fatal Offences Against the Person

Criminal Law Revision Committee, 15th Report, *Sexual Offences*, Cmnd 9213, 1984, London: HMSO

Criminal Law Revision Committee, 14th Report, *Offences Against the Person*, Cmnd 7844, 1980, London: HMSO

Gunn, M and Ormerod, D, 'The legality of boxing' (1995) 15 LS 181

Law Commission, *Consent in the Criminal Law*, Law Com 139, 1995, London: HMSO

Leigh, LH, 'Sado-masochism, consent and the reform of the criminal law' (1976) 39 MLR 130

Reed, A, '*Contra bonos mores*: fraud affecting consent in rape' (1995) 145 NLJ 174

Tyler, L, 'Towards a redefinition of rape' (1994) 144 NLJ 860

Wells, C, 'Stalking: the criminal law response' [1997] Crim LR 463

Williams, G, 'Force, injury and serious injury' (1990) 140 NLJ 1227

INDEX